Clinical Neuropsychology

Clinical Neuropsychology

A POCKET HANDBOOK for ASSESSMENT

edited by
Peter Jeffrey Snyder
Paul David Nussbaum

American Psychological Association
Washington, DC

Copyright © 1998 by the American Psychological Association. All rights reserved. Except as permitted under the United States Copyright Act of 1976, no part of this publication may be reproduced or distributed in any form or by any means, or stored in a database or retrieval system, without the prior written permission of the publisher.

First printing August 1998
Second printing February 1999
Third printing September 2000

Published by
American Psychological Association
750 First Street, NE
Washington, DC 20002

Copies may be ordered from
APA Order Department
P.O. Box 92984
Washington, DC 20090-2984

In the UK, Europe, North Africa, and the Middle East, copies may be ordered from
American Psychological Association
3 Henrietta Street
Covent Garden, London
WC2E 8LU England

Typeset in Stone Serif by Harlowe Typography, Cottage City, MD

Printer: Edwards Brothers, Ann Arbor, MI
Cover designer: Berg Design, Albany, NY
Technical/production editor: Tanya Y. Alexander

Library of Congress Cataloging-in-Publication Data
Clinical neuropsychology: a pocket handbook for assessment / edited by Peter Jeffrey Snyder and Paul David Nussbaum.
    p.   cm.
Includes bibliographical references and index.
ISBN 1-55798-514-6 (pbk.)
1. Neuropsychological tests—Handbooks, manuals, etc.   2. Clinical neuropsychology—Handbooks, manuals, etc.   I. Snyder, Peter J., 1964– .   II. Nussbaum, Paul David.
    [DNLM: 1. Nervous System Diseases—diagnosis handbooks. 2. Diagnosis, Differential handbooks.   WL 39 C641 1998]
RC386.6.N48C527   1998
616.8´0475—dc21
DNLM/DLC
for Library of Congress   98-21293
                                        CIP

Printed in the United States of America

For my grandmother, Belle Jacobs,
whose strength, wisdom, love, and guidance
cannot possibly be repaid

PJS

For Andrew Paul

PDN

Contents

PART II

Pediatric Psychology

Contributors

Norman Abeles, PhD
Past-President, American Psychological Association, and
Professor, Department of Psychology
Michigan State University
East Lansing, MI

Daniel N. Allen, PhD
Psychology Service (116B)
Highland Drive Veterans Administration Medical Center, and
Visiting Instructor of Clinical Neurology
University of Pittsburgh School of Medicine
Pittsburgh, PA

Russell M. Bauer, PhD, ABPP/ABCN
Professor of Psychology and Neurology
Department of Clinical Psychology
University of Florida Health Science Center, Gainesville

James T. Becker, PhD
Neuropsychology Research Program
University of Pittsburgh School of Medicine
Pittsburgh, PA

Susan R. Beers, PhD
Department of Psychiatry
University of Pittsburgh School of Medicine
Western Psychiatric Institute & Clinic
Pittsburgh, PA

Pelagie M. Beeson, PhD
National Center for Neurogenic Communication Disorders
University of Arizona, Tucson

Arthur L. Benton, PhD
Iowa City, Iowa

Jennifer J. Bortz, PhD
Assistant Professor of Neurology
Barrow Neurological Institute
St. Joseph's Hospital & Medical Center
Phoenix, AZ

Meryl A. Butters, PhD
Assistant Professor of Psychiatry
University of Pittsburgh School of Medicine
Western Psychiatric Institute & Clinic
Pittsburgh, PA

Daniel X. Capruso, PhD, ABCN
Clinical Neuropsychology Section
Neurodiagnostic Laboratory
The Buffalo General Hospital
Buffalo, NY

Nicole A. Ceravolo
Allegheny Neurological Associates
Pittsburgh, PA

Ronald A. Cohen, PhD
Director of Neuropsychology
The Miriam Hospital
Providence, RI

Robert B. Fields, PhD
Coordinator, Geriatric Psychiatry Program
Department of Psychiatry
Allegheny General Hospital
Pittsburgh, PA

Michael D. Franzen, PhD
Director, Psychology and Neuropsychology Section
Department of Psychiatry, Allegheny General Hospital
Pittsburgh, PA

Elizabeth L. Glisky, PhD
Department of Psychology
University of Arizona, Tucson

Gerald Goldstein, PhD
Research Neuropsychologist
Highland Drive
Veterans Administration Medical Center
Pittsburgh, PA

Leslie J. Gonzalez-Rothi, PhD
Audiology/Speech Pathology Service
Department of Veterans Affairs Medical Center
Gainesville, FL

Katherine Hammond, PsyD
Pittsburgh, PA

Kerry deS. Hamsher, PhD
Milwaukee, WI

Kenneth M. Heilman, MD
Professor of Neurology
Neurology Service (151)
Department of Veterans Affairs Medical Center
Gainesville, FL

Grant L. Iverson, PhD
University of Oklahoma Health Sciences Center
Oklahoma City

Melissa A. Jenkins, PhD
The Miriam Hospital
Providence, RI

Howard R. Kessler, PhD
Freeport, Maine

Sarah R. Kortenkamp, PhD
Department of Clinical Psychology
University of Florida, Gainesville

Rhonda K. B. Landis, PhD
Behavioral Health Services
Du Bois Regional Medical Center
Du Bois, PA

Oscar L. Lopez, MD
Neuropsychology Research Program
Pittsburgh, PA

John A. Lucas, PhD
Department of Psychiatry and Psychology
Mayo Medical School
Mayo Clinic Jacksonville
Jacksonville, FL

Paul F. Malloy, PhD
Director, Clinical Neuropsychology Section
Butler Hospital
Providence, RI

Harry W. McConnell, MD, FRCP(C)
The Centre for Epilepsy
Mapother House Neurosciences
Maudsley Hospital
Denmark Hill, London, England

Mark D. Morin
Behavioral Neurology Unit
Beth Israel Hospital
Boston, MA

Lisa A. Morrow, PhD
Western Psychiatric Institute & Clinic
University of Pittsburgh School of Medicine
Pittsburgh, PA

Paul David Nussbaum, PhD
Director, Aging Research & Education Center
Lutheran Affiliated Services/St. John Specialty Care Center
Mars, PA

Margaret G. O'Connor, PhD
Behavioral Neurology Unit
Beth Israel Hospital
Boston, MA

Steven Z. Rapcsak, MD
Neurology Service (127)
V.A. Medical Center
Tucson, AZ

Graham Ratcliff, D.Phil
HEALTHSOUTH Harmarville Rehabilitation Hospital
Pittsburgh, PA

Christopher M. Ryan, PhD
Department of Psychiatry
University of Pittsburgh School of Medicine
Western Psychiatric Institute & Clinic
Pittsburgh, PA

Judith Saxton, PhD
University of Pittsburgh School of Medicine
Western Psychiatric Institute & Clinic
Pittsburgh, PA

Thomas F. Scott, MD
Medical College of Pennsylvania and Hahneman University
Allegheny General Hospital
Pittsburgh, PA

Gregory Slomka, PhD
University of Pittsburgh School of Medicine
Western Psychiatric Institute & Clinic
Pittsburgh, PA

Peter Jeffrey Snyder, PhD
Director, Division of Behavioral Neurology
Department of Neurology, Allegheny General Hospital
Pittsburgh, PA

Elizabeth M. Soety
University of Pittsburgh School of Medicine
Western Psychiatric Institute & Clinic
Pittsburgh, PA

Christopher Starratt, PhD
Department of Psychology
Barry University
Miami Shores, FL

Glenn T. Stebbins, PhD
Section of Cognitive Neurosciences
Department of Neurological Sciences
Rush Medical College
Chicago, IL

Rodney A. Swenson, PhD, ABPN
University of North Dakota School of Medicine
MeritCare Neuroscience Clinic, Fargo

Alexander I. Tröster, PhD
Department of Neurology
University of Kansas Medical Center, Kansas City

Mieke Verfaellie, PhD
Memory Disorders Research Center
Department of Veterans Affairs Medical Center (151A)
Boston, MA

Robert T. Watson, MD
Department of Neurology
University of Florida College of Medicine, Gainesville

Amy Weinstein, PhD
Department of Neurology
University of Rochester
Rochester, NY

Robert S. Wilson, PhD
Department of Neurological Sciences
Rush-Presbyterian-St. Luke's Medical Center
Chicago, IL

Foreword

Clinical neuropsychology has advanced rapidly as a field over the past 30 years. In 1970 there were only two journals that could be identified as neuropsychological in nature. By 1960, there were more than a dozen such journals, and the number of books in neuropsychology had increased from 1 or 2 per year in 1970 to more than 20 per year in 1990. Indeed, the late Nelson Butters (1992) suggested that as recently as 1970, psychologists were still in the Dark Ages of clinical assessment of memory, noting that the Wechsler Memory Scale was still in its 1945 form and failed to separate memory from attention. Then, from 1970 to 1990, much work was done applying models of normal memory to patients suffering from hippocampal and diencephalic amnesias.

With an increase in the sophistication and number of diagnostic tests available, an area of debate with regard to neuropsychological assessment has surfaced concerning the merits of the fixed battery versus the flexible battery approach. Although the modern-day neuropsychologist is blessed with a veritable treasure chest of measures from which to choose the components of a fixed battery, it is doubtful whether any fixed battery, no matter how comprehensive, can answer all the questions that arise in clinical practice. The flexible approach, in which the battery is determined by the referral question and by clinical observations made during testing, pushes the examiner to think about what precisely is required to answer practical questions. On the debit side, however, is the danger that a flexible approach might miss unexpected performance patterns that would be picked up by the use of a standard fixed battery.

This volume helps to steer the clinical neuropsychologist through the challenges of the assessment process. It is a readily available handbook for clinicians in hospital settings, and I believe that it represents a logical extension of the advancement of neuropsychology as a field and the rapid move of the field into the mainstream of hospital practice. There has been a marked increase in the use of neuropsychological services in hospitals, and readily available information is needed for neuropsychology interns, postdoctoral fellows, and practicing clinicians. In particular, students—no matter how broad based their predoctoral clinical experiences—will be faced with entirely new situations when they start their clinical internships. They, in conjunction with their supervisors, will have to make rapid, efficient, and rational decisions concerning the assessment techniques they will use. Leading experts have provided such advice in this comprehensive handbook, and I see it as an important and vital source of readily available information. Carry it with you, and consult it often!

> Norman Abeles, PhD
> **Past President, American Psychological Association**

REFERENCE

Butters, N. (1992). Memory remembered: 1970–1991. *Archives of Clinical Neuropsychology, 7,* 285–295.

About This Handbook

The field of clinical neuropsychology has grown over the past quarter century at a phenomenal rate. In many departments of neurology, neurosurgery, and psychiatry, at major teaching hospitals across North America and much of Europe, neuropsychologists are listed as members of the professional staff. In fact, many hospitals and clinics have created autonomous departments of psychology (or neuropsychology) to meet an increasing demand for such services, across a variety of inpatient departments.

Within primary-care settings, neuropsychologists often consult in emergency departments (i.e., for patients with traumatic brain injury); oncology departments (e.g., for patients with oncogenic central nervous system [CNS] tumors); infectious disease programs (e.g., for the diagnoses of neuropsychological dysfunction in patients with AIDS-related and other viral encephalopathies); cardiology departments (e.g., to evaluate patients who have suffered strokes, anoxic events, or multiple infarcts of CNS tissue); and most frequently in departments of neurology, neurosurgery, and psychiatry. In addition, within tertiary-care settings (e.g., rehabilitation hospitals), the neuropsychologist is widely recognized as a necessary member of the multidisciplinary teams that are charged with the design and implementation of programs that serve to improve the quality of life of patients suffering from a wide array of neurological and neuropsychological illnesses.

Indeed, over the past 10 years, many internship and postdoctoral programs have been created to train a new generation of neuropsychologists, and more neuropsychologists than ever before now list inpatient hospital settings as their primary places of employment. The growth of strong national and international scientific and professional organizations; the creation of several well-respected scientific journals; and the rapid move toward formal recognition of neuropsychology internships, postdoctoral programs, and board certification requirements all attest to the development of a mature and intellectually rewarding health care specialty.

Concomitant with the expansion of clinical neuropsychological services, including consultation and liaison practice and treatment planning for a truly diverse mixture of clinical conditions and patient populations, has been the development of a large collection of neuropsychological tests and measures. Perhaps the most well-respected compendium of clinical instruments, Lezak's textbook *Neuropsychological Assessment* (1995), lists more than 600 tests and assessment techniques for the evaluation of intellectual, verbal, visuoperceptual, visuoconstructive, memory, conceptual, attentional, and executive functions.

With many hundreds of tests and assessment techniques to choose from, how can the practicing neuropsychologist or doctoral-level trainee begin to select a specific diagnostic strategy that will address the particular needs of and referral questions for individual patients? One well-accepted method is to administer a standard "battery" of tests to all patients, no matter what specific clinicopathological questions arise. Although this method has its advantages, including a generally high level of sensitivity for identifying the presence or absence of neurological impairment, such batteries generally lack a high degree of specificity for the determination of precise types of neuropathological conditions. Alternatively, many neuropsychologists choose to design unique or flexible batteries of tests for differing types of patients or to address specific clinical concerns. It is the latter method that the editors of this handbook choose to rely on, both for the training and supervision of students and for the examination of patients themselves.

It is a relatively simple matter for the experienced clinician to determine an appropriate diagnostic strategy and then to select appropriate tests and measures to address specific clinical concerns, especially from the comfort of his or her office, which typically is replete with textbooks (such as Lezak's) and journals that are used to guide such decisions. But what about the busy clinician who needs to make these decisions rapidly while working on the hospital inpatient unit (or in any clinical setting in which such library collections are unavailable)? More important, what handy references are available to guide the intern or fellow, on the ward or in the clinic, when supervisors are not always readily available?

In virtually every other medical or health care specialty, there is a fairly simple solution to this problem: the diagnostic guide that fits into the lab coat pocket. Such manuals "for the house officer" (at least one for each specialty) provide a ready source of information to aid in the differential diagnoses of relevant clinical syndromes. With this edited volume, it is our attempt to provide a readily available handbook for neuropsychology interns, postdoctoral fellows, and practicing clinicians.

For many interns and fellows who are still in training, their current training site may be their first exposure to working on staff in a hospital setting, because many graduate PhD programs do not include such exposure as part of their training programs. For these students, chapters are included that provide helpful suggestions for the rapid and efficient reading of a patient's medical chart, proper chart noting, how to understand a neurologist's notes (and stick figures) detailing his or her neurological findings, and the psychological and behavioral correlates of various types of blood and other laboratory tests. In addition, chapters are included that contain effective approaches to the clinical interview and the bedside neuropsychological exam.

Chapters are also included that cover the major differential diagnoses that neuropsychologists are routinely asked to make, ranging from the dementias and depression to nonepileptic seizure disorders to neurotoxic exposure. It is hoped that these chapters will be useful to the student and attending psychologist alike. Several chapters are included that focus on treatment options, such as cognitive rehabilitation techniques for memory dysfunction following traumatic brain injuries. The decision was made to include several chapters on treatment, which allows for the presentation of various treatment options, to provide highly pertinent information for the busy clinician who is practicing within hospital settings.

The chapters have been designed to be brief (outline format) and easily scanned at times when decisions must be made quickly. Although it is exceedingly difficult in an edited volume such as this one, we have attempted to structure all chapters as similarly as possible, to facilitate the efficiency with which any one chapter may be scanned for pertinent information when the reader is under pressure to make rapid decisions. A few chapters do provide more extensive background information than others because such detail was felt to be necessary given the state of the science in that field. Some areas, of course, owing to the nature of the disorder, do not have clear-cut assessment procedures outlined. As in many clinical investigations, providing areas of potential exploration is more realistic. Each chapter concludes with a short bibliography of primary references for further reading; these references are not meant to be complete but rather to steer the reader toward the relevant literature. Although many tests and measures are suggested for use in the differential diagnoses of specific clinical syndromes, the instructions for their administration and scoring, as well as their normative data, are not provided. In short, the author or authors of each chapter were asked to present their "best advice" for students and trainees for each topic that is covered. Rather than presenting a "dry" list of relevant tests and normative data, the authors endeavored to provide synopses of relevant concepts, their "decision trees" for making the differential diagnoses, and the methods by which they rule out competing diagnoses.

The reader should be aware that bibliographic citations for the most common and well known of assessment tests (e.g., the Wechsler Adult Intelligence Scale) are not provided, because such information is readily available elsewhere. Bibliographic citations are provided, however, for less well-known tests and measures, as well as for specific sets of normative data that are recommended for use in lieu of normative data provided in original test manuals.

We have not included chapters on the value of structural or functional neuroimaging technologies, specialized neurophysiology, or nocturnal polysomnography for differential diagnosis by the neuropsychologist. We strongly believe, however, that such recent technological advances (e.g., in functional magnetic resonance imaging) will increasingly become integral components of clinical practice and that it is critically important for neuropsychologists in acute-care settings to become active in the clinical and research applications of these diagnostic aids. We have also refrained from including chapters on the pharmacological management of patients who are treated for neuropsychological syndromes (often with psychiatric comorbidity), although we expect that such information will become increasingly important for neuropsychological practice in future years.

It is our hope that this handbook will be of interest to anyone seeking specialty training in psychiatry and neurology, as well as neuropsychology. It is intended for use by students and clinicians with a strong background in neuropathology, including a familiarity with neuroanatomy and neurophysiology. Additionally, we assume that the readers of this book will have had formal training in clinical psychology, especially in the area of psychopathology, as well as in test theory, design, and measurement. As Lezak noted in her comprehensive text, "Even to know what constitutes a neuropsychologically adequate review of the patient's mental status requires a broad understanding of brain function and its neuroanatomical principles" (1995, p. 102). We could not agree with her more!

REFERENCE

Lezak, M. D. (1995). *Neuropsychological assessment* (3rd ed.). New York: Oxford University Press.

Astasia-abasia. An unusual lurching gait of psychogenic ataxia.

Hand–face drop test. Used in patients with coma who appear flaccid; if the hand is held over the face and dropped, the patient in psychogenic coma often avoids letting the hand hit the face with subtle motor movements to the side.

Splitting the tuning fork. Patients with psychogenic sensory disturbance beginning at the midline face have a very sharply demarcated loss of sensation to the midface and may also complain of lack of vibratory sensation on the affected side of the forehead, with intact vibratory sensation on the unaffected side of the forehead.

IV. SENSORY EXAMINATION

Like the rest of the neurological examination, the sensory examination is an organized assessment of neuroanatomic structures and systems. It is reserved for last because findings related to cognition and higher cortical functions will color its interpretation. Besides testing the integrity of the peripheral nervous system and spinal cord tracts, tests involving light touch and pinprick may be used to assess the presence of a cortical lesion, such as the test for extinction in parietal lobe lesions (neglect of sensory stimuli contralateral to a parietal lobe lesion when bilateral stimuli are presented). The sensory examination is usually documented simply as a response to five modalities: pinprick, light touch, vibration, position, and temperature. The tools used for these tests consist of a safety pin or other sharp object, a cotton swab, a 128-Hz tuning fork, an ice bag or metal object such as a tuning fork placed over a cooling vent, and calipers, which may be used to test two-point discrimination.

A. Temperature and Pinprick

Perception of sharp versus dull and hot versus cold objects requires integrity of unmyelinated peripheral nerves (which originate as bipolar neurons in the dorsal root ganglia), the spinothalamic tracts of the spinal cord and brain stem, the ventral posterolateral and ventral posteromedial thalami, and thalamic projections to the parietal lobes. Sensation of light touch is transmitted similarly, but it is also likely to be transmitted through the posterior columns. Sensory loss to light touch and pinprick may occur in the distribution of a single nerve, nerve will become increasingly important for neuropsychological practice in future years.

It is our hope that this handbook will be of interest to anyone seeking specialty training in psychiatry and neurology, as well as neuropsychology. It is intended for use by students and clinicians with a strong background in neuropathology, including a familiarity with neuroanatomy and neurophysiology. Additionally, we assume that the readers of this book will have had formal training in clinical psychology, especially in the area of psychopathology, as well as in test theory, design, and measurement. As Lezak noted in her comprehensive text, "Even to know what constitutes a neuropsychologically adequate review of the patient's mental status requires a broad understanding of brain function and its neuroanatomical principles" (1995, p. 102). We could not agree with her more!

REFERENCE

Lezak, M. D. (1995). *Neuropsychological assessment* (3rd ed.). New York: Oxford University Press.

PART I

CLINICAL NEUROPSYCHOLOGY: GENERAL ISSUES

CHAPTER 1

Peter J. Snyder and Nicole A. Ceravolo

The Medical Chart: Efficient Information-Gathering Strategies and Proper Chart Noting

A patient's hospital medical chart serves several critical purposes. First, it is a vehicle of communication among all health care providers, serving to document and coordinate, in a systematic and integrated manner, all care administered to an individual patient. Without this vehicle of communication, the multidisciplinary approach to patient care in a hospital setting would be impossible. Second, the medical chart is a repository of accurate information concerning an individual patient's medical history and his or her response to various clinical interventions (pharmacological, surgical, psychological, rehabilitative, and so on). Finally, the medical chart serves as the storehouse of raw data for any and all retrospective clinical research studies, hundreds of which take place every day at virtually any medical center. Despite the critical importance that the medical chart plays in coordinating and documenting all facets of patient care, there are relatively few sources of information that describe the basics of proper chart review and chart noting for neuropsychologists who practice in a hospital setting.

I. THE CHART REVIEW

Most neuropsychology interns, postdoctoral fellows, and attending medical staff, like other hospital-based health care specialists, have little time during the regular day for a leisurely read-through of several 4-in.-thick medical charts. Most have several patients to examine on any given day, in addition to special consults, outpatient appointments, administrative duties, teaching responsibilities, research projects, supervision appointments, clinical treatment team meetings, grand rounds and lectures, and perhaps a bit of lunch once in a while. There is a clear need to develop a routine that is comfortable and efficient and that will minimize the total amount of time necessary to read through any medical chart and at the same time maximizing the amount of pertinent information retrieved from the record.

Most experienced clinicians have developed their own step-by-step method for extracting pertinent information from a new chart quickly and efficiently, but like anything else, this takes time and practice. Following is an approach that works well for us, which we hope will be of help to graduate students and clinical interns who are beginning their professional lives in hospital settings.

A. Reading the Chart: 10 Steps

1. Receive or obtain a clear referral question. Referral questions such as "Is there any organicity?" are vague and meaningless. Because everything that is biologically based is also ultimately "organic" at some reductionistic level, the answer to this question is invariably "yes." Questions such as the following are appropriate: What are the major reasons for the present hospital admission? What are the primary symptoms? What differential diagnoses have been offered for ruling out thus far? Is the patient being referred for assistance in localizing a putative central nervous system (CNS) lesion, to determine if he or she is competent to make informed personal medical decisions, or to determine if there are any neuropsychological sequelae of a recent concussive head injury?

2. Determine the appropriateness of the referral. A referral request to make a differential diagnosis, between a progressive organic dementia and a dementia syndrome of depression would be highly appropriate. A request to predict accurately the extent of neuropsychological recovery after a recently sustained moderate concussive head injury, in a patient with long-standing alcoholism and other potential complicating factors, would be inappropriate.

3. Make an imprint of the patient's hospital identification card on an index card. Check to make sure the imprint is legible and contains all basic identification and billing information (name, age, date of birth, referral source or attending physician, medical records or other hospital identification number, insurance carrier, insurance policy number).

4. Read through the admission history and physical examination report. This will be found at the front of the section labeled Progress Notes. Determine how the patient arrived at the hospital (elective admission or emergency transport by ambulance) and when he or she arrived. What were the presenting complaints listed by the patient or family? If the patient arrived by way of the hospital emergency department, look for the ambulance and emergency room records. What was the patient's Glasgow Scale score at the time that the emergency medical technicians (EMT) arrived at the accident scene, and what was the score on admission to the hospital? Are there any descriptions available about the onset and course of the illness, or about events that transpired during an accident, from family members, friends, or bystanders? Carefully read through the entire section of intake notes, the summary of background information and past medical history, and the initial diagnostic impressions offered in the initial History and Physical Examination (H&P).

5. Read through the initial few entries in the section labeled Nursing Progress Notes. These notes are useful because they may provide a fairly detailed description of the patient's behavior on admission, level of cooperation with hospital staff, and arousability and alertness, as well as of any socially inappropriate or potentially hazardous behaviors.

6. Review all prior consultation reports from the medicine, neurology, radiology, neurosurgery, and psychiatry services. Recent consultation reports are likely to be found at the very front of the chart, with older (perhaps by a day or more) reports moved to the proper section within the chart. In chapter 2, this volume, Scott provides an excellent review of the organization and writing of standard neurological consultation and progress notes.

7. Look through the laboratory data section for any abnormally high or low critical blood or urine test values, liver function tests, as well as for positive results of drug screen tests. In chapter 3, McConnell provides an excellent review of how such important laboratory studies should be read and interpreted by the neuropsychologist.

8. Look for the section that is usually mislabeled X-Ray to locate reports pertaining to relevant neuroimaging studies: computed tomography (CT), magnetic resonance imaging (MRI), single photon emission computed tomography (SPECT), position emission tomography, and cerebral angiography. Those who have been trained to read any of these types of imaging studies and have a special clinical or research interest can certainly read them. Also, read any available EEG or neurosurgical reports available in the chart.

9. Look through the physician's orders to determine current medications and dosages as well as whether the patient recently has been taken off or started on a medication that might have a negative impact on neuropsychological functioning.

10. Review the most recent progress notes (those written within the past 48 hours), and determine whether there have been any recent changes in mental status, worsening or improvement of target symptoms, or changes in psychological functioning.

B. Sources of Confusion

There are two major unintentional forms of data encryption to be aware of so that the notes may be deciphered correctly. First, many important chart notes are illegibly written. As discussed previously, the medical chart is an archival record that is critically important for the coordination of efforts among hospital staff to provide proper patient care. Everyone has a responsibility to convey data, diagnoses, recommendations, and treatment plans legibly enough so that others can read their notes.

The second source of potential confusion is the seemingly limitless list of medical abbreviations and acronyms in current use. The appendix at the back of this text provides a listing of the more common abbreviations, but most hospitals publish their own lists of abbreviations that are approved for use in medical charting at that institution. If such a list is available, obtain a copy and familiarize yourself with it. For instance, is the abbreviation LOC used at your hospital as shorthand for "loss of consciousness" or "level of consciousness"?

II. THE PROGRESS NOTE

A. Who Should Write One, When, and Why?

Any persons who are either on the medical staff or otherwise employed by the hospital and who have direct care responsibilities for particular patients (whether purely consultative or treatment oriented) should write a progress note in the medical chart every time they examine or administer care to those patients. The only exception is made for nursing staff, who may enter and leave a patient's room dozens of times each day and who have their own guidelines and procedures to follow with regard to documentation in medical charts. For the most part, it is considered unethical and, in most states, illegal for a health care provider to evaluate or administer care to a patient without leaving a written record in the chart. This rule applies to students as well (e.g., clinical neuropsychology interns), although their notes must be cosigned and approved by a supervising licensed psychologist who has medical staff privileges at the hospital. In fact, this rule also applies to (bachelor's or master's degree level) psychometrists, who must also have their notes and clinical contacts supervised by an attending psychologist.

Why is this rule so important, as it pertains to neuropsychology? Although neuropsychologists often provide consultative or treatment services across many hospital units (e.g., pediatrics, oncology, pain medicine), a majority of our patients present with a wide range of neurological trauma or illness. The prevalence rate of psychiatric comorbidity in this population is quite high, for obvious reasons, and it is this population that may enter the hospital with an increased risk for self-harm, aggressive or violent behavior, delirium, paranoid ideation, poor judgment, executive dyscontrol, and so on. Hence, these patients are at risk of posing a threat to themselves or others for a wide variety of reasons. It is important for every clinician, therapist, or psychometrist to be trained to assess the following important variables each time they visit a patient at bedside:

- Risk of self-harm
- Risk of harm to others (staff or patients)
- Level of arousal
- Any marked change in condition or mental status since last observation by clinician

- Level of cooperation during examination or treatment
- Occurrence of any unusual events during patient contact (e.g., seizure)
- Mood and affect

Does this mean that a patient should be asked if he or she has suicidal thoughts every single time that a staff member enters the room? Of course not! To suggest that patients should be asked if they have such thoughts 50 times in one day would be absurd. Rather, such an assessment should be made by qualified personnel soon after admission, and if any suicidal ideation is present, regular monitoring for increased or decreased frequency of such thoughts, the presence of a plan, and the possibility of immediate intent should be documented. If the last person to see a patient failed to document that the patient appeared to be more agitated and emotionally labile and that he expressed a clear intent for self-harm (and failed to take appropriate steps to ensure patient safety), and if the patient proceeded to injure himself, that practitioner would be open to a legitimate malpractice claim or to other disciplinary action by the hospital or state regulatory agency.

B. What Should Be Written in a Progress Note?

1. Any brief progress note left by a psychometrist should contain clear statements of the following:
   a. Whether the patient was or was not seen for an examination
   b. Level of arousal and orientation (to time, place, person)
   c. Level of cooperation
   d. Rough assessment of mood (angry, sad, inappropriately happy) and affect (flat or blunted, depressed, normal range, jubilant)
   e. Whether emotional tone was appropriate for testing situation
   f. Evidence of any possible delusional or hallucinatory behaviors
   g. Threats of harm to self or others offered spontaneously by the patient
   h. Unusual events or behaviors (described in detail, avoiding any tendency to "diagnose")

       i. Whether or not further neuropsychological assessment is to follow

       j. The name and pager number for the attending neuropsychologist

Chart notes written by a psychometrist should be read and cosigned by the attending neuropsychologist within 24 hours.

2. In addition to the points listed, any progress note left by a neuropsychology intern, postdoctoral fellow, or attending neuropsychologist should contain brief statements that address the following:

    a. Assessment of mental status

    b. Resolution of or increase in severity of target symptoms

    c. Continued monitoring for possible harm to self or others (when appropriate)

    d. Formal assessment of mood and affect

    e. Preliminary feedback on results of examination, if possible, with direct supervision of attending neuropsychologist

3. The following are important in preparing any progress note:

    a. Clearly state the purpose of your contact with the patient.

    b. Be exact in noting date, time, and observations (see preceding lists).

    c. Describe precisely what you saw, felt, or heard—this is the wrong place for mere surmise.

    d. Document any refusal of participation or treatment.

III. ADDITIONAL IMPORTANT ISSUES

Never make any attempt to alter or falsify or otherwise alter any portion of the medical record, including previous notes of your own. Once a note is written, it immediately becomes part of that patient's archival medical record, and it is technically the property of the patient. It is illegal and unethical to make any substantive changes in previous records, even if they were written only minutes ago!

Second, never leave undated or intentionally backdated chart entries. Such a practice would immediately raise the eyebrow of an attorney searching for a reason to suspect an attempt to alter the record to hide errors or negligence.

If you do make an error while writing (e.g., misspellings, incorrect drug names), do not simply scratch out the error or use "white-out" correctional fluid. The proper procedure to correct any such error is to cross out the error, print the word *error* above or next to this, and sign your initials in the same place.

Always strive to leave a progress note immediately after your contact with the patient. Most hospitals have well-delineated regulations regarding the length of time permissible between a patient contact and the entry of a progress note (e.g., a 12-hour limit). Other types of chart entries may have different time limits for when they must be written (e.g., 24-hour admission notes, 48-hour surgical procedure summaries).

Finally, always remember that the ability to read and write in a patient's chart is a privilege as well as a great responsibility. Confidentiality should always be maintained, in accordance with the strict ethical guidelines subscribed to by psychologists.

CHAPTER 2
Thomas F. Scott

The Neurological Examination

The purpose of this chapter is to acquaint the reader with the elements of a standard neurological examination and their documentation, so that the reader will be able to understand the examination as it is typically documented in patients' charts. The neurological examination is primarily a bedside tool that allows clinicians to localize lesions in the nervous system. Usually it is a combination of multiple findings on the examination that allows this localization, even with single lesions. If the results suggest multiple lesions, the implications of each lesion must be considered both individually and in combinations, and evidence of systemic disease (disease involving more than one organ system) must be taken into account. Thus, the neurological examination must be incorporated into the context of the patient's overall health history and general physical condition.

A standard neurological examination begins with a brief assessment of mental status, followed by testing of cranial nerve function, motor skills, deep tendon reflexes, sensory modalities, and pathological reflexes (generally presented in that order in documentation). In some clinical situations the examination may be abbreviated; in other situations, portions of the examination may be expanded to address a specific complaint.

I.   MENTAL STATUS EXAMINATION

The mental status examination is performed and documented as the first part of the neurological examination because it colors the remainder of the testing in terms of reliability. Patients with abnormal affect, for example, may be more likely to show signs of functional (somatoform) illness, and demented or encephalopathic patients may not be able to cooperate fully with the examination. Unfortunately, owing to time constraints the reporting of a patient's mental status is often abbreviated, sometimes reduced to a single phrase such as "patient alert and a good historian." Such limited documentation may make changes in mental status difficult to assess during the course of a hospitalization. Ideally, the record also reflects the patient's baseline mental functioning prior to hospitalization.

Level of alertness is noted first as either alert, drowsy, stuporous (tending to drift into sleep during testing or arousable only for brief periods), or comatose (with or without spontaneous or purposeful movements). An assigned number on a coma scale is no substitute for a precise description. Next, a comment concerning affect should be made, perhaps in the context of the patient's general behavior and insight during the interview and examination. Orientation is checked in four "spheres": person (self and others), place, time, and purpose. The remainder of the mental status examination varies greatly among clinicians, but several of the following tests are usually performed at the bedside routinely: naming presidents, "serial sevens," registration and memory of three objects at 5 minutes, digit span forward and backward, interpretation of proverbs and similarities, complex figure drawing, spelling "world" forward and backward, and naming five cities. A standardized mental status examination such as the Folstein Mini-Mental State Examination (MMSE) is occasionally used by the neurologist. Determination of probable moderate-to-severe dementia is often made with only a brief neurological examination employing these maneuvers.

More specific bedside testing of higher cortical functions is often added to the mental status examination in patients with evidence of focal lesions. Delineation of aphasias may involve detailed testing but is usually limited to gross observation of speech output, conduction (ability to repeat), and comprehension. Bedside testing should include object naming, awareness of right–left, and testing for visual and sensory neglect (especially important in parietal and thalamic lesions).

II.   CRANIAL NERVE EXAMINATION

An abnormality on cranial nerve examination could relate to one or more lesions in the cortex, deep gray matter (thalamus, for example), or brain stem (including nuclei), or along the course of a cranial nerve through soft and bony tissues. Certain patterns of cranial nerve dysfunction allow clinicians to localize lesions to these areas, and many such patterns are considered to be "classic" findings related to specific anatomic substrates. It is often necessary to combine a cranial nerve finding with other neurological deficits to localize a lesion precisely (see Figure 1).

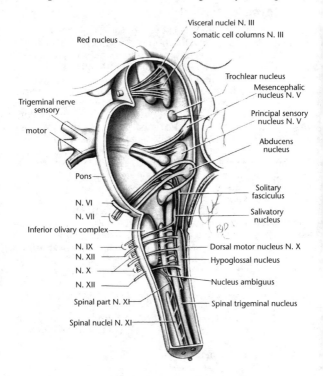

Figure 1. Brain stem and cranial nerves.

A. Cranial Nerve I

Although the first cranial nerve is often omitted as part of the routine examination, a deficit of smell is often an important clue to a diagnosis. Lesions of the olfactory groove (classically, meningiomas) may present with both psychiatric symptoms related to frontal lobe injury and loss of smell owing to compression of the olfactory nerves. Loss of smell is also common after head trauma, owing to shearing of the branches of the olfactory nerves as they pass through the cribriform plate.

B. Cranial Nerve II

Visual disturbances are listed as part of the cranial nerve examination regardless of the location of the lesion. A visual field disturbance related to hemispheric injury, for example, such as a homonymous hemianopsia, would be noted. Lesions limited to the optic nerve produce monocular visual disturbance. Precise visual acuity is rarely recorded. In patients with near blindness, the distance at which the patient can count fingers is sometimes noted. A funduscopic examination is routinely done and reported as negative if the retina, retinal vessels, and optic discs are free of lesions. Papilledema is a classic finding of increased intracranial pressure owing to tumor, hydrocephalus, or other causes. Visual field neglect, seen frequently contralateral to parietal lesions, is usually noted as part of the mental status examination or under the topic of "higher cortical functions."

When they are intact, many optic nerve functions are summarized by the abbreviation PERRLA (pupils equal, round, and reactive to light and accommodation). The swinging flashlight test may reveal a consensual response despite a relatively poor direct response ipsilaterally, owing to an optic nerve lesion (Marcus-Gunn pupil).

Some classic findings that may be listed under cranial nerve II in the report of the neurological examination are as follows:

1. **The visual field defect homonymous hemianopsia:** large hemispheric lesion or lesion of lateral jenicula ganglion.
2. **Bitemporal hemianopsia:** lesion of the pituitary area compressing the chiasm.
3. **Central scotomat:** lesions of the optic nerve, seen classically with optic neuritis.

4. **Superior quadrantanopsia:** contralateral temporal lobe lesion.
5. **Hollenhorst plaque:** bright-appearing cholesterol or atheromatous emboli seen on funduscopic examination of the retinal vessels, implying an embolic process.

C. Cranial Nerves III, IV, and V

Cranial nerves that control eye movements are usually largely noted by the abbreviation EOMI (extraocular muscles intact). Palsies of these nerves may be localized to specific nerves or muscles by the experienced examiner, who sometimes uses a red glass lens at bedside. Cranial nerve III and sympathetic fibers are responsible for eye opening, so that a ptosis, with or without Horner's syndrome, is recorded as part of the extraocular muscle test (although the pupil abnormalities associated with these syndromes may be recorded with the visual examination). A classic finding of ocular motility referred to as an **internuclear ophthalmoplegia** (INO) is seen with lacunar infarcts of the medial longitudinal fasciculus (MLF) or with multiple sclerosis plaques in the MLF. Ipsilateral adduction is lost.

D. Cranial Nerve VI

Facial sensation is tested to light touch, pinprick, and temperature. If an abnormality respects only one or two divisions of V1–V3, this is recorded; it implies a lesion distal to the gasserian ganglion. Distinct splitting of sensory function at the midline face is unusual and may imply a functional disorder. Vibration is not tested, but an examiner may look for splitting of vibratory sensation across the forehead or skull as further evidence of a functional component to a patient's clinical presentation.

E. Cranial Nerve VII

Seventh nerve lesions are referred to as either peripheral or central. In central lesions, located caudal to the seventh nerve nucleus and contralateral to the resulting facial droop, the upper face (periorbital and forehead) is relatively spared. The palpebral fissure may be slightly larger ipsilateral to the face droop. In peripheral lesions weakness is ipsilateral to the lesion of the seventh nucleus or nerve. Other brain-stem signs are seen when the lesion involves the nerve nucleus, and the term **Bell's palsy** is most often reserved for lesions of the nerve distal to the nucleus. Eye closure may be lost in severe cases of peripheral seventh nerve lesions. Hyperacusis is due to loss of seventh nerve influence on the stapes.

F. Cranial Nerve VIII

The eighth nerve consists of an auditory component and a vestibular component. Deafness rarely results from cortical lesions; more often, there is difficulty with sound localization. Common bedside testing involves comparison for gross symmetry with a high-pitched tuning fork or finger rubbing near the ear, and the Weber and Rinne tests (for air conduction compared to bone conduction of sound). Lesions of the vestibular nuclei and of the vestibular portion of the eighth nerve both produce vertigo, nausea, vomiting, and nystagmus.

G. Cranial Nerves IX and X

The examiner records symmetry of palatal elevation and gag reflex, both of which are subserved by these cranial nerves. Hoarseness and dysphagia may be seen with unilateral or bilateral injury to cranial nerve X (vagus); however, lesions of cranial nerve IX may be undetectable clinically.

H. Cranial Nerve XI

Strength of the sternocleidomastoid and trapezius muscles is tested with resistance to head turning and shoulder shrug. The loss of strength is often greater with nuclear or peripheral lesions as opposed to supranuclear injury.

I. Cranial Nerve XII

A unilateral weak tongue deviates toward the side of weakness (and toward the side of the lesion in nuclear or peripheral injury but opposite the side of supranuclear lesions). Nuclear and peripheral lesions are associated with atrophy when chronic.

III. MOTOR SYSTEM EXAMINATION

A. Tone and Power

Normal muscle tone refers to the slight tension present in muscles at rest. Tone may be increased in both pyramidal and extrapyramidal disturbances. Acute central nervous system lesions often produce hypotonia; this evolves over days to produce hypertonicity, referred to as spasticity, which is a velocity-dependent increase in tone, waxing and waning through range of motion. In opposition to these general rules, hypertonicity may be seen acutely in brain-stem lesions (decorticate, decerebrate posturing), and hypotonicity may remain chronically in neuromuscular disease.

Muscle power is manually tested at bedside, with individual muscle groups graded on a scale of 0–5 (0 = *no contraction*, 3 = *movement against gravity*, 5 = *normal*). The neurological history and examination can usually localize weakness to either muscle, the neuromuscular junction, lower motor neuron, or upper motor neuron (see Table 1). Proximal predominant weakness or atrophy when symmetrical usually suggests a myopathic condition. Flabby or flaccid weak muscles, often atrophic, are seen in lower motor neuron disorders and are associated with a decrease in deep tendon reflexes (e.g., peripheral neuropathy, spinal muscle atrophy). Upper motor neuron disorders are distinguished by spasticity, increased tone, and increased deep tendon reflexes.

Spasticity may be produced by lesions of the motor cortex, internal capsule, or pyramidal tract within the brain stem or spinal cord. The degree of spasticity may be influenced by the degree of extrapyramidal system involvement. In some neurological disorders, a mixture of upper motor neuron and lower motor neuron dysfunction evolves over time, producing seemingly conflicting upper motor neuron and lower motor neuron findings in the same patient (e.g., amyotrophic lateral sclerosis, vitamin B12 deficiency).

B. Coordination

Equilibrium refers to coordination and balance of the whole body, and when impaired, it is referred to as **truncal ataxia**. This is tested at bedside by observing sitting and standing balance and gait (classically "wide-based" in cases of mild-to-moderate ataxia). The examination is refined with testing of tandem walk (placing one heel directly in front of the opposite toes) and by testing for the Romberg sign, which may produce swaying and truncal movements (eyes are closed after the feet are placed together, arms down).

Limb ataxia (appendicular ataxia) may be present in a single extremity (usually an arm), but it is often seen in an ipsilateral arm and leg pattern, with the patient exhibiting a tendency

Table 1. Changes in Motor Function

Lesion or disorder	Loss of power	Tone	Atrophy	Fasciculations	Ataxia
Spinomuscular lesion					
a. Anterior horn cell	Focal	Flaccid	Present	Present	Absent
b. Nerve root, plexus, peripheral nerve	Focal or segmental	Flaccid	Present	Occasionally present	Absent
c. Neuromuscular junction	Diffuse	Usually normal	Usually normal	Absent	Absent
d. Muscle	Diffuse	Flaccid	Present but later than in a and b	Absent	Absent
Extrapyramidal lesion	None or mild	Rigid	Absent	Absent	Absent
Corticospinal tract lesion	Generalized, incomplete	Spastic	Absent	Absent	Absent
Cerebellar lesion	None; ataxia may stimulate loss of power	Hypotonic (ataxia)	Absent	Absent	Absent
Psychogenic disorder	Bizarre; no true loss of power; may stimulate any type	Normal or variable; often increased	Absent	Absent	Absent (may simulate ataxia)

(Continued)

Lesion or disorder	Reflexes	Abnormal movements	Pathological associated movements
Spinomuscular lesion a. Anterior horn cell	Decreased or absent	None except for fasciculations	Absent
b. Nerve root, plexus, peripheral nerve	Decreased or absent	None except for fasciculations	Absent
c. Neuromuscular junction	Usually normal	None	Absent
d. Muscle	Decreased	None	Absent
Extrapyramidal lesion	Muscle stretch reflexes normal or variable Superficial reflexes normal or slightly increased No corticospinal tract responses	Present	Absent
Corticospinal tract lesion	Muscle stretch reflexes hyperactive Superficial reflexes diminished to absent Corticospinal tract responses	None	Absent

Table 1. Changes in Motor Function *(Continued)*

Lesion or disorder	Reflexes	Abnormal movements	Pathological associated movements
Cerebellar lesion	Muscle stretch reflexes diminished or pendular Superficial reflexes normal No corticospinal tract responses	May be present (intention tremor and ataxia)	Absent
Psychogenic disorder	Muscle stretch reflexes normal or increased (range) Superficial reflexes normal or increased No corticospinal tract responses	May be present	Absent

to fall to that side. When combined with weakness, the term **ataxic hemiparesis** applies (classic for an internal capsule or pontine lacunar stroke when seen as a pure motor syndrome). Limb ataxia is demonstrated by testing finger-to-nose and heel-to-shin movements. Although limb ataxia may be seen in sensory disorders (pseudoathetosis), it is classic for lesions of the cerebellar system, producing intention tremor (see the following section) and disdiadochokinesia (impairment of rapid alternating movements). Limb ataxia in the absence of weakness implicates a lesion of the cerebellar hemispheres and its projections, whereas truncal ataxia in isolation implicates a lesion of midline cerebellar structures and their projections.

C. Abnormal Movements

1. TREMOR

a. **Essential or physiologic tremor** (usually 8–11 Hz) may be a normal finding demonstrated by having the examinee forcibly extend the arms and digits, although these terms may also be used to denote a pathological idiopathic high-frequency tremor, which is often familial. Essential tremor may be accentuated or attenuated by drugs and disease states. The term *tremulousness* generally refers to transient high-frequency tremor associated with acute illness or anxiety. In severe metabolic disturbances, tremor may coexist with other abnormal movements such as myoclonus (rapid and tense contractions of large muscle groups) and asterixis (intermittent lapses of tone interrupting voluntary movements).

b. **Intention tremor** refers to to-and-fro motions that increase in amplitude as the examinee approaches a target; it is usually demonstrated on finger-to-nose testing in patients with lesions of cerebellar hemispheres and their projections into the brain stem and ventral posterolateral thalami.

c. **Parkinsonian tremor** is usually at lower frequency than essential tremor and is often described as "pill-rolling." Unlike the "action" tremors previously described, tremor in Parkinson's disease is always present at rest (at least intermittently), is variably affected by changes in position, and is associated with stiffness (hence the term cogwheel rigidity) and bradykinesia.

2. BRADYKINESIA, DYSKINESIA, AND AKINESIA

a. **Bradykinesia** is a reduction of normal spontaneous or unconscious semipurposeful movements such as blinking, shifting movements, and facial expressions. Although it is classic for Parkinson's disease, bradykinesia is also seen in other neurodegenerative syndromes, the multistroke state, and depression.

b. **Akinetic mutism** is a condition of extreme lack of movement and interaction, verbal and nonverbal, seen in patients with brain-stem lesions or bilateral hemispheric or deep gray matter lesions. It is also seen in end-stage neurodegenerative disorders. **Catatonic mutism** is a similar condition, seen as a manifestation of severe psychiatric disturbance rather than of structural lesions, and it generally is associated with waxy flexibility or rigidity.

c. **Dyskinesia** is a nonspecific term for complex irregular involuntary movements involving multiple muscle groups. At present most patients with dyskinesia suffer from medication-induced side effects of neuroleptics and antiparkinsonian drugs containing L-dopa. **Tardive dyskinesia** refers to neuroleptic-induced choreoathetoid movements primarily of the face, head, shoulders, and upper trunk.

Rapid dyskinetic movements are often termed **choreiform**, and this term may accurately describe the involuntary movements of many patients with tardive dyskinesia as well as with Huntington's disease and Sydenham's chorea. Dystonic movements are slower and associated with increased tone or rigidity (e.g., dystonia musculorum deformans); they may be seen in Parkinson's disease as well as in acute reactions as to neuroleptics. Athetoid movements are intermittent in speed between chorea and dystonia and have a writhing or a more rhythmic quality or both.

3. MISCELLANEOUS ABNORMAL MOVEMENTS

a. **Ballismus** refer to flailing motions of an extremity, usually occurring after stroke involving the subthalamic nucleus.

b. **Tics** refer to rapid movements that are stereotyped and repetitive; these are classic for Tourette's syndrome but may also be seen in mental retardation.

c. **Akathisia**, which may be considered the opposite of bradykinesia, is an increase in the normal spontaneous movements seen in the waking state. Patients with akathisia are fidgety and often pace.

4. DEEP TENDON REFLEXES AND MISCELLANEOUS SIGNS

Deep tendon reflexes are listed by percussion over tendon insertions producing a rapid muscle stretch. These reflexes are mediated by reflex arcs originating in intramuscular organs, which are sensitive to stretching and transmit impulses to alpha motor neurons within the spinal cord producing a contraction of the percussed muscle. When deep tendon reflexes are increased or hyperactive, reflex spread occurs to other local muscles, and increased speed of reflexes and intensity of muscle contraction occurs. Deep tendon reflexes are generally graded on a 0–4+ (0, +, ++, +++, ++++) basis: 0 implies that reflexes are not elicited; "+" refers to reflexes being present only with Jendrassik's maneuver or other means of accentuating deep tendon reflexes; ++ implies a normal reflex; +++ designates reflexes that appear to be hyperactive but are not necessarily pathological; and ++++ refers to reflexes that are believed strongly to be pathological, or clonus.

a. **Babinski reflex.** Plantar stimulation with a blunt object may produce extension of the great toe and fanning of the other toes, which is believed to be a sign of upper motor neuron disease. Essentially, this sign is synonymous with **plantar response.** Other methods of eliciting an "upgoing toe" involve stimulation of the lateral foot (Chaddock's sign) or pinprick over the dorsum of the foot (Bing's sign).

b. **Cutaneous reflexes** consist of abdominal reflexes, elicited by stimulation of the skin over the four quadrants of the abdomen; cremasteric reflex, elicited by stimulation of the skin over the scrotal area; and anal wink.

c. **Hoffmann's sign** is a sign of hyperreflexia in the upper extremities, elicited by tapping distal digits in the hand and observing for abduction of the thumb.

d. **Frontal release signs** consist of the glabellar tap reflex, the snout reflex, the suck reflex, and the palmomental reflex. These signs indicate usually bilateral frontal lobe disease.

e. Some of the **more common signs of psychogenic neurological dysfunction** are as follows:

Hoover's sign. The examiner places one hand under each heel with the patient in the supine position. The patient is asked to raise one leg; the examiner should feel downward pressure on the opposite leg if voluntary effort is intact.

Astasia-abasia. An unusual lurching gait of psychogenic ataxia.

Hand–face drop test. Used in patients with coma who appear flaccid; if the hand is held over the face and dropped, the patient in psychogenic coma often avoids letting the hand hit the face with subtle motor movements to the side.

Splitting the tuning fork. Patients with psychogenic sensory disturbance beginning at the midline face have a very sharply demarcated loss of sensation to the midface and may also complain of lack of vibratory sensation on the affected side of the forehead, with intact vibratory sensation on the unaffected side of the forehead.

IV. SENSORY EXAMINATION

Like the rest of the neurological examination, the sensory examination is an organized assessment of neuroanatomic structures and systems. It is reserved for last because findings related to cognition and higher cortical functions will color its interpretation. Besides testing the integrity of the peripheral nervous system and spinal cord tracts, tests involving light touch and pinprick may be used to assess the presence of a cortical lesion, such as the test for extinction in parietal lobe lesions (neglect of sensory stimuli contralateral to a parietal lobe lesion when bilateral stimuli are presented). The sensory examination is usually documented simply as a response to five modalities: pinprick, light touch, vibration, position, and temperature. The tools used for these tests consist of a safety pin or other sharp object, a cotton swab, a 128-Hz tuning fork, an ice bag or metal object such as a tuning fork placed over a cooling vent, and calipers, which may be used to test two-point discrimination.

A. Temperature and Pinprick

Perception of sharp versus dull and hot versus cold objects requires integrity of unmyelinated peripheral nerves (which originate as bipolar neurons in the dorsal root ganglia), the spinothalamic tracts of the spinal cord and brain stem, the ventral posterolateral and ventral posteromedial thalami, and thalamic projections to the parietal lobes. Sensation of light touch is transmitted similarly, but it is also likely to be transmitted through the posterior columns. Sensory loss to light touch and pinprick may occur in the distribution of a single nerve, nerve root, plexus pattern, hemicord pattern, transverse cord pattern, or crossed brain-stem pattern, or it may occur somatotropically, corresponding to lesions above the brain stem (e.g., contralateral face-arm-leg). A lesion may be confidently localized to the brain stem when sensory loss occurs on one side of the face and contralateral body. A "stocking–glove" pattern is usually seen in patients with polyneuropathy, often owing to diabetes.

Perception of vibratory and position sense requires integrity of myelinated nerve fibers (originating as bipolar neurons in the dorsal root ganglion), the posterior columns, the medial lemniscus, the ventral posterolateral nucleus of the thalamus, and the cortex. Classically, lesions of the posterior columns are demonstrated by loss of vibratory and position sense out of proportion to loss of other modes (e.g., in vitamin B12 deficiency). Vibratory sensation is best tested with a 128-Hz tuning fork, and position sense is tested by employing small excursions of the distal digits.

B. Examples of Examinations

Following are two examples of the results of neurological examinations as they might appear in a hospital chart either in a typed, dictated form or in a handwritten form. Handwritten notes tend to be replete with commonly used abbreviations, which the neophyte will quickly become acquainted with.

1. EXAMINATION 1

The following represents a normal neurological examination (Figure 2 provides an abbreviated and diagrammatic summary of this examination): Patient is alert and oriented times four. Affect appropriate. Names presidents back to Carter easily, registers three out of three complex objects and recalls them at 5 minutes. Proverbs and serial sevens intact. Digit span six or seven numbers forward and backward.

Cranial nerves are intact (pupils equal, round, and reactive to light and accommodation; extraocular muscles intact; face, gag, and palate elevation symmetrical; facial sensation intact in all divisions of cranial nerve V), and fundi are benign. Strength is 5/5 with normal tone and bulk. No pronator drift. Finger-to-nose testing and fine finger movements normal. Gait testing including heel, toe, and tandem walk intact. Heel-to-shin intact.

Deep tendon reflexes are 2+ throughout and symmetrical with downgoing toes. No pathological reflexes.

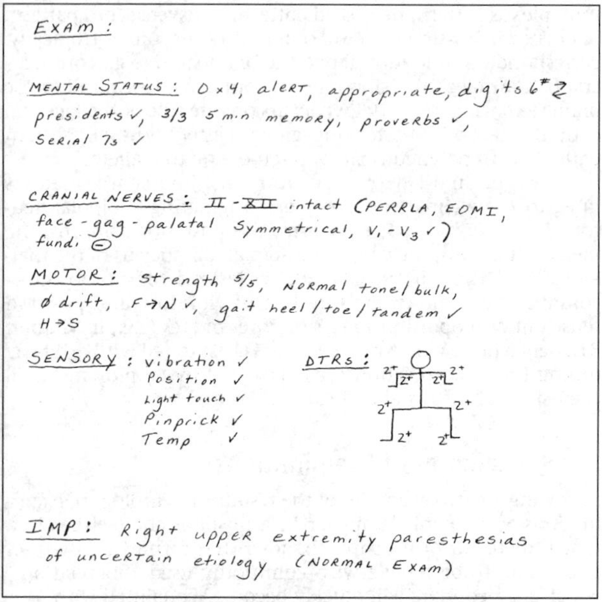

EXAM :

MENTAL STATUS : O x 4, alert, appropriate, digits 6# ↔
presidents ✓, 3/3 5 min memory, proverbs ✓,
serial 7s ✓

CRANIAL NERVES : II - XII intact (PERRLA, EOMI,
face - gag - palatal symmetrical, V₁ - V₃ ✓)
fundi ⊖

MOTOR : strength 5/5, normal tone/bulk,
∅ drift, F→N ✓, gait heel/toe/tandem ✓
H→S

SENSORY : vibration ✓   DTRs :
         Position ✓
         Light touch ✓
         Pinprick ✓
         Temp ✓

IMP : Right upper extremity paresthesias
of uncertain etiology (NORMAL EXAM)

Figure 2. Chart note for a normal neurological examination: $O \times 4$ denotes orientation in four spheres; digits 6# ← → denotes digit span; PERRLA denotes pupils, equal, round, and reactive to light and accommodation; EOMI denotes extraocular muscles intact; V_1–V_3 denotes intact fifth nerve; $\emptyset$ drift denotes no pronator drive; F→N denotes finger-to-nose testing; H→S denotes heel-to-shin testing; and stick figure denotes basic deep tendon reflexes, for example, 2^+ over the knee means that the knee is normal, whereas 1^+ means trace reflexes, and $\emptyset$ denotes loss of reflexes.

Sensory exam is intact to vibration, position, light touch, pinprick, and temperature.

2. EXAMINATION 2

The following neurological examination notes could be recorded in a patient with an acute right middle cerebral territory infarct and moderate idiopathic Parkinson's disease: *Mental Status Examination reveals the patient is slightly drowsy. Patient is oriented to place, year, and season but not to month, day of the week, or time of day. Patient does not know how long he has been in the hospital or the reason for hospitalization. Patient refuses to consider the possibility that he might have some left-sided weakness owing to stroke (anosognosia or denial). Patient seems to neglect visually the left field.*

Patient can name only one recent president. Patient knows his address and phone number but has trouble naming his four children. He is unable to register three complex objects. He is unable to perform simple calculations.

On cranial nerve examination, the patient has a left central seventh nerve palsy and some mild tongue deviation on tongue protrusion. Sensory examination of nerves VI through III is not reliable. Patient does not cross the midline with conjugate gaze. Gag intact. Patient is noted to have a snout and glabellar tap.

On motor examination, the patient has increased tone and cogwheel rigidity on the right, and he is flaccid on the left upper extremity. The left lower extremity is remarkable for trace proximal movements to command and proximal and distal withdrawal movements to deep pain. Bilateral Babinskis are present, and deep tendon reflexes are symmetrical and 2+. All sensory modalities are decreased on the left versus neglect on the left. Patient distinguishes different sensory modalities on the right, but reliability is questionable.

V. CONCLUSION

Students of neurology will find a lot of variability in the performance and documentation of the neurological examination as they rotate through ward services. Each physician lends his or her own style to the execution of the examination, although the standard elements of the examination remain. What constitutes an adequate neurological examination differs with the clinical situation. For instance, an internist caring for a patient with a gastrointestinal problem might limit the neurological examination to observance of speech and motor movements and might limit documentation to the phrase "neurologically intact." Of course, a neurology consultant will perform and document a more detailed examination.

Taken together with the history, the neurological examination allows localization of lesions in the nervous system. Localization is needed to formulate rationally a differential diagnosis of neurological disease.

BIBLIOGRAPHY

Adams, R. D., Victor, M. (1985). *Principles of neurology* (3rd ed.). New York: McGraw-Hill.

Carpenter, M. B. (1985). *Core text of neuroanatomy* (3rd ed.). Baltimore: Williams & Wilkins.

Haerer, A. F. (1992). *DeJong's the neurologic examination* (5th ed.). Philadelphia: Lippincott.

Mancall, E. (1981). *Alpers and Mancall's essentials of the neurologic examination* (2nd ed.). Philadelphia: Davis.

Rowland, L. P. (1995). *Merritt's textbook of neurology* (9th ed.). Baltimore: Williams & Wilkins.

CHAPTER 3
Harry W. McConnell

Laboratory Testing in Neuropsychology

This chapter focuses on the role of laboratory testing in assisting the neuropsychologist in the diagnosis and treatment monitoring of patients. Although in most institutions it is the psychiatrist or physician who routinely orders such testing, it is also important that the neuropsychologist be aware of and actively participate in the ordering of such tests, because their results may greatly affect the results of neuropsychological testing. The neuropsychologist may also have important input into the ordering of such tests as a result of insight gained from the neuropsychological examination. For example, the neuropsychologist examining a patient with epilepsy must be aware of the antiepileptic drugs (AEDs) that the patient is taking, because a number of AEDs are well-known to affect neuropsychological function. He or she must also be aware of the relevance of the AED blood levels and, possibly, relevant metabolites (e.g., 10,11-epoxide levels in patients taking carbamazepine), because AED toxicity can greatly influence the results of neuropsychological testing. Conversely, the results of cognitive impairment found on testing may be compatible with a pattern seen in AED toxicity and may thus be a reason to check laboratory parameters.

I discuss, first, the general use of some tests and then look at their use in specific psychiatric presentations. Although much of this information may be considered more relevant to the treating psychiatrist than the neuropsychologist, the neuropsychologist, as an active member of the treatment team concerned with the mental status of the patient, should be aware of any factors that may influence the mental state, including not only psychological parameters but also laboratory indices.

I.   BLOOD TESTS

A. Hematologic Tests

The main tests to be looked at with respect to neuropsychology are the complete blood count (CBC) and erythrocyte sedimentation rate (ESR). The CBC consists of the red blood cell (RBC), white blood cell (WBC), and platelet counts, as well as the WBC differential (which has to be ordered separately in many laboratories) and the hemoglobin (Hb), hematocrit (Hct), RBC indices (e.g., mean corpusculor volume, MCV; see Table 1), and peripheral blood smear. These tests are useful for (a) detection of anemia, polycythemia, infection, or an inflammatory state that might present with an alteration of mental state and (b) monitoring of possible toxic effects of medications (e.g., carbamazepine, clozapine), which can cause bone marrow toxicity and thus may affect these indices. Other hematologic tests of use in neuropsychology include tests for folate and vitamin B12 (deficiency of which may cause marked mental state changes even in the absence of anemia) and of ferritin and total iron-binding capacity (TIBC), which are all of use in the routine evaluation of anemia. Coagulation tests are useful in evaluating liver disease and in monitoring anticoagulation therapy. These tests are outlined in Table 1.

B. Endocrinologic Tests

Disturbances of endocrine function may present with virtually any type of mental state change. Table 2 summarizes the main endocrinologic tests used in evaluating mental state changes. The most important of these is the testing of thyroid status, which should be done in every patient presenting with psychiatric illness for the first time, because thyroid disorder is an important and common reversible cause of psychiatric illness, presenting as depression, psychosis, dementia, or essentially any change in mental state.

Table 1. Hematological Tests of Relevance in Neuropsychology

Test	Comments
White blood cell (WBC) count and differential	Important for evaluating the possibility of (a) infectious diseases, (b) leukemia, and (c) leukopenia from certain psychotropic medications. The WBC differential test is important for evaluating any abnormality of the WBC count, characterizing the individual components of the WBC count.
Red blood cell (RBC) count	Important for evaluating anemia and polycythemia.
Hemoglobin (Hb)	Important for evaluating anemia.
Hematocrit (Hct)	Important for screening, follow-up, and evaluation of anemia and polycythemia.
Mean corpuscular volume (MCV)	Average volume of a RBC; useful in establishing whether an anemia is macrocytic (i.e., increased, such as in alcoholism, folate or B12 deficiency) or microcytic (i.e., decreased, such as in iron deficiency anemia).
Mean corpuscular hemoglobin concentration (MCHC)	Concentration measured in grams per liter of hemoglobin; similar in use to mean corpuscular hemoglobin (MCH) in evaluating anemia.

(Continued)

Table 1. Hematological Tests of Relevance in Neuropsychology *(Continued)*

Test	Comments
Red cell distribution width (RDW)	Used in evaluating whether an anemia is a combination of microcytic and macrocytic anemias.
Peripheral blood smear	Characterizes abnormal RBCs, platelets, and WBCs such as the atypical lymphocytes seen in mononucleosis, the hypersegmented neutrophils seen in folate and B12 deficiency, and abnormal RBCs such as in sickle cell disease.
Reticulocyte count	Gives an indication of RBC production and, hence, of bone marrow activity; increased in anemias secondary to blood loss or hemolysis; decreased in anemias secondary to impairment of RBC maturation (e.g., folate, B12, or iron deficiency anemias prior to treatment).
Platelets	May be decreased owing to drugs (e.g., valproate, clozapine, phenothiazines) or to medical illness, either on its own or along with other cell lines (pancytopenia).
Erythrocyte sedimentation rate (ESR)	Nonspecific index of inflammation; elevated in infectious, neoplastic, and inflammatory (e.g., vasculitis, systemic lupus erythematosus) illness.
Coagulation tests	May be elevated in liver disease of many causes; prothrombin time (PT) used to monitor warfarin therapy; partial thromboplastin time (PTT) and activated partial thromboplastin time (APTT) used to monitor heparin therapy.

Folate and vitamin B12 levels	Serum levels of folate and B12 used to screen for deficiency of these important vitamins; deficiency may present with or without concomitant anemia with a variety of mental state changes or neurological sequelae; deficiency may be due to impaired absorption, deficient intake, or medication effects (e.g., antiepileptic drugs); the Schilling test and serum intrinsic factor are useful in evaluating B12 deficiency caused by pernicious anemia; it is important to monitor both B12 and folate because treatment with folate alone may reverse hematological abnormalities (macrocytic anemia) without reversal of neurological deficits; RBC folate is more indicative of overall status than serum levels.
Serum iron (Fe)	Used to evaluate iron deficiency anemia along with total iron-binding capacity (TIBC) and ferritin levels.

Table 2. Endocrinologic Tests of Use in Neuropsychology

Test	Comments
Thyroid function tests	Thyroid-stimulating hormone (TSH) is best screening test; serum triiodothyronine (T3), thyroxine (T4), reverse T3, T3 resin uptake (T3RU), free T4, free thyroxine index (FTI), and antithyroglobulin antibodies and microsomal antibodies are also useful in the evaluation of thyroid illness. Both hypothyroidism and hyperthyroidism may present with psychiatric illness including depression, hypomania, cognitive changes, personality changes, anxiety, delirium, and psychosis. Improvement in mental state often lags behind improvement in biochemical parameters; thyroid testing should also be done to evaluate possible medication-induced thyroid disease (e.g., carbamazepine, lithium).
Thyrotropin-releasing hormone stimulation test	Has been suggested by some as useful in the evaluation of "subclinical" hypothyroidism or in patients with depression.
Plasma cortisol level	Useful in assessment of adrenal function, especially in evaluation of Addison's disease (low cortisol) and Cushing's disease (high cortisol), both of which frequently present with mental status changes.
Dexamethasone supression test (DST)	Measurement of serum cortisol checked at specific times prior to and after the administration of 1 mg of dexamethasone, thought by some to be a biological marker for depression; a normal response, however, does not rule out the possibility of depression, and an abnormal response must similarly be interpreted in the clinical context; may be useful in some ambiguous situations.

Prolactin level	Useful in evaluating patients on antipsychotics with galactorrhea or to evaluate compliance because antipsychotics characteristically increase prolactin; may be of limited use in evaluating nonepileptic seizure-like events (NESLEs) if psychotropics are controlled for and if sample is obtained within 20 minutes of a suspected seizure; a normal value, however, should not be interpreted as representing a NESLE, because there may not be a rise in levels in seizures related to epilepsy. A clear rise in baseline within 20 minutes of a seizure is useful as an indication of suggestion of epilepsy.
Plasma catecholamine levels	Plasma epinephrine and norepinephrine levels are useful in evaluating pheochromocytoma, which may present with paroxysmal anxiety or other mental state changes.
Osmolality, vasopressin level	May be useful in evaluating hyponatremia, which may be secondary to psychogenic polydipsia or to the syndrome of inappropriate secretion of antidiuretic hormone (SIADH), often caused by illness, surgery, or psychotropic medication.
Parathyroid hormone level	Useful in evaluating mental state changes related to hypo- or hypercalcemia or related to changes in phosphorous levels; sometimes occurs after thyroid surgery.
Insulin and C-peptide levels	Useful in the evaluation of paroxysmal hypoglycemia to rule out insulinoma, a rare tumor that may present with paroxysmal anxiety or other mental state changes.

Table 3. Biochemical and Immunologic Evaluation Relevant to Neuropsychology

Test	Comments
Electrolytes	Sodium (Na^+), potassium (K^+), chloride (Cl^-), and bicarbonate (HCO_3^-) are useful screening tests in psychiatric illness and should also be monitored in patients on psychotropics (especially carbamazepine and antidepressants), which may cause hyponatremia; hyponatremia is also seen in various medical illnesses and in SIADH and psychogenic polydipsia; hypokalemia is common in people with bulimia and anorexia related to laxative and diuretic abuse and to bingeing, in which elevations in bicarbonate and decreased chloride may also be seen.
Liver function tests	Useful screening test in psychiatric patients; also should be monitored in patients on psychotropics (especially antiepileptic drugs); includes alanine aminotransferase (ALT), aspartate aminotransferase (AST), alkaline phosphatase (AP), gamma-glutamyl transaminase (GGT), and lactate dehydrogenase (LDH), which has five isoenzymes and may be elevated in other medical conditions as well; GGT is the most sensitive of these; bilirubin (total, direct, and indirect) is useful in evaluation of hepatobiliary disease and hemolytic anemia and is ordered separately in some laboratories.
Renal function tests	Blood urea nitrogen (BUN) and creatinine are elevated in renal failure; should be monitored in patients on lithium and amantadine; electrolytes also frequently abnormal in renal failure, especially hyperkalemia; BUN also elevated in dehydration.

Amylase and lipase levels	Used to evaluate pancreatitis and pancreatic carcinoma; should be screened in patients on valproate with any gastrointestinal symptoms; because amylase is also elevated in disease of the salivary glands, it is helpful to monitor serum lipase levels as well, which are more specific to pancreatic abnormalities; amylase levels are also elevated in patients with bulimia and may be used in this population to monitor compliance concerning binge behaviors.
Glucose level	Important in evaluating the possibility of diabetes mellitus or hypoglycemia, which has many causes and may present with a variety of intermittent mental state changes, including delirium and psychosis.
Creatinine phosphokinase (CPK) level	Useful in evaluating possible neuroleptic malignant syndrome (NMS), a severe toxic reaction to antipsychotic medications; also elevated in acute muscle injury, after exercise or intramuscular injections and from muscle disease of many etiologies; CPK isoenzyme MM is used to evaluate skeletal muscle elevations, and the MB fraction is used to evaluate patients with suspected myocardial infarction.
Copper and ceruloplasmin levels	Used to diagnose and evaluate Wilson's disease, an inherited alteration in copper metabolism that presents with personality changes, altered cognition, affective symptoms, or psychosis associated with a movement disorder, usually in adolescents and young adults.

(Continued)

Table 3. Biochemical and Immunologic Evaluation Relevant to Neuropsychology *(Continued)*

Test	Comments
Porphyrins	Porphobilinogen (PBG), aminolevulinic acid (ALA), and other porphyrins and metabolites are used to diagnose porphyria, an inherited metabolic disorder that can present with intermittent psychosis, seizures, and other neuropsychiatric manifestations.
Lupus erythematosus (LE) prep	Used along with other tests, including antinuclear antibodies (ANA), anti-DNA antibodies, lupus anticoagulant, and complement levels in the diagnosis of systemic lupus erythematosus (SLE), which may present with depression, delirium, psychosis, or dementia; phenothiazines, among other drugs, may cause false positive results.
RBC transketolase level	Test for the diagnosis of Wernicke's encephalopathy (WE); WE is a medical emergency, commonly occurring in alcoholics (but also in other groups) deficient in thiamine; usually presenting with mental status changes; sometimes associated with ophthalmoplegia, ataxia, or both; because transketolase and thiamine levels take days or weeks to obtain, WE should be diagnosed and treated on clinical grounds in the emergency room, with the tests as confirmatory; glucose should not be given until parenteral thiamine and other B vitamins have been administered.
Rapid plasma reagin test (RPR)	Screening test for syphilis; also used is the venereal disease research laboratories (VDRL) test for screening; important screening test because neurosyphilis presents with many neurological and psychiatric symptoms.

Human immunodeficiency virus (HIV) antibody testing	Screening test for HIV infection, which has been termed the "great masquerader" because it can cause so many different neurological and psychiatric symptoms and thus mimic many syndromes; pre- and posttest counseling must be given to the individual, and consent must be obtained.
Toxicology screens	Multiple drugs can be screened for at once; useful for suspected drug abuse and for suspected overdoses of an unknown substance; specific drugs may also be requested.
Drug levels	Quantitative values with reference range of therapeutic drugs; in the case of psychotropics, they are particularly useful in assessment of compliance and in patients with a poor response to standard doses; reference ranges for lithium and for the standard AEDs may be more useful in guiding dosage but should not be interpreted apart from the individual's response and tolerance of the drug.
Heavy metal screens	Many neuropsychiatric symptoms have been associated with lead, mercury, manganese, arsenic, and aluminum poisoning; these should be tested if a patient with psychiatric presentation has any suggestion of a history of exposure to them.

Note. SIADH = syndrome of inappropriate antidiuretic hormone; RBC = red blood cell; AED = antiepileptic drugs.

C. Biochemical and Immunologic Tests

Disturbances of electrolytes are common in psychiatric patients either as a presenting cause of mental status change (e.g., delirium in hyponatremia) or as secondary to the disease (e.g., hypokalemia in bulimic patients, related to bingeing) or its treatment (e.g., hyponatremia with carbamazepine). Liver and renal disease may also be a primary cause of presentation (e.g., hepatic or uremic encephalopathy) or, alternatively, secondary to the primary illness (e.g., liver failure in alcoholism) or its treatment (e.g., liver dysfunction secondary to use of AEDs). The serum glucose may give valuable information in cases of suspected diabetes mellitus or hypoglycemia presenting with mental status changes. All these tests, outlined in Table 3, are quickly obtained (often within a matter of minutes if requested urgently), are inexpensive, and provide valuable routine laboratory screening and follow-up information in psychiatric populations. The remainder of tests discussed in Table 3 are commonly obtained as well in a neuropsychiatric population, but they are generally reserved for more specific clinical situations rather than used for general screening purposes.

II. CEREBROSPINAL FLUID TESTS

The cerebrospinal fluid (CSF) is a valuable adjunct to diagnosis in specific clinical situations. It offers little information in the setting of routine screening of general psychiatric or neurological populations. The cerebrospinal fluid bathes the entire central nervous system (CNS) and thus has the potential of offering a unique window into the biochemistry of various neuropsychiatric disorders. It is obtained by means of lumbar puncture for analysis; a small needle is inserted at the level of approximately L3–4.

A. Contraindications

Lumbar puncture is contraindicated in the following circumstances:

1. If there is suspicion of increased intracranial pressure with a mass lesion or ventricular obstruction; in such instances, neuroimaging should always be obtained first.
2. In the presence of complete spinal subarachnoid block.
3. In the presence of significant coagulation defects.
4. If there is evidence of local infection at the site of the lumbar puncture.

In the case of known bacteremia, one should also be extra careful with lumbar puncture because it has been associated with the occurrence of secondary meningitis.

B. Indications

Currently the major indication for lumbar puncture in neurology and psychiatry is to exclude CNS infection. Although many hundreds of studies have been done in psychiatric patients, there is still no recognized indication clinically for the procedure in the field of psychiatry except to exclude neurological illness. However, because meningitis and encephalitis often present with mental status changes, patients with these diseases may see a psychiatrist or neuropsychologist first in the evaluation process.

1. In adults, lumbar puncture is indicated in the evaluation of the following conditions:

   a. Suspected infections or postinfectious illness (bacterial, tuberculous, viral, and fungal meningitis; aseptic meningitis, infectious polyneuritis, cysticercosis, toxoplasmosis and rickettsia infections, amebic infections, neurosyphilis, Lyme borreliosis, rubella panencephalitis, subacute sclerosing panencephalitis [SSPE], HIV and herpes simplex encephalitis, encephalitis of uncertain cause).

   b. Multiple sclerosis (most useful tests: oligoclonal bands, IgG index, and myelin basic protein).

   c. Intracranial hemorrhage (better evaluated in the first instance with neuroimaging; CSF may be diagnostic for subarachnoid hemorrhage even if neuroimaging is negative, however).

   d. Meningeal malignancy (pleocytosis, protein, glucose, specific tumor markers).

   e. Paraneoplastic syndromes (specific neuronal nuclear and Purkinje cell antibodies are detectable).

   f. Pseudotumor cerebri (requires lumbar puncture to diagnose and confirm increased pressure and to exclude meningitis).

   g. Normal pressure hydrocephalus (lumbar puncture sometimes is useful in prediction of response to shunting).

   h. Amyloid angiopathy (cystatin C, amyloid beta-protein).

   i. Neurosarcoidosis (CSF angiotensin converting enzyme).

    j. Evaluation of dementia.

    k. Stroke (better evaluated in the first instance with neuroimaging; CSF is useful in suspected subarachnoid hemorrhage, when CNS vasculitis is suspected, if septic emboli are suspected, in patients with positive syphilis or HIV serologic studies, and in young patients with unexplained strokes).

    l. Other (systemic lupus erythematosus, hepatic encephalopathy, vitamin B12 deficiency; occasionally in seizures to exclude CNS infection or bleeding, and for intrathecal therapy).

  2. In children, lumbar puncture is indicated in the following clinical situations:

    a. Suspected meningitis (CSF changes may be less specific and initially normal in children).

    b. Other infections (as in adults; most show nonspecific changes except for antibody titers in SSPE, measles, rubella, and progressive rubella panencephalitis).

    c. Febrile seizures (only if clinical evidence of meningitis is present, except in infants younger than 12 months, in whom clinical signs may be absent and CSF should be examined).

    d. Intracranial hemorrhage in neonates.

    e. Pseudotumor cerebri.

    f. Lead encephalopathy.

    g. CNS neoplasia (as in adults; best evaluated in the first instance with neuroimaging).

    h. Lysosomal storage diseases (measurement of specific glycosphingolipids).

    i. Therapeutic lumbar puncture (intrathecal therapy).

The CSF is made up primarily of water and has been termed a "modified tap water"; its study in schizophrenia has been likened to the augurs' examination of animal entrail. Although it is true that 99% of the CSF composition is water and that the many hundreds of studies looking at neurotransmitters and other markers in schizophrenia have not to date produced any useful clinical test, the remaining 1% of its composition has the potential to provide vast amounts of information to the clinician.

Although it has been more than a century since the first lumbar puncture, the routine clinical tests performed on the CSF have not changed from the first one performed. The color, pressure, cell count, protein, and glucose levels are measured routinely with every specimen and together give the "CSF profile," indicating more specific diagnoses. In bacterial meningitis, in which the lumbar puncture is most useful, an increase in pressure, WBC count, and protein is seen, as well as a decrease in glucose. The WBC count is usually greater than $1,000/mm^3$ with a predominance of polymorphonuclear cells. In viral meningitis, there is predominantly monocytic CSF pleocytosis with normal glucose levels and modest elevations in protein. Fungal and tuberculous meningitis are characterized by a predominant lymphocytic pleocytosis with increased protein and decreased glucose levels. Specific staining techniques and cultures along with measurement of antibodies, antigens, or both; other immunologic tests; and the use of the newer polymerase chain reaction (PCR) also help to differentiate the various causes of infection of the CNS. In suspected neurosyphilis, the CSF profile is nonspecific, but the CSF VDRL is a specific test used for making the diagnosis.

Apart from infections, CSF finds its greatest use in the evaluation of demyelinating disease, especially multiple sclerosis and acute and chronic inflammatory polyradiculoneuropathies. Within psychiatry, examination of the CSF is indicated in acute mental status changes when an infectious or other neurological cause is suspected and neuroimaging has ruled out the possibility of increased intracranial pressure.

III. URINE TESTS

The most common test of urine used in psychiatric patients is the routine urinalysis and culture to detect infection or renal disease. The test reveals the cell count (increased with infections), the protein (increased in renal disease) and glucose (increased in diabetes mellitus) levels, as well as the specific gravity and microscopic analysis. Urine culture is often needed to establish the cause of infection and the susceptibility of the organism to various antibiotics. Detection of urine infections is important because their presence may exacerbate other changes in mental state and may, in the elderly, even present with delirium and other acute mental state changes. The creatinine clearance test is also checked frequently in psychiatric patients when starting lithium therapy as a sensitive baseline of renal function should the question of renal impairment arise on follow-up. This is particularly important in patients with a history of renal disease. The creatinine clearance is calculated from a 24-hour urine collection using serum values as well.

Other, more specific tests of urine of use in neuropsychiatry include urine toxicology (for suspected drug abuse), trimethylamine (for trimethylaminuria), porphyrin screens (for porphyria), catecholamine and metabolites (for pheochromocytoma), osmolality (for the syndrome of inappropriate antidiuretic hormone [SIADH]), and urine myoglobin (in suspected rhabdomyolysis, such as in neuroleptic malignant syndrome, severe electrical shock, or muscle crush injury).

IV. ELECTROENCEPHALOGRAPHY

Electroencephalography (EEG) is a measure of electrical activity taken from surface electrodes on the scalp. In certain circumstances (e.g., in the evaluation of patients for epilepsy surgery), intracranial electrodes may also be used. Anterior temporal and sphenoidal electrodes may also be helpful in evaluating suspected complex partial seizures. Photic stimulation, sleep, and hyperventilation are all useful activation procedures. Although hundreds of EEG studies have been done in primary psychiatric illness, the abnormalities found are generally nonspecific, and the EEG is used primarily to exclude neurological illness within psychiatry. The EEG is the one test that relates directly to attention and to mental state, however, and therefore it is of particular interest to neuropsychologists.

The EEG is not clinically indicated for general screening of psychiatric patients or for the evaluation of primary psychiatric illness, although it is of some academic interest in these conditions. During electroconvulsive therapy (ECT), EEG monitoring is useful to establish seizure duration and may also be useful in evaluation of patients prior to ECT. The EEG is also useful in suspected drug toxicity and in evaluating suspected lithium toxicity in patients who develop mental symptoms at therapeutic levels, suspected AED toxicity, and suspected intoxication from other psychotropic drugs.

The main indication for an EEG, however, is in the evaluation of suspected epilepsy. It is also useful in the evaluation of episodic behavioral disorders when epilepsy is in the differential diagnosis (e.g., atypical panic attacks, atypical paroxysmal affective or psychotic symptoms, or transient cognitive impairment or inattention in children). Ambulatory or video EEG is often helpful as well in these situations; these tools provide the opportunity for prolonged monitoring and for correlating the EEG findings with the clinical behavior. Sphenoidal or anterior temporal leads are used if a temporal focus is suspected. It should be noted that a normal EEG does not rule out epilepsy, nor does an abnormal EEG rule it in, and the results of an EEG must always be taken within the clinical context. Deep foci, especially frontal, may have normal surface EEG findings even ictally.

Another indication for the EEG in psychiatry is the evaluation of the acute confusional state. In these situations, the EEG is useful for establishing the diagnosis and following the course of delirium. In the assessment of other cognitive impairment, the EEG is useful in the diagnosis of dementia and of cognitive impairment related to depression or to medication effects.

There are also a variety of other illnesses presenting with psychiatric symptoms for which an EEG is indicated, particularly when findings in the history, mental state examination, physical examination, or laboratory tests suggest a neurological or medical basis for the patient's symptoms; examples include an unusual course of illness (unusual onset, rapid deterioration), a history of known neurological illness such as epilepsy, and atypical mental state findings or focal abnormalities on neurological examination. Table 4 shows the primary EEG findings in psychiatric disorders and in neurological illness presenting with psychiatric symptoms.

V.   NEUROIMAGING

The main neuroimaging tests of clinical use are computed tomography (CT) and magnetic resonance imaging (MRI). Both types of neuroimaging have distinct advantages and disadvantages. The advantages of MRI over CT are a higher degree of resolution, particularly in evaluating white matter in demyelinating disorders; in searching for the seizure focus in epilepsy when resolution of the hippocampal region in particular is well delineated; and in dementia, infarction, neoplastic disease, vascular malformations, and degenerative disease. It also images the posterior fossa, spinal cord, and brain stem to a much greater degree. It has the other advantage of avoiding radiation and, in patients allergic to iodine, the use of contrast materials to which they might be sensitive. MRI, like CT, may be enhanced by the use of contrast with gadolinium. CT scanning, on the other hand, has the advantage of being much more available, much less expensive, and applicable when MRI is contraindicated owing to the presence of ferromagnetic mate-

Table 4. Primary EEG Findings in Psychiatric and Neurological Illness Presenting with Psychiatric Symptoms

Condition	EEG findings
Schizophrenia	Nonspecific findings; low mean alpha frequency, nonspecific findings in sleep staging.
Depression	Nonspecific changes in waking EEG. Sleep EEG's more useful than awake EEG; decrease in REM (rapid eye movement) latency often seen, especially if delusions and depression are present; also decreases in Stages III and IV and in sleep continuity.
Anxiety disorders	Nonspecific changes in anxiety disorders, often with predominant muscle artifact. Although the EEG changes in panic disorder are also nonspecific, it is worth remembering that panic may also occur as an ictal phenomenon; ambulatory monitoring is helpful to differentiate, especially in cases refractory to traditional treatment and atypical cases.
Delirium	Severity relates to extent of slow wave abnormality. Causes include various medical and neurological conditions: toxic, metabolic, vascular, infectious, postsurgical, traumatic.

Dementia	Nonspecific slowing most common. EEG relates somewhat to degree of impairment (mild: 40%; moderate: –65%). Lag behind cognitive impairment in Alzheimer's disease and EEG changes. Focal EEG changes suggest multi-infarct dementia or normal pressure hydrocephalus. Changes often mild or absent in Pick's disease. Characteristic triphasic complexes in Creutzfeldt-Jakob disease.
Epilepsy	Ictal EEG changes useful in assessing diagnosis and location of focus. Sharp and slow activity may also be seen interictally. Interictal changes generally do not correlate with psychiatric symptoms. Ambulatory and video-EEG monitoring often useful.
Tumors	Focal slowing may be seen. Psychiatric presentations and EEG findings depend on location and nature of tumor.
Metabolic and toxic conditions	Triphasic waves in hepatic and renal coma. Nonspecific EEG abnormalities in vitamin B12 deficiency, with cognitive impairment and nonspecific slowing in hypothyroidism.
Infections	Herpes encephalitis: temporal sharp complexes. Diffuse slowing in encephalitis of various causes. Focal or generalized slowing or paroxysmal discharges in AIDS. Localized slow waves over area of abscess in localized CNS infection. EEG findings do not generally correlate with psychiatric symptoms.

Note. From "The EEG in Psychiatry," by H. W. McConnell and J. Andrews, 1997, in *Clinical Neurophysiology*, by C. D. Binnie (Ed.). Copyright 1997 by Blackwell Scientific. Adapted with permission.

rial (e.g., aneurysm clip, pacemaker). It is superior to MRI in a few specific situations: evaluation of meningeal tumors, calcified lesions, acute intracranial hemorrhage, and acute parenchymal infarction. Both types of neuroimaging thus have a valuable place in clinical practice, and careful consideration should be given to the type of imaging used on an individual basis. Quantitative and functional MRI also promise to have an increasing clinical role in the future.

Other types of neuroimaging that are being used increasingly are single photon emission computed tomography (SPECT) and positron emission tomography (PET). These offer a functional image, and although they are still largely research tools, they are promising technologies. SPECT has the advantage of being routinely available and being much less expensive, whereas PET is still largely restricted to research institutes. Both are most useful clinically in the evaluation of epilepsy and dementia.

VI. USE OF TESTING IN SPECIFIC PSYCHIATRIC PRESENTATIONS

Laboratory testing must always be considered within the context of the clinical presentation. The appropriate ordering of tests depends on an accurate assessment of each individual presentation. Some of the most difficult clinical evaluations in neuropsychology are the evaluation of dementia, atypical affective disorder, and atypical psychosis. Exhibits 1 and 2 show the laboratory evaluation of these clinical conditions, which must be individualized depending on the nature of the presenting symptoms. In some instances a more detailed assessment than that noted in the table would be indicated, such as when there is a family history of a certain metabolic or degenerative disorder that may present with psychosis or affective disturbance, or when there is an indication from either the history or the physical examination of other CNS disease.

Other psychiatric presentations may require a different emphasis from that noted in Exhibits 1 and 2. Although the tests in Exhibit 2 would be appropriate for the evaluation of atypical anxiety disorder, a history of atypical panic attacks might warrant the use of ambulatory EEG, because complex partial seizures may present in this manner. The occurrence of symptoms seen commonly in seizure disorders with a temporal lobe focus would indicate further evaluation with EEG. If the history elucidated the finding of urine changing color, a porphyria screen may be appropriate; if a history of drug abuse

Exhibit 1. Laboratory Evaluation of Dementia

Assessment of dementia in the elderly

Blood tests:
CBC, ESR, electrolytes, glucose, calcium and phosphorus, TSH, serum B12, RBC folate, RPR

Neuroimaging:
CT or MRI

Systemic tests:
Chest X-ray, ECG, urinalysis

Optional tests:
Lumbar puncture
EEG
SPECT
Antiphospholipid antibodies
HIV testing
Toxicology screen
Heavy metal screening

Assessment of dementia in children and young adults

Preceding tests as in older adults

Blood tests:
Serum cholestanol (cerebrotendinous xanthomatosis)
Serum copper and ceruloplasmin (Wilson's disease)
Serum HIV antibodies (AIDS dementia)
Serum very long chain fatty acids (adrenoleukodystrophy)
Serum lactate and pyruvate levels (mitochondrial encephalopathies)
WBC arylsulfatase A (metachromatic leukodystrophy)
WBC galactocerebroside beta galactosidase (Krabbe's disease)
WBC sphingomyelinase (Niemann-Pick disease)
WBC Gm1 beta-galactosidase (GM1 gangliosidosis)
WBC hexosaminidase A (GM2 gangliosidosis)
WBC alpha galactosidase (Fabry's disease)
WBC alpha-*N*-acetylglucosaminidase (mucopolysaccharidosis)

(Continued)

Exhibit 1. Laboratory Evaluation of Dementia
(Continued)

> *Urine:*
> Urinary dolichols (ceroid lipofuscinosis)
> *Other:*
> Skin biopsy (polycystic lipomembranous osteodysplasia; pseudoxanthoma elasticum)
> Liver biopsy (Lafora's disease, Niemann-Pick disease)
> Skeletal muscle biopsy (Lafora's disease)
> Brain biopsy (ceroid lipofuscinosis)
> Hand X-rays (polycystic lipomembranous osteodysplasia)
> Nerve conduction studies (neuroacanthocytosis)

Note. ESR = erythrocyte sedimentation rate; TSH = thyroid-stimulating hormone; RPR = rapid plasma reagin; SPECT = single photon emission computed tomography. From *Neuropsychiatry and Behavioral Neurology,* by J. L. Cummings and M. R. Trimble, 1995, Washington, DC: American Psychiatric Association. Copyright 1995 by the American Psychiatric Association. Adapted with permission.

Exhibit 2. Laboratory Tests to Consider in the Evaluation of Atypical Psychosis or Affective Disorder

> *Blood tests:*
> CBC, electrolytes, glucose, renal and liver function tests, thyroid function tests, serum B12 and RBC folate, RPR, calcium and phosphorus, HIV serology in those with risk factors, serum cortisol
> *Systemic tests:*
> Chest X-ray
> ECG
> *Urine tests:*
> Urinalysis
> Urine toxicology
> Urine porphyrin screen
> *Neurophysiological assessment:*
> EEG
> *Neuroimaging*
> CT, MRI, or both

Note. CBC = complete blood count; RBC = red blood cell; RPR = rapid plasma reagin.

were suspected, a toxicology screen would be important. If the presentation were extremely atypical with an excess of autonomic signs, such as hypertension, associated with episodes of behavioral disturbance, the clinician should consider measuring serum and urine catecholamines and metabolites to evaluate the patient for possible pheochromocytoma, a rare tumor that may present with such symptoms. It is clearly not practical or cost efficient (or clinically necessary), however, to screen every patient with panic attacks, which is one of the most common psychiatric presentations, for rare tumors. The laboratory workup must be geared toward the history and physical findings to avoid the ordering of unnecessary tests.

The age of the patient is also an important consideration in the laboratory assessment. The evaluation of dementia in children and young adults, for example, is very different from that of elderly adults with the same clinical presentation. This is because different disorders tend to start at different ages, and the evaluation should be geared toward the possible causes for the relevant age group. It would be inappropriate, for example, to screen an older adult presenting with psychosis or dementia for congenital metabolic illness that presents only in childhood. The differential diagnosis is not the same in these situations, and the laboratory evaluation should always be geared around the differential diagnosis for an individual patient, rather than set protocols for every patient with a given presentation. Protocols do have a use in routine screening of psychiatric patients, such as set laboratory tests ordered on admission to a psychiatric hospital. In these instances, one can be sure that certain common treatable causes of psychiatric illness (e.g., hypothyroidism) will not be missed, but these tests should not replace a full clinical evaluation including a history and physical examination.

VII.   CONCLUSION

It is important for the neuropsychologist to be aware of laboratory testing because he or she is one of the principal members of the team involved in the evaluation of the patient's mental state. Both the ordering and interpretation of laboratory tests must be done within the clinical context of the patient, with patient consent and following an appropriate history and mental status, neurological, and physical examination. This chapter has summarized the major laboratory tests of interest to the neuropsychologist. The bibliography contains further readings concerning the specificity, sensitivity, indications, and contraindications for various laboratory tests.

In this time of "managed care" and "health care reform," it is of particular importance for all members of the treatment team to be aware of the spectrum of laboratory tests available and to be wary of third-party payer algorithms for the laboratory evaluation of neuropsychological illness. Whereas screening protocols have some use in this population, it is important to consider laboratory tests for individual patients within the context of their presenting symptoms, age, family history, past medical and psychiatric history, and clinical examination and to put this information in the context of a differential diagnosis and management plan for the patient.

BIBLIOGRAPHY

Aminoff, M. J. (1992). *Electrodiagnosis in clinical neurology.* Edinburgh, Scotland: Churchill Livingstone.

Andreasen, N. C. (Ed.) (1989). *Brain imaging: Applications in psychiatry.* Washington, DC: American Psychiatric Press.

Cummings, J. L., & Trimble, M. R. (1995). *Neuropsychiatry and behavioral neurology.* Washington, DC: American Psychiatric Press.

Daniel, D. G., Zigun, J. R., & Weinberger, D. R. (1992). Brain imaging in neuropsychiatry. In S. Yudofsky & R. Hales (Eds.), *Textbook of neuropsychiatry* (pp. 165–186).Washington, DC: American Psychiatric Press.

Jacobs, D. S., Kasten, B. L., Demott, W. R., & Wolfson, W. (1990). *Laboratory test handbook.* Baltimore: Williams & Wilkins.

Lishman, A. (1987). *Organic psychiatry.* Oxford, England: Blackwell Scientific.

Matthews, P. M., & Arnold, D. L. (1991). *Diagnostic tests in neurology.* Edinburgh, Scotland: Churchill Livingstone.

McConnell, H. W., & Andrews, J. (1998). The EEG in psychiatry. In C. D. Binnie (Ed.), *Clinical neurophysiology.* Oxford, England: Blackwell Scientific.

McConnell, H. W., & Bianchine, J. R. (1994). *Cerebrospinal fluid in neurology and psychiatry.* London: Chapman & Hall.

Peter, J. B. (1994). *Use and interpretation of laboratory tests in neurology.* Santa Monica, CA: Specialty Laboratories.

Rosse, R. B., Giese, A. A., Deutsch, S. I., & Morihisa, J. M. (1989). *Laboratory testing in psychiatry.* Washington, DC: American Psychiatric Press.

Strub, R. L., & Black, F. W. (1993). *The mental status examination in neurology.* Philadelphia: Davis.

CHAPTER 4

Howard R. Kessler

The Bedside Neuropsychological Examination

Neuropsychological assessment of patients at bedside presents a number of unique challenges in comparison to the standard, more extensive (outpatient) neuropsychological examination. Patients seen at the hospital bedside typically present with an acute rather than a chronic or progressive illness.

Patients are assessed for a variety of reasons. Perhaps the most difficult and challenging of referral questions is the differential diagnosis among depression or some other condition of functional origin versus delirium versus dementia. This is the primary focus of the chapter. Other referral questions include issues of capacity (competency) for informed decision making, capability for independent living (and assessing the level of supervision needed in assisted living), and elucidation of neuropsychological strengths and weaknesses for treatment planning purposes (be they medical, rehabilitative, pharmacological, or other).

I. DISORDERS OF COMMON REFERRAL POPULATIONS

Patients with a number of conditions may be referred for bedside assessment, each of which presents unique barriers to assessment. These conditions include the following:

A. Stroke

Patients with middle cerebral artery strokes may be hemiparetic (limiting the use of tests requiring significant motor or visual function), may be aphasic (limiting the use of any task requiring language for response or comprehension of task demands), or may present with visual hemineglect (requiring changes in the manner in which test materials are presented in space). Patients with posterior circulation strokes may suffer from hemianopsia (requiring an assessment of their capacity to compensate; hence the examiner needs to make allowances by presenting test materials in the unaffected field). Patients with anterior circulation strokes (e.g., hemorrhage of anterior communicating artery aneurysm) may be anergic or akinetic (limiting the patient's capacity to expend sufficient effort during testing).

B. Traumatic Brain Injury

Patients suffering from acute traumatic brain injury (TBI) likely suffer from posttraumatic amnesia, and accompanying agitation and inattention may interfere with test administration; because these patients perform at an artificially depressed level as a result of these symptoms, formal tests should not be administered until the patients are well oriented in all spheres. These patients also may change or progress rapidly over the course of even a few days, so that the examiner must determine the optimal time for formal test administration.

C. Dementia

A wide variety of diseases, both systemic and neurological, may result in progressive cognitive decline. Differential diagnoses often need to be made among various classes of dementia, between delirium and dementia, or between dementia and depression. Systemic diseases such as poorly controlled hypertension or diabetes mellitus also may cause progressive decline owing to chronic vascular insufficiency. Because the genesis of the disorder is often a crucial diagnostic marker, the clinician may need to go to great lengths to acquire accurate historical information from family members.

D. Delirium

Delirious patients may demonstrate a fluctuating level of consciousness as well as fluctuating levels of orientation and cognitive capacity. These patients often need to be examined across a number of days, at various times of the day, for an accurate diagnostic impression to be obtained. Their variability in cognitive function often masks other underlying disease states such as dementia.

E. Postsurgical Deficits

Patients may demonstrate acute neuropsychological deficits immediately after invasive, nonneurological surgery. A determination must be made as to whether changes in cognitive function are due to the effects of anesthesia, medications, or an intraoperative event such as stroke during or after coronary artery bypass graft (CABG). This may be an extremely difficult differential diagnosis because of the acuity of these patients, and there is a high false positive rate of diagnosis. For example, although CABG may result in stroke, the vast majority of patients demonstrating acute cognitive deficit after such surgery spontaneously remit.

F. Systemic Illness

Chronic conditions such as diabetes mellitus and hypertension can result in neurological disease, particularly if they are poorly controlled. Liver or kidney disease may present with symptoms of encephalopathy or delirium, whereas patients undergoing renal dialysis may demonstrate a fluctuating course. In these patients, it is important to be able to discriminate between transient and relatively permanent impairments. Furthermore, computed tomography (CT) scanning is often not helpful in these patients, because of its insensitivity to subtle small vessel disease.

II. REVIEWING THE MEDICAL RECORD

A. History and Physical Examination

In addition to checking the history and physical examination findings for the patient's admitting diagnosis, it is important to look for comorbid conditions that may have an impact on neuropsychological presentation. The clinician should look for common medical problems such as hypertension, diabetes mellitus, or cardiac or other organ conditions. In addition, certain related conditions may affect neuropsychological functioning.

A prime example is peripheral vascular disease (which often results in amputation); this condition is often accompanied by cognitive deficit owing to widespread vascular insufficiency which may also affect cerebral functioning (see chap. 1, this volume).

B. Relevant Laboratory Findings

The results of particular laboratory tests can be useful in rendering differential diagnoses of, for example, delirium or acute confusional state. Electrolyte levels (e.g., sodium, potassium, chloride, calcium) should be examined. Levels that are grossly outside of the normal range are typically sufficient to provoke delirium. Measures of kidney function (e.g., uric acid, blood urea nitrogen [BUN], creatinine), liver function (bilirubin, alkaline phosphatase, LDL cholesterol), and protein status (e.g., protein, albumin) should also be ascertained (see chapter 3, this volume).

C. Neuroimaging Results

The three most commonly used imaging procedures are electroencephalography (EEG), CT, and magnetic resonance imaging (MRI). EEG may be useful in identifying seizure disorders or space-occupying tumors. More typically, however, the neuropsychologist is called in to see patients with more diffusely represented results, such as "slowing of the background rhythm" or "diffuse bifrontal slowing." Such findings often possess little diagnostic value to the clinician beyond demonstrating that something is amiss in the central nervous system (CNS). Furthermore, even localizing features on the EEG may not indicate the presence of a localized phenomenon unless there are corroborating results from CT or MRI.

Care must also be taken in evaluating the results of CT and MRI. CT is often insensitive to subtle disease states, particularly those involving the subcortical white matter. In particular, such conditions as subtle TBI or vascular insufficiency are often better identified by neuropsychological or other behavioral tests. Although the MRI is more sensitive to many conditions than is CT, it nonetheless is not perfect. MRI can overestimate CNS involvement in some conditions. For example, T2 weighted images tend to overestimate the presence of periventricular white matter disease. CT and MRI, therefore, should not be depended on (in isolation) for making differential diagnoses.

They are often more helpful in explaining the severity (or lack thereof) of a patient's condition or in making predictive and prognostic statements.

D. Medications

It is particularly important to be able to account for the effects of a variety of psychoactive medications on test performance. This is crucial in testing elderly patients, in whom polypharmacy can present a hindrance to test performance and interpretation. The psychoactive effects of many common drug classes are summarized in Table 1. (This table is meant to provide only a rough guide; more detailed surveys of side effects may be found in the *Physician's Desk Reference* or the text *Drug Facts and Comparisons*.) It is also important to look at interactions between drugs and their side effects in the context of a patient's particular illness. For example, patients with hepatic disease may experience heightened effects of neuroleptics (such as haloperidol [Haldol]), because they are metabolized by the liver; similarly, benzodiazepines may have increased effects on patients with renal disease, and anticholinergics (such as tricyclic antidepressants) may have heightened effects on patients with cardiovascular or cerebrovascular disease.

III. CONDUCTING THE BEDSIDE EXAMINATION

A. Background History and Clinical Interview

The interview and history taking should be a standard part of the bedside assessment. Formats for history taking can be found in many sources and are not reviewed in depth here. (One of the best sources is Strub and Black's (1993) *The Mental State Examination in Neurology*.) In the case of the bedside assessment, certain background factors are particularly critical and often require that a reliable informant (other than the patient) be identified to provide corroborating information. These factors include the following:

1. GENESIS OF THE DISORDER

Was onset rapid or progressive? If progressive, was it gradual or stepwise? Was onset associated with some medical, psychosocial, or environmental event?

Table 1. Examples of Psychoactive Effects of Medications

Class	Specific drug	Mental side effects
Antiarrythmics	Propranolol (Inderal)	Depression, weakness, catatonia, hallucinations, liability
	Nifedipine (Procardia)	Hypotensive effects, mood changes
	Digoxin (Lanoxin)	Drowsiness, depression, fatigue, hallucinations, confusion, psychosis
Anticholinergics	Scopolamine (Transderm-Scōp)	Nervousness, drowsiness, mental confusion (in the elderly)
Anticonvulsants	Phenytoin (Dilantin)	Ataxia, incoordination, slurred speech, mental confusion, nervousness
	Carbamazepine (Tegretol)	Confusion, ataxia (less common than with phenytoin)
Antihistamines	Diphenhydramine hydrocholoride (Benadryl)	Drowsiness, incoordination, euphoria, hallucinations, irritability, confusion
Antihypertensives	Clonidine hydrochloride (Catapres)	Drowsiness, depression, anxiety, other behavioral changes
Antimicrobial	Sulfamethoxazole (Septra)	Depression, hallucinations

(Continued)

Table 1. Examples of Psychoactive Effects of Medications *(Continued)*

Class	Specific drug	Mental side effects
Antiparkinsonians	Levodopa-carbidopa (Sinemet)	"Dementia," hallucinations, hypomania, involuntary movements, excessive perspiration
Bronchodilators	Aminophylline	Irritability, anxiety
Cholinergics	Physostigmine salicylate (Eserine)	Confusion, slurred speech, ataxia, weakness or paralysis
Central nervous system stimulants	Methylphenidate hydrochloride (Ritalin)	Nervousness, tremors, tics
Diuretics	Furosemide (Lasix)	Tinnitus, deafness
Hormones	Prednisone (Deltasone)	Euphoria, depression, psychosis
	Levothyroxine sodium (Synthroid)	Hyperexcitability, hypomania, depression, fatigue, increased psychomotor activity
	Insulin preparations	Weakness, irritability, confusion

Hypnotics	Flurazepam hydrochloride (Dalmane)	Oversedation, ataxia, agitation, depression (long-term use)
Narcotic analgesics	Morphine sulfate, propoxyphene (Darvon)	Drowsiness, confusion, sedation, hallucinations, disorientation
NSAIDs	Naproxen (Naprosyn)	Nervousness, insomnia, depression
Oral antidiabetics	Chlopropamide (Diabinese), glyburide (Micronase)	Drowsiness, delirium, mimic of neurological disorders
Parasiticidals	Metronidazole (Flagyl)	Ataxia, confusion, depression
Anxiolytics (benzodiazepines)	Diazepam (Valium), lorazepam (Ativan), alprazolam (Xanax)	Sedation, drowsiness, fatigue, ataxia, confusion, depression, dysarthria, disinhibition (rare)
Antidepressants Tricyclics	Amitryptiline (Elavil)	Drowsiness, agitation, restlessness, tremor, hallucinations, psychosis, cerebellar symptoms, seizures
MAO inhibitors	Phenelzine sulfate (Nardil)	Agitation, anxiety, mania, weakness, drowsiness
Mood stabilizers	Lithium carbonate	Confusion, tremor, ataxia, chorea, seizures

(Continued)

Table 1. Examples of Psychoactive Effects of Medications *(Continued)*

Class	Specific drug	Mental side effects
SSRIs	Fluoxetine (Prozac) Paroxetine (Paxil)	Anxiety, sedation, akathisia
Antipsychotics	Haloperidol (Haldol)	Extrapyramidal effects, restlessness, anxiety, drowsiness, sedation, depression

Note. NSAIDs = nonsteroidal antiinflammatory drugs; MAO = monoamine oxidase; SSRIs = selective serotonin reuptake inhibitors. From *Atlas of Drug Reactions*, by R. D. Collins, 1985. Copyright 1985 by Churchill Livingstone. Adapted with permission.

2. SELF-CARE

Has the patient been compliant with his or her medications? If hypertension or diabetes is present, how stable or brittle has the condition been? Has the patient been well nourished? Has the patient conformed to dietary restrictions? Is there risk of inadvertent self-harm at home (e.g., from falls or burns)?

3. PRIOR CNS INSULTS

Mild TBI often goes unnoticed and is rarely found in the patient's medical record. Is there a history of head banging associated with loss of consciousness, retrograde or anterograde amnesia, or posttraumatic sequelae? Is there a history of brief interruptions of function or consciousness (e.g., fugue, episodes, or frank loss of consciousness), which may indicate some ongoing or episodic process, such as cerebrovascular disease or seizures? Is there a history of excessive alcohol, drug, or tobacco use, which may cause or contribute to neurological disease or, in the case of withdrawal, provoke a quite florid but possibly temporary alteration in cognitive function?

4. INSIGHT, AWARENESS, AND CONCERN

It is important during the course of the interview to determine the patient's level of awareness of his or her medical state, as well as his or her insight into cognitive and physical limitations. Lack of awareness alone is not necessarily pathognomonic of cognitive decline. For example, it is not unusual for a patient to be unaware of medical subtleties because the condition has not been adequately explained. However, poor awareness in combination with neuropsychological deficits is often helpful in neuropsychological diagnosis. In particular, patients with dementia, traumatic brain injury, and various right hemisphere or frontal lobe disorders present with various degrees of anosognosia; when they present with good awareness, they may demonstrate a rather striking lack of concern (anosodiaphoria); alternatively, those with delirium or depression usually have relatively spared awareness and concern.

5. MOOD

A full survey of the patient's mood should routinely be undertaken. This should include investigation of the patient's subjective emotional experience and of particular sources of emotional stress. Neurovegetative symptoms need to be surveyed but also need to be confirmed by a chart review (e.g., checking nurses' notes for information on nutritional intake and sleep patterns). Mood also needs to be assessed in light of the patient's degree of insight, because this relationship has ramifications for the source of the depression (reactive vs. endogenous), which gives the clinician additional information for the differential diagnosis. Finally, mood exerts a significant effect on cognitive functions that require significant effort (attention, memory, executive functions), particularly in the elderly.

B. Behavioral Observations

Inferences regarding observations of behavior are generally no different from those generated in other types of neuropsychological assessments. In the special circumstance of bedside assessment, the most common concern is with fatigue, which is very common in acutely hospitalized patients and may be attributable to a variety of factors, including sleep deprivation, fever or infection, and medication effects. This factor by itself could be sufficient to cause impaired performance. Whereas most outpatients can be counted on to inform the examiner of subjective feelings of fatigue, inpatients are not necessarily as reliable. Furthermore, inpatients may be less likely to push themselves to their absolute level of tolerance because of their infirmities, so they may require more prodding and encouragement from the examiner.

A second factor, which may be more helpful in differential diagnosis, is that of identifying emotional lability (i.e., emotional incontinence vs. pseudobulbar palsy). Lability has a unique quality, separate from emotional disturbances, in that it is easily provoked and not necessarily tied directly to an emotional stimulus. Furthermore, it has an impulsive quality, best described as "turning a faucet on, then suddenly off," and tends to be more stereotyped than are emotionally laden expressions. Lability can be helpful in differentiating between depression and an acquired neurological syndrome, as well as in the diagnosis of specific neurological syndromes (e.g., stroke).

C. Approach to Assessment

Because of the acuteness of the patient's medical–neurological status, the principles of bedside assessment differ from those of less acute environments. Steps must be taken to ensure economy as well as an adequate examination. The means of accomplishing this differs on the basis of the patient population. In performing more comprehensive outpatient assessments, limit testing is an integral part of the examination. It is not unusual to begin by administering more complex tasks; if these are performed adequately, it is unnecessary to administer simpler tasks to identify the particular mechanisms involved when the patient has failed (at which time, limit testing becomes integral). The luxury of such an approach is often unavailable in bedside assessment. The clinician often is not afforded the time to perform additional tests, making qualitative and pattern interpretation of results that much more crucial. Furthermore, the classic limit-testing approach is ill suited for certain hospitalized patients, especially the elderly, in whom failure on more complex instruments is far more likely. In such cases, it is often more fruitful to begin with an assessment of basic abilities and move upward toward the more complex. By so doing, less time is wasted, and the emotional effects on the patient of failure are minimized.

D. Choice of Assessment Instruments

Performing the bedside examination usually requires a great deal of flexibility on the part of the examiner. Examiners should have some instruments in their armamentarium that they administer to nearly every patient unless extraordinary circumstances, such as aphasia, intervene. This allows for comparisons among patients and serves to minimize the possibility of confirmation bias. Optimal tests for such purposes are those that tap a variety of abilities, possess good normative data, and have demonstrated discriminant validity. Orientation to time, place, and circumstance should be routinely tested. Although performance on such tasks alone may possess poor diagnostic accuracy, fluctuating levels of orientation may be diagnostic. Furthermore, comments in the medical chart regarding orientation (e.g., "alert and oriented x 3") should not be trusted unless they are clearly explained. It is also useful to have some kind of omnibus test available; these often can be administered with brevity, and they yield overall summary scores that are useful in test–retest comparisons. Furthermore, they allow time for the administration of more specialized tests to hone in on the abilities that appear to be particularly compromised.

1. OMNIBUS TESTS

Many such tests exist for use in neuropsychology; some, such as the Wechsler Adult Intelligence Scale–Revised (WAIS-R) or the Wechsler Memory Scale (WMS-III), are geared toward broadly assessing one specific area of function, whereas others, such as the Mattis Dementia Rating Scale (MDRS; Mattis, 1976) or the Neurobehavioral Cognitive Status Examination (NCSE; Kiernan, Mueller, Langston, & Van Dyke, 1987; Schwann, Van Dyke, Kiernan, Merrin, & Mueller, 1987), are geared toward broader surveys of multiple functions. When brevity is of the essence, the former tend to be less useful than the latter, because they often require too much time for administration. They are typically better normed, however, and often allow for a wider range of variability in performance than do the latter. It may be preferable to use portions of these tests, therefore, either as short forms (e.g., the Satz-Mogel short form of the WAIS-R, which correlates highly with IQ estimates) or by choosing selected subtests (e.g., the Information subtest as an estimate of premorbid capacity or the Digit Span and Arithmetic subtests as measures of immediate memory span, attention, and concentration) as an adjunct to broader surveys.

The MDRS is an excellent test for purposes of bedside assessment. It is easy enough that floor effects (a major concern with acutely ill patients) are successfully avoided; it possesses reasonable norms; it has demonstrated discriminant validity (e.g., in Huntington's vs. Alzheimer's disease); it correlates highly with functional capacity (e.g., in Alzheimer's disease); and it correlates highly with laterality of function (e.g., in regional cerebral blood flow [rCBF] studies). It is also rapid to administer and lends itself easily to limit testing. The MDRS is designed to allow the examiner to skip easier test items when more complex ones are passed. However, clinical practice suggests that the entire test should be administered to all patients, because differential diagnosis is often aided by observation of patient performance on tasks of varying levels of difficulty. This also allows for more reliable test–retest comparisons when repeat testing is required.

Similarly, the NCSE is designed with brevity in mind. It is a more difficult test than the MDRS, so it is more appropriate for younger patients. It is also more useful in that it taps a wider range of neuropsychological functions. Like the MDRS, the NCSE is also designed to allow the examiner to eliminate easier test items when more difficult ones are successfully performed. Again, it is preferable to administer the entire test for the reasons stated previously.

Neither the MDRS nor the NCSE is sufficient for the purposes of a comprehensive bedside assessment. In particular, briefer neuropsychological test instruments tend to have higher false negative than false positive rates, so that adequate performance does not reflect intactness of function. This requires the examiner to make two accommodations: (a) It is usually necessary to supplement these omnibus tests with more specialized, detailed tests of narrower neuropsychological realms, and (b) one must consider the qualitative interpretation of test performance crucial, because there may not be the luxury of administering a variety of additional tests to identify a clear pattern of strengths and weaknesses.

2. SPECIALIZED TESTS

There is, of course, a vast array of tests for assessing individual neuropsychological functions. Care needs to be taken in choosing those that are best tailored for bedridden patients. In general, tests chosen must be brief enough to allow for economy yet still yield meaningful information for interpretation of function and differential diagnosis. For example, verbal memory should be assessed using brief tasks that may nonetheless be sensitive: Rather than using 15- or 16-word lists such as those on the Rey Auditory Verbal Learning Test (AVLT) or the California Verbal Learning Test (CVLT), 12-word lists such as those on the Buschke Verbal Selective Reminding Procedure or Hopkins Verbal Learning Test ought to be used. Similarly, the Babcock-Levy Story Recall Test is a briefer narrative recall test than the WMS-III Logical Memory subtest. Using such a test selection strategy may not appear appreciably to affect economy in testing a given function; however, when one considers the use of such a strategy across many tests and abilities, the time saved becomes appreciable. Furthermore, the use of briefer tests helps to minimize the effects of interruptions, which are frequent in acute settings. It is often inadvisable to use tests that are heavily multidimensional (e.g., the Tactual Performance Test), because such instruments are likely to result in floor effects as well as to necessitate a great deal more limit testing and thus time investment. Finally, when short forms of some tests are unavailable, they may be designed and used with relative reliability (e.g., short forms of the Hooper Visual Organization Test [VOT] or some of the Benton tests, such as Visual Form Dis-

Table 2. Sample Core Bedside Neuropsychological Test Battery for Adults

Type of test	Specific tests
Omnibus	**Neurobehavioral Cognitive Status Examination**
General cognitive	WAIS-R Short Form (individual subtests or Satz-Mogel, depending on referral question)
Speech–language	**Boston Naming Test**
	Writing–spelling sample (BDAE Cookie-Theft, writing to dictation, WRAT-3 spelling items)
	Reading sample (Gray Oral Reading Test paragraphs, WRAT-3 reading items)
	Comprehension (complex logical questions)
	Brief screening of repetition and ability to follow commands (administer if any of the preceding skills are impaired)
	Language-mediated tasks (Benton left–right orientation, WAB praxis, finger gnosis)
Attention–memory	**Digit span**
	Stroop Neuropsychological Screening Test
	Paced Auditory Serial Addition Test (PASAT)

	Spatial span (WMS-R)
	Visual search tasks (letter cancellation)
	Verbal list learning (Buschke Verbal Selective Reminding, Hopkins Verbal Learning, with delayed recall and recognition)
	Figural recall (design recall, such as Rey-Osterrieth or WMS-III designs, with delayed recall and recognition)
	Narrative recall (administer if list learning is impaired; Babcock-Levy, WMS-R Logical Memory, with delayed recall)
	Visual recognition (administer if figural recall is impaired; Continuous Visual Memory Test)
	Three Words/3 Shapes (Mesulam) for lower functioning patients
Spatial–construction	**Drawing** (Rey-Osterrieth, BVRT-copy)
	Construction (WAIS-R Block Design)
	Visual discrimination, for patients with poor constructional performance (Benton tests)
	Visual integration (Hooper VOT)
Executive	**Hypothesis testing and concept formation (Wisconsin Card Sort** or Category Test, short forms)
	Reasoning (WAIS-R Similarities, proverb interpretation)
	Set shifting (Trails B, Trails A)

(Continued)

Table 2. Sample Core Bedside Neuropsychological Test Battery for Adults *(Continued)*

Type of test	Specific tests
	Verbal fluency (abbreviated versions of letter and category, e.g., one or two trials of each)
	Motor programming tasks (Luria Contrasting Programmes/Go-No-Go Paradigm, Manual Position Sequencing)
	Graphomotor programming (mn, ramparts)
Sensorimotor	**Psychomotor speed and coordination** (Grooved Pegboard)
	Psychomotor speed (finger tapping)
	Strength and effort (Dynamometer)
Mood and affect	**Beck Scales** (Depression, Anxiety)
	Depression scale (Yesavage, Zung, Hamilton)
	MMPI-2

Note. Standard tests are in **bold type;** others are optional or for limit testing. WAIS-R = Wechsler Adult Intelligence Scale–Revised; BDAE = Boston Diagnostic Aphasia Battery; WRAT-3 = Wide Range Achievement Test; WAB = Western Aphasia Battery; WMS-R = Wechsler Memory Scale–Revised; BVRT = Benton Visual Retention Test; VOT = Visual Organization Test; MMPI-2 = Minnesota Multiplication Personality Inventory–Revised.

Table 3. Sample Core Bedside Neuropsychological Test Battery for Geriatric Patients

Type of test	Specific tests
Omnibus	**Mattis Dementia Rating Scale**
Speech–language	**Boston Naming Test** (short form) Writing sample (BDAE Cookie-Theft or WAB kite picture) Following commands (up to four steps)
Attention–memory	**Digit span** (expanded version of MDRS digits) Visual search (Mesulam or other) Stroop Neuropsychological Screening Test **3 Words/3 Shapes** (Mesulam) Narrative recall (e.g., WMS-R Logical Memory, with delay, Babcock-Levy) Figural recall (e.g., WMS-R Visual Reproduction, with delay)
Spatial–construction	**Visual Form Discrimination** (Line Orientation, Facial Recognition, BVRT–copy trial) Visual integration (Hooper VOT)
Executive	Set shifting (Trails A, Trails B)

(Continued)

Table 3. Sample Core Bedside Neuropsychological Test Battery for Geriatric Patients *(Continued)*

Type of test	Specific tests
	Hypothesis testing and concept formation (Wisconsin Card Sort, 64-card version)
	Reasoning (WAIS-R Similarities)
	Verbal fluency (letters only)
Sensorimotor	**Psychomotor speed (finger tapping)**
	Pathognomonic sign (synkinesia)
	Strength–effort (Dynamometer)
	Psychomotor speed and coordination (Grooved Pegboard)
	Motor programming (Luria Contrasting Programmes/Go-No-Go Paradigm)
Sensory	**Pathognomonic sign (Double Simultaneous Stimulation)**
Mood–affect	Yesavage Geriatric Depression Survey

Note. Standard tests are in bold type; others are optional or for limit testing.

crimination). Sample bedside assessment test batteries are found in Tables 2 and 3.

IV. INTERPRETATION OF TEST RESULTS AND RENDERING OF THE FINAL DIAGNOSIS

Because the bedside assessment tends to be briefer than office-based evaluations, qualitative analysis of data, along with integration of a wide variety of variables, becomes more crucial to the diagnosis. The general principles for data analysis and interpretation are outlined elsewhere in this volume. In this regard, it is important to determine whether the pattern of test findings makes sense from the point of view of a neurological syndrome, or whether they are inconsistent and thus reflective of a process that is not clearly neurogenic. In the case of bedside assessment, special attention needs to be paid to the wide variety of variables mentioned elsewhere in this chapter. It is important for the clinician to be able to assess neuropsychological test findings in light of working hypotheses regarding the possible source of the patient's deficits; the history, pattern of performance, patient's mood and effort, and comorbid conditions are then integrated to generate a differential diagnosis. On the basis of these variables, the clinician then uses a set of decision trees in making the final differential diagnosis. Sample decision trees can be found in Exhibit 1. It needs to be borne in mind that the diagnosis often needs to be tentative, because the patient's status may be quite variable. However, by using the many types of information available, the clinician can usually narrow the differential diagnosis down to one or two prime possibilities, which can then be the focus of attention for other members of the treatment team. Because the differential diagnosis is often tentative, it may be necessary to recommend a reassessment sometime in the future or to continue to follow the patient through his or her hospital course to elucidate the status further. Follow-up evaluations may also be useful in tracking change over time, with special attention to disease progress or recovery and efficacy of medical interventions.

V. CONCLUSION

The bedside neuropsychological examination presents a number of unique challenges to the neuropsychologist, requiring the integration of a wide variety of variables not necessarily common to outpatient or broader assessments. This data integration needs to be accomplished with brevity, economy, and efficiency to account for both the patient's unique status and the changing demands of the health care environment.

Exhibit 1. Sample Decision Trees for Differential Diagnosis

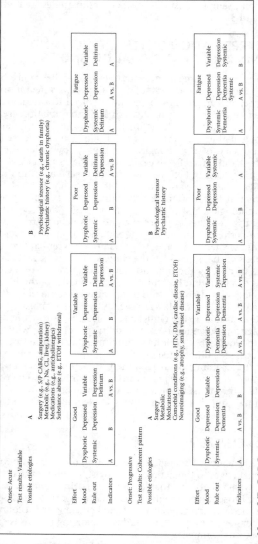

Note. S/P CABG = status-post coronary artery bypass graft; ETOH = Ethyl Alcohol; HTN = hypertension; DM = Diabetes Mellitus.

BIBLIOGRAPHY

Berg, R. A., Franzen, M., & Wedding, D. (1994). *Screening for brain impairment* (2nd ed.). New York: Springer.

Collins, R. D. (1985). *Atlas of drug reactions.* New York: Churchill Livingstone.

Kastrum, E. K. (1988). (Ed.). *Drug facts and comparisons* (updated monthly). St. Louis, MO: Facts and Comparisons, Lippincott.

Kiernan, R. J., Mueller, J., Langston, J. W., & Van Dyke, C. (1987). The neurobehavioral cognitive status examination: A brief but differentiated approach to cognitive assessment. *Annals of Internal Medicine, 107,* 481–485.

Lezak, M. D. (1995). *Neuropsychological assessment* (3rd ed.). New York: Oxford University Press.

Mattis, S. (1976). Mental status examination for organic mental syndrome in the elderly patient. In L. Bellak & T. Karasu (Eds.), *Geriatric psychiatry* (pp. 77–101). New York: Grune & Stratton.

Schwamm, L. H., Van Dyke, C., Kiernan, R. J., Merrin, E. L., & Mueller, J. (1987). The Neurobehavioral Cognitive Status Examination: Comparison with the Cognitive Capacity Screening Examination and the Mini-Mental State Examination in a neurosurgical population. *Annals of Internal Medicine, 107,* 486–491.

Strub, R. L., & Black, F. W. (1993). *The mental status examination in neurology* (3rd ed.). Philadelphia: Davis.

CHAPTER 5

Glenn T. Stebbins and Robert S. Wilson

Estimation of Premorbid Intelligence in Neurologically Impaired Individuals

An important aim of neuropsychological assessment is to identify impairment in higher cognitive, or intellectual, functioning. Because neuropsychological test data are rarely available for the premorbid period, the clinician usually must estimate, implicitly or explicitly, prior level of intellectual functioning. Although normative tables provide an estimate of an individual's premorbid performance on a given test, the specificity of normative-based estimates is rather low, because a wealth of potentially relevant information is not incorporated. Methods that allow for incorporation of this added information have been developed. Estimates derived from these methods are typically based on one or both of the following sources of information: (a) life history variables believed to be correlated with measures of intelligence (e.g., years of education); and (b) measures of current cognitive functioning that are highly correlated with measured intelligence but are relatively unaffected by brain damage (e.g., reading). Information from these sources may be used to form clinical impressions about premorbid intelligence, or actuarial methods may be used. In this chapter, a few of the principal approaches to estimation of premorbid intellectual function are reviewed, with consideration given to both the strengths and the limitations of each method.

I.   LIFE HISTORY APPROACHES

A. Conceptual Basis

Life history information can be used to form a clinical impression of premorbid intellectual level or to provide a numerical estimate of premorbid IQ. Estimates derived from this source of information are based on the empirically established relationship between many life history variables and performance on intellectual assessment measures. Life history information relevant to these determinations includes indices of socioeconomic status (e.g., educational attainment, occupational achievement), past medical history (e.g., birth and early development), other demographic variables (e.g., age, race), and other sources (e.g., previous testing results).

B. Life History Measures

1. INDICES OF SOCIOECONOMIC STATUS

a. Academic progress

Educational attainment. The number of years of formal education is highly correlated with measured intelligence, with simple correlations typically in the .5–.7 range (Matarazzo, 1972). Therefore, education is the best single predictor of performance on intelligence tests. For individuals who did not complete high school but did receive a general equivalency diploma (GED), it is customary to add 12 to years of completed schooling and divide the sum by 2 (e.g., 8 years of formal education plus GED = $[8 + 12]/2 = 10$).

Academic honors or difficulties. Failed or repeated grades in early educational history may reflect learning disabilities or significant attentional problems. Skipped grades or advanced placement may reflect higher intellectual abilities.

Grades and teacher comments. Summary measures of academic achievement, such as grade point average, are correlated with measured intelligence, but the correlations are typically modest. Teacher comments about academic performance and behavior may also help form a clinical impression of prior intellectual functioning. In general, however, such indices should be interpreted cautiously.

b. Occupational indices

Highest occupational position attained. Occupation is substantially related to measured intelligence, although somewhat less so than is education. Estimates of premorbid intellectual function are typically based on the highest occupation attained prior to the onset of injury or illness (e.g., Wilson, Rosenbaum, & Brown, 1979). A variety of occupational coding schemes exist (Wilson et al., 1979).

Other occupational information. Qualitative information about past occupations may be relevant. A history of declining performance within occupation or of shifts to less skilled work may be especially helpful.

2. PAST MEDICAL HISTORY

a. Birth and early development

Some abnormalities at birth and in early development may adversely affect intellectual functioning. Important information includes gestational age, birth weight, Apgar scores, perinatal trauma, and attainment of developmental milestones.

b. Comorbid conditions that affect cognitive function

This information includes history of specific congenital conditions (e.g., phenylketonuria [PKU], Williams syndrome) and acquired conditions (e.g., pervasive developmental delay, seizure disorder, head trauma). The presence of such conditions, depending on their nature, severity, onset, and duration, can add further complexity to the task of estimating prior level of intellectual functioning.

3. OTHER DEMOGRAPHIC VARIABLES

Other demographic variables, such as age, gender, race, and region of residence, have been shown to have some predictive value in multivariate analyses (e.g., Barona, Reynolds, & Chastain, 1984). However, these correlations are not as robust as those for educational and occupational accomplishments.

4. OTHER SOURCES

In some instances, standardized performance test results may be available from school, employment, military, or other records. Although these test results may aid in estimating prior level of intellectual functioning, caution is urged in interpreting these data. Tests are usually designed to measure something other than general intelligence (e.g., academic achievement), and such tests may be based on outdated norms that bear an uncertain relation to those relied on for current IQ measures. Furthermore, it is often difficult to evaluate whether these prior tests were administered and scored properly.

C. Estimation Methods

1. CLINICAL ESTIMATION

Information from the life history can be helpful in generating a global impression of premorbid intelligence. The clinician attempts to integrate this information to estimate a general level of function, such as below average, average, or above average. The principal advantage of this method is that the clinician can draw on all available information. The principal shortcoming of this approach is the lack of a standardized method of integrating this diverse information.

2. ACTUARIAL ESTIMATION

A number of formulas have been empirically developed that permit point estimates of measured intelligence on the Wechsler scales on the basis of socioeconomic and demographic variables. Typically, the formulas are developed by regressing summary IQ measures on predictive variables (e.g., age, education, occupation, gender) using the normative sample employed in the original development of the test. These formulas provide empirically based estimates of measured intelligence that do not depend on clinical judgment. The principal limitation of these formulas is that the resulting estimates are less accurate than one would wish, especially for persons with extreme levels of premorbid ability, for whom accurate estimates are most needed. These formulas provide point estimates of IQ, which must be considered in conjunction with the standard error of estimate for the formula. Presently, actuarial formulas have been developed for the Wechsler Adult Intelligence Scale–Revised (WAIS-R) and the Wechsler Intelligence Scale for Children–Revised (WISC-R), and validation studies have generally supported the clinical usefulness of actuarial formulas (Eppinger, Craig, Adams, & Parsons, 1987; Karzmark, Heaton, Grant, & Matthews, 1985).

a. WAIS-R estimates

Barona et al. (1984) regressed Verbal IQ (VIQ), Performance IQ (PIQ), and Full-Scale IQ (FSIQ) on age (as a categorical variable), education (as a categorical variable), occupation (as a categorical variable), gender, race, geographic region of residence, and urban–rural residence using the 1981 WAIS-R standardization sample. Variables that did not significantly contribute to IQ prediction (i.e., urban–rural residence for PIQ and

FSIQ; geographic region of residence for IQ) were not included in the final equations. The resultant regression formulas accounted for 38%, 24%, and 36% of the variance in WAIS-R VIQ, PIQ, and FSIQ scores, respectively. In an attempt to improve prediction, Barona and Chastain (1986) restricted the 1981 WAIS-R standardization sample to individuals who were older than 19 years of age and whose race was either African American or Caucasian. In addition, age and education were treated as continuous variables. These authors also added birth order and handedness as predictor variables, although those variables did not significantly contribute to the statistical solution and were not included in the final formulas. The new regression formulas were improved and accounted for 47%, 28%, and 43% of the variance in VIQ, PIQ, and FSIQ scores, respectively. The standard errors of estimate reported for the modified VIQ, PIQ, and FSIQ formulas were 11.0, 12.9, and 11.5, respectively. Because these modified formulas provide slightly better IQ prediction, they are recommended over the original formulas when applicable.

Paolo, Ryan, Tröster, and Hilmer (1996) developed regression formulas for WAIS-R subtest scores from the 1981 WAIS-R standardization sample and a sample of 130 elderly persons (age 75–96 years) stratified for age, education, gender, and race. The resultant regression formulas accounted for a modest amount of subtest variance (maximum, 48% for Digit Symbol; minimum, 22% for Digit Span). The reported standard errors of estimate for the formulas ranged from a high of 2.66 (for Picture Completion) to a low of 2.31 (for Information). The authors generated one-tailed confidence intervals at the 90% and 95% levels for each subtest estimate. The 90% confidence interval for all subtests (rounded to the nearest whole number) was 3, and the 95% confidence interval was 4. The clinical usefulness of these formulas has not been studied.

b. WISC-R estimate

Reynolds and Gutkin (1979) regressed VIQ, PIQ, and FSIQ on head of household's occupation, gender, race, urban–rural region, and geographic region of residence using the 1974 WISC-R standardization sample of 2,200 children age 6–16.5 years (Wechsler, 1974). They could not include age or education in the regression equations owing to design restrictions of the WISC-R. The resultant regression formulas accounted for little variance in summary IQs (14%–19%), and they had substantial standard errors of estimate (13.5–14.0). As a result, these formulas have not proved to be clinically useful.

II. PRESENT ABILITY APPROACH

A. Conceptual Basis

Brain damage does not affect all aspects of intelligence equally. In the present ability approach, measures of putatively less vulnerable abilities are administered to the patient and current performance on such tests is used to estimate past performance on an intelligence test. An effective measure must be both highly correlated with measured intelligence and relatively unaffected by damage to the brain, and therein lies the principal difficulty with this approach: Because all cognitive abilities are intercorrelated, it seems implausible that performance on a cognitive task can be highly related to intelligence yet unaffected by a neurological condition that alters intelligence. Nonetheless, such measures are widely used in neuropsychological assessment.

B. Methods

1. HISTORICAL BASIS

Babcock (1930) noted that measures of vocabulary tended to show less decline following mental deterioration than other measures. Wechsler (1958) extended this finding by developing a deterioration index composed of tests that "hold" with age in a cross-sectional sample and tests that do not. Subsequent studies of the deterioration index were not supportive (e.g., Larrabee, Largen, & Levin, 1985; Matarazzo, 1972), principally because performance on all Wechsler IQ subtests appears to be impaired, albeit to different degrees, in clinical samples of persons with a variety of neurological conditions. That is, Wechsler "hold" tests do not hold.

2. CURRENT METHODS

a. National Adult Reading Test (NART)

The NART is a British test of word reading and pronunciation that developed from the observation that reading ability was less impaired than vocabulary knowledge in a sample of patients with dementia (Nelson, 1982; Nelson & O'Connell,

1978). The test consists of 50 stimulus words that the patient reads aloud. The words violate common rules of phoneme production (e.g., aisle, bouquet). The use of these irregular words was intended to maximize the importance of past experience with the words and to minimize the impact of more recent experience. In the original standardization study, Nelson and O'Connell selected a sample of 120 medical inpatients with nonneurological conditions. These participants were given a prorated WAIS. Summary IQ measures were regressed on the number of errors committed on the NART. The regression formulas accounted for 60%, 32%, and 55% of the variance in VIQ, PIQ, and FSIQ scores, respectively (Crawford, Parker, Stewart, Besson, & DeLacey, 1989). The NART has been updated for predicting WAIS-R IQ measures in persons over 74 years of age (Ryan & Paolo, 1992). In the latter study, summary WAIS-R IQ measures were regressed on NART errors using a standardization sample of 85 elderly persons. The regression formulas were cross-validated on a sample of 41 elderly persons. The resultant regression formulas derived from the standardization sample accounted for 69%, 16%, and 55% of the variance in VIQ, PIQ, and FSIQ, respectively. Final regression formulas were derived from the standardization and cross-validation samples combined and resulted in standard errors of estimate of 7.7, 12.1, and 8.8 for VIQ, PIQ, and FSIQ, respectively.

b. National Adult Reading Test–Revised (NART-R)

Blair and Spreen (1989) revised the NART by adding 54 new stimulus words and applying North American pronunciation rules. In a standardization sample of 66 Canadians and Americans, they reduced the number of stimuli to 61 words and regressed WAIS-R VIQ, PIQ, and FSIQ on the number of pronunciation errors. The resultant regression formulas accounted for 69%, 16%, and 56% of the variance in VIQ, PIQ, and FSIQ, respectively. The standard errors of estimate reported for the VIQ, PIQ, and FSIQ estimates were 6.6, 10.7, and 7.6, respectively.

c. Wide Range Achievement Test–Revised (WRAT-R; Jastak & Wilkinson, 1984)

The WRAT-R Reading subtest has also been used to estimate IQ. This test contains words that conform to phonemic pronunciation rules as well as words that violate such rules. The score on the Reading subtest can be converted to standard scores that, like Wechsler summary IQs, have a mean of 100 and standard deviation of 15. Wiens, Bryan, and Crossen (1993) compared IQ estimates derived from the NART-R and WRAT-R standard scores to WAIS-R VIQ, PIQ, and FSIQ scores in a sample of 302 healthy individuals age 20–54 years. They found that the correlations of NART-R and WRAT-R Reading subtest to WAIS-R FSIQ were almost identical (NART-R to WAIS-R FSIQ = .46; WRAT-R Reading to WAIS-R FSIQ = .45) and highly significant. The WRAT-R estimate performed better than the NART-R at lower actual IQ ranges (e.g., did not overestimate low IQs), but it was similar to the NART-R in underestimating higher actual IQs.

d. Combined life history and present ability approaches

In an attempt to address the limitations of both the life history and present ability approaches, researchers have investigated the benefit of combining these two methods. The results indicated that IQ prediction is generally improved by using selected life history variables in conjunction with measures of current reading ability. Although the combined approach improves IQ prediction, these estimates still depend, in large part, on current performance on reading tests. To the extent that such performance is adversely affected by brain damage, these combined estimates will be inaccurate.

Combined NART and life history variables. Crawford and colleagues (cf. Crawford, Cochrane, Besson, Parker, & Steward, 1990; Crawford, Stewart, Parker, Besson, & Cochrane, 1989) developed and cross-validated regression formulas for estimating WAIS IQ measures from combined NART performance and demographic variables of gender, social class, and years of education. In a standardization sample of 151 healthy adults (age 16–88 years) the authors regressed WAIS IQ measures on the number of NART errors, gender, social class, and years of education. The resultant formulas improved estimations based on either NART or demographic variables alone. The amount of variance accounted for in WAIS VIQ, PIQ, and FSIQ by the estimates was 78%, 39%, and 73%, respectively. The standard errors of estimate reported for VIQ, PIQ, and FSIQ estimates were 6.8, 9.2, and 6.7, respectively.

Combined American version of the National Adult Reading Test (AMNART) and life history variables. Grober and Sliwinski (1991) employed a modified version of the NART (Schwartz & Saffran, 1987), which replaced 23 words unfamiliar to American participants with familiar words, and the demographic variable of years of education in a regression model to predict prorated WAIS-R VIQ. They standardized and double cross-validated the regression formula on a sample of more than 200 healthy elderly participants with an approximate mean age of 75 years. The resultant regression formula, based on a subset of 216 persons, accounted for 58% of the variance in prorated WAIS-R VIQ, with a standard error of estimate of 7.8. In a validation study presented in the same article, the authors compared AMNART and prorated WAIS-R VIQ performance in 25 patients with dementia and 58 nondemented control participants. The mean estimated IQ was not significantly different between groups, and the authors concluded that in mildly demented patients without significant language disturbance, the estimate appears promising.

e. Critique of present ability and combined methods

Nelson (1982; Nelson & O'Connell, 1978) hypothesized that the ability to read irregular words would be less vulnerable to brain damage because such knowledge was apt to have been acquired early through repeated encounters. She was wrong. In fact, persons with mild dementia have proportionally more difficulty reading irregular, compared to regular, words (Patterson, Graham, & Hodges, 1994). Furthermore, it has been clearly established that the ability to read words aloud, however measured, is impaired in persons with brain damage (cf. Grober & Sliwinski, 1991; Ryan & Paolo, 1992; Stebbins, Wilson, Gilley, Bernard, & Fox, 1990). Estimates of premorbid IQ based on current reading performance, therefore, depend on uncertain factors such as the extent of reading impairment and the correspondence between the individual's premorbid IQ and premorbid reading level. Combined methods are subject to the same criticism, but few empirical studies have been done. In summary, at present there is limited empirical support for estimating premorbid IQ from reading tests or other measures of present ability.

III. CONCLUSION

Knowledge regarding premorbid intellectual functioning is an important consideration in neuropsychological assessment. Because measures of premorbid IQ are rarely available, the clinician must estimate; estimates of premorbid IQ may be based on life history information, performance on tests believed to be relatively unaffected by brain damage, or both. The resultant estimates may be based on clinical judgment or an empirically derived regression formula.

All approaches to estimating premorbid IQ are subject to error. Clinical judgments of premorbid ability lack standardized methods of integrating diverse sources of information into a global estimate. Actuarial methods of estimating IQ from life history information do not permit precise prediction, especially for persons with very high or low premorbid intelligence. Present ability measures used to estimate premorbid IQ have been repeatedly shown to be affected by brain damage. In our view, the most empirically defensible approach, at present, is the use of actuarial formulas based on life history information in conjunction with test norms to guide decisions about premorbid IQ and intellectual impairment.

BIBLIOGRAPHY

Babcock, H. (1930). An experiment in the measurement of mental deterioration. *Archives of Psychology, 28* (Serial No. 117), 1–105.

Barona, A., & Chastain, C. R. (1986). An improved estimate of premorbid IQ for Blacks and Whites on the WAIS-R. *International Journal of Clinical Neuropsychology, 8,* 169–173.

Barona, A., Reynolds, C. R., & Chastain, R. (1984). A demographically based index of premorbid intelligence for the WAIS-R. *Journal of Consulting and Clinical Psychology, 52,* 885–887.

Blair, J. R., & Spreen, O. (1989). Predicting premorbid IQ: A revision of the National Adult Reading Test. *Clinical Neuropsychologist, 3,* 129–136.

Crawford, J. R., Cochrane, R. H. B., Besson, J. A. O., Parker, D. M., & Stewart, L. E. (1990). Premorbid IQ estimates obtained by combining the NART and demographic variables: Construct validity. *Personality and Individual Differences, 11,* 209–210.

Crawford, J. R., Parker, D. M., Stewart, L. E., Besson, J. A. O., & DeLacey, G. (1989). Prediction of WAIS IQ with the National Adult Reading Test: Cross-validation and extension. *British Journal of Clinical Psychology, 28,* 267–273.

Crawford, J. R., Stewart, L. E., Parker, D. M., Besson, J. A. O., & Cochrane, R. H. B. (1989). Estimating of premorbid intelligence: Combining psychometric and demographic approaches improves predictive accuracy. *Personality and Individual Differences, 10,* 793–796.

Eppinger, M. G., Craig, P. L., Adams, R. L., & Parsons, O. A. (1987). The WAIS-R index for estimating premorbid intelligence: Cross-validation and clinical utility. *Journal of Consulting and Clinical Psychology, 55,* 86–90.

Grober, E., & Sliwinski, M. (1991). Development and validation of a model for estimating premorbid verbal intelligence in the elderly. *Journal of Clinical and Experimental Neuropsychology, 13,* 933–949.

Jastak, S., & Wilkinson, G. S. (1984). *WRAT-R: Wide Range Achievement Test administration manual.* Los Angeles: Western Psychological Services.

Karzmark, P., Heaton, R. K., Grant, I., & Matthews, C. G., (1985). Use of demographic variables to predict full-scale IQ: A replication and extension. *Journal of Clinical and Experimental Neuropsychology, 7,* 412–420.

Larrabee, G. J., Largen, J. W., & Levin, H. S. (1985). Sensitivity of age-decline resistant ("hold") WAIS subtests to Alzheimer's disease. *Journal of Clinical and Experimental Neuropsychology, 7,* 497–504.

Matarazzo, J. D. (1972). *Wechsler's measurement and appraisal of adult intelligence* (5th ed.). Baltimore: Williams & Wilkins.

Nelson, H. E. (1982). *National Adult Reading Test (NART) test manual.* Windsor, England: NFER–Nelson Publishing.

Nelson, H. E., & O'Connell, A. (1978). Dementia: The estimation of premorbid intelligence levels using the New Adult Reading Test. *Cortex, 14,* 234–244.

Paolo, A. M., Ryan, J. J., Tröster, A. I., & Hilmer C. D. (1996). Demographically based regression equations to estimate WAIS-R subtest scaled scores. *Clinical Neuropsychologist, 10,* 130–140.

Patterson, K., Graham, N., & Hodges, J. R. (1994). Reading in dementia of the Alzheimer's type: A preserved ability? *Neuropsychology, 8,* 395–407.

Reynolds, C. R., & Gutkin, T. B. (1979). Predicting the premorbid intellectual status of children using demographic data. *Clinical Neuropsychology, 1,* 36–38.

Ryan, J. J., & Paolo, A. M. (1992). A screening procedure for estimating premorbid intelligence in the elderly. *Clinical Neuropsychologist, 6,* 53–62.

Schwartz, M., & Saffran, E. (1987). *The American-NART: Replication and extension of the British finding on the persistence of word pronunciation skills in patients with dementia.* Unpublished manuscript.

Stebbins, G. T., Wilson, R. S., Gilley, D. W., Bernard, B. A., & Fox, J. H. (1990). Use of the National Adult Reading Test to estimate premorbid IQ in dementia. *Clinical Neuropsychologist, 4,* 18–24.

Wechsler, D. (1974). *Wechsler Intelligence Scale for Children—Revised: Manual.* New York: Psychological Corporation.

Wechsler, D. (1958). *The measurement and appraisal of adult intelligence* (4th ed.). Baltimore: Williams & Wilkins.

Wiens, A. N., Bryan, J. E., & Crossen, J. R. (1993). Estimating WAIS-R FSIQ from National Adult Reading Test—Revised in normal subjects. *Clinical Neuropsychologist, 7,* 70–84.

Wilson, R. S., Rosenbaum, D., & Brown, G. (1979). The problem of premorbid intelligence in neuropsychological assessment. *Journal of Clinical Neuropsychology, 1,* 49–53.

CHAPTER 6
Michael D. Franzen and Grant L. Iverson

Detecting Negative Response Bias and Diagnosing Malingering:
The Dissimulation Exam

The average clinician will consider a formal evaluation for malingered performance or negative response bias only when suspicion is already raised regarding the amount of effort put forth on a clinical neuropsychological examination. These cases may include instances in which information derived from the evaluation is not in agreement with information from the chart review (e.g., the patient presents with dementia after a minor head injury), when the situation includes the possibility of external motivation for negatively biasing performance (e.g., cases of evaluation for criminal responsibility), or when behavioral observations indicate less than optimal effort. However, the subjective determination of negatively biased responding is as fraught with error as any of the tasks involving clinical intuition and judgment. As a result, it is useful to include objective indices of response style in most clinical neuropsychological examinations.

An important distinction needs to be made. Although the term *malingering* is frequently used to describe both behavior and a clinical condition, the diagnosis can be separated from the detection of the behavior related to the disorder. That is, to make a diagnosis of malingering, it is necessary both to determine that nonoptimal effort or exaggeration of symptoms has occurred and to ensure that the other diagnostic criteria of malingering are met. The many so-called malingering tests only determine the probability that nonoptimal effort or intentionally poor performance has been exhibited.

I. DEFINITION OF MALINGERING

Malingering is the intentional production of false or greatly exaggerated symptoms for the purpose of attaining some identifiable external reward (American Psychiatric Association, 1994). People may malinger to receive more money in a personal injury lawsuit, to receive workers' compensation or disability benefits, to obtain prescription medications, to avoid prosecution for criminal activities, or to avoid criminal responsibility (i.e., to be held not guilty by reason of insanity).

Within the context of a psychological or neuropsychological examination, malingering is the willful production of poor performance on measures of psychological function for the purpose of obtaining some externally recognized gain or benefit. Malingering is a highly specific diagnostic term. On the other hand, *negative response bias is the production of more pathological or deficient scores than would be expected on the basis of the skill level of the person.* Negative response bias, a more general term than malingering, can be associated with a variety of clinical situations and conditions. In addition to the motivational situations mentioned previously in connection with malingering, less than optimal performance can be associated with fatigue, disinterest, anxiety states, or depressive conditions. In each of these situations it is important to obtain some estimate of the degree to which optimal effort was expended.

The concept of malingering as a disorder is not empirically well documented. However, there are several ways in which malingering behavior may develop or become apparent. In the acute phase of treatment, it is possible for malingering to be chosen as a course of action prior to hospitalization. There are individuals who feign illness or injury to receive monetary compensation or material gain. Although the incidence is not known, this variant may represent a minority of the cases. Another form of malingering may occur when individuals admitted to the hospital for a legitimate reason decide to fabricate or magnify their difficulties to forestall discharge, to avoid responsibility, or to gain financial benefit.

It is essential to note that malingering behavior does not necessarily occur in the absence of neurologically based impairment. Malingering may occur as an exaggeration of existing deficits or as a behavioral response to an actual, although minor injury. There are no specific neuroanatomic correlates of malingering. However, the behavior may be more common in situations in which objective documentation is difficult to obtain, for example, in cases of mild head injury, subtle seizure disorders, or low-level neurotoxin exposure.

II. SUSPICION OF MALINGERING

Pankratz (1988) has listed instances in which the **suspicion of negative response bias should be raised.** We have revised that list as follows:

1. Consistently giving nearly correct responses to test items

2. A marked discrepancy between obtained scores and scores expected on the basis of premorbid background and medical diagnosis

3. Inconsistency between symptoms reported by the patient and symptoms observed by the clinician or other staff

4. Bizarre or unlikely answers to test items

5. Differences between results on tests of similar constructs that cannot be explained by variable attention, motivation, or medication status, or by psychometric properties of the tests

6. Behavior that is inconsistent with the obtained test results

In addition to knowing the situations under which malingered deficits may occur, it is useful to know the **content areas in which malingered performance can be exhibited.** These include the following:

1. Memory

2. Motoric and cognitive skills

3. Sensory-perceptual skills

4. Academic skill areas such as arithmetic

5. Abstract problem-solving skills

6. Fund of information

Of course, exhibiting behavior that arouses suspicion does not indicate that malingering has taken place. The clinician needs to **rule out other possible explanations for the data** such as the following:

1. Is there a medical complication that can explain the discrepancies in the data; for example, does the patient use narcotic medication or have unmedicated orthopedic pain?

2. Does the patient have a psychiatric disorder that can partially explain the test results; for example, can a generalized anxiety disorder in combination with an anoxic episode account for variable attention and low visual–spatial test scores?

3. Is there some personological variable that can account for variable or low effort; for example, is the patient impulsive, sociopathic, or uncooperative?

III. DIAGNOSIS

A. Differential Diagnoses

The diagnostic differentials exist across the entire gamut of clinical possibilities. First, it is necessary to rule out the possibility that the test results represent the actual level of skill impairment. Additionally, it is necessary to rule out the interactive effects of cognitive impairment with medication side effects, with psychiatric disorder, and with apathy or lack of motivation. There are three rule-out categories that need attention:
1. Actual cognitive impairment
2. Medication side effects
3. Psychiatric disorders

B. Neuropsychological Examination: An Overview

The basic notion in the evaluation of malingered performance is to make some decision related to whether the exhibited performance is possible given the history, medical condition, and psychiatric situation of the patient. Therefore, the first stages of the examination involve obtaining accurate information related to these variables. The chart review, clinical interview and history, and interview of collateral sources are important here. In fact, the most important thing to remember is that the examination for malingered performance is not different from the typical examination, although some specialized instruments and techniques may be included. The main goal is to obtain an accurate interpretation of the assessment results.

The clinician must first obtain an adequate history including information related to academic performance, prior brain insults or injuries, and familial instances of neurological disease. The medical history is frequently well documented in inpatient consultation services, but this should not be taken for granted. In particular, the patient's history should be obtained for the presence of diabetes, hypertension, stroke, or seizure. In cases of alleged mild traumatic brain injury, it is helpful to obtain ambulance crew and emergency department records because circumstances reported at a later time may be inaccurate.

The clinical neuropsychologist's observations of the patient during testing can be informative. Attending behavior and normal-appearing effort are not always indicative of adequate motivation, but exaggerated signs of effort combined with very poor scores may be an indication of malingered performance. Analog malingerers report that they may show poor cooperation and general confusion, aggravation and frustration, and slow response times with frequent hesitations during testing (Iverson, 1995).

The testing should be conducted in such a manner that optimal performance is likely. This principle may be difficult to implement in an inpatient hospital setting. However, poor performance should be the result of the patient's effort, not the result of lack of examiner effort to ensure an adequate environment.

Much has been said in the clinical literature regarding inconsistency and its relation to negative response bias. Inconsistency can include a discrepancy between the results expected on the basis of history and the obtained results, a discrepancy between performances separated by time, or a discrepancy between observations by different staff persons. Genuine impairment is diagnosed on the basis of observed inconsistencies, mainly inconsistencies between performance expected on the basis of premorbid estimates and present function, although inconsistencies across time can also be diagnostic of attentional difficulties. The interpretation of test performance as involving malingered impairment or other forms of negative response bias is made partly on the basis of ruling out other hypothetical reasons for the obtained inconsistency in results.

C. Clinical Model for Assessment

The following is a general overview suggested as a format for evaluating the presence of biased reponding. Subsequently, we review various tests that can be used within this assessment.

1. Complete a careful background review.

2. Conduct the clinical and collateral interviews.

3. Observe the patient's behavior in more than one situation, for example, with staff and family, in the interview, and during testing.

4. Administer screening procedures for biased effort at the beginning of the examination.

5a. If screening procedures reveal suspicious performance, conduct a comprehensive examination of level of effort and symptom exaggeration. This assessment should include at least one additional procedure designed to identify biased responding (e.g., digit memory tests such as the PDRT, Hiscock & Hiscock procedure, and the Victoria Symptom Validity Test, or other forced-choice procedures).

5b. If screening procedures do not reveal suspicious performance, conduct a comprehensive examination of level of effort only if there are other reasons for clinical suspicion.

6. Examine scores on standard neuropsychological instruments to identify suspicious scores (e.g., Recognition Memory Test scores below 30) or patterns of performance (e.g., average-to-low average Wechsler Memory Scale–Revised [WMS-R] General Memory Index with an impaired Attention–Concentration Index).

7. If suspicious scores or patterns are observed during testing, return to Step 5a.

D. Specific Assessment Procedures

There are many specific test procedures designed to detect negative response bias. This section provides an overview of these procedures as well as general recommendations for their use. Specific cutoff scores are not provided. This is a growing and developing area, and the current literature should always be consulted when making clinical decisions. We are merely pointing the clinician to the relevant literature and potential procedures.

1. 21-ITEM TEST

The 21-Item Test takes approximately 5 minutes to administer and score. This test can be used at the beginning of the evaluation as a rapid screen for biased effort. The 21-Item Test (Iverson, Franzen, & McCracken, 1991, 1994) consists of 21 words that are presented orally, following which the patient is instructed to recall freely as many words as possible. The patient is then instructed to identify the target words within a two-alternative forced-choice procedure. In analog studies, the rates of detecting experimental malingerers have ranged from 20% to 80% depending on which cutoff scores were used (Frederick, Sarfaty, Johnston, & Powel, 1994; Iverson & Franzen, 1996; Iverson et al., 1991, 1994).

2. REY MEMORY FOR 15 ITEMS TEST

The Rey Memory for 15 Items Test (Rey, 1964) can be used at the beginning of the examination as a rapid screen. The test consists of 15 items presented in a matrix of three columns by five rows. Patients are told that they will have just 10 seconds to study the items, following which they will have to reproduce the items from memory. The test is quite simple given that the items are arranged in logical, easy-to-remember rows (e.g., numbers, letters, and shapes). The most frequently calculated scores are the total number of correct items and the number of correctly reproduced rows.

Clinicians must know the following about this test: First, there are different methods of administration and scoring. The most widely used administration is to request recall immediately after exposure. Second, the test has limited sensitivity to analog malingering with variability in detection rates. Third, there are several different cutoff scores that have been recommended. Finally, the test is likely to be even less sensitive if it is administered after other memory procedures because its simplicity will be even more obvious.

3. 16 ITEMS TEST

The 16 Items Test can also be used at the beginning of the examination as a rapid screen. It is a modification of the Rey Memory for 15 Items Test. Paul, Franzen, Fremouw, and Cohen (1992) eliminated the geometric designs and added one item to the remaining four sets to make the test simpler and more specific to negative response bias. The test has variable sensitivity but relatively high specificity to negative response bias (Iverson & Franzen, 1996).

4. SYMPTOM VALIDITY TESTING

Symptom validity testing (SV) is best applied in situations in which more sophisticated procedures or empirically derived cutoff scores are not available. Often it is used in cases involving claimed impairment for a sensory function. Loren Pankratz was the leading proponent of symptom validity testing within neuropsychology. Early studies using this method consisted of case reports of individuals who were feigning sensory (Pankratz, Fausti, & Peed, 1975) or memory (Pankratz, 1983) deficits. Patients are exposed to a large number of trials of the stimulus (e.g., sound, tactile sense, or simple memory task) that they claim they cannot experience or remember. Given a two-alternative forced-choice response format, persons who are grossly exaggerating their symptoms may score below the probable range of chance—that is, below the confidence interval surrounding random responding (50% correct). Symptom validity testing is sensitive to blatant exaggeration, but it may not be as sensitive to more subtle or sophisticated approaches to exaggeration.

To address the issue of low sensitivity, there have been many refinements and extensions of the SVT paradigm. In review articles and chapters, these measures are often classified broadly as forced-choice procedures. Popular refinements include digit memory procedures, word lists, and adaptations of existing tests into two-alternative forced-choice paradigms.

5. HISCOCK AND HISCOCK PROCEDURE

The Hiscock and Hiscock (1989) procedure should be used when a more comprehensive assessment for potential negative response bias in memory is clinically indicated. The shortened version of the test appears to have comparable sensitivity and specificity to the full procedure. Hiscock and Hiscock refined the simple SVT memory procedure to create a digit recognition test. The patient is shown a card with a five-digit number and then, following a delay interval, asked to choose the number in a two-alternative forced-choice task. The test appears to be getting more difficult as the delay interval between digit presentation and recognition response increases from 5 to 10 to 15 seconds. The test contains three blocks of 24 trials for a total of 72 items. In the initial report, Hiscock and Hiscock (1989) demonstrated that a severely demented patient with Alzheimer's disease performed within the probable range of chance, whereas a patient suspected of malingering performed significantly below chance.

The Hiscock and Hiscock procedure has been applied to analog and clinical samples with excellent results. Patients with unequivocal brain damage generally obtain scores greater than 90% correct on the procedure, whereas suspected clinical malingerers and experimental malingerers perform much more poorly (Guilmette, Hart, & Giuliano, 1993; Prigatano & Amin, 1993). High sensitivity and specificity to experimental malingering has been reported in a shortened version (36 vs. 72 items) of the test (Guilmette, Hart, Giuliano, & Leininger, 1994).

6. PORTLAND DIGIT RECOGNITION TEST

The Portland Digit Recognition Test (PDRT; Binder, 1990) is a digit memory procedure that is an extension of the SVT paradigm and a refinement of the Hiscock and Hiscock (1989) procedure. The PDRT should be used when a more comprehensive assessment for potential negative response bias is clinically indicated. Because of the amount of time required to perform the original version, it may have limited use in an acute care hospital. It can also be administered in a shortened version and in a computer version, both of which have shown promise as clinical assessment tools. In this test, patients are presented a string of digits auditorily followed by intervals of interpolated activity (i.e., counting backward). After the interval (5, 15, or 30 seconds), the patient is presented with a two-alternative forced-choice task and instructed to choose the target digits. The PDRT differs from the Hiscock and Hiscock (1989) procedure in three ways: (a) The digits are presented auditorily; (b) the delay interval is filled with an interpolating activity; and (c) the third delay interval is 30 seconds as opposed to 15 seconds. The PDRT takes approximately 45 minutes to administer.

The PDRT is sensitive and specific to negative response bias. Blatant exaggeration is identified by below-chance performance. More sophisticated exaggeration is revealed by scores falling below empirically derived cutoffs for persons with unequivocal brain damage.

a. Short form

For the short form version, Binder (1993) provided clinical decision rules for discontinuing the PDRT in patients who are showing normal performance. For this abbreviated version, the first 36 "easy" items are administered. If the patient scores below the cutoff of 19, the entire test is administered. If the patient correctly answers 7 of the first 9 difficult items or 12 of the first 18 difficult items, the test is discontinued.

b. Computerized version

Rose and colleagues developed a computerized version of the PDRT (Rose, Hall, & Szalda-Petree, 1995). The primary advantage of this version is the ability to compute item response latencies. Differences in response latencies have been shown to be a marker of negative response bias in several studies.

7. VICTORIA SYMPTOM VALIDITY TEST

The Victoria Symptom Validity Test (VSVT), a refinement of the Hiscock and Hiscock (1989) procedure, has advantages over both the original Hiscock and Hiscock test and the PDRT in that it is substantially shorter and is computer administered and scored. It can be used in most evaluations in which negative response bias is suspected. The VSVT is a 48-item computer-administered digit memory procedure consisting of three blocks of 18 items, with each block containing 8 easy and 8 difficult items. The primary dependent variables for the test are the total number correct, number of correct easy items, number of correct difficult items, total response time for easy items, and total response time for difficult items. The test takes approximately 15 minutes to administer, and it is computer scored. The test is sensitive to the negative response bias of experimental malingerers, and nonlitigating persons with closed head injuries are not misclassified on the basis of the cutoff scores (Slick, Hopp, Strauss, Hunter, & Pinch, 1994).

8. FORCED-CHOICE TEST OF NONVERBAL ABILITY

The Forced-Choice Test of Nonverbal Ability should be used when a more comprehensive assessment for potential negative response bias is clinically indicated in the assessment of nonverbal abstraction or general intellectual skills. Frederick and Foster (1991) modified the Test of Nonverbal Intelligence by combining the two 50-item forms and eliminating two of the four response choices. Thus, the revised test is a 100-item two-alternative forced-choice procedure. The most obvious score is a comparison to chance. However, the test yields several more sophisticated scores including slope, consistency ratio, slope × consistency ratio, and correlation between test performance and item difficulty. These scores appear to be reasonably sensitive and specific to negative response bias (Frederick et al., 1994).

E. Suggestions for Use of General Instruments

1. MINNESOTA MULTIPHASIC PERSONALITY INVENTORY (MMPI-2)

The MMPI-2 is best suited for the detection of grossly exaggerated symptoms of psychological dysfunction. To this end, the standard validity scales and several other validity indices are clinically useful. Two careful, thorough, and thoughtful meta-analyses and reviews have provided some guidance for the clinician (Berry, Baer, & Harris, 1991; Rogers, Sewell, & Salekin, 1994). Berry and colleagues (1991) found that the largest effect sizes were associated with the F scale, the original Dissimulation scale, and the F-K index. Rogers et al. (1994) determined that F, F-K, and the Obvious minus Subtle score demonstrated the greatest effect sizes for both normal controls and psychiatric comparison groups. On the basis of their review, Rogers and colleagues (1994) offered two sets of cutoff scores for clinical practice.

The following set represents the mean cutoff scores in their meta-analysis and can be used to raise the clinician's index of suspicion regarding possible negative response bias:

a. F-scale raw score greater than 23
b. F-scale T score greater than 81
c. F-K index greater than 10
d. Obvious minus Subtle score greater than 83

It is important to note that these scores should be used only to raise one's index of suspicion. The scores are likely to classify falsely a substantial minority of patients with genuine complaints. Extreme elevations on the validity scales and indices are considerably more specific to negative response bias. More conservative cutoff scores suggested by Rogers and colleagues (1994) are as follows: (a) F-scale raw score greater than 30, (b) F-K index greater than 25;, and (c) Obvious minus Subtle score greater than 190.

2. WECHSLER MEMORY SCALE–REVISED

An approach proposed by Mittenberg, Azrin, Millsaps, and Heilbronner (1993) was to compare the WMS-R Attention–Concentration (AC) Index score with the General Memory (GM) Index score. These researchers operated under the assumption that it is unlikely for someone with normal memory (GM Index) to have impaired attention and concentration (AC Index). Therefore, large GM–AC discrepancies should be unlikely in genuinely memory-impaired patients, whereas previous research has demonstrated a propensity for analog malingering participants to suppress their performance on attentional tasks such as Digit Span (Bernard, 1990; Iverson & Franzen, 1996). Mittenberg and colleagues (1993) found that participants instructed to malinger concerning memory suppressed their Attention-Concentration Index ($M = 71$) to a greater extent than their General Memory Index ($M = 85$), whereas patients with genuine problems associated with closed head injuries demonstrated the opposite pattern (Mittenberg et al., 1993). These discrepancy scores may be relatively specific to negative response bias.

Large GM–AC Index score discrepancies may reflect negative response bias. This finding should be followed up by a more careful examination of level of effort.

3. RECOGNITION MEMORY TEST

The Recognition Memory Test should be used as a within-evaluation assessment of effort. This test appears sufficiently difficult to be unaffected by order of test administration. The Recognition Memory Test consists of two 50-item subtests: recognition memory for words (RMW) and recognition memory for faces (RMF). The test appears to be sensitive to exaggeration in both analog and clinical settings. Iverson and Franzen (1996) found that cutoff scores for both RMW and RMF were sensitive and specific to analog malingering. Millis (1994) demonstrated that litigating patients with mild head injuries scored much lower on both subtests than nonlitigating patients with moderate-to-severe head injuries. Because the subtests are in a two-alternative forced-choice format, patients' scores can be compared to the probable range of chance and to empirically derived cutoff scores. A score of 19 or less on either subtest is significantly below chance ($p < .04$).

IV. CONCLUSION

The recent interest in the detection of malingering is part of the larger clinical concern with establishing whether nonoptimal effort has occurred and determining the validity of the scores obtained from standardized testing. Although this can be a difficult assessment issue, it can be addressed by paying close attention to the history, clinical presentation, and pattern of obtained test scores, as well as by the use of procedures specifically designed to evaluate level of effort and biased responding.

BIBLIOGRAPHY

American Psychiatric Association. (1994). *Diagnostic and statistical manual of mental disorders,* (4th ed). Washington, DC: Author.

Bernard, L. C. (1990). Prospects for faking believable memory deficits on neuropsychological tests and the use of incentives in simulation research. *Journal of Clinical and Experimental Neuropsychology, 12,* 715–728.

Berry, D. T. R., Baer, R. A., & Harris, M. J. (1991). Detection of malingering on the MMPI: A meta-analysis. *Clinical Psychology Review, 11,* 585–598.

Binder, L. M. (1990). Malingering following minor head trauma. *Clinical Neuropsychologist, 4,* 25–36.

Binder, L.M. (1993). An abbreviated form of the Portland Digit Recognition Memory Test. *Clinical Neuropsychologist, 7,* 104–107.

Frederick, R. I., & Foster, H. G. (1991). Multiple measures of malingering on a forced-choice test of cognitive ability. *Psychological Assessment, 3,* 596–602.

Frederick, R. I., Sarfaty, S. D., Johnston, J. D., & Powel, J. (1994). Validation of a detector of response bias on a forced-choice test of nonverbal ability. *Neuropsychology, 8,* 118–125.

Guilmette, T. J., Hart, K. J., & Giuliano, A. J. (1993). Malingering detection: The use of a forced-choice method in identifying organic versus simulated memory impairment. *Clinical Neuropsychologist, 7,* 59–69.

Guilmette, T. J., Hart, K. J., Giuliano, A. J., & Leininger, B. E. (1994). Detecting simulated memory impairment: Comparison of the Rey Fifteen-Item Test and the Hiscock Forced-Choice procedure. *Clinical Neuropsychologist, 8,* 283–294.

Hiscock, M., & Hiscock, K. C. (1989). Refining the forced-choice method for the detection of malingering. *Journal of Clinical and Experimental Neuropsychology, 11,* 967–974.

Iverson, G. L. (1995). Qualitative aspects of malingering. *Brain Injury, 9,* 35–40.

Iverson, G. L., & Franzen, M. D. (1996). Using multiple objective memory procedures to detect simulated malingering. *Journal of Clinical and Experimental Neuropsychology, 18,* 38–51.

Iverson, G. L., Franzen, M. D., & McCracken, L. M. (1991). Evaluation of an objective assessment technique for the detection of malingered memory deficits. *Law and Human Behavior, 15,* 667–676.

Iverson, G. L., Franzen, M. D., & McCracken, L. M. (1994). Application of a forced-choice memory procedure designed to detect experimental malingering. *Archives of Clinical Neuropsychology, 9,* 437–450.

Millis, S. R. (1994). Assessment of motivation and memory with the Recognition Memory Test after financially compensable mild head injury. *Journal of Clinical Neuropsychology, 50,* 601–605.

Mittenberg, W., Azrin, R., Millsaps, C., & Heilbronner, R. (1993). Identification of malingered head injury on the Wechsler Memory Scale–Revised. *Psychological Assessment, 5,* 34–40.

Pankratz, L. (1983). A new technique for the assessment and modification of feigned memory deficit. *Perceptual and Motor Skills, 57,* 367–372.

Pankratz, L. M. (1988). Malingering on intellectual and neuropsychological measures. In R. Rogers (Ed.), *Clinical assessment of malingering and deception* (pp. 169–192). New York: Guilford Press.

Pankratz, L., Fausti, S. A., & Peed, S. (1975). A forced-choice technique to evaluate deafness in the hysterical or malingering patient. *Journal of Consulting and Clinical Psychology, 43,* 421–422.

Paul, D., Franzen, M. D., Fremouw, W., & Cohen, S. (1992). Standardization and validation of two tests used to detect malingering. *International Journal of Clinical Neuropsychology, 14,* 1–9.

Prigatano, G. P., & Amin, K. (1993). Digit Memory Test: Unequivocal cerebral dysfunction and suspected malingering. *Journal of Clinical and Experimental Neuropsychology, 15,* 537–546.

Rey, A. (1964). *L'examen clinique en psychologie.* Paris: Presses Universitaires de France.

Rogers, R., Sewell, K. W., & Salekin, R. T. (1994). A meta-analysis of malingering on the MMPI-2. *Assessment, 1,* 227–237.

Rose, F. E, Hall, S., & Szalda-Petree, A. D. (1995). Portland Digit Recognition Test-Computerized: Measuring response latency improves the detection of malingering. *Clinical Neuropsychologist, 9,* 124–134.

Slick, D., Hopp, G., Strauss, E., Hunter, M., & Pinch, D. (1994). Detecting dissimulation: Profiles of simulated malingerers, traumatic brain-injury patients, and normal controls on a revised version of Hiscock and Hiscock's Forced-Choice Memory Test. *Journal of Clinical and Experimental Neuropsychology, 16,* 472–481.

PART II

PEDIATRIC
NEUROPSYCHOLOGY

CHAPTER 7
Christopher M. Ryan, Katherine Hammond,
and Susan R. Beers

General Assessment Issues for a Pediatric Population

Behaviorally and cognitively, children are so different from adults that the assessment of pediatric patients places special and challenging demands on those who evaluate their neuropsychological status. This is evident in each of the four major components of an evaluation: obtaining information about the child, building rapport and maintaining the child's cooperation during testing, interpreting assessment results, and communicating those results to others.

History taking requires an approach that is quite unlike that routinely used with adults, primarily because children—particularly those under the age of 10—tend to be poor historians. They have difficulty identifying and describing salient symptoms or problems in a clear and reliable fashion, and they often have trouble recounting the sequence of events. For these reasons, obtaining current and past medical and psychosocial information about the child requires a much greater reliance on surrogates—hospital staff, old medical records, and reports from teacher and parent—than is the case with adult patients.

We thank Rick Hendrickson and Dorothy Sandstrom for their helpful comments on an earlier draft of the manuscript.

Eliciting and maintaining the typical child's cooperation with an assessment, especially on an inpatient unit, also requires more effort and attention than is usually the case when assessing adults. Sitting for any extended time period and answering what the child may perceive as "dumb" questions or attempting to complete frustrating tests often challenges the patience of children, and may result in inattention, acting out, or even outright refusal. To reduce these problems, the clinician must first encourage the resistant child to participate in the evaluation and then work diligently to maintain the child's motivation and cooperation over the course of the assessment. This is not a trivial task, especially if one is not completely comfortable with children or has not spent much time around them.

Interpreting results of a neuropsychological assessment is complicated by the fact that, unlike adults or older adolescents, the child has a central nervous system that is not developmentally static but is still maturing. Not only are developmental differences in brain maturation evident between children of the same age, but also different brain areas may mature at different rates in any given child. Both of these facts mean that it is far more difficult for the neuropsychologist to distinguish developmental *delay* from stable or progressive brain *damage* in children and challenge the professional's ability to make strong inferences about the nature and extent of brain dysfunction in the child. Heterogeneity in brain development, coupled with cultural and experiential differences, further reinforces the view that each child is truly unique, necessitating a cautiously idiographic, or "*N* of 1," approach when interpreting test results. Neuropsychologists make an egregious error when they take a purely nomothetic, or actuarial, approach that simply compares the child's scores with published test norms and identifies performance as falling inside or outside of the "normal" range. Rather, conclusions must be based on a thorough clinical *integration* of age-appropriate test scores, qualitative features of performance, and the wealth of historical and behavioral data gathered during the course of the assessment.

Providing useful feedback is a critical part of any assessment, yet this may be a particularly complex and time-consuming process when children are involved, not only because there are so many diverse parties with a "need to know," but also because each party may expect the evaluation to answer a different set of questions. Certainly, there should be a common core of information communicated to everyone that includes a general description of the child's cognitive and behavioral strengths and weaknesses. In addition, the physician may want information about etiology or specific disorders ruled out; other members of the hospital treatment team may want suggestions that can help them with patient management, and teachers may want recommendations about educational placement and suggestions about strategies to help the child perform better in the classroom. Psychologists, social workers, and family members may want all of this information, as well as some discussion of the long-term implications for the child's well-being, but distilled in such a way that it is truly understandable and relevant. Finally, the child will require sufficient age-appropriate feedback so that he or she can understand enough of what is going on to participate fully in whatever treatment recommendations are implemented in the future.

The remainder of this chapter elaborates on each of these major components and provides lists of practical information that can help the clinician cope with typical problems encountered when evaluating a child or adolescent in a hospital setting that includes both psychiatric and medical patients. The initial issue, however, which is not unique to pediatric assessment, is the need to clarify the referral question prior to planning the assessment.

I. CLARIFYING THE REFERRAL QUESTION

Referral requests are frequently so vague or ambiguous (e.g., "This child's behavior seems odd to me—what do you think is going on?" or "She's had a recent history of academic decline—why?") that understanding why a particular patient has been referred for a neuropsychological evaluation often requires a level of clairvoyance that most clinicians do not possess. Because managed care now permits relatively little time for assessments, it is critical to work closely with the referring professional from the outset *to ensure that the planned assessment answers the question of interest.* Understanding the professional's rationale for the assessment helps to generate a series of reasonable hypotheses as to what types of problems might be manifested by the child during the neuropsychological evaluation, and that, in turn, guides in the selection of specific neuropsychological tests. The following steps usually occur after receipt of the initial consultation request.

A. Formulation of the Question

1. Speak *directly* with referring health professionals

a. What behaviors or symptoms have they observed that triggered this request?

b. What medical or psychosocial disorders do they think could explain the child's problems?

2. Formulate primary goals that may include the following:

a. Detailed description of neuropsychological strengths and weaknesses

b. Clarification of diagnostic issues

c. Improvement in patient management

d. Recommendations for additional evaluations, treatment, or rehabilitation

B. Developing Testable Neuropsychological Hypotheses to Guide Assessment

Hypotheses should be practical, should be based on information that can actually be obtained by the clinician, and should specifically address issues raised by the referring professional. Neuropsychologists are frequently criticized in the clinical setting for providing reports that have little relevance to the child's treatment.

II. INFORMATION GATHERING

To understand fully the kinds of problems a child is having, it is necessary to consult *multiple* information sources prior to initiating an assessment. Relying on any single source (e.g., medical records *or* parent reports) is likely to provide an incomplete or even biased picture of the child's medical and psychosocial problems and of the available resources for overcoming such difficulties. Obtaining as complete a picture as possible about the child's current and previous functioning provides a context in which to interpret the test results and generate treatment or placement recommendations that are reasonable and feasible.

Various sources of information are usually available to the clinician. It is important to review current and past medical records to ascertain medical or psychosocial problems that could affect the child's performance, explain the etiology of the child's problem, and help interpret results of the assessment. Admission and discharge summaries often provide salient information on developmental history, medical disorders, accidents, and medications. One must be especially alert to comments about academic or behavioral problems in the classroom and medical or psychosocial problems within the child's extended family. Because performance on neuropsychological tests is affected by previous exposure to the instrument, particularly within the past 6 months, it is important to review the results of any previous neuropsychological evaluation.

The process of obtaining information regarding children on an inpatient unit is somewhat different from that associated with outpatient evaluations. An inpatient hospitalization provides the clinician with an opportunity to observe the child directly as he or she interacts with peers and adults, whereas with outpatients, more time is usually available to gather the information prior to the evaluation, and there is more opportunity for parent involvement.

The following activities should be completed prior to the formal neuropsychological assessment of the child.

A. For Inpatients

1. Observe the child's interactions with staff.
2. Elicit staff's description of the child's behavior and child–family interactions.
3. Evaluate the child's readiness for formal assessment (e.g., not acutely ill, settled into unit, cooperative with other procedures).
4. Ascertain the patient's estimated length of stay to determine feasibility of completing the evaluation.

B. For Outpatients

1. Obtain all relevant records from physicians and other health professionals.
2. Discuss the purpose of the assessment with a family member (usually completed by phone).
3. Provide an opportunity for the child to talk with you about the assessment.
4. Ask parents to bring school records to the evaluation.

C. Interview

Information gathering continues during the initial clinical interview and usually includes input from both the parents and the child.

1. Ascertain the family's understanding of the need for this assessment.

2. Obtain the parent's view of the child's medical, developmental, social, and academic history (see the following section).

3. Have the parent complete a standard developmental history form (e.g., Pediatric Neuropsychology Questionnaire) and a standard behavior checklist (e.g., Child Behavior Checklist [CBC], Behavior Assessment System for Children [BASC]).

4. Obtain a release of information to contact the child's teachers and other relevant professionals.

D. Developmental History

For both inpatients and outpatients, information about the child's development and academic history are particularly important to a neuropsychological assessment. This is usually provided by a family member, typically the mother.

1. Obtain a brief description of medical, psychosocial, and academic problems.

2. Define behavioral symptoms:

a. Mood swings or tantrums

b. Staring spells

c. Attentional problems

d. Relationship difficulties ("teasing" or frequent fighting with peers)

e. Sleep problems

3. Review pre-, peri-, and postnatal history (see Exhibit 1).

4. Review developmental history (see Table 1).

5. Review family history:

a. Was this child's development different from that of other children in the family?

b. Was there a history of psychiatric or neurological problems (e.g., learning disability, attention deficit disorder) in other family members (e.g., sibs, parents)?

III. THE CLINICAL INTERVIEW

The amount of truly useful anamnestic information that can be obtained directly from children is largely dependent on their overall level of cognitive maturity (usually indexed by age), the nature and severity of their medical or psychiatric disorder, their ability to sustain attention, their degree of comfort with strange environments and adults, and their overall level of

Exhibit 1. Key Development History Issues
to Be Reviewed

1. Difficulties during gestation
2. Prenatal exposure to toxins or drugs (e.g., nicotine, alcohol, cocaine)
3. Difficulties during labor and delivery
4. Method of delivery
5. Perinatal illness or critical-care issues (e.g., hospitalization in intensive care unit)
6. Developmental milestones (see Table 1)
7. History of febrile illnesses or seizures
8. History of other major childhood illnesses
9. History of head injuries (with or without unconsciousness) or other neurological problems

motivation. Surrogates provide the most reliable information about the child's problems and strengths, but it is also important to hear the child's view of the problem. Observing the child directly during the clinical interview also yields valuable information. Particular attention should be paid to language, motor coordination, sensory problems (e.g., hearing), ability to sit still, social appropriateness, and mood. This permits the clinician to see how the child behaves in an unfamiliar, at times quite stressful, situation. During this informal, relatively unstructured conversation, the clinician usually learns enough about the child's interests and develops sufficient rapport that a comfortable and valid neuropsychological evaluation can be completed.

A. The Testing Environment

1. Whenever possible, conduct formal neuropsychological testing in a testing room or a private office designed for evaluating children (e.g., age-appropriate seating, all testing materials organized and "ready to use").

2. Help the child become comfortable in this testing space.

3. If testing *must* be conducted in the child's room, ensure that there will be sufficient privacy, without nursing interruptions.

Table 1. Selected Neuromotor and Language Milestones

Skill	Age 2	Age 3	Age 4	Age 5
Gross motor	Runs well; kicks ball; goes up and down stairs (one step at a time)	Stands on one foot; pedals tricycle; goes up stairs (alternating feet)	Hops on one foot; stands on one foot (5 s); goes down stairs (alternating feet)	Stands on one foot (10 s); may be able to skip
Fine motor	Builds tower of six cubes; turns book pages singly	Copies circle; copies cross	Copies square; uses scissors; draws persons with two to four parts	Copies triangle; prints some letters; draws person with body
Comprehension	Follows simple commands; identifies body parts; points to common objects	Understands spatial relationships (in, on, under); knows functions of common objects	Follows two-part commands; understands same and different	Follows three-part commands; recalls parts of a story; understands number concepts
Expression	Speaks two- or three-word sentences; labels common objects	Speaks three- to four-word sentences; uses regular plurals; can count three objects; can tell age, sex, and full name	Speaks four- to five-word sentences; can tell story; uses past tense; can count four objects; names one color	Speaks sentences of five or more words; uses future tense; can count 10 or more objects; names four colors

Note. From *"Developmental-Behavioral Pediatrics"* (2nd ed.), by M. D. Levine, W. B. Carey, & A. C. Crocker, 1992, Philadelphia: Saunders. Copyright 1994 by W. B. Saunders. Adapted with permission.

Table 2. Useful Assessment Measures

Area	Specific tests
Attention	WISC-III Digit Span
	Continuous Performance Test
	Halstead-Reitan (HR) Rhythm Test
Motor speed, eye-hand coordination, and fine motor praxis	HR Fingertapping
	Grooved Pegboard or Purdue Pegboard
Psychomotor efficiency	WISC-III Coding
Learning and memory	Wide Range Assessment of Memory and Learning (WRAML) screening
	Test of Memory and Learning (TOMAL)
Visuoconstructional skills	WISC-III Block Design
	WISC-III Object Assembly
	Rey-Osterreith Complex Figure
Mental flexibility and executive functions	Trail Making (or Reitan Progressive Figures Test, for younger children)
	WISC-III Mazes
	HR Tactual Performance

(Continued)

Table 2. Useful Assessment Measures *(Continued)*

Area	Specific tests
Reasoning (hypothesis testing)	Wisconsin Card Sorting Test (WCST; preferably on computer)[a]
Academic achievement	Wechsler Individual Achievement Test (WIAT)
	Wide Range Achievement Test (WRAT-3)
General Intelligence	Information, Comprehension, Picture Completion, Block Design[b]
	Test of Nonverbal Intelligence (TONI-2)
Language comprehension[c]	HR Aphasia Screening Test
	Token Test
	Sections of the Boston Diagnostic Aphasia Examination (BDAE)

Note. WISC-III = Wechsler Intelligence Scale for Children

[a]If testing requires the child to work quietly on his or her own (e.g., WRAT-3 Arithmetic; WCST administered by computer), the examiner should remain, unobtrusively, in the room.

[b]See Sattler (1988) for a more complete discussion of short-form estimates.

[c]If there is reason to suspect language problems, the clinician should consider consultation with the speech–language service, a formal audiological examination, or both.

Exhibit 2. A Sample Introduction

> *"Dr. Smith told me that you fell out of your tree fort and hurt your head pretty bad, and she asked me to take some time this afternoon to see how you're doing."* Following some rapport building and "small talk," testing is introduced: *"Now I have some interesting things for you to do. [Depending on the child's level of understanding and motivation] I'm going to ask you to do things like put pegs in holes as quickly as possible, look at pictures and tell me what's missing or odd about them, put together some jigsaw puzzles, answer general information questions, draw some designs for me, and so on. Some of these are easy and fun. And some of them are hard. Everybody has trouble with some of these tasks. But that's OK. I want to see how you're doing, and I want you just to try your best for me. We're going to be working together for the rest of the morning [or part of the afternoon as appropriate]. Let me know if you need a drink of water or if you have to go to the bathroom. OK? Do you have any questions? Are you ready?"*

B. Introducing the Evaluation

Avoid using terms like "play games" when describing the testing. Provide the child with an *age-appropriate* introduction to testing including the following elements:

1. Who asked for this assessment
2. What will happen during this assessment
3. Approximately how long the assessment will take
4. Review of "ground rules"

Exhibit 2 provides a sample introduction to the testing situation.

C. Dealing With Parents

It is customary to begin the outpatient clinical interview with parent and child together. After some rapport has been established, the family should be asked to leave so that the testing can begin. Parents are often reluctant to leave their child and may wish to remain in the testing room. Except for very young children, this is not good clinical practice. A typical response to parent concerns might be as follows: "It's very important that I have an opportunity to work with your child alone, without any distractions. This is a highly standardized testing situation, and working with the child alone is a necessary part of our assessment procedure."

IV. MAINTAINING THE CHILD'S COOPERATION DURING TESTING

Some children are so engaged by the testing situation that the examiner can administer the entire battery smoothly and efficiently. Unfortunately, other children find the process of being evaluated—or just sitting still for a few hours—so onerous that completing each task becomes a battle that can be won only if the examiner remains calm and maintains control over the testing situation by giving the child the *illusion* of control.

Start the assessment with a task the child is likely to enjoy, perhaps something he or she mentioned during the clinical interview. Do not get involved in a discussion with the child while administering a test. If the child asks, "Is that right?" after a specific item, provide a reassuring but nonspecific response ("You're really trying" or "Boy, some of these really make you think, don't they? Let's keep on going, and try your best for me"). If a child persistently demands feedback after specific items, an appropriate response might be "We'll talk about it later" or "Let's finish this set of questions [or tasks] first; then we can talk." Children often do not ask for more detailed feedback following this initial request, and the clinician should not volunteer additional information *during* the testing session.

If, after completing the test, the child reiterates his or her request for feedback, provide some *brief, but accurate,* feedback (e.g., "You did better on some things than on others, but that's how it is for most kids"). After completion of the entire session, ask the child if he or she has any questions about anything that occurred during the session. This procedure helps "debrief" the child and allows the clinician to correct any misconceptions about the nature of the assessment or performance. In addition, the ensuing discussion can provide additional insights about how the child thinks and feels.

A. Dealing With Off-Task Behaviors During the Assessment

As the test session continues, the child's attention may wander. This can be prevented to some extent by maintaining a comfortably structured testing situation.

1. Become well practiced and comfortable with the testing materials before working with any child.

2. Move quickly from one test to another.

3. Do not engage in lengthy chats with the child between tests.

4. Do not provide an elaborate introduction to each new test.

5. Improve on-task behavior by implementing a contingency contract.

6. Provide a short break.

7. Keep the session brief.

The best way to prevent a child's attention from wandering is to ensure that the test session is brief. This means that the clinician has selected the *minimal number* of tests needed to answer the referral question and has integrated data from both record review and observation of the child during the clinical interview. To facilitate this, testing behavior must be well practiced and the testing space must be sufficiently organized so that one can move quickly and effortlessly from one test to another. Although the goal is to complete testing in one session, a second session often is necessary, especially for younger or very impaired children.

B. Early Termination of the Assessment

For any number of reasons, it may not be possible to complete the assessment. In that case, a good rule of thumb is to get as much information as possible from a formal assessment as well as from less formal observations, incorporate that information in the report, clearly detail why the assessment was not completed (or not initiated), and make recommendations as to what should be done in the future (e.g., evaluate on an outpatient rather than inpatient basis, delay until the child has recovered from acute illness or trauma). One might consider terminating the assessment session early when the child passively "refuses" by manifesting little effort (e.g., giving "I don't know" responses to questions he or she should be able to answer), by making extremely careless or impulsive responses that are out of character with other behaviors, or by being directly oppositional (e.g., "I don't want to do this! This is stupid!").

If the child is so inattentive that he or she cannot focus on a task for more than a few minutes at one time, one should attempt to continue the assessment on another day. If the child continues to refuse, a brief report should be prepared that summarizes one's observations, results, and impressions; discusses the extent to which these impressions or conclusions are valid (based on the child's level of cooperation); and makes recommendations for future evaluations, if indicated, with suggestions as to when and how they ought to be structured.

V. SELECTING A BATTERY OF TESTS

How to choose a series of neuropsychological tests is an art that cannot be taught easily. The specific tests selected are determined by a host of factors, including the environment in which one is working (e.g., pediatric unit, psychiatric unit), the neuropsychological "culture" of that clinic (e.g., Halstead-Reitan, Luria-Nebraska, Process Approach), the clinician's level of experience, the nature of the referral question, the age and level of cognitive maturity of the child, and the amount of time available for the assessment. Regardless of one's theoretical approach to assessment, however, one should attempt to develop a "core" battery that can be used with all patients and add other tests to this battery when confronted with specific referral questions that may require more information or a different type of information (e.g., academic achievement). The application of a standard core battery is quite useful in improving diagnostic skills insofar as it allows one to observe how different medical and psychiatric disorders influence performance on the same set of neuropsychological tests.

Any test used as part of a formal neuropsychological assessment must have good norms, span a reasonable age range, and be psychometrically sound (i.e., have good validity and test–retest reliability). Clinicians should rely on measures that have good, age-appropriate norms so they can document the child's cognitive strengths and weaknesses—the first, and perhaps most important, goal for any neuropsychological evaluation. However, as suggested in the following section, clinical interpretation requires more than comparing a child's test scores to the published norms and determining whether they fall within "normal limits" or within the "brain damaged" range. Most clinicians prefer tests that are readily available and used widely, so that another neuropsychologist will be able to evaluate the patient at some time in the future and compare their results with those of the earlier assessment. Serial assessment remains the best way to differentiate developmental delays or the effects of transient situations (e.g., acute psychiatric disorder) from permanent brain damage.

There continues to be no consensus as to what specific tests ought to be incorporated into the "ideal" brief battery, and organizing specific tests by "cognitive domain" also remains controversial. Table 2 provides a listing of instruments found to be quite useful on a general pediatric medicine unit. This is not an inclusive list but is meant to provide the names of some tests that are available for measuring each domain.

VI. INTERPRETING TEST RESULTS

Neuropsychological tests may be sensitive to brain damage in children, but they are not specific. That is, performance on any single test or series of tests can be influenced by a host of factors, most of which are unrelated to central nervous system dysfunction. As a consequence, it is difficult to make strong diagnostic statements about the presence or absence of brain damage or about underlying neuropathology, particularly if the child has been evaluated briefly and at only one point in time. One method favored by clinicians is to use a hypothesis-testing strategy to interpret results.

A. Steps in Hypothesis Testing

1. Prepare a summary of results organized by domain.
2. Identify cognitive strengths and weaknesses:

a. Place emphasis on domains (e.g., memory) or subdomains (e.g., verbal–nonverbal distinctions) rather than on specific tests.

b. Discuss specific test results only to emphasize a point that has direct relevance to hypothesis testing.

3. Generate a series of hypotheses to explain the pattern of results (see Exhibit 3).

4. Evaluate each hypothesis systematically, integrating all relevant data.

5. Make a decision about the plausibility of each hypothesis.

6. Present the most reasonable interpretations in the report:

a. Summarize empirical data (e.g., test scores, observations) to support the interpretation.

b. Consider mentioning possible alternative interpretations that have been rejected, and present reasons for the rejection.

7. List any limitations or problems associated with this assessment, including any omissions in the data (e.g.,

Exhibit 3. Possible Explanations for Pattern of Neuropsychological Test Results

---

1. Poor motivation
2. Inadequate exposure to certain experiences or information that are tapped by particular tests (e.g., from impoverished environment)
3. Psychosocial discomfort in testing or social situation (e.g., test-taking anxiety, social phobia)
4. Acute physical illness
5. Attentional problems
6. Serious psychopathology (e.g., depression)
7. Developmental delay in the maturation of certain cognitive processes (e.g., language or motor delay)
8. Brain damage[a]

---

[a]The nature and extent (e.g., focal vs. diffuse) and possible etiology should be discussed in the report.

missing school records) or distractions (e.g., hallway noise or interruptions).

VII. PROVIDING FEEDBACK

A. Communicating Results

To make the neuropsychological assessment truly useful, feedback should be given to all parties who will be making decisions about the child's short- and long-term welfare. The written report serves as the "core" material for providing information to anyone who has a need to know about the patient. The term *feedback* in this context is almost always an *oral* communication whereby results are interpreted in a way that can be understood by each person asking for information.

B. The Feedback Process

1. Discuss results with the referring health professional:
a. Answer the referral question.
b. Review etiologic issues (if relevant).
c. Make treatment recommendations (if relevant).

d. Make reevaluation recommendations (if appropriate).

e. Address any other issues raised by the referral source.

2. Review results with other members of the treatment team:

a. Provide a brief summary of results and interpretation.

b. Indicate whether the patient should be referred to other professionals for evaluation or treatment.

c. Discuss treatment recommendations and long-term prognosis.

3. Summarize findings to parents:

a. Discuss the child's strengths and weaknesses.

b. Educate parents about the diagnostic and treatment implications.

c. Provide information on available resources.

d. Help parents develop a plan to discuss results with their child.

4. Provide feedback to school officials (usually teacher), if requested:

a. Review the child's school placement.

b. Discuss strategies to improve the child's classroom performance.

c. Explain why the child may be having trouble in school.

d. Be sensitive to the parents' concerns about revealing personal information.

5. Maximize opportunities to highlight the child's strengths. Remind parents, child, and educators that this child has a number of strengths that can serve as the cornerstone for developing new educational and behavioral skills as well as compensatory strategies.

VIII. CONCLUSION

Like any other skill, pediatric neuropsychological assessment improves with specialized training, and practice; exposure to as many different patients as possible is helpful. Moreover, each clinician has a somewhat different view of how to proceed. This chapter highlights an approach that is drawn from collective experiences in a variety of medical and psychiatric settings. The recent explosion of books about pediatric neuropsychology can provide the clinician with a wealth of wisdom that can accelerate the development of clinical acumen. Although it is by no means exhaustive, a listing of several books that may be particularly helpful is provided in the bibliography.

One of the most common errors made by novice neuropsychologists is the tendency to overdiagnose brain damage.

Low scores that are consistent with brain dysfunction are interpreted as unequivocal evidence that the brain has been damaged by some insult or disorder. In making strong statements about the integrity of any patient's central nervous system, one needs to be cautious when that conclusion is based on a one-time evaluation with a brief battery of neuropsychological tests. This chapter has emphasized the need to obtain as much information as possible about the child from myriad sources and to integrate that information clinically. It is this overall pattern—and not any single element—that provides the most accurate characterization of the child's neuropsychological status. The diagnosis of brain damage, when based on neuropsychological test results, must necessarily be a diagnosis of exclusion. Before concluding that any individual's behavior is a direct consequence of structural damage to the central nervous system, all other possible interpretations of the neuropsychological data must be considered by the clinician, and discarded.

BIBLIOGRAPHY

Neuropsychological Issues

Baron, I. S., Fennell, E. B., & Voelker, K. K. S. (1995). *Pediatric neuropsychology in the medical setting.* New York: Oxford University Press.

Cantwell, D., & Baker, L. (1987). *Developmental speech and language disorders.* New York: Guilford Press.

Pennington, B. (1991). *Diagnosing learning disorders: A neuropsychological framework.* New York: Guilford Press.

Reitan, R. M., & Wolfson, D. (1992). *Neuropsychological evaluation of older children.* South Tucson, AZ: Neuropsychology Press.

Reynolds, C. R., & Fletcher-Janzen, E. (Eds.). (1989). *Handbook of clinical child neuropsychology.* New York: Plenum Press.

Reynolds, C. R., & Kamphaus, R. W. (Eds.). (1990). *Handbook of psychological and educational assessment of children: Intelligence and achievement.* New York: Guilford Press.

Rourke, B. P., Fisk, J. L., & Strang, J. D. (1986). *Neuropsychological assessment of children: A treatment-oriented approach.* New York: Guilford Press.

Sattler, J. M. (1992). *Assessment of children* (3rd ed., rev.). San Diego, CA: Jerome M. Sattler

Developmental Considerations

Behrman, R. E., Kliegman, R. M., & Arvin, A. M. (1996). *Nelson textbook of pediatrics* (15th ed.). Philadelphia: Saunders.

Levine, M. D., Carey, W. B., & Crocker, A. C. (1992). *Developmental-behavioral pediatrics* (2nd ed.). Philadelphia: Saunders.

Attention Deficit Hyperactivity Disorder

Attention deficit hyperactivity disorder (ADHD) is the diagnostic term used to describe children and adults who are unable to modulate attention, impulse control, and motor activity appropriately. The current formulation of the American Psychiatric Association (1994) diagnostic nosology *(DSM–IV)* uses a syndromic–descriptive approach in the differential diagnosis of these disorders. Three specific subtypes include the (a) inattentive, (b) impulsive–hyperactive, and (c) combined types. In addition, the classification "ADHD not otherwise specified" is used to describe behavioral presentations that do not meet the full criteria for one of three subtypes of ADHD. The *DSM–IV* lists 18 symptoms that are categorized across two primary domains: inattention (nine symptoms) or hyperactivity–impulsivity (six symptoms of hyperactivity and three symptoms related to impulsivity). Subtyping is based on decision rules related to the individual clustering of these primary symptoms.

Other required inclusion criteria for this spectrum of behavioral disorders include an age of onset prior to age 7, primary symptoms observable in at least two different social contexts (e.g., home and school, home and workplace), and an adverse effect of symptoms on social, occupational, or academic achievement. It is well understood that each of these core features varies substantially in expression across age or developmental demands. Exclusionary criteria for a diagnosis of ADHD include the presence of other pervasive developmental disorders, schizophrenia, or other psychoses.

I. EPIDEMIOLOGY

The incidence of ADHD is estimated at 3%–5% (American Psychiatric Association, 1994), and it is one of the most common psychiatric conditions in childhood (Ross & Ross, 1982). In terms of socioeconomic status, there appears to be small but nonsignificant variability in primary expression of the disorder. Increased problems with comorbidity, however, are related to adverse psychosocial stressors. The prevalence of ADHD in males, compared to females, is disproportional, with rates in males four times those for females in the general population and nine times those seen in clinically referred populations (American Psychiatric Association, 1994).

II. ETIOLOGY

ADHD may occur as a result of multiple biologically based etiologic factors. Genetic predisposition may account for up to 50% of the variance expressed in these conditions (Goodman & Stevenson, 1989). Exposure to a variety of early central nervous system insults (e.g., perinatal and neonatal hypoxia, obstetric trauma, intrauterine exposure to infection, early childhood heavy metal exposure) further predisposes some individuals to the development of ADHD. Because multiple neural systems contribute to attentional functioning and behavioral self-regulation, even subtle developmental perturbations may lead to attentional dysfunction. In addition, ADHD symptoms tend to be exacerbated by stress, are more prevalent in unstructured situations, and may be exacerbated by high-demand situations. Psychosocial factors can produce a phenotype of this condition in which there is absence of any neurobiological etiology (Pennington, 1991). In most cases, the etiology of ADHD remains cryptogenic.

III. DEVELOPMENTAL COURSE

Prior to the overt expression of ADHD, young children might show such premorbid behavioral characteristics as excessive motor activity, behavioral irritability, and difficulty in establishing consistent sleep schedules in infancy. Although such early developmental signs are not by themselves specific to the later development of ADHD, a child may be at greater risk if these characteristics persist into the preschool years and additional cognitive and behavior problems emerge. By age 3 or 4, a distinct behavioral phenotype is identifiable. Difficulties maintaining age-appropriate behavioral self-regulation, excessive motor activity, and a limited capacity to adapt to unexpected changes in the child's environment are seen. On entering elementary school, greater demands are placed on children to conform to rule-governed behavior, and a poor capacity for sustained attention leads children who are predisposed to ADHD to express overt symptoms in greater numbers. Other disruptive behavior disorders and academic difficulties may also be seen, because children at this stage are expected to function with increased self-directed learning, independence, and autonomy.

The emergence of the inattentive subtype of ADHD appears to be harder to detect, because the external structure common in the early elementary grades may mollify the expression of symptoms until middle childhood. It is only at this stage that greater demands are imposed for self-directed learning, and the amount and complexity of academic burden increase. Children with this subtype also tend to develop internalizing behavior disorders or adjustment disorder problems or both (as opposed to disruptive behavior disorders).

With the progression from middle childhood into adolescence, symptoms of overt hyperactivity tend to improve, whereas residual cognitive and attentional deficits are more prone to persist. Approximately 20% do not display primary symptoms by adulthood. For the majority, however, a variable pattern of primary and subclinical symptoms persists. Approximately 75% of these individuals continue to suffer from some form of social–emotional difficulties as well. In summary, ADHD disorders represent a class of conditions that affect early development and have the potential to influence adversely social, scholastic, and emotional adjustment in adulthood.

IV. ADHD SUBTYPES

In a review of multiple studies of children with predominantly hyperactive versus primary attentional dysfunction, Goodyear and Hynd (1992) identified multiple features distinguishing these subgroups (see Exhibit 1).

Exhibit 1. Distinguishing Characteristics Associated with ADHD Subtypes

ADD With Hyperactivity	ADD: Inattentive Type
Motorically overactive	Tendency toward a sluggish personal tempo
"Sustained" attentional problems	"Selective" attentional problems
Impulsivity	Disorganization
Problems with behavior and adaptation in academic setting	Academic deficiencies related to underlying cognitive dysfunction
	Higher incidence of co-occurring learning disabilities
	Greater susceptibility to performance anxiety

In a subsequent review, Dykman and Ackerman (1993) concluded that youngsters with ADHD that is characterized by predominant hyperactive–impulsive behaviors exhibited more problems related to impulse control and aggressive–defiant characteristics (i.e., externalizing behavior disorder traits). In contrast, youngsters with ADHD of the inattentive type expressed greater overanxious, dysthymic, depressed, and interpersonal withdrawal symptoms (i.e., internalizing behavior disorder characteristics). Barkley (1994) summarized data that reflect a dissociation between ADHD subtypes and suggest that the inattentive subtype may represent a primary deficit in the focus–execute dimensions of attention, whereas the hyperactivity subtype may represent primary deficits in response inhibition and the capacity to maintain focused or sustained attention. Thus, ADHD subtypes appear to be dissociable along dimensions of both cognition and behavior.

Whereas there is a general acceptance of ADHD subtypes along the dimension of primary symptom attributes (i.e., with or without hyperactivity), research efforts continue to focus on the delineation of more discrete forms based on other behavioral characteristics. It is common practice, however, to treat related emotional–behavioral findings by describing and ranking these associated symptoms using the multiaxial criteria for other specific clinical conditions.

V. COMORBID CONDITIONS

ADHD exists among a continuum of other developmental disorders of childhood. Because primary symptoms are seen early in childhood, potential adverse influences both on general psychosocial adaptation and on learning and academic adjustment must be anticipated. ADHD is considered independent of general intellectual ability and, therefore, is prevalent among both intellectually gifted and impaired individuals. Still, there is a clear association between ADHD and specific developmental learning disorders. In addition, there are a number of other developmental, medical, and neurological conditions that can result in similar behavioral symptoms. For instance, undiagnosed hearing or vision impairments may result in impaired sensory integration, which often leads to apparent deficits in attention. Other specific conditions such as (but not limited to) thyroid disorders, other metabolic disorders, systemic lupus erythematosus, diabetes, acquired neurological insults, certain types of seizure disorders, hypoxic or anoxic cerebral events, hypoglycemia, and HIV-I are also associated with specific deficits in attentional functioning. Furthermore, iatrogenic effects of various medication therapies (e.g., phenobarbital, theophylline) may mimic ADHD features.

The disruptive behavior disorders (oppositional–defiant disorder, conduct disorder) are the most thoroughly investigated of comorbid conditions. ADHD is grouped along with these disorders under the disruptive disorders category within *DSM–IV*. The overlap among these disorders can be so extensive that the question has been raised as to whether hyperactivity is synonymous with both ADHD and conduct disorder. Oppositional and conduct disorders occur in up to two thirds of children with ADHD. Barkley (1994) argued that a common pathway for the expression of both hyperactivity and other disruptive behavior disorders may be through perturbations in neural systems for inhibition and delayed responding.

Anxiety and mood disorders are expressed in upward of 25%–30% of this population. Adjustment disorder evolving into dysthymia or major depression may occur as a consequence of impaired adaptation to residual ADHD symptoms, which may remain untreated or undiagnosed. Primary depression may be associated with cognitive blunting, deficits in attention–concentration, and limitations associated with everyday working memory, all of which may mimic the inattentive features of ADHD. It is possible, however, to discern differences in the temporal course or natural history of these disorders.

The co-occurrence of anxiety disorders requires careful differential diagnosis. The existence of symptoms of anxiety, mood disorder, or obsessive–compulsive disorder affects the appropriate selection of psychopharmacological interventions. Because internalizing disorder symptoms are more prevalent in the inattentive subtype of ADHD, neuropsychological evaluation may prove especially helpful in patients with that subtype in ruling out other competing diagnoses such as generalized anxiety disorder.

Bipolar features may mimic ADHD characteristics. Although the former condition is usually viewed as primary when the coincidence of conditions is suspected, the two conditions frequently are indistinguishable. The establishment of ADHD characteristics earlier in childhood has not been found to be a differentiating factor between these two conditions. Only a careful delineation of the relevant contributory history may be helpful. Whereas the individual with ADHD typically displays rapid mood shifts that tend to be "reactive," in bipolar disorder a more cyclic pattern is established that is defined by more protracted periods of excitability or expansiveness.

Along with other developmental disorders, the ADHD-related conditions form a heterogeneous group of conditions that may vary in their expression as a function of primary subtype, age, developmental level, and comorbid conditions. In the differential diagnosis for ADHD, as in any of the developmental disorders of childhood, it is necessary to consider further the matrix of psychosocial and individual factors that may be contributory. Therefore, a flexible, multivariate method of assessment for purposes of differential diagnosis is required. With the identification of any of the factors cited previously, additional medical, psychiatric, and neurological consultations may be required.

VI. ADHD AND LEARNING

The relationship between ADHD and other learning problems requires special attention, because marginal academic performance has been found in nearly 80% of this population (Anderson, Williams, McGee, & Silva, 1987). Prospective studies have documented disproportionate rates of school failure and dropout. Whereas most children with ADHD fall within the normal range with regard to overall intelligence, some investigators have reported 7- to 15-point discrepancies on IQ measures between ADHD and control groups (Barkley, 1990).

An overview of the primary difficulties in the scholastic areas of reading, spelling, arithmetic, and handwriting is provided by Zentall (1993). Although it is not uncommon to find discrepancies of at least 1 standard deviation on academic achievement tests, approximately 9%–63% of children with ADHD may also be diagnosed with a specific learning disability (LD; Fiore, Becker, & Nero, 1993). Estimates of the existence of ADHD within populations of learning-disabled children have been reported in the ranges of 26%–41% (Silver, 1981) and as high as 80% (Safer & Allen, 1976).

Both cognitive and behavioral complications associated with ADHD presentations impose obvious limitations on academic skill acquisition. Denckla (1996) stressed two sources of vulnerability that potentially affect the educational development of children with ADHD: (a) deficits in the encoding and acquisition of new information secondary to limited use of metacognitive skills that are essential for the development of working memory and (b) a form of developmental output disorder (i.e., deficits associated with planning and organization). Thus, deficits in central executive as opposed to modality-specific information processing may be unique to this population. More specific forms of learning disability can be identified if, in addition to attentional dysfunction, specific deficits in other domains of information processing are discerned. Additional problems may arise as a result of the reciprocal effects of a repeated pattern of academic failure and the development of low self-esteem. The presence of comorbid conduct or oppositional disorder presents the need to rule out effects of disadvantageous psychosocial adjustment as well as any possible predisposition toward language-mediated cognitive deficits. To date, the long-term effects of treatment on academic development remain to be elucidated (Carlson & Bunner, 1993), and disentangling the characteristics of combined ADHD-LD presentations remains a clinical challenge. A comprehensive method for differential diagnosis, as described in chapter 9, this volume, is necessary when comorbid LD-ADHD is suspected.

VII. NEUROBIOLOGY OF ADHD

Although the ontogeny of ADHD remains incompletely understood, increasing evidence suggests that, for many, this is a disorder of anterior brain system functioning, primarily involving the orbital–frontal areas and connections to the caudate, striatum, and other limbic structures (see Barkley, 1994, p. 25 for discussion). Support for such a hypothesis has been culled from the single photon emission computed tomography (SPECT) studies of Lou and colleagues (Lou, Henriksen, & Bruhn, 1984; Lou, Henriksen, Bruhn, Borner, & Nielsen, 1989) as well as the positron emission tomography (PET) studies of Zametkin et al. (1990). In addition, quantitative EEG studies in boys with ADHD have shown increased slow wave activity in frontal regions and decreased beta activity in the temporal regions relative to controls (Mann, Lubar, Zimmerman, Miller, & Muenchen, 1992).

Studies involving structural brain imaging remain inconclusive. Although atypicalities in caudate and basal ganglia volumes have been implicated (Hynd, Semrud-Clikeman, Lorys, Novey, & Eliopulos, 1990; Castellanos et al., 1994), results have been inconsistent. Other findings have implicated decreased frontal width measurements in children with ADHD in comparison to normal controls (Hynd, Marshall, & Gonzales, 1993), as well as select differences in the size of the corpus callosum. Right hemisphere contributions to attentional dysfunction are also possible (Heilman, Voeller, & Nadeau, 1991). Investigations have also centered on the brain stem, the reticular activating system, the cerebellum, and the locus coeruleus as sources of attentional dysfunction.

The ontogeny of ADHD symptoms remains ill defined, although multiple cortical and subcortical systems have been implicated. At this stage in the understanding of these conditions, there are no neurodiagnostic studies that aid in making a differential diagnosis, and the consensus of opinion focuses on multifactorial etiologies.

VIII. NEUROPSYCHOLOGICAL ASSESSMENT

A variety of neuropsychological studies of ADHD have been undertaken, and overviews provided by Barkley (1990), Pennington (1991), and DuPaul and Stoner (1994) have highlighted a broad array of potential neurocognitive correlates of this disorder. It is difficult to draw general conclusions from this literature, however, because selection of study participants has typically included mixed ADHD subtypes or primarily hyperactive subtypes.

"Attention" as a construct relates to a variety of cognitive processes. The integrity of attentional systems is critically important for the successful development of diverse higher cognitive functions (Kinsbourne, 1992). The development of age-appropriate attentional faculties permits incremental increases in "processing capacity," which, in turn, facilitate the ability to decode selectively complex information, allocate or deploy processing strategies, and monitor the quality of ongoing cognitive performance. The increased capacity to allocate and sustain attention flexibly is in response to an ongoing maturational demand that remains crucial over the course of cognitive development.

That attention represents a multivariate construct is not subject to debate. What remains less well defined are the components of attentional dysfunction that have the greatest potential usefulness for aiding not only in the differential diagnosis of ADHD but also in delineating specific subtypes. More important, questions remain as to how these features should be evaluated to contribute in an ecologically valid fashion to the development of remedial or compensatory strategies to support an individual's general adaptation. Surveying the literature, one notes three to five dimensions of attentional functioning that are commonly addressed within comprehensive treatment-oriented neuropsychological assessment batteries. These approaches typically include direct measures of focus–execute, shift, sustain and encoding abilities (Mirsky, Anthony, Duncan, Dhearn, & Kellam, 1991). Sohlberg and Mateer (1989) used additional measures of alternating and divided attention in addition to the focus, sustain, and select continuum. Mapou and Spector (1995) offered a hybridization of these measures that adds components involving the expanded assessment of executive functioning as well as modality-specific new learning and memory. Empirical validation of any of these or other strategies awaits the test of time. Table 1 provides a representative selection of neuropsychological assessment tests that evaluate the relative integrity of these specific domains of attentional functioning.

Selecting from among a sampling of representative measures in order to complete a multifactoral assessment of attention permits an opportunity to ostensibly "map" individual differences within aspects of performance. When combined with measures of general intellectual and academic ability as well as the assessment of sensory, motor, higher cognitive functioning, one can dissociate the relative contribution of attentional dysfunction from other sources of neuropsychological disintegrity. It remains important to recognize that until broader validation of such attentional batteries is achieved, such an assessment strategy serves only as paradigm for the appreciation of the potential cognitive ramifications of attentional dysfunction upon social, scholastic, and emotional adaptation.

Table 1. Multivariate Assessment of Attention

Domain	Child measures
Focused attention	Wechsler Intelligence Scale for Children, 3rd ed. (WISC-III) Coding Smith Symbol Digit Modalities Test Trail Making Test A Contingency Naming Test Parts 1 and 2 Underlining Tests Visual Memory Subtest of the Test of Visuo-Perceptual Skills (Nonmotor)
Sustained attention	Tests of Variables of Attention Connors Continuous Performance Test
Shift or alternating attention	WISC-III Digits Backwards Trail Making Test Part B Contingency Naming Tests Parts 3 and 4 Wisconsin Card Sorting Test

(Continued)

Table 1. Multivariate Assessment of Attention *(Continued)*

Domain	Child measures
Encoding	WISC-III Digits Forward
	Trail 1 of the California Verbal Learning Test–Children's Version (CVLT-C)
	Wide Range Assessment of Memory and Learning (WRAML) Story Memory
	Visual Sequential Memory Subtest of the TVPS-NM
	WRAML Picture Memory
Executive functions	Wisconsin Card Sorting Test
	Rey-Osterreith Complex Figure
	CVLT-C Semantic Versus Serial Clustering Score

Note. All tests with the exception of the Test of Visuo-Perceptual Skills and the Contingency Naming Test are referenced in the *Handbook of Neuropsychological Assessment* (Lezak, 1995). Tests not referred to in the text are cited in the bibliography at the end of this chapter.

The use of a limited neuropsychological screening battery that is augmented by domain specific tests of attention, and combined with traditional psychoeducational testing (intelligence and achievement testing), offers a unique opportunity to aid in the process of differential diagnosis by:

1) delineating patterns of attentional dysfunction which may be at variance with normative expectations;

2) documenting any comorbidity in the form of acquired cerebral dysfunction or patterns of associated developmental learning disorders; and

3) elucidating the functional ramifications of ADHD on general adaptive skills, especially as they pertain to new learning demands.

The ultimate goal of any such assessment is the description of the structure and organization of cognitive abilities for an individual at a particular developmental stage.

IX. BEHAVIORAL ASSESSMENT

The evaluation of ADHD driven by *DSM–IV* diagnostic criteria has placed primary emphasis not on the cognitive attributes of attentional dysfunction, but rather on associated behavioral features. Hence, any reasonable examination must include a variety of behavioral assessment methods, which typically rely on a thorough clinical history as well as observer ratings of the presence or absence, and frequency or severity, of recognizable ADHD behavioral characteristics. Any comprehensive assessment of ADHD should reflect integrated, combined data from both sources (i.e., behavioral and cognitive). In terms of applied behavioral analysis, a number of screening measures have been shown to be useful. More time-consuming multidimensional behavioral symptom inventories provide increased breadth of coverage of ADHD-related symptoms and thereby enhance the psychometric validity of clinical decision making. Highlighted in Figure 1 is a hierarchical strategy for integrating behavioral assessment data.

Overviews of these and other behavioral assessment methods are provided by DuPaul and Stoner (1994) as well as Barkley (1988). In addition, structured or semistructured interview schedules can be used to objectify and standardize clinical decision making. The ADHD Parent Interview, developed by Barkley (1990), surveys a variety of developmental and psychosocial factors in combination with behaviors relevant to general adjustment. Other interview schedules offer coverage

Figure 1. Behavioral Assessment Protocol

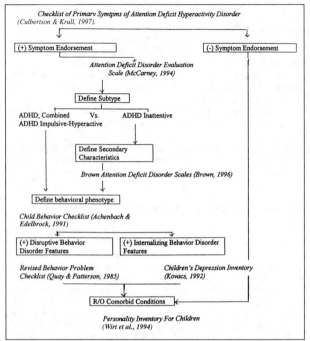

of ADHD complicity within the rubric of other emotional behavior disorders: the Diagnostic Interview for Children–Parent Form (Costello, Edelbrock, Kalas, Kessler, & Klaric, 1982) and the Diagnostic Interview for Children and Adolescents (Herjanic, Brown, & Wheatt, 1975). However, these two interview schedules predate the current *DSM–IV* nosology. A number of direct observational methods are also available to provide context-specific descriptors of the impact of attentional skill inefficiencies in both structured (e.g., classroom) and open (e.g., the playground or other social contexts) settings. The Classroom Observation of Conduct in ADD Scale (Atkins, Pelham, & Licht, 1985), the ADHD Behavior Coding System (Barkley, 1990), and the Child Behavior Checklist Direct Observation Form (Achenbach, 1986) are representative of such strategies.

X. CONCLUSION

A multimodal assessment approach for ADHD begins with a limited core battery that is sufficient to permit differential diagnosis. Specific areas of attentional defects are subsequently assessed in greater detail. A battery should include repeatable measures of attentional functioning so that the data obtained can be used as a benchmark to evaluate response to treatment. Assessment is further directed at understanding emotional, motivational, and psychosocial factors that may be contributory. Finally, an attempt is made to define etiology within the matrix of individual developmental and psychosocial factors that each child presents with. These steps reflect an adaptation of the "biobehavioral system" approach to neuropsychological assessment endorsed by Taylor and Fletcher (1990).

BIBLIOGRAPHY

Achenbach, T. M. (1986). *Manual for the Child Behavior Checklist–Direct Observation Form.* Burlington: University of Vermont, Department of Psychiatry.

American Psychiatric Association. (1994). *Diagnostic and statistical manual of mental disorders* (4th ed.). Washington, DC: Author.

Anderson, J. C., Williams, S., McGee, R., & Silva, P. (1987). DSM-III disorders in preadolescent children: Prevalence in a large sample from the general population. *Archives of General Psychiatry, 44,* 69–76.

Atkins, M. S., Pelham, W. E., & Licht, M. H. (1985). A comparison of objective classroom measures and teacher ratings of attention deficit disorder. *Journal of Abnormal Child Psychology, 13,* 155–167.

Barkley, R. A. (1988). Attention. In M. Tramontana & S. Hooper (Eds.), *Issues in child clinical neuropsychology* (pp. 145–176). New York: Plenum Press.

Barkley, R. A. (1990). *Attention deficit hyperactivity disorder: A handbook for diagnosis and treatment.* New York: Guilford Press.

Barkley, R. A. (1994). The assessment of attention in children. In G. R. Lyon (Ed.), *Frames of reference for the assessment of learning disabilities* (pp. 69–102). Baltimore: Paul H. Brooks.

Barkley, R. A. (1994). Impaired delayed responding: A unified theory of attention deficit hyperactivity disorder. In D. K. Routh (Ed.), *Disruptive behavior disorder in children: Essays honoring Herbert C. Quay* (pp. 11–57). New York: Plenum Press.

Brown, T. E. (1996). *Brown Attention Deficit Disorder Scales.* San Antonio, TX: Psychological Corporation.

Castellanos, F. X., Geidd, J. N., Eckburg, P., Marsh, W.L., Vaitusis, A., et al. (1994). Quantitative morphology of the caudate nucleus in attention deficit hyperactivity disorders. *American Journal of Psychiatry, 151,* 1791–1796.

Carlson, C. L., & Bunner, M. R. (1993). Effects of methylphenidate on the academic performance of children with attention-deficit hyperactivity disorder and learning disabilities. *School Psychology Review, 22,* 184–196.

Costello, A. J., Edelbrock, C. S., Kalas, R., Kessler, M., & Klaric, S. (1982). *The NIMH Diagnostic Interview Schedule for Children (DISC),* Unpublished manuscript.

Courchesne, E. (1994). A new finding: Impairment in shifting attention in artutic cerebellar patients. In S. R. Broman & J. Graffman (Eds.), *Atypical cognitive deficits in developmental disorders: Implications for brain function.* Hillsdale, NJ: Erlbaum.

Denckla, M. B. (1996). Biological correlates of learning and attention: What is relevant to learning disability and attention deficit hyperactivity disorder? *Developmental and Behavioral Pediatrics, 17*(2), 114–119.

DuPaul, G. J., & Stoner, G. (1994). *ADHD in the schools.* New York: Guilford Press.

Dykman, R. A., & Ackerman, P. T. (1993). Behavioral subtypes of attention deficit disorder. *Exceptional Children, 60,* 132–141.

Epstein, M. A., Shaywitz, S. E., Shaywitz, B. A., & Woolston, J. L. (1991). The boundaries of attention deficit disorder. *Journal of Learning Disabilities, 24,* 78–86.

Fiore, T. A., Becker, E. A., & Nero, R. C. (1993). Educational interventions for students with attention deficit disorder. *Exceptional Children, 60,* 163–173.

Goodman, R., & Stevenson, J. (1989). A twin study of hyperactivity-II. The etiological role of genes, family relationships and perinatal adversity. *Journal of Child Psychology and Psychiatry, 5,* 691–709.

Goodyear, P., & Hynd, G. (1992). Attention deficit disorder with (ADD-H) and without (ADD-W) hyperactivity: Behavioral and neuropsychological differentiation. *Journal of Clinical Child Psychology, 21,* 273–305.

Heilman, K. M., Voeller, K. K., & Nadeau, S. E. (1991). A possible pathophysiological substrate of attention deficit hyperactivity disorder. *Journal of Child Neurology 6* (Suppl.), 576–581.

Herjanic, B., Brown, F., & Wheatt, T. (1975). Are children reliable reporters? *Journal of Abnormal Child Psychology, 3,* 41–48.

Hynd, G. W., Marshall, R., & Gonzales, J. J. (1993). *Asymmetry of the caudate nucleus in ADHD: An exploratory study of gender and handedness effects.* Paper presented at the annual meeting of the Society for Research in Child and Adolescent Psychopathology, Santa Fe, New Mexico.

Hynd, G. W., Semrud-Clikeman, M., Lorys, A. R., Novey, E. S., & Eliopulos, D. (1990). Brain morphology in developmental dyslexia and attention deficit disorder/hyperactivity. *Archives of Neurology, 47,* 919–926.

Kinsbourne, M. (1992). Development of attention and metacognition. In S. J. Segalowitz and I. Rapin (Eds.), *Handbook of neuropsychology* (Vol. 7, pp. 261–278). Amsterdam: Elsevier.

Lezak, M. (1995). Neuropsychological assessment (3rd ed.). Oxford, England: Oxford University Press.

Loge, D. V., Staton, R. D., & Beatty, W. W. (1990). Performance of children with ADHD on tests sensitive to frontal lobe dysfunction. *Journal of the American Academy of Child and Adolescent Psychiatry, 29,* 540–545.

Lou, H. C., Henriksen, L., & Bruhn, P. (1984). Focal cerebral hyperfusion in children with dysphasia and/or attention deficit disorder. *Archives of Neurology, 41,* 825–829.

Lou, H. C., Henriksen, L., Bruhn, P., Borner, H., & Nielsen, J. B. (1989). Striatal dysfunction in attention deficit and hyperkinetic disorder. *Archives of Neurology, 46,* 48–52.

Mann, C. A., Lubar, J. F., Zimmerman, A. W., Miller, C. A., & Muenchen, R. A. (1992). Quantitative analysis of EEG in boys with attention-deficit hyperactivity disorder: Controlled study with clinical implications. *Pediatric Neurology, 8,* 20–36.

Mirsky, A. F., Anthony, B. J., Duncan, C. C., Dhearn, M. B., & Kellam, S. G. (1991). Analysis of the elements of attention: A neuropsychological approach. *Neuropsychology Review, 2,* 109–145.

Pennington, B. F. (1991). *Diagnosing learning disorders. A neuropsychological framework.* New York: Guilford Press.

Quay, H. C., & Peterson, D. R. (1983). *Interim manual for the revised behavior problem checklist.* Unpublished manuscript, University of Miami.

Ross, D. M., & Ross, S. A. (1982). *Hyperactivity: Research, theory, and action* (2nd ed.). New York: Wiley.

Safer, D. J., & Allen, R. D. (1976). *Hyperactive children: Diagnosis and management*. Baltimore: University Park Press.

Silver, L. B. (1981). The relationship between learning disabilities, hyperactivity, distractability and behavior problems. A clinical analysis. *Journal of the American Academy of Child Psychiatry, 20,* 285–397.

Sohlberg, M. M., & Mateer, C. A. (1989). *Introduction to cognitive rehabilitation*. New York: Guilford Press.

Taylor, H. G., & Fletcher, J. M. (1990). In M. Hersen & G. Goldstein (Eds.), *Handbook of psychological assessment* (2nd ed., pp. 228–255). New York: Pergamon Press.

Wirt, R. D., Lachar, D., Klinedinst, J. K., & Seat, P. D. (1989). *Multi-dimensional description of child personality*. Los Angeles, CA: Western Psychological Services.

Zametkin, A. J., Nordaha, T. E., Gross, M., King, A. C., Sempk, W. E., Rumsey, J., Hamburger, S., & Cohen, R. M. (1990). Cerebral glucose metabolism in adults with hyperactivity of childhood onset. *New England Journal of Medicine, 323,* 1361–1366.

Zentall, S. S. (1993). Research on the educational implications of attention deficit hyperactivity disorder. *Exceptional Children, 60,* 143–153.

CHAPTER 9

Gregory Slomka

Learning Disorders

The neuropsychological study of learning disabilities has a relatively short history, dating back to the 1960s. Advances in the understanding of the neurological bases for these disorders and in the empirical validation of specific subtypes have firmly shown neuropsychological evaluation to be a valuable tool in their diagnosis. Because learning disabilities are recognized as discrete disorders that have impact extending beyond limitations in academic progress, such assessment serves to delineate the functional implications of these oftentimes subtle neurodevelopmental disorders.

There exists great heterogeneity in types of patients who present with learning disabilities, which is related to: (a) comorbidity, (b) their association with variable patterns of cognitive deficits, and (c) the reciprocal effects of a developmental disorder affecting successful social and emotional maturation. The latter effects are not limited to academic or adjustment problems; deficits in information processing may significantly affect general psychosocial development as well.

Although approximately 20% of the population experience difficulties in academic performance, an estimated 3%–7% of individuals with otherwise average intelligence struggle with severe impediments to learning in one or more academic domains. Between 5% and 10% of vocational rehabilitation caseloads consist of adults with learning disabilities. Although these conditions have been attributed to a variety of causal mechanisms, their precise etiologies remain unknown.

I. DIFFERENTIAL DIAGNOSES OF LEARNING DISORDERS

Multiple classification schemes have been used to define learning disabilities, but in this chapter *DSM-IV* terminology is followed. The neuropsychologist should be familiar with other classification systems, however, especially state and local standards for the psychoeducational definitions of learning disabilities. Commonalities identifiable within these classification systems include (a) a failure to achieve in one or more areas of academic proficiency, (b) documentation of a severe discrepancy between aptitude and achievement test scores, (c) the presence of associated psychological process disorders, and (d) the exclusion of other conditions that could adversely affect development (e.g., primary sensory disintegrity, medical–neurological complications, or psychosocial or emotional factors).

Diagnosis in any field is driven by a search for consistent patterns. The major contribution of neuropsychology as a discipline to the investigation of learning disabilities has been the application of methods that permit the mapping of underlying cognitive-processing deficits that characterize these disorders. The application of this inside-to-outside approach, as described by Denkla (1996), distinguishes the neuropsychologist from other diagnosticians. The establishment of a severe discrepancy criterion is only the first step in an assessment method geared toward treatment. The identification of primary and secondary strengths and weaknesses in perceptual, cognitive, and learning abilities forms the foundation for remedial and accommodative interventions.

II. NEUROANATOMIC CORRELATES

Neurobiological foundations of reading disability have been derived from two forms of investigation: postmortem–cytoarchitectonic studies and structural brain imaging as well as electrophysiological studies (reviewed by Semrud-Clikeman & Hynd, 1994). More recently, functional brain imaging has heralded a new epoch in neuroanatomic correlation. Neuroanatomic variations include left cerebral hemisphere abnormalities in laminar structure, decreased size of magnocellular thalamic nuclei, symmetry in the planum temporale (larger plana in right hemisphere), symmetrical or reversed asymmetry in parieto-occipital regions, rightward asymmetry in prefrontal regions, and atypicalities in the structure of the corpus callosum. For the present, neuroradiological and neurometric techniques remain of limited use in the diagnosis of reading disorder, but from a research perspective they offer important linkages to the formulation of neurocognitive models of reading. Key in these findings is the inextricable linkage of reading impairment and atypicalities in systems mediating phonology and language.

Math disorders have not received the attention relegated to the investigation of reading disorders. The examination of acquired disorders of mathematics in adults has not yielded lesion studies evocative of specific math disability. Lesions in both hemispheres as well as select subcortical involvement have been attributed to impairment in mathematics. With the exception of conditions in which math disability is secondary (e.g., etiologies associated with the nonverbal learning disability subtype, in which early hydrocephaly, congenital syndromes, and other acquired neurological conditions affect subcortical white matter), studies of neuroimaging correlates remain of limited use.

III. ASSESSMENT APPROACHES

Regardless of the learning disability subtype under consideration, there are core components of the assessment battery that are consistent. Typically, a thorough assessment involves the following three separate parts:

Psychoeducational assessment, consisting of intelligence and achievement tests (Wechsler Intelligence Scale for Children, 3rd ed. [WISC-III] and the Wechsler Individual Achievement Test [WIAT]), to do the following:

1. Establish a level of performance from which outcomes on achievement and neuropsychological measures can be contrasted.

2. Delineate the academic skill profile

3. Quantify the nature and extent of any aptitude–achievement discrepencies

Behavioral assessment, consisting of the Child Behavior Checklist (Parent and Teacher Versions) as well as the Attention Deficit Disorders Evaluation Scale, to accomplish the following:

1. Identify any secondary behavior or adjustment disorder features
2. Rule out comorbid psychiatric disorders

Neuropsychological assessment, using any of the fixed methods (age-appropriate versions of the Halstead-Reitan or Luria-Nebraska battery) or a flexible battery, to accomplish these purposes:

1. Identify associated patterns of sensory–perceptual motor and cognitive dysfunction underlying the learning disability
2. Rule out specific cerebral dysfunction

Each of the fixed batteries has demonstrated efficacy in supporting the differential diagnosis of learning disabilities. An advantage of the flexible battery approach is that it provides economy as well as a means to examine in greater detail areas of deficit. A prototypical battery, consisting of core screening measures and probes, is summarized in Table 1.

In the discussion that follows, characteristics associated with learning disability subtypes, assessment strategies, and interpretive formulations are described.

IV. READING DISORDER

Unlike other language functions, which unfold naturally in a fairly predictable fashion, reading represents an acquired skill. As such, not only constitutional but also environmental determinants must be considered when any failure occurs. Disparities in the development of reading competencies hold significant implications for success across other academic domains, and reading disorders frequently coexist with other disabilities in spelling and math.

A. Etiology

The specific neurodevelopmental causes of reading disorders are unknown. Evidence for a genetic predisposition for some individuals with reading disorders has been derived from multiple sources. Although heterogeneity in the transmission of reading disability is presumed, the primary attribute linked to heritability is phonological coding (Olson, Wise, Conness, Rack, & Fulker, 1989; Pennington, 1991).

B. Reading Development

Without an explicit model of normal reading development, patterns of impairment cannot be described. The mastery of

Table 1. Neuropsychological Battery for Learning Disabilities

Domain	Core measure	Supplemental probes
Tactile sensory integration	LNNB-C Items 43, 53, 54, 55, 56, 57, 58 LNNB Items 64, 65, 74, 75, 82, 83, 84, 85	HRNB finger agnosia, bilateral simultaneous stimulation, astereognosis, fingertip number writing
Auditory discrimination	LNNB-C Items 66, 68, 70, 93	WJR Sound Patterns, TOLD-II Primary Auditory Discrimination, HRNB Speech Sounds Perception Test, Seashore Rhythm Test
Motor skills	HRNB Lateral Dominance Examination, Purdue Pegboard Test	Finger Tapping, Grooved Pegboard Test, LNNB Motor Sequencing Tasks, DTVP-II Eye-Hand Coordination Test, Grip-Strength Test, cerebellar screening, tandem walking, disdiadokokinesia examination
Visual discrimination	TVPS-R Visual Discrimination	Remaining subtests of the Test of Visuoperceptual Skills–R or Upper Extension or Benton Visual Discrimination Test

(Continued)

Table 1. Neuropsychological Battery for Learning Disabilities *(Continued)*

Domain	Core measure	Supplemental probes
Visuospatial processing	TVPS-R Visual Spatial Relations and Visual Figure-Ground subtests, and Hooper Visual Organizational Test	Remaining subtests of the Test of Visuoperceptual Skills–R or Upper Extension (seven subtests), DTVP-II Spatial Relations, Benton Judgment or Line Orientation Test, Block Rotation subtest of the LNNB
Visuomotor skills	WISC-III Block Design and Object Assembly, Developmental Test of Visuomotor Integration	Stanford-Binet Pattern Analysis, DTVP-II Design Copying, DTVP-II Spatial Relations, Rey-Osterreith Complex Figure
Language	Peabody Picture Vocabulary Test, Expressive One Word Picture Vocabulary Test, Controlled Oral Word Associaton Test, TOLD-II Primary Grammatic Understanding Test or Syntactic Comprehension Test, WRAML Sentence Repetition Test	TOLD-II Primary or Intermediate or CELF-III
Attention	WISC-III Digit Span, TVPS-R Visual Memory and Visual Sequential Memory, Underlying Tests 4, 9, and 12, Continuous Performance Test	Refer to chapter 8, Figure 2, multivariate assessment of attention

Cognitive flexibility and speed	WISC-III Coding, Contingency Naming Test (Parts I, II, and III), Trail Making Test	Smith Symbol Digit Modalities Test, Stroop Test
Memory	WRAML Visual Memory, Design Memory, Verbal Learning, and Story Memory subtests	Memory Scale of McCarthy Scales Test of Children's Abilities, CVLT-C (or CVLT), Children's Stories Memory Test, WMS-III
Conceptual abilities	WISC-III Similarities and Test of Nonverbal Intelligence	DTLA-II Picture Abilities and Conceptual Matching, TOLD-II Generals, Children's Category Test
Executive functions	Wisconsin Card Sorting Test, Contingency Naming Test, Part IV	LNNB Go-No-Go items, Stroop Test, Rey-Osterreith Complex Figure, CVLT-C Semantic vs. Serial Clustering Score

Note. LNNB = Luria-Nebraska Neuropsychological Battery; WRAML = Wide Range Achievement of Memory and Learning; TOLD-II = Test of Language Development, 2nd ed.; CELF-II = Clinical Evaluation of Language Fundamentals, 2nd ed.; WISC-III = Wechsler Intelligence Scale for Children, 3rd ed.; TVPS-R = Test of Visuo-perceptual Skills–Revised; CVLT-C = California Verbal Learning Test–Children's Version; WMS-III = Wechsler Memory Scale, 3rd ed.; DTLA-II = Detroit Test of Learning Ability, 2nd ed.

basic phonological correspondence (i.e., sound–symbol association skills) develops from systematic instruction and opportunities for overpractice. Under normal conditions, these skills develop rapidly. The mechanisms of early reading have been traditionally categorized across component skills that must be mastered early in the course of reading development. These have been described in dual- and multiroute models of reading that involve a phonological as well as a direct lexical route in which whole-word, or orthographic, recognition skills facilitate the act of word recognition.

The earliest stages of development of prereading competencies are marked by the mastery of the visual–orthographic properties of letters, the memorization of a limited repertoire of sight words, and the use of visual associative skills to foster word recognition from pictures that accompany text. In the subsequent "alphabetic phase," sound–symbol associative skills develop predicated on a child's ability to (a) decompose speech into component structures (phonological awareness) and (b) learn to associate visual symbols (graphemes) with their corresponding sound equivalents (phonemes). With increasing experience, direct orthographic associative competency is established and familiar words are recognized on sight. Confrontation with low-frequency word forms requires some combination of orthographic and phonological decoding. By the fourth grade, skilled readers rely primarily on automatized orthographic skills in reading. Phonological processing becomes relegated primarily to the processing of less familiar words. A skilled reader develops additional proficiency with the incorporation of morphological cues, as well as lexical–semantic and other contextual cues, to facilitate word recognition.

C. Specific Deficits Associated With Reading Disabilities

Impaired reading ability is associated with deficits in the following areas:

1. Language
   a. Phonemic discrimination
   b. Sound blending and sound segmentation
   c. Receptive vocabulary
   d. Naming
   e. Oral word fluency (word retrieval)
   f. Semantic knowledge
   g. Grammatical and syntactical analysis

2. Perception
   a. Rapid auditory processing
   b. Rapid visual processing
   c. Auditory discrimination
3. Attention
   a. Auditory sequencing
   b. Sentence recall
4. Verbal memory

Converging evidence suggests that among the multivariate contributions to reading proficiency, language-based competencies account for the majority of the variance (Fletcher et al., 1994; Shaywitz et al., 1996). Catts (1989) further specified higher rates of speech deficits, including early histories of articulation inefficiencies, among the reading disabled. The commonalities associated with these deficits involve the processing of the sound patterns of language. These deficits have been broadly conceived as evidence that specific maturational lags in systems supporting language development represent a major secondary source of deficit expressed by disabled readers. The relevancy of language vulnerabilities is conveyed by Tallal's finding (1987) that 85% of children expressing these disorders in the preschool years developed language-related learning disabilities.

Because reading represents a language-based activity in which visual features are transformed into an auditory code through the use of grapheme–phoneme correspondence rules, a substantial portion of early research focused on the relative contribution of visual–perceptual processing deficits. Although low-level visual deficits have been identified among reading-disabled populations (e.g., rapid visual processing; Lovegrove et al., 1986), research has yet to elucidate specifically how deficiencies in aspects of visual feature analysis, pattern recognition, and visual attention may be contributory.

Cognitive models of reading development go beyond tacit word recognition and analytic skills (see Chase & Tallal, 1991, for review). These models provide a heuristic for understanding how metalinguistic awareness, selective attention, and working memory support reading comprehension. Although phonological analysis represents the most widely studied aspect of reading development, an increasing body of knowledge has linked other types of linguistic-rule knowledge (semantic, morphological, and syntactic conventions) to the development of higher level reading skills, such as comprehension monitoring. Thus, empirically driven assessment methods must explore both phonological skills and higher level linguistic competencies.

D. Subtypes of Reading Disorder

Despite more than 2 decades of effort, no one classification schema has gained general acceptance as a means to classify reading disorder subtypes. Converging lines of research emanating from the early subtyping literature identified three broad categories of reading impairment: (a) auditory–linguistic deficits, (b) visual-processing deficits, and (c) combined deficits (Hynd & Cohen, 1983). Still, considerable heterogeneity is expressed among the reading disabled. It is presumed that the constitutional, environmental, and behavioral characteristics of this population, along with a high incidence of complex comorbidity, preclude easy classification of many of these individuals within conventional subtyping schemas. As such, multiple investigators have questioned the functional usefulness of subtyping (Stantovich, 1986; Taylor, 1989; Vellutino, 1979).

Stantovich (1988) proposed an alternative means to explain the variability expressed among impaired readers: the **phonological-core variable-deficit model.** It begins with the tenet that all impaired readers manifest a phonological processing deficit. The most severe forms of reading disability are characterized by a fundamental deficit in the ability to establish grapheme–phoneme correspondence. Mildly impaired readers reveal less deficiency in this area or develop compensatory strategies. The term *variable* is attributed to information-processing deficits outside the domain of phonological processing (see the preceding section, "Specific Deficits Associated With Reading Disabilities"). Conceived in this fashion, the goal of assessment becomes the definition of the individual array of strengths and weaknesses expressed by any reader. This represents an alternative to models that posit more discrete subtypes of disabled readers and permits a means to conceive of reading on a continuum from normal variability in reading proficiency to the heterogeneous expression of impaired reading development.

E. Assessment

1. DISCREPANCY ANALYSIS

Reading impairments have traditionally been "categorically" classified. The goal has been to distinguish children with reading disabilities from "garden variety poor readers" (Stantovich,

1988). Boundaries between normal and impaired readers have been specified by decision rules, such as aptitude–achievement discrepancies on standardized tests. These strategies have been criticized on statistical and methodological grounds (see Berninger & Abbott, 1994, for review). Limiting assessment to use of psychoeducational measures for purposes of classification contributes minimally to the task of discerning etiology. The discrepancy criterion represents only the first phase of the assessment process.

2. MULTIFACTORIAL DESCRIPTION OF READING IMPAIRMENT

Linkage of assessment to intervention requires the analysis of tacit reading skills at four levels: phonemic analysis, word identification, reading fluency, and reading comprehension. A two-stage assessment approach is recommended. An initial probe consisting of age appropriate reading measures is first administered:

a. Level I assessment (screen)

Below age 8 (component skills: tests):
- Letter recognition: Woodstock Reading Mastery Test–Revised (WRMT-R) Letter Recognition
- Word analysis: WRMT-R Word Identification
- Vocabulary comprehension: WRMT-R Word Comprehension
- Reading comprehension: WRMT-R Passage Comprehension

Age 8 or older (component skills: tests):
- Word analysis: WRMT-R Word Identification
- Reading Comprehension: Gray Oral Reading Test III or Gates-MacGinitie Reading Comprehension subtests

If performances below normative expectations are obtained on any of these screening measures, follow-up probes from Level II measures can be applied in an age or developmentally appropriate sequence to specify areas of deficit.

b. Level II assessment (probes)

Visual sequencing: Informal observations of visual tracking

Letter recognition deficits
- Perceptual constancy: Jordan Left-Right Reversals Test
- Phonemic awareness: Rosner Auditory Analysis Test; Test of Language Development–Second Edition (TOLD-II) Auditory Discrimination Test

- Grapheme–phoneme correspondence (pseudoword reading): WRMT-R Word Attack Test
- Word identification: WRMT-R Word Identification; Boder Reading Test (graded word lists distinguishing phonologically regular and irregular word forms)

Vocabulary comprehension

- Synonym–antonym: WRMT Word Comprehension
- Cloze procedures: WRMT Passage Comprehension
- Word association: Gates-MacGinitie Reading Test, Vocabulary Subtest; Nelson Denny Reading Test, Vocabulary Subtest

Reading fluency

- Reading speed: Gray Oral Reading Test–Third Edition (GORT-III) Reading Rate; Nelson Denny Reading Test (older subjects); GORT-III Reading Fluency

In addition to the reading measures cited, supplementary language measures that tap semantic knowledge, linguistic short-term memory, auditory comprehension, and grammatical and syntactical analysis are required. If the neuropsychological examination includes only a cursory dysphasia screening, any of the following (depending on the patient's age) represents an adequate strategy for defining the extent of associated language impairment.

C. **Supplementary language measures**

- Test of Language Development-2 (Primary)
- Test of Language Development-2 (Intermediate)
- Test of Adolescent and Adult Language
- Clinical Evaluation of Language Fundamentals-III

V. MATHEMATICS DISORDER

Mathematics disorder is defined as a discrepancy in the development of computation or math reasoning relative to general aptitude. It results in functional limitations in the development of arithmetic skills appropriate for age and circumstance. Its prevalence is estimated at approximately 6%. Definitive data delineating a gender ratio remain unavailable at present. The etiology of developmental mathematics disorder remains unknown. Multifactorial contributions to the display of impaired math performances are presumed.

The complexity of the subject matter, overreliance on a spiral curriculum, and other factors related to instructional technology have been blamed for trends indicating lower overall math achievement in American children during the last 2 decades. Factors associated with math underachievement include performance anxiety, attributional issues, and motivation. Math disabilities clearly supersede such risk factors in terms of impact. The influence of genetic and other constitutional factors remains ill defined.

A. Comorbidity

Although mathematics disorder may be expressed as a unitary condition, it more frequently is associated with other learning disabilities, including reading disorders, expressive and receptive language disorders, and developmental coordination disorder. Attention deficit hyperactivity disorder (ADHD) represents the most commonly found comorbid AXIS I diagnosis. In addition, social immaturity, school and personal adjustment problems, social skill deficits, anxiety, and depression are often seen.

B. Development of Mathematical Abilities

A number of informal mathematical concepts and skills are acquired through spontaneous interaction with the environment during the preschool years. These include concepts of more and less, conservation, additive and subtractive qualities within events, rudimentary counting, and numeration (Ginsburg, 1987a). It appears there is development of an informal knowledge base derived from experience prior to any conventional learning. Levine, Jordan, and Huttenlocher (1992) demonstrated that as early as age 4, math strategy is driven primarily by nonverbal conceptual abilities. It is not until age 5 or 6 that conventional number fact or story problems can begin to be assimilated. During elementary school years, the mastery of elementary conventions associated with number facts (counting and grouping), the alphanumeric symbol code of integers, number alignment, and place is established. These skills permit mastery of written calculation. With advancing age, mastery of more complex computational algorithms is possible, and the curriculum includes greater emphasis on concept development, mathematical theory, and applied problem solving (refer to Ginsburg, 1987b, for further discussion).

C. Specific Deficits Associated With Mathematics Development

1. Skill acquisition and mastery vary as a function of developmental stage, teaching strategies used, and a variety of intrinsic

and extrinsic factors. **Vulnerabilities in the following neuropsychological skills** have been identified as adversely affecting math skill development (for review, see Keller & Sutton, 1991):

    a. Visuoperceptual
    b. Visuomotor
    c. Visual sequential memory
    d. Verbal association
    e. Sequential information
    f. Verbal comprehension
    g. Abstract concept formation

    2. The **expression of these vulnerabilities** may take the form of specific problems with the following:

    a. Decoding symbols
    b. Writing and copying numbers
    c. Appropriate sequencing and alignment of numbers
    d. Fact mastery
    e. Acquisition of the semantics of mathematics
    f. Memorization
    g. Capacity to convey multistep sequenced cognitive operations
    h. Monitoring the quality of ongoing performance
    i. Higher level linguistic competencies related to both reading and segmental language
    j. Applied reasoning and abstract conceptual abilities

Heterogeneity in the expression of mathematics disabilities tends to be the rule rather than the exception.

D. Subtypes of Mathematics Disorder

A paucity of clinically applicable classification strategies exists for delineating mathematics disorders. Spreen and Haaf (1986) and Rourke and colleagues (see Rourke, 1993, for review) have provided a synopsis of the limited research in this area. It is rare to identify mathematics disability in isolation from the following neurodevelopmental disorders.

    1. **Neurodevelopmental disorders** that co-occur with mathematics disability:

    a. Generalized academic dysfunction
    b. Reading disability
    c. Language disorder
    d. Attention or executive function disorder
    e. Visuoperceptual or visuospatial dysfunction
    f. Nonverbal learning disability

Despite the multiplicity of expression of mathematics disorders, Geary's (1993) taxonomy of mathematics disorders offers a useful clinical heuristic for categorizing areas of shared variance. Summarizing clinical and experimental studies of math disabilities, Geary (1993) identified three error patterns that are useful in conceptualizing information-processing deficits and strategies for intervention.

2. **Subtypes of mathematics disorder**

a. **Subtype 1. Semantic memory deficits:** These are deficits in the representation and retrieval of arithmetic facts in semantic memory. Despite drill, memorization of math facts (e.g., multiplication tables) remains incomplete. When facts are retrieved, they are contaminated by high error rates. These deficits are attributed to left cerebral hemisphere dysfunction. This subtype correlates most highly with the expression of comorbid reading disabilities.

b. **Subtype 2. Procedural deficits:** Immature development of strategies associated with the conveyance of math algorithms, the display of high-frequency execution errors, and limited appreciation of procedural concepts represent predominant errors. Neuropsychological correlates are presumed to reflect effects of generalized verbal and nonverbal information-processing inefficiencies.

c. **Subtype 3. Visuospatial deficits:** Difficulties using visuospatial skills for the representation or interpretation of numerical information predominate. Procedurally these problems concern borrowing and carrying, the conveyance of algorithms requiring columnar organization of operations, and errors of perception and place value. These deficits are attributed to right cerebral hemisphere dysfunction.

E. Assessment

Assessment of math disorders is developmentally driven. It requires knowledge of the developmental sequences of math concept development and an understanding of the typical academic curriculum structure for each age cohort. One must transcend the skills related to the conveyance of rote, overlearned math algorithms (computation) and capture both the conceptual and communication demands children face within contemporary math curricula.

A core battery of achievement tests assesses (a) computational arithmetic; (b) conceptual understanding, conceptual proficiency, and skill applications; and (c) the integration of qualitative error analysis and clinical interview procedures. The measures permit normative comparisons that are essential for establishing severe discrepancy criteria and the pattern of analysis errors. Strategy permits insights into errors in thinking and strategy use.

Reliance on methods restricted to computational measures (i.e., the Wide Range Achievement Test, 3rd ed. [WRAT-III]) is insufficient for diagnosis or description of mathematics disabilities. Rather, an individual diagnostic math achievement test is required. Examples of several current tests of this type follow:

1. **Formal tests**

a. Key Math–Revised: A Diagnostic Inventory of Essential Mathematics (Connolly, 1988).

b. Test of Mathematical Abilities (Brown & McEntire, 1984).

c. The Test of Early Mathematics Ability (2nd ed.; Ginsburg & Baroody, 1990)

These assessment tests offer the opportunity for multiple observations of performance across age-appropriate measures of conceptual understanding, computational skills, and applied problem solving.

2. In addition, the following **informal strategies** are required to aid in defining the nature of procedural deficits or problem analysis:

a. Error analysis provides a means to determine whether systematic errors are committed in computational arithmetic.

b. Clinical interview and a "testing of limits" procedure (Ginsburg, 1987b) provide insights into the nature of problem analysis and conceptualization.

c. Structured interviewing (Levine, 1994) is used to pinpoint further the person's appreciation of the nature of underlying math inefficiencies.

The augmentation of an assessment battery with various neuropsychological measures provides a means to (a) correlate the manifest disabilities with cognitive skill deficits that may contribute to learning problems, (b) define the procedural math deficits from an information-processing perspective, and (c) establish a database from which remediation and accommodations can be developed.

VI. DISORDERS OF WRITTEN EXPRESSION

Disorders of written expression are defined by a demonstrable lag in the development of writing competencies. They may be characterized by deficits in spelling, punctuation, grammatical form and structure, or composition and organization. Manifestations of spelling deficits or legibility problems alone do not constitute a diagnosis of this disorder. Despite the inherent simplicity of current DSM-IV diagnostic criteria, describing this form of learning disability has been challenging owing to the multifactorial nature of writing. Intraindividual expression of writing disorders varies as a function of impairment in any of the following areas: (a) handwriting, (b) spelling, (c) language, (d) attention and memory, (e) written narrative organizational skills, and (f) metacognitive abilities.

Diagnosis requires establishment of a significant discrepancy in writing abilities, associated functional impairment in the ability to mediate academic and life skills in which writing is required, and determination of associated cognitive-processing deficits. Determination of whether the deficits are primary or secondary to language disabilities is integral for differential diagnosis. The occurrence of isolated disorders of written language is comparatively rare. The multidimensional nature of the neuropsychological underpinnings of writing suggests that deficits in any of the areas sufficient to affect writing would also affect other domains of academic performance. The evaluator must be prepared to identify a variety of potential comorbid conditions, including not only other learning disabilities, but ADHD, depression, low academic self-esteem, anxiety, or thought disorder.

No data are available that formally characterize the prevalence of this disorder. Gender influences remain ill defined. Hooper and colleagues (1994) suggested that the prevalence likely parallels closely the expression of developmental language disorder. Written language deficits may represent the most prevalent minor disability in communication skills seen in children.

A. Development of Writing Abilities

Developmentally, writing has been conceived as the final stage in the ontogeny of language. Levine (1987) has provided a heuristic three-stage model describing the progression of writing skills. Stage 1 involves prewriting behaviors, including drawing, tracing, and coloring as well as attempts at protowriting in play, set the stage for imitative writing training in the first grade. Stage 2, graphic presentation, involves the enhancement of the basic orthographic skills related to letter and word formation as well as the establishment of greater graphomotor control. Stage 3, beginning in late second grade, is characterized by the progressive incorporation of appropriate capitalization, punctuation, syntax, and grammar in writing. It is at this stage that cursive writing is introduced. In the automatization stage, progressive mastery of primary competencies permits greater capacity for self-monitoring of the written product, expansion in the length of written expression, and the use of more complex structural forms. In addition, planning and organizational skills begin to be incorporated. In the elaboration stage (Grades 7 through 9), the act of writing is presumed to be sufficiently automatized to permit its use as a means to develop ideas. Greater capacity for ideational integration is expressed, and summarization skills develop. Capacity to form and express a viewpoint is then developed. In the final stage (Grade 9 and beyond), diversification in writing style is achieved, and writing increases in versatility and as a means to support reasoning as well as creative expression.

B. Subtypes of Writing Disorder

Although intraindividual variability in skills underlying writing deficits can be readily specified with the use of a comprehensive assessment approach, the specification of interindividual variability, or how patterns or subtypes of writing disorders are manifest, remains incompletely understood. The data presented below represent a preliminary attempt at subtype analysis.

By relying on a clustering algorithm based on an analysis of teacher ratings of writing impairment and on eight domains of neuropsychological performance, Sandler et al. (1992) delineated four discrete clusters within a sample of children exhibiting writing disorders (see Table 2).

C. Assessment

Six separable components of writing should be examined (Berninger, 1994). Depending on the developmental or instructional stage at which a child presents, greater or lesser emphasis should be placed on any of these assessment domains:

    a. Handwriting quality (legibility)

    b. Writing fluency (number of words copied within time constraints)

    c. Spelling from dictation

    d. Spelling accuracy within composition

    e. Compositional fluency (number of words produced within time constraints)

    f. Computational quality (content, cohesiveness, and organization of written narrative material)

Table 2. Features of Four Clusters of Writing Disorders

Frequency (%)	Primary features	Secondary features
50	Fine motor and linguistic deficits	Phonetic spelling errors Slow writing rate Punctuation– capitalization errors
35	Spatial organization problems Compromised legibility	Lanuage and reading skills intact
10	Visual attention– visual memory problems	Spelling problems Poor self-monitoring Poor quality of written output
10	Sequencing problems	Poor legibility Math deficits

The prominence of handwriting deficiencies (graphomotor immaturity or dyspraxia) requires focused assessment of motor, perceptual, and visuomotor integrative competencies and ruling out any specific developmental output failure (refer to specific recommendations for assessment of handwriting disorders by Bain, 1991). Requisite skills essential in spelling include the mastery of grapheme–phoneme correspondence, overlearning of the orthographic representation of word structures, and development of morphological knowledge. Strategies for assessment in this area have been discussed in the section of this chapter on reading disorders (refer to phonological awareness and linguistic measures).

Comprehensive assessment requires, in addition to accrual of graphomotor samples and analysis of spelling errors, the evaluation of language competencies and reading skills. Proficiency in oral language has traditionally marked the starting point for the investigation of written language. Semantic and general linguistic competencies (grammar and syntax) are prerequisites for the conveyance of ideas in written form. Strategies outlined in the assessment of linguistic contributions to reading disorders are equally appropriate for screening at this level.

Berninger (1994) specified how developmental output failure in writing may be a reflection of deficits in other aspects of higher cognitive functioning. Attentional inefficiencies may be expressed as a function of input or output faculties. Deficits in capacity to self-monitor the quality of ongoing cognitive performances clearly affect writing demands, placing a premium on simultaneous information-processing abilities. In the same way, executive function deficits would be expected to contribute to deficits in planning and organizational skills essential in orchestrating complex ideation in a logical, coherent form.

In terms of measures applicable in the assessment of writing abilities, Larsen (1987) provided a review of 13 individual and group-administered achievement tests summarized according to methods of administration, test formats, and breadth of coverage. The majority of these tests have been criticized as providing only a cursory evaluation of writing abilities. Among traditional general-purpose academic achievement tests, the revised Woodcock-Johnson (1989) tests of academic achievement offer the broadest coverage of conventional writing skills. The WIAT-R, although less comprehensive in assessment of core competencies related to the mechanics of writing, offers a means to evaluate narrative writing within a standardized format.

Unfortunately, the typical psychoeducational screening battery applied to the assessment of learning disabilities is limited in sensitivity toward the identification of writing disorders. If writing disorder is suspected, a screening battery consisting of the following measures could be administered:

Domain	Method
Spelling	WRAT-III
Mechanics	Woodcock-Johnson Proofing subtest
Written grammar	Woodcock-Johnson Writing Samples subtest
Narrative organization	WIAT Narrative Writing subtest

Poor performance on any of these measures serves to identify areas for more comprehensive testing. Unfortunately, the range of standardized tests designed to assess written language remains restricted. No single standardized assessment method comprehensively evaluates the heterogeneous language and cognitive deficits that characterize this disorder (Gregg, 1992). In terms of standardized writing assessment batteries for formally probing a writing disorder, two of the most frequently used tests are briefly summarized:

1. **Test of Written Language** (Hammill & Larsen, 1995). This instrument, standardized for use with children ages 7-6

through 17-11, samples both spontaneous and contrived writing abilities. Eight subtests tap spelling, punctuation and capitalization, applications of semantic knowledge, syntax, and grammatical cohesiveness. Factors relevant to story construction and thematic maturity are also tapped. The protocol provides an overall index of written language competency that can be contrasted with other standard scores related to intellectual ability or language mastery.

2. **Test of Early Written Language** (Hresko, Herron, & Peak, 1995). This tool, a downward extension of the Test of Written Language–Third Edition (TOWL-III), is designed to capture emergent writing abilities. In addition to sampling linguistic skills, it taps discrimination of verbal and nonverbal representational forms as well as handwriting abilities. Like the TOWL-III, it provides a ready means for profile analysis.

A major disadvantage of direct assessment methods is that they are time consuming. In addition, challenges associated with scoring can be intimidating. Given the labor intensity of these direct assessment methods, an alternative is the Core Battery for Writing Assessment by Berninger (1994). This battery uses the Writing Samples and Dictation subtests of the Woodcock-Johnson battery to assess handwriting; the WRAT-III Spelling Test; the handwriting fluency, spontaneous spelling, and compositional fluency subtests, which are hybrid measures for which norms are available for Grades 1 through 9 (refer to Berninger & Hart, 1992); and the Woodcock-Johnson Writing Samples and Writing Fluency subtests to tap compositional quality and fluency.

VII. LEARNING DISORDER NOT OTHERWISE SPECIFIED

In the *DSM-IV* nomenclature, learning disorder; not otherwise specified (NOS) has been reserved as a category for disorders of learning that do not meet criteria for the aforementioned categories. Spelling disorder is subsumed within this category and is no longer a distinct *DMS-IV* condition. The most prevalent condition attributed to the learning disorder; NOS designation is the nonverbal learning disability (NLD). This variant was first described by Johnson and Mykelbust (1971). Weintraub and Mesulam (1983) and Voller (1986) subsequently described patterns of social and learning problems associated with the predominance of right cerebral hemisphere dysfunction. Recognition of the role of the right cerebral hemisphere in the processing of extrapersonal information and deficits in social adaptation displayed by such individuals led Denckla (1985) to characterize this condition as a social–emotional learning disability. More formal elaboration of the functional correlates of this condition has been advanced by Rourke (1989, 1995), who extended conceptualizations of the disorder beyond presumptive dysfunction in right cerebral hemisphere functioning to include disruption of cerebral white matter in general.

A. Nonverbal Learning Disability: Developmental Correlates

Characteristically, pragmatic vocabulary skills and the development of general declarative knowledge represent early strengths in children with this disorder. Tacit language skills appear adequate. Within early elementary school years, a reasonably favorable academic adjustment pattern tends to be conveyed. It is rare for these youngsters to be identified as learning disabled during those years. The inherent structure afforded students in the first three grades serves as a "buffer." By early middle childhood, when more fluid–synthetic, integrative skills are required, increasing weaknesses in higher level cognitive abilities become apparent. Tasks demanding tactile as well as complex visuoperceptual skills, integrated motor output, and higher level spatial–analytic abilities reflect areas of greatest vulnerability. It is not uncommon to see organizational problems. Although these inefficiencies may be subtle, more prominent are difficulties associated with the development of graphomotor skills essential in writing and drawing. In addition, although tacit language faculties are intact, prosodic anomalies and pragmatic deficits are discernible. By the middle school years, when demands for increasing "automaticity" in lower level faculties and simultaneous information processing are confronted, evidence of "disorganization" is more discernible. Many such youngsters display a phenotype similar to the ADHD, inattentive type.

In terms of general problem solving, relatively pragmatic rote memory skills are usually a strength. Within this context, verbally mediated rote learning tends to exceed nonverbal learning proficiencies. Academically, reading inefficiencies are not characteristically displayed. In fact, in a number of youngsters hyperlexia may be expressed. With advancing age, subtle reading problems may emerge in perspective taking or inferring complex ideation from text. Math skill inefficiencies represent the earliest and most persistent challenge. The extent of math inefficiencies displayed is variable. Many youngsters are able to compensate in early years by exploiting rote memorization skills. The increasing complexity of math algorithms as middle childhood is approached represents a distinct foil. Rourke (1995) indicated that computational math abilities typically do not exceed sixth-grade ability levels. Writing problems, particulary deficits in narrative organization, represent the second most prominent academic deficit.

Whereas in early years these youngsters readily compensate through the structure and redundancy available within their academic programs, the conveyance of larger amounts of new information, demands for self-directed learning and discovery of new information, as well as an emphasis on written as opposed to oral transmission of factual knowledge combine to complicate scholastic adjustment in the late middle-childhood years. By the time these youngsters reach preadolescence, more superordinate deficits in metacognitive development become apparent. Deficits associated with the ability to convey complex schedules are not unusual. These youngsters appear to be more structure bound than average and more dependent on the superimposition of supports from adults or peers for the conveyance of routine activities. Homework organization and follow-through as well as test preparation may be quite problematic.

This condition holds implications beyond the predictable pattern of scholastic inefficiencies (mathematics, narrative writing, and metacognitive abilities); deficits in simultaneous–synthetic information processing have the potential to affect psychosocial adjustment as well. Because up to 65% of social communication involves the processing of nonverbal stimuli, a youngster with a deficit in this mode of information processing is at a disadvantage in complex social situations. Many of the nuances of social discourse may be ignored, misperceived, or misinterpreted. As the demands for negotiating an ever-increasing social milieu are met with advancing age, it is not uncommon to see anxiety or withdrawal exhibited. Novelty and ambiguity associated with social situations may prove anxiety provoking. These children function best in social situations that are familar and readily "scripted." They are typically on the periphery of the social matrix of the school or of large-scale social situations. In some instances the deficits in social processing are severe, and a distinctly asocial or avoidant adaptational style develops. In general, a greater proclivity toward the expression of internalizing behavior disorder characteristics has been associated with this population.

B. Differential Diagnosis

Although the etiology is unkown, characteristics associated with the NLD syndrome may occur secondary to a variety of congenital, developmental, or acquired neurological disorders. In terms of pervasive developmental disorders, high-functioning autism and, to a greater extent, Asperger's syndrome reflect a similar cognitive profile. Although ADHD; inattentive type and NLD may share elements of a behavioral phenotype, NLD is readily discernible as a function of the underlying cognitive profile. Early hydrocephaly, callosal dysgenesis, and acquired neurological conditions affecting white matter result in varying degrees of this condition. Early stages of demyelinating disorders present in a similar manner. Rourke (1995, p. 486) has provided a hierarchical model characterizing the phenotypic similarity of a variety of such conditions to levels of expression of the NLD subtype.

C. Assessment

Differential diagnostic criteria proposed for this condition include the following:

1. A history of early tactile sensory–integrative problems
2. Residual motor skill inefficiencies
3. Weaknesses expressed across task demands involving higher level visuoperceptual, visuospatial, and visuomotor integrative skills
4. Comparative integrity of tacit linguistic competencies relative to deficits in pragmatics and prosody
5. The preponderance of math as opposed to other academic inefficiencies
6. Deficits in nonverbal conceptual ability

A comprehensive neuropsychological battery is capable of distinguishing these primary symptom characteristics. Unfortunately, standardized methods appropriate for the assessment of prosodic elements of language, social perception, and interpretation of complex social situations remain experimental in nature. Existence of these deficits is largely inferred from clinical history taking.

VIII. CONCLUSION

The neuropsychological evaluation of learning disabilities poses numerous challenges to the clinician. First, the competency of the practitioner requires knowledge of brain maturation, brain behavior relationships, developmental psychology, and educational psychology, as well as of the general field of neuropsychology. Second, evaluation entails the understanding of the efficacy and appropriateness of the plethora of psychoeducational as well as psychosocial treatments presently available. Third, the examination process itself requires skill, patience, and the ability to integrate a large amount of information such that a comprehensive understanding of the individual is obtained in the context of interactions within a psychosocial environment.

Conceptualizations of learning disabilities remain in flux. There is a substantial contribution that can be made from the discipline of neuropsychology by advancing the description of these disorders beyond the categorical. Discussion of remedial support and accommodation lies beyond the scope of this chapter. For the interested reader, reviews are provided by Jordan and Goldsmith-Phillips (1994) and Lyon (1994). For the reader more specifically interested in accommodative strategies for adults, Gregg, Hoy, and Gay (1996) have provided discussion.

BIBLIOGRAPHY

Bain, A. M. (1991). Handwriting disorders. In A. M. Bain, L. Lyons-Bailet, & L. Cook-Moats (Eds.), *Written language disorders: Theory into practice.* Austin, TX: Pro Ed.

Berninger, V. W. (1994). Future directions for research on writing disabilities: Integrating endogenous and exogenous variables. In G. R. Lyon (Ed.), *Frames of reference for the assessment of learning disabilities: New view on measurement issues* (pp. 419–440). Baltimore: Paul H. Brooks.

Berninger, V. W., & Abbott, R. D. (1994). Redefining learning disabilities. In G. R. Lyon (Ed.), *Frames of reference for the assessment of learning disabilities. New views on assessment issues* (pp. 163–184). Baltimore: Paul H. Brooks.

Berninger, V., & Hart, T. (1992). A developmental neuropsychological perspective for reading and writing acquisition. *Educational Psychologist, 27,* 415–434.

Bookheimer, S. Y., & Dapretto, M. (1996). Functional neuroimaging of language in children: Current directions and future challenges. In R. W. Thatcher, G. R. Lyon, & K. Krasnegor (Eds.), *Developmental Neuroimaging: Mapping the development of brain and behavior* (pp. 143–152). San Diego, CA: Academic Press.

Brown, V. L., & McEntire, E. (1984). *Test of mathematical abilities*. Austin, TX: Pro Ed.

Catts, H. W. (1989). Speech production deficits in developmental dyslexia. *Journal of Speech and Hearing Disorder, 54*, 422–428.

Chase, C. H., & Tallal, P. (1991). Cognitive models of developmental reading disorders. In J. E. Obrzut & G. W. Hind (Eds.), *Neuropsychological foundations of learning disabilities* (pp. 199–231). San Diego, CA: Academic Press.

Connolly, A. J. (1988). *Key Math Revised: A diagnostic inventory of essential mathematics*. Circle Pines, MN: American Guidance Service.

Denckla, M. B. (1985). The neuropsychology of social-emotional learning disability. *Archives of Neurology, 40*, 461–462.

Denckla, M. B. (1996). Biological correlates of learning and attention: What is relevant to learning disability and attention-deficit hyperactivity disorder. *Developmental and Behavioral Pediatrics, 17*, 114–119.

Fletcher, J. M., Shaywitz, S. E., Shankweiler, D. P., Katz, L., Liberman, I. Y., Stuebing, K. K., Francis, D. J., Fowler, A. E., & Shaywitz, D. A. (1994).Cognitive profiles of reading disability: Comparisons of discrepancy and low achievement definition. *Journal of Educational Psychology, 86*, 6–23.

Geary, D. C. (1993). Mathematical disabilities: Cognitive, neuropsychological, and genetic components. *Psychological Bulletin, 114*, 345–362.

Ginsburg, H. P. (1987a). *Assessing the arithmetic abilities and instructional needs of students*. Austin, TX: Pro Ed.

Ginsburg, H. P. (1987b). The development of arithmetic thinking. In D. D. Hammill (Ed.), *Assessing the abilities and instructional needs of students* (pp. 423–440). Austin, TX: Pro Ed.

Ginsburg, H. P., & Baroody, A. J. (1990). *Test of Early Mathematics Ability* (2nd ed.). Austin, TX: Pro Ed.

Gregg, N. (1992). Expressive writing disorders. In S. R. Hooper, G. W. Hynd, & R. E. Mattison (Eds.), *Developmental disorders: Diagnostic criteria and clinical assessment*. Hillsdale, NJ: Erlbaum.

Gregg, N., Hoy, C., & Gay, A. F. (1996). *Adults with learning disabilities: Theoretical and practical perspectives*. New York: Guilford Press.

Hammill, D. D., & Larsen, S. C. (1995). *Test of Written Language* (3rd ed.). Austin, TX: Pro Ed.

Hooper, S. R., Montgomer, J., Swartz, C., Reed, M. S., Sandler, A. D., Levine, M. D., Watson, T. E., & Wasileski, T. (1994). Measurement of written language expression. In G. R. Lyon (Ed.), *Frames of reference for the assessment of learning disabilities: New views on measurement issues*. Baltimore: Paul H. Brooks.

Hresko, W. P., Herron, S. R., & Peak, P. K. (1995). *Test of Early Written Language* (2nd Ed.). Austin, TX: Pro Ed.

Hynd, G. W., & Cohen, M. J. (1983). *Dyslexia: Neuropsychological theory, research, and clinical differentiation.*

Johnson, D. J., & Mykelbust, H. R. (1971). *Learning disabilities.* New York: Grune & Stratton.

Jordan, N. C., & Goldsmith-Phillips, J. (1994). *Learning disabilities: New directions for assessment and intervention.* Boston: Allyn & Bacon.

Keller, C. E., & Sutton, J. P. (1991). Specific mathematics disorders. In J. E. Obrzut & G. W. Hynd (Eds.), *Neuropsychological foundations of learning disabilities.* San Diego, CA: Academic Press.

Larsen, S. C. (1987). Determining the presence and extent of writing problems. In D. D. Hammill (Ed.), *Assessing the instructional abilities and instructional needs of students.* Austin, TX: Pro Ed.

Levine, M. D. (1987). *Developmental variation and learning disorders.* Cambridge, MA: Educators Publishing Service.

Levine, M. (1994). *Educational care: A system for understanding and helping students with learning problems at home and in school.* Cambridge, MA: Educators Publishing Service.

Levine, S. C., Jordan, N. C., & Huttenlocher, J. (1992). Development of calculation abilities in young children. *Journal of Experimental Child Psychology, 53,* 72–103.

Lovegrove, W., Martin, F., & Slaghuis, W. (1986). A theoretical and experimental case for a visual defect in specific reading disability. *Cognitive Neuropsychology, 3,* 225–267.

Lyon, G. R. (1994). *Frames of reference for the assessment of learning disabilities: New views on measurement issues.* Baltimore: Paul H. Brooks.

Myklebust, H. R. (1975). Nonverbal learning disabilities: Assessment and intervention. In H. R. Myklebust (Ed.), *Progress in learning disabilities* (Vol. 3). New York: Grune & Stratton.

Olson, R., Wise, B., Conness, F., Rack, J., & Fulker, D. (1989). Specific deficits in component reading and language skills: Genetic and environmental influences. *Journal of Learning Disabilities, 22,* 339–348.

Pennington, B. F. (1991). *Learning disorders: A neuropsychological framework.* New York: Guilford Press.

Pennington, B. F., Gilger, J. W., Pauls, D., Smith, S. A., Smith, S. D., & De Fries, J. C. (1991). Evidence for major gene transmission of developmental dyslexia. *Journal of the American Medical Association, 266,* 1527–1534.

Rourke, B. P. (1989). *Nonverbal learning disabilities: The syndrome and the model.* New York: Guilford Press.

Rourke, B. P. (1993). Arithmetic disabilities, specific and otherwise: A neuropsychological perspective. *Journal of Learning Disabilities, 26,* 214–226.

Rourke, B. P. (1995). *Syndrome of nonverbal learning disabilities: Neurodevelopmental manifestations.* New York: Guilford Press.

Sandler, A. D., Watson, T. E., Footo, M., Levine, M. D., Coleman, W. L., & Hooper, S. R. (1992). Neurodevelopmental study of writing disorders in middle childhood. *Developmental and Behavioral Pediatrics, 13,* 17–25.

Semrud-Clikeman, M., & Hynd, G. W. (1994). Brain-behavior relationships in dyslexia. In N. C. Jordan & J. Goldstein-Phillips (Eds.), *Learning disabilities: New directions for assessment and intervention.* Boston: Allyn & Bacon.

Shamra, M. C. (1986). Dyscalculia and other learning problems in arithmetic: A historical perspective. *Focus on Learning Problems in Mathematics, 8,* 7–45.

Shaywitz, B. A., Shaywitz, S. E., Pugh, K. R., Skudlarski, P., Fulbright, R. K., Constable, R. T., Bronen, R. A., Fletcher, J. M., Liberman, A. M., Shankweiler, D. P., Katz, L., Lacadie, C., Marchione, K. E., & Gore, J. C. (1996). Functional magnetic resonance imaging as a tool to understand reading and reading disability. In R. W. Thatcher, G. R. Lyon, J. Rumsey, & N. Krasnegor (Eds.), *Developmental neuroimaging.* San Diego, CA: Academic Press.

Spreen, O. (1989). The relationship between learning disabilities, emotional disorders and neuropsychology: Some results and observations. *Journal of Clinical and Experimental Neuropsychology, 11,* 117–140.

Spreen, O., & Haaf, R. G. (1986). Empirically derived learning disability subtypes: A replication attempt and longitudinal patterns over 15 years. *Journal of Learning Disabilities, 19,* 170–180.

Stantovich, K. E. (1986). Matthew effects in reading: Some consequences of individual differences in the acquisition of literacy. *Reading Research Quarterly, 21,* 360–406.

Stantovich, K. E. (1988). Explaining the differences between the dyslexic and the garden-variety poor reader: The phonological-core variable-deficit model. *Journal of Learning Disabilities, 21,* 590–604.

Tallal, P. (1987). *Developmental language disorders.* Interagency committee on learning disabilities. Report to the U.S. Congress.

Taylor, H. G. (1989). Learning disabilities. In E. J. Mash & L. G. Terdal (Eds.), *Behavioral assessment of childhood disorders.* New York: Guilford Press.

Vellutino, F. (1979). *Dyslexia: Theory and research.* Cambridge, MA: MIT Press.

Vellutino, F., & Scanlon, D. (1987). Phonological coding, phonological awareness, and reading ability: Evidence from a longitudinal and experimental study. *Merrill-Palmer Quarterly, 33,* 321–363.

Voller, K. K. S. (1986). Right-hemisphere deficit syndrome in children. *American Journal of Psychiatry, 143,* 1004–1009.

Weintraub, S., & Mesulam, M. M. (1983). Developmental learning disabilities of the right hemisphere. *Archives of Neurology, 40,* 463–486.

Woodcock, R., & Johnson, M. (1989). *The Woodcock-Johnson Psycho-Educational Battery–Revised.* Allen, TX: Developmental Learning Materials Teaching Resources.

GERIATRIC NEUROPSYCHOLOGY

CHAPTER 10

Paul David Nussbaum

General Assessment Issues for a Geriatric Population

Thirty million Americans are at least 65 years of age and considered elderly. As a percentage of the population, the elderly represent the fastest growing age cohort. For example, at present seniors make up approximately 12% of the total population of the United States, but by the year 2030, this figure will increase to 20% (Albert & Moss, 1989). The health care delivery system will certainly be challenged to meet the increased medical, psychological, and social needs of the older adult.

For clinical neuropsychologists, there is a clear need for specialized training in geriatrics that will facilitate understanding of the effects of the aging brain on behavior. This chapter provides a brief overview of issues regarding the basic clinical assessment of the geriatric inpatient (age 65 and older).

I. MEDICAL AND NEUROPSYCHOLOGICAL DISORDERS OF THE OLDER ADULT

A. Medical Disorders

Chronic or disabling health problems increase significantly with age. At least 80% of individuals over age 65 have one chronic medical illness, and many have multiple conditions. Primary health problems include heart disease, cancer, and stroke. Additionally, an estimated 48% of older adults suffer from arthritis, 17% from orthopedic conditions, 30% from hearing loss, and 10% from visual impairment (LaRue, 1992).

Older adults fall victim to hospitalization at least twice as often as younger adults. The elderly also account for more outpatient visits to physicians and use twice as many prescription drugs as younger adults. Elderly with chronic medical problems who require highly skilled care generally reside in nursing homes. Indeed, an estimated 5% of the elderly population reside in nursing homes, but the lifetime risk for nursing home placement is estimated to be 52% for women and 30% for men age 65 and older (LaRue, 1992).

B. Neuropsychological Disorders

Mental illness also represents a significant problem for older adults, with prevalence estimates varying dependent on the setting of the sample studied. For example, prevalence rates of mental illness are 12.3% for community-based residents, 70% for nursing home residents, and 50% for patients in acute-care hospitals. A one month prevalence rate for all types of mental illness was found to be 12% for individuals 65 years of age and older compared to 17% for those aged 25 to 44 years (see LaRue, 1992).

Depression and a variety of cognitive impairments are two of the most frequently occurring psychological and neuropsychological problems of older adults (Blazer, 1993; LaRue, 1992). It is important to note that multiple clinical reports have found the prevalence of major depression in community-dwelling elderly to be between 2% and 8%, depending on the method of calculation. In contrast, medical inpatients have consistently demonstrated somewhat higher rates (18%–40%) of major depression. There is little doubt that depression is a serious problem for the elderly (Blazer, 1993). Cognitive impairments in the elderly similarly are more prevalent in medical inpatient (30%) and nursing home (84%) settings than in the community (5%).

The effects of the aging brain on behavior are well documented and relate to many different neuropsychological disorders. The most problematic of these is dementia, with an estimated prevalence of 15% in the population age 65 and older. It is well known that the incidence of dementia increases significantly with age, which is of concern given the fact that individuals are living longer. Dementia has more than 50 causes, some of which are progressive (e.g., Alzheimer's disease [AD]), whereas others are reversible (e.g., vitamin B12 deficiency). A frequent referral issue for neuropsychologists is the differential diagnosis of dementia syndrome of depression (DSD; see Nussbaum, 1995), which is a reversible dementia, versus AD (see Table 1 for a guide to differential diagnosis, Table 2 for qualitative features in memory testing, Table 3 for neurophysiological measures to differentiate AD from DSD, and Table 4 for different etiologies of dementia). Thus, the importance of accurate differential diagnosis is underscored. Some of the common causes of progressive and reversible dementias are listed in Table 4, ordered by frequency (Katzman & Rowe, 1992).

II. BRIEF NEUROPSYCHOLOGICAL ASSESSMENT OF THE GERIATRIC INPATIENT

The clinical neuropsychologist assists in the important process of accurate diagnosis, treatment intervention, and long-range placement and care of the elderly inpatient (Lovell & Nussbaum, 1994). The neuropsychological evaluation of the geriatric inpatient is crucial to this process because it provides a window to the functional integrity of the brain, thereby permitting accurate diagnostic and treatment decisions. Following is a general outline of key steps to a proper brief neuropsychological evaluation of the geriatric inpatient. This approach can be generalized to most inpatient health care settings where similar questions regarding health of the patient's central nervous system are posed to the attending neuropsychologist.

Typical referral questions include the following:
1. Does the patient have dementia?
2. Does the patient have organicity?
3. Does the patient have cognitive impairment?
4. Does the patient have depression or dementia?
5. Is the patient competent?
6. Can the patient live alone?
7. Does the patient have Alzheimer's disease?

These and other referral questions need to be addressed quickly by the neuropsychologist. A brief flexible neuropsychological battery is proposed as the best method of providing a thorough assessment of the older patient's neuropsychological

Table 1. Differentiating Alzheimer's Disease (AD) From Depression Syndrome of Dementia (DSD): Historical and Clinical Markers

Marker	AD	DSD
1. Symptom duration at time of seeking medical attention	Long	Short
2. Previous psychiatric history	Unusual	Usual
3. Progression of symptoms	Slow	Rapid
4. Patient complaint of deficit	Unusual	Frequent
5. Emotional reaction	Variable	Distress
6. Patient self-appraisal	Variable	Diminished
7. Awareness of deficit	Diminished	Intact
8. Behavior congruent with cognitive deficit	Usual	Unusual
9. Delusions	Mood independent	Mood congruent
10. Mood disorder	Environmentally responsive	Persistent

11. Night confusion	Common	Variable
12. Early morning awakening	Variable	Common
13. Topographical disorientation	Common	Unusual
14. Temporal disorientation	Persistent	Fluctuating
15. Dress apraxia	Common	Unusual
16. Loss of libido	Variable	Severe

Note. From "Differential Diagnosis of Dementia and Depression," by A. W. Kaszniak and G. D. Christenson, in *Neuropsychology Assessment of Dementia and Depression in Older Adults* (p. 98), by M. Storandt and G. R. Vandenbos (Eds.), 1995, Washington, DC: American Psychological Association. Copyright 1995 by the American Psychological Association. Adapted and expanded with permission.

Table 2. Differentiating Alzheimer's Disease (AD) From Depression Syndrome of Dementia (DSD): Qualitative Features in Memory Test Performance

Test feature	AD	DSD
1. Free verbal recall	Poor	Variable
a. Learning curve	Flat	Reduced U-Shaped
b. Primacy effect	None	Reduced
c. Recency effect	Impaired	Near normal
d. Extra-list errors	Frequent	Infrequent
e. Don't know errors (controversial)	Unusual	Usual
f. Perseveration errors	Common	Uncommon
2. Recognition memory	Impaired	Relatively intact
a. False positive recognition memory errors	Common	Uncommon
3. Semantic organization	Unhelpful	Helpful
4. Prompting	Unhelpful	Helpful
5. Effort in attempting to perform tasks	Good	Poor
6. Performance on "automatic" encoding tasks	Impaired	Intact
7. Performance on "effortful" encoding tasks	Impaired	Impaired

8. Performance on tasks of similar difficulty	Consistent	Variable
9. Memory complaint	Relatively rare	Extreme
10. Memory complaint versus memory performance	Underachieves	Overachieves
11. Rate of forgetting	Rapid	Relatively normal
12. Frequent reminders of task directions	Needed	Unusual

Note. From "Differential Diagnosis of Dementia and Depression," by A. W. Kaszniak and G. D. Christenson, in *Neuropsychology Assessment of Dementia and Depression in Older Adults* (p. 104), by M. Storandt and G. R. Vandenbos (Eds.), 1995, Washington, DC: American Psychological Association. Copyright 1995 by the American Psychological Association. Adapted and expanded with permission.

Table 3. Differentiating Alzheimer's Disease (AD) From Depression Syndrome of Dementia (DSD): Neurophysiological Measures

Measure	AD	DSD
Cerebral metabolism PET	Bilateral Temporoparietal Hypometabolism	Bilateral frontal lobe Hypometabolism
Cerebral perfusion SPECT	Bilateral Temporoparietal Hypoperfusion	Bilateral frontal lobe Hypoperfusion
Magnetic resonance imaging	Cortical atrophy Enlarged sulci Leukoaraiosis[a]	White matter Hyperintensities Typical in basal ganglia Periventricular area
Computerized EEG	Abnormal	Normal

Note. PET = positron emission tomography; SPECT = single photon emission computed tomography; EEG = electroencephalography.

[a]Diminution in the density of the brain's white matter (Hachinski et al., 1987).

Table 4. Etiology of Dementia

Disease	Prevalence estimate (%)
Progressive dementias	85–90
Alzheimer's disease	50–70
Other	15–17
Vascular disease	
Huntington's disease	
Parkinson's disease	
Posttraumatic	
Postanoxic-carbon monoxide	
Progressive nuclear palsy	
Creutzfeldt-Jakob disease	
Postencephalitic	
AIDS dementia	
Amyotrophic lateral sclerosis	
Reversible dementias	1–10
Hydrocephalus	
Tumor	
Alcohol	
Drug toxicity (polypharmacy)	
Metabolic	
Depression	
Thyroid	
Subdural hematoma	
Epilepsy	
Vitamin B12 deficiency	

status (see Lovell & Nussbaum, 1994). A systematic approach to the assessment is needed and includes the following four steps.

A. Four Steps of a Systematic Assessment

1. OBTAIN BACKGROUND INFORMATION ON THE PATIENT

The goal of the first step is to gather all reasonably available information on the patient to be assessed. The background information aids the examiner in answering questions and provides a necessary context for interpreting results of the examination. This step can be best accomplished by using the following protocol, which outlines the key strategies:

a. Generate impressions from the primary caregiver and identify the exact referral question

(1) Contact the referral source to determine the precise referral question.

(2) Travel to the patient's hospital unit and identify the primary nurse.

(3) Request the patient's chart and solicit the nurse's impressions of the behaviors of the patient during his or her inpatient stay. Specific issues to address include the patient's level of cooperation, orientation, memory and language capacity, sleep and appetite, activities of daily living, social support network, and disposition plan, as well as any abnormal behaviors displayed by the patient.

b. Conduct a thorough chart review

(1) Gather information on demographics of patient:
(a) Name
(b) Date of admission
(c) Age and date of birth
(d) Handedness
(e) Education (grades, learning disability)
(f) Occupation
(g) Marital status
(h) Developmental history
(i) Military experience
(j) Criminal and legal history
(k) Nutritional status
(2) Gather information on medical history:
(a) Current medications
(b) Past and current medical conditions
(c) History of cardiac illness, stroke, hypertension, diabetes, epilepsy, head injury, loss of consciousness, and so on
(d) Past surgical interventions
(e) Laboratory (i.e., blood work) findings
(f) Magnetic resonance imaging, computerized tomography, electrocardiogram, and electroencephalogram findings
(g) History of alcohol and drug abuse
(h) Family medical history
(i) History of medical compliance
(j) Presence of sensory deficit
(3) Gather information on psychiatric history:
(a) Current medications

(b) Past and current psychiatric conditions
(c) Past psychiatric hospitalizations
(d) Past psychiatric treatment including electroconvulsive therapy
(e) Past and current suicidal ideation and intent
(f) Family psychiatric history
(g) Acuteness or chronicity of problem
(h) Important recent losses
(i) Appetite and sleep behavior
(j) Description of behavior in nurses' notes
(k) Level of arousal, orientation, cooperation
(l) Evidence for hopelessness, helplessness, somatization, and social withdrawal
(m) Cognitive problems including memory

2. INTERVIEW THE PATIENT AND CONDUCT A MENTAL STATUS EXAMINATION

This step permits the examiner to meet, observe, and interact with the patient. The purpose of this step is to develop early ideas regarding the patient's neuropsychological status.

a. Background information

Speak loud and slow, and repeat questions to patient. Also, permit breaks as needed and make sure lighting and privacy are adequate. Ask for spelling of full name, age, date of birth, date of admission, education, handedness, marital status, and history of medical and psychiatric illness (correlate with chart review data). Ask the patient to provide a reason for hospitalization (i.e., to ascertain awareness of deficit).

b. Appearance

Take note of the patient's grooming, clothing, level of arousal (alert, lethargic, obtundent, stuporous), level of cooperation, language comprehension, oral expression, ability to follow conversation, memory capacity (is the patient forgetting rapidly?), effort to answer questions, and rate of response.

c. Mood and affect

Take note of the patient's affect and seek information pertaining to mood. Besides ruling out suicidal and homicidal behavior, check for the following indicators of mood:
(1) Depression
(2) Anger
(3) Frustration

(4) Happiness
(5) Irritability

d. Psychotic behavior

Rule out the presence of psychotic behavior. Is the patient experiencing any of the following?
(1) Hallucinations
(2) Paranoia
(3) Illusions
(4) Delusions (mood congruent or incongruent)

e. Language functioning

Assess the patient's language for the following:
(1) Comprehension
(2) Expression
(3) Volume
(4) Tempo and prosody
(5) Content
(6) Word-finding ability

f. Motor functioning

Assess patient's motor functions for the following:
(1) Gait
(2) Posture
(3) Resting or action tremor
(4) Slowness of movement

g. Estimate of premorbid intellect

Estimate patient's premorbid level of intellect using the following:
(1) Educational level
(2) Grades in school
(3) Information regarding learning disability
(4) Occupational history
(5) Vocabulary used by patient in conversation

3. CONDUCT A BRIEF NEUROPSYCHOLOGICAL EVALUATION (2 HOURS)

The brief evaluation provides empirical support for the clinician's early ideas regarding neuropsychological status and provides answers to the referral question. Some of the instruments listed in this section provide information that is important to more than one cognitive domain.

a. General intellect

An initial assessment of the patient's ability to communicate, attend to, and process information is obtained. The clinician can begin to develop working hypotheses regarding cognitive impairment as it relates to neuroanatomic substrates. The clinician can monitor the patient's approach to problem solving focusing on strengths and weaknesses. More thorough assessment of cognitive deficits can be conducted on the basis of an examination of general intellect. Afterward, a preliminary judgment is made regarding whether the patient's cognitive functioning has declined from estimated premorbid levels.

General intellect includes cognitive functions related to global neuroanatomic parameters: The dominant hemisphere (usually left hemisphere) relates primarily to language-based functions, and the nondominant hemisphere (usually right hemisphere) relates primarily to visuospatial capacity. The following tools may be used for assessment of general intellect:

1. *Language-based functions*
   (a) Folstein Mini-Mental State Examination.
   (b) Wechsler Adult Intelligence Scale–Revised (WAIS-R): Information, Vocabulary, and Similarities subtests.
   (c) These WAIS-R subtests assess academic knowledge thought to be resistant to progressive dementia, as well as verbal abstraction skill.

2. *Visuospatial and constructional functions*
   (a) WAIS-R subtests: Block Design, Object Assembly, Digit Symbol.
   (b) These WAIS-R subtests provide a measure of visuospatial and constructional skill; the results can be compared to results obtained on measures of language integrity.

b. Attention and concentration

Although the clinical interview and assessment of general intellect provide information pertaining to the patient's attentional capacity, a formal examination is needed. Attention represents an important cognitive domain and one that is particularly vulnerable in the older patient. Poor attention can compromise performance on the neuropsychological examination and may indicate delirium. Attention is generally regarded as an active cognitive process more complex than arousal and limited in capacity. The following tools can be used for assessment of attention and concentration:

1. ***Attention and Concentration Index Score (Wechsler Memory Scale–Revised [WMS-R]).*** This measure provides standardized norms with mean of 100 and standard deviation of 15. This permits easy comparison to other measures of cognitive capacity with identical scaling properties (e.g., WAIS-R).

2. ***Trail Making Test–Part A.*** This instrument measures simple rapid visual sequencing of information and demands both visual scanning and attention.

c. Memory

Memory is an important cognitive domain to be examined, particularly because degenerative diseases of advanced age typically affect memory first. Memory is not a unitary construct (nor are any of the other cognitive domains), and it should be examined from a process approach that permits assessment of the patient's strategies for encoding, consolidating, and retrieving information. Poor encoding and consolidation of new information have been related to the medial temporal lobe and diencephalic brain regions (Squire, 1987), whereas intact encoding but poor retrieval relates more to subcortical–frontal regions. Dissociating the processes of memory can, therefore, assist in differential diagnosis. Finally, psychiatric disturbances (e.g., depression) can reduce the patient's ability to perform well on memory tasks. However, the analysis of the memory performance (encoding vs. retrieval) can help to distinguish progressive from reversible disturbances. The following tools can be used for the assessment of memory.

1. ***WMS-R: Logical Memory I and II; WMS-R: Visual Reproduction I and II.*** (Retention score = delay divided by immediate [%].) The WMS-R permits an analysis of language-based recall versus visual recall. It is important to note, however, that "verbal and visual recall" from the WMS-R correlate with each other and likely measure an identical construct. The retention score is critical because it permits a measure of forgetting. The patient's rate of forgetting generally assists in differential diagnosis (i.e., normal forgetting versus probable Alzheimer's disease).

2. ***Hopkins Verbal Learning Test (HVLT; with 20-minute delay).*** The HVLT provides a brief free recall measure that is perhaps more complex than WMS-R verbal passages. The HVLT provides measures of learning across repeated trials, semantic clustering, intrusion errors, "don't know responses," recognition performance, and potentially a 20-minute delay recall.

3. *Rey Complex Figure Test (with 20-minute delay).* Because the WMS-R does not adequately measure visual recall, the Rey is recommended. A copy, immediate recall, and 20-minute delay recall of the figure are encouraged. This permits analysis of visuoperceptual capacity, approaches to problem solving, and the patient's capacity to process gestalt (nondominant hemisphere function) versus details (dominant hemisphere function).

d. Visuoconstructional skill

Assessment of visuoconstructional skill is vital with older adults because AD, the most frequently occurring type of dementia, manifests early with visuospatial and constructional dysfunction (thought to be related to bilateral parietal lobe damage). The instruments selected permit assessment of visuomotor construction, visuointegration, and visual organization without a motor component. The patient's performance on these tasks assists in ruling out parietal lobe involvement and permits preliminary analysis of executive (frontal lobe) functions. The following tools can be used for assessment of visuoconstructional skill:

1. *Block Design (WAIS-R).* The Block Design subtest measures rapid visuoconstructional capacity using a visual prompt for guidance.

2. *Object Assembly (WAIS-R).* This subtest measures rapid visuointegrational skill without visual prompt.

3. *Clock drawing.* This task permits analysis of organizational skill, visuospatial skill, and vulnerability to perseveration and concrete response style.

4. *Hooper Visual Organization Test.* This instrument measures visual organizational skill, concrete response style, and ability to integrate fragmented pictures into a gestalt.

e. Language

Assessment of language is a highly specialized area of neuropsychology. Dementia and other disease processes of late life (e.g., stroke) impair language. The tests selected include a measure of object naming with relatively good normative data for age and educational levels. The Boston Naming Test permits a measure of the patient's ability to produce words given semantic prompts that might assist in determining integrity of the semantic lexicon, which is typically decompensated with AD. The verbal fluency task permits a measure of rapid spontaneous word generation. A measure of fluency is generated using phonemic prompts (F-A-S or C-F-L) and semantic prompts (animal naming). Verbal fluency likely reflects ability to access semantic lexicon and is thought to be related to the left anterior cortex. The following tools can be used in the assessment of language:

1. *Boston Naming Test.* This test permits a relatively quick assessment of object-naming ability and can be useful for identifying early signs of progressive dementia.

2. *Verbal fluency (F-A-S or C-F-L and Grocery Story Test).* Fluency is useful for measurement of an individual's ability to access semantic lexicon (word library) and assists in understanding the integrity of the lexicon to be accessed. Inability to access an intact lexicon may indicate depression or frontal lobe disorder, whereas a diminished lexicon is likely more related to progressive dementia.

f. Executive functions

Measurement of frontal lobe function remains less developed in neuropsychology compared to measures of temporal or parietal lobe function. However, the measures selected provide data pertaining to functions related to the frontal lobe. These include cognitive flexibility, rapid word generation, verbal abstraction, and novel problem solving. Measurement of executive functions may be related to the patient's capacity to make sound decisions, exhibit good judgment, and maintain independence of living, all crucial to older adults. Use the following tools for assessment of general functioning:

1. *Trail Making Test–Part B.* Measures rapid complex visual sequencing and represents a useful assessment of cognitive flexibility.

2. *Verbal fluency (F-A-S or C-F-L and Grocery Store Test).* See description in the preceding section on language.

3. *Wisconsin Card Sorting Test (one deck).* Measures novel problem-solving skill. One-deck administration is recommended with older inpatients, particularly because normative data exist for this procedure.

4. *Similarities (WAIS-R).* Measure of verbal abstraction skill.

g. Motor skill

Measurement of gross motor skill of the older inpatient may be difficult for the neuropsychologist. However, attention should be given to any lateral weakness or asymmetries. Tremor and posture may be observed, and gait can be measured by asking the individual to walk across the room. Care should be taken to assist the older inpatient, who will likely be frail. Simply asking the inpatient to squeeze your two index fingers with each hand permits a gross measure of hand strength. Also, by asking the inpatient to smile and raise both eyebrows, an indication for facial asymmetry may be obtained. The best tool for assessment of motor skill is the **Finger Oscillation Test**, which provides a quick measure of cerebral lateralization that can assist in highlighting hemispheric deficiencies.

h. Mood

Mood is always important to assess with older adults, particularly older inpatients. Accurate diagnosis of depression or other mood disorder can permit appropriate treatment and result in earlier discharge with fewer complications. The best tool for assessment of mood is the **Geriatric Depression Scale**, from which it is best to read the questions to the patient.

The Geriatric Depression Scale is a 30-item yes/no-based questionnaire that has demonstrated usefulness in measurement of depression in older adults with psychiatric and neurological disorders. It also has demonstrated use with patients who have AD. It is important to read each question to the patient to maximize validity, particularly for patients who have dementia.

4. COMMUNICATE THE RESULTS OF THE EVALUATION

This step enables the patient to hear and understand results. Treatment options are explored with the patient, and information is provided to the referring agent. Exhibit 1 provides suggestions for what to do during this stage.

III. CONCLUSION

Expertise in the effects of aging and brain–behavior relations has become a specialization within clinical neuropsychology. Indeed, neuropsychologists employed in general medical facilities are now required to provide important diagnostic and prognostic information concerning older patients suffering from many different disease processes, all of which may affect the central nervous system.

To meet the challenges of an increasing number of elderly patients, clinical neuropsychology must continue to promote specialization in aging. This chapter attempts to provide the attending neuropsychologist with a basic framework for systematic assessment of the elderly inpatient. Key components of the neuropsychological examination have been highlighted,

Exhibit 1. Steps for Patient Referral and Treatment

---

1. Provide feedback to referring physician and primary nurse. (Interpretation of results is based on the patient's current cognitive performance compared to same-age peers and to the patient's estimated premorbid intellect.)

2. Document results and interpretations in chart.

3. Prepare a formal report and send to referring physician.

4. Provide treatment recommendations:
   a. Disposition needs
   b. Need for neuroimaging
   c. Psychotherapy and psychosocial needs
   d. Medication suggestions
   e. Family education
   f. Legal and financial planning
   g. Additional neuropsychological testing

---

and the clinician is guided through appropriate solicitation of important clinical information. Although the chapter is not designed to be exhaustive, it enables the attending clinical neuropsychologist to conduct a reasonably thorough examination of the elderly inpatient, thereby promoting accurate diagnosis, treatment, and disposition.

BIBLIOGRAPHY

General Sources

Albert, M. S., & Moss, M. B. (1989). *Geriatric neuropsychology.* New York: Guilford Press.

Blazer, D. G. (1993). *Depression in late life* (2nd ed.). St Louis, MO: Mosby.

Hachinski, V. C., Potter, P., & Merskey, H. (1987). Leukoaraiosis. *Archives of Neurology, 44*, 21–23.

Kaszniak, A. W., & Christenson, G. D. (1995). Differential diagnosis of dementia and depression. In M. Storandt & G. R. Vandenbos (Eds.), *Neuropsychology assessment of dementia and depression in older adults* (pp. 81–118). Washington, DC: American Psychological Association.

Katzman, R., & Rowe, J. W. (1992). *Principles of geriatric neurology.* Philadelphia: Davis.

LaRue, A. (1992). *Aging and neuropsychological assessment.* New York: Plenum Press.

Lezak, M. (1995). *Neuropsychological assessment* (3rd ed.). New York: Oxford Press.

Lovell, M., & Nussbaum, P. D. (1994). Neuropsychological assessment. In C. E. Coffey & J. L. Cummings (Eds.), *Textbook of geriatric neuropsychiatry* (pp. 129–144). Washington, DC: American Psychiatric Press.

Nussbaum, P. D. (1995). Pseudodementia: A slow death. *Neuropsychology Review, 4,* 71–90.

Ruff, R. M., Light, R. H., & Parker, S. B. (1996). Benton controlled oral word association test: Reliability and updated norms. *Archives of Clinical Neuropsychology, 11,* 329–338.

Spreen, O., & Strauss, E. (1991). *A compendium of neuropsychological tests: Administration, norms, and commentary.* New York: Oxford University Press.

Squire, L. R. (1987). *Memory and brain.* New York: Oxford University Press

References for Older Adult Norms[1]

Clinical Neuropsychologist. (1992). Vol. 6, supplement for older age normative data.

Lezak, M. (1995). *Neuropsychological assessment* (3rd ed.). New York: Plenum Press.

Spreen, O., & Strauss, E. (1991). *A compendium of neuropsychological tests: Administration, norms, and commentary.* New York: Oxford University Press.

---

[1]The references in this group provide normative data for persons older than 75. The clinician is encouraged to make cautious interpretations of test results without norms appropriate to the patient population being examined.

CHAPTER 11
Graham Ratcliff and Judith Saxton

Age-Appropriate Memory Impairment

There is good evidence that many aspects of memory deteriorate with increasing age. The decline affects recent memory (also known as long-term or secondary memory) more than immediate (short-term or primary) or remote (tertiary) memory, and it cannot be entirely explained by other age-related changes in cognition and behavior. This effect of age in otherwise healthy, normally aging individuals is compounded by the fact that many disease states that cause memory impairment are considerably more prevalent in the elderly. The net result of these changes is that the ability to encode new information into memory, hold it in store, and recall it after an interval is typically reduced in older individuals. On the other hand, although the processes involved in remembering become less effective, the content of memory that constitutes the individual's knowledge base can continue to increase. Older people may, therefore, perform nearly as well as young people on tests assessing general knowledge or vocabulary, which require well-learned, factual information or semantic knowledge rather than memory for a specific event, but they perform less well on tests requiring delayed recall of recently presented material that exceeds immediate memory spans.

The effect of age on memory is large enough to be clinically significant, and age has a major effect on neuropsychological test performance. For example, the scores of people age 35–44 in the normative sample for a standard test of recent memory, the Wechsler Memory Scale–Revised (WMS-R; Wechsler, 1987), were up to 50% higher than those of 70- to 74-year-olds. As in other cognitive tasks, memory for nonverbal material seems to be somewhat more affected by aging than memory for verbal material, and delayed recall is affected more than immediate recall.

I. VARIETIES OF AGE-RELATED MEMORY DISORDER

Three general classes of age-related memory disorders have been identified: those that are age appropriate and can be regarded as a usual consequence of normal aging, those that are age inappropriate in that they involve more severe memory loss than is typical for an individual of a given age but are not known to be progressive or malignant, and those that are signs of a disease that is significantly impairing brain function. These varieties of age-related memory disorder have not been clearly distinguished in the literature, even conceptually, and the terminology is vague and inconsistent (for a more detailed review, see Ratcliff & Saxton, 1994). Differentiating between them in the clinic is important; indeed, assigning the patient's memory impairment to one of these categories is the goal of many evaluations. Unfortunately, there is no simple algorithm for doing so, and the clinician must weigh the balance of the evidence and use clinical judgment in reaching a conclusion.

A. Age-Appropriate Memory Decline

This category is defined in terms of either memory test performance that is worse than expected of a young adult (e.g., age-associated memory impairment [AAMI]; Crook et al., 1986) or memory test performance in an average range for the individual's age (age-consistent memory impairment [ACMI]; Blackford & LaRue, 1989) in the absence of pathological conditions sufficient to explain the memory loss. The criteria for AAMI are particularly well defined (Crook et al., 1986). Briefly they are as follows:

1. Memory test performance 1 standard deviation below that of a young adult
2. Average vocabulary
3. Subjective complaints of forgetfulness
4. Objective evidence of impairment on a standard test of delayed recall for verbal information
5. Absence of an extensive list of conditions that might potentially affect memory including dementia and depression.

These criteria are useful for some research purposes, but they are too restrictive to be helpful in most clinical situations because most elderly individuals fail to meet the exclusion criteria and are ineligible for the diagnosis even though their memory impairments are the result of "usual aging" in the sense of Rowe and Kahn (1987).

For clinical purposes, age-appropriate memory decline can be considered normal aging and can be diagnosed in usually aging individuals, even if they are not entirely free of common diseases that could affect memory. The rationale for this is that a number of disease states that can affect memory (e.g., hypertension, other forms of cardiovascular disease, and depression) are prevalent enough in the elderly that they might be regarded as part of usual aging. Moreover, at the level of severity typically encountered in community-resident individuals, their effects on memory are usually quite small. Although one must always take the patient's medical state into account, moderate levels of cardiovascular disease or depression are not usually a sufficient explanation for clinically significant memory impairment. The specific term AAMI should be reserved for the relatively few individuals who meet the strict diagnostic criteria set out by Crook et al. (1986). Conversely, the clinician should be prepared to identify normal, age-appropriate memory decline in normally aging individuals who are not perfectly healthy, as well as in the unusually healthy, successfully aging persons who are eligible for the diagnosis of AAMI. In other words, the category of age-appropriate memory decline includes but is not limited to AAMI.

In our experience, roughly half of community-resident individuals over the age of 65 seem to have experienced a decline in memory that could cause their memory test scores to drop by an amount equivalent to 1 standard deviation of the distribution of memory test scores in young adults. As might be expected for an age-related change, the prevalence of age-appropriate memory decline seems to increase with increasing age, but there is no clear evidence that it has any particular prognostic significance.

B. Age-Inappropriate Memory Impairment

These disorders imply memory impairment worse than that expected of a person of the affected individual's age. There is also an implicit requirement that memory be more affected than other cognitive domains; otherwise, other diagnoses should be considered, such as mild cognitive disorder (World Health Organization, 1978), questionable dementia (Hughes, Berg, Danzinger, Coben, & Martin, 1982), or dementia as defined in DSM-IV (American Psychiatric Association, 1994). There is also an implicit presumption, weaker than that in the construct of age-appropriate decline, that the disorder is not the result of some known, specific pathology, although the affected individual does not have to be completely free of disease. Age-inappropriate memory impairment should therefore be suspected when the following are found:

1. Memory test performance is impaired relative to age peers.

2. Other cognitive domains are unimpaired (or significantly less impaired than memory).

3. The impairment is not presumed to be the direct result of known, specific disease.

When it has been specified, the criterion for deviation from normality is again 1 standard deviation below the mean, but the comparison group here is composed of people of the affected individual's own age. Examples of the construct of age-inappropriate memory impairment are benign senescent forgetfulness (Kral, 1958), senescent forgetfulness (Larrabee, Levin, & High, 1986), late-life forgetfulness (Blackford & LaRue, 1989), and age-inappropriate forgetfulness (Ratcliff & Saxton, 1994). The prevalence of age-inappropriate impairment does not seem to increase with increasing age within the population of individuals older than 65. The clinical significance of age-inappropriate memory impairment is not clear, partly because of the confusing terminology and varying criteria used in the literature. However, there are increasing suggestions that it is sometimes an early manifestation of dementia or that individuals exhibiting it are at risk for progressing to dementia, although this is certainly not universally true.

C. Malignant Memory Impairment Associated With Disease

This category reflects the memory impairment of dementia or, less frequently, organic amnesic syndromes. It is typically more severe than the preceding two categories, frequently associated with other cognitive deficits, and usually progressive. Qualitatively, memory impairment is particularly likely to be a sign of brain disease if recognition as well as recall is affected (Branconner, Cole, Spear, & DeVitt, 1972), if delayed recall is more impaired than the amount initially learned, and if learning is not helped by cues (Petersen, Smith, Kokmen, Ivnik, & Tangalos, 1992), although none of these are necessary conditions.

II. DIFFERENTIAL DIAGNOSIS AND DECISION PROCEDURES

In order to distinguish among the disorders discussed, the clinician needs to take a history, assess memory and other cognitive functions, and review medical records.

A. Taking a History

The usual demographic, psychosocial, and medical history that constitutes the background against which neuropsychological test results are viewed needs to be supplemented by specific inquiries about memory function, memory failures, and risk factors for age-related memory impairment. The history given by the patient should be compared with information from a collateral source wherever possible. The purposes of the inquiry are as follows:

1. To discover whether the patient is forgetful and, if so, the objective severity of the problem.

2. To distinguish the actual severity of the problem from its perceived severity in the eyes of the patient.

3. To determine whether this represents a change for the patient and, if so, whether it occurred gradually or suddenly, whether it is getting worse or getting better, and whether onset coincided with any medical or social event that might have constituted a precipitating factor.

4. To establish whether memory impairment is the chief (or even sole) complaint or whether it is simply part of a larger problem.

5. Finally, to check whether the patient has had a recent neuropsychological evaluation elsewhere that might provide relevant data or contraindicate repetition of some tests. In the rehabilitation context, it is quite common for patients to have had previous testing elsewhere that is not documented in the

fragmentary records available and that they do not mention until specifically asked.

To achieve these goals, it is helpful to ask for specific examples of memory problems. This serves several purposes. First, it allows the examiner to check whether the problems appear to be attributable to memory impairment. It is not at all uncommon, for example, to hear complaints about difficulty "remembering" words the patient wants to use, a problem that is usually classified as language rather than memory impairment. Similarly, praxic or attentional problems are sometimes described by patients in terms of forgetfulness. Second, the type and frequency of problems described and the ease with which the patient and informant come up with examples can provide insight into the severity of the problem. If the only examples are stereotyped, involving the same failures as are described in other examiners' reports, or if the examples refer to trivial or common occurrences, one may suspect that the perception is worse than the reality, alerting one to the possibility of a depressive or factitious component or simple worry. In this context, we find it helpful to check whether patients have recently had such phenomena as Alzheimer's disease brought to their attention (e.g., because a friend or family member has been so diagnosed or because of coverage of the disorder in the media); this can lead to overconcern about normal memory failures. Conversely, when relatives report trivial successes (e.g., "He is doing OK—he remembered where we were going today"), one suspects a severe problem. Finally, in the rehabilitation setting, specific examples can be translated into specific functional goals. We find that use of a formal questionnaire (see the following section) can be a useful, structured way of obtaining this information.

We also recommend asking what initially caused the patient to seek professional care (i.e., either from the psychologist directly or from the physician or agency that initiated the chain of referrals culminating in the neuropsychological evaluation) and whether there have been any changes in the patient's activities of daily living, work performance, leisure activities, or habits. In both cases, the question may elicit important information that the patient or informant would not have considered relevant. Information about the progression of the disorder can often best be obtained by asking for comparison with a specific landmark in the past (e.g., How does it compare with last Thanksgiving, or with your 65th birthday?).

B. Choosing a Memory Test

Assessment must involve some form of objective memory test rather than subjective report alone, and the minimum requirement for such a test is that it involve delayed recall of a sufficient amount of recently presented information that it is not subject to a marked ceiling effect. Norms for elderly individuals should be available, and a comprehensive evaluation should also include a way of comparing the encoding, retention, and recall of information (e.g., through immediate and delayed recall trials); use of both verbal and nonverbal material; and a measure of multitrial learning as well as recall. Unfortunately, the three-word memory test on the Mini Mental State Examination (MMSE) (Folstein, Folstein, & McHugh, 1975) is too simple to detect mild-to-moderate memory impairment, and no other single test meets all of these requirements.

The test of choice depends to some extent on the referral question. Some useful measures selected from the large number available are shown in Table 1. The Logical Memory and Visual Reproduction subtests of the WMS-R (Wechsler, 1987) are useful general-purpose memory measures and are included in most of our evaluations. Norms for individuals up to age 97 are now available (Ivnik et al., 1992b). We tend to rely on the Logical Memory more than Visual Reproduction subtest because the latter is confounded with constructional ability. Also, Logical Memory is one of the more ecologically valid memory tests in general use (Sunderland, Harris, & Baddeley, 1983); it can serve as a guide to everyday functional memory and is reasonably sensitive to memory deficit. Most memory impairments are not material specific, and even when they are, verbal memory impairments are more readily demonstrable. Nevertheless, the Visual Reproduction subtest is available when memory for nonverbal material is an issue. The Recognition Memory Test (Warrington, 1984) can also be used when the difference between verbal and nonverbal memory is of particular interest.

We regard delayed recall as the most useful measure of memory. Although comparison of immediate and delayed recall scores is certainly informative, we do not favor reliance on a percentage recall score or other such measure of forgetting as an index of memory impairment. Moderate memory impairments can affect immediate as well as delayed recall on most memory tests because the memoranda exceed span; these impairments are not reflected in forgetting scores although delayed recall scores remain informatively low. Thus, delayed recall is more sensitive than forgetting in some situations, and

Table 1. Suggested Memory Tests and Alternatives

Test	Features
Basic memory assessment	
Wechsler Memory Scale–Revised (Wechsler, 1987)	Standard, norms for elderly, face validity
Logical Memory I and II	
Visual Reproduction I and II	Nonverbal, confounded with constructional skills
Rey Auditory Verbal Learning Test (Rey, 1964)	Sensitive, norms for elderly
Rivermead Behavioural Memory Test (Wilson et al., 1985)	Ecological validity, prospective memory, fair norms for elderly, parallel forms
Alternative instruments	
Recognition Memory Test (Warrington, 1984)	Simple responses, verbal versus nonverbal comparison
California Verbal Learning Test (Delis et al., 1987)	Sensitive, norms to age 80
Hopkins Verbal Learning Test (Brandt, 1991)	Slightly easier, parallel forms
CERAD Word List Learning Task (Morris et al., 1989)	Easiest
Fuld Object Memory Evaluation (Fuld, 1980)	Concrete, some norms for nursing home residents, selective reminding, avoids floor effects

(Continued)

Table 1. Suggested Memory Tests and Alternatives *(Continued)*

Test	Features
Subjective Memory Questionnaires	
Everyday memory questionnaire (Sunderland et al., 1983)	User-friendly scale, concrete examples
MAC-S (Crook & Larrabee, 1990)	Extensive validity data

Note. CERAD = Consortium to Establish a Registry of Alzheimer's Disease. MAC-S = Memory Assessment Clinics Subjects Scale.

although the two are subject to different limitations on specificity, delayed recall is reasonably specific for memory impairment in most settings. When it is not (e.g., when the impairment is secondary to other cognitive or language deficits), this is usually obvious. However, it is clearly sensible to use all the information available and not tie oneself to any single index of impairment in a clinical setting.

We find the other WMS-R subtests much less useful and tend to substitute the Rey Auditory Verbal Learning Test (RAVLT; Rey, 1964), the Hopkins Verbal Learning Test (HVLT; Brandt, 1991), or the CERAD Word List Learning Task (Morris et al., 1989) for the paired-associate subtest on the WMS-R. The CERAD task is shorter and simpler and is appropriate when the more severe memory impairment of dementia is suspected or to follow the progress of patients with significant memory deficits (Welsh, Butters, Hughes, Mohs, & Heyman, 1991). The HVLT is also relatively brief and has the advantage of six parallel forms if repeated assessment is anticipated (e.g., after a trial of pharmacotherapy). The RAVLT is the most extensive, provides more information than the others, and is probably more sensitive; however, it takes longer to administer and is more taxing for the patient. RAVLT norms are now available for individuals up to the age of 97 (Ivnik et al., 1992a). The California Verbal Learning Test (CVLT; Delis, Kramer, Kaplan, & Ober, 1987) is an extensive word list learning task designed to allow the examiner to analyze the patient's learning strategies; norms are available up to age 80, separately for males and females.

The Rivermead Behavioural Memory Test (RBMT; Wilson, Cockburn, & Baddeley, 1985) is particularly useful if prediction of everyday memory function is required. It has four parallel forms and includes prospective memory items (i.e., items in which the patient is required to "remember to remember" to do something at a prearranged time or signal). Prospective memory is at the root of many patient complaints of forgetfulness, and informal prospective memory tasks of the kind used in the RBMT can usefully be inserted into an evaluation on an informal basis (e.g., by asking the patient to do something when an alarm sounds, to "remind" the examiner to give the patient his or her business card before leaving, or to check with the receptionist after the evaluation). Ecological validity is particularly important in the rehabilitation context, where the improvement of the patient's functional capacity is the goal.

A formal subjective memory questionnaire can also help to identify treatment goals as well as illustrate the severity of the problem in the eyes of the patient and, when filled out by a significant other, those of an observer. We find a questionnaire based on that used by Sunderland et al. (1983) convenient because it asks for frequency ratings for concrete, easily targeted types of memory failure and because it has a user-friendly rating scale that seems to be well understood by patients. Another well-documented questionnaire, the Memory Assessment Clinics Subjects Scale (MAC-S), is described by Crook and Larrabee (1990). Other memory questionnaires are reviewed by Zelinski and her colleagues (Zelinski, Gilewski, & Thompson, 1980; Zelinski & Gilewski, 1988).

The patient's self-report of memory problems should not be taken as evidence of memory impairment without supporting data, even if it is dignified by presentation in the form of a scorable response to a formal questionnaire. This is particularly true when the issue is diagnosis rather than rehabilitation planning. There is considerable evidence to show both that individuals with significant memory impairments may not be aware of them and that patients' reports of memory problems are typically correlated more closely with their affective state than with the severity of memory impairment as determined by neuropsychological testing. An intriguing exception to this rule is reported in an article by Larrabee, West, and Crook (1991), who found that MAC-S questionnaire responses were related to performance on a series of memory tests that appear to be sensitive to everyday memory functioning. This finding opens up the possibility that patients' subjective reports sometimes give accurate information about everyday memory problems to which standard memory tests are not sensitive. Jonker, Launer, Hooijer, and Lindeboom (1996) also reported that subjective complaints are a valid indicator of memory impairment. However, these remain minority findings, and it is certainly the case that everyday remembering can be affected by other deficits (including depression and attentional problems) as well as by impairments of what is typically described as "memory" in a clinical context. Hence, our view that patients' subjective reports need to be treated with great caution, particularly when one is exploring a differential diagnosis in which presence or absence of memory impairment is crucial rather than assessing everyday functioning for rehabilitation planning or evaluation of disability.

Incidental memory can be assessed by asking patients to recall the symbols from the Digit Symbol subtest of the Wechsler Adult Intelligence Scale–Revised (WAIS-R) without prior warning that they will be required to do this. Patients can be asked simply to draw as many symbols as they can or to pair the symbols with the correct number. One disadvantage of this procedure is that to ensure that all patients have the same exposure to the stimuli, all patients must complete the full Digit Symbol subtest, which can be time-consuming for older individuals.

C. Choosing Norms

In most clinical situations, the first question is whether the results are abnormal, which implies comparison with a demographically appropriate normative population, particularly with respect to age, education (or some other index of overall intellectual achievement), and gender. The Mayo's Older Americans Normative Studies (MOANS) are useful in this regard because they extend the normative base for the WMS-R (Ivnik et al., 1992b) up to the age of 94 and for the RAVLT (Ivnik et al., 1992a) up to the age of 97. MOANS norms call for slightly higher scores on average than the WMS-R norms, possibly because of differences in the demographics of the study samples, and we have also found that our sample of community-resident individuals performed better than the WMS-R normative population, probably because they are somewhat more educated.

Normative data that account for both age and education in elderly samples are not generally available for memory tests. When they are not available, we tend to use a rule of thumb based on the results of our recent study of 989 elderly persons in Pittsburgh and Hagerstown, Maryland (Ratcliff & Saxton, 1994). Regression analysis indicated that age and education both significantly affected memory test performance in this sample, and looking at the slope of the regression line, one can deduce that the weighted delayed recall score on the WMS-R declined by about 1.24 points, or nearly 2% with each additional year of age after 64. Because the standard deviation of weighted delayed raw scores in the sample was 16.56, this corresponds to a decrease of about three fourths of a standard deviation with every 10 years of increasing age. Verbal memory scores declined slightly less and visual memory scores slightly more than this amount. Scores increased by roughly 2%–4% with each additional year of education.

Generalizing from these data, one can estimate the degree to which the expected memory test score for an individual whose age or education is not typical of the normative sample would differ from the average score of the group. The rule of thumb is that every 6 to 8 years of increasing age shifts the distribution of memory scores down by about one half of a standard deviation, and every 4 additional years of education moves it up by a similar amount. The age effect is somewhat larger for visual than verbal memory, whereas the reverse is true for education. The figures for participants in our study expressed in terms of change in total raw score per year are shown in Table 2.

Of course these data can serve only as a rough guide. They probably become less reliable for very old individuals and may not work well for extremes of education. The figures also may be different for other memory tests, although the effects of age and education are so widespread and robust that they will probably be of the same order of magnitude. We also found that women tended to score higher on memory tests than men in our study, possibly because they tended to be healthier, but we do not routinely make any formal attempt to allow for this relatively small effect in our clinical work.

D. Choosing a Cutoff for Impairment

Several cutoff scores have been proposed in different contexts. One standard deviation below the mean is commonly quoted in the age-associated memory literature, but the 5th and 10th percentiles have been found to be sensitive and specific criteria for impairment in community-based studies of dementia epidemiology (Ganguli et al., 1993), and 2 standard deviations below the mean is recommended as a critical level in some neuropsychological tests. We believe that the appropriate criterion varies depending on whether the clinical situation makes it more important to avoid false positives or false negatives and with the base rates of disorder in the population. Less stringent criteria seem to be appropriate in older individuals, in whom impairment is more common, or when the purpose of the evaluation is to screen individuals prior to possible referral for more elaborate workup. In general, we regard as significant a score that is at least 1 standard deviation away from expected levels of performance, operationalized either as the average level for a person of the individual's age and education, or a score that is more than 1 standard deviation lower than scores on nonmemory tests. To facilitate these comparisons, it is clearly helpful to convert scores into z or T scores.

E. Decision Guidelines

Although there are explicit research diagnostic criteria for AAMI, the rules for making clinically important distinctions

Table 2. Effects of Age and Education on Performance on the Wechsler Memory Scale–Revised

Weighted raw score			Change in raw score per additional year				
	Mean Score for 65–74-year-olds with mean education of 13.26 years		Age		Education		
Subscales	(N = 639)	SD	Raw	%	Raw	%	
Verbal Memory	65.17	15.08	-0.903	1.39	2.205	3.38	
Visual Memory	46.54	9.31	-0.756	1.62	1.213	2.61	
General Memory	111.79	21.04	-1.658	1.48	3.418	3.05	
Attention/Concentration	62.05	11.01	-0.435	0.70	1.413	2.27	
Delayed Recall	62.6	16.56	-1.241	1.98	2.318	3.70	

Note. Table is based on the performance of 989 community-resident elderly individuals tested in a laboratory.

between different forms of age-related memory disorder are less hard and fast. The following general guidelines should be applied; they are shown schematically in Figure 1.

1. Is memory test performance significantly worse than expected for age and educational background?

a. **If no,** the patient's memory is age appropriate. It may reflect a decline from young-adult levels, meriting a diagnosis of AAMI, but it does not constitute evidence of pathology. Consider whether the complaint is out of proportion to the objective severity. If it is, consider the influence of nonclinical factors, depression, or nonmnemonic cognitive impairment that may be affecting everyday functioning.

b. **If yes,** evaluate further.

2. Is there evidence for age-inappropriate impairment in other cognitive domains, particularly language or executive function?

a. **If no,** the patient has isolated age-inappropriate memory impairment. Look for potential precipitating factors (e.g., history of stroke, cardiac bypass surgery, head trauma). Consider whether the disorder is of sudden or insidious onset. Unless the disorder has a known cause and is clearly nonprogressive, recommend following the patient on an annual basis or as clinically indicated to rule out a developing dementia.

b. **If yes,** this is not just age-related memory decline.

3. Is there evidence of a decline from a higher premorbid level?

a. **If no,** consider the possibility of below-average intellectual function.

b. **If yes,** consider the possibility of dementia, polypharmacy, severe depression, or other general medical causes of cognitive decline.

III. CONCLUSION

An age-related decline in memory is common but not universal. For clinical purposes, the task is to distinguish putatively normal, usually mild age-related changes from abnormal, usually more severe memory impairments. Within the latter category, it is important to distinguish isolated memory impairments that may or may not be progressive from the memory impairments that form part of a more global dementing illness. This can be accomplished by comparing the patient's memory test performance with appropriate normative data and with performance in other cognitive domains; the results must be considered in the light of a careful history.

Figure 1. Algorithm for assessing age-related memory disorders. CABG = coronary artery bypass graft.

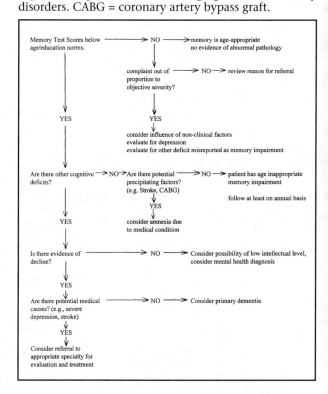

BIBLIOGRAPHY

American Psychiatric Association. (1994). *Diagnostic and statistical manual of mental disorders* (4th ed.). Washington, DC: Author.

Blackford, R. C., & LaRue, A. (1989). Criteria for diagnosing age associated memory impairment: Proposed improvements from the field. *Developmental Neuropsychology, 5,* 295–306.

Branconner, R. J., Cole, J. O., Spear, K. F., & DeVitt, D. R. (1972). Recall and recognition as diagnostic indices of malignant memory loss in senile dementia: A Bayesian analysis. *Experimental Aging Research, 4,* 189–193.

Brandt, J. (1991). The Hopkins Verbal Learning Test: Development of a new memory test with six equivalent forms. *Clinical Neuropsychologist, 5,* 125–142.

Crook, T., Bartus, R. T., Ferris, S. H., Whitehouse, P., Cohen, G. D., & Gershon, S. (1986). Age-associated memory impairment: Proposed diagnostic criteria and measures of clinical change: Report of a National Institute of Mental Health Work Group. *Developmental Neuropsychology, 2,* 261–272.

Crook, T. H., & Larrabee, G. J. (1990). A self-rating scale for evaluating memory in everyday life. *Psychology and Aging, 5,* 48–57.

Delis, D. C., Kramer, J. H., Kaplan, E., & Ober, B.A. (1987). *California Verbal Learning Test.* San Antonio, TX: Psychological Corporation.

Folstein, M. F., Folstein, S. E., & McHugh, P. R. (1975). Mini-Mental State: A practical method of grading the cognitive state of patients. *Psychiatric Research, 12,* 189–198.

Fuld, P. A. (1980). Guaranteed stimulus processing in the evaluation of memory and learning. *Cortex, 16,* 255–272.

Ganguli, M., Belle, S., Ratcliff, G., Seaberg, E., Huff, F. J., Porter, K., & Kuller, L. (1993). Sensitivity and specificity for dementia of population-based criteria for cognitive impairment: The MoVIES project. *Journal of Gerontology: Medical Sciences, 48,* M156–161.

Hughes, C. P., Berg, L., Danzinger, W. L., Coben, L. A., & Martin, R. L. (1982). A new scale for the staging of dementia. *British Journal of Psychiatry, 140,* 566–572.

Ivnik, R. J., Malec, J. F., Smith, G. E., Tangalos, E. G., Petersen, R. C., Kokmen, E., & Kurland, L. T. (1992a). Mayo's older Americans normative studies: Updated AVLT norms for ages 56–97. *Clinical Neuropsychologist, 6,* 83–104.

Ivnik, R. J., Malec, J. F., Smith, G. E., Tangalos, E. G., Petersen, R. C., Kokmen, E., & Kurland, L. T. (1992b). Mayo's older Americans normative studies: WMS-R norms for ages 56–94. *Clinical Neuropsychologist, 6,* 49–82.

Jonker, C., Launer, L. J., Hooijer, C., & Lindeboom, J. (1996). Memory complaints and memory impairment in older individuals. *Journal of the American Gerontological Society, 44,* 44–49.

Kral, V. A. (1958). Neuropsychiatric observations in an old peoples' home. *Journal of Gerontology, 13,* 169–176.

Larrabee, G. J., Levin, H. A., & High, W. M. (1986). Senescent forgetfulness: A quantitative study. *Developmental Neuropsychology, 2,* 373–385.

Larrabee, G. J., West, R. L., & Crook, T. H. (1991). The association of memory complaint with computer-simulated everyday memory performance. *Journal of Clinical and Experimental Neuropsychology, 13,* 466–478.

Morris, J. C., Heyman, A., Mohs, R. C., Hughes, J. P., van Belle, G., Fillenbaum, G., Mellits, E. D., Clark, C., & the CERAD Investigators. (1989). The consortium to establish a registry for Alzheimer's disease (CERAD): Part I. Clinical and neuropsychological assessment of Alzheimer's disease. *Neurology, 39,* 1159–1165.

Petersen, R. C., Smith, G., Kokmen, E., Ivnik, R. J., & Tangalos, E. G. (1992). Memory function in normal aging. *Neurology, 42,* 396–401.

Ratcliff, G., & Saxton, J. (1994). Age associated memory impairment. In C. E. Coffey & J. L. Cummings (Eds.), *Textbook of geriatric neuropsychiatry* (pp. 145–158). Washington, DC: American Psychiatric Press.

Rey, A. (1964). *L'examen clinique en psychologie* [Clinical examinations in psychology]. Paris: Presses Universitaires de France.

Rowe, J. W., & Kahn, R. L. (1987). Human aging: usual and successful. *Science, 237,* 143–149.

Sunderland, A., Harris, J. E., & Baddeley, A. D. (1983). Do laboratory tests predict everyday memory? A neuropsychological study. *Journal of Verbal Learning and Verbal Behavior, 22,* 341–357.

Warrington, E. K. (1984). *Recognition memory test.* Windsor, England: NFER-Nelson.

Wechsler, D. (1987). *The Wechsler Memory Scale–Revised manual.* New York: Harcourt Brace Jovanovich.

Welsh, K., Butters, N., Hughes, J., Mohs, R., & Heyman, A. (1991). Detection of abnormal memory decline in mild cases of Alzheimer's disease using CERAD neuropsychological measures. *Archives of Neurology, 48,* 278–281.

Wilson, B., Cockburn, J., & Baddeley, A. (1985). *The Rivermead Behavioural Memory Test.* Reading, England: Thames Valley Test Company.

World Health Organization. (1978). *Mental disorders: Glossary and guide to their classification in accordance with the ninth revision of the International Classification of Diseases.* Geneva, Switzerland: Author.

Zelinski, E. M., & Gilewski, M. J. (1988). Assessment of memory complaint by rating scales and questionnaires. *Psychopharmacology Bulletin, 24,* 523–529.

Zelinski, E. M., Gilewski, M. J., & Thompson, L. W. (1980). Do laboratory tests relate to self assessment of memory ability in the young and old? In L. W. Poon, J. L. Fozard, L. S. Cermak, D. Arenberg, & I. W. Thompson (Eds.), *New directions in memory and aging: Proceedings of the George A. Talland Memorial Conference* (pp. 519–544). Hillsdale, NJ: Erlbaum.

The Dementias

The neuropsychological evaluation of dementia involves three components: (a) a working knowledge of the diagnostic criteria, base rates, and neuropsychological characteristics of the major causes of dementia and the conditions that may present with similar symptoms; (b) the use of a flexible neuropsychological battery that assesses cognitive domains relevant to the diagnosis of dementia and that contains appropriate tests and norms; and (c) a systematic approach to interpretation that takes into account factors such as the patient's history and current circumstances and that addresses the real-life consequences of the test results.

I. WORKING KNOWLEDGE OF DEMENTIAS

A. Definitions and Diagnostic Criteria

The term *dementia* refers to a deterioration in mental capacities that goes beyond the changes expected to occur with the normal aging process. Dementia is both a behavioral syndrome and a diagnostic classification. As a **behavioral syndrome**, dementia is characterized by the presence of generalized and persistent cognitive impairment that (a) represents a change from a previous level of functioning, (b) occurs without a disruption in consciousness, (c) is of sufficient severity to influence daily functioning, (d) cannot be explained by situational stress, and (e) may be the result of a variety of conditions, some of which are reversible.

Memory impairment is the hallmark feature of dementia; however, the syndrome of dementia is distinguished from conditions such as amnestic disorder by the presence of memory impairment in combination with deficits in other areas of cognitive functioning (e.g., language, visuospatial processing, problem solving). Because most dementias are not reversible, another common feature is deterioration over time. During the course of this deterioration, changes in cognitive capacities occur, so that patients at different points along the continuum of dementia severity may present with different patterns of deficits.

Changes in functional capacity, mood, personality, and behavior also occur in dementia and are also associated with severity of impairment. For example, anxiety and depression may be present at the very early stages of dementia, when compromised learning and problem-solving capacities result in difficulty keeping up with the demands of a job. As deficits in memory and executive functioning worsen, problems may develop in areas such as driving a car and managing medication or finances, and patients with dementia may display increased gullibility, vulnerability, apathy, and disregard for societal norms and expectations. Later in the course of dementia, when recall of recent events becomes severely impaired, relatively benign confabulations may be replaced by delusions of persecution or infidelity. Similarly, agitation may occur when an individual's memory loss and perceptual distortions result in incorrect comprehension of his or her circumstances (e.g., striking out at a caretaker who is misidentified as an intruder).

As a **diagnostic classification**, dementia is defined as follows in the fourth edition of the Diagnostic and Statistical Manual of Mental Disorders (DSM-IV; American Psychiatric Association, 1994): a "group of disorders whose essential feature is the development of multiple cognitive deficits" (p. 134). The criteria for all DSM-IV diagnoses of dementia include the following three components:

A. The development of multiple cognitive deficits manifested by both
   1) memory impairment (impaired ability to learn new information or to recall previously learned information), and

    2) one (or more) of the following cognitive disturbances:
      a) aphasia (language disturbance)
      b) apraxia (impaired ability to carry out motor activities despite intact motor function)
      c) agnosia (failure to recognize or identify objects despite intact sensory function)
      d) disturbance in executive functioning (i.e., planning, organization, sequencing, abstracting).

B. The cognitive deficits in Criteria A1 and A2 each cause significant impairment in social or occupational functioning and represent a significant decline from a previous level of functioning.

C. The deficits do not occur exclusively during the course of a delirium.

Subtypes of dementia are classified on the basis of additional criteria including (a) characteristic symptoms and history, (b) presumed etiology, (c) age of onset, and (d) psychiatric features (e.g., uncomplicated or with delirium, delusions, or depression). The presence of behavioral disturbance (e.g., wandering, aggression) is noted in the diagnosis with the specifier "with behavioral disturbance," but it is not coded in the diagnostic subtype.

The specific subtypes of dementia included in DSM-IV are as follows:

1. Dementia of the Alzheimer's type
2. Vascular dementia (formerly, multi-infarct dementia)
3. Dementia owing to HIV disease
4. Dementia owing to head trauma
5. Dementia owing to Parkinson's disease
6. Dementia owing to Huntington's disease
7. Dementia owing to Pick's disease
8. Dementia owing to Creutzfeldt-Jakob disease
9. Dementia owing to a general medical condition
10. Substance-induced persisting dementia
11. Dementia owing to multiple etiologies
12. Dementia not otherwise specified

B. Conditions That Cause Dementia

A recent review (American Psychiatric Association, 1997) revealed the following prevalence rates for dementia: age 65 and older, 5%–8%; age 75 and older, 15%–20%; age 85 and older, 25%–50%. Alzheimer's disease (AD) is still thought to be the most common cause of dementia. Cerebrovascular disease appears to be the second most common cause, and recent studies have suggested that Lewy body disease may account for more cases of dementia than previously thought. Diseases that cause dementia are not mutually exclusive, so that some patients have dementia due to mixed, or multiple, causes.

Less prevalent are dementias caused by conditions such as Parkinson's disease and "Parkinson's plus" disorders (e.g., progressive supranuclear palsy), frontal lobe disease (e.g., Pick's disease), normal pressure hydrocephalus, and chronic alcoholism, but these conditions occur frequently enough that they should be considered in the differential diagnosis. Even less prevalent are conditions such as prion disease (i.e., "prion" for proteinaceous infectious particle). Creutzfeldt-Jakob disease (CJD) is an example of a prion disease with a prevalence rate of 1 in 1 million (Roberts, Leigh, & Weinberger, 1993). Although it is rare, CJD generates interest because it is transmissible (e.g., in humans through corneal transplantation) and because there are variants in other species (e.g., bovine spongiform encephalopathy in cows, or "mad cow disease").

Exhibit 1 provides a summary of the characteristics of the most frequent causes of dementia (i.e., Alzheimer's disease, cerebrovascular disease, Lewy body disease, frontal and frontotemporal lobe diseases, and subcortical diseases) as well as two other conditions that can cause cognitive impairment (i.e., delirium and depression). Although the conditions that cause dementia share common features, it is often possible to identify the probable cause on the basis of information such as type of onset, course of deterioration, pattern of neuropsychological deficits, and behavioral symptoms.

For example, although there appear to be subtypes of **Alzheimer's disease**, the typical patient with AD has (a) an insidious onset, (b) initial symptoms of memory impairment (e.g., deficient consolidation, rapid forgetting of new information) and executive dysfunction, and (c) a gradual course of generalized deterioration in cognitive capacities. In contrast, dementia caused by **cerebrovascular disease** is often associated with an abrupt onset and fluctuating course as well as more focal neurological and neuropsychological deficits. Patients with **Lewy body disease** are more likely to have detailed visual hallucinations, Parkinsonian motor symptoms, greater sensitivity to antipsychotic medications, and significant fluctuations in functioning, whereas patients with **frontal lobe disease** are more likely to present with changes in personality and behavior prior to the onset of deficits in memory. Finally, patients

Exhibit 1. Summary of Conditions That Can Cause Cognitive Impairment

---

Dementia owing to Alzheimer's disease (AD)

Prevalence: 50% (or more) of all cases of dementia.

Major risk factors: advanced age; family history of AD, Parkinson's disease or Down's syndrome; genetic factors (e.g., homozygous for the apolipoprotein E–ε4 allele); history of head injury.

Onset and course: insidious onset, progressive deterioration. Early onset is associated with genetic causes and more rapid course.

Neuropsychological features: Early features include deficits in memory (e.g., deficient consolidation and storage, rapid forgetting of new information, recall and recognition deficits, impaired incidental learning) and executive dysfunction. As the disease progresses, there is global deterioration of cognitive capacities with intellectual decline, aphasia, agnosia, and apraxia.

Behavioral features: Early features may include subtle personality changes such as decreased energy, social withdrawal, indifference, and impulsivity. Insight is usually limited, and complaints about memory problems are less frequent than in patients with depression. Severe depression is uncommon, and mood can change on the basis of patients' experience of their environment. Later features include apathy, emotional blunting, mood-independent delusions, decreased sleep and appetite, and increased motor activity (e.g., restlessness and wandering).

Recent reviews: Butters et al., 1994; Miller et al., 1994; Salmon & Bondi, 1997.

Dementia owing to cerebrovascular disease (CVD)

Prevalence: 15%–25% of all cases of dementia.

Major risk factors: advanced age, stroke, smoking, obesity, alcoholism, hypertension, diabetes.

Onset and Course: Average age of onset is earlier than in AD. Type of onset and course vary depending on the type of stroke (e.g., abrupt following large infarct, insidious in small vessel disease).

Neuropsychological features: focal, multifocal, or "patchy" deficits that correspond to the location of the infarcts.

(Continued)

Exhibit 1. Summary of Conditions That Can Cause Cognitive Impairment *(Continued)*

Behavioral features: Compared to patients with AD, patients with CVD are more likely to display depression, affective lability, focal neurological signs, pseudobulbar palsy, gait disturbance, weakness, fluctuating course, and nocturnal exacerbation of confusion.

Recent reviews: McPherson & Cummings, 1997; Peskind & Raskind, 1996.

Dementia owing to Lewy body disease (LBD)

Prevalence: estimated from 7% to 26% of dementia cases.

Major risk factors: advancing age, Alzheimer's disease (approximately 20% of patients with AD have a Lewy body variant of AD, with Lewy bodies in the brain stem and cortex).

Onset and course: Onset is similar to AD; however, course appears to be more rapid.

Neuropsychological features: similar to AD, but with relatively greater deficits in attention, visuospatial and constructional capacities, psychomotor speed, and verbal fluency.

Behavioral features: generally similar to AD, but distinguished by the presence of (a) a subset of mild Parkinsonian or extrapyramidal motor symptoms (e.g., masked facies, bradykinesia, and gait abnormality, but not extreme rigidity, flexed posture, or resting tremor), (b) earlier and more prominent visual hallucinations than in AD, (c) increased sensitivity to the extrapyramidal effects of antipsychotic medication, and (d) the presence of significant fluctuations in cognitive functioning (i.e., relatively good functioning on some days and very impaired functioning on others).

Recent reviews: McKeith et al., 1994; Roberts et al., 1993.

Dementia owing to frontal or frontotemporal lobe disease (FLD)

Prevalence: less than 5% of all cases of dementia.

Major risk factors: advanced age, family history of FLD.

Onset and course: usually insidious and progressive; earlier average age of onset than in patients with AD (i.e., mid-50s); slightly more rapid course than AD.

Exhibit 1. Summary of Conditions That Can Cause Cognitive Impairment *(Continued)*

Neuropsychological features: early on, selective executive dysfunction (e.g., perseveration and deficits in the regulatory aspects of cognition such as selective attention, set shifting, concept and strategy formation, planning, abstraction, self-monitoring, mental flexibility, and response inhibition) in the presence of relatively intact memory, language, and motor capacities. Later, there are deficits in memory (e.g., problems with organizing and retrieving material), language (e.g., decreased fluency), and selective attention. Parkinsonian motor changes may also occur.

Behavioral features: Changes in personality and social behavior (e.g., apathy, withdrawal, and disinterest in some, and disinhibition, poor frustration tolerance, overactivity, and impaired judgment in others) are the hallmark early features of these disorders. Frontal release signs, weakness, and motor perseveration or impersistence may occur as the disease progresses. The late stages of FLD are often difficult to differentiate from AD but may include mutism and increased rigidity.

Recent reviews: Miller et al., 1994; Usman, 1997.

Dementia owing to subcortical disease

Examples: Parkinson's disease, progressive supranuclear palsy, Huntington's disease, subcortical vascular disease (e.g., thalamic infarcts, lacunar state, Binswanger's disease).

Prevalence: less than 10% of all cases of dementia.

Major risk factors: depends on the specific disease (e.g., Huntington's—family history; subcortical vascular—cerebrovascular risk factors), advanced age.

Onset and course: Average age of onset is variable depending on the type of disorder (e.g., Huntington's—age 35–45; Parkinson's—70s). Course is also variable.

Neuropsychological features: also variable, but the pattern can usually be distinguished from conditions such as AD by the presence of memory retrieval deficits (i.e., with better performance on recognition than recall tests and less temporal grading of retrograde amnesia) and impairment in executive functioning, sustained attention,

(Continued)

Exhibit 1. Summary of Conditions That Can Cause
Cognitive Impairment *(Continued)*

visuospatial skills, and motor speed, with relative sparing of language.

Behavioral features: also variable, but distinguishable from
conditions such as AD by the presence of bradyphrenia,
gait and balance disturbance, movement disorder,
dysarthria, apathy, and frequently depression.

Recent reviews: Cummings, 1990.

Delirium

Prevalence: in inpatient medical settings, up to 50%.

Major risk factors: advanced age, hospitalization for medical
disorder, medications that affect the central nervous system, multiple medications, residing in an institution,
preexisting cognitive impairment, dehydration, infection, pain, sensory loss.

Onset and course: typically abrupt onset (although not
always in the elderly) with fluctuations in symptoms, can
last weeks or months if the source is not treated.

Neuropsychological features: deficits in capacities that
require intact arousal, attention, and perception, such as
orientation, attention, memory, language, construction,
and motor and executive functions.

Behavioral features: Fluctuations in arousal and consciousness are hallmark symptoms of delirium and distinguish
it from conditions such as dementia owing to AD. Other
features include attentional dysfunction, stimulus-bound
responses, perseveration, perceptual disturbances (e.g.,
visual and tactile hallucinations), and change in activity
level (i.e., increased, reduced, or mixed).

Recent reviews: McConnell (chap. 3, this volume); Tune &
Ross, 1994.

Dementia syndrome of depression

Prevalence: Approximately 20% of older adults with depression display impairments on neuropsychological testing.

Major risk factors: depression plus evidence of structural
brain changes.

Onset and course: Cognitive deficits begin slowly, escalate
rapidly in conjunction with increased symptoms of
depression, and improve as depressive symptoms

Exhibit 1. Summary of Conditions That Can Cause
Cognitive Impairment *(Continued)*

> improve. Symptoms of cognitive impairment as part of
> the syndrome of depression may reflect the presence of
> an early dementia.
>
> Neuropsychological features: no consistent impairment in
> language, perception, or visuospatial processing; some-
> what variable test performance, often with deficits in
> attention and short-term recall; better performance on
> recognition memory tests than recall memory tests.
>
> Behavioral features: more complaints of memory problems
> than in patients with AD, more "don't know" answers,
> fewer false positive answers, and poorer effort than in
> patients with AD, persistent mood disturbance that is not
> responsive to the environment; delusions (when present)
> are typically mood congruent.
>
> Recent reviews: Kazniak & Christenson, 1994.

with disorders that primarily affect **subcortical** structures (e.g.,
brain stem, thalamus, basal ganglia) or the tracts connecting
frontal lobe and subcortical areas often display a constellation
of symptoms that is different from that seen in other types of
dementia. These symptoms include bradyphrenia, memory
retrieval deficits, executive dysfunction, and deficits in sustained attention and visuospatial skills in the absence of language deficits. A consensus statement regarding the diagnosis
and treatment of Alzheimer's disease and related disorders was
recently published by the American Association for Geriatric
Psychiatry, the Alzheimer's Association, and the American Geriatrics Society (Small et al., 1997).

In addition to the disorders listed in Exhibit 1, numerous
other conditions can cause the syndrome of dementia. Among
them is **normal pressure hydrocephalus (NPH)**, a type of
hydrocephalic dementia that is associated with normal
intracranial pressure; impaired absorption of the cerebrospinal
fluid; and the clinical triad of dementia, gait disturbance, and
urinary incontinence. Although the disorder is relatively rare, it
is important to consider NPH in the diagnostic workup because
early detection may lead to symptomatic improvement with
treatment (i.e., through serial lumbar punctures or cerebroven-
tricular shunting).

The most common form of **substance-induced persisting
dementia** is caused by alcohol, and it remains a somewhat con-

troversial diagnosis. Dementia owing to alcoholism has been associated with deficits in anterograde and retrograde memory, abstract problem solving, and visuoperceptual capacities. These patients have more neurological findings (e.g., peripheral neuropathy), fewer naming deficits, and less progression over time than patients with AD. It remains open to debate whether this syndrome is uniquely related to prolonged alcohol toxicity or is the consequence of nutritional deficiency, hemorrhagic lesions in the diencephalon, hepatic encephalopathy, or alcohol-related head injury. (See Franklin & Frances, 1992, for a review.)

C. Conditions That Present With Cognitive Impairment

Disrupted cognitive processing in the elderly can be the result of numerous conditions. Examples include specific neurological lesions (e.g., amnesia caused by herpes simplex encephalitis; see chapter 21, this volume), medical disorders (e.g., acute delirium; see chapter 3, this volume), medication (e.g., subacute delirium), psychiatric conditions (e.g., depression), long-standing developmental disorders (e.g., mental retardation, learning disability), and age-related changes (e.g., age-associated memory impairment; see chapter 11, this volume).

Two of these conditions are particularly important to consider and are summarized in Exhibit 1. **Delirium** is a common, generally transient, condition that affects cognitive processing and is often underdiagnosed among older adults. It is particularly common among elderly patients on medical units and those receiving multiple medications. In one study (Levkoff et al., 1992), for example, well over half of an older adult sample (i.e., age 65 and over) admitted to a general medical unit either met diagnostic criteria for delirium or displayed symptoms of delirium during their hospitalization. Medications with anticholinergic effects can be especially problematic among the elderly, but any medication that affects the central nervous system can potentially cause delirium.

Although the exact prevalence is unknown, approximately 20% of older adults with **depression** display impairments on neuropsychological tests (LaRue, D'Elia, Clark, Spar, & Jarvik, 1986). Formerly referred to as "pseudodementia" because the cognitive deficits often resolve as the symptoms of mood disturbance improve, this syndrome has more recently been termed the **dementia syndrome of depression** (see chap. 10, this volume, by Nussbaum). Although still a somewhat controversial finding, the presence of cognitive deficits during an episode of depression may predict future dementia.

II. NEUROPSYCHOLOGICAL EVALUATION OF DEMENTIA

A. Under Ideal Conditions

Ideally, the evaluation of possible dementia should include the following:
1. An interview with the patient and a knowledgeable collateral source (to obtain patient and family history)
2. A thorough medical examination with diagnostic and laboratory testing by a physician trained in geriatric medicine, neurology, or neuropsychiatry (to rule out cognitive impairment owing to delirium from medical illness)
3. A screening examination for primary psychiatric disorders (e.g., depression)
4. A review of the medication regimen by a professional with expertise in geriatric pharmacology (to rule out delirium owing to medication effects or interactions)
5. An assessment of functional capacities by an occupational therapist
6. Serial neuropsychological assessments using tests with appropriate norms under ideal conditions (e.g., medication free and illness free)

B. Under Real-World Conditions

Neuropsychological examinations under real-world conditions (e.g., inpatient medical settings with limited history and limited time) can be most useful if the examiner attempts to follow a basic outline and to obtain relevant data by using tests (a) with appropriate norms, (b) that can be tolerated by the patient, and (c) that assess domains of cognitive functioning relevant to the differential diagnosis and the specific referral question. These domains include arousal, orientation, learning and memory, attention and concentration, motor capacities, language, perception, visuospatial processing, executive functioning, mood, and comportment (i.e., the ability to adapt behavior to the appropriate social context).

C. Recommended Approach to Testing

Step 1. Brief screening battery
    a. Review of available data (e.g., medical chart)
    b. Patient interview and observations
    c. Mini-Mental State Examination
    d. Clock Drawing Test
    e. Delirium Rating Scale

The purpose of the chart review and patient interview is to obtain information about premorbid functioning, onset and course of impairment, and factors that may affect test performance and help establish diagnosis (e.g., delirium, depression).

The Mini-Mental State Examination (MMSE; Folstein, Folstein, & McHugh, 1975) was chosen because it is the most widely used dementia-screening test. The advantages of the MMSE are its widespread use, the availability of norms based on age and education (Crum, Anthony, Bassett, & Folstein, 1993; see Table 1), and its brief administration time. Among its many disadvantages are the limited number of cognitive domains sampled, the widespread acceptance of one cutoff score without taking into account factors such as age and education, differences in administration and scoring among examiners, and its insensitivity to deficits in right hemisphere and frontal lobe capacities. Examples of differences in test administration include: inconsistent use and scoring of serial sevens and differences in the amount of time that lapses between asking the examinee to register and then to recall the three words on the memory portion of this test. The inclusion of a 4- or 5-minute delay is critical in the assessment of the patients for whom rapid forgetting may be the most important finding of the entire exam.

The Clock Drawing Test (Freedman et al., 1994) is a useful addition to a brief screening battery because it can provide information about several domains of functioning (e.g., ability to follow directions, motor capacity, planning, organization, stimulus-bound responses, perseveration) and because it is usually well tolerated. One set of instructions and scoring criteria for the Clock Drawing Test are presented in Exhibit 2.

Because the prevalence of delirium is so high among elderly medical inpatients, a delirium rating scale is also recommended for the initial screen (e.g., Delirium Rating Scale; Trzepacz, Baker, & Greenhouse, 1987; Confusion Assessment Method; Inouye et al., 1990). Recently (Solomon et al., 1998), a brief "7-minute" battery of four cognitive screening tests (i.e. temporal orientation, clock drawing, verbal fluency, and

Table 1. Norms for the Mini-Mental State Examination by Age and Education

Education	\multicolumn{8}{c}{Age range}
	50–54	55–59	60–64	65–69	70–74	75–79	80–84	85+
0–4 years								
M	23	22	23	22	22	21	20	19
SD	2.6	2.7	1.9	1.7	2.0	2.2	2.9	2.3
5–8 years								
M	27	26	26	26	26	25	25	23
SD	2.4	2.9	2.3	1.7	1.8	2.1	1.9	3.3
9–12 years								
M	28	28	28	28	27	27	25	26
SD	2.2	2.2	1.7	1.4	1.6	1.5	2.3	2.0
13 or more years								
M	29	29	29	29	28	28	27	27
SD	1.9	1.5	1.3	1.0	1.6	1.6	0.9	1.3

Note. From "Population-Based Norms for the Mini-Mental State Examination by Age and Educational Level," by R. M. Crum, J. C. Anthony, S. S. Bassett, and M. F. Folstein, 1993, *Journal of the American Medical Association, 269,* p. 2389. Copyright 1993 by the American Medical Association. Adapted with permission.

enhanced cued recall) was shown to have excellent sensitivity and specificity in the differentiation of patients with probable Alzheimer's disease from normal elderly. The utility of this battery as a valid screening tool among more heterogeneous samples of older adults is not yet known.

Step 2. Additional assessment based on results of screening battery

On the basis of the referral question and the results of the initial screening examination, additional testing is often useful in establishing a diagnosis, monitoring changes in cognitive functioning, and assessing severity of impairment. Following are four options for further testing:

Option a. Serial screening battery
    (1) Benton Temporal Orientation Test
    (2) Mini-Mental State Examination
    (3) Clock Drawing Test
    (4) Delirium Rating Scale

Option b. Lower level battery
    (1) Cognistat (formerly the Neurobehavioral Cognitive Screening Examination) or Mattis Dementia Rating Scale
    (2) Hopkins Verbal Learning Test
    (3) Controlled Oral Word Association Test or Executive Interview or Frontal/Subcortical Assessment Battery

Option c. Higher level battery
    (1) Orientation: Benton Temporal Orientation Test
    (2) Memory: Wechsler Memory Scale (revised or 3rd edition), California Verbal Learning Test (or Hopkins Verbal Learning Test), Rey Complex Figure–Recall
    (3) Attention: Digit Span, Visual Memory Span, Trails A
    (4) Language: Boston Naming Test, Controlled Oral Word Association Test, Tokens Test
    (5) Verbal intellectual capacities: WAIS-R Information, Similarities
    (6) Visual perception: Hooper Visual Organization Test
    (7) Nonverbal intellectual capacities: WAIS-R Block Design, Object Assembly
    (8) Motor capacities: Grooved Pegboard
    (9) Executive functioning: Trails B, Wisconsin Card Sort Test (or Short Booklet Category Test), Rey Complex Figure
    (10) Mood: Geriatric Depression Scale

Exhibit 2. Instructions and Scoring Criteria for the Clock Drawing Test

Instructions: Draw the face of a clock, put in all of the numbers, and make the hands of the clock say "11:10."

Scoring:
  Integrity of the clock face (maximum = 2 points)
    2 = present without gross distortion
    1 = incomplete or some distortion
    0 = absent or totally inappropriate

Presence and sequencing of the numbers (maximum = 4 points)
    4 = all present in the right order and at most minimal error in the spatial arrangement
    3 = all present but errors in spatial arrangement
    2 = missing or added numbers but no gross distortions of the remaining numbers
        numbers placed in counterclockwise direction
        numbers all present but gross distortion in spatial layout (e.g., hemineglect, numbers outside the clock)
    1 = missing or added numbers and gross spatial distortions
    0 = absence or poor representation of numbers

Presence and placement of hands (maximum = 4 points)
    4 = hands are in correct position and the size difference is respected
    3 = slight errors in the placement of the hands or no representation of the size difference between the hands
    2 = major errors in the placement of the hands (significantly out of course, including 10 to 11)
    1 = only one hand or poor representation of two hands
    0 = no hands or perseveration on hands

Interpretation:
    9–10 = normal
       8 = borderline impairment
    6–7 = mild impairment
    4–5 = moderate impairment
    0–3 = severe impairment

Note. From "Quantitative and Qualitative Analyses of Clock Drawings in Alzheimer's Disease and Huntington's Disease," by I. Rouleau, D. P. Salmon, N. Butters, C. Kennedy, and K. McGuire, 1992, *Brain and Cognition, 18,* p. 75. Copyright 1992 by Academic Press. Adapted with permission.

Option a is recommended if Step 1 suggests the presence of delirium. In this case, serial monitoring of cognitive status (on a daily basis in an inpatient setting) is recommended, using a screening battery that is brief and quantifiable, until the patient's scores plateau.

If the patient's cognitive screening test performance is significantly impaired (e.g., MMSE below 18) and delirium is not present, **Option b** is to administer a "lower level" battery. The goals of this battery include documenting the severity of impairment, determining the pattern of impairment (e.g., generalized vs. focal or multifocal), gathering information about specific capacities to provide feedback to caregivers, and establishing a baseline for future evaluations. The Dementia Rating Scale (DRS; Mattis, 1988) and the Cognistat (formerly the Neurobehavioral Cognitive Status Examination; Kiernan, Mueller, Langston, & Van Dyke, 1987) are good choices to use in a lower level battery because they sample more cognitive domains than does the MMSE.

When the patient's cognitive screening test performance is relatively good (e.g., MMSE at least 18) and delirium is not present, **Option c** involves the administration of a "higher level" battery to assess the aforementioned cognitive domains. Examples of tests that provide the most information, have appropriate norms, and have acceptable floors and ceilings are included in Table 2. More comprehensive lists of tests with norms for older adults are available elsewhere (e.g., Erickson, Eimon, & Hebben, 1994).

Finally, for patients whose level of impairment is severe, behavioral rating scales of self-care capacities (e.g., London Psychogeriatric Rating Scale; Hersch, Kral, & Palmer, 1978) and measures such as the Severe Impairment Battery (Saxton, McGonigle-Gibson, Swihart, Miller, & Boller, 1990) can be used to assess specific cognitive domains and to quantify severity of impairment.

D. Interpretation of Test Results

Interpreting neuropsychological test results for dementia involves answering four basic questions: (a) Does impairment exist? (b) How severe is the impairment? (c) Does the pattern of impairment in the context of the patient's history suggest a diagnosis? (d) What are the real-life consequences of this impairment?

Table 2. Neuropsychological Tests With Norms for Older Adults

Strategy or domain	Test	Reference with geriatric norms
Estimating premorbid capacity	Wilson/Barona method	Barona et al., 1984
		Helmes, 1996
	NART/AMNART/NART-R	Blair & Spreen, 1989
		Ivnik et al., 1996
	WRAT-R Reading	Ivnik et al., 1996
		Johnstone et al., 1996
Cognitive screening	Mini-Mental State Examination	Crum et al., 1993
	Clock Drawing Test	Freedman et al., 1994
Lower level battery		
General screening	Mattis Dementia Scale	Mattis, 1988
	Cognistat (NCSE)	Kiernan et al., 1987
Memory	HVLT	Brandt, 1991
Executive functions	Controlled Oral Word	Ivnik et al., 1996
	Association Test	Spreen & Strauss, 1991

(Continued)

Table 2. Neuropsychological Tests With Norms for Older Adults *(Continued)*

Strategy or domain	Test	Reference with geriatric norms
	Executive Interview	Royall et al., 1992
	Frontal/Subcortical Assessment Battery	Rothlind & Brandt, 1993
Higher level battery		
Orientation	Temporal orientation	Benton et al., 1994
Memory		
Immediate and delayed recall	WMS-R Logical Memory and Visual Reproductions	Ivnik et al., 1992b
Learning & recall versus recognition	WMS-III	Wechsler, 1997b
	CVLT	Delis et al., 1987
		Libon et al., 1996
	HVLT	Brandt, 1991
Incidental learning	Rey Complex Figure–Recall	Spreen & Strauss, 1991
Attention	Digit Span	Ivnik et al., 1992b
	WMS-III Digit Span	Wechsler, 1997b
	Visual Memory Span	Ivnik et al., 1992b
	WMS-III Spatial Span	Wechsler, 1997b

Domain	Test	Reference
	Trails A	Ivnik et al., 1996
		Spreen & Strauss, 1991
Language	Boston Naming Test	Ivnik et al., 1996
		Spreen & Strauss, 1991
	Controlled Oral Word Association Test	Ivnik et al., 1996
	Tokens Test	Spreen & Strauss, 1991
		Ivnik et al., 1996
Construction	Rey Figure	Spreen & Strauss, 1991
	Cognistat Construction	Kiernan et al., 1987
	WAIS-R Block Design	Ivnik et al., 1992a
	WAIS-III Block Design	Wechsler, 1997a
Executive functioning	Trails B	Ivnik et al., 1996
		Spreen & Strauss, 1991
	WAIS-R Similarities	Ivnik et al., 1992a
	WAIS-R Similarities, Matrix Reasoning	Wechsler, 1997a
	WCST	Spreen & Strauss, 1991

(Continued)

Table 2. Neuropsychological Tests With Norms for Older Adults *(Continued)*

Strategy or domain	Test	Reference with geriatric norms
Motor speed	WAIS-R Digit Symbol	Ivnik et al., 1992a
	WAIS-III Digit Symbol	Wechsler, 1997a
	Finger Tapping	Spreen & Strauss, 1991
Mood	Geriatric Depression Scale	Yesavage et al., 1983

Note. NART = National Adult Reading Test; AMNART = American Version of the National Adult Reading Test; NART-R = National Adult Reading Test–Revised; WRAT-R = Wide Range Achievement Test–Revised; NCSE = Neurobehavioral Cognitive Status Examination; HVLT = Hopkins Verbal Learning Test; WMS-R = Wechsler Memory Scale–Revised; WAIS-R = Wechsler Adult Intelligence Scale–Revised; WAIS-III = Wechsler Adult Intelligence Scale–Third Edition; WMS-III = Wechsler Memory Scale–Third Edition.

The answer to the first two questions requires an awareness of expected changes with normal aging as well as an individual's background (e.g., education, vocational history). The use of tests that have norms based on age and educational level helps address the degree of departure of an individual's test score from the expected performance of his or her peer group. For example, the usual "cutoff" score for impairment on the MMSE (i.e., 23/30) is 1 standard deviation *above* the mean for 80-year-olds with a fourth-grade education but 4 standard deviations *below* the mean for 80-year-olds with a college degree (Crum et al., 1993; see Table 1).

Estimating level of premorbid intellectual capacity can be accomplished using criteria such as demographic variables (Barona, Reynolds, & Chastain, 1984) and sight-reading vocabulary (e.g., Wide Range Achievement Test–Revised, Reading subtest or National Adult Reading Test). Similarly, information regarding living situation, social support network, recent losses or environmental changes, recent medication changes, lifelong personality style, and functional capacities (e.g., driving, paying bills, shopping, cooking) can be used to develop a template for expected neuropsychological test performance for particular patients.

Answering the third question requires knowledge of the unique features of the different dementias as well as a systematic approach to test interpretation. Adapted from a model proposed by Weintraub (1995), one such approach uses a hierarchical step-by-step method to assess the integrity of capacities (e.g., arousal, attention, mood, language) on which the assessment of other capacities (e.g., memory) depends. The use of this type of interpretation strategy to suggest hypotheses about diagnosis is as follows:

Level 1 assessment: Arousal. Deficits in arousal suggest the presence of delirium or subcortical dysfunction and limit the usefulness of comprehensive tests of higher level functions such as memory and executive functioning.

Level 2 assessment:

a. **Attention.** Deficits in attention suggest delirium or subcortical–frontal dysfunction.

b. **Mood and motivation.** Abnormalities in mood or motivation suggest conditions such as depression or dementia owing to vascular or frontal lobe disorders.

Level 3 assessment: Language, motor, visuoperceptual and visuospatial skills. Focal deficits (e.g., aphasia, visual field deficits, unilateral motor impairment) suggest more circumscribed areas of impairment owing to vascular or other disorders (e.g., tumor) and limit the ability to assess higher level capacities that are dependent on these capacities (e.g., verbal memory in a patient with language impairment, visuospatial planning and organization in a patient with motor coordination deficits).

Level 4 assessment: Memory, executive functioning, comportment. Deficits in these areas are critically important for the differential diagnosis of early dementia, but they cannot be adequately assessed without knowledge of the integrity of other mental functions.

The final question is often the most difficult to answer. Recommendations regarding real-life consequences of the neuropsychological test deficits generally fall into three categories: (a) need for further assessment, (b) need for treatment, and (c) need for assistance or supervision in specific areas.

E. Recommendations for Further Assessment

1. Need for additional neuropsychological testing (e.g., to assess focal visuospatial deficits following a small stroke)
2. Need for medical–neurological evaluation (e.g., in outpatients who have no primary physician or who present with specific medical–neurological symptoms or complaints)
3. Need for psychiatric evaluation (e.g., in patients with depressive or psychotic symptoms)
4. Need for occupational therapy assessment of specific functional capacities (e.g., to provide caretakers with information about specific self-care skills)
5. Need for evaluation by a social worker or visiting nurse of living situation and family–community resources.

F. Considerations for Treatment

1. Medications for memory loss (e.g., Aricept [Donepezil])
2. Psychiatric medication as well as individual or family psychotherapy or both
3. Environmental change (e.g., making adjustments to the home environment such as in-home assistance, calendars, message boards, reminder signs in the house, or relocation)

G. Considerations for Specific Capacities (e.g., decision making, living independently, driving)

1. Because neuropsychological tests measure general domains of cognitive functioning (e.g., verbal reasoning, perceptual–motor capacities) rather than specific capacities (e.g., the ability to make decisions about medical procedures or to drive safely in one's neighborhood), their use in this area is limited. This is especially true for patients whose overall level of impairment is mild.

2. The answers to specific questions for an individual patient may require a functional assessment of that specific capacity. Recently published procedures such as those designed to assess capacity to give informed consent or write advance directives (Hopkins Competency Assessment Test; Janofsky, McCarthy, & Folstein, 1992), to comply with medication regimen (Fitten, Coleman, Siembieda, Yu, & Ganzell, 1995), and to consent to electroconvulsive therapy (Competency Interview Schedule; Bean, Nishisato, Rector, & Glancy, 1994) offer the clinician help in this area (as do tests of adaptive living skills such as the Kohlman Evaluation of Living Skills; Kohlman-Thomson, 1992), but more assessment tools are clearly needed. The best method of assessing driving safety remains an *in vivo* road test. Although none of these assessment techniques is foolproof, the importance of evaluating specific capacities is underscored by a recent study in which physicians with expertise in geriatrics demonstrated significant disagreement when judging the competency of mildly impaired patients with Alzheimer's disease (Marson, McInturff, Hawkins, Bartolucci, & Harrell, 1997).

H. General Considerations

The diagnosis of dementia is often devastating for patients and families. Neuropsychological test results can be of tremendous assistance to referring clinicians, patients, and families by providing documentation of areas of impairment and explanations of the consequences of these impairments. These test results are often most helpful if written summaries and face-to-face feedback sessions are provided and follow-up assistance is offered.

Ultimately, ensuring the safety of a cognitively impaired patient becomes the top priority in working with families of these patients over time. Quality of life is the second priority. At present, there is not sufficient information to provide definitive criteria based on neuropsychological test results for exactly when an individual is no longer able to live independently, drive, or make medical and financial decisions. However, on the basis of knowledge of neuropsychiatric disorders, the availability of neuropsychological test data, and the application of behavioral and family systems principles, there is probably no discipline better equipped than clinical neuropsychology to help patients and their families understand, plan for, and cope with the day-to-day consequences of the condition.

III. CONCLUSION

Dementia is a syndrome of generalized and persistent cognitive impairment that (a) represents a deterioration from a previous baseline, (b) occurs without a disruption in consciousness, (c) is of sufficient severity to influence daily functioning, (d) cannot be explained by normal aging or situational stress, and (e) may be the result of a variety of conditions, some of which are reversible. Familiarity with the base rates and neuropsychiatric characteristics of conditions whose presentation includes cognitive impairment is the first step in the evaluation of possible dementia. The second step is the selection of tests with appropriate norms to sample domains of cognitive processing that are of relevance to the differential diagnosis of possible dementia and the specific referral question. These domains include arousal, orientation, memory (i.e., learning, rate of forgetting, recall vs. recognition), executive functioning, motor capacity, attention, language (e.g., naming, fluency, comprehension), and visuospatial processing.

The third step is an interpretation of the test results in the context of a patient's history and current circumstances. For example, "mildly impaired" test performance probably does not reflect dementia in an elderly individual with limited education who lives independently, manages his or her finances, and is able to take public transportation to an appointment. In contrast, "below average" memory test scores with rapid forgetting of new information in an individual with a graduate degree whose performance on tests of intellectual functioning is in the average-to-above-average range may be evidence of an early stage of dementia.

Finally, it should be remembered that the diagnosis of dementia can be devastating to patients and families and that, at present, the ability of neuropsychological tests to predict some of the specific real-world consequences of this diagnosis is limited (e.g., ability to drive safely in a familiar neighborhood or make informed decisions about medical or financial matters). As a result, it is often helpful to consider the neuropsychological evaluation as an opportunity to establish an ongoing relationship with patients, families, and referring clinicians to help them understand and deal with the consequences of the cognitive and behavioral symptoms of dementia. Although it is not often taken, it is a role for which clinical neuropsychologists are uniquely suited.

BIBLIOGRAPHY

American Psychiatric Association. (1994). *Diagnostic and statistical manual of mental disorders* (4th ed.). Washington, DC: Author.

American Psychiatric Association. (1997, May). Practice guideline for the treatment of patients with Alzheimer's disease and other dementias of late life. *American Journal of Psychiatry, 154* (Suppl.), 1–39.

Barona, A., Reynolds, C., & Chastain, R. (1984). A demographically based index of premorbid intelligence for the WAIS-R. *Journal of Consulting and Clinical Psychology, 52,* 885–887.

Bean, G., Nishisato, S., Rector, N. A., & Glancy, G. (1994). The psychometric properties of the competency interview schedule. *Canadian Journal of Psychiatry, 39,* 368–376.

Benton, A. L., Sivan, A. B., Hamsher, K. D., Varney, N. R., & Spreen, O. (1994). *Contributions to neuropsychological assessment* (2nd ed.). New York: Oxford University Press.

Blair J., & Spreen, O. (1989). Predicting premorbid IQ: A revision of the National Adult Reading Test. *Clinical Neuropsychologist, 3,* 129–136.

Brandt, J. (1991). The Hopkins Verbal Learning Test: Development of a new memory test with six equivalent forms. *Clinical Neuropsychologist, 5,* 125–142.

Butters, M. A., Salmon, D. P., & Butters, N. (1994). Neuropsychological assessment of dementia. In M. Storandt & G. R.

VandenBos (Eds.), *Neuropsychological assessment of dementia and depression in older adults: A clinician's guide* (pp. 33–59). Washington, DC: American Psychological Association.

Crum, R. M., Anthony, J. C., Bassett, S. S., & Folstein, M. F. (1993). Population-based norms for the Mini-Mental State Examination by age and educational level. *Journal of the American Medical Association, 269,* 2386–2391.

Cummings, J. L. (1990). *Subcortical dementia.* New York: Oxford University Press.

Delis, D. C., Kramer, J. H., Kaplan, E., & Ober, B. A. (1987). *The California Verbal Learning Test.* New York: Psychological Corporation.

Erickson, R. C., Eimon, P., & Hebben, N. (1994). A listing of references to cognitive test norms for older adults. In M. Storandt & G. R. VandenBos (Eds.), *Neuropsychological assessment of dementia and depression in older adults: A clinician's guide* (pp. 183–197). Washington, DC: American Psychological Association.

Fitten, L. J., Coleman, L., Siembieda, D. W., Yu, M., & Ganzell, S. (1995). Assessment of capacity to comply with medication regimens in older patients. *Journal of the American Geriatrics Society, 43,* 361–367.

Folstein, M. F., Folstein, S. E., & McHugh, P. R. (1975). Mini-mental state: A practical method for grading the cognitive state of patients for the clinician. *Journal of Psychiatric Research, 12,* 189–198.

Franklin, J. E., & Francis, R. J. (1992). Alcohol induced organic mental disorders. In S. C. Yudofsky & R. E. Hales (Eds.), *Textbook of neuropsychiatry* (pp. 563–583). Washington, DC: American Psychiatric Press.

Freedman, M., Leach, L., Kaplan, E., Winocur, G., Shullman, K. I., & Delis, D. C. (1994). *Clock drawing: A neuropsychological analysis.* New York: Oxford University Press.

Helmes, E. (1996). Use of the Barona method to predict premorbid intelligence in the elderly. *Clinical Neuropsychologist, 10,* 255–261.

Hersch, E., Kral, V., & Palmer, R. (1978). Clinical value of the London Psychogeriatric Rating Scale. *Journal of the American Geriatrics Association, 26,* 348–354.

Hughes, C. P., Berg, L., Danziger, W. L., Coben, L. A., & Martin, R. L. (1982). A new clinical scale for the staging of dementia. *British Journal of Psychiatry, 140,* 566–572.

Inouye, S. K., van Dyck, C. H., Alesi, C. A., Balkin, S., Siegal, A. P., & Horwitz, R. I. (1990). Clarifying confusion: The confusion assessment method: A new method for detection of delirium. *Annals of Internal Medicine, 113,* 941–948.

Ivnik, R. J., Malec, J. F., Smith, G. E., Tangalos, E. G., & Peterson, R. C. (1996). Neuropsychological tests' norms above age 55: COWAT, BNT, MAE Token, WRAT-R Reading, AMNART, STROOP, TMT, and JLO. *Clinical Neuropsychologist, 10,* 262–278.

Ivnik, R. J., Malec, J. F., Smith, G. E., Tangalos, E. G., Peterson, R. C., Kokmen, E., & Kurland, L. T. (1992a). Mayo's older Americans normative studies: WAIS-R norms for ages 56–97. *Clinical Neuropsychologist, 6*(Suppl.), 1–30.

Ivnik, R. J., Malec, J. F., Smith, G. E., Tangalos, E. G., Peterson, R. C., Kokmen, E., & Kurland, L. T. (1992b). Mayo's older Americans normative studies: WMS-R norms for ages 56–94. *Clinical Neuropsychologist, 6*(Suppl.), 49–82.

Janofsky, J. S., McCarthy, R. J., & Folstein, M. F. (1992). The Hopkins Competency Assessment Test: A brief method for evaluating patients' capacity to give informed consent. *Hospital and Community Psychiatry, 43,* 132–136.

Johnstone, B., Callahan, C. D., Kapila, C. J., & Bouman, D. E. (1996). The comparability of the WRAT-R reading test and NAART as estimates of premorbid intelligence in neurologically impaired patients. *Archives of Clinical Neuropsychology, 11,* 513–519.

Kazniak, A. W., & Christenson, G. T. (1994). Differential diagnosis of dementia and depression. In M. Storandt & G.R. VandenBos (Eds.), *Neuropsychological assessment of dementia and depression in older adults: A clinician's guide* (pp. 81–117). Washington, DC: American Psychological Association.

Kiernan, R. J., Mueller, J., Langston, J. W., & Van Dyke, C. (1987). The Neurobehavioral Cognitive Status Examination: A brief but differentiated approach to cognitive assessment. *Annals of Internal Medicine, 107,* 481–485.

Kohlman-Thomson, L. (1992). *The Kohlman Evaluation of Living Skills* (3rd ed.). Rockville, MD: American Occupational Therapy Association.

LaRue, A., D'Elia, L. F., Clark, E. O., Spar, J. E., Jarvik, L. F. (1986). Clinical tests of memory in dementia, depression, and health aging. *Journal of Psychology and Aging, 1,* 69–77.

Levkoff, S. E., Evans, D. A., Liptzin, B., Cleary, P. D., Lipsitz, L. A., Wetle, T. T., Reilly, C. H., Pilgrim, D. M., Schor, J., & Rowe, J. (1992). Delirium: The occurrence and persistence of symptoms among elderly hospitalized patients. *Annals of Internal Medicine, 152,* 334–340.

Libon, D. J., Mattson, R. E., Glosser, G., Kaplan, E., Malamut, B. L., Sands, L. P., Swenson, R., & Cloud, B. S. (1996). A nine-word dementia version of the California Verbal Learning Test. *Clinical Neuropsychologist, 10,* 237–244.

Marson, D. C., McInturff, B., Hawkins, L., Bartolucci, A., & Harrell, L. E. (1997). Consistency of physician judgments of capacity to consent in mild Alzheimer's disease. *Journal of the American Geriatrics Society, 45,* 453–457.

Mattis, S. (1988). *Dementia Rating Scale (DRS).* Odessa, FL: Psychological Assessment Resources.

McKeith, J. G., Fairbarn, A. F., Perry, R. H., & Thompson, P. (1994). The clinical diagnosis of senile dementia of Lewy body type (SDLT). *British Journal of Psychiatry, 165,* 324–332.

McPherson, S. E., & Cummings, J. L. (1997). Vascular dementia: Clinical assessment, neuropsychological features, and treatment. In P.D. Nussbaum (Ed.), *Handbook of neuropsychology and aging* (pp. 177–188). New York: Plenum Press.

Miller, B. L., Chang, L., Orophilla, G., & Mena, I. (1994). Alzheimer's disease and frontal lobe dementias. In C. E. Coffey & J. L. Cummings (Eds.), *Textbook of geriatric neuropsychiatry* (pp. 389–404). Washington, DC: American Psychiatric Press.

Peskind, E. R., & Raskind, M. A. (1996). Cognitive disorders. In E. W. Busse & D. G. Blazer (Eds.), *Textbook of geriatric psychiatry* (pp. 213–234). Washington, DC: American Psychiatric Press.

Roberts, G. W., Leigh, P. N., & Weinberger, D. R. (1993). *Neuropsychiatric disorders.* London: Wolfe Publishing.

Rothlind, J. C., & Brandt, J. (1993). A brief assessment of frontal and subcortical functions in dementia. *Journal of Neuropsychiatry and Clinical Neurosciences, 5,* 73–77.

Rouleau, I., Salmon, D. P., Butters, N., Kennedy, C., & McGuire, K. (1992). Quantitative and qualitative analyses of clock drawings in Alzheimer's disease and Huntington's disease. *Brain and Cognition, 18,* 70–87.

Royall, D. R., Makurin, R. K., & Gran, K. F. (1992). Bedside assessment of executive cognitive impairment: The executive interview. *Journal of the American Geriatrics Society, 40,* 1221–1226.

Salmon, D. P., & Bondi, M. W. (1997). The neuropsychology of Alzheimer's disease. In P. D. Nussbaum (Ed.), *Handbook of Neuropsychology and Aging* (pp. 141–158). New York: Plenum Press.

Saxton, J., McGonigle-Gibson, K. L., Swihart, A. A., Miller, V. J., & Boller, F. (1990). Assessment of the severely impaired patient: Description and validation of a new neuropsychological test battery. *Psychological Assessment, 2,* 298–303.

Small, G. W., Rabins, P. V., Barry, P. B., Buckholtz, N. S., Dekoskky, S. T., Ferris, S. H., Finkel, S. I., Gwyther, L. P., Khachaturian, Z. S., Lebowitz, B. D., McRae, T. D., Morris, J. C., Oakley, F., Schneider, L. S., Streim, J. E., Sunderland, T., Teri, L. A., & Tune, L. E. (1997). Diagnosis and treatment of Alzheimer disease and related disorders: Consensus statement of the American Association for Geriatric Psychiatry, the Alzheimer's Association, and the American Geriatrics Society. *Journal of the American Medical Association, 278,* 1363–1371.

Solomon, P. R., Hirschoff, A., Kelly, B., Relin, M., Brush, M., DeVeaux, R. D., & Pendlebury, W. W. (1998). A 7 minute neurocognitive screening battery highly sensitive to Alzheimer's disease. *Archives of Neurology, 55,* 349–355.

Spreen, O., & Strauss, E. (1991). *A compendium of neuropsychological tests.* New York: Oxford University Press.

Trzepacz, P. T., Baker, R. W., & Greenhouse, J. (1987). A symptom rating scale for delirium. *Psychiatry Research, 23,* 89–97.

Tune, L., & Ross, C. (1994). Delirium. In C. E. Coffey & J. L. Cummings (Eds.), *Textbook of geriatric neuropsychiatry* (pp. 351–365). Washington, DC: American Psychiatric Press.

Usman, M. A. (1997). Frontotemporal dementias. In P. D. Nussbaum (Ed.), *Handbook of neuropsychology and aging* (pp. 159–176). New York: Plenum Press.

Wechsler, D. (1997a). Wechsler Adult Intelligence Scale–Third edition. San Antonio, TX: Psychological Corporation.

Wechsler, D. (1997b). Wechsler Memory Scale–Third edition. San Antonio, TX: Psychological Corporation.

Weintraub, S. (1995). Examining mental state. In M. A. Samuels & S. Feske (Eds.), *Office practice of neurology* (pp. 698–705). New York: Churchill Livingstone.

Yesavage, J. A., Brink, T. L., Rose, T. L., Lum, O., Huang, V., Adey, M., & Leirer, V. O. (1983). Development and validation of a geriatric depression screening scale: A preliminary report. *Journal of Psychiatric Research, 17,* 37–49.

PART IV

NEUROLOGICAL DISORDERS

CHAPTER 13

John A. Lucas

Traumatic Brain Injury and Postconcussive Syndrome

Traumatic injuries represent the leading cause of death and disability in young adults in the United States and other industrialized countries. When head trauma is sufficient to cause alterations in consciousness, neurological impairment, or cognitive deficits, an injury to the brain is assumed.

The clinical assessment of patients with traumatic brain injuries should focus on two main goals. First, the clinician must carefully construct a history of the injury. Information regarding the nature of the event, the amount of time that has passed since the injury, and the clinical course of symptoms should be gathered from several sources, including the patient, family members, and medical records. This information will guide the choices of measures administered and allow consideration of the types of questions that can be answered by the assessment.

The second goal of assessment is to ensure that the full nature of the disorder is determined. Head injuries may result in focal, multifocal, or diffuse cerebral dysfunction, often involving structures and systems beyond the site of initial impact. Moreover, contributions from preexisting conditions, psychological sequelae, and other factors may obscure or exacerbate cognitive symptoms. Knowledge of both the mechanisms underlying traumatic brain injury and the potential effects of nonorganic sequelae is therefore essential for competent assessment of neurocognitive status.

I. CLASSIFICATION OF HEAD INJURY

Brain injury resulting from head trauma is a dynamic process, not only evolving over the hours and days following the injury, but continuing over the course of weeks and months. Neuropsychological results may vary depending on the time of assessment, the nature and location of the trauma, the estimated severity of brain injury, and the extent of secondary effects, such as metabolic alterations, interruption of blood flow, and cerebral swelling.

A. Open Versus Closed Head Injury

Head injuries may be broadly classified as either open or closed, depending on whether or not the integrity of the skull has been breached. The term **open head injury** most often refers to traumas in which the skull is crushed or penetrated by a foreign object. The majority of fatalities following head trauma are seen in patients with open head injury. In **closed head injuries** (also called blunt or nonpenetrating injuries), the skull remains relatively intact. Impact injuries that involve skull fractures are technically considered open head injuries; however, their clinical presentation is typically more consistent with that of closed head injuries.

The neuropathological effects of head injury typically occur as a result of two processes. The **primary injury** is the damage to the brain caused by the penetrating object or impact forces at the time of trauma. Although the primary injury is usually focal and time limited in nature, it sets in motion a series of physiological and metabolic processes that produce **secondary effects.** These effects are often as damaging to brain tissue as the primary injury, if not more so. Some secondary effects invariably occur (e.g., edema), whereas others may or may not develop, depending on the nature, location, and extent of the primary injury. The more common consequences of primary injury and potential secondary effects are reviewed in the following sections.

1. PENETRATING HEAD INJURIES

The majority of penetrating brain injuries are missile injuries caused by bullets. As a bullet travels, air is compressed in front of it, leading to an explosive effect on entering the body. When the missile is of low velocity (i.e., less than 1,000 ft/s), brain damage is typically restricted to the missile track and the victim frequently remains conscious. With higher velocity missiles, however, damage typically extends well beyond the missile track, and victims are usually rendered unconscious.

a. Primary injury

1. Destruction of brain tissue at the site of entry and along the path of object
2. Intracranial bleeding owing to damaged blood vessels
3. Meningeal and cerebral laceration

b. Potential secondary effects

1. Destruction of brain tissue during surgical removal of foreign object and during cleansing (i.e., debridement)
2. Ischemia (i.e., interruption of blood flow to tissue)
3. Edema (i.e., reactive swelling of brain tissue). Note that both ischemia and edema are much worse if the brain is penetrated by a high-velocity missile
4. Brain infection (e.g., meningitis, abscess)
5. Posttraumatic epilepsy

2. CLOSED HEAD INJURIES

Brain damage caused by closed head injuries also occurs in two stages. The damage incurred at the time of impact, also known as the primary injury, sets in motion a series of physiological processes that may produce secondary effects.

a. Primary injury

1. Brain contusions (bruises) are typically seen at the site of impact (i.e., coup lesion). In addition, pressure during impact often causes the brain to rebound and hit the skull opposite the initial blow. This typically results in a larger contusion (i.e., **contrecoup** lesion) than at the site of impact.
2. Contusions of the inferior surface of brain are caused by the brain's rubbing against the base of the skull. The orbitofrontal and anterior temporal regions are the most common sites of contusion.
3. Diffuse axonal injury is common following closed head injury and may be responsible for persistent neurologic deficits.

b. Potential secondary effects

1. Ischemia
2. Edema

3. Subdural hematoma
4. Intracerebral bleeding
5. Increased intracranial pressure and herniation
6. Hypoxia
7. Obstructive hydrocephalus
8. Posttraumatic epilepsy

3. SKULL FRACTURES

Closed head injuries with skull fractures may present with additional primary and secondary features, including the following:

a. Primary injury

1. Cranial nerve damage and related palsies
2. Damage to vasculature entering or leaving base of skull
3. Pituitary stalk damage (if basilar skull is fractured near the sella)

b. Potential secondary effects

1. Collection of air in the cranial cavity (i.e., aerocele)
2. Infection
3. Cerebrospinal fluid leakage
4. Endocrine–hormonal dysfunction (if pituitary stalk is damaged)

B. Measurement of Severity of Injury

Several indices may be used to gauge the severity of a head injury. Two of the most important indicators are the length of time the victim is unconscious and the degree of posttraumatic amnesia experienced. In addition, clinical instruments have been developed to sample patient behavior during acute recovery and provide summary indices reflecting the extent of the head injury.

1. LOSS OF CONSCIOUSNESS

At the moment of impact, victims of head injury typically demonstrate immediate loss of consciousness (LOC), suppression of reflexes, and brief changes in cardiopulmonary functions. Although most vital signs return to normal and stabilize within a few seconds following the injury, the victim may remain unconscious (i.e., comatose). The amount of time it takes a patient to regain consciousness is often used as an indication of the severity of the brain injury. The patient may not be able to provide reliable information regarding the length of

LOC, and in such cases, collateral information from a witness to the injury, police reports, or emergency medical service records should be sought.

Several systems of grading LOC have been published; however, there is little consensus among the writers. The Mild Traumatic Brain Injury Committee (MTBIC) of the Head Injury Interdisciplinary Special Interest Group of the American Congress of Rehabilitation Medicine (1993) has classified head injuries as follows:

a. Mild injury: LOC for 30 minutes or less
b. Moderate-to-severe injury: LOC longer than 30 minutes

2. POSTTRAUMATIC AMNESIA

A disturbance of memory for events that occur immediately following a head injury is called posttraumatic amnesia (PTA). This is caused by the interruption of mechanisms responsible for ongoing encoding and memory storage. Length of PTA is typically more accurate than length of coma in predicting recovery of function, with longer periods of PTA associated with more severe brain injuries and poorer recovery of function.

Length of PTA may be elicited by asking the patient to describe his or her first memories after the accident. It is important, however, to distinguish between episodic and semantic memories of the injury. For example, "memories" of the series of events that took place following the injury may be based on information provided to the patient after full return to alert consciousness (i.e., a semantic memory). Only true episodic memories of the injury should be used to estimate length of PTA. The typical PTA grading system is as follows:

a. Mild injury: PTA less than 1 hour
b. Moderate injury: PTA for 1–24 hours
c. Severe injury: PTA longer than 24 hours

Others have supplemented the preceding criteria to include finer scaling at the extremes. These include very mild (PTA less than 5 minutes), very severe (PTA for 1–4 weeks), and extremely severe (PTA longer than 4 weeks) injuries. Guidelines of the MTBIC (1993), however, include all patients with less than 24 hours of PTA under the classification of mild head injury.

3. GLASGOW COMA SCALE

The most commonly used clinical method for measuring the severity of brain injury is the Glasgow Coma Scale (GCS; Teasdale & Jennett, 1974). The GCS rates verbal responses, eye-opening behavior, and best motor responses on a scale ranging from 3 to 15 points (see Table 1).

Table 1. Glasgow Coma Scale

Response	Score
Verbal response	
None	1
Incomprehensible sounds	2
Inappropriate words	3
Confused	4
Oriented	5
Eye opening	
None	1
To pain	2
To speech	3
Spontaneously	4
Best motor response	
None	1
Abnormal extension	2
Abnormal flexion	3
Withdraws	4
Localizes	5
Obeys	6

Note. From "Assessment of Coma and Impairment of Consciousness: A Practical Scale," by G. Teasdale and B. Jennett, 1974, *Lancet, 2*, p. ?? Copyright 1974 by ?? Reprinted with permission.

The GCS is sensitive to moderate and severe head injuries and is useful for predicting neurobehavioral outcome (i.e., the higher the score, the better the prognosis). Sensitivity at the milder end of the spectrum, however, is less impressive. Head injuries are classified as follows:

a. Mild injury: at least 13 points
b. Moderate injury: 9–12 points
c. Severe injury: 8 or fewer points

4. GALVESTON ORIENTATION AND AMNESIA TEST

The Galveston Orientation and Amnesia Test (GOAT; Levin, O'Donnell, & Grossman, 1979) is a mental status examination composed of 10 questions. Eight of the 10 questions assess orientation to person, place, and time. The remaining two questions require that the patient describe the first memory recalled after the injury (to detect PTA) and the last memory recalled prior to the injury (to detect retrograde amnesia). The GOAT is scored on a scale of 0–100 and may be administered repeatedly to assess recovery from LOC and posttraumatic confusion. Higher scores reflect better functioning:

    a. Normal: 76–100 points

    b. Borderline: 66–75 points

    c. Impaired: 65 or fewer points

C. Concussion

Defined as an alteration in mental status induced by mechanical forces affecting the brain, a concussion is typically manifested as LOC, PTA, or some other transient disruption in neurological function such as being "stunned" (Binder & Rattok, 1989). Some of the more frequently observed behavioral features of patients during acute concussion include vacant stare, delayed responding, inability to focus attention, disorientation, confusion, slurred or incoherent speech, motor incoordination, excessive emotionality, and forgetfulness.

Following recovery from acute cerebral concussion, a wide variety of subjective neurocognitive, somatic, and psychological symptoms may be observed. Studies have demonstrated that these symptoms do not occur all at once, but are often reported in stages (Rutherford, 1989).

1. EARLY SYMPTOMS

Early symptoms develop immediately after the patient regains consciousness or by the following morning. These include the following:

    a. Headache

    b. Dizziness

    c. Vomiting

    d. Nausea

    e. Drowsiness

    f. Blurred vision

Nausea, vomiting, drowsiness, and blurred vision are typically short-lived complaints, whereas headache and dizziness may persist for weeks or longer.

2. LATE SYMPTOMS

The onset of some behavioral symptoms may be delayed for several days to weeks after the head injury. These include the following:

    a. Irritability

b. Anxiety
c. Depression
d. Poor memory
e. Impaired concentration
f. Insomnia
g. Fatigue
h. Visual and auditory complaints

3. POSTCONCUSSIVE SYNDROME

Nearly 15% of patients with mild head injury continue to complain of postconcussive symptoms 1 year after their injury (Rutherford, 1989). Until recently, the prevailing model of concussion depicted a transitory alteration of consciousness without any associated pathological changes in the brain. Because of this view, it was believed that behavioral symptoms in patients with no obvious brain damage should be brief in duration. Organic bases for persistent complaints were therefore dismissed in favor of psychological or motivational explanations. More recent studies, however, have demonstrated that structural and metabolic changes take place in the brain following mild head injury and that these changes may underlie the persistence of cognitive sequelae.

The exact nature of the postconcussive syndrome (PCS) remains controversial. The proportion of patients with mild head injury who complain of PCS 1 year after their injury more than doubles (i.e., 34%) if litigation is involved (Rutherford, 1989), and data such as these are often used to highlight the potential role of nonorganic factors. The neuropsychologist who evaluates patients with persistent PCS must therefore be prepared to examine the relative roles of both organic and nonorganic factors.

4. SECOND IMPACT SYNDROME

A rare but catastrophic complication of head injury can occur when an individual suffers repeated concussions over a relatively brief time interval. Observed in contact sports such as boxing, football, and ice hockey, this phenomenon is called **second impact syndrome.** Typically, the individual sustains a second head injury while still symptomatic from an earlier concussion. Even if the second head injury is mild, the victim demonstrates rapid deterioration from an alert, conscious state to coma and possibly death, all within minutes to hours following the trauma.

Autopsy studies indicate that victims of second impact syndrome lose autonomic regulation of blood vessel diameter, causing cerebral blood volume to rise. This, in turn, increases intracranial pressure, diminishes cerebral perfusion, and increases risk of fatal brain herniation. A similar phenomenon, observed in children following an initial head injury, is known as **acute brain swelling** or **malignant brain edema syndrome**.

II. NEUROANATOMIC CORRELATES OF HEAD INJURY AND CONCUSSION

A. Pathophysiological Changes

Recent studies have indicated that even mild head injury can cause structural damage to the brain. Subsequent to head trauma, diffuse damage may be seen in long, large-caliber neuronal fibers (Goodman, 1994). Previously, it was believed that this damage was caused by axonal tearing; however, it now appears that compression or stretching of axons is the mechanism of injury (Povlishock, 1993). Axonal compression or stretching creates a focal abnormality on the surface membrane of the axon, which within 3 hours after the injury is sufficient to impair axoplasmic transport. This leads to accumulation of organelles and axoplasm at the site of the abnormality, resulting in swelling (i.e., edema). The swollen axon then separates. The proximal section remains attached to the cell body, and the distal segment collapses and undergoes phagocytosis by nearby glial cells. Axonal swellings may persist unchanged, or the axons may attempt to regenerate. In the regenerative process, sprouting and growth-cone formation are observed at or near the site of the swelling. Over the course of several weeks, the sprouts elongate, extend through the parenchyma, and enter the myelin sheaths of the detached distal axonal segments that had previously collapsed. If axons do not regenerate, reactive deafferentation (i.e., death of "downstream" neurons owing to lack of synaptic input) is observed within 60 days of the head injury.

B. Neurochemical Changes

Cells that are not mechanically damaged as a result of a head injury are nonetheless exposed to significant metabolic and ... rochemical changes. The cascade of changes following head injury begins with a sharp, transient increase in concentrations of acetylcholine and excitatory amino acids such as glutamate. The acute release of glutamate causes widespread neuronal depolarization and ionic flux of potassium across the membrane into the extracellular space. Within 2 minutes of a mild injury, the concentration of extracellular potassium increases 2-fold; 10-fold increases are observed following moderate injury (Katayama, Becker, Tamura, & Hovda, 1990). Changes in potassium concentration cause increased glycolysis, which, in turn, results in accumulation of lactic acid within the cells. This leads to a state of metabolic depression (i.e., decreased metabolism and cerebral blood flow). In animals, the presence and severity of metabolic depression is correlated strongly with behavioral changes.

III. DIAGNOSTIC ISSUES REGARDING POSTCONCUSSIVE SYNDROME

The etiology of persistent postconcussive complaints in patients who show no obvious neuroradiological abnormalities is often difficult to determine. This difficulty arises in part because the majority of postconcussive complaints are nonspecific in nature. Although structural abnormalities in the form of diffuse axonal injury suggest a potential organic cause, the roles of preexisting symptoms, medication effects, psychological sequelae, and motivational factors must also be considered.

A. Nonspecific Symptoms

The majority of symptoms associated with PCS are nonspecific and are readily endorsed by patients with other medical disorders, as well as by medically healthy individuals (Dikmen, McLean, & Temkin, 1986; Lees-Haley & Brown, 1993). Consequently, all potential sources of these symptoms should be ruled out.

1. PREEXISTING MEDICAL CONDITIONS

A variety of medical conditions may produce nonspecific symptoms such as headache, dizziness, irritability, or cognitive complaints. Some of the more common conditions include the following:

- a. Hypertension
- b. Diabetes
- c. Hypoglycemia
- d. Thyroid dysfunction
- e. Psychiatric disorder

2. PREMORBID SUBSTANCE ABUSE

The relationship between alcohol abuse and head injury is well documented (Kraus & Nourjah, 1989). The physical and cognitive sequelae of abuse and withdrawal may confound the postinjury symptom picture and test performances in patients with a dual diagnosis of substance abuse and head injury. Symptoms and cognitive deficits typically associated with primary alcohol abuse are reviewed elsewhere in this volume.

3. DEVELOPMENTAL DISORDERS

A history of learning disability or attention deficit disorder should be ruled out, because these may result in subtle impairment of attention or new learning.

4. MEDICATION SIDE EFFECTS

Irritability, agitation, anxiety, drowsiness, dizziness, nausea, inattention, and memory complaints are common side effects of numerous medications. The examiner should be especially aware of any narcotic analgesic use, because these medications may be associated with changes in mental status.

B. Psychological Factors

Psychological reactions to head injury may exacerbate PCS. Adjustment disorders with depressed or anxious mood or both are common following head trauma and may contribute to complaints of fatigue, irritability, insomnia, poor concentration, and impaired memory. A more complete discussion of psychological and psychiatric components to head injury is presented later in this chapter.

C. Motivational Factors

The question of secondary gain invariably arises when patients complain of persistent postconcussive symptoms. A recent study of patients with PCS beyond 6 months after the injury revealed that motivational factors may have adversely affected neuropsychological test performances in approximately half of the participants (Youngjohn, Burrows, & Erdal, 1995). One should also be especially vigilant if the patient is planning, or currently involved in, litigation regarding the injury.

The rewards of financial compensation following head injury are not the only potential motivations for persistent cognitive complaints and poor neuropsychological test performance. Head injuries may elicit behaviors from others that, in turn, serve to reinforce disability. It is therefore important to identify potential secondary gain derived from changes in the nature of interpersonal relationships at home or in the work environment.

Motivational factors may be conscious or unconscious, and their involvement does not necessarily rule out organic cerebral dysfunction. Understanding motivational factors, however, can help one to discern a more accurate representation of the patient's true cognitive abilities. Careful observation of test behaviors and consistency of effort put forth by the patient throughout the assessment often provides clues to the role of motivational factors in test performance. More formal evaluations of dissimulation and malingering are reviewed later in this chapter and elsewhere in this volume.

IV. NEUROIMAGING DATA

Increasingly sophisticated techniques of neural, metabolic, and electrophysiological imaging have permitted improved identification of cerebral abnormalities following head injury, even when damage is subtle.

A. CT and MRI

Gross brain pathology associated with moderate-to-severe head trauma is typically well visualized on both computed tomography (CT) and magnetic resonance imaging (MRI) scans. Abnormalities following mild head injury, however, are more readily identified by MRI than CT. Mild orbitofrontal and temporal lobe contusions are commonly missed by CT scanning because of bone artifact. In addition, CT is poor in visualizing diffuse axonal injury and trauma-induced lesions in the basal ganglia. The one advantage that CT holds over MRI is the ability to detect hemorrhage soon after the injury. At 3 weeks postinjury, however, MRI often detects residual hemorrhage missed by CT.

B. EEG

Electroencephalographic (EEG) studies indicate that posttraumatic epilepsy is common following penetrating brain injury, with incident estimates approaching 50% (Adams, Victor, & Ropper, 1997; Grafman & Salazar, 1996; Salazar et al., 1985). The overall risk of posttraumatic epilepsy following closed head injury is comparatively low (2%–5%), with a higher incidence associated with more severe injury (11%), skull fracture (15%), and hematoma (31%; Annegers et al., 1980; Jennett & Teasdale, 1981).

Nonspecific, nonepileptic electroencephalographic abnormalities may be detected following mild head injury. The EEG tends to be most abnormal when performed soon after the injury and when there is alteration of consciousness associated with the injury. In approximately 10% of patients with cerebral concussion, slight diffuse EEG abnormalities may persist beyond 3 months.

C. Brain-Stem Auditory Evoked Potentials

Abnormal brain-stem auditory evoked potentials (BAEPs) are most often found in patients with more severe head injuries; however, approximately 10%–20% of patients with mild head injury also demonstrate abnormal BAEPs. Abnormalities are more prevalent in patients who suffered longer periods of unconsciousness, but they do not appear to be related to performance on neurocognitive measures.

D. Positron Emission Tomography

In general, head-injured patients tend to demonstrate reduced cerebral blood flow and widespread abnormalities in cerebral glucose metabolism beyond any structural abnormalities identified on CT or MRI. These metabolic abnormalities tend to be most severe closer to the time of injury and tend to improve with clinical recovery. Evidence of metabolic depression can be found in some patients as long as 6 months postinjury.

V. NEUROPSYCHOLOGICAL ASSESSMENT

A decision-making model of assessment of head-injured patients is presented in Figure 1. With the exception of brief screening measures (e.g., Mini-Mental State Examination, GOAT) or informal bedside testing, neuropsychological assessment of head-injured patients should be deferred until after the postacute stage of injury. The dynamic nature of symptoms over the days and weeks immediately following injury makes assessment during this time invalid for most purposes. Moreover, most head-injured patients are not able to tolerate the demands of extensive neuropsychological testing during the initial stages of recovery. A 6-week waiting period is usually adequate; however, the exact time frame may vary depending on the severity of the injury.

The diagnostic focus of the neuropsychological assessment differs depending on the nature of the injury. Typically, the initial assessment of patients with moderate-to-severe head injury focuses primarily on gauging the severity and extent of neu-

Figure 1. Decision-making in neuropsychological assessment of head-injured patients. MMSE = Mini Mental State Examination; GOAT = Galveston Orientation and Amnesia Test; PTA = posttraumatic amnesia; LOC = loss of consciousness; GCS = Glasgow Coma Scale; R/O = rule out.

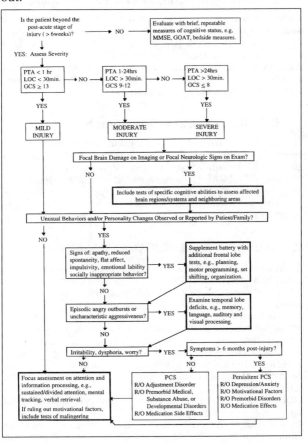

rocognitive dysfunction. Repeated assessments can then provide information regarding recovery of function and the efficacy of cognitive rehabilitation.

The diagnostic focus of neuropsychological assessment of patients with mild head injury should be on identifying changes that may be associated with diffuse axonal injury. This typically calls for more specialized assessment of attention and information-processing abilities.

A. Assessing Moderate-to-Severe Head Injury

Patients with moderate-to-severe head injury can display the full spectrum of impairment across all cognitive domains. Very severely injured individuals are likely to show general impairment of all cognitive abilities; however, less severely impaired patients demonstrate unique patterns of preserved and impaired abilities consistent with the focal (or multifocal) nature of brain damage incurred. A complete assessment, therefore, includes screening for deficits in all cognitive domains. Deficits identified on the screening examination can then be pursued with more detailed assessment.

1. MECHANICAL COMPLICATIONS

Knowing of the presence of skull fractures, structural brain damage (e.g., cerebral contusion, laceration), cerebrovascular complications (e.g., hematoma, intracerebral hemorrhages), or pressure effects (e.g., severe edema, obstructive hydrocephalus) prior to assessment often guides the choice of measures administered. Needless to say, cognitive domains associated with the damaged area and surrounding brain regions should be thoroughly examined.

2. FOCAL NEUROLOGICAL DEFICITS

Special attention must be paid to the presence of any focal neurological deficits, such as motor, sensory, or language impairment (e.g., hemiplegia, hemianopia, anosmia, aphasia), because they may (a) provide information regarding focal brain dysfunction, (b) guide more detailed assessment of affected brain regions, and (c) dictate modifications of test administration (e.g., ensuring placement of visual stimuli in the intact hemispace of a patient with a homonymous hemianopia).

Table 2. Recommended Neuropsychological Measures for Assessment of Cognitive Dysfunction Following Mild Head Injury

Domain	Measures
Reaction time	Continuous-performance tests
Vigilance	Digit Vigilance Test
	Visual Search and Attention Test
	Continuous-performance tests
Divided attention	Paced Auditory Serial Addition Test
	Paced Auditory Serial Attention Task
Mental tracking	Digits Backward
	Serial calculations
	Stroop Test
	Trail Making Test
Verbal retrieval	Boston Naming Test
	WAIS-R NI (multiple-choice modifications of Information, Vocabulary, and Similarities subtests)
	Word fluency
	California Verbal Learning Test

Note. WAIS-R = Wechsler Adult Intelligence Scale–Revised; NI = neuropsychological instrument.

3. COMMON COGNITIVE DEFICITS

Certain cognitive deficits are relatively common following moderate-to-severe closed head injury. A high incidence of orbitofrontal and anterior temporal lobe contusions is associated with these injuries, and they typically produce the following:

a. Attention deficits and distractibility
b. Slowed cognitive processing and behavioral responding

c. Impaired learning and retrieval of new information
d. Deficits in auditory or visual processing
e. Frontal lobe signs (e.g., initiation deficits, poor planning and organization, impaired motor programming, preservation, anosognosia, impulsivity)

B. Assessing Mild Head Injury

The most common cognitive sequelae of mild head injury are diffuse reductions in attention and information processing. Use of measures with sufficient sensitivity to detect these changes is therefore recommended (see Table 2). The majority of patients with mild head injury improve to within normal limits on most neuropsychological measures within 30 days; however, a subset of patients continue to demonstrate impairment beyond this time.

1. REACTION TIME

Reaction time (RT) tests measure the time it takes a patient to respond to presented stimuli. **Simple RT** is typically measured by asking patients to look at a blank screen and press a keypad as soon as a stimulus is presented. A variation of this paradigm is the **Choice RT** test, in which both target stimuli and foils are presented in random order and the patient must respond only when the target stimulus is detected. Choice RT is one way of measuring **selective attention**, which is the capacity to focus on certain stimuli while ignoring or suppressing awareness of competing, distracting stimuli (Lezak, 1995).

Given the rapid and precise requirements for measurement, RT tests are typically administered by computer. Most of the commercially available continuous-performance tests (CPT) include simple and choice RT paradigms as well as more complex measures of attention. CPTs were originally developed for use with children; however, use with adults has increased in recent years. The nature of the test stimuli, presentation rates, length of the test, and paradigms offered vary depending on the instrument used; most can be customized to measure whatever variables are of interest. Normative data for adults, however, are somewhat limited and typically based on standard administration paradigms.

2. VIGILANCE

Vigilance refers to the ability to sustain selective attention. Typically, stimuli are presented sequentially over time and the patient is required to indicate when a target is perceived. This can be evaluated on a CPT or by any number of paper-and-pencil measures. Cancellation tests, such as the Digit Vigilance Test (Lewis & Rennick, 1979) and Visual Search and Attention Test (VSAT; Trennery, Crosson, DeBoe, & Leber, 1990), are common measures of vigilance. Patients are instructed to scan rows of letters, numbers, or symbols and cross out specified targets. These tests are typically scored for time to completion and accuracy (i.e., number of targets missed).

3. DIVIDED ATTENTION

The ability to divide one's attention between two or more concurrent tasks places significantly greater demand on information-processing capacity than do tests of selective or sustained attention. Reaction time paradigms can be used to measure divided attention by requiring participants to perform an unrelated task (e.g., counting backward) while responding to target stimuli. The Paced Auditory Serial Addition Test (PASAT; Gronwall, 1977) is another measure of divided attention. A string of single digits is presented sequentially on a taped recording, and the patient must continuously add the most recently presented number to the one presented immediately before it. The rate of presentation of numbers increases steadily over four trials from one every 2.4 seconds to one every 1.2 seconds. The PASAT places a great deal of stress on patients, and some clinicians prefer not to use it because of this. The test is highly sensitive to information-processing deficits associated with diffuse cerebral dysfunction, however, and is therefore appropriate for assessment of patients with mild head injury. A proprietary version of the PASAT, entitled the Paced Auditory Serial Attention Task (Cegalis & Birdsall, 1995), is available for computer administration.

4. MENTAL TRACKING

In this complex attentional process, the individual is required to maintain a cognitive or perceptual set over time. Simple measures of mental tracking include repeating digits backward and performing serial calculations. The complexity of a tracking task can be increased, however, by requiring participants to attend to more than one stimulus, alternately, or sequentially (Lezak, 1995). Other common mental-tracking measures include the Stroop paradigm (Stroop, 1935) and the Halstead-Reitan Trail Making Test (TMT; Reitan & Wolfson, 1985).

5. VERBAL RETRIEVAL

Some patients with mild head injury experience verbal

retrieval deficits. Mild word-finding problems or difficulty accessing previously stored information may be assessed by comparing free and cued response trials. Phonemic cueing on the Boston Naming Test (Kaplan, Goodglass, & Weintraub, 1983) and multiple-choice modifications of the verbal subtests of the Wechsler Adult Intelligence Scale–Revised (WAIS-R) as a neuropsychological instrument (WAIS-R NI; Kaplan, Fein, Morris, & Delis, 1991) provide means of assessing semantic knowledge while minimizing retrieval requirements. Other measures of verbal retrieval include tests of word fluency and of verbal learning and memory that employ both free recall and recognition paradigms.

6. TESTS OF MALINGERING

Patients who present with cognitive complaints may have conscious or unconscious motivations to perform poorly on neuropsychological tests. The nature and assessment of malingering are addressed elsewhere in this volume and are not reviewed in detail here. Forced-choice measures (also known as symptom validation tests) are probably the most commonly used techniques; they include measures such as the Portland Digit Recognition Test (Binder, 1993) and the Hiscock Forced-Choice Procedure (Hiscock & Hiscock, 1989).

VI. PSYCHIATRIC AND PSYCHOSOCIAL SEQUELAE OF HEAD INJURY

The emotional impact of head injury can be devastating to victims and their families. Alterations of personality, mood, and behavior may be organically based, reactive to the trauma and its sequelae, or a combination of both processes.

A. Moderate-to-Severe Injury

Psychiatric symptoms following moderate-to-severe head injury are usually of organic etiology. This does not exclude the possibility of additional reactive symptoms; however, such reactions are typically less prominent than organically based changes. Approximately two thirds of patients with moderate-to-severe head trauma continue to demonstrate personality changes up to 10 years posttrauma. Although the severity of some of these changes lessens over time, the symptoms continue to be viewed by family members as significant problems (Bond, 1986).

1. PERSONALITY CHANGES

Alterations of personality following moderate-to-severe

closed head injury typically reflect damage to the frontal or temporal lobes. This type of injury results in exaggerated, muted, or poorly regulated affect.

a. Frontal lobe personality changes

When the frontal lobe is injured, personality may change in one of two ways. Patients may become more activated and excitable than before the injury or may demonstrate markedly reduced activation.

1. Excitability can be manifested as (a) impulsivity, (b) emotional lability and mood swings, (c) socially inappropriate behaviors, or (d) childishness.

2. Symptoms of reduced activation include (a) apathy, (b) decreased spontaneity or abulia, (c) lack of interest, or (d) emotional blunting.

b. Temporal lobe personality changes

Damage to temporal lobe limbic structures following head injury is typically associated with episodic emotional dyscontrol, including the following:

1. Episodic hyperirritability
2. Angry or aggressive outbursts
3. Sudden onset of dysphoric mood states

2. PSYCHIATRIC DISORDERS

Psychiatric diagnoses are more common in patients with moderate-to-severe head injuries than in the population at large. Some of the more frequent disorders are as follows:

a. Mania
b. Paranoia
c. Psychosis with predominantly negative symptoms (e.g., flattened affect, suspiciousness, social withdrawal)
d. Depression with or without anxiety

B. Mild Head Injury

Fatigue, irritability, and physical discomfort are postconcussive sequelae of mild head injury that are often sufficient to produce dysphoric mood. This response may be compounded further by the patient's reaction to cognitive sequelae associated with diffuse axonal injury. Victims of mild head injury are often acutely aware of their attention problems and reduced information-processing capacity. Tasks that were once automatic now require effort and concentration, and the ability to perform or track multiple tasks simultaneously is severely limited, if not absent.

Adjustment reactions are common and may develop into clinical syndromes of depression and anxiety if not addressed early. Without proper education concerning the natural evolution of postconcussive sequelae, patients with mild head injury may quickly lose self-confidence, worry excessively about the long-term consequences of the injury, and become distressed by their own irritability and low frustration tolerance.

Other sources of stress that may contribute to dysphoric mood states include alteration of appearance from the injury; role changes within the family or in other interpersonal relationships in response to the injury; and frequent dealings with insurance companies, medical professionals, or lawyers. It is important to identify any and all potential stressors and psychological symptoms, because these may exacerbate cognitive symptoms and contribute to the persistence of cognitive complaints beyond physiological recovery from mild head injury.

VII. CONCLUSION

The neuropsychological sequelae of traumatic brain injury vary greatly with the nature of the trauma, location and severity of brain involvement, and extent of secondary effects. Deficits in attention, information processing, executive functions, new learning, and verbal retrieval are common following most head injuries, but they tend to be more subtle following mild head injury. Personality changes following head injury are also common and may reflect an organic process, a psychological reaction to the head injury, or a combination of both.

BIBLIOGRAPHY

Adams, R. D., Victor, M., & Ropper, A. H. (1997). *Principles of neurology.* New York: McGraw-Hill.

Anneegers, J., Grabow, J., Groover, R., Laws, E. J., Elveback, L., & Kurland, L. (1980). Seizures after head trauma: A population study. *Neurology, 30,* 683–689.

Binder, L. M. (1993). An abbreviated form of the Portland Digit Recognition Test. *Clinical Neuropsychologist, 7,* 104–107.

Binder, L. M., & Rattok, J. (1989). Assessment of the postconcussive syndrome after mild head trauma. In M. D. Lezak (Ed.), *Assessment of the behavioral consequences of head trauma* (pp. 37–48). New York: Alan R. Liss.

Bond, M. R. (1986). Neurobehavioral sequelae of closed head injury. In I. Grant & K. Adams (Eds.), *Neuropsychological assessment of neuropsychiatric disorders* (pp. 347—373). New York: Oxford University Press.

Cegalis, J. A., & Birdsall, W. (1995). *Paced Auditory Serial Attention Task.* Nashua, NH: ForThought.

Dikmen, S., McLean, A., & Temkin, N. (1986). Neuropsychological and psychosocial consequences of mild head injury. *Journal of Neurology, Neurosurgery, and Psychiatry, 49,* 1227–1232.

Goodman, J. C. (1994). Pathologic changes in mild head injury. *Seminars in Neurology, 14,* 19– 24.

Grafman, J., & Salazar, A. (1996). Traumatic brain injury. In B. S. Fogel, R. B. Schiffer, & S. M. Rao (Eds.), *Neuropsychiatry* (pp. 935–946). Baltimore: Williams & Wilkins.

Gronwall, D. M. A. (1977). The Paced Serial Addition Task: A measure of recovery from concussion. *Perceptual and Motor Skills, 44,* 367–373.

Hiscock, M., & Hiscock, C. K. (1989). Refining the forced-choice method for the detection of malingering. *Journal of Clinical and Experimental Neuropsychology, 11,* 967–974.

Jennett, B., & Teasdale, G. (1981). *Management of head injuries.* Philadelphia: F. A. Davis.

Kaplan, E., Fein, D., Morris, R., & Delis, D. C. (1991). *WAIS-R as a neuropsychological instrument.* San Antonio, TX: Psychological Corporation.

Kaplan, E. F., Goodglass, H., & Weintraub, S. (1983). *The Boston Naming Test* (2nd ed.). Philadelphia: Lea & Febinger.

Katayama, Y., Becker, D. P., Tamura, T., & Hovda, D. A. (1990). Massive increases in extracellular potassium and the indiscriminate release of glutamate following concussive brain injury. *Journal of Neurosurgery, 73,* 889–900.

Kraus, J. F., & Nourjah, P. (1989). The epidemiology of mild head injury. In H. S. Levin, H. M. Eisenberg, & A. L. Benton (Eds.), *Mild head injury* (pp. 8–22). New York: Oxford University Press.

Lees-Haley, P. R., & Brown, R. S. (1993). Neuropsychological complaint base rates of 170 personal injury claimants. *Archives of Clinical Neuropsychology, 8,* 203–209.

Levin, H. S., O'Donnell, V. M., & Grossman, R. G. (1979). The Galveston Orientation and Amnesia Test: A practical scale to assess cognition after head injury. *Journal of Nervous and Mental Disease, 167,* 675–684.

Lewis, R. F., & Rennick, P. M. (1979). *Manual for the Repeatable Cognitive-Perceptual-Motor Battery.* Clinton Township, MI: Ronald F. Lewis.

Lezak, M. D. (1995). *Neuropsychological assessment* (3rd ed.). New York: Oxford University Press.

Mild Traumatic Brain Injury Committee of the Head Injury Interdisciplinary Special Interest Group of the American Congress of Rehabilitation Medicine. (1993). Definition of mild traumatic brain injury. *Journal of Head Trauma Rehabilitation, 8,* 86–87.

Povlishock, J. T. (1993). Pathobiology of traumatically induced axonal injury in animals and man. *Annals of Emergency Medicine, 22,* 41–47.

Reitan, R. M., & Wolfson, D. (1985). *The Halstead-Reitan Neuropsychological Test Battery.* Tucson, AZ: Neuropsychology Press.

Rutherford, W. H. (1989). Postconcussion symptoms: Relationship to acute neurological indices, individual differences, and circumstances of injury. In H. S. Levin, H. M. Eisenberg, & A. L. Benton (Eds.), *Mild head injury* (pp. 217–228). New York: Oxford University Press.

Salazar, A., Jabbar, B., Vance, S., Grafman, J., Amin, D., & Dillon, J. (1985). Epilepsy after penetrating head injury. I: Clinical correlates. *Neurology, 35,* 1406–1414.

Stroop, J. R. (1935). Studies of interference in serial verbal reactions. *Journal of Experimental Psychology, 18,* 643–662.

Teasdale, G., & Jennett, B. (1974). Assessment of coma and impairment of consciousness: A practical scale. *Lancet, 2,* 81–84.

Trennery, M. R., Crosson, B., DeBoe, J., & Leber, W. R. (1990). *Visual Search and Attention Test.* Odessa, FL: Psychological Assessment Resources.

Youngjohn, J. R., Burrows, L., & Erdal, K. (1995). Brain damage or compensation neurosis? The controversial post-concussion syndrome. *The Clinical Neuropsychologist, 9,* 112–123.

CHAPTER 14

Alexander I. Tröster

Assessment of Movement and Demyelinating Disorders

Neuropsychologists are rarely asked to make differential diagnoses among movement and demyelinating disorders. Indeed, such an endeavor is beyond the scope of neuropsychology. At this time there is no "diagnostic" test (neuropsychological or otherwise) for many of the conditions outlined in this chapter. Many of the identified differences in neuropsychological profiles associated with different movement disorders are based on group studies. Such studies do not reveal the diagnostic sensitivity and specificity of neuropsychological test profiles. Consequently, it is advisable to report on the consistency of neuropsychological test results with particular conditions. Neuropsychologists are, however, asked to assist in differential diagnosis when there is a suspicion of a psychogenic movement disorder or, in individuals with dementia, to determine whether

Editors' Note. Dr. Tröster agreed to the difficult task of preparing a chapter that includes both demyelinating and movement disorders. These two disease types are considered together because their neuropsychological profiles overlap considerably. It is important to note, however, that the pathophysiology, clinical signs, and symptoms of movement and demyelinating disorders are distinct, and thus they are typically considered separately in textbooks of neurology. Although this chapter concentrates on the most common the dementia is associated with a movement or demyelinating disorder, depression, or some other neurological condition such as Alzheimer's disease. Referrals also are often made to obtain a baseline neuropsychological evaluation, enabling the physician to determine with repeat evaluation whether a dementia is evolving, if a particular drug treatment is associated with cognitive and behavioral change, or if an individual is likely to require assistance with activities of daily living. More recently, with the reemergence of neurosurgical treatments for movement disorders, neuropsychologists are increasingly being asked to determine possible cognitive and behavioral contraindications to surgical intervention and to document cognitive and behavioral changes as a result of such treatments (for a review, see Wilkinson & Tröster, in press).

I. MOVEMENT DISORDERS

A. Definitions and Description of the Disorders

1. DEFINITIONS

a. Abnormal movements

Extrapyramidal movement disorders (invariably affecting the basal ganglia) are of two broad types: **akinetic** (involving paucity of voluntary movement) and **hyperkinetic** (involving excessive, involuntary movements).

Terms pertaining to **paucity of movement** include the following:

a. **Akinesia:** loss or reduction of voluntary movement
b. **Hypokinesia:** slowing in the *initiation* of movements
c. **Bradykinesia:** slowing in the *execution* of movements

---

of these disorders, of necessity it is a bit longer and more comprehensive than would typically be expected in a handbook such as this one. Less frequently encountered conditions and syndromes whose neuropsychological sequelae are poorly described in the literature are mentioned only briefly and listed as potential differential diagnoses.

The author thanks Donald A. Eckard, MD, Department of Diagnostic Radiology, University of Kansas Medical Center, for provision of magnetic resonance images, and Julie A. Fields, Department of Neurology, University of Kansas Medical Center, for assistance with figure and table preparation.

Abnormalities involving **excessive movements** include the following:

a. **Tremor:** rhythmic, repetitive, oscillating movements of a body part. **Resting tremor** is one occurring at rest; **action (kinetic or intention)** tremor occurs during movement; **postural tremor** is observed when the affected body part is voluntarily held against gravity.

b. **Chorea** (choreiform movements): asynchronous, irregular movements that appear to proceed semipurposively from one body part to another.

c. **Ballismus:** an irregular, unilateral, choreiform movement, typically affecting an upper limb. The limb appears to move in a "flinging" fashion.

d. **Dystonia:** prolonged muscle contraction, often painful, causing abnormal posture, twisting, or repetitive movements.

e. **Tic:** repetitive, sudden, transient, and stereotyped movements, with a limited distribution. When prolonged, tics are described as dystonic.

f. **Athetosis:** peripheral dystonic movements that have the appearance of "writhing," typically iatrogenic in origin.

g. **Dyskinesia:** strictly refers to any involuntary movement; most often used to describe complex, choreiform, dystonic movements of iatrogenic origin. Not only seen after chronic neuroleptic treatment, dyskinesias can develop as a side effect of dopaminergic agonist treatment for parkinsonism.

h. **Myoclonus:** brief, repetitive, shocklike muscle contractions of central nervous system (CNS) origin, typically affecting the same muscles. It can be of cortical or subcortical origin. When of subcortical origin, myoclonic movement is generalized; when of cortical origin, it is typically focal or multifocal.

i. **Fasciculation:** visible as "twitches" beneath the skin; caused by random, repetitive contractions of groups of muscle fibers.

b. Parkinsonism

Parkinson's disease (PD) and parkinsonism are not synonymous. PD refers to a specific disease entity, whereas **parkinsonism** refers to a syndrome consisting of four motor signs: tremor, rigidity, bradykinesia, and postural abnormalities. This syndrome is seen in Parkinson's disease, but it can also be a manifestation of numerous other conditions (see Table 1), including neurodegenerative, vascular, metabolic, toxic, infectious, and even psychogenic disorders (Koller, Marjama, & Tröster, 1998; Koller & Megaffin, 1994).

Table 1. Conditions That Can Produce Parkinsonism

Type of condition	Condition or disorder
Structural	Hydrocephalus, chronic subdural hematoma, arteriovenous malformation, tumor
Vascular	Multiple infarcts, amyloid angiopathy, Binswanger's disease, basal ganglia infarct
Toxin-induced	Manganese, mercury, carbon monoxide, carbon disulfide, cyanide, 1-methyl-4-phenyl-1,2,3,6-tetrahydropiridine (MPTP)
Drug-induced	Lithium, neuroleptics
Infectious	Creutzfeldt-Jakob disease, viral encephalitis, syphilis, encephalitis lethargica (von Economo's disease), HIV, sarcoid, toxoplasmosis, cryptococcosis
Traumatic	Dementia pugilistica

(Continued)

Table 1. Conditions That Can Produce Parkinsonism *(Continued)*

Type of condition	Condition or disorder
Psychogenic	Factitious and somatoform disorders, malingering
Neurodegenerative	Parkinson's disease, olivopontocerebellar atrophy, Shy-Drager syndrome, progressive supranuclear palsy, striatonigral degeneration, corticobasal ganglionic degeneration, Parkinson-ALS-dementia complex of Guam, pallidoponto-nigral degeneration, dentato-rubro-pallido-luysian atrophy, Alzheimer's disease, diffuse Lewy body disease (also called Lewy body variant of Alzheimer's disease and Lewy body dementia), Huntington's disease, Pick's disease, Fahr's disease (familial, idiopathic basal ganglia calcification), multiple sclerosis, neuroacanthocytosis
Inherited metabolic	Wilson's disease, Gaucher's disease, Hallervorden-Spatz disease, GM_1 gangliosidosis

Note. Table from Parkinson's Disease and Parkinsonism, 1994, by W. C. Koller & B. B. Megaffin, in C. E. Coffey and J. L. Cummings (Eds.), *Textbook of Geriatric Neuropsychiatry.* Copyright 1994 by American Psychiatric Press. Adapted with permission.

2. DESCRIPTION OF DISORDERS AND EVOLUTION OF DISEASE STATES

a. Parkinson's disease

Age-adjusted prevalence estimates of PD in the United States range from 98 to 175 per 100,000 (Zhang & Romàn, 1993). PD accounts for about 75% of extrapyramidal movement disorders, and idiopathic PD accounts for approximately 75% of parkinsonism. All four signs of parkinsonism rarely emerge simultaneously, and typically PD has a unilateral onset. Indeed, some have suggested that PD might involve a long prodromal phase. This, coupled with the fact that PD can first present with nonmotor signs and symptoms, makes early diagnosis difficult. The diagnosis is typically not made until at least two of four parkinsonian symptoms are evident, and some clinicians do not make the diagnosis until there has been a clear progression of symptoms. No uniform set of diagnostic criteria exists. Diagnostic accuracy for PD (verified at autopsy) is approximately 75%.

Although PD most often becomes symptomatic during the sixth decade of life (see Wichmann, Vitek, & DeLong, 1995), juvenile and young-onset forms occur. Early in the course of PD, cognitive abnormalities (including deficits in conceptual reasoning, memory, attention, and visuospatial perception) are ascribed to a dysexecutive syndrome attributable to frontostriatal dysfunction. Dementia evolves only in a minority of patients, with the most commonly reported prevalence estimates falling into the 20%–40% range (Mohr, Mendis, & Grimes, 1995). The dementia, typically of the "subcortical" type, is characterized by predominant impairments in attention and executive functions, visuospatial disturbance, and memory. Language and praxis are typically relatively preserved.

b. Parkinson-plus syndromes

Perhaps the conditions from which it is most difficult to differentiate PD are of the class of disorders known as **parkinson-plus syndromes** (see Cohen & Freedman, 1995). Among parkinson-plus syndromes are **progressive supranuclear palsy** (PSP; also known as Steele-Richardson-Olszewski syndrome), the **multiple system atrophies** (olivopontocerebellar atrophy [OPCA]; striatonigral degeneration [SND]; Shy-Drager syndrome [SDS]), and, according to some authors, **corticobasal ganglionic degeneration** (CBGD; also referred to as corticobasal degeneration, corticonigral degeneration, or corticodentatonigral degeneration with neuronal achromasia).

Progressive supranuclear palsy (Steele-Richardson-Olszewski syndrome). No adequate population-based incidence and prevalence estimates exist for this syndrome. A recent study suggested a minimum prevalence of about 1.5 per 100,000 (Golbe, 1996). Unlike PD, symptoms typically are symmetrical at onset, resting tremor is minimal, and gait disturbance (postural imbalance) is an early prominent sign. Dysarthria may also appear earlier than in PD. Symptoms typically respond poorly to dopaminergic medications. Later combinations of signs of PSP are more characteristic of the disease: prominent vertical gaze palsy, disproportionate axial versus limb rigidity, prominence of gait disturbance, facial spasticity, and impairment of saccadic eye movements. Age at onset is narrower than in PD, with few cases (about 5%) having onset before age 50. The typical onset, as in PD, is in the sixth decade of life. Progression of the disease is more rapid than in PD, with immobility occurring a median of 6 years after diagnosis. Unfortunately, underdiagnosis of the condition often results in formal diagnosis about 3.5 years after symptom onset. No uniform set of diagnostic criteria exists, and in a recent study, investigators evaluating four sets of neurological criteria with autopsy-proven cases found reasonably good diagnostic specificity but poor sensitivity (Litvan et al., 1996).

Some have suggested cognition is unaffected in PSP and that overdiagnosis of dementia is attributable to patients' bradyphrenia, emotional changes, and visual dysfunction. There is no consensus concerning the prevalence of dementia in PSP, and in different patient series dementia was reported to occur in from 50% to 80% of cases. The dementia is of the subcortical type, with pronounced executive dysfunction. A good, recent review of cognitive changes in PSP has been provided by Grafman, Litvan, and Stark (1995).

Multiple system atrophies. This is a heterogeneous group of disorders (for a brief review, see Quinn & Wenning, 1995). **Olivopontocerebellar atrophy** is not a unitary disorder but refers to several inherited and sporadic disorders characterized by progressive ataxia and additional neurological signs. Typical prevalence estimates are in the range of 2 per 100,000, although some regional prevalence estimates are as high as 184 per 100,000. Age at onset for familial and sporadic forms of OPCA is the late 20s or early 30s and the late 40s or early 50s, respectively. Almost invariably, early signs involve cerebellar ataxia. Other signs are more variable, but if rigidity and dementia occur early, they are thought to remain dominant symptoms throughout the course of the disease. Cognitive impairments (and their existence) reported in the literature are highly heterogeneous. Some have described an early onset of dementia in OPCA; others have reported that dementia develops only in the middle or late stages of the diseases.

Striatonigral degeneration has not been studied extensively from a neuropsychological standpoint. The disease is sporadic and marked by bradykinesia and rigidity. Tremor is minimal, and symptoms fail to respond adequately to dopaminergic therapy.

Shy-Drager syndrome, like SND, responds poorly to dopaminergic therapy, and among motor signs, rigidity and bradykinesia predominate. SDS is distinguished by early dysautonomia (i.e., signs and symptoms of autonomic nervous system dysfunction such as orthostatic hypotension, constipation, impotence, and pupillary dysfunction).

Corticobasal ganglionic degeneration. CBGD has an insidious onset late in adulthood and is slowly progressive. Its prevalence and incidence have not been reported, and although several sets of diagnostic criteria have been formulated, none have been adequately validated. The initial presentation is typically asymmetrical; occasionally "alien limb" syndrome is evident, and both cortical and subcortical deficits (of which apraxia is a key cortical feature) are often present. The patient's most typical initial complaint involves clumsiness, stiffness, and jerkiness of one arm, and less frequently, difficulty walking due to clumsiness of one leg (Rinne, Lee, Thompson, & Marsden, 1994). The most common early movement problems are akinesia and rigidity. Dementia is thought to occur late in the disease (although this is debated), and to reveal both cortical and subcortical deficits.

c. Wilson's disease

A disorder of copper metabolism, Wilson's disease (WD) is inherited through an autosomal recessive gene on chromosome 13. The disease can become symptomatic between ages 5 and 50, although most cases present between 8 and 16 years of age. Prevalence is estimated at 3 per 100,000 (Pfeiffer, 1997). Presentation is highly variable but most often involves liver disease (more often in females) or neurological signs and symptoms (more often in males). Kayser-Fleischer (copper corneal) rings are not specific to WD and do not occur in all cases of WD. Neurological signs and symptoms most commonly include dysarthria and poor coordination, but patients can also have postural abnormalities, dystonia, chorea, and the full parkinsonian syndrome. Treatments aimed at restriction of copper intake and enhanced copper elimination are thought to be effective in reversing hepatic, renal, and cerebral dysfunction.

d. Huntington's disease

A disorder inherited in autosomal dominant manner, Huntington's disease (HD) symptoms typically emerge in the mid-30s to mid-40s. Initial manifestations of HD include personality change and adventitious movements, which are followed by the gradual emergence of chorea and cognitive impairment progressing to dementia. In the juvenile form (onset before age 20), resting tremor and rigidity may predominate. Prevalence is estimated at 5 to 10 per 100,000 (Marshall & Shoulson, 1997). The course of the disease spans 10 to 30 years, and death is usually attributable to complications (e.g., pneumonia). The characteristic subcortical dementia associated with HD has been well characterized elsewhere (Bondi, Salmon, & Kaszniak, 1996).

3. VARIANTS OF DISORDERS

Postencephalitic parkinsonism, drug (1-methyl-4-phynyl-1,2,3,6-tetrahydropiridine [MPTP]) induced parkinsonism, and Parkinson-dementia complex of Guam are rarely encountered. Cognitive deficits in MPTP-parkinsonism resemble those seen in PD (Stern & Langston, 1985).

4. NEUROPATHOLOGICAL CORRELATES

a. Parkinson's disease

Idiopathic PD is characterized by pigmented cell loss in the substantia nigra (particularly the ventrolateral aspect) and the presence of Lewy bodies in the substantia nigra, locus caeruleus, substantia innominata, and dorsal vagal nucleus. Dopamine is reduced in nigrostriatal system structures (putamen more than caudate) and projections to the frontal cortex and limbic system. There is loss of noradrenergic cells in the locus caeruleus, and serotonergic cell loss in the raphe and dorsal vagal nuclei. Nucleus basalis cell loss is also observed and is associated with cholinergic depletion.

b. Progressive supranuclear palsy

Four pathological findings are consistently evident in PSP: astrocytic gliosis, loss of nerve cells, presence of neurofibrillary tangles (NFTs), and granulovacuolar nerve cell degeneration. Unlike PD, PSP involves the entire substantia nigra. The NFTs are different from those observed in Alzheimer's disease. Other loci of pathology include the globus pallidus, subthalamic nucleus, dentate nucleus, red nucleus, periaqueductal gray, and pontine tegmentum. Cholinergic depletion is evident in the nucleus basalis and laterodorsal tegmental nucleus, but cortical cholinergic loss is mild. Dopamine is comparably reduced in the caudate and putamen, as well as in the substantia nigra.

c. Multiple system atrophies

Cell loss and gliosis are evident in the striatum (especially putamen), substantia nigra, inferior olives, pons, and cerebellum. Lewy bodies, except for incidental ones, are absent, but oligodendroglial cytoplasmic inclusions are widespread. Sporadic OPCA-associated lesions most often affect substantia nigra and striatum; less commonly, they affect locus caeruleus and dentate nucleus. There might be increased putaminal iron deposition in SND.

d. Corticobasal ganglionic degeneration

No accepted set of neuropathological criteria for CBGD diagnosis exists. Although "ballooned neurons" are almost always found in CBGD, they also occur in Pick's disease and other neurodegenerative conditions. In CBGD they are observed in cortex (most often in an asymmetrical, frontoparietal distribution) and substantia nigra. With greater variability, they are found among gray matter structures such as the subthalamic nucleus, globus pallidus, dentate nucleus, locus caeruleus, and lateral thalamus. Neuronal loss and gliosis are also evident in the structures outlined previously, and there is depigmentation of the substantia nigra.

e. Wilson's disease

In the hepatolenticular degeneration of WD, there is striking red pigmentation of the basal ganglia. Spongy degeneration and astrocytosis can be observed in the putamen and frontal cortex. Basal ganglia may show neuronal loss and axonal degeneration. Degenerative changes are less evident in dentate and substantia nigra.

f. Huntington's disease

Early changes are limited to subcortical structures, but at autopsy cortical and caudate atrophy are prominent. There is loss especially of the medium-sized spiny neurons and their gamma-aminobutyric acid (GABA-ergic) efferents in the caudate and putamen. The consequent atrophy of striatopallidal and striatonigral fiber bundles is thought to be responsible for the movement abnormalities in HD. Reactive gliosis is observed in affected areas.

B. Functional Neuroanatomic Correlates

Understanding of the neuroanatomic bases of motor and non-motor deficits in movement disorders requires knowledge of frontosubcortical neural circuitry (see review by Mega & Cummings, 1994). The frontal cortex and basal ganglia appear to be linked by five parallel but anatomically and functionally segregated circuits that share common structures (frontal cortex, striatum, globus pallidus, substantia nigra, subthalamic nucleus, and thalamus) and involve the same neurotransmitters. In addition, each circuit has direct and indirect connections between the striatum and the internal globus pallidus and substantia nigra. These circuits retain their relative anatomic positions within their shared neuroanatomic structures. For example, the dorsolateral circuit projects to the dorsolateral aspect of the caudate, from there to the lateral dorsomedial globus pallidus, and from there to the dorsomedial and ventral anterior thalamus.

Each of these circuits is a "closed" loop (i.e., circuits remain segregated), although each circuit has open components allowing it to communicate with other areas of the brain involved in similar functions. The five circuits are named according to their function or site of frontal origin: the **motor circuit** originating in the supplementary motor area; the **oculomotor circuit** originating in the frontal eye field; and the **lateral orbitofrontal, anterior cingulate,** and **dorsolateral prefrontal circuits.** The first two circuits are important in motor function, whereas the latter three circuits (Figure 1) are important in cognition and behavior.

Behavioral deficits associated with pathology of the three circuits have been outlined by Mega and Cummings (1994):

1. **Dorsolateral circuit:** poor organizational and memory search strategies, stimulus-bound behavior, impaired cognitive flexibility, dissociations in verbal and manual behavior

2. **Orbitofrontal circuit:** personality change, mood disorders, environmental dependency, and obsessive–compulsive behavior

3. **Anterior cingulate circuit:** impaired motivation and ineffective response inhibition

Figure 1. Simplified schematic of the three frontosubcortical circuits implicated in behavior and cognition. GABA = gamma (γ)-aminobutyric acid; D1 = dopamine acting on dopamine 1 subtype receptor; D2 = dopamine acting on dopamine 2 subtype receptor.

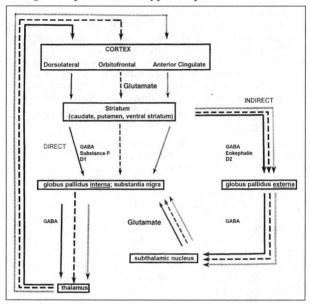

Several points bear emphasizing regarding these functional correlates of frontosubcortical circuit dysfunction. First, in neurodegenerative conditions, cognitive and behavioral syndromes are likely to be complex because multiple circuits are often disrupted. Second, although broad statements about anatomic–functional correlates can be advanced, details are less well worked out and are controversial. For example, there is little debate that patients with PD often demonstrate executive dysfunction (e.g., Taylor & Saint-Cyr, 1995). What remains debated is to what extent executive deficits account for other (e.g., memory) deficits (Tröster & Fields, 1995). Third, the fact that each circuit has open components allows for the possibility that cognitive dysfunction reflects disruption of afferent or efferent connections, or both, between the open component and another structure. For example, several of the cognitive and behavioral deficits observed in HD might be attributable to disconnection of the caudate from the limbic system.

C. Competing Diagnoses

Neuropsychologists are rarely asked to distinguish among movement disorders; neuropsychological tests lack the needed specificity. Rather, referral questions often center on whether a suspected dementia is associated with the movement disorder, Alzheimer's disease, or depression. Occasionally, referrals are for the purpose of confirming that a patient is experiencing delirium or that neuropsychological evaluation supports (or does not support) a diagnosis of psychogenic movement disorder.

1. PARKINSON'S DISEASE VERSUS ALZHEIMER'S DISEASE

Often this differential diagnosis is made easily: In typical PD and AD, the dementias conform to patterns of "subcortical" and "cortical" dysfunction, respectively (see Bondi, Salmon, & Kaszniak, 1996; Bondi & Tröster, 1997). The issue becomes more difficult when the patient presents with extrapyramidal signs and a mixture of cortical and subcortical cognitive dysfunction. It is possible, then, that the patient has one of the disorders in the spectrum of diffuse Lewy body diseases (see Olichney, Galasko, Corey-Bloom, & Thal, 1995) or corticobasal degeneration. Unfortunately, these conditions have only recently begun to receive the attention of neuropsychologists, and the characterization of cognitive deficits for these disorders (Table 2) should be considered highly preliminary.

Reviews of neuropsychological features of autopsy-confirmed and clinically diagnosed diffuse Lewy body disease (DLBD) (Salmon & Galasko, 1996; Salmon et al., 1996) indicate that there are probably subtle cognitive differences between cases of pure DLBD and cases demonstrating pathology of AD and DLBD (which constitute the majority of DLBD cases). In general, DLBD is associated with marked deficits in attentional, visuoperceptual, and constructional functions. Pure DLBD cognitive impairment resembles that of PD, whereas the cognitive profile in cases with DLBD and AD pathology resembles a superimposition of PD cognitive deficits on those of AD.

Cognitive deficits in corticobasal ganglionic degeneration have not been well characterized (see Massman, Kreiter, Jankovic, & Doody, 1996; Pillon et al., 1995). Two hallmarks are a pronounced, early apraxia and the alien hand sign, which

Table 2. Patterns of Cognitive Impairments in Movement Disorders and Alzheimer's Disease

Area of cognitive impairment	PD	PD + dementia	DLBD	CBGD	AD
Attention	0/-	-/—	—	-/—	-
Problem solving, conceptualization, and cognitive flexibility	-	—	-/—	—	-/-
Speech (e.g., dysarthria)	-	-	0/-	-	0
Language					
Visual confrontation naming	0/-	-	-/-	-	—
Letter fluency	0/-	-	-/-	-/-	-
Category fluency	-	-	-/-	?	-/-
Word knowledge	0/-	0/-	?	0	-
Anterograde memory					
Encoding	0/-	-	-	0/-	-/-
Storage	0	0/-	-	0/-	—
Retrieval	-	—	—	-/-	0/-
Proactive interference	0	-	0/-	?	—

(Continued)

Table 2. Patterns of Cognitive Impairments in (*Continued*)

Area of cognitive impairment	PD	PD + dementia	DLBD	CBGD	AD
Retrograde memory	0	-	?	0/-?	—
Praxis	0	0/-	-	—	-
Alien-hand sign	0	0	0	—	0
Visuoperceptual functions	-	-/—	—	0/-?	-
Visuoconstructional functions	0/-	-	—	?	-/—

Note. PD = Parkinson's disease; DLBD = diffuse Lewy body disease; CBGD = corticobasal ganglionic degeneration; AD = Alzheimer's disease; 0 = unimpaired; - = mild-to-moderate impairment; — = moderate-to-severe impairment; ? = unknown or to-be-confirmed.

typically develops within 1–2 years of disease onset. Cognitive impairment patterns reflect asymmetrical cortical and subcortical pathology.

2. DEMENTIA VERSUS DEPRESSIVE DEMENTIA IN PARKINSON'S DISEASE

Depression is common in PD, with lifetime prevalence estimated to be about 40%. Depression is a risk factor not only for PD itself, but also for the evolution of dementia in PD (Fields, Norman, Straits-Tröster, & Tröster, in press). Recent research has suggested that depression probably affects the severity rather than the pattern of cognitive impairment in PD (Tröster, Stalp, Paolo, Fields, & Koller, 1995). Given the similar pattern of cognitive impairment in depressed and nondepressed patients with PD, it is difficult to determine from a single assessment the extent to which a dementia in a patient with PD and depression reflects PD as opposed to depression. The implication, however, is important. Cognitive impairment due to depression is likely to resolve with successful treatment of the depression, whereas the cognitive impairment of PD does not resolve. Thus, I recommend that etiologic determination be deferred until adequate treatment for depression has been undertaken. Repeat assessment is then likely to reveal the cause of the cognitive impairment in the patient with PD and depression.

3. PSYCHOGENIC MOVEMENT DISORDERS

Neuropsychological evaluation cannot adequately differentiate *psychogenic* from *organic* movement disorders. Even neurological criteria lack specificity, and as many as 6%–30% of patients diagnosed with a psychogenic disorder are ultimately found to have an organic movement disorder. Misdiagnosis of an organic as a psychogenic movement disorder is more likely than the converse. A neuropsychological profile consistent with PD, for example, is more helpful in directing one *away* from a psychogenic diagnosis than a normal evaluation is in directing one *to* a psychogenic diagnosis. Use of personality inventories (e.g., Minnesota Multiphasic Personality Inventory [MMPI] or MMPI-II) is fraught with difficulty, because both organic and psychogenic movement disorders are likely to show "1-3" elevations. In other words, the *Hypochondriasis* and *Hysteria* scales, which contain items dealing with somatic concerns, physical competence, denial of physical health, and denial of emotional problems, might be elevated because patients with organic movement disorders actually do experience many of the symptoms addressed by the scales' items. Proposed "correction" factors have not been evaluated in movement disorders. If a psychogenic movement disorder is suspected, it is imperative that the nature of the psychological condition be identified (e.g., factitious, somatoform, or malingering).

D. Medical History and Laboratory Data

The history should always be scrutinized for recreational and medicinal drug use. Because several movement disorders are heritable, family history should always be investigated. In young individuals with movement abnormalities (e.g., chorea), especially when a recreational intravenous drug use history is present, questioning about HIV risk factors or diagnosis is indicated. With regard to laboratory data, the following information is relevant:

1. **Parkinson's disease:** Laboratory tests are typically not used in the diagnosis of PD. If an infectious condition is suspected as a cause of parkinsonism, cerebrospinal fluid (CSF) studies are obtained. Laboratory tests are more likely to be done in juvenile-onset or young-onset parkinsonism to rule out metabolic, toxic, and inherited conditions. In cases with suspected toxic etiology, urine is typically screened for heavy metals (e.g., mercury, manganese) and recreational drugs (e.g., cocaine, narcotics). For metabolic conditions, urinalysis can be used to screen for dolichols, amino acids, oligosaccharides, and organic acids.

2. **Progressive supranuclear palsy:** Biochemistry, urinalysis, and hematology are normal. CSF findings are not specific.

3. **Multiple system atrophies:** In autosomal dominant OPCA, the genotype can be determined by genetic linkage and polymerase chain reaction (PCR) methods. Electromyography and nerve conduction velocity studies are typically used when OPCA is associated with amyotrophy and lower motor neuron involvement.

Autonomic dysfunction tests are used in SDS, possibly including blood pressure response to standing up or head tilt, heart rate response to standing, sphincter electromyography, and gastrointestinal swallow and emptying studies. Laboratory tests are generally not helpful in the diagnosis of SND.

4. **Corticobasal ganglionic degeneration:** Biochemistry, hematology, and urinalysis are normal.

5. **Wilson's disease:** Family history should be investigated. Prior liver disease and gastrointestinal symptoms may be noted in the history. Urinalysis for copper (typically increased

to 100–1,000 μg per 24-hour sample), slit-lamp examination for Kayser-Fleischer rings, and measurement of copper content of a liver biopsy specimen (the most important in diagnosis) are helpful.

6. **Huntington's disease:** DNA analysis for this disease is possible, and family history of the disorder must be present. Biochemistry, urinalysis, and hematology are all normal.

E. EEG and Neuroimaging Correlates

Electroencephalographic (EEG) studies in movement disorders are generally unhelpful. Abnormal findings are nonspecific. EEG is helpful if Creutzfeldt-Jakob's disease is suspected as a cause of parkinsonism: It shows characteristic generalized slowing and pseudoperiodic sharp wave activity.

Neuroimaging studies vary in their helpfulness. Of course, if hydrocephalus, tumors, hematoma, infarcts, basal ganglia calcification, or infections are suspected as causing parkinsonism, computed tomography (CT) or magnetic resonance imaging (MRI) is helpful in demonstrating this. Imaging studies are also recommended when parkinsonism is accompanied by rapid cognitive deterioration. In PD, PSP, and HD, both MRI and CT studies are normal early in the course. MRI reveals narrowing of the high signal region between substantia nigra and the red nucleus in some patients with PD. PSP, later in the disease, is likely to be associated with increased signal in the periaqueductal region, dilation of the cerebral aqueduct, and reduction of midbrain diameter. In intermediate-to-advanced HD, a reduction in atrophy of the caudate and putamen, and decreased pallidal signal, might be evident on T1-weighted MRI. Putaminal signal loss on MRI might indicate that SND is more likely than PD. Cerebellar and brain-stem atrophy are observed in multiple systems atrophies (MSA) but not PD. MRI is often helpful in Wilson's disease: T2-weighted MRI may reveal the characteristic "face of the giant panda" sign (i.e., hypointensity of superior colliculus, preserved signal from lateral substantia nigra pars reticulata, and high signal intensity in the tegmentum with exception of the red nucleus). MRI is also likely to reveal cerebral atrophy, ventricular dilation, and lenticular signal hyperintensity.

Numerous functional imaging studies using positron emission tomography (PET) or single photon emission computed tomography (SPECT) have been carried out, but their clinical usefulness remains unclear. PET-visualized glucose hypometabolism in the frontal and striatal regions is more likely to be observed early in SND and PSP than in PD. Unilateral temporoparieto-occipital hypometabolism is observed on PET in CBGD, but this can also be seen in cases of asymmetrical AD. The diffuse cortical and striatal hypometabolism seen on PET in HD is likely to be nonspecific.

F. Areas of Emphasis Within the Neuropsychological Evaluation

Clinicians who administer lengthy, fixed batteries of tests need to be particularly cognizant of fatigue effects common in PD as well as of the fluctuation of symptoms (on–off phenomenon) and iatrogenic dyskinesias to which some PD patients are prone. Ideally, PD patients should be evaluated during the "on" phase (but in the absence of dyskinesias), permitting them to perform optimally. A lengthy neuropsychological test battery administered during both on and off phases is likely to yield a pattern of strengths and weaknesses that is difficult to interpret meaningfully.

Regardless of the type of movement disorder, the neuropsychological profile often resembles that of frontosubcortical dysfunction, and if dementia is present, the profile is expected to conform to one associated with "subcortical" dementias (for reviews, see Bondi & Tröster, 1997; McPherson & Cummings, 1996). Because most of the movement disorders discussed in this chapter are associated with progressive cognitive dysfunction, it is important to obtain estimates of premorbid functioning. Finally, although a cognitive screening examination might not yield useful information early in the course of these diseases, it is still advisable to obtain a baseline on a screening measure; this will facilitate monitoring of cognitive function once the patient can no longer cooperate with a lengthy neuropsychological test battery.

Because many movement disorders are associated with a "frontosubcortical" cognitive dysfunction pattern, emphasis is placed on the evaluation of attention and executive functions (e.g., conceptual flexibility, abstraction, planning, monitoring of behavior). Because visuoperceptual–spatial dysfunction is often observed early in PD and HD, these functions are also thoroughly evaluated. Priority is given to memory tests that permit differentiation of recall and recognition deficits. Language tests sensitive to word search inefficiency (e.g., verbal fluency, visual confrontation naming) are given more emphasis than repetition and comprehension tests. Because mood disturbance is common, assessment of depression and anxiety is imperative.

G. Neuropsychological Measures Helpful in Differential Diagnosis

Mohr, Mendis, and Grimes (1995) listed tests commonly used in the evaluation of cognition in parkinsonian disorders, chosen on the basis of their review of 50 articles published between 1983 and 1993. Table 3 contains a list of some of the tests listed by Mohr et al. and by Raskin, Borod, and Tweedy (1990), along with tests that I have found helpful in evaluating movement disorders. This listing should not be viewed as prescriptive or exhaustive; rather, test selection must be made on the basis of the referral question and the patient's ability to cooperate with the tests.

Although these measures are less likely to be helpful in differential diagnosis among movement disorders, several measures are helpful in differentiating between PD with dementia and HD, on the one hand, and CBGD and AD, on the other hand. In particular, measures of language (fluency and visual confrontation naming), praxis, and memory are helpful in this regard. It is emphasized that the sensitivity and specificity of different patterns of performance among these patient groups remain to be empirically demonstrated.

With respect to verbal fluency, single-letter (e.g., the Controlled Oral Word Association Test; COWAT) and semantic category fluency (e.g., the Animal Naming Test from the Boston Diagnostic Aphasia Examination) tasks are helpful. Patients with movement disorders are likely to perform particularly poorly on letter fluency tasks, whereas patients with AD perform extremely poorly on tasks of semantic and letter fluency. Patients with PD have only mild if any difficulty with visual confrontation naming (e.g., on the Boston Naming Test; BNT). Although visual confrontation naming deteriorates as dementia evolves in patients with PD, the impairment is more severe in AD. Normative data for fluency and naming tests are still being published for the elderly. Norms from Spreen and Strauss (1991, 1998) are helpful. The publications by Ivnik et al. (1996) of age-corrected standard scores for individuals 55 years and older, for a host of tests including the BNT and COWAT, are likely to facilitate greatly interpretation of scores on these tests. Normative data for the BNT for individuals up to 88 years old were published by Tombaugh and Hubley (1997). Tombaugh, Kozak, and Rees (in press) have also provided noramtive data up to age 95 years for two verbal fluency tasks (FAS and animal naming). These scores can be further corrected for education using provided formulas.

Table 3. Tests Frequently Used or Recommended in the Evaluation of Movement Disorders

Type of test	Specific test
Estimate of premorbid function	North American Adult Reading Test (except if patient has a marked dysarthria), Barona Demographic Equations
General cognitive functioning	Raven's Progressive Matrices, Wechsler Adult Intelligence Scale–Revised (WAIS-R Ward 7 subtest, short form, except in patients with marked motor dysfunction), Mattis Dementia Rating Scale
Language	Controlled Oral Word Association Test, Boston Diagnostic Aphasia Examination's Animal Naming and Boston Naming Tests
Attention and executive functions	Stroop Color and Word Interference Test, Brief Test of Attention, Wechsler Memory Scale–Revised (WMS-R): Digit and Visual Memory Span subtests, Wisconsin Card Sorting Test, Cognitive Estimation Test, WAIS-R: Similarities and Comprehension subtests
Memory	Benton Visual Retention Test, WMS-R: Logical Memory I & II subtests, Rey-Osterreith Complex Figure Test (not for patients with notable motor impairment), Rey Auditory Verbal Learning Test, California Verbal Learning Test (not for patients with less than 12

	years of formal education), Kaufman Adolescent & Adult Intelligence Test: Famous Faces subtest
Motor	Finger Tapping, Grooved Pegboard (both are used only in patients with mild movement disorder)
Visuoperceptual–spatial	Benton Judgment of Line Orientation, Money Map Test, Benton Right-Left Orientation, Benton Facial Recognition Test, Benton Visual Discrimination Test, State–Trait Anxiety Inventory
Mood	Profile of Mood States, Beck Depression Inventory, Zung Depression Index
Quality of life	Sickness Impact Profile, Parkinson's Disease Questionnaire

Sources: Mohr, Mendis, and Grimes (1995) and Raskin, Borod, and Tweedy (1990).

On memory tests such as the Wechsler Memory Scale–Revised (WMS-R) Logical Memory and Visual Reproduction subtests, the patient with AD is likely to demonstrate much more rapid rates of forgetting over the 30-minute delay than is the patient with a movement disorder (Tröster et al., 1993). Helpful norms (standard scores), stratified by age and education, and based on the WMS-R standardization sample, have been provided for forgetting rates (percentage retained) by Ledbetter and Prifitera (1994). For individuals older than 74, the norms provided by Ivnik et al. (1992b) are recommended. On the Visual Reproduction subtest, at least in the early stages of dementia, individuals with AD are far more likely to commit intrusion errors than are persons with HD (Jacobs, Salmon, Tröster, & Butters, 1990). Patients with PD are also less likely than those with AD to commit intrusion errors. When comparing the difference between the Attention/Concentration Index (ACI) and the General Memory Index (GMI), the difference is likely to be greater in AD (at least, as a group) than in HD, with the GMI much lower than the ACI (Tröster, Jacobs, Butters, Cullum, & Salmon, 1989). Norms for the WMS-R have been extended above age 74 years by Ivnik et al. (1992b).

The third edition of the Wechsler Memory Scale (WMS-III) was recently published. The technical manual for the test (The Psychological Corporation, 1997) describes performance patterns for small samples of HD ($n = 15$) and PD ($n = 10$) and in AD ($n = 35$). These data suggest that the test will likely be useful in distinguishing among the memory impairments of patients with different neurodegenerative diseases, but confirmatory research with much larger samples is still required. There is little doubt, however, that the extension of norms to age 89 years in the WMS-III will make this test more useful than its predecessors in assessing memory in elderly individuals.

Subgroups of patients with PD demonstrating patterns of cortical and subcortical dementia on the California Verbal Learning Test (CVLT) likely exist (Filoteo et al., 1997), but those with PD without dementia are likely to demonstrate only mild, if any, impairment on recall and to perform fairly normally on recognition (Levin & Katzen, 1995). The patient with AD is likely to demonstrate equally impaired recall and recognition, and to make many intrusion and perseveration errors. Norms for the CVLT have been extended to the elderly by Paolo, Tröster, and Ryan (1997). Clinicians using the Rey Auditory Verbal Learning Test (AVLT) will find norms for the elderly provided by Ivnik et al. (1992a) to be helpful. Given the variety of means by which recognition is tested in the AVLT, clinicians wishing to use the Ivnik et al. (1992a) norms should be sure that they evaluate recognition in a manner identical to that used by Ivnik et al. A wide variety of norms (including those for alternate forms and foreign language versions of the AVLT) have been summarized by Schmidt (1996).

In terms of apraxia, patients with PD with or without dementia are likely to perform normally. Patients with AD and CBGD both show impairments, but those with CBGD do so early in the disease. A useful test for screening is the apraxia test from the Western Aphasia Battery.

Clinicians often seek a Wisconsin Card Sorting Test (WCST) short form for administration to individuals with movement disorders or dementia. Two short forms have been found to be sensitive to AD, HD, and PD with and without dementia: Nelson's (1976) short form (e.g., Paulsen et al., 1995) and a version employing traditional administration and scoring methods but using only 64 cards (Paolo, Axelrod, Tröster, Blackwell, and Koller, 1996).

Among cognitive screening examinations, the Dementia Rating Scale (DRS; Mattis, 1988) can be helpful because performance patterns of AD, HD, and PD have been characterized on this test. Compared with patients with AD, patients with HD perform significantly worse on the Initiation/Perseveration subtest; and patients with PD perform worse on the Construction subtest. In contrast, patients with AD perform significantly worse on the Memory subtest than do patients with HD or PD (Paolo, Tröster, Glatt, Hubble, & Koller, 1995; Salmon, Kwo-on-Yuen, Heindel, Butters, & Thal, 1989). When patients with PD are depressed, their performance deteriorates, especially on the Initiation/Perseveration and Memory subtests (Norman, Tröster, Fields, & Brooks, 1997).

For estimation of premorbid IQ, Ivnik, Malec, Smith, Tangalos, and Petersen (1996) have provided norms for the elderly on an oral reading test. Wechsler Adult Intelligence Scale–Revised (WAIS-R) norms for individuals older than 74 years are provided by Ivnik et al. (1992) and by Ryan, Paolo, and Brungardt (1990). The new WAIS-III has norms to age 89 years.

H. Psychiatric Morbidity in Movement Disorders

Depression is common among individuals with HD and PD. In HD, it is estimated that 30% of individuals experience major depressive episodes, 5% have dysthymia, and many more experience episodes of dysphoria (Cummings, 1995). Suicide prevalence is considerably greater in patients with HD than in the general population (approximately a four- to sixfold increase) and greater than in those with other neurological disorders that are frequently accompanied by depression. Individuals with HD and depression, particularly those older than 50, appear to be especially vulnerable. Other psychiatric disorders in HD include personality changes, which frequently are evident many years before diagnosis. Such changes might include irritability, lability, social disinhibition, and apathy. HD patients with intermittent explosive disorder and antisocial personality disorder appear to be more prone to aggressive outbursts. Estimates of psychosis range from 5% to 25%. The psychosis often resembles that observed in schizophrenia.

Estimates of the prevalence of depression in PD vary greatly, ranging between 7% and 90%. The preponderance of estimates indicates that about 30%–40% of individuals with PD experience depression. Half of this number of patients meet criteria for major depression, and the other half for dysthymia. Anxiety symptoms are a prominent feature among PD patients with depression. Diagnosis of depression in PD is difficult, given that symptoms such as fatigue, psychomotor slowing, and appetite changes occur in PD without depression. Although the Beck Depression Inventory has been shown empirically to be a valid measure of depression in PD, it is a good idea to interview the patient in detail about the nature and evolution of self-reported symptoms.

Psychosis characterized by paranoid delusions, hallucinations, and confusion is estimated to occur in 20%–30% of patients. Psychosis often relates to treatment with dopaminomimetics. Although anticholinergics on their own rarely produce acute confusional states, elderly patients with PD are particularly vulnerable to acute confusional states when treated with a combination of anticholinergics and dopaminomimetics.

II. DEMYELINATING DISORDERS

A. Definitions and Description of Disorders

1. DESCRIPTION OF DISORDERS AND EVOLUTION OF DISEASE STATES

Demyelinating conditions include **multiple sclerosis** (MS), **concentric sclerosis** (or **Baló's disease**, a variant of MS characterized by rings of demyelination in cerebral white matter), **Schilder's disease** (a variant of MS involving diffuse sclerosis characterized by a monophasic course, affecting younger patients), **Devic's disease** (a variant of MS characterized by a single spinal, typically cervical, demyelinating lesion, accompanied by signs of demyelination in the optic pathway), **central pontine myelinolysis**, and **Marchiafava-Bignami disease** (which involves primary degeneration of the corpus callosum). Other, very rare conditions include **acute disseminated encephalomyelitis** (usually occurring in relation to acute hemorrhagic leucoencephalitis) and **acute hemorrhagic leucoencephalitis**, which is characterized by sudden onset of severe neurological disturbance, rapid progression, and frequently death. Multiple sclerosis is by far the most common among these conditions, and the only condition that has been adequately studied from a neuropsychological perspective. Consequently, this review focuses on MS. Readers interested in case reports of the neuropsychological aspects of Marchiafava-Bignami disease are referred to an article by Kalckreuth, Zimmermann, Preilowski, and Wallesch (1994).

The incidence and prevalence of MS vary geographically, with few cases near the equator and larger numbers of cases in northern and southern latitudes (ranging approximately from 60 to 300 per 100,000). Although there are estimated to be between 250,000 and 350,000 persons with MS in the United States, residents north of latitude 40° N. are about 3 times as likely to have MS as are residents of southern regions of the United States. The disease is about twice as likely to affect women as men and has its onset typically in the 30s (Beatty, 1996).

Initial symptoms vary greatly but most often include one or more of the following: sensory disturbances, weakness, gait and balance disturbance, dysarthria, and, extremely rarely, cognitive changes. After the first episode of symptoms, complete remission typically ensues. Subsequent episodes are unpredictable, occurring weeks to years later, and symptoms associated with them remit less completely or not at all. Relapses themselves may last days to weeks or, more rarely, hours or months. Typically, MS runs its course over 1 or more decades; rarely does death from MS-related complications ensue within months of disease onset.

Previously, MS was classified into two major disease-course types: the relapsing–remitting and chronic progressive types. A newer classification scheme is outlined in Table 4. There is no diagnostic sign or test for MS. Ultimately, the diagnosis is made on the basis of clinical judgment and a variety of test results. Approximately 45%–65% of persons with MS experience cognitive impairment, but only 20%–30% experience cognitive impairment severe and extensive enough to qualify for the

Table 4. Taxonomy of Multiple Sclerosis Disease Courses

Type	Disease Course
Benign sensory	One to two lifetime episodes consisting mainly of sensory symptoms
Benign relapsing–remitting	Periodic relapses followed by almost complete recovery
Progressive relapsing–remitting	Periodic relapses followed by incomplete recovery
Chronic progressive	Slow, steady deterioration without substantial recovery
Acute progressive	Rapid deterioration (often leading to death)

Note. Table adapted from Multiple Sclerosis, by W. W. Beatty, in R. L. Adams, O. A. Parsons, J. L. Culbertson, and S. J. Nixon (Eds.), *Neuropsychology for Clinical Practice: Etiology, Assessment, and Treatment of Common Neurological Disorders.* Copyright 1996 by the American Psychological Association. Adapted with permission.

diagnosis of dementia. Dementia in MS is characterized by a subcortical dementia pattern of cognitive impairments, at least regarding groups of patients (Rao, 1995). As Beatty (1996) pointed out, however, there is considerable heterogeneity among individuals' cognitive impairments, and only 10%–15% of persons with MS might exhibit all of the cognitive deficits associated with "subcortical dementia."

2. NEUROPATHOLOGICAL CORRELATES

Demyelination occurs in the form of plaques, which appear as ill-defined, pale, pink–yellow lesions in the unfixed brain. Myelin is broken down within the plaque, and this phagocytosis is accompanied by astrocytosis. At autopsy, plaques are most often seen in the corpus callosum, in the temporal and occipital lobes, and around the lateral ventricles. Plaques are also found in white matter regions of thalamus, hypothalamus, and basal ganglia, as well as in the brain stem and spinal cord.

B. Functional Neuroanatomic Correlates

Because lesion size and distribution are highly variable in MS, there is no one pattern of cognitive dysfunction that might be considered "typical." Early in the course of MS (typically, in suspected but unconfirmed MS), neurobehavioral deficits might be a manifestation of a single lesion (and cognitive deficits depend on the lesion's location). Early in confirmed MS, the neurobehavioral deficit pattern is often consistent with multifocal lesions. Deficits consistent with diffuse pathology (e.g., a "subcortical dementia") typically develop later in the disease, although such a pattern of deficits may be present early. Conversely, a patient who has had MS for some time might be quite intact cognitively. It should be noted that disease type (course) and disease duration are not good predictors of cognitive deficits in patients. Rather, cognitive deficits tend to be proportional to MRI-visualized total lesion load and to cortical and callosal atrophy.

C. Competing Diagnoses

Competing neurological diagnoses include the variants of MS, acute disseminated encephalomyelitis, and leukoencephalitis, in which neuropsychology is not helpful given the lack of empirical literature. Sometimes the most difficult differential diagnosis is a conversion reaction, given the often strange nature and course of symptoms in MS. The MMPI is generally not helpful in making this differential diagnosis because Scales 1, 3, and 8 are elevated (and to a lesser extent, Scale 2) owing to endorsement of "true" neurological symptoms. Even correction attempts have not been very useful, and experimental MMPI scales designed to separate patients with "organic" from those with "pseudoneurological" conditions have poor sensitivity and specificity in MS (ranging approximately from 40% to 60%).

D. Medical History and Laboratory Data

Medical history is typically noncontributory. In the patient with isolated "visual" symptoms, it is wise to inquire about recent infections or vaccinations. A history of systemic disease is helpful in differentiating MS from lupus erythematosus. No test is diagnostic of MS in itself, and multiple, corroborating laboratory data need to be carefully interpreted. Presence of abnormal oligoclonal bands in the CSF and abnormal immunoglobulin (IgG) synthesis rates are most helpful for making the diagnosis. During the active phase of the disease, CSF examination shows evidence of an inflammatory reaction (increased number of lymphocytes and macrophages) and an elevated protein level.

E. EEG and Neuroimaging Correlates

Nonspecific MRI findings characteristically seen in MS include white matter lesions that are larger than 6 mm in diameter, occur below the tentorium, and occur close to the ventricles in a poorly demarcated pattern. It is estimated that 80% of patients with MS (excluding those with monosymptomatic disease) have abnormal results on MRI (Rolak, 1996). Figures 2 and 3 illustrate, respectively, typical and atypical demyelination patterns in MS.

Evoked potential studies have lower sensitivity than MRI and CSF studies. Abnormalities on these studies are seen in 20%–80% of patients, and visual and somatosensory evoked potential studies are helpful in confirming the neural basis of vague symptoms. Evoked potential studies serve no useful diagnostic purpose in the patient with known optic neuritis or spinal cord lesions (Rolak, 1996).

F. Areas of Emphasis Within the Neuropsychological Evaluation

Because MS is characterized by heterogeneous cognitive findings, a test battery sampling multiple areas of cognitive functions is helpful. The battery should be kept relatively brief (2–3 hours) given the fatigability of individuals with MS. Memory is the domain of cognition most often affected in MS, so that a battery of tests examining working memory, immediate and delayed recall, and recognition should always be included. To evaluate the potential contribution of attentional and executive impairments to memory dysfunction, card-sorting tasks such as the WCST and tests of selective attention such as the Brief Test of Attention are helpful. Digit span is often unimpaired. Visuoperceptual–spatial test results, although often abnormal, are difficult to interpret, and such tests are unlikely to be helpful in the patient with double vision or optic neuritis. Because depression and anxiety are relatively common in MS, an assessment of mood state is useful to include.

Measures of motor speed and intelligence are probably most helpful early in the disease to establish a baseline. Dis-

Figure 2. A T-2-weighted magnetic resonance imaging (MRI) scan (axial section) from a 38-year-old male presenting with symptoms of optic neuritis. Several areas of increased signal intensity in the periventricular white matter, typical of multiple sclerosis, are visible.

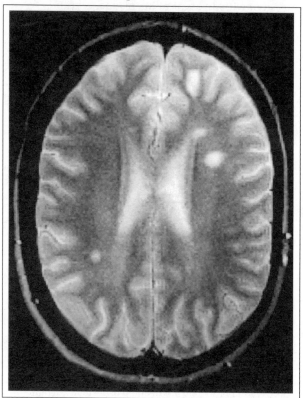

Figure 3. A T-1-weighted, post-contrast (gadolinium DTPA) MRI scan (coronal section) from a 35-year-old female presenting with complaints of left-sided numbness. A peripherally enhancing lesion, which at biopsy was found to represent an area of demyelination consistent with an atypical MS plaque, is visible

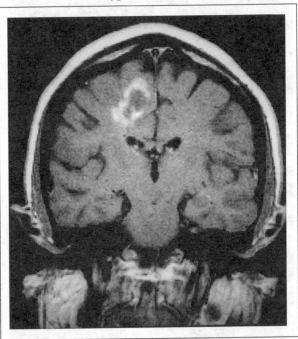

crepancies between Verbal and Performance IQs (the latter being lower) are of little value because interpretation of the finding is complicated by motor and sensory deficits commonly observed in MS. Language is typically intact (although letter and semantic fluency, and less often visual confrontation naming, can be impaired in MS secondary to bradyphrenia and executive deficits). Brief cognitive screening instruments have generally been shown to lack sensitivity, and their use is not advocated. Instead, Beatty (1996) recommended the brief screening battery proposed by Rao, Leo, Bernardin, and Unverzagt (1991), which takes 20 minutes to administer and includes the COWAT, the PASAT, the 7/24 Spatial Recall Test, and the Selective Reminding Test.

G. Neuropsychological Measures Helpful in Differential Diagnosis

Differential diagnosis is rarely requested in cases of MS. Rather, characterization of cognitive deficits and their potential impact on social and occupational functioning, as well as the assessment of change over time, is a common reason for neuropsychological referral. One may select from among the many tests available for assessing movement disorders (see Table 3) depending on the referral question, the patient's sensory and motor limitations, and his or her level of fatigue and ability to cooperate.

Tests of learning and memory often reveal poor recall and better recognition. Evidence of encoding deficiencies is equivocal, although encoding is frequently normal. Sensitivity to proactive interference is typically normal. Remote memory might be affected; if so, patients perform better on recognition than free recall tasks of remote memory (Beatty, 1996).

Although speech abnormalities such as dysarthria and hypophonia are observed often in MS, aphasia is not. Similarly, alexia, agraphia, and apraxia are extremely rare (Mahler, 1992). On attention tasks such as the PASAT and the oral version of the Symbol Digit Modalities Test, MS patients are often impaired. Visuoperceptual–spatial task impairments that might be observed on the Hooper Visual Organization Test, the Benton Facial Recognition Test, and the Benton Judgment of Line Orientation Test are difficult to interpret, and data obtained from visuoconstructional measures are even more difficult to interpret.

H. Psychiatric Morbidity in Multiple Sclerosis

Although symptoms of anxiety and depression are common among patients with MS, a careful interview is needed to clarify whether the symptoms reflect a mood disturbance or a somatic manifestation of MS. A recent survey indicated that patients with MS had approximately a 50% lifetime risk for depression (Sadovnick et al., 1996). One group reported a suicide rate 7.5 times higher in patients with MS than in the general population (Sadovnick, Eisen, Paty, & Ebers, 1991). It is interesting that the relationship between depression and greater cognitive impairment typically observed in PD has not been reported in MS. Only very weak relationships have been reported between depression and neuropsychological test performance. Psychosis is rare. Bertween 10% and 25% of patients experience euphoria during the course of the disease.

III. CONCLUSION

This chapter reviewed the epidemiology, phenomenology, and neuropathology of the most common movement and demyelinating disorders. The utility of various diagnostic tests (including laboratory and radiologic studies) was reviewed. Typical cognitive and behavioral impairment patterns were outlined, and tests for the evaluation of cognition and behavior were suggested. Neuropsychological evaluation is of importance especially in assisting with the differential diagnosis of dementia in the person with a movement or demyelinating disorder. Increasing importance is being attached to the neuropsychological evaluation of persons with movement disorders who seek stereotactic and functional neurosurgical treatment. Neuropsychology is likely to find increased application in evaluating outcomes of medical and surgical treatments for movement and demyelinating disorders. A future goal for neuropsychology is to translate assessment information into a form useful for the rehabilitation specialist and to document empirically the value of neuropsychological evaluation and intervention.

BIBLIOGRAPHY

Beatty, W. W. (1996). Multiple sclerosis. In R. L. Adams, O. A. Parsons, J. L. Culbertson, & S. J. Nixon (Eds.), *Neuropsychology for clinical practice: Etiology, assessment, and treatment of common neurological disorders* (pp. 225–242). Washington, DC: American Psychological Association.

Bondi, M. W., Salmon, D. P., & Kaszniak, A. W. (1996). The neuropsychology of dementia. In I. Grant & K. M. Adams (Eds.), *Neuropsychological assessment of neuropsychiatric disorders* (2nd ed., pp. 164–199). New York: Oxford University Press.

Bondi, M. W., & Tröster, A. I. (1997). Parkinson's disease: Neurobehavioral consequences of basal ganglia dysfunction. In

P. D. Nussbaum (Ed.), *Handbook of neuropsychology and aging* (pp. 216–245). New York: Plenum Press.

Cohen, S., & Freedman, M. (1995). Cognitive and behavioral changes in the parkinson-plus syndromes. In W. J. Weiner & A. E. Lang (Eds.), *Advances in neurology: Vol. 65. Behavioral neurology of movement disorders* (pp.139–157). New York: Raven Press.

Cummings, J. L. (1995). Behavioral and psychiatric symptoms associated with Huntington's disease. In W. J. Weiner & A. E. Lang (Eds.), *Advances in neurology: Vol. 65. Behavioral neurology of movement disorders* (pp. 179–186). New York: Raven Press.

Fields, J. A., Norman, S., Straits-Tröster, K. A., & Tröster, A. I. (in press). The impact of depression on memory in neurodegenerative disease. In A. I. Tröster (Ed.), *Memory in eurodegeneorodite disease: Biological, cognitive, and clinical perspectives.* Cambridge, England: Cambridge University Press.

Filoteo, J. V., Rilling, L. M., Cole, B., Williams, B. J., Davis, J. D., & Roberts, J. W. (1997). Variable memory profiles in Parkinson's disease. *Journal of Clinical and Experimental Neuropsychology, 19,* 879–888.

Golbe, L. I. (1996) The epidemiology of progressive supranuclear palsy. In L. Battistin, G. Scarlato, T. Caraceni, & S. Ruggieri (Eds.), *Advances in neurology: Vol. 69. Parkinson's disease* (pp. 25–31). New York: Raven Press.

Grafman, J., Litvan, I., & Stark, M. (1995). Neuropsychological features of progressive supranuclear palsy. *Brain and Cognition, 28,* 311–320.

Ivnik, R. J., Malec, J. F., Smith, G. E., Tangalos, E. G., & Petersen, R. C. (1996). Neuropsychological tests' norms above age 55: COWAT, BNT, MAE Token, WRAT-R Reading, AMNART, STROOP, TMT, and JLO. *Clinical Neuropsychologist, 12,* 262–278.

Ivnik, R. J., Malec, J. F., Smith, G. E., Tangalos, E. G., Petersen, R. C., Kokmen, E., & Kurland, R. T. (1992). Mayo's Older Americans Normative Studies: WAIS-R norms for ages 56 to 97. *Clinical Neuropsychologist, 6*(Suppl.), 1–30.

Ivnik, R. J., Malec, J. F., Tangalos, E. G., Petersen, R. C., Kokmen, E., & Kurland, L. T. (1992a). Mayo's Older Americans Normative Studies: Updated AVLT norms for ages 56 to 97. *Clinical Neuropsychologist, 6*(Suppl.), 83–104.

Ivnik, R. J., Malec, J. F., Tangalos, E. G., Petersen, R. C., Kokmen, E., & Kurland, L. T. (1992b). Mayo's Older Americans Normative Studies: WMS-R norms for ages 56 to 94. *Clinical Neuropsychologist, 6*(Suppl.), 49–82.

Jacobs, D., Salmon, D. P., Tröster, A. I., & Butters, N. (1990). Intrusion errors in the figural memory of patients with Alzheimer's and Huntington's disease. *Archives of Clinical Neuropsychology, 5,* 49–57.

Kalckreuth, W., Zimmermann, P., Preilowski, B., & Wallesch, C. W. (1994). Incomplete split-brain syndrome in a patient with chronic Marchiafava-Bignami disease. *Behavioral Brain Research, 64,* 219–228.

Koller, W. C., Marjama, J., & Tröster, A. I. (1998). Psychogenic movement disorders. In J. Jankovic & E. Tolosa (Eds.), *Parkinson's disease and movement disorders* (3rd ed., pp. 859–868. Baltimore: Williams & Wilkins.

Koller, W. C., & Megaffin, B. B. (1994). Parkinson's disease and parkinsonism. In C. E. Coffey & J. L. Cummings (Eds.), *Textbook of geriatric neuropsychiatry* (pp. 433–456). Washington, DC: American Psychiatric Press.

Ledbetter, M. F., & Prifitera, A. (1994). Education-adjusted percent retention scores based on the Wechsler Memory Scale-Revised standardization sample [Abstract]. *Archives of Clinical Neuropsychology, 9,* 154.

Levin, B. E., & Katzen, H. L. (1995). Early cognitive changes and nondementing behavioral abnormalities in Parkinson's disease. In W. J. Weiner & A. E. Lang (Eds.), *Advances in neurology: Vol. 65. Behavioral neurology of movement disorders* (pp. 85–95). New York: Raven Press.

Litvan, I., Agid, Y., Jankovic, J., Goetz, C. Brandel, J. P., Lai, E. C., Wenning, G., D'Olhaberriague, L., Verny, M., Chaudhuri, K. R., McKee, A., Jellinger, K., Bartko, J. J., Mangone, C. A., & Pearce, R. K. B. (1996). Accuracy of clinical criteria for progressive supranuclear palsy (Steele-Richardson-Olszewski syndrome). *Neurology, 46,* 992–930.

Mahler, M. E. (1992). Behavioral manifestations associated with multiple sclerosis. *Psychiatric Clinics of North America, 15,* 427–438.

Marshall, F. J., & Shoulson, I. (1997). Clinical features and treatment of Huntington's disease. In R. L. Watts & W. C. Koller (Eds.), *Movement disorders: Neurologic principles and practice* (pp. 491–502). New York: McGraw-Hill.

Massman, P J., Kreiter, K. T., Jankovic, J., & Doody, R. S. (1996). Neuropsychological functioning in cortical-basal ganglionic degeneration: Differentiation from Alzheimer's disease. *Neurology, 46,* 720–726.

Mattis, S. (1988). *Dementia Rating Scale.* Odessa, FL: Psychological Assessment Resources.

McPherson, S., & Cummings, J. L. (1996). Neuropsychological aspects of Parkinson's disease and parkinsonism. In I. Grant

& K. M. Adams (Eds.), *Neuropsychological assessment of neuropsychiatric disorders* (2nd ed., pp. 288–311). New York: Oxford University Press.

Mega, M. S., & Cummings, J. L. (1994). Frontal-subcortical circuits and neuropsychiatric disorders. *Journal of Neuropsychiatry and Clinical Neurosciences, 6,* 358–370.

Mohr, E., Mendis, T., & Grimes, J. D. (1995). Late cognitive changes in Parkinson's disease with an emphasis on dementia. In W. J. Weiner & A. E. Lang (Eds.), *Advances in neurology: Vol. 65. Behavioral neurology of movement disorders* (pp. 97–113). New York: Raven Press.

Nelson, H. E. (1976). A modified card sorting test sensitive to frontal lobe deficits. *Cortex, 12,* 313–324.

Norman, S., Tröster, A. I., Fields, J. A., & Brooks, R. (1997). The effects of depression and Parkinson's disease on cognitive functioning [Abstract]. *Archives of Clinical Neuropsychology, 12,* 376–377.

Olichney, J. M., Galasko, D., Corey-Bloom, J., & Thal, L. J. (1995). The spectrum of diseases with diffuse Lewy bodies. In W. J. Weiner & A. E. Lang (Eds.), *Advances in neurology: Vol. 65. Behavioral neurology of movement disorders* (pp. 159–170). New York: Raven Press.

Paolo, A. M., Axelrod, B. N., Tröster, A. I., Blackwell, K. T., & Koller, W. C. (1996). Utility of a Wisconsin Card Sorting Test short form in persons with Alzheimer's and Parkinson's disease. *Journal of Clinical and Experimental Neuropsychology, 18,* 892–897.

Paolo, A. M., Tröster, A. I., Glatt, S. L., Hubble, J. P., & Koller, W. C. (1995). Differentiation of the dementias of Alzheimer's and Parkinson's disease with the Dementia Rating Scale. *Journal of Geriatric Psychiatry and Neurology, 8,* 184–188.

Paolo, A. M., Tröster, A. I., & Ryan, J. J. (1997). California Verbal Learning Test: Normative data for the elderly. *Journal of Clinical and Experimental Neuropsychology, 19,* 220–234.

Paulsen, J. S., Salmon, D. P., Monsch, A. U., Butters, N., Swenson, M. R., & Bondi, M. W. (1995). Discrimination of cortical from subcortical dementias on the basis of memory and problem-solving tests. *Journal of Clinical Psychology, 51,* 48–58.

Pillon, B., Blin, J., Vidailhet, M., Deweer, B., Sirigu, A., Dubois, B., & Agid, Y. (1995). The neuropsychological pattern of corticobasal degeneration: Comparison with progressive supranuclear palsy and Alzheimer's disease. *Neurology, 45,* 1477–1483.

Pfeiffer, R. F. (1997). Wilson's disease. In R. L. Watts & W. C. Koller (Eds.), *Movement disorders: Neurologic principles and practice* (pp. 623–637). New York: McGraw-Hill.

The Psychological Corporation. (1997). *WAIS-III/WMS-III technical manual*. San Antonio, TX: Author.

Quinn, N., & Wenning, G. (1995). Multiple system atrophy. *Current Opinion in Neurology, 8*, 323–326.

Rao, S. M. (1995). Neuropsychology of multiple sclerosis. *Current Opinion in Neurology, 8*, 216–220.

Rao, S. M., Leo, G. J., Bernardin, L., & Unverzagt, F. (1991). Cognitive dysfunction in multiple sclerosis, I: Frequency, pattern and predictions. *Neurology, 41*, 685–691.

Raskin, S. A., Borod, J. C., & Tweedy, J. (1990). Neuropsychological aspects of Parkinson's disease. *Neuropsychology Review, 1*, 185–221.

Rinne, J. O., Lee, M. S., Thompson, P. D., & Marsden, C. D. (1994). Corticobasal degeneration: A clinical study of 36 cases. *Brain, 117*, 1183–1196.

Rolak, L. A. (1996). The diagnosis of multiple sclerosis. *Neurologic Clinics, 14*, 27–43.

Ryan, J. J., Paolo, A. M., & Brungardt, T. M. (1990). Standardization of the WAIS-R for persons 75 years and older. *Psychological Assessment, 2*, 404–411.

Sadovnick, A. D., Eisen, K., Paty, D. W., & Ebers, G. C. (1991). Cause of death in patients attending multiple sclerosis clinics. *Neurology, 41*, 1193–1196.

Sadovnick, A. D., Remick, R. A., Allen, J., Swartz, E., Yee, I. M. L., Eisen, K., Farquhar, R., Hashimoto, S. A., Hooge, J., Kastrukoff, L. F., Morrison, W., Nelson, J., Oger, J., & Paty, D. W. (1996). Depression and multiple sclerosis. *Neurology, 46*, 628–632.

Salmon, D. P., & Galasko, D. (1996). Neuropsychological aspects of Lewy body dementia. In E. K. Perry, R. H. Perry, & I. G. McKeith (Eds.), *Lewy body dementia* (pp. 99–113). Cambridge, England: Cambridge University Press.

Salmon, D. P., Galasko, D., Hansen, L. A., Masliah, E., Butters, N., Thal, L. J., & Katzman, R. (1996). Neuropsychological deficits associated with diffuse Lewy body disease. *Brain and Cognition, 31*, 148–165.

Salmon, D. P., Kwo-on-Yuen, P. F., Heindel, W. C., Butters, N., & Thal, L. J. (1989). Differentiation of Alzheimer's disease and Huntington's disease with the Dementia Rating Scale. *Archives of Neurology, 46*, 1204–1208.

Schmidt, M. (1996). *Rey Auditory and Verbal Learning Test: A handbook*. Los Angeles: Western Psychological Services.

Spreen, O., & Strauss, E. (1991). *A compendium of neuropsychological tests: Administration, norms, and commentary*. New York: Oxford University Press.

Spreen, O., & Strauss, E. (1998). *A copendium of neuropsychological tests* (2nd ed.). New York: Oxford University Press.

Stern, Y., & Langston, J. W. (1985). Intellectual changes in patients with MPTP-induced parkinsonism. *Neurology, 35,* 1506–1507.

Taylor, A. E., & Saint-Cyr, J. A. (1995). The neuropsychology of Parkinson's disease. *Brain and Cognition, 28,* 281–296.

Tombaugh, T. N., & Hubley, A. M. (1997). The 60-item Boston Naming Test: Norms for cognitively intact adults aged 25 to 88 years. *Journal of Clinical and Experimental Neuropsychology, 19,* 922–932.

Tombaugh, T. N., Kozak, J., & Rees, L. M. (in press). Normative data stratified by age and education for two measures of verbal fluency: FAS and Animal naming. *Archives of Clinical Neuropsychology.*

Tröster, A. I., Butters, N., Salmon, D. P., Cullum, C. M., Jacobs, D., Brandt, J., & White, R. F. (1993). The diagnostic utility of savings scores: Differentiating Alzheimer's and Huntington's diseases with the Logical Memory and Visual Reproduction tests. *Journal of Clinical and Experimental Neuropsychology, 15,* 773–788.

Tröster, A. I., & Fields, J. A. (1995). Frontal cognitive function and memory in Parkinson's disease: Toward a distinction between prospective and declarative memory impairments? *Behavioural Neurology, 8,* 59–74.

Tröster, A. I., Jacobs, D., Butters, N., Cullum, C. M., & Salmon, D. P. (1989). Differentiating Alzheimer's disease from Huntington's disease with the Wechsler Memory Scale–Revised. *Clinics in Geriatric Medicine, 5,* 611–632.

Tröster, A. I., Stalp, L. D., Paolo, A. M., Fields, J. A., & Koller, W. C. (1995). Neuropsychological impairment in Parkinson's disease with and without depression. *Archives of Neurology, 52,* 1164–1169.

Wichmann, T., Vitek, J. L., & DeLong, M. R. (1995). Parkinson's disease and the basal ganglia: Lessons from the laboratory and from neurosurgery. *Neuroscientist, 1,* 236–244.

Wilkinson, S. B., & Tröster, A. I. (in press). Surgical interventions in neurodegenerative disease: Impact on memory and cognition. In A. I. Tröster (Ed.), *Memory in neurodegenerative disease: Biological, cognitive, and clinical perspectives.* Cambridge, England: Cambridge University Press.

Zhang, Z. X., & Romàn, G. C. (1993). Worldwide occurrence of Parkinson's disease: An updated review. *Neuroepidemiology, 12,* 195–208.

CHAPTER 15

Peter J. Snyder

Epilepsy

Epilepsy is a common neurological disorder characterized by sudden, brief attacks that may alter motor activity, consciousness, and sensory experiences. Convulsive seizures are the most common type of paroxysmal event, but any recurrent seizure pattern is considered "epilepsy." Many forms of epilepsy have been linked to viral, fungal, or parasitic infections of the central nervous system; known metabolic disturbances; the ingestion of toxic agents; brain lesions; tumors or congenital defects; or cerebral trauma. Although the direct causes of seizures are not always readily observable, with the advent of sophisticated histological, neuroimaging, and biochemical techniques, it is becoming increasingly possible to diagnose the causes of seizure disorders that have, in the past, been difficult to identify (e.g., microscopic brain lesions).

Because it can result from a myriad of differing types of insults to the nervous system, ranging from identifiable structural pathology including space-occupying lesions (e.g., brain tumors, vascular malformations) to pathological processes of unknown etiology and indiscernible by current neurodiagnostic techniques, epilepsy is best thought of as a class of symptoms rather than a "disease" per se. Exhibit 1 contains a glossary of terms used in this chapter.

Exhibit 1. Glossary of Terms

Clonic alternating contraction and relaxation of muscles

Convulsion paroxysms of involuntary muscular contractions, relaxations, or both

Epileptogenic focus a discrete area of the brain wherein the electrical discharges that give rise to seizure activity originate

Gliosis a proliferation of neuroglial tissue (largely nonnervous, supporting tissue of the brain and spinal cord) in the central nervous system

Ictus the period of time during which an epileptic seizure occurs

Paroxysm a sudden, periodic attack or recurrence of symptoms; a sudden spasm or convulsion of any kind

Seizure a recurrent paroxysmal event that is characteristic of epilepsy; may or may not include impairments of consciousness or convulsions

Tonic increased muscle tone sustained over a given length of time, such as during a seizure

Uncus a hook-shaped anterior portion of the hippocampal gyrus, within the temporal lobe of the brain

I. PREVALENCE

Approximately 2% of the population will have at least one seizure sometime during their lives, and many of these individuals will develop chronic seizure disorders. Although 70% of persons with epilepsy are successfully treated with available medications, about 30% develop chronic seizures that do not respond completely or satisfactorily to anticonvulsant medications.

The existence of this smaller yet sizable group of people with epilepsy supports the hypothesis that early seizures may serve to intensify any latent predisposition of an individual's central nervous system to produce further seizure discharges (an idea first advanced by the British neurologist William Gowers in 1881), and for some patients suboptimal seizure control may lead to a disorder that becomes progressively more resistent to pharmacologic treatment.

II. MEDICALLY REFRACTORY SEIZURE DISORDERS

From 30% to 45% of patients with epilepsy are medically refractory to conventional antiepileptic pharmacotherapy; at any time in the United States, at least 240,000 patients suffer from inadequate seizure control. Most epileptologists agree that the first few seizures serve to intensify any predisposition of the central nervous system to produce further paroxysmal discharges. Reynolds, Elwes, and Shorvon (1983) suggested that any patient who has experienced a seizure be placed immediately on therapeutic dosages of an anticonvulsant instead of the common approach of waiting for another seizure to occur and then building up the systemic level of the drug slowly.

When noninvasive treatments (e.g., antiepileptic medication) have not been successful in controlling a seizure disorder, surgical removal of the discharging tissue is typically considered. Patients may be suitable candidates for surgical intervention if the epileptogenic discharge originates in a localized area of the brain and if the seizures are of such severity and frequency that they seriously interfere with the patient's quality of life. The prognosis for such surgical intervention, with regard to reducing the frequency and severity of seizures, depends largely on the size and location of the discharging foci. The incidence of unsuccessful alleviation of seizures increases in patients with multiple or bilateral epileptogenic foci and in cases of incomplete resection of the discharging tissue.

III. ETIOLOGY AND CLASSIFICATION OF THE EPILEPSIES

Epilepsy has been classified by both seizure type and etiology. Several types of seizures are associated with specific cerebral locations of discharging epileptogenic foci. The differential diagnoses of various seizure disorders are important areas of ongoing research and debate.

Because of the myriad of different ways of classifying a complex set of phenomena (with a wide range of possible motor, sensory, psychological, and behavioral symptoms), dramatic refinements in seizure classification did not occur until the Commission on Classification and Terminology of the International League Against Epilepsy (ILAE) introduced a formal classification system for seizure types in 1970. The ILAE classification system, last revised in 1985, separates seizures that are primarily generalized in their origin from within the brain from those that are localized (partial) in their origin. A further separation may be made on the basis of whether individual types of seizures involve convulsions or not. A modified and abbreviated version of the ILAE classification scheme is shown in Exhibit 2.

A. Types of Seizures

1. GENERALIZED SEIZURES

Approximately one third of all patients with epilepsy suffer from generalized seizure disorders, including a variety of generalized motor and "absence" seizure types. In primary generalized seizures, in which the seizure does not begin as a partial seizure (see the following section), the paroxysmal discharges typically arise from deep structures located in the base and middle of the brain (brain stem or thalamus). Unlike many patients with partial seizures, patients with generalized seizures do not experience any psychic or sensory disturbances at the start of the seizure (aura), and there are no focal motor behaviors elicited by the seizure (e.g., automatic motor movements of limbs on only one side of the body).

Generalized motor seizures are divided into subtypes (e.g., tonic, clonic) depending on the motor sequence observed during the seizure event (see Exhibit 2), and collectively they represent the most common of the primary generalized epilepsies. There is some evidence pointing to a genetic basis for some of the subtypes of this group of seizure disorders.

Typical absence (petit mal) seizures usually occur in childhood, between the ages of 4 and 12, and only rarely persist into adulthood. These seizures are associated with a brief (5- to 30-second) staring spell and a highly characteristic electroencephalographic (EEG) pattern.

2. SIMPLE- AND COMPLEX-PARTIAL SEIZURES

Of the 2% of the population with epilepsy, two thirds have simple- or complex-partial seizure disorders. Partial seizures begin in one part of the brain and may or may not spread to other regions; they usually consist of specific motor, sensory, or psychic alterations. The psychic changes are often accompanied by stereotyped automatic movements (leading to the term **psychomotor**) such as lip smacking, chewing, or eye blinking. These seizures often originate from one or both of the temporal lobes (usually from the hippocampus or amygdala, structures that are buried

Exhibit 2. Abbreviated Classification of Epileptic Seizures

I. CONVULSIVE SEIZURES
- A. GENERALIZED SEIZURES
  1. Myoclonic seizures
  2. Clonic seizures
  3. Tonic seizures
  4. Tonic–clonic seizures (grand mal)
  5. Atonic seizures
- B. PARTIAL SEIZURES EVOLVING TO SECONDARILY GENERALIZED SEIZURES
  1. Simple-partial seizures evolving to generalized seizures
  2. Complex-partial seizures evolving to generalized seizures
  3. Simple-partial seizures evolving to complex partial seizures and then to generalized seizures

II. NONCONVULSIVE SEIZURES
- A. GENERALIZED SEIZURES
  1. Absence seizures (petit mal)
- B. SIMPLE PARTIAL SEIZURES
  1. With motor symptoms
  2. With somatosensory or special sensory symptoms
  3. With autonomic symptoms
  4. With psychic symptoms
- C. COMPLEX-PARTIAL SEIZURES
  1. Beginning as simple-partial seizures and progressing to impairment of consciousness
     a. With no other features
     b. With features as in II.B.1–4
     c. With automatisms
  2. With impairment of consciousness at onset (psychomotor)
     a. With no other features
     b. With features as in II.B.1–4
     c. With automatisms

within the temporal lobes), and they are often accompanied by emotional changes that are quite variable from one person to another. The most common of these emotional changes is fear, but sadness, pleasure, or "deja vu" feelings are frequently reported as well. Hallucinations or misperceptions are also common ictal phenomena of simple- and complex-partial seizures. These sensory experiences can be auditory, tactile, visual, or olfactory.

In **simple-partial epilepsy**, there is no alteration in consciousness as a result of the seizure discharge. In **complex-partial epilepsy**, impaired consciousness results directly from the seizure discharge. Although both simple-partial and complex-partial seizures typically result from a localizable seizure focus, the electrical discharge may spread to other cortical areas and trigger discharges from other possible epileptogenic foci, resulting in secondarily generalized seizures. Often the specific ictal motor and sensory phenomena exhibited by individual patients correspond to the cerebral localization, or focus, of the epileptic discharge, and the progression of symptoms may indicate the degree of spread of abnormal electrocerebral activity during a seizure. Should this electrocerebral activity spread widely enough, it will be associated with readily apparent alterations in consciousness (complex-partial seizures).

B. Temporal Lobe Epilepsy

Of the approximately 2% of the population with epilepsy, 40%–60% have simple-partial or complex-partial seizures (with or without secondary generalization) of temporal lobe origin. Glaser (1978) estimated that seizures of temporal lobe origin are found in approximately 25% of children and 50% of adults with epilepsy.

Many investigators have reported specific cognitive deficits, such as memory disturbances, that differentiate patients with temporal lobe epilepsy (TLE) from those with other types of epilepsy (cf. Jones-Gotman, 1991). The duration of the disorder in years has been shown to be positively correlated with the degree of preoperative neurocognitive dysfunction (Strauss, Hunter, & Wada, 1995). Patients with TLE often present with the following:

- A longer history of seizure disorder
- Febrile seizures in infancy (Berg, Levy, Novotny, & Shinnar, 1996)
- Early anoxic episodes in childhood
- Family history of epilepsy

Because temporal lobe epilepsy is the largest single type of seizure disorder, and because it is most frequently associated with cognitive, emotional, personality, and behavioral alterations (both during and between seizures), most of the following sections of this chapter concentrate primarily on this type of epilepsy.

IV. MULTIDISCIPLINARY APPROACH TO DIAGNOSIS

A variety of diagnostic techniques are routinely used to infer the location of epileptogenic foci, ranging from **structural brain-imaging techniques** (e.g., computed tomography [CT], magnetic resonance imaging [MRI]) to the **imaging of brain function** or metabolism (e.g., measurements of regional cerebral blood flow [rCBF] with positron emission tomography [PET], single photon emission tomography [SPECT], MRI spectroscopy [fMRI], EEG, and neuropsychological examination). All of these techniques are highly complex, and no single diagnostic approach, in isolation, provides definitive data that can be used to guide surgical decisions. The proper diagnostic evaluation of patients whose seizures are not easily controlled by medications requires the collective efforts of a multidisciplinary team, all members of which are typically on staff at an epilepsy center. At the very least, these teams consist of a neurologist, neurosurgeon, neuropsychologist, social worker, and neurological nurses.

V. THE NEUROPSYCHOLOGICAL EXAMINATION

A. Functions

The neuropsychological examination serves three functions. First, it is useful in determining the locus of an epileptogenic lesion that is not observable with standard (structural) neuroimaging techniques and for which EEG data are equivocal. Second, because most patients with epilepsy present with temporal or frontotemporal epileptogenic foci or both, they are at risk for developing iatrogenic impairments in speech and memory functions following any planned surgical treatment. To diminish this risk, cortical and subcortical regions that are crucial for cognition, in particular, for speech and memory, must be identified presurgically.

Third, the neuropsychological examination has proved its value with the subset of patients who have left temporal lobe epileptogenic foci and whose seizure disorders are of childhood origin. For these patients, certain relatively uncommon features of cortical organization have been found to occur more often than in the general population. These features are broadly seen as reflecting either intra- or interhemispheric cortical reorganization (Strauss, Wada, & Goldwater, 1992). The former kind would be reflected in speech representation beyond the conventional, or usual, perisylvian zones of the left hemisphere; the latter are reflected in right hemisphere dominance for speech. For such individuals, the possibility of anomalous functional topography for speech and other higher cognitive functions can make the usual diagnostic rules, based on studies of adult-onset brain lesions, only partly applicable or even frankly misleading.

In addition to the recording of seizures by 24-hour EEG-CCTV telemetry and the identification of focal neuropathology with neuroradiological studies (when possible), the neuropsychological examination (including administration of the Intracarotid Amobarbital Procedure, or Wada Test) may provide corroborating evidence for unilateral temporal lobe dysfunction and thus further help to localize the epileptogenic focus. Finally, the neuropsychological examination is useful in the presurgical identification of surgical candidates who are likely to suffer debilitating functional impairments following surgery.

An overview of the methods by which the neuropsychological examination contributes to the comprehensive preoperative evaluation of epilepsy patients is detailed in the following sections. It is important to remember that in most epilepsy surgery programs, the presurgical neuropsychological evaluation typically occurs prior to invasive electrophysiological procedures (e.g., depth EEG, cortical grid mapping). Hence, any neuropsychological test battery must be designed not merely to detect unilateral mesiotemporal or lateral temporal lobe dysfunction, but also to aid in the detection of focal dysfunction throughout the neocortex.

B. Step-By-Step Guide

The selection of a battery of assessment tests must be determined not by isolating the neurocognitive functions that are typically subsumed by the neocortical region that contains the epileptogenic focus, but rather by the range of adaptive behaviors potentially affected by surgery. Multiple levels of each function must be examined, and both intact and impaired functions must be appraised to determine potential adverse/iatrogenic effects of surgery. For any patient, the type and extent of behavioral and cognitive impairments that are expected to result from surgical intervention determine both surgical candidacy and type and extent of surgical resection.

Standard, "off-the-shelf" neuropsychological test batteries, such as the Halstead-Reitan Neuropsychological Battery (HRB), do not reliably differentiate among patients with TLE, schizophrenia, bipolar disorder, and "brain damage." That is, although the HRB might be sensitive to the detection of central nervous system dysfunction in a general sense, it lacks the diagnostic specificity required for use in the comprehensive evaluation of medically refractory epilepsy patients. Several suggestions are offered in the following sections to aid in the construction of a useful neuropsychological examination battery.

1. PATIENT HISTORY AND CLINICAL INTERVIEW

In taking a patient's developmental, family, past medical, social, and occupational histories, careful attention must be paid to identifying possible precipitating or etiologic factors, age at seizure onset, age of onset of chronic seizures, and occurrence of febrile convulsions in infancy. The data obtained from answers to these questions will aid in the interpretation of late achievement of developmental milestones, childhood learning disorders, employment history with various levels of occupational complexity, and social functional level. The clinical interview with both the patient and his or her family forms an integral part of the neuropsychological evaluation, therefore, and the information provided often leads to a more focused assessment that may target specific areas of deficit in greater detail. Furthermore, for patients with complex-partial seizures or generalized seizure disorders, the description of the ictal behaviors (or semiology) by family and friends is important to obtain because such descriptions often lead to the first piece of evidence linking the seizures to a focal area of neurological dysfunction.

Finally, it is important for the neuropsychologist to obtain an accurate history of current antiepileptic drug (AED) therapy, as well as of the timing and duration of prior AED mono- or polytherapy trials. The problem of behavioral toxicity, that is, impairment of cognitive functions secondary to AED treatment in the absence of frank neurotoxic side effects, is an important issue to consider when evaluating the data obtained from a neuropsychological examination. For example, the speed of access to information in short-term memory storage is sensitive to phenobarbital concentration, whereas the speed of access to information held in long-term memory storage is much less affected. Several excellent reviews of neuropsychological side effects of both the older and the "new generation" AEDs have been recently published (cf. McConnell & Duncan, 1998).

2. OBSERVATION OF ICTAL SEMIOLOGY

In interviewing the patient, it is important to observe his or her facial morphology carefully. Facial asymmetries may be noticeable in 50%–80% of patients with TLE, in comparison with about 30% of matched controls. It is also important to note any obvious speech disturbances, especially during a seizure discharge. When the seizure discharge involves the language areas located within the perisylvian region of the dominant hemisphere for speech, there is typically a transient epileptic aphasia during and immediately postictus. Rarely, this transient epileptic aphasia is due to seizure activity in the supplementary motor area.

If the opportunity to observe the patient during a seizure presents itself, it is important to observe the occurrence of any motoric automatisms. For example, *forced* (versive) turning of the head and eyes and dystonic posturing of a limb at seizure onset are reliably contralateral to the side of the epileptogenic focus; therefore, this behavioral observation provides a good indicator of laterality of the focus in patients with focal onset of seizure activity. However, not all unusual ictal psychomotor activity is limited to TLE. Spencer, Spencer, Williamson, and Mattson (1983), in their sample of 61 patients with medically refractory complex-partial seizures, found four patients (all with seizure foci restricted to the frontal lobes) who displayed ictal sexual automatisms (e.g., masturbatory activity), whereas none of their patients with temporal lobe seizure foci displayed any sexual automatisms. This finding disconfirms the belief that ictal sexual automatisms, for which the patient is later amnestic, are found solely in temporal lobe disease.

The observation of ictal semiology may assist in providing evidence to support or reject a diagnosis of psychogenic seizure-like events. For example, it is highly unlikely for a patient to have his or her eyes shut during a generalized tonic–clonic seizure; rather, the eyes are invariably open, the eyebrows are raised, and the mouth is typically open during the tonic phase of the event. In contrast, it is often the case that patients with psychogenic (convulsive) seizures show an opposite pattern. A heavy reliance on behavioral observations made during a seizure may also be quite misleading; for example, the ictal behaviors typically seen in the average adult patient do not necessarily apply for children (Wyllie, 1995) or the elderly (Tinuper et al., 1996).

The presence of peri-ictal auras just prior to seizure onset, which may be reported by the patient or family, is often indicative of TLE. Compared to patients with extratemporal foci, those with TLE have reported a higher incidence of visceral, complex, and olfactory–gustatory auras and automatic behaviors (Gloor, Olivier, Quesney, Andermann, & Horowitz, 1982). Gloor et al. found that 18 of 29 patients with TLE reported experiential phenomena (e.g., memory flashbacks, visual hallucinations) concomitant with either seizure discharge or evoked stimulation of the amygdala by stereotactically placed depth electrodes. They found that for such phenomena to occur, electrical stimulation or seizure discharge always involved limbic structures but did not necessarily involve the temporal neocortex (verified by depth EEG).

3. UPPER-EXTREMITY MOTOR EXAMINATION

This portion of the evaluation is useful in discerning lateralized dysfunction of the prefrontal cortex; it also may be helpful in distinguishing patients with TLE from those with other types of seizure disorders. For example, although patients with complex-partial seizures and a unilateral temporal lobe epileptogenic focus often show a clear deficit in motor performance as measured by finger-tapping and pointing tasks, patients with focal involvement of the caudal aspect of the primary motor strip also show a profound defect on measures of fine motor praxis with the contralateral upper extremity. **Recommended tests and measures include (a) the Rapid Finger Oscillation Test, (b) the Purdue Pegboard Test, and (c) the Grooved Pegboard Test.**

4. SENSORY–PERCEPTUAL EXAMINATION

The typical sensory–perceptual examination involves the separate assessment of visual–perceptual functions and simple audition, an informal visual fields examination, and a tactile sensory examination. The use of visual-searching procedures to evaluate the relative efficiency with which a patient searches or attends to left versus right visual space may lead to the observation of a visual field cut or hemineglect, both of which have clear localizing significance. Likewise, various deficits in auditory processing (e.g., for environmental sounds, rhythmic pattern discrimination) are suggestive of focal involvement of primary or tertiary auditory centers or both in or near the superior temporal gyri of one or both hemispheres. In addition, the careful analysis of tactile sensory–perceptual deficits (typically involving double simultaneous stimulation of the face and upper extremities) may lead to evidence suggestive of focal dysfunction of unilateral primary sensory areas. **Recommended** tests and measures include (a) single and double simultaneous tactile stimulation, (b) informal tests of visual fields and audition, and (c) the Mesulam and Weintraub Visual Scanning Task.

5. ATTENTIONAL CONTROLS, CONCENTRATION, AND "EXECUTIVE" FUNCTIONS

The evaluation of these important neurobehavioral domains may require a diverse set of procedures, such as design fluency and continuous-performance tests (Jones-Gotman, 1991). Many of these tests are now computer administered to provide for the accurate measurement of various psychophysical variables, such as reaction time. Deficits in the maintenance of sustained concentration, focused attention, divided attentional controls, and both response inhibition and the production of frequent perseverative errors all may lead to the suggestion of focal frontal lobe involvement (Jones-Gotman, 1991). Furthermore, the pattern of performance across this range of tests often leads to the prediction of left versus right and mesial versus lateral frontal lobe involvement. However, the potential for eliciting false localizing signs is quite high, and both false positive and false negative diagnostic errors are frequently made. For example, poor performance on several of these measures may be secondary to anticonvulsant toxicity. As is usually the case, such diagnostic impressions require independent corroborative evidence from other sources. **Recommended tests and measures include (a) the Trail Making Test, Parts A and B, (b) the Ruff Figural Fluency Test, (c) the Working Memory Index of the Wechsler Memory Scale (WMS-III), (d) the Benton Serial Digit Learning Test, (e) the Wisconsin Card Sorting Test, and (f) Competing Programs and Go/No-Go tasks.**

6. SPEECH AND LANGUAGE EXAMINATION

Expressive speech functions may be assessed by a myriad of techniques including controlled oral word production, confrontation naming, sentence repetition, and rapid rote reading (with and without distractors). A common interictal "memory" impairment in patients with left TLE, but not those with right TLE, is the presence of dysnomia. Additionally, patients with left temporal or frontotemporal foci often show a clear deficit in the fluidity of speech production, as well as a transient aphasia secondary to ictal events with focal onset in the perisylvian region. **Recommended tests and measures include (a) single-letter and category-level verbal fluency tests and (b) the Boston Naming Test.**

For patients who are candidates for surgical intervention, the accurate determination of hemispheric dominance for speech is extremely important, and the intracarotid amobarbital procedure (IAP; also called the Wada Test) currently provides the least ambiguous method for accomplishing this. In a well-known study, Milner (1975) found that in patients with evidence of early damage to the left cerebral hemisphere, 81% of right-handed and 30% of left- or mixed-handed individuals demonstrated left hemisphere speech dominance, whereas 51% of left-handed patients with early damage to the left cerebral hemisphere lateralized speech function to the contralateral side. Milner (1975) also reported evidence of mixed speech dominance in 15% of the left- or mixed-handed patients in her series ($N = 122$).

The preceding finding regarding the prevalence of mixed speech dominance (MSD) in an epileptic population is inconclusive, however, for three reasons. First, several other investigators have reported very different estimates of MSD in their samples (see review by Snyder, Novelly, & Harris, 1990). Second, there is little agreement among researchers at centers that perform the IAP as to what the criteria should be for determining the presence of speech production from the "minor" hemisphere. Finally, it may be that MSD can never be determined with certainty using the IAP as long as there is no definitive method for determining complete unilateral anesthetization of the perioper-cular speech zones (Snyder et al., 1990). In short, although the IAP provides the most definitive method of determining unilateral speech dominance in epilepsy surgery candidates, its usefulness in the determination of MSD remains unresolved.

Receptive language functions may be assessed by various techniques, ranging from speech-sounds discrimination tests to dichotic-listening procedures. Specific deficits in the areas of word reading, reading comprehension, and the appropriate use of syntax and grammar all are diagnostically significant. Zaidel (1985) argued that the right hemisphere in a normal population has limited but measurable competence for comprehending both spoken and written language, but that it is generally impoverished in its ability to produce meaningful verbal expression. Such preclinical research findings, along with the demonstration of specific functions known to be primarily mediated by the right hemisphere (e.g., modulation of prosodic speech, appropriate interpretation of emotional tone in speech), have specific implications with regard to the determination of the extent of any planned surgical resection in the right frontotemporal and temporoparietal regions. **Recommended tests and measures** include an informal assessment of prosody of speech as well as the following subtests of the Boston Diagnostic Aphasia Examination (BDAE): (a) Commands, (b) Passive Subject–Object Discrimination, (c) Complex Ideational Material, and (d) Reading Sentences and Paragraphs.

7. EXAMINATION OF MNESTIC FUNCTIONS

The neural networks underlying memory encoding, storage, and retrieval are complex and well integrated, branching to many areas of the brain that only recently have been recognized as important in memory function. A common theme running throughout the research in this area is the paramount importance of the hippocampi and adjacent parahippocampal gyri (at least in humans) for the encoding and retrieval of new learning. Jasper (1962) correctly noted that the amnesia that is a common characteristic of temporal lobe ictal automatisms seems "most likely due to a functional or paralytic blockade of the normal functions of the hippocampus and related neuronal systems which seem essential to mechanisms for the recording of immediate experience." This finding is crucial in the diagnostic workup of patients in whom epilepsy surgery is being considered, because in many instances, both hippocampi (and adjacent neocortex) do not contribute equally to the overall integrity of the complex neural network for memory. Rather, a preponderance of such patients have a unilateral distribution of memory patency owing to an early, lateralized brain injury. Thus, if the only remaining functional hippocampus is epileptogenic, removal of this structure may eliminate the seizure activity but would be akin to a bilateral hippocampectomy, with disastrous results for memory functioning.

In addition to guarding against such a tragic neuropsychological syndrome, a comprehensive memory examination is useful in assisting in the localization of focal neurological dysfunction and, perhaps, the epileptogenic focus. Clear impairment in short-term recall for verbal information, with relatively intact verbal-reasoning abilities (e.g., no significant verbal IQ–performance IQ [VIQ–PIQ] split), is highly suggestive of focal *left* temporal lobe dysfunction. Unfortunately, for reasons discussed later, we do not currently have comparable neuropsychological measures for the reliable detection of focal *right* temporal lobe dysfunction.

8. VERBAL MEMORY EXAMINATION PROCEDURES

The impairment in the encoding, storage, and recall of verbal information may be measured through story narratives or with serial list learning procedures. In the former task, the patient is afforded the benefit of processing information that is embedded in a salient social context, whereas in the latter type of task, the patient must remember a list of words that may not share any obvious contextual relationship. Impaired performance across these broad sets of measures is often observed in patients with left temporal lobe epilepsy. Furthermore, the use of certain types of verbal memory measures (e.g., paired-associate learning paradigms) might afford greater diagnostic specificity than other types (e.g., story learning; Loring, 1994). Two types of verbal memory tests (i.e., paired-associate learning and story learning) appear to correlate reasonably well with histopathological disturbances in the left CA1 and CA3 hippocampal subfields, as well as in the parahippocampal gyrus. **Recommended tests and measures include (a) two subtests of the WMS-III: Verbal Paired Associates and Logical Memory I and II and (b) the California Verbal Learning Test.**

9. EXAMINATION OF MEMORY FOR VISUALLY PRESENTED INFORMATION

The assessment of "visual memory" is typically conducted by observing the immediate and delayed recall production of novel graphic designs. Several clinical studies have shown that patients with right TLE perform significantly worse than those with left TLE in their recall of fairly complex line drawings and that those with right TLE are more impaired than patients with right frontal epileptogenic foci in their ability to recall very simple drawings after a 30-minute delay (although other studies have failed to show such group differences). In addition, patients with right TLE (but not left TLE) sometimes (but not always) show impairments on tests of immediate recall for human faces, an observation that highlights the role of the right inferotemporal cortex in higher order visual processing for the faces of conspecifics.

Despite these encouraging clinical findings, there have been numerous conflicting studies showing that most current tests of visual memory suffer from significant problems of face validity. Although the tests appear to measure one's ability to rely on nonverbal mediation for the encoding and later recall of novel stimuli, virtually all of these tests allow for verbal mediation as well. Essentially, none of the widely used visual memory tests have been shown to have a satisfactory degree of construct validity and reliability. The search for nonverbalizable graphic designs for use in constructing memory tests with greater construct validity and reliability remains elusive. It is equally important to develop a new generation of "true" visual memory tests that are equivalent to matched verbal memory measures in terms of task difficulty. **Recommended tests and measures include (a) the Visual Reproduction I and II subtests of the WMS-III, (b) the Rey-Osterreith Complex Figure Test, (c) the Denman Facial Recognition Memory Test (Denman, 1984), and (d) the Biber Figure Learning Test.**

10. ROLE OF THE INTRACAROTID AMOBARBITAL PROCEDURE IN THE ASSESSMENT OF MEMORY

The assessment of memory functions in the awake, fully conscious patient often leads to false lateralizing signs depending on whether the epileptogenic lesion is situated more laterally or mesially in the temporal lobe, because the mesial temporal structures are essentially non–material specific for new learning (Helmstaedter, Grunwald, Lehnertz, Gleißner, & Elger, 1997). Rather, it is the left versus right overlying temporal neurocortex that appears to be material specific for the encoding of new verbal versus visual information, respectively.

For this reason, among others, the IAP has long been known to be extremely important for the reliable determination of unilateral hemispheric patency for mnestic functions (see historical review by Snyder & Harris, 1997). Accordingly, the IAP has become a key part of the neuropsychologist's repertoire within epilepsy centers (Loring, Meador, Lee, & King, 1992; Snyder et al., 1990). Essentially, if IAP results indicate that the suspected epileptogenic focus is unable to be resected without significant risk of global amnesia, there is no justification for continuing with presurgical evaluation.

11. INTELLECTUAL–CONCEPTUAL MEASURES

In general, standard measures of verbal–conceptual compared to visual–performance intellectual functioning (e.g., VIQ-PIQ differences on the revised Wechsler Adult Intelligence Scale [WAIS-R]) are poor indicators of left versus right temporal lobe epilepsy, although an early age of seizure onset is associated with lower IQ scores across all domains. In a recent study by Hermann et al. (1995), only the Vocabulary subtest of the WAIS-R (and none of the other 10 subtests) reliably discriminated between patients with left versus right TLE. Performance across virtually all measures of intellectual functioning is linearly related to seizure frequency. Patients with an early age of seizure onset, long duration of epilepsy, and a high seizure frequency demonstrate significantly greater cognitive dysfunction in comparison to those with a later age of seizure onset, a shorter duration of epilepsy, and a lower seizure frequency. This pattern of deficit associated with seizure activity is supported by histopathological study of the hippocampal–dentate complex, suggesting that wide variation in the degree of cytoarchitectural changes across patients with varying durations of the disorder implies a continual degenerative process, rather than one due to a single cortical insult prior to the onset of the disorder (Scheibel, Crandall, & Scheibel, 1974). Although several investigators have reported a negative correlation between the presence of epilepsy and intelligence in children, Ellenberg, Hirtz, and Nelson (1986) studied children both before and after the onset of seizures and found that the occurrence of seizures is not causally related to lower IQs. They claimed that the lower IQs commonly observed in epileptic children are accounted for by other, associated neurological deficits.

Finally, a complete neuropsychological evaluation of patients with epilepsy requires the selection of independent measures of reasoning and judgment to supplement intelligence testing (e.g., the Wisconsin Card Sorting Test), because patients with extratemporal dysfunction demonstrate great difficulty on untimed, trial-and-error tasks in which they are required to use feedback from their previous response to guide their next choice. **Recommended tests and measures include (a) the WAIS-III or Wechsler Intelligence Scale for Children (WISC-III) and (b) the Wisconsin Card Sorting Test.**

12. PERSONALITY EXAMINATION

Personality measurement procedures have long been regarded as an important component of the neuropsychological examination. Much work has been reported on the so-called epileptic personality. Psychometric methods of personality assessment, however, may easily reflect the occurrence of perceptual distortion owing to ictal events experienced during the test administration, leading to an increased probability of false positive profiles of psychopathology. Projective test procedures are especially problematic in the presence of focal central nervous system pathology affecting language and visual–perceptual systems.

In 1977, Bear and Fedio reviewed research that indicated a long interval of approximately 15 years between seizure onset in TLE and the observation of a "schizophrenia-like psychosis," which occurs in some patients. This finding suggests that the psychiatric disorder is a secondary and atypical effect of the major underlying neurological process. Bear and Fedio (1977) noted that there is no compelling reason why any type of psychosis should accurately describe the behavioral sequelae of a neurological process at a specific locus in the brain. This may be why standard personality tests, such as the Thematic Appercation Test and the Rorschach Inkblot Test, which are based on psychodynamic principles and normed on psychiatric populations, have yielded inconsistent results in categorizing patients with TLE. For this reason, actuarial–inventory procedures such as the Minnesota Multiphasic Personality Inventory (MMPI-2) are recommended. Trimble (1983), however, noted that although many comparative studies with the MMPI have been conducted, many of them failed to differentiate among groups of patients with various seizure types and epileptogenic foci. These findings imply that even if epileptic patients suffer from an increased prevalence of psychopathology, it may be attributable to other factors (e.g., anoxic events, head injury, related developmental distrubances) that are only indirectly associated with epilepsy. Recently, however, the MMPI-2, used in conjunction with other measures of dissimulation or malingering, has been shown to be quite helpful in the differential diagnosis of nonepileptic seizures of psychogenic origin (see chapter 16, this volume).

It is often felt that patients with TLE show a poorer response to most treatments and a higher incidence of psychiatric difficulties than do patients with other types of epilepsy. In fact, a centuries-old historical association exists between TLE and hysteria (Glaser, 1978). Flor-Henry (1969) found that in TLE, psychotic disturbances were significantly increased in patients in whom the epileptogenic foci were lateralized to the dominant hemisphere for speech. He also found a significant correlation between left temporal lobe seizure foci and schizophrenic syndromes, and between right-sided foci and bipolar syndromes (Flor-Henry, 1969). Although a number of database studies of patients with TLE at various surgery programs have supported the position that psychoses that are not attributable solely to peri-ictal behavioral and sensory disturbances are prevalent among these patients, other empirical studies have not confirmed this relationship.

Bear and Fedio (1977) attempted to determine the effects of unilateral temporal lobe foci on specific aspects of psychosocial behavior. These authors identified 18 traits previously associated with interictal behavior (e.g., humorlessness) obtained mostly by previous report. Limited support for 4 of the 18 personality traits identified by Bear and Fedio, in distinguishing between patients with TLE and those with primary generalized epilepsy, was offered by Hermann and Riel (1981). Other investigators have not been able to offer reliable corroborative support for any of these "TLE traits" reported by Bear and Fedio.

13. PSYCHOSOCIAL ADJUSTMENT AND QUALITY-OF-LIFE ISSUES

In recent years, greater attention has been paid to the formal evaluation of the role that epilepsy plays in a patient's psychosocial development as well as in the quality of interpersonal relationships and social adjustment. It has now become the "standard of care" to monitor quality of life in a broad sense that is not limited to the reduction of seizure frequency and severity prior to and following surgical intervention. Accordingly, several inventories that measure the quality of life of epilepsy patients across a wide range of indices have been developed in recent years (cf. Perrine et al., 1995). **Recommended tests and measures include (a) the MMPI-2 (the first 400 items, to provide basic scale scores), (b) the Spielberger State-Trait Anxiety Inventory, (c) the Beck Depression Inventory, and (d) the Quality of Life in Epilepsy Inventory, 31-item version (QOLIE-31).**

VI. PSYCHOSOCIAL ISSUES FOR PATIENTS WITH EPILEPSY

A. Social Stigma

Most people with epilepsy are able to enjoy interesting and happy lives as active members of the societies in which they live. As I have shown, however, some people with epilepsy show a broad range of alterations in personality and in emotional, cognitive, intellectual, sensory, and motor functioning as a result of their seizure disorders. In addition, some face further problems in coping with epilepsy in their homes and communities: All patients with epilepsy are at risk of suffering from social stigma, prejudice, or even hostility, which typically result from a lack of information and understanding.

This lack of understanding varies across racial and cultural groups, with some cultures persisting to this day in viewing epilepsy as either infectious, "dirty," or caused by pernicious supernatural influences. Although Western cultures no longer subscribe to this belief system, persons with epilepsy continue to encounter negative attitudes in many areas here, too, ranging from immediate family and school environments to the job market.

B. Epilepsy and the Law

The law in most Western societies serves both to discriminate against and to protect people with epilepsy. For example, people with uncontrolled epilepsy are prohibited from operating motor vehicles. Although this regulation is entirely reasonable and prudent from a public safety perspective, it is a hard restriction to accept for someone whose social life and employment opportunities are disrupted as a result. There are considerable differences among states concerning legal restrictions. Patients with epilepsy have also been discriminated against in their attempts to procure health and life insurance policies, although there has been moderate improvement in this legal arena over the past 2 decades.

Special services for patients with epilepsy, including financial assistance, housing, education for handicapped children, and legal assistance services, have recently become more widely available. In the United States, the single most active resource center and organization for people with epilepsy and their families is the Epilepsy Foundation of America, Inc. (4351 Garden City Drive, Landover, MD 20785). This organization maintains a library that is open to any interested person (persons with epilepsy and their families, students, and health care providers) as well as a toll-free telephone number for information: 1-800-EFA-4050.

VII. CONCLUSION

The clinical neuropsychological examination provides a special contribution to the comprehensive detection and localization of focal cerebral dysfunction, and the neuropsychologist is now considered to be a "core member" of the multidisciplinary team within any epilepsy center. The neuropsychologist relies on the analysis of a broad range of neurobehavioral and cognitive functions, and thus his or her diagnostic impression complements those obtained from the analyses of anatomic and physiological distrubances by other specialists. Hence, the neuropsychological examination is often able to supply evidence of focal cerebral dysfunction before any structural or electrochemical lesion can be demonstrated. However, the neuropsychological examination may lead to a diagnosis of central nervous system pathology that is unrelated to epileptogenicity of the pathological tissue, thereby increasing the possibility of false positive errors in the identification of epileptogenic foci.

BIBLIOGRAPHY

Bear, D. M., & Fedio, P. (1977). Quantitative analysis of interictal behavior in temporal lobe epilepsy. *Archives of Neurology, 34*, 454–467.

Berg, A. T., Levy, S. R., Novotny, E. J., & Shinnar, S. (1996). Predictors of intractable epilepsy in childhood: A case-control study. *Epilepsia, 37,* 24–30.

Denman, S. B. (1984). *Denman Neuropsychology Memory Scale.* Charleston, SC: Sidney B. Denman.

Ellenberg, J. H., Hirtz, D. G., & Nelson, K. B. (1986). Do seizures in children cause intellectual deterioration? *New England Journal of Medicine, 314,* 1085–1088.

Flor-Henry, P. (1969). Schizophrenic-like reactions and affective psychoses associated with temporal lobe epilepsy: Etiological factors. *American Journal of Psychiatry, 126,* 400–403.

Glaser, G. H. (1978). Epilepsy, hysteria, and "possession": A historical essay. *Journal of Nervous and Mental Disease, 166,* 268–274.

Gloor, P., Olivier, A., Quesney, L. F., Andermann, F., & Horowitz, S. (1982). The role of the limbic system in experiential phenomena of temporal lobe epilepsy. *Annals of Neurology, 12,* 129–144.

Gowers, W. R. (1881). *Epilepsy and other chronic convulsive diseases.* London: Churchill.

Helmstaedter, C., Grunwald, T., Lehnertz, K., Gleißner, U., & Elger, C. E. (1997). Differential involvement of left temporolateral and temporomesial structures in verbal declarative learning and memory: Evidence from temporal lobe epilepsy. *Brain and Cognition, 35,* 110–131.

Hermann, B. P., Gold, J., Pusakulich, R., Wyler, A. R., Randolph, C., Rankin, G., & Hoy, W. (1995). Wechsler Adult Intelligence Scale–Revised in the evaluation of anterior temporal lobectomy candidates. *Epilepsia, 36,* 480–487.

Hermann, B. P., & Riel, P. (1981). Interictal personality and behavioral traits in temporal lobe and generalized epilepsy. *Cortex, 17,* 125–128.

Jasper, H. H. (1962). Mechanisms of epileptic automatism. *Epilepsia, 3,* 381–390.

Jones-Gotman, M. (1991). Localization of lesions by neuropsychological testing. *Epilepsia, 32*(Suppl. 5), S41–S52.

Loring, D. (1994). Neuroanatomic substrates of clinical memory measures. In Symposium II: Hippocampus, memory and epilepsy. *Epilepsia, 35*(Suppl. 8), 79.

Loring, D. W., Meador, K. J., Lee, G. P., & King, D. W. (1992). *Amobarbital effects and lateralized brain function: The Wada Test.* New York: Springer-Verlag.

McConnell, H. W., & Duncan, D. (1998). Behavioral effects of antiepileptic drugs. In H. W. McConnell & P. J. Snyder (Eds.), *Psychiatric comorbidity in epilepsy* (pp. 245–361). Washington, DC: American Psychiatric Association Press.

Milner, B. (1975). Psychological aspects of focal epilepsy and its neurosurgical management. In D. P. Purpura, J. K. Penry, & R. D. Walter (Eds.), *Advances in neurology* (Vol. 8, pp. 299–321). New York: Raven Press.

Perrine, K., Hermann, B. P., Meador, K. J., Vickrey, B. G., Cramer, J. A., Hays, R. D., & Devinsky, O. (1995). The relationship of neuropsychological functioning to quality of life in epilepsy. *Archives of Neurology, 52,* 997–1003.

Reynolds, E. H., Elwes, R. D. C., & Shorvon, S. D. (1983). Why does epilepsy become intractable? Prevention of chronic epilepsy. *Lancet,* 952–954.

Scheibel, M. E., Crandall, P. H., & Scheibel, A. B. (1974). The hippocampal-dentate complex in temporal lobe epilepsy: A Golgi study. *Epilepsia, 15,* 55–80.

Snyder, P. J., & Harris, L. J. (1997). The intracarotid amobarbital procedure: An historical perspective. *Brain and Cognition, 33,* 18–32.

Snyder, P. J., Novelly, R. A., & Harris, L. J. (1990). Mixed speech dominance in the intracarotid sodium Amytal procedure: Validity and criteria. *Journal of Clinical and Experimental Neuropsychology, 12,* 629–642.

Spencer, S. S., Spencer, D. D., Williamson, P. D., & Mattson, R. H. (1983). Sexual automatisms in complex partial seizures. *Neurology, 33,* 527–533.

Strauss, E., Hunter, M., & Wada, J. (1995). Risk factors for cognitive impairment in epilepsy. *Neuropsychology, 9,* 457–463.

Strauss, E., Wada, J., & Goldwater, B. (1992). Sex differences in interhemispheric reorganization of speech. *Neuropsychologia, 30,* 353–359.

Tinuper, P., Provini, F., Marini, C., Cerullo, A., Plazzi, G., Avoni, P., & Baruzzi, A. (1996). Partial epilepsy of long duration: Changing semiology with age. *Epilepsia, 37,* 162–164.

Trimble, M. R. (1983). Personality disturbances in epilepsy. *Neurology, 33,* 1332–1334.

Wyllie, E. (1995). Developmental aspects of seizure semiology: Problems in identifying localized-onset seizures in infants and children. *Epilepsia, 36,* 1170–1172.

Zaidel, E. (1985). Language in the right hemisphere. In D. F. Benson & E. Zaidel (Eds.), *The dual brain: Hemispheric specialization in humans* (pp. 205–231). New York: Guilford Press.

CHAPTER 16

Jennifer J. Bortz

Nonepileptic Seizures

Nonepileptic seizures (NES) are clinical spells that resemble epileptic seizures (ES) but are most often behavioral and emotional manifestations of psychological distress, conflict, or trauma. Broadly considered, any such spell that is not produced by an electrophysiologically based event (e.g., syncope) could be regarded as a **nonepileptic seizure**. However, the term **NES** is used throughout this chapter to refer to **psychologically based spells** that have no identifiable electrographical or neurological correlate. This chapter is intended to provide a brief overview of NES diagnostic and treatment issues. For comprehensive review of this topic, the reader is referred to two recently published texts: *Imitators of Epilepsy* (Fisher, 1995) and *Nonepileptic Seizures* (Rowan & Gates, 1993).

I.   EPIDEMIOLOGY

A. Incidence

Approximately 5%–20% in outpatient settings and up to 40% in comprehensive epilepsy centers (Gates & Mercer, 1995).

B. Risk Factors

More common in young adults, in women (3:1 ratio), and in patients with histories of sexual or other forms of physical abuse (Alper, Devinsky, Perrine, Vazquez, & Luciano, 1993). No clear relationship has been found between educational level, intellectual ability, personality profiles, or neuropsychological status and NES; however, certain aspects of the neuropsychological evaluation may identify risk factors that can assist in differential diagnosis and treatment of NES.

II. TERMINOLOGY

The terms used to refer to NES are as varied and confusing as the disorder itself. Far from simplifying communication between professionals and patients, terms for NES that include the word *epilepsy or seizure* often foster confusion regarding the disorder and its important distinction from epileptic seizures (see Exhibit 1). To avoid this problem, my colleagues and I use the descriptive term **episodic stress reaction** in clinical discussions with patients who have NES and their families seen at our center.

III. DIFFERENTIAL DIAGNOSIS

A. NES Versus Epilepsy

The primary imitator of epilepsy is NES, and vice versa. John Hughlings Jackson defined a seizure as a symptom caused by

Exhibit 1. Historical and Current Terminology for NES

Nonepileptic events
Nonepileptic attacks
Nonepileptic seizures
Nonelectrical seizures
Pseudoseizures
Pseudoepileptic seizures
Psychogenic seizures
The Sacred Disease (Hippocrates)
Hysteroepilepsy (Charcot)
Hysterical epilepsy (Freud)

"an occasional, excessive, and a disorderly discharge of nerve tissue." Seizures are produced by a virtual storm of uncontrolled electrical impulses in the brain. Epilepsy is a chronic brain disorder characterized by recurrent seizures. The etiology of ES is diverse and includes infection, tumor, vascular disease, traumatic brain injury, neurodegenerative disease, congenital malformations, and idiopathic disease. Electroencephalographic (EEG) abnormalities remain the gold standard in their diagnosis. A broader discussion of the classification, semiology, and differential diagnosis of seizure disorders is provided in chapter 15, this volume.

Specialists in the field of epileptology find it difficult to differentiate epileptic from nonepileptic seizures, primarily because of the high degree of overlap between the phenomenology of these two disorders. Patients' subjective experience and clinical behavior are frequently quite similar, if not indistinguishable. Patients who present with either ES or NES may show the following symptoms:

1. Alterations in consciousness and periods of unresponsiveness
2. Motor and sensory symptoms (e.g., motor automatisms)
3. Postictal confusion
4. Spells that appear to arise during sleep
5. Self-injury during ictal or behavioral events
6. Similar types of cognitive and mood disturbances, including memory impairment, attention and concentration deficits, slowed thinking, and emotional lability

The psychiatric sequelae of ES can be quite severe and can result in significant functional disability. A high incidence of depression, as well as of anxiety, adjustment difficulties, characterological problems, thought disturbances, and ictal-related auditory and visual hallucinations, has been well documented in this population. Additional overlap between ES and NES lies in the fact that a significant number of patients with NES have concomitant histories of neurological insult, electrographic seizures, and other nonspecific EEG abnormalities. Moreover, the reported incidence of epilepsy in patients with NES has ranged from 10% to 80%, and from 5.9% to 40% of patients with well-documented epilepsy have coexisting NES (see review by Ramsay, Cohen, & Brown, 1993).

Frontal lobe epilepsy is perhaps the most difficult seizure disorder to differentiate from NES. Ictal discharges originating deep in the frontal lobes may not be detected by conventional surface EEG, resulting in a completely normal record throughout a clinical spell. Ictal behaviors are often bizarre and less stereotyped than those associated with more common forms of epilepsy (e.g., screaming, pelvic thrusting, asymmetrical tonic posturing, desynchronous or "bicycling" movements). Thus, a combination of atypical ictal behavior and the absence of EEG abnormality places patients with frontal lobe epilepsy at particularly high risk for being misclassified as having NES or other primary psychiatric conditions (cf. Boon & Williamson, 1993).

In many cases, admission to an epilepsy-monitoring unit is the only means by which documentation of NES can be accomplished. As described by Snyder in chapter 15, this volume, this setting allows for on-line correlation of behavioral events or clinical spells through simultaneous video and EEG recordings. The diagnosis remains one of exclusion, however, requiring thorough investigation of organic causes. Physical and psychiatric disorders that commonly mimic NES are listed in Exhibit 2 and are briefly described later.

Exhibit 2. Common Physiological and Psychiatric Disorders That Mimic Nonepileptic Seizures

Physiological
Epilepsy
Orthostatic hypotension
Cardiac arrhythmias
Syncope
Migraine
Transient ischemic attacks
Paroxysmal movement disorders
Sleep disorders
Hypoglycemia
Hyperventilation
Psychiatric
Somatoform disorders
Conversion disorder
Somatization disorder
Dissociative disorders
Panic disorders
Affective disorders
Posttraumatic stress disorder
Psychotic disorders
Factitious disorder with physical symptoms
Malingering

B. NES Versus Other Paroxysmal Disorders

Although the greatest overlap in clinical signs and symptoms occurs between NES and ES, other organic disorders can convincingly mimic NES. As shown in Exhibit 2, symptoms similar to NES may result from many other paroxysmal disorders besides epilepsy, including cardiovascular events (e.g., orthostatic hypotension), cerebrovascular episodes, paroxysmal movement disorders (e.g., benign essential myoclonus), sleep disorders (e.g., hypnagogic myoclonic jerks), acute and chronic hyperventilation, and hypoglycemia. (For the neurological and psychological signs and symptoms of hyperventilation, see Exhibit 3.)

C. Psychiatric Disorders

The psychological characteristics associated with NES can be quite varied, making presenting signs, symptoms, and course of the disorder difficult to integrate into formal classification

Exhibit 3. Neurological and Psychological Signs and Symptoms of Hyperventilation

---

Neurological
    Headache, pressure, fullness or warmth in the head
    Blurred or tunnel vision, flashing lights, diplopia
    Vertigo, faintness, giddiness, unsteadiness
    Tinnitus
    Paresthesias; coldness of face, extremities, or trunk
    Muscle spasms or stiffness, carpopedal spasm, generalized tetany, tremor
    Ataxia, weakness
    Syncope, seizures
Psychological
    Impairment of concentration and memory
    Feelings of unreality or distortion, confused or dream-like state, déjà vu
    Hallucinations
    Anxiety, apprehension, tension, crying, agoraphobia, phobia, panic

---

Note. From "Neurologic Aspects of Hyperventilation Syndrome," by R. W. Evans, 1995, *Seminars in Neurology, 15*(2), p. 116. Copyright 1995 by Thieme Medical Publishers, Inc. Adapted with permission.

schemes (Gates, Luciana, & Devinsky, 1991). Features of NES can meet diagnostic criteria for multiple psychiatric diagnoses, although NES most commonly holds true to its historical classification as a conversion disorder. According to the fourth edition of the American Psychiatric Association's (1994) *Diagnostic and Statistical Manual of Mental Disorders (DSM-IV)*, **conversion disorder** is characterized by the following:

- motor or sensory symptoms/deficits that are typically associated with medical illness;
- symptoms that are psychologically-based and involuntarily produced;
- not due to either a medical disorder, the effects of pharmacologic substances, or culturally-based experience;
- result in significant distress and/or impairment in daily functioning;
- are not restricted to pain or sexual dysfunction; and
- do not occur only within the course of Somatization Disorder (American Psychiatric Association, 1994, p. 457).

NES is the second most frequent symptom profile among conversion disorders, occurring in approximately 15% of patients with that disorder (Toone, 1990). Several other psychiatric conditions, however, are commonly associated with NES (for review, see Gates, 1998).

In a recent study, Bowman and Marland (1996) formally determined psychiatric diagnoses of 45 adult patients with NES seen in a tertiary-care video-EEG facility. Application of standardized instruments and *DSM-III-R* diagnostic criteria revealed the following patient distribution: 89% somatoform disorders, 91% dissociative disorders, 64% affective disorders, 62% personality disorders, and 49% posttraumatic stress disorder (PTSD). Forty-seven percent of patients met criteria for other types of anxiety disorders. Of note, a high lifetime rate of other conversion symptoms was documented in 18 patients observed to demonstrate ictal conversion symptoms, suggesting that NES is likely one of many conversion symptoms manifested in the course of the disorder. In rare cases, patients present with a factitious disorder in which symptoms are intentionally produced to maintain a sick role (Gates, 1998). Factitious disorders are differentiated from malingering, in which material gains motivate simulation or exaggeration of symptoms.

IV. NEUROANATOMIC CORRELATES

There are no known neuroanatomic correlates of NES. However, studies examining central nervous system and autonomic nervous system involvement in other psychiatric disorders may

eventually lead to the discovery of biological substrates underlying NES. For example, Rausch and colleagues recently documented hypermetabolism by positron emission tomography
(PET) in right-sided limbic, paralimbic, and visual cortical areas,
as well as left inferior frontal and middle temporal cortex in
patients with PTSD undergoing experimental induction of
acute anxiety states (Rausch et al., 1996). Differential changes
in regional cerebral blood flow (rCBF) have similarly been documented in patients with simple phobias, obsessive–compulsive disorder, and primary affective disorders (cf. Rausch et al.,
1995). At this time, any conclusions regarding functional neuroanatomic correlates of NES remain purely speculative.

V. NEUROPSYCHOLOGICAL FINDINGS

Probably because of the heterogeneity of this patient population and the vast overlap of signs and symptoms, there have
been no consistent differences that reliably separate patients
with NES from those with well-defined epilepsy either on formal tests of neuropsychological functioning or on tests of personality and emotional functioning, such as the Minnesota
Multiphasic Personality Inventory (MMPI).

Several investigators have attempted to separate or otherwise classify NES patients according to neuropsychological profiles. Varied results have been reported; some studies have indicated that patients with NES evidence greater impairment in
intellectual and problem-solving abilities (i.e., Wechsler Adult
Intelligence Scale–Revised [WAIS-R] profiles) and in other
domains of cognitive functioning relative to patients with ES,
whereas other investigators have failed to replicate such findings (see review by Hermann, 1993).

Highlighting difficulties in separating these clinical groups
is a study conducted by Hermann (1993), who obtained
detailed neuropsychological data from 12 patients who presented with a diagnosis of NES from other facilities. No epilep-
tiform abnormalities were evidenced during behavioral spells
in previous workups. Patients in this study consented to invasive EEG monitoring with subdural strip electrodes. Review of
video-EEG findings associated with patients' typical spells
revealed epileptic seizures in 6 of the 12 patients and NES in the
remaining 6 patients. No significant differences emerged
between the two groups on measures of neuropsychological
functioning, again underscoring the amount of overlap
between these two patient groups.

In light of the difficulties in identifying consistent *quantitative* differences between NES and ES groups, my colleagues

and I investigated the question of whether *qualitative* characteristics of patients' performance on a recognition memory task could differentiate NES and ES groups (Bortz, Prigatano, Blum, & Fisher, 1995). In responses to the **California Verbal Learning Test (CVLT)**, we found that patients with NES (compared to those with ES) produced a negative response bias on the Recognition Memory subtest, characterized by (a) a tendency to recognize explicitly fewer target words and (b) generation of relatively few false positive responses. A CVLT response bias cutoff score below 0 (i.e., a negative response bias) showed a sensitivity of 61% and a specificity of 91% in the correct classification of patients with NES. An important caveat to these data, however, is that we have found a similar response pattern in patients with frontal lobe epilepsy. Moreover, this tendency appears to be distinct from that seen in patients with "static" frontal lobe lesions, who show the expected leniency, or positive response bias (Bortz, Wong, Blum, Prigatano, & Fisher, 1997). Replication and extension of these findings may prove useful in identifying differential response patterns in these patients.

It is notable that the nature and length of the neuropsychological examination afford a unique opportunity to establish a meaningful working alliance with patients presenting with a complex psychological disturbance. It has been my group's experience that abuse and trauma histories are often elicited during the neuropsychological evaluation, even though patients are routinely asked about such risk factors in other clinical settings and may have denied such experiences. This history has frequently been revealed during attempts to clarify the reason for unexpectedly low WAIS-R Information and Vocabulary scores that are inconsistent with psychosocial history and achievement or other test scores. Histories of academic underachievement, truancy, and frequent or extended absences from school may raise a red flag of significant emotional distress during childhood or adolescence. Obtaining a detailed history of these problems is crucial, because patients with longstanding ES may have similar patterns of test performance owing to academic difficulties, school absences, and attention or memory deficits secondary to their seizure disorder.

VI. PERSONALITY ASSESSMENT

Numerous studies have examined usefulness of MMPI profiles in the differential diagnosis of NES. Wilkus and colleagues published several papers concerning a series of decision rules used to differentiate NES from ES (cf. Wilkus & Dodrill, 1989). Empirical application of these criteria by other investigators has yielded varying degrees of specificity and sensitivity, with considerable overlap between ES and NES groups (see review in Rowan & Gates, 1993). Recently, Mason, Mercer, Risse, and Gates (1996) reported a 60% correct classification rate for NES and 30% incorrect classification for ES using a set of decision rules revised for the MMPI-II. The "sizable error rate" led these authors to question the predictive value of previously established MMPI decision rules.

Although the reliability of various categorization rules remains controversial, MMPI somatization profiles have assisted in identifying key NES risk factors. For example, Connell and Wilner (1996) found that a higher mean Scale 3 elevation, combined with earlier onset of seizures, differentiated groups of patients with NES versus those with ES; in their study, the highest diagnostic "hit rate" was derived from Scale 3 for NES and from age at onset for ES (90% and 83%, respectively). Other investigators have identified Scale 3 elevations, either in isolation or in conjunction with other variables, as differentially characteristic of NES (e.g., Snyder et al., 1997; Derry & McLachlan, 1996). In all, it appears that MMPI findings play an important role in identifying risk factors associated with NES and that differential diagnosis can be significantly enhanced by clinical exploration of these factors (i.e., stress and emotional conflict issues) and integration with other diagnostic information. MMPI data are also valuable in treatment planning for patients with both NES and ES.

VII. PROVOCATIVE TESTING PROCEDURES

Placebo induction, or provocative testing procedures, are often used to support a diagnosis of NES. The goal of these procedures is to evoke a behavioral spell identical to the patient's spontaneous episodes. Clinical techniques include photic stimulation, hyperventilation, tactile compression, injection of physiologic saline or other chemical placebos, placement of epidural patches soaked in alcohol, and hypnotic suggestion. Although such tests may provide useful diagnostic information, consideration of several risks and caveats is warranted.

A major risk associated with these procedures is the potential threat to the therapeutic alliance established between patients and clinicians. Specifically, techniques in which patients are directly given false information, or in which they may later perceive that they have been misled or manipulated, could potentially cause additional distress and resentment in an already emotionally fragile patient. Rather, when an induction is deemed appropriate, permission should be obtained from the patient to try a procedure that may produce a clinical spell similar to those occurring spontaneously. Consent allows the patient to be an active participant in, rather than a subjugated object or victim of, the diagnostic process.

At the center I work in, my colleagues and I typically use a combination of hyperventilation, photic stimulation, and suggestion involving the verbal elaboration of clinical signs and symptoms manifested during the procedure in an attempt to evoke a behavioral spell. If the induction is positive, patients and family members are asked to rate the degree to which the induced spell resembled a "typical" seizure. Induced spells that are highly similar to typical events are considered supportive of the NES diagnosis. However, a positive clinical finding (i.e., elicitation of a subjectively and behaviorally typical spell in the absence of concomitant EEG abnormalities) does not confirm a diagnosis of NES; careful consideration of several additional factors is required. One factor is the fact that the base rate of the frequency of a positive induction in patients with well-documented ES has not yet been sufficiently explored. Second, the possibility of a mixed disorder remains; patients with more than one type of spell may have both NES and underlying ES (Gates, 1998). Third, patients with either type of disorder may be unaware of what their typical spells are like, and they may not be able to estimate reliably the degree of similarity between an induced and a spontaneous spell or seizure. With the patient's consent, it is often helpful to review videotaped spells with someone who has witnessed these events to have him or her assess the extent to which the spell resembles previous events.

VIII. PATIENT EDUCATION AND TREATMENT

At my center, patients with known or suspected risk factors for NES are told of this possibility early in the diagnostic process. This "inoculation technique" gives patients additional time to gather and process relevant information in a manner intended to promote understanding and acceptance of psychological aspects of the disorder. In this way, treatment of NES begins early by (a) presenting the diagnosis in a therapeutic manner, (b) dispelling misconceptions and addressing personal and social stigma concerning the diagnosis, and (c) providing educational information for patients and families.

In presenting the diagnosis, the clinician must fully consider the emotional fragility of most patients with NES. NES is a manifestation of relatively primitive and ineffective coping mechanisms. The contribution of enmeshed or otherwise dysfunctional interpersonal relationships to the disorder is often complex. Fear of abandonment, including loss of the physician–patient relationship, can be overwhelming to these patients.

As described by others in the literature (e.g., Gates & Mercer, 1995), my colleagues and I present the diagnosis of NES to patients and their families in a "good news" format, intended to convey a genuine sense of accomplishment in the collaboration required to make the diagnosis, the desire to form a strong therapeutic working alliance, and optimism about therapeutic outcome. Several points are emphasized, including (a) the importance of arriving at an accurate diagnosis; (b) the opportunity to plan for successful treatment; (c) the chance to discontinue antiepileptic drugs and eliminate related side effects; and (d) the likelihood that memory, attention, and other cognitive and affective problems will improve with remission of the disorder. For higher functioning patients, the possibility of being able to drive, to resume daily activities, and to return to school or work serves as a primary reinforcer for therapeutic intervention.

Patients' initial reaction to hearing the diagnosis is often one of confusion, embarrassment, or defensiveness. Two important misconceptions that require early discussion include the fact that, in the vast majority of cases, patients are not consciously "faking" their spells and that they are usually unable to control their symptoms armed only with identification of the disorder. In accordance with the "good news" perspective, patients are given examples of how physical symptoms may be exacerbated by stress (e.g., migraine headaches worsening with stress-induced muscle tension). Examples of how cognitive processes can occur outside the realm of conscious awareness may also further understanding and acceptance of the diagnosis (e.g., the inability to recall information on an examination or the inability to recall the name of an old friend until it seemingly emerges "out of nowhere," when one least expects it).

Last, understanding and acceptance of the diagnosis is frequently enhanced by review of the diagnostic process and discussion of educational information with family members. In select cases, family participation in the therapeutic process can significantly enhance treatment efficacy.

IX. TREATMENT AND PROGNOSIS

As a conversion disorder, NES has historically been viewed within a psychodynamic framework in which unresolved internal conflicts elicit and maintain pathological states. However, the extent of repression and denial exhibited by many NES patients, as well as their inability to tolerate intense affect, can restrict the efficacy of traditional dynamic approaches. Given these barriers, symptom management is often needed to establish a strong therapeutic alliance and to effect more immediate behavioral improvement. Early progress in alleviating target symptoms with known physiological components (e.g., hyperventilation, insomnia) can provide a strong therapeutic foundation, with realization of relatively short-term gains effecting patients' sense of increased control and self-efficacy. Central issues may then emerge once more primitive defenses are weakened. Although patients vary in their ability to work through primary conflicts, tolerating this type of work is often key to avoiding symptom substitution and to achieving full resolution of the disorder.

Literature regarding prognosis and outcome following diagnosis of NES is extremely sparse. Five favorable prognostic factors were identified by Meierkord, Will, Fish, and Shorvon (1991) in a study of 110 patients with video-EEG confirmed NES: female gender, an independent lifestyle, higher intelligence, normal EEG findings, and no prior history of psychotherapy. Unfavorable prognostic factors included a chronic history of NES or other psychiatric disorders, family history of epilepsy, unemployment, and evidence of co-existing epilepsy. Approximately 40% of study patients had full remission of NES symptoms at a mean 5-year followup. Prospective outcome studies, including controlled studies of the independent and combined efficacy of psychotherapeutic and pharmacologic interventions, and their respective effects on medical use, quality of life, and employment status are clearly warranted.

X. CONCLUSION

Assessment, diagnosis, and treatment of NES are complex, with differential diagnoses spanning a broad spectrum of neurological and psychiatric disorders. Diagnostic and therapeutic processes are often aided by the neuropsychological evaluation; however, quantitative findings alone are of limited use owing to the high degree of overlap between cognitive and psychological profiles of patients with NES and ES. Neuropsychological data are most useful in the context of a thorough review of the patient's medical and psychosocial history and a thoughtful integration of findings from the neurological examination, EEG, and neuroimaging studies. Neuropsychology often plays an important therapeutic role through clinicians' involvement in provocative testing procedures; by providing "good news" regarding cognitive integrity and the likelihood of reversible memory and other cognitive inefficiencies; and by providing educational, treatment, and referral information to patients and family members.

BIBLIOGRAPHY

Alper, K., Devinsky, O., Perrine, K., Vazquez, B., & Luciano, D. (1993). Nonepileptic seizures and childhood sexual and physical abuse. *Neurology, 43*, 1950–1953.

American Psychiatric Association. (1994). *Diagnostic and statistical manual of mental disorders* (4th ed.). Washington, DC: Author.

Boon, P. A., & Williamson, P. D. (1993). The diagnosis of pseudoseizures. *Clinical Neurology and Neurosurgery, 95*,1–8.

Bortz, J. J., Prigatano, G. P., Blum, D., & Fisher, R. S. (1995). Differential response characteristics in nonepileptic and epileptic seizure patients on a test of verbal learning and memory. *Neurology, 45*, 2029–2035.

Bortz, J. J., Wong, J., Blum, D., Prigatano, G. P., & Fisher, R. S. (1997). Differential verbal learning and memory characteristics in frontal lobe epilepsy. *Journal of the International Neuropsychological Society, 3*(1), 73–74.

Bowman, E. S., & Marland, O. M. (1996). Psychodynamics and psychiatric diagnoses of pseudoseizure subjects. *American Journal of Psychiatry, 153*, 57–63.

Connell, B. E., & Wilner, A. M. (1996). MMPI-2 distinguishes intractable epilepsy from pseudoseizures: A replication. *Epilepsia, 37*(5), 19.

Crosson, B., Sarton, K. J., Jenny, A. B., Nabors, N. A., & Moberg, P. J. (1993). Increased intrusions during verbal recall in traumatic and nontraumatic lesions of the temporal lobe. *Neuropsychology, 7*, 193–208.

Derry, P. A., & McLachlan, R. S. (1996). The MMPI-2 as an adjunct to the diagnosis of pseudoseizures. *Seizure, 5*(1), 35–40.

Fisher, R. S. (1995). *Imitators of epilepsy*. New York: Demos Press.

Gates, J. R. (1998). Diagnosis and treatment of nonepileptic seizures. In H. W. McConnell & P. J. Snyder (Eds.), *Psychiatric comorbidity in epilepsy*. Washington, DC: American Psychiatric Press.

Gates, J. R., Luciano, D., & Devinsky, O. (1991). The classification and treatment of nonepileptic events. In O. Devinsky & W. A. Theodore (Eds.), *Epilepsy and behavior* (pp. 251–263). New York: Wiley-Liss.

Gates, J. R., & Mercer, K. (1995). Nonepileptic events. *Seminars in Neurology, 15*, 167–174.

Heinrichs, T. F., Tucker, D. M., Farha, J., & Novelly, R. A. (1988). MMPI indices in the identification of patients evidencing pseudoseizures. *Epilepsia, 21*, 184–187.

Hermann, B. P. (1993). Neuropsychological assessment in the diagnosis of non-epileptic seizures. In A. J. Rowan & J. R. Gates (Eds.), *Nonepileptic seizures* (pp. 221–232). Stoneham, MA: Butterworth-Heinemann.

Hermann, B. P., Wyler, A. R., Bush, A. M., & Tabatabai, F. R. (1992). Differential effects of left and right anterior temporal lobectomy on verbal learning and memory performance. *Epilepsia, 33*, 289–297.

Mason, S. L., Mercer, K., Risse, G. L., & Gates, J. R. (1996). Clinical utility of the MMPI-II in the diagnosis of non-epileptic seizures (NES). *Epilepsia, 37*(Suppl. 5), 18.

Meierkord, H., Will, B., Fish, D., & Shorvon, S. (1991). The clinical features and prognosis of pseudoseizures diagnosed using video-EEG telemetry. *Neurology, 41*, 1643–1647.

Ramsay, R. E., Cohen, A., & Brown, M. C. (1993). Coexisting epilepsy and non-epileptic seizures. In A. J. Rowan & J. R. Gates (Eds.), *Nonepileptic seizures* (pp. 47–54). Stoneham, MA: Butterworth-Heinemann.

Rausch, S. L, Savage, C. R., Alpert, N. M., Miguel, E. C., Baer, L., Breiter, H. C., Fischman, A. J., Manzo, P. A., Moretti, C., & Jenike, M. A. (1995). A positron emission tomographic study of simple phobic symptom provocation. *Archives of General Psychiatry, 52*, 20–28.

Rausch, S. L., van der Kolk, B. A., Fisler, R. E., Alpert, N. M., Savage, C. R., Fischman, A. J., Jenike, M. A., & Pitman, R. K. (1996). A symptom provocation study of posttraumatic stress disorder using positron emission tomography and script-driven imagery. Archives of *General Psychiatry, 53,* 380–387.

Rowan, A. J., & Gates, J. R. (Eds.). (1993). *Nonepileptic seizures.* Stoneham, MA: Butterworth-Heinemann.

Saygi, S., Katz, A., Marks, D. A., & Spencer, S. S. (1992). Frontal lobe partial seizures and psychogenic seizures: Comparison of clinical and ictal characteristics. *Neurology, 42,* 1274–1277.

Snyder, P. J., Martin, R. C., Ceravolo, N., Turrentine, L., Franzen, M. D., Valeriano, J., Kelly, K. M., Faught, E., Gilliam, F., & Kuzniecky, R. (1997). Neuropsychological and clinical indicators for rapid identification of patients with nonepileptic seizures [Abstract]. *Epilepsia, 38*(Suppl. 8), 170.

Toone, B. K. (1990). Disorders of hysterical conversion. In C. Bass (Ed.), *Somatization: Physical symptoms and psychological illness* (pp. 207–234). London: Blackwell.

Vanderzant, C. W., Giordani, B., Berent, S., Dreifuss, F. E., & Sackellares, J. C. (1986). Personality of patients with pseudoseizures. *Neurology, 36,* 664–668.

Warner, M. H., Wilkus, R. J., Vossler, D. G., Wyler, A. R., & Abson, D. L. (1996). MMPI-2 profiles in differential diagnosis of epilepsy vs. psychogenic seizures. *Epilepsia, 37*(5), 19.

Wilkus, R., Dodrill, C. B., & Thompson, P. M. (1984). Intensive EEG monitoring and psychological studies of patients with pseudo-epileptic seizures. *Epilepsia, 25*(1), 100–107.

Wilkus, R., & Dodrill, C. B. (1989). Factors affecting the outcome of MMPI and neuropsychological assessments of psychogenic and epileptic seizure patients. *Epilepsia, 30,* 339–347.

CHAPTER 17

Oscar L. Lopez and James T. Becker

HIV Infection and Associated Conditions

Human immunodeficiency virus (HIV) is a nontransforming retrovirus that produces a cytopathic or lytic effect on T lymphocytes. The exact mechanisms for this process are not completely known, although it is currently recognized that the CD4+ receptor is the principal target site of HIV. Consequently, HIV causes a severe disruption of cellular immunity that permits the development of latent infections as well as of true opportunistic infections. One of the most important aspects of this infection is that HIV replicates within the central nervous system (CNS). Therefore, the CNS clinical symptoms of HIV infection may arise as a result of diffuse or focal brain involvement, caused either by HIV or by opportunistic infections. Autopsy studies have reported that 80%–90% of HIV-infected individuals had neuropathological evidence of CNS involvement (Navia, Jordan, & Price, 1986). The variety of HIV-related CNS diseases is shown in Table 1 (Levy & Berger, 1993). These

Preparation of this chapter was supported in part by a grant from the National Institute of Mental Health (MH-45133). James T. Becker is the recipient of a Research Scientist Development Award Level II (MH-01077) and Oscar L. Lopez received a Minority Scientist Supplement through the University of Pittsburgh Alzheimer's Disease Research Center (AG-05151).

Table 1. HIV-1-Related Nervous System Diseases

Type of disease	Specific illness or agent
Primary viral (HIV-1 syndromes)	HIV-1 encephalopathy Atypical aseptic meningitis Vacuolar myelopathy Peripheral motor–sensory neuropathy HIV myopathy Polyradiculopathy
Opportunistic viral illnesses	Cytomegalovirus Herpes simplex virus, Types 1 and 2 Varicella zoster virus Papovavirus (progressive mult-focal leukoencephalopathy) Adenovirus Type 2
Nonviral infections	*Toxoplasma gondii* *Cryptococcus neoformans* *Candida albicans* *Aspergillus fumigatus* *Coccidioides immitis* *Mucormycosis* *Rhizopus sp.* *Acremonium alabamensis* *Histoplasma capsulatum* *Mycobacterium hominis tuberculosis* *Mycobacterium avium-intracellulare* *Listeria monocytogenes* *Nocardia asteroides* *Streptococcus pneumonia* *Hemophilus influenza*
Neoplasms	Primary CNS lymphoma Metastatic systemic lymphoma Metastatic Kaposi's sarcoma
Cerebrovascular	Ischemic–hemorrhagic infarction Hemorrhage Vasculitis

Note. From "HIV and HTLV Infections of the Nervous System," by R. M. Levy and J. R. Berger, 1993, in *Infectious Diseases of the Central Nervous System* (p. 93), K. L. Tyler and J. B. Martin (Eds.). Copyright 1993 by F. A. Davis. Adapted with permission.

infections reflect a diminished immunocompetence, and the CD4+ cell count is generally below 200/1 mm. However, a specific diagnosis made on the basis of neurological or neuropsychological symptoms is sometimes difficult in these patients, even in cases with available laboratory data. This chapter is an overview of the neuropsychiatric and cognitive syndromes that develop in HIV-infected individuals. We examine the most frequent opportunistic infections that occur in HIV-infected individuals, although we have chosen to emphasize the signs and symptoms that are directly related to HIV encephalopathy.

I. EPIDEMIOLOGICAL FEATURES

The Centers for Disease Control and Prevention (CDC) has reported that from the beginning of the acquired immunodeficiency syndrome (AIDS) epidemic through December 1, 1995, approximately 476,899 cases of AIDS have been diagnosed in the United States and approximately 295,473 (62%) of these patients have died (CDC, 1995). The World Health Organization estimated that 16,000,000 adults and 1,000,000 children are infected with the HIV and that 4,000,000 people have developed AIDS around the world since the epidemic began. The largest number of estimated AIDS cases is in sub-Saharan Africa (more than 2.5 million). However, as the epidemic has expanded, there has been an increase in the number of AIDS cases in Asia, from 30,000 to 250,000 in 1994 (World Health Organization; WHO, 1995).

Although the patterns of AIDS-defining illnesses appear to be consistent in different cultures, the frequency and prevalence of many disorders can be influenced by racial or ethnic factors, age, and characteristics of the risk group. Premorbid exposure to infectious agents, diagnosis and reporting of infectious diseases, and access to care and therapy also appear to affect the manifestations of HIV.

In terms of CNS infections, cryptococcal meningitis is more common among Blacks than among Whites and in intravenous drug users than in non-drug users (Levy, 1988). Neuropathological studies have shown that HIV encephalopathy is more frequent in Europe (Martinez et al., 1995) and the United States (de la Monte, Ho, & Schooley, 1987) than in South America (Chimelli, Rosemberg, & Hahn, 1992). Toxoplasmic encephalitis is more common in Europe, South America, and Miami (Moskowitz, Hensley, & Chan, 1984) than on the U.S. West Coast (Anders, Guerra, & Tomiyashu, 1986). Cytomegalovirus (CMV) encephalitis is more common on the U.S. East Coast (Petito, Cho, Lemann, Navia, & Price, 1986) than the West

Coast. Primary CNS lymphoma is more frequent in Europe than in the United States (Martinez et al., 1995).

II. HIV CNS INFECTION

Although the majority of patients have abnormal cerebrospinal fluid (CSF) at the time of seroconversion, only a small number of them exhibit CNS symptoms. These symptoms include headaches, encephalitis, meningitis, myopathy, and plexitis, which usually subside within weeks. A few patients develop acute HIV meningitis, but the clinical symptoms are indistinguishable from any aseptic meningitis. The CSF shows elevated proteins, increased cellularity, immunoglobulins, and viral antigens (McArthur, 1994).

As the infection progresses, more than 65% of patients develop neurological disease involving every level of the neuraxis. In the CNS, HIV infection gives rise to encephalitis, meningitis or meningoencephalitis, and vacuolar myelopathy. The meningitis can start at the time of seroconversion, and it may become chronic or recurring. Despite the frequency with which the virus is cultured from the CSF in the early stages of the infection, HIV encephalopathy does not usually develop until later stages, when the immunologic disturbances are significant.

HIV-related peripheral nervous system involvement includes polyneuropathy, inflammatory demyelinating polyradiculopathies, and mononeuritis multiplex. In this chapter, we do not examine the clinical features of peripheral nervous system damage or of vacuolar myelopathy.

III. HIV NEUROBEHAVIORAL DISORDERS

Early observations of HIV-infected individuals led to the identification of a triad of psychomotor slowing, slow thinking, and flat affect, which was termed *AIDS-dementia complex* (Navia et al., 1986). The CDC (1987) diagnostic criteria for HIV encephalopathy resemble the symptoms of the AIDS-dementia complex described by Navia and colleagues. However, more recent observations have indicated that at least two types of neurobehavioral disorders can occur in HIV-infected patients (Grant & Martin, 1994). The more severe disorder is HIV dementia (HIV-D), in which there is a significant deterioration of the activities of daily living; the other is a milder disorder, which is frequently identified with neuropsychological testing and has a lesser effect on life activities.

Consequently, these clinical criteria were revised to capture the whole spectrum of cognitive impairment seen in HIV-infected patients. The American Academy of Neurology (AAN) AIDS Task Force (AAN, 1991) published diagnostic criteria for the HIV-associated cognitive–motor complex (see Exhibit 1). These patients exhibited a dementia syndrome with severe impairment of the activities of daily living, consistent with the clinical symptoms of the HIV-dementia complex. For less severe cases, in which the activities of daily living are not affected but there is mild neuropsychological deficit, the diagnosis of HIV-associated minor cognitive–motor disorders is given. Price and Brew (1988) provided a clinical staging scheme similar to the Clinical Dementia Rating for Alzheimer's disease, specifically for HIV-related impairments (see Table 2).

One of the current problems in the study of HIV-D is the lack of information about the natural course of the disease. Although an important step was taken when the syndrome was dichotomized to differentiate between frank dementia and minor cognitive changes, information is provided only from these two extremes of the spectrum.

A. HIV Dementia

The prevalence of HIV-D has been estimated at between 6% and 30% among adult patients with AIDS. The introduction of antiviral treatments and a better definition of HIV-D may explain the discrepancy between prevalence in early (Navia et al., 1986) and more recent reports (McArthur et al., 1993; Portegies et al., 1989; Qureshi, Hanson, Jones, & Jansson, 1998). Risk factors included anemia, constitutional symptoms, and low weight before developing AIDS, suggesting that the sickest patients develop dementia (McArthur, 1994).

The most salient aspect of HIV-D is an insidious decline in cognitive function. In early stages, patients complain of difficulty coordinating previously routine tasks. As the disease progresses, they develop apathy, symptoms of depression, moderate-to-severe cognitive and psychomotor slowing, impaired concentration and attention, and memory deficits (Navia et al., 1986; Price et al., 1988). With advancing dementia, memory deteriorates further, and the patient becomes slower and exhibits language disorders. These symptoms produce a pattern of cognitive and motor impairment similar to that found in other dementias resulting from predominantly subcortical involvement, such as Parkinson's disease and Huntington's disease. The terminal stage of the syndrome is characterized by

Exhibit 1. Criteria for Clinical Diagnosis of HIV Dementia (Cognitive–Motor Complex) in Adults and Adolescents

All of the following require laboratory evidence for systemic HIV-1 infection (ELISA test confirmed by Western Blot, polymerase chain reaction, or culture).

I. Sufficient for diagnosis of AIDS: HIV-1-associated dementia complex

  A. *Probable* (must have *each* of the following):

   1. Acquired abnormality in at least two of the following cognitive abilities (present for at least 1 month): attention–concentration, speed of processing of information, abstraction–reasoning, visuospatial skills, memory–learning, and speech–language). The decline should be verified by reliable history and mental status examination. In all cases, when possible, history should be obtained from an informant, and examination should be supplemented by neuropsychological testing.

   2. Cognitive dysfunction causing impairment of work or activities of daily living (objectively verifiable or by report of a key informant). This impairment should not be attributable solely to severe systemic illness.

   At least *one* of the following:

    a. Acquired abnormality in motor function, performance, or both, verified by clinical examination (e.g., slowed rapid movements, abnormal gait, limb incoordination, hyperreflexia, hypertonia, weakness), neuropsychological tests (e.g., fine motor speed, manual dexterity, perceptual-motor skills).

    b. Decline in motivation or emotional control or change in social behavior characterized by any of the following: change in personality with apathy, inertia, irritability, emotional lability, or new onset of impaired judgment characterized by socially inappropriate behavior or disinhibition.

   3. Absence of clouding of consciousness during a period long enough to establish the presence of diagnostic criteria No. 1.

   4. Evidence of another causal condition, including active central nervous system opportunistic infection

or malignancy, psychiatric disorder (e.g., depressive disorder), active alcohol or substance abuse, or acute or chronic substance withdrawal, must be sought from history, physical and psychiatric examination, and appropriate laboratory and radiological investigation (e.g., lumbar puncture, neuroimaging). If another potential cause (e.g., major depression) is present, it must not be the cause of the preceding cognitive, motor, or behavioral symptoms and signs.

B. *Possible* (must have *one* of the following):

1. Other potential cause present (must have each of the following):

   a. Meets preceding criteria (see A. *Probable*) Nos. 1, 2, and 3.

   b. Other potential cause is present, but uncertain.

2. Incomplete clinical evaluation (must have *each* of the following):

   a. Meets preceding criteria (see A. *Probable*) Nos. 1, 2, and 3.

   b. Cause cannot be determined (appropriate laboratory or radiological investigations not performed).

II. Not sufficient for diagnosis of AIDS: HIV-1-associated minor cognitive–motor disorder

A. *Probable* (must have *each* of the following):

1. Cognitive–motor–behavioral abnormalities (must have *each* of the following):

   a. At least *two* of the following acquired cognitive, motor, or behavioral symptoms (present for at least 1 month) verified by reliable history (when possible, from an informant):

      (1) Impaired attention or concentration

      (2) Mental slowing

      (3) Impaired memory

      (4) Slowed movements

      (5) Incoordination

      (6) Personality change, irritability, or emotional lability

   b. Acquired cognitive–motor abnormality verified by clinical neurological examination or neuropsycho-

(Continued)

Exhibit 1. Criteria for Clinical Diagnosis of HIV Dementia (Cognitive–Motor Complex) in Adults and Adolescents *(Continued)*

logical testing (e.g., fine motor speed, manual dexterity, perceptual–motor skills, attention–concentration, speed of processing of information, abstraction–reasoning, visuospatial skills, memory–learning, or speech–language).

2. Disturbance from cognitive–motor–behavioral abnormalities (see No. 1) causes mild impairment of work or activities of daily living (objectively verifiable or by report of a key informant).

3. Does not meet criteria for HIV-1-associated dementia complex or HIV-1-associated myelopathy.

4. *No* evidence of another cause, including active central nervous system opportunistic infection, malignancy, or severe systemic illness, determined by appropriate history, physical examination, and laboratory and radiological investigation (e.g., lumbar puncture, neuroimaging). The preceding features should not be attributable solely to the effects of active alcohol or substance use, acute or chronic substance withdrawal, adjustment disorder, or other psychiatric disorders.

B. *Possible* (must have *one* of the following):

1. Other potential cause present (must have *each* of the following):

   a. As in the preceding (see A. *Probable*) Nos. 1, 2, and 3.

   b. Other potential cause is present, and the cause of the cognitive–motor–behavioral abnormalities is uncertain.

2. Incomplete clinical evaluation (must have *each* of the following):

   a. As in the preceding (see A. *Probable*) Nos. 1, 2, and 3.

   b. Cause cannot be determined (appropriate laboratory or radiological investigations not performed).

Note. From "Nomenclature and research case definitions for the neurological manifestations of human immunodeficiency virus type-1 infection," by the American Academy of Neurology, 1991, *Neurology, 41.* Copyright 1991 by the American Academy of Neurology. Reprinted with permission.

Table 2. Clinical Staging of the AIDS Dementia Complex

Stage	Characteristics
Stage 0 (normal)	Normal mental and motor function.
Stage 0.5 (equivocal or subclinical)	Absent, minimal, or equivocal symptoms *without impairment of work or capacity to perform ADL*. Mild signs (snout response, slowed ocular or extremity movements) may be present. Gait and strength are normal.
Stage 1 (mild)	Able to perform *all but the more demanding aspects of work or ADL* but with unequivocal evidence (signs or symptoms that may include performance on neuropsychological testing) of functional intellectual or motor impairment. Can walk without assistance.
Stage 2 (moderate)	Able to perform *basic activities of self-care* but cannot work or maintain the more demanding aspects of daily life. Ambulatory but may require a single prop.
Stage 3 (severe)	*Major intellectual incapacity* (cannot follow news or personal events, cannot sustain complex conversation, considerable slowing of all output) *or motor disability* (cannot walk unassisted, requiring walker or personal support, usually with slowing and clumsiness of arms as well).
Stage 4 (end stage)	*Nearly vegetative*. Intellectual and social comprehension and output are at a rudimentary level. Nearly or absolutely mute. Paraparetic or paraplegic with urinary and fecal incontinence.

Note. Staging definition revised as of September 21, 1988. ADL = activities of daily living. From "The AIDS Dementia Complex," by R. W. Price & B. J. Brew, 1988, *Journal of Infectious Diseases, 158.* Copyright 1988 by the University of Chicago Press. Reprinted with permission.

global cognitive impairment and severe psychomotor retardation. These symptoms often progress rapidly over a few weeks or months, and there is a mean survival of 6 months (Price & Brew, 1988).

Neuropsychologically, timed tasks measuring psychomotor speed and mental flexibility are most sensitive. In contrast to other dementia criteria, such as the DSM-IV (American Psychiatric Association, 1994) or the ICD-10 (WHO, 1991), criteria for HIV-D require an impairment in at least two cognitive areas, but *memory deficits are not strictly necessary* (Becker, Martin, & Lopez, 1994). Nevertheless, memory can be affected in early stages, with a discrepancy between recall and recognition memory: Recognition is often unimpaired. Language and simple concentration tasks remain unimpaired until more advanced stages of the disease.

These cognitive symptoms are associated with neurological signs including hyperreflexia, slowing of rapid movements of the eyes and limbs, and release signs. As the dementia progresses, these patients exhibit increased muscle tone, especially in lower limbs (which may reflect a vacuolar myelopathy), clonus, exaggerated tremors, ataxia, myoclonus, incontinence, and seizures (Navia et al., 1986; Price et al., 1988).

B. HIV With Mild Neuropsychological Impairment

Current research suggests that HIV-infected individuals with mild neuropsychological deficit do not always progress to HIV-D (Selnes et al., 1995). This deficit is usually mild in medically asymptomatic patients and worsens as the disease progresses. It affects attention, speed of information processing, and learning; psychiatric, substance abuse, or constitutional problems cannot explain its presence. The pattern suggests an early dysfunction of frontal–subcortical systems (Heaton et al., 1995). This cluster of neuropsychological symptoms can be seen at any stage of the infection, although it is more frequent in later stages of the disease.

There are numerous questions about mild neuropsychological deficits in HIV-infected individuals. It is still unknown whether there are specific predictors for development of such mild deficits before development of AIDS-defining illnesses. Although constitutional symptoms at the time of AIDS diagnosis appear predictive of later HIV-D (McArthur et al., 1993), it is unclear whether such symptoms relate to mild neuropsychological impairment in HIV-infected patients with or without AIDS. Another issue of significant public health relevance is whether mild neuropsychological deficits are present in otherwise medically asymptomatic HIV-infected persons. Grant et al. (1987) reported in a small sample that up to 44% of asymptomatic HIV-infected individuals had neuropsychological deficits. This report received considerable attention, and it was suggested that even asymptomatic HIV-infected pilots should be medically disqualified from flying (Association, 1992). However, others have found no neuropsychological differences between asymptomatic HIV-infected individuals and seronegative controls (Miller, Selnes, & McArthur, 1990). Nevertheless, more recent studies conducted in a large number ($N = 500$) of HIV-infected individuals, using detailed neuropsychological assessment, have revealed cognitive deficits in 30.5% of the asymptomatic patients of the CDC-A group, 44.5% of the CDC-B group, and 55.6% of the CDC-C group (Heaton et al., 1995).

C. HIV With Psychiatric Symptoms

1. DELIRIUM

The most common psychiatric symptom in hospitalized patients with HIV (e.g., 43% according to Maj, Starace, & Sartorius, 1993), delerium is characterized by an abrupt onset of confusion, agitation, attentional deficits, incoherent speech, language deficits, and sometimes psychosis. It can be caused by a single or various medical abnormalities, such as systemic opportunistic infections, medication toxicity, metabolic imbalance (i.e., electrolyte imbalance), or a primary CNS lesion. Because delirium in HIV-positive patients has a high rate of morbidity, it is important to initiate a rapid workup to determine the cause; neuroimaging and lumbar puncture are most helpful for ruling out secondary CNS infection.

2. DEPRESSION

Depressed mood has been reported in up to 76% of HIV-infected individuals, and major depression in 10%–15% (Atkinson, Grant, & Kennedy, 1988; Dew et al., 1997; Maj et al., 1994). Because HIV affects cerebral structures (e.g., frontal–subcortical systems) that are involved in human behavior, especially affective behaviors, the mood disorders in HIV may be related, at least in part, to actual CNS lesions rather than solely a reaction to illness or comorbid stressors (Zorrilla, McKay, Luborsky, &

Schmidt, 1996). Recent longitudinal studies have shown that depression is associated with HIV serostatus, even when other risk factors for depression were controlled (Dew et al., 1997). The depressive effect of medications such as steroids, antineoplastic drugs, or antibiotic–antifungal drugs must also be taken into consideration when determining the etiology of depressive disorders in patients with HIV. Finally, the neuropsychological performance of these patients improves after antidepressant therapy is initiated (Buckingham & Van Gorp, 1994).

3. PSYCHOSIS

Psychotic symptoms are rare in HIV-infected individuals (Busch, 1989), and their cause is sometimes difficult to determine. The presence of psychotic symptoms is often interpreted in the context of delirium (secondary to metabolic imbalance, systemic opportunistic infection, or medication), end-stage dementia, or pre- or comorbid psychiatric conditions, such as schizophrenia, paranoid states, depression with psychotic features, or a brief reactive psychosis to a severe life stressor.

4. MANIA

Several HIV-positive patients with mania or hypomania have been reported on in the literature (Boccellari, Dilley, & Shore, 1988; Smith, 1990). As in psychosis, the major methodological problem in the study of these symptoms in HIV infection is that the onset of the infection (e.g., age 20–45 years) is coincidental with the onset of major affective disorder in the general population. The onset of new mania is a strong predictor of subsequent dementia (Lyketsos et al., 1993). In some cases, it has been noted that mania or hypomania was related to the use of antiviral agents (e.g., ddI, AZT; see section VII. **Treatment**). However, in other cases there appears to be a relationship between the HIV infection and manic syndrome. It has been noted that HIV-positive patients with mania can have meningeal enhancement on magnetic resonance imaging studies, indicating a meningeal inflammation.

IV. NEUROPSYCHOLOGICAL ASSESSMENT OF HIV-D

Although HIV-D appears as a motor, cognitive, and behavioral syndrome, the neuropsychological profile remains the core feature. Many researchers have emphasized the use of comprehensive neuropsychological batteries (Butters, Grant, & Haxby, 1990) to increase sensitivity to mild cognitive deficits, provide a better characterization of the cognitive pattern, and determine possible relationships with medical or psychosocial conditions. As noted by Selnes and Miller (1994), neuropsychological batteries in HIV-infected individuals should be sensitive to a wide variety of impairments; the tests should already have demonstrated sensitivity to HIV-related changes; and the overall testing period should be relatively brief. The latter issue is particularly important because patients become more impaired and more physically disabled. Indeed, the extent and breadth of the test battery directly affect the likelihood of finding HIV-related deficits in asymptomatic individuals (White, Heaton, & Monsch, 1995). Although they may be overly inclusive, the recommendations of the National Institute of Mental Health (NIMH) Workgroup (Butters et al., 1990) are still valid and useful. (see Table 3).

V. NEUROPATHOLOGY OF HIV DEMENTIA

HIV has a propensity to invade the CNS, especially subcortical areas. Kure, Weidenheim, Lyman, and Dickson (1990) showed that the highest concentrations of gp41 staining were in the globus pallidus, thalamus, corpus striatum, ventral midbrain, and dentate nucleus. In addition, neuronal loss, synaptic loss, and dendritic simplification have been observed in the neocortex, especially in the frontal areas (Everall, Luthert, & Lantos, 1991; Wiley et al., 1991). This tropism of HIV for subcortical areas, and especially for frontal–subcortical systems, may explain the typical neuropsychological pattern of attentional and memory deficits, difficulty performing complex cognitive tasks, and slowed information processing.

The relationship between CNS abnormality and dementia is not as clear-cut as in other dementia syndromes. The presence of certain neuropathological features (such as multinucleated giant cells) is sensitive but nonspecific. That is, whereas patients with HIV-D are likely to have one or more of these features, patients without HIV-D are also likely to have them. By contrast, diagnosis of HIV encephalitis appears to be both sensitive and specific. Indeed, if abnormal CNS viral burden is included in the diagnosis, the 90% of HIV-D can be so classified with no false positives (Wiley et al., 1991).

One of the proposed mechanisms of neuronal damage is the production of several neurotoxins released by infected or activated macrophages within the CNS or outside the CNS but able to cross the brain–blood barrier (BBB; Giulian, Vaca, & Noonan, 1990; Power et al., 1993). Cytokines released by HIV infection may play a crucial role in this process. High levels of

Table 3. Domains of the NIMH Core Neuropsychological Battery

Domain	Tests
Indication of premorbid intelligence	Vocabulary (WAIS-R) National Adult Reading Test (NART)
Attention	Digit Span (WMS-R) Visual Span (WMS-R)
Speed of processing	Sternberg Search Task (Sternberg, 1966) Simple and choice reaction times Paced Auditory Serial Attention Test
Memory	California Verbal Learning Test Working Memory Test Visual Reproduction Test (WMS-R)
Abstraction	Category Test Trail Making Test, Parts A and B
Language	Boston Naming Test Letter and Category Fluency Test
Visuospatial	Embedded Figures Test Money's Standardized Road-Map Test of Direction Sense Digit Symbol Substitution
Construction abilities	Block Design Test Tactual Performance Test
Motor abilities	Grooved Pegboard Finger Tapping Test Grip Strength
Psychiatric assessment	Diagnostic Interview Schedule Hamilton Depression Scale State–Trait Anxiety Scale Mini-Mental State Examination

Note. NIMH = National Institute of Mental Health; WAIS-R = Wechsler Adult Intelligence Scale–Revised; WMS-R; Wechsler Memory Scale–Revised. From "Assessment of AIDS-Related Cognitive Changes: Recommendations of the NIMH Workshop on Neuropsychological Assessment Approaches," by N. Butters, I. Grant, & J. Haxby, 1990, *Journal of Clinical and Experimental Neuropsychology, 12.* Copyright 1990 by Swets & Zeitlinger. Reprinted with permission.

cytokines including interleukin-1-beta (IL-1-beta), interleukin-6 (IL-6), and tumor necrosis factor-alfa (TNF-alfa) are present in the CSF of patients with AIDS (Lipton & Gendelman, 1995). IL-1-beta and TNF-alfa stimulate astrocytosis, and the latter increases BBB permeability and damages oligodendrocytes in vitro (Merrill, 1991; Robbins et al., 1987; Tyor et al., 1992).

VI. NEUROIMAGING AND ELECTROENCEPHALOGRAPHIC CORRELATES

Neuroimaging studies are critical in the evaluation of suspected HIV-D to exclude mass lesions (e.g., opportunistic infection, primary cerebral lymphoma, stroke). Computed tomography (CT) and magnetic resonance imaging (MRI) studies have shown more global cerebral atrophy and white matter abnormalities in HIV-infected individuals than in seronegative controls (Dal Pan et al., 1992; Gelman & Guinto, 1992; Moeller & Backmund, 1990), and they have demonstrated this atrophy to be more central (at the level of the basal ganglia) than cortical (Gelman & Guinto, 1992). Recent studies involving MRI measurement of gray matter volume reduction conducted in HIV-D individuals have shown that dementia is associated with specific volume reduction in the basal ganglia and posterior cortex, as well as with a generalized reduction of the white matter (Aylward et al., 1995).

Neither single photon emission computed tomography (SPECT) nor positron emission tomography (PET) are used frequently in HIV-D patients. Neither of these methods are widely available, and their interpretation and quantification can be difficult in the context of HIV, especially because cocaine users present similar defects to those observed in HIV infection. Nevertheless, PET studies have shown subcortical hypermetabolism in early stages of HIV-D, with later progression to cortical hypometabolism (Rottenberg, Moeller, & Strother, 1987), and normalization of PET abnormalities has been noted after antiviral therapy (Yarchoan, Berg, & Brouwers, 1987).

Electroencephalography (EEG) has less use than the methods mentioned previously in the diagnosis of HIV-D. However, EEG is always useful to rule out an epileptogenic abnormality, caused either by an opportunistic lesion or by the HIV. EEG often shows a diffuse slowing in late stages of HIV infection, but it is normal in half of the cases in the early stages (McArthur, 1987).

VII. TREATMENT

A. HIV Dementia

To inhibit HIV replication in the CNS, antiviral drugs must effectively cross the BBB and achieve adequate concentrations in the CSF. The most common drug used to treat HIV-D is azidothymidine (AZT), a nucleoside antagonist of reverse transcriptase that efficiently penetrates the BBB and antagonizes HIV replication in macrophages. AZT appears to improve neuropsychological performance and to normalize PET scans (Yarchoan et al., 1987). More important, however, is the prophylactic effect of AZT on the development of cognitive deficits. Consequently, the widespread use of AZT may be the explanation for the drop in HIV-D prevalence, from 53% before AZT was available to less than 10% in the latest reports (Portegies et al., 1989; Qureshi et al., 1998).

The efficacy of other antiretroviral agents is uncertain. Dideoxyinosine (ddI) appears to be effective in improving cognitive performance in children, but it may not be as effective in adults. The recent introduction of protease inhibitors (e.g., saquinavir, ritonavir, indinavir, nelfinavir) in the treatment of HIV has opened more therapeutic avenues for HIV-D. Long-term prospective studies have not been completed to demonstrate the benefit of this medication in HIV-D, although it seems that there are some benefits when it is administered in conjunction with AZT. Experimental medications that may have some effect on HIV-D are cytokine blockers such as pentoxifylline, calcium channel blockers such as nimodipine (Dreyer, Kaiser, Offermann, & Lipton, 1990), N-Metyl-D-Aspirate (NMDA) antagonists such as memantine (Lipton, 1992), and peptides that block gp120 toxicity such as peptide T (Bridge, Linde, Ollo, & Mayer, 1991).

B. HIV-Related Psychiatric Symptoms

Because of CNS involvement, HIV-positive patients are particularly vulnerable to the side effects of psychiatric medication. For instance, the central respiratory depression related to the use of hypnotics and anxiolytics can complicate the treatment of pulmonary infections such as *Pneumocystis carinii* pneumonia. Nevertheless, the limited use of short or intermediate-acting benzodiazepines can be effective in the treatment of anxiety. Small doses of antipsychotics, such as haloperidol or perphenazine, can be used to treat psychosis, agitation, and combativeness. Although high-potency antipsychotics are help-ful in patients with HIV infection, it is important to have in mind that these patients may have an increased tendency to develop side effects such as parkinsonism. Depression can be treated with tricyclic antidepressants or with inhibitors of neu-ronal reuptake of serotonin (e.g., fluoxetine, sertraline). Full therapeutic doses may precipitate delirium in HIV-positive patients; therefore, it is recommended that one start with smaller doses (McArthur, 1994).

VIII. OPPORTUNISTIC INFECTIONS

Multiple opportunistic infections are common in HIV-infected patients, reflecting the underlying reduced immunocompe-tence (see Table 1). It is rare to detect opportunistic infections in patients with a peripheral blood CD4+ count greater than $200/mm^2$. Approximately 15% of patients with AIDS develop opportunistic processes.

A. Nonviral Opportunistic Infections

Approximately 10% of patients with AIDS develop cryptoccocal meningitis, and in 5% this is the first recognized opportunistic infection (McArthur, 1994). HIV-infected patients with cryp-toccocal meningitis frequently present with a short history of headaches, fever, decreased mental status, and signs of meningeal irritation.

Toxoplasmosis is caused by a protozoan, *Toxoplasma gondii*, and is one of the most common infections in animals and humans. The infection is clinically evident in 5% of normal individuals. These patients develop flulike symptoms, lym-phadenopathy, splenomegaly, and hepatitis. In HIV-infected patients, the infection is generally caused by a reactivation of latent organisms in the CNS. *T. gondii* causes multiple necrotic abscesses throughout the cerebral hemispheres, and it is the most common cause of cerebral mass in patients with AIDS. Between 10% and 90% of patients with AIDS have antibodies (Ab) against *T. gondii*, and the probability of developing toxo-plasmosis is 28% in patients with *T. gondii* Ab (Grant & Heaton, 1990). These patients present with fever, lethargy, mental slow-ness, focal neurological signs, and seizures (Navia et al., 1986); the abscesses are more frequent in the basal ganglia.

Because both HIV infection and syphilis are sexually trans-mitted diseases, they are likely to coexist in particular popula-tions (Simon, 1994; Tyler, Sandberg, & Baum, 1994; Valdisseri,

Brandon, & Lyter, 1984). It has been suggested that HIV increases the risk for neurosyphilis, that coinfected patients have a more aggressive course, that false negative tests for syphilis can occur in HIV-infected patients and that coinfected patients respond differently to antibiotic therapy. Although the issue is still under debate, current evidence does not appear to support the notion that syphilis is an opportunistic infection, nor that it is more aggressive or refractory to treatment in HIV-infected individuals (Simon, 1994).

CNS mycobacterium infection is always the result of *Mycobacterium tuberculosis*. Patients with this infection can develop meningitis, encephalitis, or cerebral abscesses. Approximately two thirds of the patients present with a cerebral mass lesion, and one third with meningitis. *Mycobacterium avium* is common in patients with AIDS, although the CNS is rarely affected. These patients can present with encephalitis, meningitis, cranial nerve involvement, and peripheral neuropathy.

B. Viral Opportunistic Infections

1. PROGRESSIVE MULTIFOCAL LEUKOENCEPHALOPATHY

PML is an unusual infection caused by a reactivation of the JC papovavirus infection. It has been reported that 70% of all adults have antibodies to JC virus, indicating that the infection is common in adults and usually silent. A reactivation of this infection is often seen in immunocompromised patients (e.g., owing to leukemia, sarcoidosis, rheumatoid arthritis, postorgan transplant immunosuppression); nevertheless, AIDS is the most common cause of PML, and neuropathological studies have reported PML in up to 8% of patients with AIDS (Martinez et al., 1995). Patients with PML present with progressive dementia syndrome, aphasia, blindness, ataxia, and hemiparesis (Berger, Kaszovitz, Post, & Dickinson, 1987). These symptoms progress inexorably to death over weeks or months, although spontaneous improvements have been reported in patients with AIDS (Berger & Mucke, 1988).

2. CYTOMEGALOVIRUS

CMV can be the source of significant neurological problems in AIDS; CMV encephalitis, retinitis, and progressive radiculopathy have been reported (MacGregor et al., 1995; Snider, Simpson, & Nielsen, 1983; Vintners et al., 1989). These patients present with periventriculitis or encephalitis with a rapidly progressive cognitive deterioration.

IX. OTHER HIV-RELATED CEREBRAL LESIONS

Noninfectious causes of cognitive impairment or behavior problems must always be taken into account in the differential diagnosis of AIDS patients with cerebral mass. Primary cerebral lymphoma has been reported in up to 28% of patients with AIDS (Martinez et al., 1995), although half of the cases are clinically silent. These patients present with progressive neurological deterioration leading to death within weeks or months (Rosenblum et al., 1988).

Neuropathological series have documented cerebrovascular disease (CVD), either ischemic or hemorrhagic, in up to 17% of patients with AIDS (Martinez et al., 1995). Although there is no evidence that HIV is the cause of CVD, other, concomitant conditions such as drug use may be related to the vascular phenomenon in AIDS patients.

BIBLIOGRAPHY

American Academy of Neurology. (1991). Nomenclature and research case definitions for the neurological manifestations of human immunodeficiency virus type-1 infection. *Neurology, 41*, 778–785.

American Psychiatric Association. (1994). *Diagnostic and statistical manual of mental disorders* (4th ed.). Washington, DC: Author.

Anders, K. H., Guerra, W. F., & Tomiyashu, V. (1986). The neuropathology of AIDS: UCLA experience and review. *American Journal of Pathology, 124*, 537–558.

Association, A. M. (1992). Special committee report 1992: HIV positivity and aviation safety. *Aviation, Space, and Environmental Medicine, 63*, 375–377.

Atkinson, J. H., Grant, I., & Kennedy, C. J. (1988). Prevalence of psychiatric disorder among men infected with human immunodeficiency virus. *Archives of General Psychiatry, 45*, 859–864.

Aylward, E. H., Brettschneider, P. D., McArthur, J. C., Harris, G. J., Schlaepfer, T. E., Henderer, J. D., Barta, P. E., Tien, A. Y., & Pearlson, G. D. (1995). Magnetic resonance imaging measurement of gray matter volume reductions in HIV dementia. *American Journal of Psychiatry, 152*, 987–994.

Becker, J. T., Martin, A., & Lopez, O. L. (1994). The dementias and AIDS. In I. Grant & A. Martin (Eds.), *Neuropsychology of HIV infection* (pp. 133–145). New York: Oxford University Press.

Berger, J. R., Kaszovitz, B., Post, M. J., & Dickinson, G. (1987). Progressive multifocal leukoencephalopathy associated with human immunodeficiency virus infection: A review of the literature with a report of sixteen cases. *Annals of Internal Medicine, 107,* 78–87.

Berger, J. R., & Mucke, L. (1988). Prolonged survival and partial recovery in AIDS-associated progressive multifocal leukoencephalopathy. *Neurology, 38,* 1060–1065.

Boccellari, A., Dilley, J. W., & Shore, M. D. (1988). Neuropsychiatric aspects of AIDS dementia complex: A report on a clinical series. *Neurotoxicology, 9,* 381–390.

Bridge, P., Linde, R., Ollo, C., & Mayer, K. (1991). *Neuropsychological results of control HIV-1 trial of peptide T.* Paper presented at the VII International Conference on AIDS, Florence, Italy.

Buckingham, S. L., & Van Gorp, W. G. (1994). HIV-associated dementia: A clinician's guide to early detection, diagnosis, and intervention. *Families in Society: The Journal of Contemporary Human Services,* 333–345.

Busch, K. A. (1989, June). Psychotic states in human immunodeficiency virus illness. *Current Opinion in Psychiatry, 2,* pp. 3–6.

Butters, N., Grant, I., & Haxby, J. (1990). Assessment of AIDS-related cognitive changes: Recommendations of the NIMH workshop on neuropsychological assessment approaches. *Journal of Clinical Experimental Neuropsychology, 12,* 963–968.

Centers for Disease Control. (1987). Revision of the CDC surveillance case definition for aquired immunodeficiency syndrome. *Morbidity and Mortality Weekly Report, 36*(Suppl. 1S), 3–15.

Centers for Disease Control. (1995). AIDS statistical summary. *HIV/AIDS Surveillance Report, 1,* 14.

Chimelli, L., Rosemberg, S., & Hahn, D. (1992). Pathology of the central nervous system in patients infected with the human immunodeficiency virus (HIV): A report of 252 autopsy cases from Brazil. *Neuropathology and Applied Neurbiology, 5,* 478–488.

Dal Pan, J. G., McArthur, J., Aylward, E., Selnes, O. A., Nance-Sproson, T. E., Kumar, A. J., Mellits, E. D., & McArthur, J. C. (1992). Patterns of cerebral atrophy in HIV1-infected individuals: Results of a quantitative MRI analysis. *Neurology, 42,* 2125–2130.

de la Monte, S. M., Ho, D. D., & Schooley, R. T. (1987). Subacute encephalomyelitis of AIDS and its relation to HTLV-III infection. *Neurology, 37,* 562–569.

Dew, M. A., Becker, J. T., Sanchez, J., Caldararo, R., Lopez, O. L., Giconi, J., Dorst, S. K., & Banks, G. (1997). Prevalence and predictors of depressive, anxiety, and substance use disorders in HIV-infected and -uninfected men: A longitudinal evaluation. *Psychological Medicine, 27*, 395–409.

Dreyer, E. B., Kaiser, P. K., Offermann, J. T., & Lipton, S. A. (1990). HIV-1 coat protein neurotoxicity prevented by calcium channel antagonists. *Science, 248*, 364–367.

Everall, I., Luthert, P., & Lantos, P. (1991). Neuronal loss in the frontal cortex in HIV infection. *Lancet, 337*, 1119–1121.

Gelman, B. B., & Guinto, F. C. (1992). Morphometry, histopathology, and tomography of cerebral atrophy in the acquired immunodeficiency syndrome. *Annals of Neurology, 32*, 31–40.

Giulian, D., Vaca, K., & Noonan, C. A. (1990). Secretion of neurotoxins by mononuclear phagocytes infected with HIV-1. *Science, 250*, 1593–1596.

Grant, I., Atkinson, J., Hesselink, J., Kennedy, C., Richman, D., Spector, S., & McCutchan, J. (1987). Evidence of early central nervous system involvement in the acquired immunodeficiency syndrome (AIDS) and other human immunodeficiency virus (HIV) infections. *Annals of Internal Medicine, 107*, 828–836.

Grant, I., & Heaton, R. K. (1990). Human immunodeficiency virus-Type 1 (HIV-1) and the brain. *Journal of Consulting and Clinical Psychology, 58*, 22–30.

Levy, R. M., & Berger, J. R. (1993). HIV and HTLV infections of the nervous system. In K. L. Tyler & J. B. Martin (Eds.), *Infectious diseases of the central nervous system* (pp. 47–75). Philadelphia: Davis.

Levy, S. M. (1988). Behavioral risk factors and host vulnerability. In J. P. Bridge, A. F. Mirsky, & F. K. Goodwin (Eds.), *Psychological, neuropsychiatric and substance abuse aspects of AIDS*. New York: Raven Press.

Lipton, S. A. (1992). Memantine prevents HIV coat protein-induced neuronal injury in vitro. *Neurology, 42*, 1403–1405.

Lipton, S. A., & Gendelman, H. E. (1995). Dementia associated with the acquired immunodeficiency syndrome. *New England Journal of Medicine, 332*, 934–940.

Lyketsos, C. G., Hoover, D. R., Guccione, M., Senterfitt, W., Dew, M. A., Wesch, J., VanRaden, M. J., Treisman, G. J., & Morgenstern, H. (1993). Depressive symptoms as predictors of medical outcomes in HIV infection. *Journal of the American Medical Association, 270*, 2563–2567.

MacGregor, R. R., Pakola, S. J., Graziani, A. L., Montzka, D. P., Hodinka, R. L., Nichols, C. W., & Friedman, H. M. (1995). Evidence of active cytomegalovirus infection in clinically stable HIV-infected individuals with CD4+ lymphocyte counts below 100/ul of blood: Features and relation to risk of subsequent CMV retinitis. *Journal of Acquired Immunodeficiency Syndromes, 10*, 324–330.

Maj, M., Satz, P., Janssen, R., Zaudig, M., Starace, F., D'Elia, L., Sughondhabirom, B., Mussa, M., Naber, D., Ndetei, D., Schulte, G., & Sartorius, N. (1994). WHO Neuropsychiatric AIDS Study, Cross Sectional Phase II. *Archives of General Psychiatry, 51*, 51–61.

Maj, M., Starace, F., & Sartorius, N. (1993). *Mental disorders in HIV-1 infection and AIDS* (Vol. 5). Seattle, WA: Hogrefe & Huber.

Martinez, A. J., Sell, M., Mitrovics, T., Stoltenburg-Didinger, G., Iglesias-Rozas, J. R., Giraldo-Velasquez, M. A., Gosztonyi, G., Schneider, V., & Cervos-Navarro, J. (1995). The neuropathology and epidemiology of AIDS: A Berlin experience. A review of 200 cases. *Path Res Pract, 191*, 427–443.

McArthur, J. (1987). Neurologic manifestations of AIDS. *Medicine, 66*, 407–437.

McArthur, J. C. (1994). Neurological and neuropathological manifestations of HIV infection. In I. Grant & A. Martin (Eds.), *Neuropsychology of HIV infection* (pp. 56–107). New York: Oxford University Press.

McArthur, J. C., Hoover, D. R., Bacellar, H., Miller, E. N., Cohen, B. A., Becker, J. T., Graham, N. M. H., McArthur, J. H., Selnes, O. A., Jacobson, L. P., Visscher, B. R., Concha, M., & Saah, A. (1993). Dementia in AIDS patients: Incidence and risk factors. *Neurology, 43*, 2245–2253.

Merrill, J. E. (1991). Effects of interleukin-1 and tumor necrosis factor-x on astrocytes, microglia, oligodendrocytes, and glial precursors in vitro. *Developmental Neuroscience, 13*, 130–137.

Miller, E. N., Selnes, O. A., & McArthur, M. B. (1990). Neuropsychological test performance in HIV1-infected homosexual men: The Multicenter AIDS Cohort Study (MACS). *Neurology, 40*, 197–203.

Moeller, A. A., & Backmund, H. C. (1990). Ventricle brain ratio in the clinical course of HIV infection. *Acta Neurologica Scandinavica, 81*, 512–515.

Moskowitz, L. B., Hensley, G. T., & Chan, J. C. (1984). The neuropathology of acquired immune deficiency syndrome. *Archives of Pathology and Laboratory Medicine, 108*, 867–872.

Navia, B. A., Jordan, B. D., & Price, R. W. (1986). The AIDS dementia complex: I. Clinical features. *Annals of Neurology, 19*, 517–524.

Petito, C. K., Cho, E.-S., Lemann, W., Navia, B. A., & Price, R. W. (1986). Neuropathology of acquired immunodeficiency syndrome (AIDS): An autopsy review. *Journal of Neuropathology and Experimental Neurology, 45*, 635–646.

Portegies, P., de Gans, J., Lange, J. M., Derix, M. M., Speelman, H., Bakker, M., Danner, S. A., & Goudsmit, J. (1989). Declining incidence of AIDS dementia complex after introduction of zidovudine treatment. *British Medical Journal, 299*, 819–821.

Power, C., Kong, P. A., Crawford, T. O., Wesselingh, S., Glass, J. D., McArthur, J. C., & Trapp, B. D. (1993). Cerebral white matter changes in acquired immunodeficiency syndrome dementia: Alternations of the blood-brain barrier. *Annals of Neurology, 34*, 339–350.

Price, R. W., & Brew, B. J. (1988). The AIDS dementia complex. *Journal of Infectious Diseases, 158*, 1079–1083.

Price, R. W., Brew, B., Sidtis, J., Rosenblum, M., Scheck, A. C., & Cleary, P. (1988). The brain in AIDS: Central nervous system HIV-1 infection and AIDS dementia complex. *Science, 239*, 586–592.

Qureshi, A. I., Hanson, D. L., Jones, J. L., & Jansson, R. S. (1998). Estimation of temporal probability of human immunodeficiency virus HIV dementia after risk stratification for HIV-infected persons. *Neurology, 50*, 392–397.

Robbins, D. S., Shirazi, Y., Drysdale, B. E., Liebermann, A., Shin, H. S., & Shin, M. L. (1987). Production of cytotoxic factor for oligodendrocytes by stimulated astrocytes. *Journal of Immunology, 139*, 2593–2597.

Rosenblum, M. L., Levy, R. M., Bredesen, D. E., So, Y. T., Wara, W., & Ziegler, J. L. (1988). Primary central nervous system lymphomas in patients with AIDS. *Annals of Neurology, 23*, S13–S16.

Rottenberg, D., Moeller, J., & Strother, S. (1987). The metabolic pathology of the AIDS dementia complex. *Annals of Neurology, 22*, 700–706.

Selnes, O. A., Galai, N., Bacellar, M. A., Miller, E. N., Becker, J. T., Van Gorp, W., & McArthur, J. C. (1995). Cognitive performance after progression to AIDS: A longitudinal study from the Multicenter AIDS Cohort Study. *Neurology, 45*, 267–275.

Selnes, O. A., & Miller, E. N. (1994). Development of a screening battery for HIV-related cognitive impairment: The MACS experience. In I. Grant & A. Martin (Eds.), *Neuropsychology of HIV infection* (pp. 176–190). New York: Oxford University Press.

Simon, R. P. (1994). Neurosyphilis. *Neurology, 44*, 2228–2230.

Smith, J. (1990). *Manic psychosis as a neuropsychiatric complication of HIV infection.* Paper presented at the Satellite Meeting to the VI International Conference on AIDS, Montreal, Canada.

Sternberg, S. (1966). High speed scanning in human memory. *Science, 153*, 652–654.

Tyler, K. L., Sandberg, E., & Baum, K. F. (1994). Medial medullary syndrome and meningovascular syphilis: A case report in an HIV-infected man and a review of the literature. *Neurology, 44*, 2231–2235.

Tyor, W. R., Glass, J. D., Griffin, J. W., Becker, P. S., McArthur, J. C., Bezman, L., & Griffin, D. E. (1992). Cytokine expression in the brain during AIDS. *Annals of Neurology, 31*, 349–360.

Valdisseri, R. O., Brandon, W. R., & Lyter, D. W. (1984). AIDS surveillance and health education: Use of previously described risk factors to identify high-risk homosexuals. *American Journal of Public Health, 74*, 259–260.

Vintners, H. V., Kwok, M. K., Ho, H. W., Anders, K. H., Tomiyasu, U., Wolfson, W. L., & Robert, F. (1989). Cyto-megalovirus in the nervous system of patients with the acquired immune deficiency syndrome. *Brain, 112*, 245–268.

White, D. A., Heaton, R. K., & Monsch, A. U. (1995). Neuropsychological studies of asymptomatic human immunodeficiency virus-Type 1 infected individuals. *Journal of the International Neuropsychological Society, 1*, 304–315.

World Health Organization. (1991). *The neurological adaptation of the International Classification of Diseases (ICD-10NA)* [Draft]. Geneva, Switzerland: Author.

World Health Organization. (1995). *Pulic Information Office Global Programme on AIDS*. Geneva, Switzerland: Author.

Wiley, C. A., Masliah, E., Morey, M., Lemere, C., DeTeresa, R., Grafe, M., Hansen, L., & Terry, R. (1991). Neocortical damage during HIV infection. *Annals of Neurology, 29*, 651–657.

Yarchoan, R., Berg, G., & Brouwers, P. (1987). Response of human immunodeficiency virus-associated neurological disease to 3′-azido-3′-deoxythymidine. *Lancet, i*, 132–135.

Zorrilla, E. P., McKay, J. R., Luborsky, L., & Schmidt, K. (1996). Relation of stressors and depressive symptoms to clinical progression of viral illness. *American Journal of Psychiatry, 153*, 626–635.

CHAPTER 18
Lisa A. Morrow

Neurotoxicology

It is estimated that in the United States there are 60,000 chemicals in commercial use, many of which, such as lead, pesticides, and solvents, are known hazards to the human nervous system (Goetz, 1985). Adverse neuropsychological effects may vary, depending on a number of factors including the type and kind of exposure as well as individual characteristics. However, there is no specific pattern of cognitive deficits associated with individual chemicals (Hartman, 1995); the neuropsychological impairments are generally diffuse, with deficits reported for memory, attention, visuospatial ability, motor speed, problem solving, and mental flexibility. It has recently been suggested that advances in neuroimaging have made such techniques especially useful in assessing patients with a history of neurotoxic exposure (Morrow, Steinhauer, & Ryan, 1994). This chapter discusses parameters of exposure, the most frequently encountered neurotoxins, documentation of exposure, and neuropsychological and neurophysiological assessment techniques.

I. PARAMETERS OF EXPOSURE

Absorption into the human body is through four primary routes: inhalation, ingestion, skin absorption, and injection. The most common route of entry is through inhalation. Risk of exposure is reduced with the use of protective equipment such as respirators, gloves, proper clothing, and fume hoods, but these precautions do not always preclude a toxic exposure.

A. Acute Effects

Acute effects are distinguishable from chronic effects for most agents. For example, acute lead toxicity produces gastrointestinal symptoms, whereas chronic exposure results in central nervous system (CNS) and peripheral nervous system (PNS) changes as well as disruption of hemoglobin synthesis. In the clinical setting a patient typically presents with acute effects from a high dose of a chemical, usually in the context of an accidental spill or leak or owing to voluntary abuse (e.g., glue sniffing). Symptoms from an acute exposure may be confined to minor respiratory irritation or there may be more severe neurological effects that range from incoordination to dizziness, convulsions, coma, and death. Studies have suggested that an acute overexposure, as opposed to low-level chronic exposure, may place one at greater risk for increased neuropsychological deficits over time.

B. Chronic Effects

Chronic effects are seen in persons with a history of exposure over an extended time period. Typically, symptoms do not appear for years, but with the onset of neurobehavioral changes (e.g., memory impairment, motor slowing), deficits may be permanent and irreversible. There is some evidence that prior occupational exposure to neurotoxic chemicals may place one at greater risk for the development of dementia-type illnesses (e.g., Alzheimer's disease) in later life (Kukull et al., 1995).

II. FREQUENTLY ENCOUNTERED NEUROTOXINS

A. Heavy Metals

Lead and mercury are probably the most common heavy metal neurotoxins seen in clinical practice. Initial signs of adult lead poisoning are gastrointestinal symptoms, motor neuropathy, and generalized cognitive impairment. With very high lead levels, patients may display the classic "wrist drop." The most common way to establish lead concentration is to measure lead in whole blood. For adults, the current recommended safe level is below 25 µg/dl of blood. Initial presenting signs of lead poisoning in children are changes in mental status, gait disturbance, and onset of seizures. For children, the current recommended safe level is below 10 µg/dl of blood. Children have higher lead levels than adults in similar exposure situations, and lack of iron and minerals in the diet and use of alcohol may increase lead absorption. General signs of encephalopathy (memory loss, irrational behavior) may accompany both acute and chronic lead toxicity. Common sources of lead exposure are shown in Exhibit 1.

Symptoms of **mercury poisoning** were highlighted by the "mad hatters" syndrome in workers employed at the turn of the century in the felt-hat industry. Exposure to **inorganic mercury** produces coarse tremor (hatters shakes), salivation, motor weakness, pain, vomiting, diarrhea, and renal failure. Personality changes—increased emotional tension and irritability (erethism)—may begin before the motor changes occur. **Organic mercury** exposure is associated with ataxia, dysarthria, neuropathy, deafness, excessive sweating and salivation, tremor, mental slowing, and visual constriction. Persons exposed to mercury may also report a metallic taste in the mouth, and a brown line may be noticeable on the teeth. Neuropsychological effects may be the first signs of mercury poisoning. Studies of exposed persons have documented changes across a number of cognitive domains (memory, abstraction, visuospatial ability), and it has been suggested that mercury levels must be under 25 µg/m^3 to avoid neurotoxic effects (see Exhibit 1 for the most common sources of mercury exposure).

B. Organic Solvents

Persons with a history of acute or chronic solvent exposure (see Exhibit 1 for common sources) report a range of somatic and neurobehavioral symptoms. The most common acute symptoms are headaches, nausea, dizziness, decreased attention and concentration, and a general feeling of intoxication. Patients with long-term chronic exposure often describe symptoms during exposure but remittal on exposure termination (e.g., weekends). However, with continued chronic exposure, symptoms such as headaches and dizziness may not diminish, and

Exhibit 1. Common Sources of Exposure for Various Neurotoxins

Lead	Mercury	Organic solvents	Pesticides and insecticides	Carbon monoxide
Automobile man-ufacture and repair	Dentistry	Paints	Farming	Steel mills
Industrial and commercial painting	Farming	Varnishes	Landscaping	Coal mines
Dentistry	Metal and elec-trical work	Glues	Contaminated food	Charcoal grills
Brick making	Painting	Cleaning agents		Poorly ventilated appliances (furnace)
Plumbing	Photography	Plastics		Car exhaust
Explosives (lead-encased bullets)	Taxidermy	Textiles		Fire fighting
Refinishing wood	Alcohol brewing	Pharmaceuticals		
Pottery	Food (grain treated with fungicide)	Agricultural products		
Photography				
Chinese herbal medicines				

patients may report the onset of memory and personality changes. Many persons with chronic effects of solvents also state that their symptoms seem to increase when they are in the vicinity of noxious odors (e.g., gasoline). Threshold limit values (TLVs) have been established for many individual solvents (Proctor, Hughes, & Fischman, 1988). Because of the short half-life of solvents (24–48 hours), it is difficult to estimate body burden. Also, because solvents are highly lipophilic, there may be individual differences in absorption and clearance rates depending on the amount of fat tissue. If blood or urine samples are not taken within several hours of exposure, or if air sampling measures are not available from the workplace, the clinical interview (discussed later in the chapter) becomes the primary source for estimating duration, frequency, and dose of exposure. Prominent neuropsychological deficits include changes in memory, attention, mental flexibility, and psychomotor speed. Emotional changes are also common (e.g., depression), although studies show there is typically no correlation between emotional symptoms and neuropsychological performance (Morrow, Ryan, Hodgson, & Robin, 1990).

C. Pesticides and Insecticides

Billions of pounds of pesticides are used each year worldwide (see Exhibit 1 for common sources). Organophosphates are among the most widely used pesticides; the toxic CNS effects are produced by inhibition of acetylcholinesterase, which increases acetylcholine levels. Acute neurotoxic effects of organophosphate poisoning include a "garlic" breath odor, increased salivation and lacrimation, excessive sweating, intestinal cramps, vomiting, fatigue, ataxia, bulbar signs, muscular fasciculations, and respiratory distress. Symptoms typically occur soon after exposure but may be delayed up to 12 hours. Poisoning is verified when serum cholinesterase levels are reduced by 10%–50%. However, symptoms may occur with only a 30% drop when the exposure is quite rapid, and with chronic low-level exposure over time there may be a drop to 70% with no symptoms. Neuropathy may also occur, often with a delay, following organophosphate poisoning. CNS effects such as choreoathetosis have also been reported. The toxicity of pesticides is complicated by the fact that many have various chemical stabilizers and some are mixed with other chemical agents, such as solvents. Although applicators have a high risk of exposure, risk of poisoning may be even higher in a nonoccupational setting (e.g., spraying in the home or office) due to lack of protective equipment (e.g., respirators). As occurs with other neurotoxins, moderate-to-severe cognitive and psychiatric changes have been reported following acute and chronic exposure. Reductions in motor speed and coordination are prominent neuropsychological findings, along with reductions in memory and visuoperception. Emotional disturbances, particularly anxiety, have been reported in persons with pesticide poisoning.

D. Carbon Monoxide

Carbon monoxide (CO) is generated when organic compounds, such as wood and gas, are not completely burned (see Exhibit 1 for sources). CO is rapidly absorbed in the lungs and has an affinity for hemoglobin that is 210–240 times greater than that of oxygen. The resulting carboxyhemoglobin (COHb) impairs oxygen transport to tissue and produces hypoxia. Cigarette smokers have higher levels of COHb (average 10%–15%) than nonsmokers (average 1%). Methylene chloride—a primary ingredient in paint remover—is metabolized to CO, and elevated COHb levels may persist longer from this type of exposure than from CO exposure alone. With exposure to CO at 4,000 ppm or higher, dizziness and weakness may be the only symptoms prior to lapsing into coma. With exposure to 500–1,000 ppm, headache, dizziness, weakness, and mental confusion occur, and possibly hallucination. Levels of COHb exceeding 60% are usually fatal, whereas levels between 30% and 40% are associated with collapse and syncope. At about 25%, there may be headache, nausea, and cardiac changes. Symptoms are usually absent with levels below 15%. Body burden for carbon monoxide may vary depending on factors such as exertion, circulation, and presence or absence of anemia. Although most reports suggest that patients with CO poisoning will have only transient neurobehavioral changes, there is evidence for delayed neuropsychiatric sequelae following CO toxicity. That is, patients may manifest no symptoms for days or weeks following the exposure but then show a rapid change in cognitive function (e.g., aphasia, memory decline) and fairly severe psychiatric symptoms (e.g., psychosis; Smith & Brandon, 1970). Neuropsychological deficits have also been reported following long-term low-level chronic exposure to CO (Ryan, 1990).

III. DOCUMENTING EXPOSURE

When a patient is initially evaluated for a possible neurotoxic exposure, background information should be obtained from the patient as well as from collaterals (e.g., spouse, coworker). The interviewer should gather as much information as possible concerning symptom onset, work environment, and use of protective clothing. If the toxin is known, biological measures (e.g., heavy metal screen, COHb levels) should be obtained as soon as possible. If company records are available, these should be gathered, as well as the Material Safety Data Sheet for each suspected chemical. Finally, if the patient complains of changes in mental status, a neuropsychological evaluation is recommended as well as functional neuroimaging or neurophysiological assessment. Because many chemicals also affect the peripheral nervous system, these tests (e.g., thermal and vibratory quantitative sensory testing) may also prove helpful for diagnostic purposes.

A. Interview

The most important information is likely to be obtained from the clinical interview. Interviews with coworkers and family members may help to verify symptoms. Although the majority of patients are exposed in the workplace, exposures can occur in the home as well (e.g., carbon monoxide), and questions should be modified to apply to the environment where the exposure took place. Queries should also be made concerning coexposures from hobby equipment or other activities (e.g., furniture stripping). Following is a list of questions my colleagues and I ask all patients who come to our clinic with a history of neurotoxic exposure:

1. What type of work do you do and what are the work requirements?

2. What is your work setting like (e.g., work space, ventilation)?

3. What protective equipment do you wear and how often do you wear it (e.g., gloves [latex or cloth], respirator [mask, cartridge, airline], special clothing)?

4. What chemicals do you work with?

5. How long have you worked with each of these chemicals?

6. What type of contact did you, or do you still, have with the chemicals (inhalation, skin contact, ingestion)?

7. How often do you estimate that you come into contact with chemicals on the job (<5%, 5–15%, >30% of the time)?

8. How many days (or hours) has it been since you were last exposed to chemicals?

9. Was there ever any incident or accident in which you were suddenly exposed to a large amount of a chemical? If so, did you seek treatment?

10. What problems did you *first* notice following your exposure? Have you had changes in your physical well-being (e.g., headaches, fatigue), cognitive function (e.g., memory loss, concentration), or emotional state (e.g., depression, anxiety)?

11. What problems do you *now* have?

B. Estimating Body Burden

For many patients it is difficult or impossible to establish body burden, or the amount of chemical in tissue or blood. With the exception of some heavy metals, most chemicals are excreted from the body in a relatively short time. For example, solvents have a half-life of only 24–48 hours and the half-life elimination of carbon monoxide is approximately 5 hours when breathing air and about 90 minutes with administration of pure oxygen. For most chemical exposures, therefore, unless urine or blood measures are taken very shortly afterward, estimating body burden is problematic. In rare instances, air monitoring is done at the work site, and information regarding time weighted averages (TWAs) or the level of exposure in terms of parts per million (ppm) may be available. In many instances it is also difficult to determine the exact chemical, or mixture of chemicals, the patient was exposed to and what tests should be done. Often patients do not present for a neuropsychological evaluation until weeks or months following an exposure, and they may not know what chemicals they were exposed to. Persons who report a possible exposure should always be evaluated by a physician with training and expertise in occupational and environmental medicine.

C. Material Safety Data Sheet

All work sites are required to have an MSDS for any hazardous chemical on the property, and employers are required to make this form available to workers. Material Safety Data Sheets (MSDSs) are not uniform, and they may look quite different depending on the manufacturer; however, it is required that the following information be contained in the MSDS:

1. A list of the hazardous substances and their chemical and physical properties

2. Names used to identify the substance, including trade names and chemical names

3. Fire and explosion data and the reactivity of the chemical

4. Conditions to be avoided, as well as the general requirements for health protection (e.g., ventilation, respirators)

5. Adverse health effects that cover both acute (e.g., muscle weakness, drowsiness) and chronic (e.g., infertility, cancer) effects for different exposure routes (e.g., inhalation, ingestion)

6. First-aid measures to treat overexposure

IV. NEUROPSYCHOLOGICAL CHANGES ASSOCIATED WITH EXPOSURE

To a large extent, the neuropsychological profiles are similar for persons with acute and chronic neurotoxic exposure, although as noted previously, the presenting physical symptoms may be somewhat distinctive for different chemical agents. Generally, there is no specific pattern of impairment on cognitive tests, because the effects of most neurotoxic exposures mimic an encephalopathy. As in most incidents of general CNS damage, prominent presenting symptoms are attentional deficits and changes in personality and memory (Morrow et al., 1990; Morrow, Kamis, & Hodgson, 1993; Morrow, Robin, Hodgson, & Kamis, 1992). Often patients report difficulty reading and "getting the right word out," but documented deficits in language function (e.g., frank aphasia) are usually absent. Because many of these patients are not profoundly impaired and they often have an estimated premorbid IQ that is average or above average, a battery of sophisticated information-processing tests may provide the best measure of changes in neuropsychological function. The neuropsychological examination should be heavily weighted toward tests of learning, memory, attention, and concentration. Motor speed may also be reduced—either from CNS damage or from peripheral neuropathy—and tests assessing reaction time should be included. Tests such as the Mini-Mental State Examination or the Cognitive Evaluation Examination should be avoided because they are not sensitive to subtle neuropsychological changes. Several batteries have been developed specifically for use with exposed patients. With the exception of a battery for use in cases of acute CO exposure, these neuropsychological test batteries were developed for use in large-scale epidemiological studies or the clinical assessment of patients with some type of neurotoxic exposure. Most tests

Exhibit 2. Neuropsychological Test Batteries

Neurobehavioral Core Test Battery (NCTB)	Neurobehavioral Evaluation System (NES)	Pittsburgh Occupational Exposures Test (POET) Battery	Carbon Monoxide Neuropsychological Screening Battery
Pursuit Aiming	Finger Tapping	Verbal Paired Associative Learning and Delayed Recall	General Orientation
Simple Reaction Time	Hand-Eye Coordination		Digit Span
Digit Symbol	Simple Reaction Time	Symbol-Digit Associative Learning and Delayed Recall	Trail Making Test
Benton Visual Retention (Recognition)	Continuous Performance Test		Aphasia Screening
Digit Span	Symbol-Digit Substitution	Incidental Memory	WAIS (Digit Symbol, Block Design)
Santa Ana Dexterity	Pattern Memory	Recurring Words	
Profile of Mood States	Digit Span	Wechsler Memory Scale (Visual Reproductions, Immediate and Delayed Recall)	
	Serial Digit Learning		
	Paired Associate Learning and Delayed Recall	Embedded Figures Test	
	Visual Retention	Grooved Pegboard	
	Pattern Comparison	Trail Making Test	
	Vocabulary Test	WAIS-R (Digit Span, Digit Symbol, Information, Similarities, Picture Completion, Block Design)	
	Profile of Mood States		

Note. WAIS-R = Wechsler Adult Intelligence Scale–Revised.

within the batteries are standard neuropsychological tests. Following are brief descriptions of the most widely used batteries; the tests included in each battery are presented in Exhibit 2.

A. World Health Organization Neurobehavioral Core Test Battery

Conceived as a quick and economical battery of tests to identify neurotoxic effects, the Neurobehavioral Core Test Battery (NCTB) is targeted for both industrial and nonindustrial countries and is very brief, consisting of six tests focusing on visuospatial and visuomotor function and a brief self-report measure of mood state (Johnson, 1990). Although studies have suggested that many of the individual tests can discriminate between exposed and nonexposed persons, testing done in several European countries has shown a wide variation in test performance among the groups tested, suggesting limited use without appropriate normative data.

A computerized version of the NCTB has been developed with the addition of a visual learning test. The computerized battery, the Milan Automated Neurobehavioral System (MANS), has shown a fairly good correlation with the paper-and-pencil version and was able to discriminate between persons exposed to heavy metals and nonexposed controls (Cassitto, Gilioli, & Camerino, 1989).

B. Neurobehavioral Evaluation System

Now in its third revision, the Neurobehavioral Evaluation System (NES) was initially developed for use in epidemiological field studies of active workers at risk for developing neurobehavioral complications from workplace exposure (Baker, Letz, & Fidler, 1985). It is a computerized battery, and there is minimal interaction between the examiner and the testee. The battery includes more attention and memory tests than the NCTB, and it has been shown to be sensitive to neurobehavioral changes associated with neurotoxic exposure. The NES has also been translated into several languages. However, because the NES allows one to select specific tests and to tailor the administration on the basis of specific test situations (e.g., repeated testings), normative data must be collected for individual applications.

C. Pittsburgh Occupational Exposures Test Battery

Requiring about 90 minutes to administer, the Pittsburgh Occupational Exposures Test (POET) Battery was developed to be used primarily for clinical assessment of individual patients with a history of neurotoxic exposure (Ryan, Morrow, Bromet, & Parkinson, 1987). It is heavily weighted for assessment of learning, memory, attention, and mental flexibility. Normative data for 182 nonexposed blue-collar workers were collected, and factor analysis of the data revealed five cognitive domains (Learning and Memory, Attention and Mental Flexibility, Visuospatial Ability, Motor Speed and Eye Hand Coordination, and General Intelligence). Means and standard deviations for men age 21–59 have been published (Ryan et al., 1987). In addition, coefficients for age and education were derived for each test so that predicted test scores could be determined and compared to established cutoffs for impairment. Published studies have shown that the battery is effective in discriminating between exposed and nonexposed workers in both clinical and occupational settings (Morrow et al., 1990; Morrow, Steinhauer, Condray, & Hodgson, 1997).

D. Carbon Monoxide Neuropsychological Screening Battery

Messier and Myers (1991) developed a brief battery of six cognitive tests to assist in evaluating patients who present to an emergency room with CO poisoning. In a study comparing patients before and after treatment with hyperbaric oxygen and matched controls who were tested twice, the test battery was found to discriminate between patients and controls. Following treatment, the patients had improved test scores that exceeded expected practice effects. Use of a quick cognitive screening battery to detect subtle symptoms of acute CO poisoning may be particularly beneficial when deciding whether to implement hyperbaric oxygen treatment.

E. Recommended Tests for Use With Exposed Patients

The tests, or test battery, of choice for assessing exposed patients depends on several issues, such as whether the person is presenting for a clinical evaluation or whether testing is to be repeated over the work shift. The NES is probably the battery of choice if repeated testing is to be done (e.g., beginning and end of a work shift) and time is limited. The POET battery is probably best suited for clinical assessments, especially if the patient has a blue-collar background. My colleagues and I routinely use the POET in our clinic and supplement the battery with additional standard tests. The additional tests we find most useful are ones that assess complex information processing, divided attention, and working memory, such as the Paced Serial Addition Test (Gronwall, 1977) or the Four-Word Short-Term Memory Test (Morrow, Robin et al., 1992). Subtests from the Wechsler Memory Scale–Revised, such as Mental Control and Orientation, are less likely to detect subtle neuropsychological changes in exposed patients. An assessment of psychiatric symptoms should always be included. We typically use the Beck Depression Inventory, the Symptom Checklist 90-R, and the Millon Clinical Multiaxial Inventory (MCMI). The MCMI is particularly useful because it provides information for both Axis I and Axis II disorders and is much shorter than the Minnesota Multiphasic Personality Inventory (MMPI). Finally, as in evaluations for any disorder that may produce cognitive and psychiatric changes, one must consider possible symptom enhancement. That is, there may be gains—primary or secondary—to patients if they are diagnosed with a cognitive impairment. There are a number of paper-and-pencil tests that have been developed to detect malingering or exaggeration of symptoms, although the tests are typically validated by asking nonpatient participants to "fake bad" (cf. Rogers, 1988).

V. NEUROPHYSIOLOGICAL AND NEUROIMAGING TECHNIQUES IN EXPOSED PATIENTS

Functional imaging techniques—positron emission tomography (PET), single photon emission computed tomography (SPECT), and functional magnetic resonance imaging (FMRI)—may be particularly well suited to document quantifiable CNS damage in patients exposed to solvents and pesticides. Several studies have noted decreased blood flow to both cortical and subcortical areas in solvent-exposed patients. Patients with neurotoxic exposure show a high rate of abnormality on SPECT, with the most common areas of decreased function seen in the temporal lobes, frontal lobes, basal ganglia, and thalamus. Magnetic resonance imaging (MRI) and computed tomography (CT) are less likely to show changes in patients with solvent and pesticide poisoning, although they show the white matter changes associated with CO poisoning (lesions of the globus pallidus).

Psychophysiological measures (e.g., event-related potentials [ERPs], cardiac and pupil reactivity) have had limited use with exposed patients, but recent studies have suggested that these may be particularly sensitive to neurotoxic exposure (Morrow et al., 1994). Although impairment on neuropsychological tests may not be noted until deficits are clinically significant, subclinical levels of impairment may be seen on ERPs. Work in my group's laboratory has shown that the P300 component of the ERP is significantly delayed in persons with a history of solvent exposure (Morrow, Steinhauer, & Hodgson, 1992; Steinhauer, Morrow, Condray, & Dougherty, 1997). Both cardiac and pupillary measures have also shown abnormalities in this patient population (Morrow & Steinhauer, 1995). In addition, these measures may be helpful in assessing cognitive function unconfounded by patient motivation.

VI. CONCLUSION

Patients with complaints of neuropsychological and psychiatric changes should always be interviewed regarding a possible exposure to neurotoxins. A neurotoxic exposure can occur in the home or workplace, and symptoms may have an abrupt or a delayed onset, depending on the chemical agent. The neuropsychological evaluation should be more than a brief screening and should focus on complex tests of learning and memory, attention, information processing, mental flexibility, and emotional function. Neurophysiological testing and neuroimaging are also recommended, particularly if cognitive and physical symptoms do not subside.

BIBLIOGRAPHY

Baker, E. L., Letz, R., & Fidler, A. (1985). A computer-administered neurobehavioral evaluation system for occupational and environmental epidemiology. *Journal of Occupational Medicine, 27,* 206–212.

Cassitto, M. G., Gilioli, R., & Camerino, D. (1989). Experiences with the Milan Automated Neurobehavioral System (MANS) in occupational neurotoxic exposure. *Neurotoxicology and Teratology, 11,* 571–574.

Goetz, C. G. (1985). *Neurotoxins in clinical practice*. New York: Spectrum Publications.

Gronwall, D. M. A. (1977). Paced Auditory Serial Addition Task: A measure of recovery from concussion. *Perceptual and Motor Skills, 44*, 367–373.

Hartman, D. E. (1995). *Neuropsychological toxicology* (2nd ed.). New York: Plenum Press.

Johnson, B. L. (Ed.). (1990). *Advances in neurobehavioral toxicology: Applications in environmental and occupational health*. Chelsea, MI: Lewis.

Kukull, W. A., Larson, E. B., Bowen, J. D., Anger, W. K., Durao, A., & Yintaras, C. (1995). Solvent exposure as a risk factor for Alzheimer's disease: A case-control study. *American Journal of Epidemiology, 141*, 1059–1071.

Messier, L. D., & Myers, R. A. M. (1991). A neuropsychological screening battery for emergency assessment of carbon-monoxide-poisoned patients. *Journal of Clinical Psychology, 47*, 675–684.

Morrow, L. A., Kamis, H., & Hodgson, M. J. (1993). Psychiatric symptomatology in persons with organic solvent exposure. *Journal of Consulting and Clinical Psychology, 61*, 171–174.

Morrow, L. A., Robin, N., Hodgson, M. J., & Kamis, H. (1992). Assessment of attention and memory efficiency in persons with solvent neurotoxicity. *Neuropsychologia, 30*, 911–922.

Morrow, L. A., Ryan, C. M., Hodgson, M. J., & Robin, N. (1990). Alterations in cognitive and psychological functioning after organic solvent exposure. *Journal of Occupational Medicine, 32*, 444–450.

Morrow, L. A., & Steinhauer, S. R. (1995). Alterations in heart rate and pupillary response in persons with organic solvent exposure. *Biological Psychiatry, 37*, 721–730.

Morrow, L. A., Steinhauer, S. R., Condray, R., & Hodgson, M. J. (1997). Neuropsychological performance of journeymen painters under acute solvent exposure and exposure free conditions. *Journal of the International Neuropsychological Society, 3*, 269–275.

Morrow, L. A., Steinhauer, S. R., & Hodgson, M. J. (1992). Delay in P300 latency in patients with organic solvent exposure. *Archives of Neurology, 49*, 315–320.

Morrow, L. A., Steinhauer, S. R., & Ryan, C. M. (1994). The utility of psychophysiological measures in assessing the correlates and consequences of organic solvent exposure. *Toxicology and Industrial Health, 10*, 537–544.

Proctor, N. H., Hughes, J. P., & Fischman, M. L. (1988). *Chemical hazards of the workplace* (2nd ed.). Philadelphia: Lippincott.

Rogers, R. (Ed.). (1988). *Clinical assessment of malingering and deception.* New York: Guilford Press.

Ryan, C. M. (1990). Memory disturbance following chronic low-level carbon monoxide exposure. *Archives of Clinical Neuropsychology, 5,* 59–67.

Ryan, C. M., Morrow, L. A., Bromet, E. J., & Parkinson, D. K. (1987). Assessment of neuropsychological dysfunction in the workplace: Normative data from the Pittsburgh Occupational Exposures Test Battery. *Journal of Clinical and Experimental Neuropsychology, 6,* 665–679.

Smith, J. S., & Brandon, S. (1970). Acute carbon-monoxide poisoning: 3 years experience in a defined population. *Postgraduate Medical Journal, 46,* 65–70.

Steinhauer, S. R., Morrow, L. A., Condray, R., & Dougherty, G. (1997). Event-related potentials in workers with ongoing occupational exposure. *Biological Psychiatry, 42,* 854–858.

Cerebrovascular Disease

I. DEFINITION

Cerebrovascular disease is defined as any pathological process involving blood vessels in the brain. The vascular pathology can include lesions of the vessel wall, occlusion of the vessel, rupture of the vessel or malformation. This chapter focuses on the cerebrovascular conditions most frequently encountered by a neuropsychologist. The role of the neuropsychologist when working with this patient population is to determine changes in cognitive and emotional behavior post-CVA. Accordingly, the neuropsychologist gathers data, often at repeated intervals, to monitor the degree and course of impairment, subsequent recovery, and prognosis, and to assist in establishing suitable rehabilitation programs in collaboration with a rehabilitation team.

A. Cerebrovascular Accident

The CVA, or stroke, is the most common type of cerebrovascular disease. Approximately one-half million persons per year in the United States are expected to suffer from strokes of various causes. During the development of a stroke, a specific part of the brain does not receive adequate nutrients, specifically oxygen and glucose, owing to disrupted blood supply. After several minutes of deprived blood supply without adequate collateral blood circulation, **infarction** (areas of damaged or dead tissue) occurs. If blood supply is restored within an appropriate time limit, brain tissue remains viable and function recovers. If **ischemia** from tissue starvation owing to insufficient blood flow obstruction occurs but the ischemic tissue has sufficient collateral supply, functional impairments are temporary with eventual recovery.

B. Evolution of Disease Expression

Factors that influence the type, extent, and symptoms of a stroke include size of blood vessels (small capillaries vs. large major arteries), degree of blood vessel weakness and capacity for compensation by surrounding vessels, preexisting lesions and degree of recovery, location of lesion, and rate of symptom development.

C. Types of Cerebrovascular Disorders

Mechanisms that account for brain tissue starvation include: (a) **obstruction** of blood vessels, which causes disrupted or deficient blood flow to the brain and (b) **hemorrhage**, or arterial rupture, which causes bleeding within the brain tissue itself.

1. OBSTRUCTIVE ISCHEMIC STROKES

Blockage of a blood vessel can occur when a clot travels from its origin and becomes lodged along the way in the cerebral artery. This can occur rapidly, over hours or days, or episodically, depending on the mechanism of obstruction.

a. Cerebral thrombosis

Obstruction of blood flow can be due to buildup of **atherosclerotic plaques**, which are fat deposits within the artery walls. Obstruction of blood flow to the brain results from accumulation of clots of coagulated blood and plugs of tissue and plaques that remain at the point of formation and narrow the vessel openings, thereby restricting passage of blood flow. This type of stroke can evolve over hours or days. Because thrombotic strokes tend to evolve from plaques in the internal carotid artery and vertebral basilar arteries, regions fed by the middle cerebral artery and vertebral basilar artery are most affected.

b. Cerebral embolism

An **embolus** is either a plug of thrombus material or a fatty deposit broken away from blood vessel walls or a plug of foreign matter such as clumps of bacteria or obstructive gas bubbles. Obstruction of blood flow can be due to a blood clot, air bubble, fat plug, or small mass of cells traveling from another vessel and lodged into a smaller one, restricting circulation and causing sudden onset of symptoms.

c. Cerebral atherosclerosis

Obstruction of blood flow can occur when narrowing of the vessel results from thickening and hardening of the arteries.

d. Cerebral vasculitis

Inflammation or vasospasm (spasmodic constriction of blood vessels) can cause narrowing of the vessels and restriction of blood supply.

2. HEMORRHAGIC STROKES

This type of stroke results from massive bleeding into brain tissue. Causes of cerebral hemorrhage include hypertension, congenital cerebral artery defects, toxins, and blood disorders. Onset is abrupt with poor prognosis when loss of consciousness is beyond 2 days.

a. Spontaneous intracranial hemorrhage secondary to ruptured aneurysm

Aneurysms are balloonlike expansions from blood vessels caused by congenital defects, hypertension, arteriosclerosis, embolisms, or infections. The weakened vessel walls make them prone to rupture.

b. Intracranial hemorrhage from arteriovenous malformation

An arteriovenous malformation is a congenital collection of abnormal blood vessels with abnormal blood flow that tend to be weak and susceptible to vessel leakage.

c. Subarachnoid hemorrhage

Bleeding under arachnoid matter can cause damage to brain tissue from pressure effects and irritation.

3. LACUNAR STROKES

This type of vascular insufficiency results when small branches of the cerebral arteries become occluded. The softened infarcted tissue leaves multiple small lacunae. The resulting infarcts are so minuscule that there may be no obvious clinical symptoms, although location is a critical determinant of symptom presentation. Computed tomography (CT) and arteriography tend to have negative findings.

4. TRANSIENT ISCHEMIC ATTACKS

Usually caused by transient focal ischemia, transient ischemic attacks (TIAs) are linked to atherosclerotic thrombosis. These brief events last from a few minutes to a number of hours and typically reverse themselves. TIAs are more commonly associated with atherosclerosis and hypertension, particularly in males. They can involve any cerebral or cerebellar artery. The individual attack may resolve abruptly or gradually.

5. MULTI-INFARCT STATES

Several conditions can lead to multi-infarct states, including small vessel ischemic changes, which are often associated with atherosclerosis, diabetes, and hypertension. Small vessel changes also can be the result of cranial radiation, which has been demonstrated to affect the intimal walls of blood vessels and subsequently lead to small vessel changes. Any disorder that can lead to a hypercoagulable state can be a setup for multi-infarct states. It is not atypical for patients with these syndromes to present "acutely," but care should be taken during history taking; many times a stepwise deterioration can be evident in the behavioral history.

II. FUNCTIONAL NEUROANATOMIC CORRELATES

A. Distribution of Blood Supply to the Brain

Blood supply to the brain is transported by two carotid arteries and two vertebral arteries, with both vessels entering on each side of the body.

1. INTERNAL CAROTID ARTERIES

These arteries enter the skull at the base of the brain and branch out to form two major arteries and a number of smaller arteries.

a. Major branches

Major branches (anterior cerebral artery and middle cerebral artery) irrigate the anterior and middle regions of the cortex. The anterior cerebral artery has branches that supply the orbital frontal lobes, medial frontal lobes, cingulate gyrus, anterior fornix, parts of the corpus callosum, and the posterior parietal region. The middle cerebral artery is the greatest blood supplier of the cerebral hemispheres. Its branches supply internal nuclear masses; orbitofrontal, precentral, and anterior regions; plus anterior temporal, posterior temporal, and posterior parietal branches.

b. Minor branches

Minor branches (ophthalmic artery, anterior choroidal artery, posterior communicating artery, and anterior communicating artery) irrigate various subcortical regions. The posterior communicating artery joins the middle cerebral artery and the posterior cerebral artery on each side, and the anterior communicating artery joins the anterior and middle cerebral arteries.

2. VERTEBRAL ARTERIES

The vertebral arteries enter at the base of the brain and join to form the basilar artery, which gives off smaller arteries and then branches into the posterior cerebral artery. The vertebral arteries supply the spinal cord, brain stem (medulla, pons, midbrain), cerebellum, and posterior diencephalon.

a. Major branches

These arteries (basilar artery and posterior cerebral artery) supply parts of the temporal and occipital lobes. The posterior cerebral artery, which branches off from the vertebral system, supplies the lower surface of the temporal lobe, and large areas of the occipital lobe and visual cortex.

b. Minor branches

Interconnection of all these arteries (anterior inferior cerebellar artery and posterior inferior cerebellar artery) form the **circle of Willis.** If blockage of a vertebral or carotid artery occurs on one side, this circular connection helps compensate the half of the brain that has lost its blood supply.

3. NEUROPATHOLOGICAL AND NEUROPSYCHOLOGICAL SYMPTOM CORRELATES

Interruption of blood supply to specific brain regions is often associated with characteristic neuropsychological signs and symptoms. The distribution of the major anterior, middle, and posterior cerebral arteries irrigates both cortical and subcortical regions. Table 1 provides a review of arterial blood supply to anatomic–functional divisions of brain regions considered of primary importance from a neuropsychological perspective.

III. DIAGNOSES TO RULE OUT

Compared with cerebrovascular accidents, other causes of cognitive impairment such as tumors, progressive dimenting diseases (Alzheimer's disease, Pick's disease, and Lewy body disease), and movement disorders presenting with dementia (Parkinson's disease and Huntington's disease) typically present with a slow, progressive course. Multi-infarct dementia of vascular origin can be misdiagnosed as an Alzheimer's-type dementia because symptoms can vary depending on location of the small strokes and symptom progression. Often, multi-infarct states present in a stepwise fashion as opposed to the more insidious decline that is seen in Alzheimer's disease. Also, it is often the case that "acute" presentations of multi-infarct events are magnified by changes in the person's environmental structure. Therefore, a careful history is important in delineating all the factors that lead to behavioral changes.

Diagnostic clues from past medical history should include medical risk factors for cerebrovascular disease such as hypertension, atherosclerosis in other parts of the body, coronary heart disease, atrial fibrillation, previous CVA or TIA, carotid bruit, rheumatic heart disease, diabetes, smoking, excessive alcohol use, and use of birth control pills.

IV. RELEVANT LABORATORY, NEURORADIOLOGICAL AND ELECTROPHYSIOLOGICAL STUDIES

Other prominent neurological conditions that may be mistaken for vascular dementia include infectious processes, metabolic encephalopathies, toxic conditions, and nutritional deficien-

Table 1. Arterial Blood Supply to Functional–Anatomic Divisions of the Brain Relevant to Neuropsychology

Function	Impairment	Brain structure	Blood supply
Sensorimotor	Paralysis of contralateral face, arm, and leg	Primary motor area, precentral gyrus	Middle cerebral artery, anterior cerebral artery
	Sensory impairment over face, arm, and leg	Primary sensory area, postcentral gyrus	Middle cerebral artery, anterior cerebral artery
Language	Broca's aphasia	Inferior frontal gyrus in dominant hemisphere	Middle cerebral artery
	Wernicke's aphasia	Superior temporal gyrus in dominant hemisphere	Middle cerebral artery
Visual perception	Homonymous hemianopia	Optic radiation deep in temporal convolution	Middle cerebral artery, Posterior cerebral artery
	Visual integration, spatial neglect, visual agnosia	Parietal-occipital lobe, nondominant hemisphere	Middle cerebral artery
	Constructional apraxia, dressing apraxia	Parietal lobe, nondominant hemisphere	Middle cerebral artery
	Gerstmann's syndrome (agraphia, acalculia, alexia,	Angular gyrus of the dominant hemisphere	Middle cerebral artery

(Continued)

Table 1. Arterial Blood Supply to Functional–Anatomic Divisions of the Brain Relevant to Neuropsychology *(Continued)*

Function	Impairment	Brain structure	Blood supply
	finger agnosia, right–left confusion)		
Movement	Ideomotor and ideational apraxia	Left temporal, parietal, occipital area	Middle cerebral artery, posterior cerebral artery
Memory	Short-term and long-term memory impairment	Hippocampus, medial temporal lobes, frontal lobes, basal forebrain, medial thalamus	Medial cerebral, posterior cerebral, anterior choroidal, and posterior communicating arteries
	Working memory impairment	Dorsolateral frontal lobes	Anterior cerebral artery
Frontal–executive	Impairment in set maintenance, problem solving, planning, self-evaluation, ability to modify behavior	Dorsolateral frontal	Middle cerebral artery
	Impairment in inhibition, emotional regulation	Orbital frontal	Anterior cerebral artery
	Akinesia, bradykinesia, dyskinesia	Basal ganglia, putamen, globus pallidus, caudate nucleus, amygdaloid	Anterior choroidal artery, Middle cerebral artery

cies. Medical studies are critical to rule out or account for conditions that contribute to physical and behavioral changes.

Neuropsychologists should be familiar with relevant laboratory, neuroradiological, and electrophysiological studies in order to assist in diagnosis, neuropsychological test interpretation, and treatment recommendations. The neuropsychologist, of course, is not qualified to interpret these tests but should be knowledgeable concerning the typical laboratory values associated with these medical tests and able to discuss these test results with the physicians involved in the acute workup of the patient. Knowledge of these results might influence interpretation of the neuropsychological assessment if the tests are done at an early stage (see chap. 3, this volume). For example, diagnosis of vascular dementia is inappropriate if a patient is acutely hyponatremic, is suffering from oxygen deprivation, or has uremic poisoning owing to kidney failure.

- *Routine Laboratory Tests.* Routine laboratory studies typically include a complete blood count (CBC) Panel 20, electrolytes, and blood-clotting-factor studies.

- *Cardiac Tests.* In acute myocardial infarction (MI), cardiac enzyme levels are often requested. In infectious endocarditis, blood cultures are typically taken. Other important tests that are beneficial to consider include an electrocardiogram (EKG) to rule out possible MI or arrhythmia, a chest X-ray to rule out cardiomegaly or infection, and oxygen saturation levels or blood gases.

- *Other Relevant Laboratory Tests.* If rheumatologic or inflammatory disease is considered, the physician typically orders an erythrocyte sedimentation rate (ESR) and fluorescent antinuclear antibody (FANA). In coagulopathies, more advanced studies such as protein C and protein S as well as anticardiolipin and venereal disease resource laboratory (VDRL) studies are typically ordered. In systemic cancer, guaiac stools are often considered. Some stroke-related symptoms are due to illicit drug use; therefore, a drug screen, particularly aimed at cocaine and amphetamines, is helpful.

- *Computed Tomography.* In general, when a patient presents with symptoms of a stroke, a head CT scan is done to rule out a hemorrhage, infarct, or mass lesion. It is important to appreciate that CT scans do not always show evidence of a stroke initially because the densities on CT scans of newly acquired stroke are often similar to those of normal brain tissue. Typically, in 3–4 days after a stroke has completed, a lesion is appreciable on CT scan.

• *Magnetic Resonance Imaging.* Occasionally magnetic resonance imaging (MRI) is indicated; this type of imaging is more capable than CT of detecting small vessel, subcortical strokes. MRI scans can also be particularly helpful in patients with a newly acquired stroke because, unlike the CT scan, it enables disclosure of preexisting underlying periventricular white matter disease. Detecting the presence of coexisting white matter lesions has obvious implications for neuropsychological interpretation, prognosis, and recovery.

• *Other Diagnostic Tests.* Carotid ultrasound is of value in determining whether obstructed carotid arteries could be a source of embolus. This procedure also serves as a general screen for vascular disease. An echocardiogram or transesophageal echocardiogram, which provides better images of the heart as it pumps blood through the valves and chambers, is sometimes performed if a cardiac source is suspected.

V. NEUROPSYCHOLOGICAL ASSESSMENT

Table 2 provides an introductory review of tests recommended for basic neuropsychological assessment of patients with CVA. Administration and valid interpretation of standardized neuropsychological tests is often quite difficult in this patient population. The following section provides some hints for alternative neuropsychological testing approaches when standardized neuropsychological testing is ineffective.

Hemiparesis, visual field cuts, weakness, aphasia, and a host of other acquired behavioral syndromes in patients with stroke often tax the neuropsychologist to the point that individually customized neuropsychological assessment is often the rule and not the exception. The addition of creative testing beyond the limits of standardized tests can also be helpful in designing rehabilitation strategies that might aid the patient. The following sections provide specific examples of alternative neuropsychological testing approaches that may be used when standardized neuropsychological testing is ineffective.

Table 2. CVA-Related Neuropsychological Disorders and Tests of Assessment

Function or impairment	Suggested neuropsychological tests	References[a]
Aphasia		
Broca's aphasia	Boston Diagnostic Aphasia Examination	Goodglass & Kaplan, 1983a,b
Wernicke's aphasia	Multilingual Aphasia Examination	Benton & Hamsher, 1989
Transcortical motor aphasia	Western Aphasia Battery	Kertesz, 1979
Global aphasia		
Transcortical sensory aphasia		
Conduction aphasia		
Comprehension	Token Test	Boller & Vignolo, 1966
Naming	Boston Naming Test	Kaplan, Goodglass, & Weintraub, 1983
Vocabulary	Peabody Picture Vocabulary Test	Dunn & Dunn, 1981
Verbal fluency	Controlled Oral Word Association Test	Benton & Hamsher, 1976, 1989 Spreen & Strauss, 1991
Reading	National Adult Reading Test	Nelson, Nelson, & O'Connell, 1978
Writing	Boston Diagnostic Aphasia Examination: Cookie Theft Picture	Goodglass & Kaplan, 1983a,b

(Continued)

Table 2. CVA-Related Neuropsychological Disorders and Tests of Assessment (*Continued*)

Function or impairment	Suggested neuropsychological tests	References[a]
Visual perception		
Homonymous hemianopia	Double Simultaneous Stimulation Test	Walsh, 1987
Visual organization and integration	Hooper Visual Organization Test	Hooper, 1958; Hooper Organization Test Manual, 1983
Visual motor construction	Wechsler Adult Intelligence Scale–Revised: Block Design, Object Assembly	Wechsler, 1994, 1955, 1981 Benton, Hamsher, et al., 1983 Benton & Van Allen, 1968
Visual recognition	Visual Form Discrimination Test	Benton, Hamsher, et al., 1983
Face recognition	Test of Face Recognition	
Attention		
Auditory attention	Wechsler Adult Intelligence Scale–Revised: Digit Span	Wechsler, 1994, 1955, 1981
	Paced Auditory Serial Addition Test	Gronwell, 1977; Gronwell & Sampson, 1974
	Verbal and Nonverbal Cancellation	Mesulam, 1985, 1988 Schenkenberg et al., 1980
Visual attention and spatial neglect	Line Bisection Test	Smith, 1982
	Symbol Digit Modalities Test	

Movement

Ideomotor and ideational apraxia	Boston Diagnostic Aphasia Examination: Apraxia Test	Goodglass & Kaplan, 1983

Memory

Short-term, long-term, and working memory	Wechsler Memory Scale–Revised	Wechsler, 1945, 1987
	California Verbal Learning Test	Delis, Kramer, Kaplan, & Ober, 1987
	Buschke Selective Reminding Test	Buschke & Fuld, 1974
	Hopkins Verbal Learning Test	Brandt, 1991
	Rey Auditory Verbal Learning Test	Rey, 1964; Taylor, 1959
	Rey-Osterreith Complex Figure	Osterreith, 1944
	Benton Visual Retention Test	Benton, 1974

Frontal–executive

Set maintenance and set shifting	Trail Making Test	Army Individual Test Battery, 1944
Problem solving		
Conceptualization	Wisconsin Card Sorting Test	Berg, 1948; Grant & Berg, 1948
Response inhibition	Stroop Interference Test	Stroop, 1935; Jensen & Rohwer, 1966

[a]Neuropsychological test references cited here can be found in *Neuropsychological Assessment* (3rd ed.), by M. D. Lezak, 1995, New York: Oxford University Press.

A. Visual Neglect

In the acute assessment of a patient with right hemisphere stroke who has visual neglect, it is not helpful for the neuropsychologist to administer numerous visuospatial tests that the patient will continually fail. Rather, it is important for the neuropsychologist to minimize the problem of neglect when attempting to assess higher cortical visual perceptual functions by using methods of remediation or compensation. If such a patient is failing miserably on the block design test, for example, it is helpful to limit presentation of the blocks to the "good" right visual field. Line bisection is another difficult test for patients with right parietal dysfunction; therefore, after left hemineglect has been identified, one can structure the task by writing letters at the end of each line to be bisected. Having the patient read the letters out loud ensures that he or she attends to the entire line before bisecting it. Likewise, vertical alignment of the picture arrangement stimulus cards can overcome the barrier of visual inattention.

B. Aphasia

Patients with aphasic syndromes often perform poorly on a variety of tests simply because they are given verbal instructions that are not understood because of underlying comprehension deficits. Comprehension problems can be minimized by examiner demonstrations and use of nonverbal gesturing and facial expression to enhance communication. Expressive problems can often be overcome by multiple-choice or yes–no recognition testing in which the patient does not have to provide a complex verbal response.

C. Hemiparesis

Most neuropsychologists agree that it is of little value to test motor speed, such as finger-tapping performance, in patients with severe hemiparesis. Although patients with left hemisphere stroke who have severe right hemiparesis often are also clumsy and slow with their left hand, functional evaluation of the left hand for assessing performance on nonspeed tests would be of benefit.

VI. THE NEUROLOGICAL EXAMINATION

The neurological examination provides critical information regarding simple sensorimotor function that should be carefully reviewed by the neuropsychologist. Physical symptoms that may directly affect the neuropsychological evaluation include numbness, weakness, or paralysis of face, arm, or leg; sudden blurring, decreased vision, or double vision in one or both eyes; difficulty speaking owing to dysarthria; and dizziness, loss of balance, or loss of coordination. It is critical for the neuropsychologist to appreciate the contribution of basic sensorimotor system disturbance when assessing higher cognitive function to guide test selection and enhance accuracy of test interpretation. Poor performance on a measure of word production, for example, may be due to dysarthric speech rather than impaired semantic fluency. Neuropsychological testing in the assessment of cardiovascular disease should include attention to the following issues:

A. Timing of the Evaluation

The first thing to consider when evaluating a patient with a newly acquired stroke is the timing of the evaluation. A stroke is an evolving situation, and findings during the acute stage could definitively change in the ensuing months. Therefore, the neuropsychologist must consider the typical neurobehavioral recovery course of the stroke and point of measurement. Regardless of whether a stroke has stabilized or is evolving, a neuropsychological evaluation is critical in assisting both initial and long-term diagnostic and rehabilitative treatment planning.

B. Identifying Strengths and Weaknesses

An important perspective to take at this stage is one of identifying strengths as well as weaknesses. The purpose of the neuropsychological evaluation is not only to look at what areas of deficit are prevalent but also to identify remaining cognitive strengths that can be exploited in the rehabilitative compensatory process.

C. Test Administration and Interpretation

1. THE QUALITATIVE APPROACH

It is often necessary to adjust standardized administration procedures when evaluating stroke patients to elicit behavior and account for major deficits. It is important to look beyond final scores as a criterion for determining the degree of brain damage because the cognitive processes employed by patients as they struggle to perform neuropsychological tests are frequently more revealing than the final quantitative outcome on a test. Fine-tuned analysis of patients' qualitative behavior can measure improvement that final scores cannot convey. For example, on the Picture Arrangement subtest of the Wechsler Adult Intelligence Scale–Revised (WAIS-R), a patient with a right hemisphere stroke may perform poorly. When tested months later, the patient may continue to obtain similarly poor scores, yet instead of misarranging all of the cards as he did earlier, he now only misarranges one of four cards. This finding indicates improvement, despite an unchanged final score. The qualitative approach is important for neuropsychologists to consider when trying to document improvement as well as to provide justification for ongoing rehabilitation.

2. ECOLOGICAL VALIDITY

Neuropsychologists have to be concerned about the ecological validity of their tests. For example, if one is finding significant problems on measures of apraxia during a neuropsychological evaluation, it is important to discuss these findings with the physical and occupational therapists working with the patient to see how this deficit is affecting the patient in real-life situations.

3. ENVIRONMENTAL CONDITIONS

Environmental conditions during testing can have a notable influence on examination and rehabilitation of cognition and behavior. The neuropsychologist should always be aware that patients can show an amplification of cognitive abnormalities in unfamiliar environments with distractions and overstimulation.

4. FUNCTIONAL SIGNIFICANCE

Direct and clear communication of test results is important when working with professionals from other disciplines involved in the treatment of patients as well as with patients and family members. Whereas the training of neuropsychologists emphasizes identifying and understanding the complex cognitive processes involved in a behavior, attempts to translate these processes into functional activities often remain obtuse. It is critical to present neuropsychological data in a format that has functional meaning and significance, so that impressions and recommendations can be used by staff and family to enhance recovery.

D. Determining Patient Competency

The neuropsychologist is often faced with addressing issues of competency in stroke patients. It is important when determining competency to consider what phase of recovery the patient is in, because competency status may change rather dramatically as recovery progresses. A detailed analysis of the patient's available behavioral responses helps to clarify his or her potential for independence and self-care. Some patients with aphasia, for example, have relatively unimpaired reasoning and judgment, yet impoverished expressive language renders them unable to communicate their ideas effectively.

VII. TREATMENT ISSUES

Emotional and medical concerns should be taken into account when devising a rehabilitation strategy for patients with vascular disorders.

A. Treatment of Emotional Behaviors

It is important for the neuropsychologist to monitor emotional behavior continually in order to provide needed psychotherapeutic intervention, as well as to assist the physician or therapist in appropriately treating the behavior. The neuropsychologist should not underestimate the powerful influence of emotional factors in shaping a patient's ultimate recovery. Individual as well as family education and psychotherapy can be helpful in motivating patients to achieve their highest level of functional outcome.

Behavioral techniques such as distraction are often helpful in controlling emotional lability and can prevent the need for antidepressant drugs, which may further compromise cognitive abilities. Monitoring of neurovegetative signs and degree of participation in therapies may provide clues to whether or not psychopharmacological intervention is warranted. In some cases, medications to assist in emotional regulation or reduce symptoms of anxiety and depression can serve to facilitate the recovery process by enabling active participation in rehabilitation.

B. Medication

Drugs are often used to treat conditions that either accompany or result from cerebrovascular disease. **Anticoagulants** are drugs used to dissolve clots or prevent further clotting; **hypertensive** drugs are used to control blood pressure; and **steroid drugs** are used to reduce cerebral edema, or swelling. Familiarity with use of these and other medications in patients undergoing neuropsychological evaluation is of importance, because side effects can confound test performance and interpretation. The book *Neurotoxic Side Effects of Prescription Drugs* by John C. M. Brust (1996) is a helpful resource that can familiarize neuropsychologists with medication side effects from drugs frequently prescribed to patients with CVA.

C. Rehabilitation Strategies

Comprehensive textbooks are available to instruct the practitioner in implementation of cognitive rehabilitation strategies (see Sohlberg & Mateer, 1989a). However, every neuropsychologist working with CVA patients in an inpatient setting should be familiar with basic rehabilitative techniques.

1. VISUAL PERCEPTUAL DEFICITS

For patients with right hemisphere stroke, therapy designed to assist in orienting to the intact left visual field is helpful. It is important to distinguish among inattention, neglect, and a field cut in these patients (see chapter 23, this volume). Simple techniques such as making a brightly colored line on the left side of the page when the patient is reading may help the patient to orient to his or her left side, thereby enabling him or her to read a complete line. The neuropsychologist should work hand in hand with the occupational therapist in the rehabilitation of these types of disorders.

2. SPEECH AND LANGUAGE DEFICITS

Typically, speech pathologists are involved not only in the evaluation of speech and language disturbances but in their treatment. The neuropsychologist should be able to assist the speech pathologist with treatment efforts by helping to differentiate the nature of the language disturbance and identifying other cognitive disturbances, such as diminished initiation and impaired memory, that may contribute to overall language performance. For example, on the Token Test, a measure of verbal comprehension, impaired memory rather than aphasia may be the cause of compromised performance on the more complex multistep commands. By simplifying memory demands or training the patient in mnemonics, preserved aspects of language can be enhanced.

3. MEMORY DEFICITS

Memory disorders are variably amenable to rehabilitation strategies depending on the nature of the impairment (e.g., encoding vs. retrieval deficits). Schacter's method of vanishing cues (Schacter & Glisky, 1986), which exploits implicit memory processing, can be helpful for teaching some procedural aspects of memory, but experience has shown this to be limited and quite time consuming. For the patient who demonstrates significant retrieval problems, however, use of compensatory strategies such as a notebook and memory log can be helpful (see chap. 22, this volume).

4. EXECUTIVE FUNCTION DEFICITS

Rehabilitation of any kind is difficult unless patients have adequate attention and awareness regarding their deficits. Executive system dysfunction can lead to serious impediment of the ability to organize, sequence, plan, benefit from feedback, and carry over treatment information. Effective evaluation and rehabilitation of executive system function is necessary in all patients with stroke disorder (see chap. 28, this volume). Adding structure to a patient's environment to make it more predictable and reduce distractions can significantly improve cognitive function and emotional adjustment. Sohlberg and Mateer (1989a) provide helpful executive system rehabilitation techniques.

VIII. PSYCHIATRIC COMORBIDITY ASSOCIATED WITH STROKE

Psychological and psychiatric comorbidity often result from an acquired neurological disease. The neuropsychological examination may assist in differentiating the amplification of preexisting emotional behaviors from newly acquired primary brain-based or secondary reactive emotions (see Heilman, Bowers, & Valenstein, 1993; Starkstein & Robinson, 1992).

A. Preexisting Emotional Illness

The possibility of a preexisting psychiatric condition with subsequent poststroke amplification requires close evaluation and monitoring because inadequate coping skills and diminished emotional reserve may contribute to poor adjustment. Careful review of medical history and clinical interview with family members are critical to establish a positive psychiatric history.

B. Emotional Adjustment to Illness

An appreciation for the normal grieving process, as a reaction to the profound loss occurring with a stroke, is important. It is not uncommon for patients as well as their families to experience depressive symptoms as they begin to adjust to the condition. Experiencing the various stages of grieving is considered appropriate and even healthy because it will enable the patient and family ultimately to cope better. Early intervention with antidepressant medication is contraindicated unless depressed mood is excessively prolonged and extreme.

C. Emotional Changes Resulting From Brain Lesions

The contribution of the cortex to emotional processing is to interpret and analyze emotional information and express and regulate affective behavior.

1. HEMISPHERIC DIFFERENCES

Studies of change in mood and emotional experience as a result of brain lesions have suggested that patients with left hemisphere damage with frontal and caudate involvement are more often depressed or anxious, whereas those with right hemisphere damage tend to be indifferent or euphoric. Patients with right hemisphere lesions may have difficulty with emotional facial expression and emotional vocal prosody; hence they can appear indifferent. Depression should not automatically be assumed in patients demonstrating flattened facial and prosodic emotional expression related to frontal lobe and right hemisphere lesions. In many of these patients, internal emotional experience and mood state are discrepant with outward emotional expression. Furthermore, voluntary and involuntary expression of humor can also be misleading, because patients may demonstrate laughter in response to a joke but not when commanded to show facial and prosodic emotional affect (e.g., happy, sad, angry).

2. RIGHT HEMISPHERE

The right hemisphere contains a "vocabulary" of nonverbal affective signals (facial expressions, prosody, and gestures). Patients with right hemisphere damage, therefore, are frequently unable to discern the emotional meaning of facial, vocal, and gestural expression of emotion, as well as to engage in similar emotional expression.

3. FRONTAL AND SUBCORTICAL REGIONS

Portions of the frontal lobe are intimately bound to subcortical, primarily limbic structures. Hence, damage to frontal convexity and orbital poles can result in flattened affect, apathy, loss of social control, and overly emotional behavior. With lesions involving frontal–subcortical–basal ganglia regions, obsessive–compulsive symptoms including ruminative, checking, and perseverative behavior may also be present and might profoundly interfere with the rehabilitation process.

4. CORTICOBULBAR MOTOR PATHWAYS

Lesions that interrupt the corticobulbar motor pathways bilaterally release reflex mechanisms for facial expression from cortical control. Emotional lability (i.e., involuntary laughing or crying) results in symptoms of inappropriate emotional expression with appropriate emotional experience. Again, it is important not to interpret this stereotypical excess of emotional expression as representative of mood state.

IX. CONCLUSION

This chapter provides a general overview of the wide range of causes and types of cerebrovascular accidents, blood supply to anatomic–functional divisions of the brain, issues related to assessment of cognitive and emotional disorders resulting from CVAs, and basic rehabilitative techniques. This topic encompasses a broad range of behavioral disorders that can accompany damage to the brain by way of the vascular system; additional, more detailed and specific information beyond the scope of this general review can be found in the publications listed in the bibliography.

BIBLIOGRAPHY

Adams, G. F., & Victor, M. (1989). *Principles of neurology* (4th ed.). New York: McGraw-Hill.

Bornstein, R. A., & Brown, G. G. (1991). *Neurobehavioral aspects of cerebrovascular disease.* New York: Oxford University Press.

Brandstater, M. E. (1990). An overview of stroke rehabilitation. *Stroke, 21*(Suppl. II), II-40–II-42.

Brust, J. C. (1996). *Neurotoxic side effects of prescription drugs.* Stoneham, MA: Butterworth-Heinemann.

Goodglass, H., & Kaplan, E. (1983) *Assessment of asphasia and related disorders* (2nd ed.). Philadelphia: Lea & Febiger. (Distributed by Psychological Assessment Resources, Odessa, FL)

Heilman, K. M., Bowers, D., & Valenstein, E. (1993). Emotional disorders associated with neurological diseases. In K. M. Heilman & E. Valenstein (Eds.), *Clinical neuropsychology* (3rd ed.). New York: Oxford University Press.

Lezak, M. D. (1995). *Neuropsychological assessment* (3rd ed.). New York: Oxford University Press.

Ross, E. D. (1985). Modulation of affect and nonverbal communication by the right hemisphere. In M. M. Mesulam (Ed.), *Principles of behavioral neurology.* Philadelphia: Davis.

Schacter, D. L., & Glisky, E. L. (1986). Memory remediation: Restoration, alleviation and the acquisition of domain specific knowledge. In B. P. Uzell & Y. Gross (Eds.), *Clinical neuropsychology of intervention* (pp. 257–282). Boston: Martinus Nijhoff.

Starkstein, S. E., & Robinson, R. G. (1992). Neuropsychiatric aspects of cerebral vascular disorders. In S. C. Yudofsky & R. E. Hayes (Eds.), *Textbook of neuropsychiatry* (2nd ed., pp. 449–472). Washington, DC: American Psychiatric Press.

Sohlberg, M. M., & Mateer, C. A. (1989a). *Introduction to cognitive rehabilitation: Theory and practice.* New York: Guilford Press.

Sohlberg, M. M., & Mateer, C. A. (1989b). Training use of compensatory memory books: A three stage behavioral approach. *Journal of Clinical and Experimental Neuropsychology, 11,* 871–891.

CHAPTER 20

Pelagie M. Beeson and Steven Z. Rapcsak

The Aphasias

I. DEFINITION

Aphasia is an acquired language impairment that results from neurological damage to the language areas of the brain, which are typically located in the left hemisphere. Also referred to as **dysphasia**, aphasia is characterized by defective word selection, language production, and language comprehension. Incorrect word choice and sound substitution errors are common features of aphasic speech and are referred to as paraphasic errors, or **paraphasias**. Language comprehension deficits are present to some extent in all aphasias, but a subtle impairment may become apparent only when the patient is tested with syntactically complex sentences. Because aphasia is a central language impairment, it affects not only spoken language but also the comprehension and production of written language (i.e., reading and writing). Reading impairment is referred to as **alexia**, and writing disorders are labeled **agraphia**. The specific characteristics of aphasia and its accompanying deficits reflect the site

This work was supported, in part, by National Multipurpose Research and Training Center Grant DC - 01409 from the National Institute on Deafness and Other Communication Disorders.

and extent of neurological damage, as well as individual differences in brain organization. Various classic aphasia syndromes are characterized by identifiable constellations of language symptoms and provide a useful framework for the diagnostic evaluation of patients with aphasia.

II. ETIOLOGY

The most common cause of acute aphasia is ischemic stroke (embolic or thrombotic) in the distribution of the left middle cerebral artery, which is the main blood supplier of the perisylvian cortical language areas. Other causes of acute aphasia include cerebral hemorrhage (hypertensive, or following the rupture of an aneurysm or arteriovenous malformation) and traumatic brain injury. By contrast, slowly progressive aphasia typically occurs with brain tumors and cortical degenerative disorders (e.g., aphasia associated with dementia of the Alzheimer's type or primary progressive aphasia). Transient aphasia may be associated with transient ischemic attacks (TIAs), migraine, and seizures.

Aphasia most often results from left hemisphere lesions because about 95% of right-handed individuals and about 70% of left-handed individuals are left hemisphere dominant for language. However, aphasia can occur following right hemisphere damage in left-handed individuals, and in rare cases, right hemisphere damage in a right-handed individual results in what is called **crossed aphasia**.

III. GENERAL CLINICOANATOMIC CONSIDERATIONS

A. Perisylvian Versus Extraperisylvian Lesions

Aphasia is most often caused by damage to the perisylvian language areas of the brain (see Figure 1). The perisylvian language zone includes Broca's area, which is involved in the motor programming of speech; Wernicke's area, which is critical for the auditory comprehension of spoken words; and the arcuate fasciculus, which links these two areas and is thought to play an important role in repetition. Aphasia may also be caused by lesions that do not directly damage the perisylvian language areas but isolate them from brain regions involved in semantic processing and the production of volitional speech. The extraperisylvian aphasias are referred to as **transcortical aphasias**.

B. Fluency

Aphasic speech production can be classified as either fluent or nonfluent.

- **Fluent aphasias** are characterized by plentiful verbal output consisting of well-articulated, easily produced utterances of relatively normal length and prosody (i.e., variations of pitch, loudness, rhythm). Fluent aphasias are associated with posterior (post-Rolandic) lesions that spare anterior (pre-Rolandic) cortical regions critical for motor control for speech.
- **Nonfluent aphasias** are characterized by sparse, effortful utterances of short phrase length and disrupted prosody. Nonfluent aphasias are associated with anterior or pre-Rolandic lesions that compromise motor and premotor cortical regions involved in speech production.

C. Auditory Comprehension

Auditory processing is defective in most aphasic patients, although the severity of the impairment varies with aphasia type. Anterior lesions result in relatively mild auditory comprehension impairments, whereas posterior lesions (especially if they involve Wernicke's area) result in significant impairment of auditory processing.

D. Repetition

Aphasia types differ with regard to the preservation of repetition ability.

- Repetition of spoken utterances requires an intact perisylvian region: posterior regions (Wernicke's area) for auditory processing, anterior regions (Broca's area) for speech production, and the critical connecting fiber tracts (arcuate fasciculus). Therefore, lesions anywhere in the perisylvian region are likely to disrupt repetition.
- Extraperisylvian lesions are characterized by preserved repetition despite a severe reduction of spontaneous speech (transcortical motor aphasia) or severe comprehension disturbance (transcortical sensory aphasia), or both (mixed transcortical aphasia).

E. Naming

All individuals with aphasia exhibit naming impairment, or *anomia*, usually in combination with other language deficits.

However, naming impairment can also occur in relative isolation in patients with anomic aphasia. Owing to its ubiquitous nature, anomia is considered the least useful localizing sign in aphasia.

IV. ASSESSMENT OF APHASIA

The initial assessment of aphasia can be performed informally, as in the context of a bedside evaluation. A 15- to 30-minute interview that includes conversational interaction, as well as some structured tasks, is typically adequate to discern the presence or absence of aphasia, provide an estimate of the aphasia severity, establish a profile, and document the relative strengths and weaknesses of the patient (Exhibit 1). A more formal, in-depth assessment of aphasia is necessary for other purposes, such as designing a treatment plan, prognosticating recovery, and answering research questions.

A. Medical Chart Review

In addition to obtaining information about the patient's current and past medical history, the following information should be obtained, if possible:

- **Handedness**—to anticipate possible exceptions to left hemisphere dominance for language and to guide the assessment of writing in cases of hemiparesis (i.e., to determine whether writing will be assessed with the dominant or nondominant hand)
- **Education and occupation**—to shape assumptions regarding premorbid language, reading, and writing abilities
- **Vision and hearing status**—to determine the need for eyeglasses or sound amplification (hearing aid) during testing

B. Bedside Evaluation

To assess aphasia properly, the patient must be awake, alert, and able to engage in interaction with the intent to communicate. If the patient has diminished responsiveness or is inattentive and uncooperative, the assessment for aphasia should be delayed because the obtundent, delirious, or confused patient will not provide a valid basis for language assessment. General measures of mental status, such as the Mini-Mental State Examination, are not appropriate for assessing the mental status of

Exhibit 1. Key Questions to Consider When Examining for Aphasia

Is It Aphasia?		
• Is the patient awake and alert with the intention to communicate? *If not, assessment will be invalid.*	Y	N
• Is there evidence of word retrieval difficulty (anomia)?	Y	N
Example: _____		
• Are there paraphasic errors? phonemic semantic neologistic	Y	N
Example: _____		
• Is there evidence of comprehension difficulty?	Y	N
Example: _____		
• Is the language impairment present across all modalities? spoken language auditory comprehension writing reading	Y	N
What Is the Aphasia Profile? (Use decision tree in Figure 1.)		
• Is the verbal output fluent or nonfluent? _____		
• Is auditory comprehension significantly impaired?	Y	N
• Is repetition significantly impaired?	Y	N
What Is the Communication Status?		
• How severe is the communication impairment? mild moderate severe		
• Is the patient using compensatory strategies to achieve communication?	Y	N
gesture _____ writing _____		
drawing _____ other _____		

individuals with aphasia because of the dependence of these tests on language comprehension and production.

Bedside assessment should concentrate on four language tasks: production of conversational speech, auditory comprehension, repetition, and naming. A brief assessment of reading and writing should also be performed. Throughout the evaluation, the examiner should seek to discover the patient's successful communication strategies, as well as to reveal deficits. Particularly when the impairment is obvious and severe, the examiner should discern what level of assistance results in successful communication and how communication breakdowns are best repaired.

1. ASSESSMENT OF CONVERSATIONAL SPEECH

Begin the evaluation by conversing with the patient. While establishing rapport, listen for evidence of language impairment. Having reviewed the medical chart for background information, ask biographical questions that allow observation of the patient's ability to communicate. Ask open-ended questions to elicit a sample of connected speech. Picture description can also be used to elicit spontaneous speech. Obtain enough information to respond to the following questions:

a. Is there evidence of word retrieval difficulty?

1. Are there word-finding pauses, hesitations, or self-corrections?

2. Does the patient show circumlocution, which means talking around the topic owing to inability to retrieve specific words? Examples follow:

(a) Semantic circumlocution: "Hand me that thing over there, that thing for my nose, that wiper, you know, that ..." (facial tissue)

(b) Empty circumlocution: "It's for this one and that one, and one and two and three, and then boom, boom, boom ... and I wish I could tell you" (target unknown)

3. Are there paraphasic errors?

(a) Verbal or semantic paraphasia: an incorrect word that is related to the intended word in meaning (e.g., *girl* for *boy*)

(b) Literal or phonemic paraphasia: error of sound selection (e.g., *boap* for *boat*)

(c) Neologism: a novel utterance that bears no obvious relationship to the intended word in sound or meaning (e.g., *kleeza* for *table*)

b. Is the output fluent or nonfluent?

1. Fluent aphasia is characterized by the following:

(a) Utterance length that is typically greater than four words and may approximate a normal range of five to eight or more words

(b) Relatively normal speech prosody (i.e., pitch, loudness, and timing variations), although fluent utterances may be interrupted by occasional hesitations, word-finding pauses, and revised utterances

(c) Articulation that is relatively facile and produced without struggle

(d) Conversational speech that is lacking in informational content and may sound "empty" owing to a paucity of content words (e.g., nouns and action verbs) and an excess of grammatical functors (e.g., articles, prepositions, conjunctions) and indefinite words (e.g., "thing")

2. Nonfluent aphasia is characterized by the following:

(a) Reduced utterance length to typically less than four words per utterance; may be primarily single words

(b) Halting speech lacking normal prosodic variations of pitch, loudness, and timing

(c) Effortful articulation, although reactive or automatic responses may be surprisingly well articulated, such as "hello" or "fine" or "I don't know"

(d) Reduced grammatical complexity, with utterances consisting mostly of nouns and lacking function words, resulting in agrammatical, or "telegraphic," speech

2. ASSESSMENT OF AUDITORY COMPREHENSION

Auditory comprehension is typically impaired to some extent in all aphasias. A patient's ability to respond in a natural conversational exchange should be observed, but it is also important to evaluate responses to auditory–verbal information on more structured tasks. Response modalities may need to be adapted so that other impairments do not cause response interference (e.g., unreliable yes or no responses may require pointing to notecards with printed "yes" vs. "no" or "+" vs. "–").

a. Sample tasks

1. Word recognition: "Where's the phone?" "Show me the chair"

2. Commands of increasing complexity for the patient to carry out

(a) Simple commands: "Make a fist"

(b) Multistep complex commands: "Point to the window, the door, and then the pen"

3. Yes or no questions of increasing complexity: "Do you live in Tucson?" "Do you close your umbrella when it starts to rain?"

b. Take note of the following:

1. At what point does auditory comprehension break down: single words, short commands, complex commands?

2. How does the patient respond to auditory comprehension difficulties? Are there requests for clarification or repetition? Is there a lack of awareness of the deficit?

3. If comprehension problems are mild, they may become evident only in difficult listening situations that require divided attention or under conditions of fatigue.

3. ASSESSMENT OF REPETITION

Although the ability to repeat spoken utterances has little communicative value, repetition tasks provide an assessment of speech input and output processes and have diagnostic value for aphasia classification and lesion localization. If repetition is severely impaired, and even single words are not repeated, emotionally laden words or phrases may evoke better responses (e.g., money, I love you).

a. Sample tasks:

1. Repetition of single words (e.g., dog, apple, baseball)
2. Short phrases (e.g., a cup of coffee, salt and pepper, go for a walk)
3. Sentences of increasing length (e.g., The telephone is ringing. He saw a very good movie. I had cereal, toast, and juice for breakfast).

b. Take note of the following:

1. Is repetition better or worse than spontaneous speech?
2. Does repetition break down at the single-word level or only at the sentence level?
3. Do repetition attempts result in the production of paraphasic errors?

4. ASSESSMENT OF NAMING

Although word-finding difficulties in spontaneous speech may suggest anomia, formal testing of confrontation naming allows direct assessment of the patient's ability to retrieve specific words. The extent of naming difficulty is a good general measure of aphasia severity. Select common objects in the room for naming, and if no errors are made, probe naming of less common objects. Individuals with aphasia typically exhibit a word-frequency effect, in that more frequently used content words (e.g., shirt) are retrieved more easily than less frequently used words (e.g., collar). Naming can also be assessed in response to questions, but the questions should probe relatively common knowledge and not be dependent on higher education or extensive vocabulary. Aphasia typically results in impaired confrontation naming regardless of the modality of presentation (visual, auditory, or tactile). Naming deficits confined to a single modality suggest recognition impairment, or agnosia (see section VI).

a. Sample tasks:

1. Naming of common objects: cup, watch, table, pencil
2. Naming less common items: fingernail, collar, eraser
3. Response to questions: What do you use to tell time? What color is an apple?
4. Naming to definition: What do you call the African animal with the long neck?
5. Generative naming: Name all the animals you can think of in 1 minute. Name all the words you can think of that begin with the letter *s* in 1 minute.

b. Take note of the following:

1. What is nature of the naming errors?
2. Are there paraphasic responses? What type?
3. Can the patient produce the word if given the first sound, that is, with phonemic cueing?
4. Is there any evidence of modality-specific impairment, such as improved naming when allowed to hold the object?
5. Is there awareness of errors? Are there attempts to self-correct? Are those attempts successful?
6. Is the patient able to generate at least 12–15 animal names in 1 minute?

5. ASSESSMENT OF READING AND WRITING

A bedside evaluation of reading and writing is brief by necessity. Inquire whether or not the patient has attempted to read or write and what difficulties he or she experienced. Reading and writing abilities are generally defective in aphasia. If reading and writing are spared, the patient may not have aphasia but rather a selective impairment affecting speech input or output processes (see section VI). If aphasia is mild, and the patient is not fatigued, a more extensive exploration of reading and writing may be performed to assess the type and severity of alexia and agraphia.

a. Sample tasks:

1. Read aloud single words or sentences
2. Carry out written commands
3. Write single words to dictation (nouns, verbs, functors)
4. Write a sentence or paragraph

b. Take note of the following:

1. Is the patient able to read aloud? What kind of reading errors (paralexias) are produced in oral reading?
2. Can the patient comprehend written materials?

3. Are there motor difficulties that interfere with writing? If paralysis precludes use of the dominant hand, can writing be accomplished with the nondominant hand? Does the patient have difficulty forming legible letters even when using a non-paralyzed limb (i.e., apraxic agraphia)?

4. Are there spelling errors?

6. PRAGMATIC ASSESSMENT OF LANGUAGE

There can be considerable variation in communicative success by individuals with similar language impairments. Throughout the examination process, take note of the communication strategies used by the patient. First, note whether the patient is aware of the communication deficit. If so, what attempts are made to repair communication failures? Does the patient supplement spoken utterances with gesture or with attempts to write or draw? In the case of unintelligible or perseverative utterances, does the patient convey information through tone of voice and prosodic variations? What are the most successful communication modalities and strategies for this patient?

Figure 1. Schematic drawing of the left hemisphere.

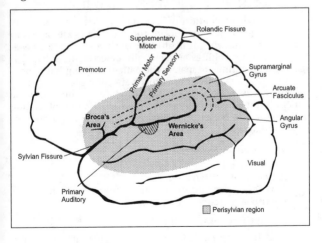

V. CLASSIC APHASIA SYNDROMES

The performance profile that emerges from the brief language assessment can be used to assign patients to one of eight classic aphasia syndromes. Classification is achieved by a series of binary decisions regarding fluency, auditory comprehension, and verbal repetition as shown in Figure 2. Various aphasia syndromes have been used for more than a century to communicate easily the profile of a patient. However, not all patients exemplify a classic aphasia type; in some cases, a patient may be distinguished by his or her divergence from a given syndrome.

Although it is important to assess reading and writing abilities, performance in those modalities does not predict aphasia type. Oral reading performance often is similar to spoken language, and written language deficits may mimic the agrammatical or paragrammatical elements of spoken language. However, there is considerable variability within a given aphasia type regarding reading and writing ability. For that reason, a description of reading and writing abilities is not included in the following summaries of the clinical characteristics of the classic aphasia syndromes.

A. Fluent Aphasias

Anomic aphasia is a fluent aphasia in which there is good auditory comprehension and repetition.

- **Conversational speech** is fluent, with normal utterance length and grammatically well-formed sentences. Word-finding difficulty in spontaneous speech may be evidenced by occasional pauses and circumlocutions.
- **Auditory comprehension** is good for everyday conversation, but there may be some difficulty with complex syntax or in difficult listening situations, such as those that require divided attention.
- **Repetition** is generally preserved, even for full-length sentences.
- **Naming** impairment, in the absence of other significant language deficits, is the hallmark of this aphasia type.
- **Lesion location.** Lesions in *acute* anomic aphasia are usually located outside the perisylvian language zone and involve the angular gyrus or the inferior temporal region. Moderate and mild aphasias of various types caused by perisylvian lesions may evolve to *chronic* anomic aphasia.

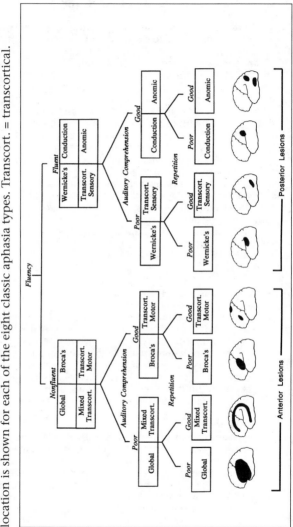

Figure 2. Decision tree for classification of aphasia on the basis of fluency, auditory, comprehension, and repetition abilities. A schematic drawing of the associated lesion location is shown for each of the eight classic aphasia types. Transcort. = transcortical.

Generalized effects of head trauma, Alzheimer's disease, and increased intracranial pressure associated with brain tumor can also result in anomia; therefore, except in the setting of acute anomic aphasia, anomia has limited localizing value.

- **Accompanying deficits.** Anomic aphasia often exists without significant concomitant neurological deficits, but when it is caused by lesions of the angular gyrus, it may be associated with the Gerstmann syndrome (finger agnosia, acalculia, agraphia, left–right confusion) and limb apraxia.
- **Prognosis.** Acute anomic aphasia frequently resolves to minimal language impairment in the form of occasional word-finding difficulty. Anomic aphasia is the most common evolutionary end point for mild-to-moderate aphasia of all types.

Conduction aphasia is a fluent aphasia in which there is good comprehension but poor repetition.

- **Conversational speech** is fluent, with relatively normal utterance length but marred by paraphasias. Phonemic paraphasic errors predominate, and self-correction attempts may result in increasingly closer phonological approximations of the desired word, referred to as *conduit d'approche*. Rate of speech may be slowed by word-finding problems and attempts to self-monitor, but the overall prosodic pattern is akin to normal. Despite word-finding difficulties and paraphasias, spontaneous speech is much more meaningful than in Wernicke's aphasia.
- **Auditory comprehension** is relatively good for casual conversation. Single-word comprehension is well preserved, but patients may have difficulty with complex syntax or multistep commands.
- **Repetition** impairment is the hallmark of conduction aphasia, despite relatively good spontaneous speech. Paraphasias tend to be particularly prominent during repetition tasks. In severe cases, patients may not be able to repeat even single words. In milder cases, single-word repetition is possible, but phrase or sentence repetition is impaired. Repetition of unfamiliar or meaningless items is especially difficult. In some cases, sentence repetition may result in semantic restatements rather than verbatim repetition (e.g., "He's gone" for "He is not coming back").
- **Naming** is always impaired. Paraphasic errors are not uncommon and are typically phonemic.

- **Lesion location.** Conduction aphasia results from posterior perisylvian lesions affecting primarily the supramarginal gyrus in the parietal lobe and the underlying white matter (arcuate fasciculus).
- **Associated deficits.** Conduction aphasia is not associated with significant motor deficit, but cortical sensory loss affecting the right side of the body may be present. Limb and buccofacial apraxia are not uncommon.
- **Prognosis.** Conduction aphasia may persist or may evolve into anomic aphasia.

Transcortical sensory aphasia (TcSA) is a fluent aphasia with impaired comprehension and preserved repetition.

- **Conversational speech** is fluent with relatively normal utterance length, but semantic paraphasias, word-finding difficulties, and circumlocutions are common. Verbal output may sound similar to that of Wernicke's aphasia in that utterances may be semantically "empty" owing to lack of content words and overuse of functors and imprecise words, but output is generally not as voluble as in Wernicke's aphasia.
- **Auditory comprehension** is significantly impaired, although usually not to the extent seen in Wernicke's aphasia.
- **Repetition** is surprisingly preserved, sometimes even for long complex utterances and unfamiliar words. Patients repeat words and sentences without evidence of comprehension and may spontaneously correct minor grammatical violations. Repetition at times cannot be inhibited (echolalia).
- **Naming** is severely impaired.
- **Lesion location.** TcSA most commonly results from lesions in the temporoparieto-occipital region, typically located posterior and deep to Wernicke's area. This posterior region is in the "watershed" zone between the posterior and middle cerebral artery territories. In a smaller number of cases, TcSA follows lesions of the parieto-occipital convexity region. Preservation of Wernicke's area and connections to anterior motor speech regions allow for repetition to be spared in TcSA. Alzheimer's disease can also result in a TcSA profile.
- **Accompanying deficits.** TcSA may be accompanied by right hemianopia and right hemisensory loss.
- **Prognosis.** TcSA owing to stroke may evolve to anomic aphasia. TcSA associated with dementing disease may

progress to Wernicke's aphasia over time and ultimately to global aphasia.

Wernicke's aphasia is a fluent aphasia with poor auditory comprehension and repetition.

• **Conversational speech** is fluent, easily articulated speech of relatively normal utterance length. Abundant semantic and phonemic paraphasias are present, as well as some neologisms. Speech may be completely meaningless to the listener, sometimes referred to as **jargonaphasia**. Utterances may be empty owing to a lack of content words (nouns, verbs), an excess of grammatical words (e.g., articles, prepositions), and overuse of imprecise words (*it*, *thing*). Word retrieval failures may result in circumlocutions. Utterances may violate the rules of syntax and grammar, resulting in paragrammatical speech (e.g., "We need the thing in the over the house"). Verbal output may be excessive and rapid, with an apparent lack of inhibition of the flow of speech, referred to as *press of speech* or **logorrhea**.

• **Auditory comprehension** is severely impaired, often even at the single-word level. Difficulty with complex syntax or multistep commands is always present. Poor self-monitoring of their own speech may make patients surprisingly unaware of their inability to produce meaningful speech and result in failure to attempt self-correction.

• **Repetition** is significantly defective; patients may not be able to repeat even single words. Repetition is similar to spontaneous speech in that it contains phonemic and semantic paraphasias.

• **Naming** attempts are often paraphasic, and severe anomia is the rule.

• **Lesion location.** Wernicke's aphasia is typically associated with large posterior perisylvian lesions encompassing the posterior superior temporal gyrus (Wernicke's area) and often extending superiorly into the inferior parietal region. A common cause is embolic occlusion of the inferior division of the left middle cerebral artery.

• **Accompanying deficits.** Right visual field defect sometimes accompanies Wernicke's aphasia. Lack of awareness of the language deficit (i.e., anosagnosia) is common in the acute stage.

• **Prognosis.** If auditory comprehension improves over time, the profile becomes more consistent with that of conduction aphasia. Other cases may evolve in the direction of TcSA. A particularly good recovery could result in residual anomic aphasia.

B. Nonfluent Aphasias

Transcortical motor aphasia (TcMA) is a nonfluent aphasia characterized by relatively good auditory comprehension and preserved repetition.

- **Conversational speech** is nonfluent, but unlike patients with Broca's aphasia, who try to communicate, patients with TcMA are generally abulic and make no attempt to produce speech spontaneously. In the acute stage, patients may be mute. When utterances are produced, usually after a long delay, they tend to be of reduced length (typically less than four words) and grammatical complexity. Articulation is generally preserved.
- **Auditory comprehension** is good for most conversational interaction, but there may be difficulty with complex syntax or multistep commands. Accurate assessment of auditory comprehension is problematic in some cases owing to prominent akinesia (i.e., the failure to initiate voluntary movement) and the tendency to perseverate.
- **Repetition** is preserved in striking contrast to the virtual absence of spontaneous conversational speech.
- **Naming** can be relatively intact. Unlike most other aphasias, in TcMA confrontation naming may be better than spontaneous speech production. Generative naming, however, is a particularly difficult task for patients with TcMA.
- **Lesion location.** Lesions producing TcMA involve the left frontal lobe. In some cases the lesions are mesial, in the distribution of the anterior cerebral artery, encompassing the supplementary motor area (SMA) and the cingulate gyrus, which play an important role in the initiation of speech. TcMA has also been described following dorsolateral frontal lesions located anterior or superior to Broca's area. These lesions are often in the "watershed" zone between the middle and anterior cerebral artery territories.
- **Associated deficits.** Mesial frontal lesions may be associated with leg weakness and urinary incontinence. Dorsolateral frontal lesions in the watershed territory may be associated with predominantly proximal weakness of the right extremities, at times sparing the face.
- **Prognosis.** TcMA may essentially resolve, or it may persist as relatively mild anomic aphasia.

Broca's aphasia is a nonfluent aphasia in which there is relatively good comprehension and poor repetition.

- **Conversational speech** is nonfluent, with slow, halting speech production. Articulatory impairment is common. Utterances are of reduced length (typically less than four words) with simplified grammar, referred to as **agrammatism**. Nouns predominate; there are some verbs and adjectives but few functors. Words often lack morphological endings, such as *-ing, -es, -ed*.
- **Auditory comprehension** is relatively good for conversational speech, but there is considerable difficulty with complex syntax or multistep commands. Especially difficult are semantically reversible or passive sentences in which word order cues alone are not sufficient for correct comprehension (e.g., "The girl was pushed by the boy").
- **Repetition** is limited to single words and short phrases, typically commensurate with the length of spontaneous utterances.
- **Naming** is always impaired to some degree, especially for low frequency words. Motor speech production deficits may interfere with intelligibility.
- **Lesion location.** Lesions restricted to Broca's area cause only transient disruption of speech production and fluency. Persistent Broca's aphasia results from much larger lesions encompassing the entire territory of the superior division of the middle cerebral artery. The lesions typically include not only Broca's area proper but also both banks of the Rolandic fissure (including the motor and sensory regions for the face), the insula, the anterior parietal lobe, and subcortical regions deep to these areas. Persistent Broca's aphasia characteristically evolves from global aphasia over several months.
- **Associated deficits.** Right hemiparesis is common, affecting the face and the arm more than the leg. Motor programming deficits, including buccofacial apraxia, apraxia of speech, and apraxia of the nonparalyzed left limb, are frequently observed.

Mixed transcortical aphasia (MTcA), also called the "isolation syndrome," is a nonfluent aphasia with poor comprehension but relatively preserved repetition.

- **Conversational speech** is similar to that found in global aphasia, in that meaningful verbal expression is severely limited or is absent altogether. Stereotyped utterances are common, as is echolalia—the inappropriate, and somewhat irrepressible, repetition of what others say.

- **Auditory comprehension** is markedly impaired, often even at the single-word level.
- **Repetition** of phrases and complete sentences is preserved, although repetition typically occurs without comprehension.
- **Naming** is significantly impaired.
- **Lesion location.** MTcA is seen in association with diffuse or multifocal lesions that result in anatomic isolation of the perisylvian language zone from surrounding cortical areas. MTcA may follow carotid artery occlusion, producing a confluent arc of infarction in the watershed region along the periphery of the middle cerebral artery vascular territory. MTcA has also been described in cortical dementia and following carbon monoxide poisoning.
- **Accompanying deficits.** Right-sided weakness or sensory loss may be present in cases of MTcA caused by stroke.
- **Prognosis.** Variable recovery occurs in MTcA; patients in whom the cause is vascular have the best chance of some recovery of language.

Global aphasia is a severe nonfluent aphasia with poor auditory comprehension and poor repetition.

- **Conversational speech** is nonfluent with slow, halting speech production. Utterances may be restricted to single words or phrases that are perseverative, such as *I can see.* Articulatory impairment is common. Some meaning may be conveyed by inflectional variations imposed on otherwise meaningless utterances (e.g., *nokeydoe, nokeydoe*).
- **Auditory comprehension** is reduced to the extent that even single-word comprehension is significantly compromised. Comprehension is markedly impaired at the phrase or sentence level.
- **Repetition** is defective, and even single words may not be repeated accurately.
- **Naming** is severely impaired.
- **Lesion location.** Lesions in global aphasia are extensive and typically involve the entire perisylvian language zone. A common cause is embolic occlusion of the main stem of the middle cerebral artery.
- **Accompanying deficits** include right hemiparesis, right hemisensory loss, and right homonymous hemianopia.
- **Prognosis.** Global aphasia may evolve to Broca's aphasia, or it may persist as global aphasia.

VI. OTHER APHASIA SYNDROMES

A. Subcortical Aphasias

Many cortical lesions extend to subcortical regions, but aphasia can also result from deep lesions that spare the cerebral cortex. There is no single subcortical aphasia profile, and there appears to be considerable variability among individuals with subcortical lesions. In general, subcortical aphasias resemble transcortical aphasias in that repetition is frequently preserved. Subcortical aphasias include thalamic aphasia and the various aphasia syndromes associated with damage to the basal ganglia and surrounding white matter pathways.

B. Aphasia Associated with Cortical Degenerative Disease

Language impairment is frequently associated with Alzheimer's disease. Language deterioration typically follows a progressive course that begins with anomic aphasia, proceeds to transcortical sensory aphasia and then Wernicke's aphasia, and ultimately becomes global aphasia. In some patients progressive language deterioration occurs without significant dementia (i.e., primary progressive aphasia).

VII. DISTINGUISHING APHASIA FROM OTHER DISORDERS

Aphasia needs to be distinguished from other disorders that impair communication. The following disorders are distinct from aphasia:

A. Input Problems

1. **Pure word deafness** refers to a selective impairment of speech input processing. Patients with pure word deafness cannot comprehend or repeat spoken language, but their spontaneous speech production and naming are intact, and they can read and write without difficulty. In some cases, recognition of environmental sounds is also preserved. Pure word deafness is a rare syndrome that usually results from bilateral damage to the auditory cortex of the temporal lobes. A unilateral deep left temporal lobe lesion may also result in pure word deafness by disconnecting Wernicke's area from auditory input.

2. **Pure alexia**, or alexia without agraphia, refers to an acquired reading impairment that occurs in the absence of significant aphasia. Language production and auditory comprehension are preserved. Patients can also write, although they are frequently unable to read what they have written. The syndrome is typically seen with left occipital infarctions within the territory of the posterior cerebral artery. The left occipital lesion often results in dense right hemianopia, denying direct visual access to the left hemisphere. Additional damage to transcallosal white matter pathways prevents written stimuli projected to right occipital cortex from reaching left hemisphere language areas as is necessary for reading.

3. **Agnosia** refers to recognition failure affecting a single sensory modality (i.e., visual, tactile, auditory). Patients with agnosia may be unable to name objects presented in a particular sensory modality, but naming is possible when the same object is presented in a different modality. For instance, a patient with visual agnosia may not be able to recognize and name an object on visual presentation, but the name of the object is easily retrieved when the individual is provided with nonvisual input (e.g., given the object to feel, or asked to name it in response to a spoken definition). By contrast, the naming impairment associated with aphasia persists regardless of the modality of presentation.

B. Production Problems

1. **Apraxia of speech** is a disturbance of motor programming for the positioning and movement of the articulators for speech production. It can exist in the absence of muscle weakness and buccofacial apraxia, that is, without a disturbance of motor control for nonspeech movements of the articulators.

2. **Dysarthria** refers to a group of motor speech disorders that result from weakness, slowness, or incoordination of speech musculature and result in imprecise articulation. Dysarthria can co-occur with aphasia, but it should be regarded as an impairment of speech rather than language.

3. **Mutism** refers to a complete inability to produce speech, caused by a wide range of neurological and nonneurological disorders. Mute patients do not talk, but they should not be considered aphasic when it can be demonstrated that auditory and reading comprehension are preserved and patients can communicate successfully in writing.

4. **Aphemia** refers to a selective impairment of the ability to articulate speech with preservation of spoken and written

language comprehension and the ability to write. Aphemia results from relatively small cortical or subcortical lesions of Broca's area, the left sensorimotor region for the face, or both. In the acute stage, the patient may be mute; over time, speech typically returns with residual disturbance of prosody and articulatory precision.

VIII. KEY NEUROPSYCHOLOGICAL TESTS

Numerous standardized tests are available for the assessment of aphasia. Most of these measures are not designed for bedside administration and are best reserved for clinical administration during the nonacute stage. Following is a sampling of tests commonly used by speech–language pathologists and clinical neuropsychologists, along with some relatively new assessment tools.

A. Examining for Aphasia

1. **Selected standardized aphasia tests:**
a. Boston Diagnostic Aphasia Examination (Goodglass & Kaplan, 1983)
b. Western Aphasia Battery (Kertesz, 1982)
c. Aphasia Diagnostic Profiles (Helm-Estabrooks, 1992)
2. **Naming:** Boston Naming Test (Kaplan, Goodglass, & Weintraub, 1983)
3. **Auditory comprehension:** Token Test of the Multilingual Aphasia Examination (Benton, deHamsher, & Siven, 1994)
4. **Reading and writing:** Psycholinguistic Assessment of Language Processing in Aphasia (PALPA; Kay, Lesser, & Coultheart, 1992)

B. Assessing the Impact of Aphasia

Tests in the preceding list primarily assess language impairment. Other assessment tools were designed to examine the disability that results from the aphasia, that is, the consequences of the impairment at a more functional level. Examples of such measures include the following:

1. American Speech-Language-Hearing Association (ASHA) Functional Assessment of Communication Skills for Adults (Frattalli, Thompson, Holland, Wohl, & Ferketic, 1995)
2. Communicative Abilities in Daily Living (Holland, 1980; Holland, Fromm, & Frattali, in press)

IX. CONCLUSION

The purpose of this chapter has been to provide an introduction to important differential diagnoses across the broad spectrum of speech and language disorders, with a focus on the inpatient bedside examination. The formal study of aphasiology is a rapidly expanding field of specialty, and the impact of new neurodiagnostic technologies will no doubt continue to expand the understanding of brain organization for speech and language.

The social consequences of aphasia can be tremendous, affecting employment, economic status, social roles, and overall sense of well-being. It is difficult to quantify such variables (and their change over time), particularly when the language impairment itself limits information exchange regarding the impact of the deficit. Appropriate measures for these social consequences, or handicaps, are limited; however, clinicians should not overlook such critical issues.

BIBLIOGRAPHY

References for Standardized Tests

Benton, A. L., deHamsher, K. S., & Siven, A. B. (1994). *Multilingual Aphasia Examination*. Iowa City, IA: AJA Associates.

Frattalli, C. M., Thompson, C. K., Holland, A. L., Wohl, C. B., & Ferketic, M. M. (1995). *ASHA Functional Assessment of Communication Skills for Adults*. Bethesda, MD: American Speech-Language-Hearing Association.

Goodglass, H., & Kaplan, E. (1983). *Boston Diagnostic Aphasia Examination*. Philadelphia: Lea & Febiger.

Helm-Estabrooks, N. (1992). *Aphasia Diagnostic Profiles*. Chicago: Riverside.

Holland, A. (1980). *Communicative Abilities in Daily Living*. Austin, TX: Pro-ed.

Holland, A. L., Fromm, D., & Frattalli, C. (in press). *Communicative Abilities in Daily Living* (2nd ed.). Austin, TX: Pro-Ed.

Kaplan, E., Goodglass, H., & Weintraub, S. (1983). *The Boston Naming Test*. Philadelphia: Lea & Febiger.

Kay, J., Lesser, R., & Coultheart, M. (1992). *Psycholinguistic Assessment of Language Processing in Aphasia*. East Sussex, England: Erlbaum.

Kertesz, A. (1982). *Western Aphasia Battery*. San Antonio, TX: Psychological Corporation.

Sources of Additional Information

Albert, M. L., Goodglass, H., Helm, N. A., Rubens, A. B., & Alexander, M. P. (1981). *Clinical aspects of dysphasia.* New York: Springer-Verlag.

Benson, D. F., & Ardila, A. (1996). *Aphasia: A clinical perspective.* New York: Oxford University Press.

Duffy, J. R. (1995). *Motor speech disorders: Substrates, differential diagnosis, and management.* St. Louis, MO: Mosby.

Goodglass, H. (1993). *Understanding aphasia.* Boston: Academic Press.

Heilman, K. M., & Valenstein, E. (Eds.). (1993). *Clinical neuropsychology.* New York: Oxford University Press.

Helm-Estabrooks, N., & Albert, M. L. (1991). *Manual of aphasia therapy.* Austin, TX: Pro-Ed.

Kertesz, A. (Ed). (1994). *Localization and neuroimaging in neuropsychology.* Boston: Academic Press.

CHAPTER 21

Margaret G. O'Connor and Mark D. Morin

Amnesic Syndromes

Memory, and difficulties associated with memory, is a complex and multifaceted subject. This chapter addresses neuroanatomical and neuropsychological dimensions of memory disorders. We begin by examining memory deficits in terms of localization of function. This information is summarized in Table 1. As summarized in Table 2, we then consider memory deficits in terms of etiology and effects on the brain. Figure 1 and Table 3 outline the proceeding discussion of neuropsychological assessment of memory deficits.

I. CLINICAL MANIFESTATIONS OF AMNESIA

A. Definitions

The purest form of amnesia is a circumscribed and dense memory deficit in which there is preserved intelligence and reasoning. Amnesic patients are unable to encode and consolidate verbal and nonverbal stimuli regardless of the modality of pre-

Preparation of this chapter was supported by a grant (NS26985) from the National Institute of Neurological Disorders and Stroke.

Table 1. Neuroanatomic Distinctions in Memory Impairment

	Location		
	Medial temporal	Diencephalic	Frontal
Cause	Anoxia, limbic encephalitis, cerebrovascular accident, Alzheimer's disease	Infarction of thalamic arteries, trauma, diencephalic tumor, Wernicke-Korsakoff syndrome	Cerebrovascular accident, tumor, surgery, anterior communicating artery aneurysm
Insight	Present	Absent	Often absent
Confabulation	Absent	Present	Often present
Deficits	Retrograde[a] declarative memory[b]	Retrograde[c]	Retrograde[d] contextual memory[e]

[a]Extent depends on the extent of the damage to the lateral temporal neocortex.

[b]Deficits in the conscious recall of facts.

[c]Often caused by deficits in the initial processing stages of memory and sensitivity to proactive interference.

[d]The degree of retrograde amnesia is variable and is often attributable to attentional deficits that adversely affect encoding and retrieval. Recognition of previously learned material is often normal, suggesting that consolidation is relatively intact.

[e]Memory for temporal and spatial aspects of events.

Table 2. Neurological Illnesses Associated With Amnesia

Illness	Lesion	Disturbance	Reference
Anterior communicating artery aneurysms	Basal forebrain (restricted damage)	Mild memory problems	Irle et al. (1992)
	Basal forebrain, striatum (extensive damage)	Severe amnesia	
Herpes simplex encephalitis	Lateral and medial temporal cortices (left or right)	Verbal learning, nonverbal learning, severe retrograde	Eslinger et al. (1993)
	Lateral temporal cortex		O'Connor et al. (1992)
Paraneoplastic limbic encephalitis	Medial temporal lobe	Retrograde, anterograde; variable effects on remote memory	O'Connor et al. (1996) Parkin & Leng (1993)
Anoxic encephalopathy	Medial temporal lobe	Anterograde; variable effects on remote memory	Zola-Morgan et al. (1989)
Posterior cerebral artery infarction	Medial temporal lobes	Material-specific memory loss in association with laterality of lesion	Benson et al. (1974); Ott & Saver (1993)
Wernicke-Korsakoff syndrome	Anteromedial, dorsomedial, and intralaminar thalamic nuclei; mammillary bodies and frontal network systems	Anterograde and temporally graded retrograde amnesia	Cramon et al. (1985); Mair (1979); Victor et al. (1989)

Figure 1. Evaluation of Amnesia

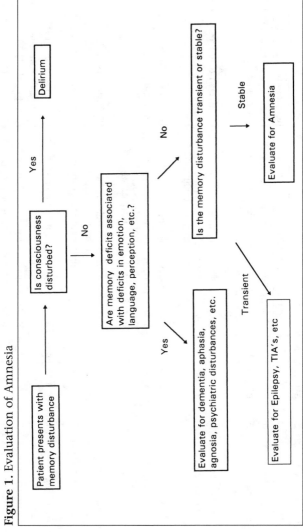

Table 3. Clinical Evaluation of Memory

Test	Focus of assessment	Reference
Brown Peterson Test	Working memory, rate of forgetting	Peterson & Peterson (1959)
Rey Auditory Verbal Learning Test	Learning curve, recency and primacy effects, proactive and retroactive interference	Rey (1964)
Rey-Osterreith Complex Figure	Nonverbal (visual) memory	Osterreith & Rey (1944)
California Verbal Learning Test	Learning curve, proactive and retroactive interference, semantic memory	Delis et al. (1987)
Continuous Visual Memory Test	Nonverbal (visual) memory	Trahan & Larrabee (1986)
Wechsler Memory Scale–Revised	Visual recognition, attention span, paragraph recall, paired-associate learning (verbal and nonverbal), figural recall	Wechsler (1987)
Wechsler Memory Scale–III	Working memory, single-trial learning, learning slope, retention, retrieval	Wechsler (1997)
Warrington Recognition Memory Test	Verbal and nonverbal recognition memory	Warrington (1984)
Autobiographical Memory Interview	Remote autobiographical memory	Kopelman et al. (1989)
Crovitz procedure	Remote memory	Crovitz & Schiffman (1974)
Famous Faces	Remote memory for public figures	Albert et al. (1979)
Transient Events Test	Remote memory for public events, recognition and recall	O'Connor (1997)

sentation (i.e., auditory or visual) or the nature of the material (i.e., verbal or nonverbal). In contrast, attention span, language functions, and logical deductive abilities are relatively preserved. Amnesic patients show the greatest deficits on tasks of **declarative memory** in that they are unable to demonstrate awareness of prior learning experiences, whereas **procedural memory** (e.g., skills, habits, and classically conditioned responses) remains intact. A wide variety of studies have shown that **semantic memory** (i.e., knowledge of facts and other general information) is intact in amnesia, whereas **episodic memory** (i.e., experiential knowledge of events) is not (Tulving, 1983). Amnesic patients are capable of normal (or near-normal) performance on tasks of **implicit memory**, in that perceptual and conceptual attributes of events modify their responses to previously presented stimuli, but they are not capable of normal performance on tasks of **explicit memory** (i.e., conscious recollection of the learning episode).

The examination of an amnesic patient should focus on both **anterograde** and **retrograde** aspects of the memory disturbance (see Figure 1 for a flow chart describing the evaluation of an amnesic patient). Anterograde amnesia (AA) refers to an inability to learn new information after the onset of amnesia. AA is present in most cases of amnesia and is typically associated with bilateral brain lesions. **Retrograde amnesia** (RA) refers to deficient recall of events preceding the onset of amnesia. Patients demonstrate various profiles of RA: In some instances, RA is limited to days, weeks, or months before the onset of memory loss; in others, it encompasses events and memories from the distant past. The RA exhibited by patients with Wernicke-Korsakoff syndrome (WKS) has been described as "temporally graded," because remote memories are better preserved than memories closer in time to the onset of amnesia. Cases of RA consisting of a loss of a lot of information over an extended period of time are usually associated with extensive neural damage in neocortical brain regions (Squire, 1994). Cases of RA in the absence of significant AA are rare but have been described (Kapur, 1993a).

B. Stability of the Clinical Presentation

In most instances, the term *amnesic* is reserved for the patient with an isolated and stable memory disorder that presents acutely and is permanent. However, some patients suffer from memory disorders that change over time. For instance, patients with amnesia secondary to anterior communicating artery

(ACoA) aneurysms may show improvement in memory and other cognitive functions in the months following surgery. Other patients present with isolated memory problems that become worse over time and that culminate in dementia with deficits in multiple cognitive domains.

Transient forms of amnesia have been described in conjunction with epilepsy and vascular dysfunction. A subgroup of patients with temporal lobe epilepsy demonstrate transient but dramatic episodes of amnesia. These episodes may occur frequently and are usually associated with subtle behavioral disturbances such as automatisms (Gallassi, Morreale, Sarro, & Lugaresi, 1992). It is interesting that performance on formal neuropsychological tests is often normal despite patients' subjective memory complaints. Some patients with epilepsy have demonstrated significant RA in comparison to mild or moderate disturbances on tasks of anterograde memory (Kapur, 1993b).

Transient global amnesia (TGA) has been described in association with decreased perfusion to medial temporal or diencephalic brain regions. Patients with TGA demonstrate profound anterograde memory problems and variable profiles of RA, perhaps owing to retrieval problems. Most researchers describe resolution of the memory problems when testing is conducted weeks or months after the episode; however, some patients with TGA demonstrate residual deficits on challenging tests of verbal long-term memory (Mazzucchi, Moretti, Caffarra, & Parma, 1980) and time estimation (Gallassi, Lorusso, & Stracciari, 1986). Semantic memory, procedural learning, and implicit memory have been described as intact during the TGA episode (Hodges, 1994).

C. Subtypes of Amnesia

Amnesic patients present with a variety of medical and psychosocial conditions that influence their patterns of memory loss and residual learning abilities. One way of reducing this variability has been to group amnesic patients according to neuroanatomic distinctions. The following information is also summarized in Table 1.

Medial temporal lobe (MTL) amnesia occurs as a consequence of anoxia, limbic encephalitis, cerebrovascular accidents, and probable Alzheimer's disease (PRAD). Historically, patients with MTL have been described as having (a) preserved insight, (b) increased rate of forgetting, (c) limited RA, and (d) lack of confabulation. Whereas some aspects of this profile are present in most patients with MTL amnesia, initial speculation that patients with MTL amnesia demonstrated accelerated forgetting relative to those with diencephalic amnesia has not been upheld in more recent studies (Freed, Corkin, & Cohen, 1987; McKee & Squire, 1992). In addition, the idea that the RA of MTL amnesia is restricted has been reexamined; recent work has underscored an association between severity of RA in the MTL patient group and extent of pathology in the hippocampus and adjacent cortices.

Diencephalic forms of amnesia result from infarction of thalamic arteries, trauma, diencephalic tumors, and Wernicke-Korsakoff syndrome (Butters & Stuss, 1989). Patients with thalamic amnesias demonstrate deficits in the initial processing stages of memory, confabulation, sensitivity to **proactive interference** (i.e., prior learning interferes with acquisition of new material), and lack of insight into the memory disturbance. Rate of forgetting may be normal in some patients with diencephalic pathology. Remote memory is minimally affected in some patients, whereas others demonstrate severe problems in the retrieval of events immediately predating the onset of amnesia. Some of the features associated with the neuropsychological profile of diencephalic patients (e.g., confabulation and lack of insight) may occur as a result of disruption of frontal networks. The memory deficits in this patient group have been attributed to damage in medial thalamic structures, the mammillary bodies, or both of these regions (Markowitsch, 1982). It is interesting that material-specific memory deficits may occur as a result of unilateral thalamic damage.

A third group includes patients with memory impairment **secondary to damage in frontal brain regions** in association with cerebrovascular lesions, tumors, surgical intervention for refractory frontal lobe seizures, and rupture and surgical repair of ACoA. These patients exhibit attentional deficits that adversely affect encoding and retrieval. Under some circumstances, recognition is normal, suggesting that consolidation is relatively intact. Patients with frontal amnesia often lack insight into their memory problems and tend to confabulate. Deficits are also seen on tasks of proactive interference, **contextual memory** (i.e., memory for the temporal and spatial aspects of events), and semantic categorization. Some frontal amnesia patients present with RA owing to impaired retrieval of previously stored information.

A number of investigators have argued that etiologically based classification systems are reductionistic and fail to capture the complex interplay between processing deficits and other factors that contribute to apparent distinctions among amnesic subgroups (Weiskrantz, 1985). In addition, questions have been raised as to whether these groups are neuroanatomically discrete: It may be that patients with medial temporal and diencephalic amnesia share common sites of neuropathology. Furthermore, it is important to note that comparisons across subtypes of amnesia are influenced by extraneous factors such as baseline intelligence, capacity for attention, and prior education. Many studies of diencephalic amnesia have been confined to patients with WKS (who have less formal education and extensive histories of alcohol abuse), whereas those with MTL amnesia are often of higher premorbid intelligence and socioeconomic status. Clearly, in addition to differences, the type of amnesia can affect performance on tasks of anterograde and retrograde memory, thereby confounding subtype comparisons.

II. NEURAL SUBSTRATES OF AMNESIA

A. The Neuroanatomy of Memory

Current information regarding brain systems involved in memory is based on lesion studies with humans and animals. Declarative memory deficits have been associated with damage in bilateral medial temporal brain regions (Scoville & Milner, 1957). Initial investigations with nonhuman primates supported the idea that new learning was dependent on two neural systems: the **hippocampal pathway** (i.e., the hippocampus, fornix, mammillary bodies, mammillothalamic tract, and cingulate cortex) and the **amygdaloid pathway** (i.e., the amygdala, dorsal medial thalamus, and orbital frontal cortex). Damage to either system was thought to result in moderate-level memory loss, whereas damage to both the hippocampal and amygdaloid systems was associated with severe amnesia (Mishkin, 1982).

More recent work concerning the neural underpinnings of declarative memory has challenged the importance of the amygdala, mammillary bodies, and fornix in the etiology of severe amnesia. In a series of articles, Zola-Morgan and colleagues underscored the hippocampus proper, parahippocampal gyrus, and entorhinal and perirhinal cortices as critical substrates for new learning (Zola-Morgan, Squire, Amaral, & Suzuki, 1989). Converging data from studies with patients and with nonhuman primates have suggested that damage restricted to the hippocampus proper is associated with mild-to-moderate memory deficits, whereas damage to the hippocampus and adjacent (entorhinal and parahippocampal) cortices results in severe amnesia.

In all likelihood, medial temporal lobe and medial thalamic structures work in concert with one another in establishing new memories. Studies of patients with WKS and other memory disorders secondary to damage in the region of the third ventricle have highlighted the contribution of diencephalic structures in memory. Postmortem analyses have shown that damage to midline thalamic (i.e., the internal medullary lamina and anteromedial or dorsomedial nuclei) and mammillary nuclei is associated with severe amnesia (Cramon, Hebel, & Schuri, 1985; Markowitsch, 1988).

The basal forebrain, including the medial septal nucleus, the diagonal band of Broca, and the nucleus basalis of Meynert, has also been studied extensively in human and animal models of amnesia. The amnesias associated with PRAD and with rupture and surgical repair of ACoA aneurysms have been viewed as by-products of basal forebrain damage. Some investigators have emphasized that damage restricted to the basal forebrain produces mild memory problems, whereas damage to basal forebrain and striatal brain regions produces severe amnesia (Irle, Wowra, Kunert, Hampl, & Kunze, 1992). Other investigators have emphasized that septal damage is the cause of true amnesia in basal forebrain lesions owing to the disruption of anatomic connections to the hippocampus (Zola-Morgan & Squire, 1993).

There is a great deal of support for the idea that medial temporal lobe and medial diencephalic structures play critical but temporary roles in new learning. Observations of intact remote memory within the context of severe amnesia have suggested that information eventually becomes independent of hippocampal and diencephalic circuitry (Squire, 1994). In their analysis of the literature, Squire and colleagues concluded that the extent of neocortical damage influences severity of remote memory loss: Limited damage to core hippocampal regions is associated with an attenuated retrograde amnesia, whereas more severe damage in neocortical brain regions may result in extreme retrograde amnesia.

B. Diseases That Give Rise to Amnesia

Amnesia occurs in conjunction with a variety of psychiatric and neurological disorders. Owing to space limitations, psychiatric causes of amnesia are not discussed in this chapter (see Kopelman, 1995, for a good review of this topic). Closed head injury and PRAD are not elaborated on because these disorders are reviewed elsewhere in this volume. What follows is a summary of neurological conditions that give rise to amnesia (see Table 1).

1. SURGICAL ABLATION

Over the last 40 years, investigations of H.M., a patient who underwent bilateral temporal lobe resection for treatment of refractory seizures, paralleled major developments and theories regarding the neuroanatomy and cognitive parameters of memory. H.M.'s clinical profile has become synonymous with definitions of the amnesic syndrome. His profound amnesia underscored the critical role of hippocampal and surrounding cortical regions in new learning. Initial neuropsychological studies with H.M. validated the distinction between short- and long-term memory. More recent work with H.M. supported theories suggesting that distinct brain systems mediate implicit versus explicit memory processes.

Fortunately, amnesia following surgical intervention for treatment of intractable epilepsy is rare. This procedure is now limited to unilateral temporal lobe removal and is typically performed after careful neuropsychological and intracarotid sodium amobarbital studies to minimize the risk of postoperative amnesia.

2. AMNESIA ASSOCIATED WITH HERPES SIMPLEX ENCEPHALITIS

Herpes simplex encephalitis (HSE) is the most common form of viral encephalitis in the United States. Diagnosis of HSE depends on laboratory values (from brain biopsy or cerebral spinal fluid studies), brain imaging studies, and clinical presentation. Patients initially present with confusion, aphasia, and agnosia that may gradually resolve to a circumscribed amnesic syndrome. In general, the memory sequelae of HSE have been attributed to damage in lateral and medial temporal cortices; however, these lesions may be distributed asymmetrically. Specific patterns of memory loss vary in conjunction with the location of the lesion; disproportionate verbal learning difficulties are associated with greater left hemisphere involvement, whereas nonverbal deficits are associated with more extensive lesions in the right hemisphere (Eslinger, Damasio, Damasio, & Butters, 1993). Patients with HSE may demonstrate extensive RA in association with lateral temporal brain damage (O'Connor, Butters, Miliotis, Eslinger, & Cermak, 1992). Semantic memory problems have also been described in this patient group (DeRenzi, Liotti, & Nichelli, 1987).

3. AMNESIA ASSOCIATED WITH PARANEOPLASTIC LIMBIC ENCEPHALITIS

Paraneoplastic limbic encephalitis (PLE) is an autoimmune response to cancer elsewhere in the body. In most instances PLE is associated with oat cell cancer of the lung, but there have been cases in association with other forms of cancer. Lesions in limbic brain areas have been identified in a number of radiological and autopsy studies (Newman, Bell, & McKee, 1990). There are only a few case studies of patients with amnesia secondary to PLE. Parkin and Leng (1993) described a case of PLE amnesia characterized by global anterograde memory deficits, confabulation, and a dense RA. We studied one patient who demonstrated profound, but atypical, AA in association with PLE; this patient was able to learn and retain information for hours at a time, but consolidation was disrupted over the course of day-long interludes of time. It was our suspicion that his amnesia was due to a combination of the disruptive effects of seizures on new learning as well as to PLE (O'Connor et al., 1997). We recently studied another patient who demonstrated a material-specific pattern of memory loss in association with PLE.

4. AMNESIA SECONDARY TO ANOXIC ENCEPHALOPATHY

Anoxic encephalopathy occurs as a result of cardiac arrest, respiratory distress, strangulation, and carbon monoxide poisoning. When oxygen saturation is depleted for 5 minutes or more, permanent brain damage occurs as a result of an accumulation of pathological excitatory neurotransmitters or lactic acid. Anoxia can result in extensive cerebral and cerebellar brain damage and in a variety of cognitive, perceptual, and motor abnormalities. However, because the medial temporal lobes are particularly sensitive to oxygen deprivation, anoxia may result in circumscribed amnesia. Area CA1 of the hippocampus has been identified as particularly sensitive to the effects of ischemia. An isolated lesion in this area can result in a moderately severe anterograde amnesia with minimal effects on remote memory (Zola-Morgan, Squire, & Amaral, 1989).

5. CEREBROVASCULAR ACCIDENTS

Amnesia secondary to bilateral **posterior cerebral artery** (PCA) **infarction** has been well described in the literature. In addition, some investigators have described patients with memory deficits in the wake of unilateral (primarily left) PCA infarction (Benson, Marsden, & Meadows, 1974; Ott & Saver, 1993). Unfortunately, many investigators have failed to include measures of nonverbal memory and rate of forgetting in their description of PCA-related amnesia. Consequently, it is difficult to determine whether the memory deficits of patients with unilateral PCA infarction are qualitatively or quantitatively different from those of other amnesics. It is important to note that deficits beyond memory loss, including visual field deficits, hemianopic alexia, pure alexia, color agnosia, and object agnosia, often occur in association with PCA strokes. The latter difficulties are more likely when the lesion extends posteriorly to include occipitotemporal cortices. Lesions in the posterior parahippocampus or collateral isthmus (a pathway connecting the posterior parahippocampus to the association cortex) are viewed as critical in the memory disturbance in this patient group (Cramon et al., 1985).

Another vascular event associated with memory loss is infarction of thalamic arteries, particularly the tuberothalamic and paramedian vessels. There is some variability in neuropsychological profiles related to location of lesion. Again, a number of cases have been described with memory loss secondary to unilateral damage.

6. WERNICKE-KORSAKOFF SYNDROME

Patients with Wernicke-Korsakoff syndrome develop amnesia as a result of chronic alcohol abuse and thiamine deficiency (Victor, Adams, & Collins, 1989). In the Wernicke phase, patients demonstrate oculomotor palsies, ataxia, and confusion. The Korsakoffian phase of WKS is accompanied by severe memory deficits and personality change. Patients with WKS are prone to irritability and apathy, problems that often undermine performance on tasks of new learning (Butters & Cermak, 1980). The neuropathology of WKS involves damage in anteromedial, dorsomedial, and intralaminar thalamic nuclei; mammillary bodies; and frontal network systems (Victor et al., 1989). The extent to which these areas separately or convergently result in amnesia is controversial. Frontal (i.e., executive) deficits also undermine WKS patients' ability to learn new information. It is important to understand that the severe alcohol abuse associated with WKS is often accompanied by long-standing social isolation and a general lack of interest in world events. These premorbid psychosocial patterns adversely affect

WKS patients' performance on tests measuring knowledge of public events.

7. RUPTURE AND SURGICAL REPAIR OF ACOA

Approximately 40% of patients who suffer rupture and undergo surgical repair of anterior communicating artery aneurysms present with memory and other behavior problems (Stenhouse, Knight, Longmore, & Bishara, 1991). Descriptions of patients with ACoA emphasize amnesia, apathy, disorientation, and confabulation; these symptoms may be related to a number of factors including subarachnoid hemorrhage, vasospasm, hematoma formation, herniation of the medial temporal lobes, hydrocephalus, and surgical intervention. Heterogeneity in the neuropsychological presentations of these patients is in all likelihood due to the fact that there is variability in the site of neural damage. Brain lesions are seen in the basal forebrain and striatal and frontal areas. It is widely assumed that basal forebrain damage is the critical underpinning of the memory deficits in this patient group, although recent work has suggested that combined basal forebrain and striatal lesions may be necessary for severe memory problems to result (Irle et al., 1992).

Patients with ACoA are often described as suffering from attentionally based memory problems. They tend to benefit from recognition cues, perhaps owing to problems in the strategic search of memory. A subgroup of these patients, particularly those with frontal damage, are prone to confabulation and diminished insight. Performance on tasks of RA varies. In a recent study, we found that patients with ACoA demonstrated a temporally graded RA on some tests, whereas their performance on the other tests of remote memory was similar to that of normal controls (O'Connor, Walbridge, D'Esposito, McGlinchey-Berroth, & Alexander, 1995).

III. NEUROPSYCHOLOGICAL EVALUATION

Evaluation of amnesia takes place within the context of a comprehensive assessment of intelligence, attention, language, perception, reasoning, and emotional status. Information regarding performance across a broad array of neuropsychological tasks is important for diagnostic and therapeutic purposes. Diagnosis of *focal* amnesia cannot be made unless it is firmly established that the individual is relatively intact in other cognitive spheres. Information regarding baseline IQ and other cognitive functions facilitates the determination of the extent and severity of the memory impairment. In addition, a comprehensive neuropsychological evaluation elucidates factors that adversely affect memory (e.g., coexisting depression) as well as strengths that should be highlighted in remediation programs.

The clinical assessment of memory has been greatly influenced by cognitive research with amnesic patients. For a period of time researchers emphasized that amnesia was the result of disruptions in various stages of learning. On the basis of their work with WKS patients, Butters and Cermak (1980) emphasized **encoding** deficits as the critical problem in amnesia. Investigations of H.M. led Milner and colleagues to speculate that amnesia was due to an inability to transfer information from short- to long-term memory, thereby highlighting **consolidation** deficits in amnesia (Milner, 1966). Warrington and Weiskrantz (1968, 1970) proposed that amnesia was due to faulty **retrieval.** More recent theories regarding information processing in amnesia emphasize the interdependence among these stages (see Cermak, 1995, for a review of this subject). Despite the fact that researchers no longer view amnesia as a unitary deficit in a specific stage of learning, the clinical assessment of amnesia still involves the discrimination between encoding, consolidation, and retrieval.

Persistent use of the stage model approach in the clinical assessment of amnesia is based on the fact that this framework is both parsimonious and clinically meaningful. Information regarding disruptions in various stages of memory can be obtained from standard tests of memory. Encoding and retrieval abilities are inferred from performance on tasks of immediate recall: If the individual fails to recall a normal amount of information, even after repetition, the examiner may assume the presence of either encoding or retrieval problems. More information regarding the relative contributions of encoding versus retrieval is gained from multiple comparisons across tasks. Retrieval abilities are judged from a comparison of performance on tasks of recognition versus free recall: A large disparity favoring recognition over free recall suggests that retrieval is relatively deficient. At the same time, normal recognition implies that encoding is intact. Information regarding consolidation (or retention) is based on a comparison of performance on tasks of immediate versus delayed recall: Relative preservation of immediate memory versus poor performance on delayed memory tasks implicates a consolidation deficit.

A. Assessment of Anterograde Memory

There are many good tests of memory, most of which are reviewed by Lezak (1995). At the Memory Disorders Research Center, Boston University School of Medicine, assessment of amnesia includes the following tests (this information is also summarized in Table 3).

1. THE REY AUDITORY VERBAL LEARNING TEST

The Rey Auditory Verbal Learning Test (RAVLT; Rey, 1964) involves presentation of a list of 15 words across five trials followed by a second (interference) list, with testing under delayed recall and delayed recognition conditions. A comparison of performance on immediate versus delayed recall provides information regarding retention, whereas comparison of free recall versus recognition highlights the status of retrieval. Use of a supraspan list (i.e., one that exceeds attention span limitations) allows for the examination of the effects of repetition on learning and for calculation of a learning curve. Serial learning (e.g., recency and primacy effects) is examined by determining whether there is a preference for initial list items over later ones. This test provides information regarding proactive inhibition (i.e., the extent to which old learning [list A] is interfering with new learning [list B]) and retroactive interference (intrusion of the first list on recall of the second list).

2. THE CALIFORNIA VERBAL LEARNING TEST

The California Verbal Learning Test (CVLT; Delis, Kramer, Kaplan, & Ober, 1987) has similar properties to the RAVLT. In addition to the information provided by the RAVLT, the CVLT yields information regarding the extent to which semantic categories facilitate memory. Sixteen words from four semantic categories are presented for five learning trials, followed by a second list. A free recall trial followed by a cued recall, using the semantic categories for cues, is conducted after a 30-minute delay interval. Patients with deficient semantic memory do not benefit from the categories of the CVLT, whereas patients with memory problems secondary to impaired organization usually benefit from the structure afforded by this test.

3. THE BROWN PETERSON TEST

The Brown Peterson Test (Peterson & Peterson, 1959) requires that the individual retain consonant or word triads while performing an interference task over short (3-, 9-, or 18-second) time intervals. This test provides an index of working memory and rate of forgetting over very short intervals of time. Some patients with severe amnesia perform normally on this task. However, patients with attentionally based memory problems perform poorly.

4. THE REY-OSTERREITH COMPLEX FIGURE

The Rey-Osterreith Complex Figure (Rey-O; Osterreith & Rey, 1944) is a test of complex visual organization abilities. Memory for the Rey-O figure yields information regarding the extent to which the individual can encode visual information that exceeds normal span limitations. The individual copies the complex figure without knowledge that memory will be examined; hence, initial recall is a measure of incidental learning. Delayed recall performance is examined relevant to rate of forgetting. A recognition component can be added to the test whereby the individual components of the figure are presented along with elements that are not part of the original figure. If the individual is able to discriminate the elements of the figure from the distracting elements, it is thought that consolidation has been preserved.

5. THE CONTINUOUS VISUAL MEMORY TEST

The assessment of nonverbal memory is often overlooked during neuropsychological testing, in part owing to the fact that there are not many good tests of nonverbal memory abilities. The Continuous Visual Memory Test (CVMT; Trahan & Larrabee, 1986) is a well-designed task measuring recognition of previously presented line drawings. An immediate recognition score is calculated, and the effects of response bias are controlled. Delayed recognition and visual discrimination scores are also obtained for this test.

6. THE WARRINGTON RECOGNITION MEMORY TEST

The Warrington Recognition Memory Test (Warrington, 1984) is used to evaluate immediate recognition of faces and words. This test is particularly important because it allows a comparison of verbal and nonverbal memory when modality of presentation and task-specific processing demands are equated. The individual is presented with a series of words, one at a time, and is then presented with pairs of words and asked to identify which of the two words he or she saw before. The same procedure is done with photographs of faces. Relative deficits in one task correlate with site of pathology in right versus left temporal areas. Scores significantly lower than that expected from random responding (i.e., less than 50% correct responses) should alert the clinician to the possibility of psychological contributions to test performance (e.g., factitious disorder).

7. THE WECHSLER MEMORY SCALE–REVISED AND WMS-III

The Wechsler Memory Scale–Revised (WMS-R; Wechsler, 1987) is a widely used and well-normed test of memory. The test consists of a variety of different subtests including measures of visual recognition, attention span, paragraph recall, paired-associate learning (verbal and nonverbal), and figural recall. Five indices of attention and memory are derived. Comparison of the General Memory, Delayed Memory, and Attention indices provides information regarding density of amnesia. The WMS-R also provides measures of verbal and nonverbal memory abilities; the nature of the material (verbal vs. nonverbal), however, is confounded with modality of presentation (auditory vs. visual), limiting the validity of this comparison. Further complicating the problem of the inconsistency of the sensory mode is the fact that many of the nonverbal memory items from the WMS-R are open to verbal mediation (visual stimuli that can be described in words).

The third edition of the Wechsler Memory Scale (WMS-III; Wechsler, 1997) represents a substantial improvement over the WMS-R. The WMS-III contains 11 subtests, 7 retained from the WMS-R and 4 new subtests. The confounding effects of modality of presentation versus nature of material are less problematic in the WMS-III. In addition, the 4 new subtests provide information regarding working memory, picture recognition, and serial list learning. A comparison of recognition versus free recall performance on WMS-III subtests allows for examination of retrieval deficits. The WMS-III yields four composite scores: Single Trial Learning and Learning Slope Composite scores are obtained by examining scores on the first learning trials and comparing them with those scores on the last trials. The Retention Composite score represents the difference between tasks of immediate versus delayed recall. The Retrieval Composite score is based on the difference between delayed recognition and delayed recall.

B. Assessment of Retrograde Amnesia

There are many factors that make formal assessment of RA difficult (see Table 3). The memories assessed are often from the remote past, and external confirmation is difficult to obtain. When memories are incorrectly recalled, it is not possible to determine whether errors are the result of inadequate storage at the time of initial exposure or disruption of the retrieval process. One method of assessing RA involves recall of public event information. The problem with this approach is that there is a great deal of heterogeneity in individuals' premorbid fund of knowledge; variations in performance may be due to differences in premorbid intelligence or interest in world events. Caution should be exercised whenever interpreting a test that is intended to assess RA.

With these caveats stated, we recommend the following for assessment of remote memory. Throughout assessment, memory for different types of information (e.g., personal history, world history, recognizing famous people) should be measured, because different classes of information break down differentially within the context of neurological disease.

1. MEMORY FOR PERSONAL EVENTS

The **Autobiographical Memory Interview** (AMI; Kopelman, Wilson, & Baddeley, 1989) is a semistructured interview that focuses on events from three time periods throughout the life span. Both semantic and episodic aspects of events are probed. Each memory is scored in terms of the amount of detail and vividness of the recollection. It is important to note that, in general, memory for autobiographical information is selective; even individuals with normal memory functions may fail to remember wedding dates, birth dates, and other events of this nature. Any assessment of autobiographical memory should be accompanied by an interview with someone who can provide a collateral source of information such as a family member or friend.

The **Crovitz procedure** (Crovitz & Schiffman, 1974) is an additional method of assessing autobiographical memory. The individual is asked to generate memories in response to a list of high-frequency words. Unique memories with specific details receive high scores on this test, whereas vague and generic recollections of past events do not. The individual is asked to estimate the date on which each episode occurred.

2. MEMORY FOR PUBLIC EVENTS

The **Famous Faces Test** (FFT; Albert, Butters, & Levin, 1979) from the Boston Remote Memory Battery requires the patient to identify photographs of famous individuals from the 1920s to the 1980s. This test has been used extensively in studies of RA; however, a problem with this test is that some of the early items (e.g., the face of Charlie Chaplin) are overlearned; hence, all items are not representative of specific temporal epochs. Despite this problem, the FFT provides useful information regarding the individual's knowledge and recall of public figures.

The **Transient Events Test** (TET; O'Connor et al., 1997) focuses on recall of information that was in the news for a discrete period of time. Events that were noteworthy but only for limited time periods were chosen to eliminate the possible effects of overlearning. Free recall and recognition questions are asked about three events from each hemidecade in the period of time from 1950 to 1994. Recall questions are worded such that the most salient aspect of the event is in the question and the individual is asked to provide more details. Recognition questions are administered in a forced-choice format in which the correct answer is paired with a distractor item.

IV. CONCLUSION

Over the past 4 decades, clinical and research investigations of amnesic patients have yielded fascinating insights regarding the psychological parameters and biological substrates of memory. Neuropsychologists have attempted to identify conditions that facilitate learning for memory-impaired patients including environmental supports, pharmacological intervention, and psychological and cognitive remediation strategies. The neuropsychological evaluation serves as a framework for the design of remediation programs and other support services that facilitate adaptation to chronic amnesia. Recommendations should be individually tailored to the patient's specific profile of cognitive and emotional need with input from the patient and family regarding the practical constraints of his or her current living circumstances. Although increasingly sophisticated and environmentally germane remediation efforts have been developed over the past few years, remediation programs often do not address the needs of severely amnesic patients. Clearly, treatment issues should be at the forefront of future investigations.

BIBLIOGRAPHY

Ahern, G. L., O'Connor, M. G., Dalmau, J., Coleman, A., Posner, J. B., Schomer, D. L., Herzog, A. G., Kolb, D. A., & Mesulam, M. M. (1994). Paraneoplastic temporal lobe epilepsy with testicular neoplasm and atypical amnesia. *Neurology, 44,* 1270–1274.

Albert, M. S., Butters, N., & Levin, J. (1979). Temporal gradients in retrograde amnesia of patients with alcoholic Korsakkoff's disease. *Archives of Neurology, 36,* 211–216.

Benson, D. F., Marsden, C. D., & Meadows, J. C. (1974). The amnesic syndrome of posterior cerebral artery occlusion. *Acta Neurologica Scandinavica, 50,* 133–145.

Butters, N., & Cermak, L. S. (1980). *Alcoholic Korsakoff's syndrome: An information processing approach.* New York: Academic Press.

Butters, N., & Stuss, D. T. (1989). Diencephalic amnesia. In F. Boller & J. Grafman (Eds.), *Handbook of neuropsychology* (pp. 107–148). New York: Elsevier Science.

Cermak, L. S. (1995). Processing deficits in amnesic patients: Nearly a full cycle? In L. S. Cermak (Ed.), *Neuropsychological explorations of memory and cognition: A tribute to Nelson Butters* (pp. 31–43). New York: Plenum Press.

Cramon, D. Y. von, Hebel, N., & Schuri, U. (1985). A contribution to the anatomical basis of thalamic amnesia. *Brain, 108,* 993–1008.

Crovitz, H. F., & Schiffman, H. (1974). Frequency of episodic memories as a function of their age. *Bulletin of the Psychonomic Society, 4,* 517–518.

Delis, D. C., Kramer, J. H., Kaplan, E., & Ober, B. A. (1987). *The California Verbal Learning Test.* San Antonio, TX: Psychological Corporation, Harcourt Brace Jovanovich.

DeRenzi, E., Liotti, M., & Nichelli, P. (1987). Semantic amnesia with preservation of autobiographical memory: A case report. *Cortex, 23,* 575–597.

Eslinger, P. J., Damasio, H., Damasio, A. R., & Butters, N. (1993). Nonverbal amnesia and asymmetric cerebral lesions following encephalitis. *Brain and Cognition, 21,* 140–152.

Freed, D. M., Corkin, S., & Cohen, N. J. (1987). Forgetting in H.M.: A second look. *Neuropsychologia, 25,* 461–471.

Gallassi, R., Lorusso, S., & Stracciari, A. (1986). Neuropsychological findings during a transient global amnesia attack and its follow-up. *Italian Journal of Neurological Sciences, 7,* 45–49.

Gallassi, R., Morreale, A., Sarro, D., & Lugaresi, E. (1992). Epileptic amnesic syndrome. *Epilepsia, 33,* S21–S25.

Hodges, J. R. (1994). Semantic memory and frontal executive function during transient global amnesia. *Journal of Neurology, Neurosurgery and Psychiatry, 57,* 605–608.

Irle, E., Wowra, B., Kunert, H. J., Hampl, J., & Kunze, S. (1992). Memory disturbance following anterior communicating artery rupture. *Annals of Neurology, 31,* 473–480.

Kapur, N. (1993a). Focal retrograde amnesia in neurological disease: A critical review. *Cortex, 29*, 217–234.

Kapur, N. (1993b). Transient epileptic amnesia: A clinical update and a reformulation. *Journal of Neurology, Neurosurgery, and Psychiatry, 56*, 1184–1190.

Kopelman, M. D. (1995). The assessment of psychogenic amnesia. In A. D. Baddeley, B. A. Wilson, & F. N. Watts (Eds.), *Handbook of memory disorders* (pp. 427–448). New York: Wiley.

Kopelman, M. D., Wilson, B. A., & Baddeley, A. D. (1989). The Autobiographical Memory Interview: A new assessment of personal and autobiographical semantic memory in amnesic patients. *Journal of Clinical and Experimental Neuropsychology, 11*, 724–744.

Lezak, M. (1995). *Neuropsychological assessment.* New York: Oxford University Press.

Markowitsch, H. J. (1982). Thalamic mediodorsal nucleus and memory: A critical evaluation of studies in animals and man. *Neuroscience and Biobehavioral Reviews, 6*, 351–380.

Markowitsch, H. J. (1988). Diencephalic amnesia: A reorientation towards tracts? *Brain Research Review, 13*, 351–370.

Mazzucchi, A., Moretti, G., Caffarra, P., & Parma, M. (1980). Neuropsychological functions in the follow-up of transient global amnesia. *Brain, 103*, 161–178.

McKee, R. D., & Squire, L. R. (1992). Equivalent forgetting rates in long-term memory in diencephalic and medial temporal lobe amnesia. *Journal of Neuroscience, 12*, 3765–3772.

Milner, B. (1966). Amnesia following operation on the temporal lobes. In C. W. M. Whitty & O. L. Zangwill (Eds.), *Amnesia* (pp. 109–133). London: Butterworths.

Mishkin, M. (1982). A memory system in the monkey. *Philosophical Transactions of the Royal Society of London, 298*, 85–95

Newman, N. J., Bell, I. R., & McKee, A. C. (1990). Paraneoplastic limbic encephalitis: Neuropsychiatric presentation. *Biological Psychiatry, 27*, 529–542.

O'Connor, M. G., Bachna, K., Kaplan, B., Cermak, L. S., & Ransil, B. (1997). *Long-term retention of transient events.* Manuscript submitted for publication.

O'Connor, M. G., Butters, N., Miliotis, P., Eslinger, P. J., & Cermak, L. (1992). The dissociation of anterograde and retrograde amnesia in a patient with herpes encephalitis. *Journal of Clinical and Experimental Neuropsychology, 14*, 159–178.

O'Connor, M. G., Sieggrreen, M. A., Ahern, G., Schomer, D. L., & Mesulam, M. M. (1997). Accelerated forgetting in association with temporal lobe epilepsy and paraneoplastic limbic encephalitis. *Brain and Cognition, 35*, 71–84.

O'Connor, M. G., Walbridge, M., D'Esposito, M., McGlinchey-Berroth, R., & Alexander, M. (1995). *An investigation of the remote memory abilities of patients with rupture and surgical repair of ACoA aneurysms.* Paper presented at the meeting of the International Neuropsychological Society, Seattle, WA.

Osterreith, P., & Rey, A. (1944). Le test de copie d'une figure complexe [The test of copying a complex figure]. *Archives de Psychologie, 30,* 206–356.

Ott, B. R., & Saver, J. L. (1993). Unilateral amnesic stroke: Six new cases and a review of the literature. *Stroke, 24,* 1033–1042.

Parkin, A. J., & Leng, R. C. (1993). *Neuropsychology of the amnesic syndrome.* Hillsdale, NJ: Erlbaum.

Peterson, L. R., & Peterson, M. J. (1959). Short-term retention of individual verbal items. *Journal of Experimental Psychology, 58,* 193–198.

Rey, A. (1964). *L'examen clinique en psychologie* [The clinical exam in psychology]. Paris: Presses Universitaires de France.

Scoville, W. B., & Milner, B. (1957). Loss of recent memory after bilateral hippocampal lesions. *Journal of Neurology, Neurosurgery and Psychiatry, 20,* 11–12.

Squire, L. (1994). Memory and forgetting: Long-term and gradual changes in memory storage. *International Review of Neurobiology, 37,* 243–269.

Stenhouse, L. M., Knight, R. M., Longmore, B. E., & Bishara, S. N. (1991). Long-term cognitive deficits in patients undergoing surgery on aneurysms in the anterior communicating artery. *Journal of Neurology, Neurosurgery, and Psychiatry, 54,* 909–914.

Trahan, D. M., & Larrabee, G. (1986). *Continuous Visual Memory Test.* Odessa, FL: Psychological Assessment Resources.

Tulving, E. (1983). *Elements of episodic memory.* New York: Oxford University Press.

Victor, M., Adams, R. D., & Collins, G. H. (1989). *The Wernicke-Korsakoff syndrome and related neurologic disorders due to alcoholism and malnutrition* (2nd ed.). Philadelphia: Davis.

Warrington, E. K. (1984). *Recognition Memory Test.* London: NFER-Nelson.

Warrington, E. K., & McCarthy, R. A. (1988). The fractionation of retrograde amnesia. *Brain and Cognition, 7,* 184–200

Warrington, E. K., & Weiskrantz, L. (1968). A new method for testing long-term retention with special reference to amnesic patients. *Nature, 217,* 972–974.

Warrington, E. K., & Weiskrantz, L. (1970). The amnesic syndrome: Consolidation or retrieval? *Nature, 228*, 628–630

Wechsler, D. (1987). *WMS-R manual*. New York: Psychological Corporation.

Wechsler, D. (1997). *WMS-III manual*. New York: Psychological Corporation.

Weiskrantz, L. (1985). Issues and theories in the study of the amnesic syndrome. In N. M. Weinberger, K. F. Berham, & G. Lynch (Eds.), *Memory systems of the brain* (pp. 380–415). New York: Guilford Press.

Zola-Morgan, S., & Squire, L. R. (1993). Neuroanatomy of memory. *Annual Review of Neurosciences, 16*, 547–563.

Zola-Morgan, S., Squire, L. R., & Amaral, D. G. (1989). Lesions of the hippocampal formation but not lesions of the fornix or the mammillary nuclei produce long-lasting memory impairment in monkeys. *Journal of Neuroscience, 9*, 898–913.

Zola-Morgan, S., Squire, L. R., Amaral, D. G., & Suzuki, W. A. (1989). Lesions of the perirhinal and parahippocampal cortex that spare the amygdala and hippocampal formation produce severe memory impairment. *Journal of Neuroscience, 9*, 4355–4370.

CHAPTER 22

Meryl A. Butters, Elizabeth M. Soety,
and Elizabeth L. Glisky

Memory Rehabilitation

Difficulty with memory and learning is the most frequent complaint of individuals with neuropsychological disorders. Moreover, people typically find that memory impairment is particularly disabling in their everyday lives. For this reason, strategies that focus on the alleviation of real-world memory problems are likely to be of greatest benefit. The optimal strategies for any individual depend on both the nature and the level of memory impairment and the family- and self-reported difficulties in everyday life. This chapter provides an outline of some of the aspects of memory assessment that are especially important for rehabilitation planning and some practical methods for enhancing everyday memory functioning and solving some of the problems of daily living that people with memory disorders commonly experience. Before outlining important aspects of assessment and rehabilitation, we provide a brief review of relevant concepts.

In the preparation of this chapter, Meryl A. Butters was supported in part by the Mental Health Clinical Research Center for the study of Late Life Mood Disorders (Charles F. Reynolds III, MD, PI; PHS Grant MH 52247-01A1) and by a Veterans Administration Rehabilitation Research Development Service Award (Steven Graham, MD, PI; VA Grant B785-RC).

I. MEMORY PROCESSES AND CONCEPTS

Memory is often **retrospective**, a term that refers to retrieval of past experiences both recent and remote. Memory can also be **prospective**, or concerning the retrieval of future intentions, such as remembering to keep an appointment, remembering to take medication, or remembering to turn off the stove. Although the bulk of research on memory rehabilitation has focused on retrospective memory, remembering to perform an action in the future is often critical to everyday functioning.

The act of remembering depends on at least four basic processes and can fail as a result of a breakdown in any one of them. These processes include the following:

A. Attention

A multicomponent process that is critical for ensuring the entry of information into the system. Attentional processes are responsible for these behaviors:
- **Selecting** goal-relevant information from the range of stimuli in the environment
- **Focusing** on relevant information
- **Inhibiting** irrelevant information
- **Sustaining** focus until all relevant information has been selected and processed

B. Encoding

Initial processing of information that results in the formation of a memory trace. Semantic, or meaningful, analyses during encoding (i.e., deep processing) result in more durable memory traces.

C. Storage

The retention of information in the system through the process of consolidation.

D. Retrieval

The process of accessing the information in storage and bringing it to mind. The act of retrieval may be conscious, resulting in recollection of information from the past, in which case it is termed **explicit memory.** Information may come to mind or influence current behavior even when a person has no conscious recollection of its prior occurrence, in which case it is termed **implicit memory.**

II. MEMORY ASSESSMENT

To develop and initiate an effective memory rehabilitation program, determination of both the nature and the level of memory deficits through a thorough assessment is critical. The evaluation should focus on attention, retrospective verbal and visual memory, and prospective memory. In addition to differentiating between verbal and visual memory impairment, the results of the assessment can be used to identify specific encoding, storage, and retrieval deficits, as well as areas of strength that might later be exploited for rehabilitation purposes.

A. Attention

Individuals with attentional deficits may report difficulty recalling why they have entered a room or whether they have completed a task. Attentional capacity should be assessed independently of memory. Testing may reveal difficulty focusing or concentrating on relevant information and ignoring distractions, slowed information processing, and difficulty retaining material over even short intervals as well as staying on task for extended periods of time. Following are the attentional components and examples of appropriate measures that should be included in an assessment.

- **Selective attention:** digit span forward and recitation of automatic sequences (e.g., alphabet, months of the year)
- **Concentration:** digit span backward and mental arithmetic problems
- **Inhibition:** Stroop Color–Word Interference Task and Trail Making Test Part B
- **Sustained attention:** continuous-performance tests (e.g., Vigil Continous Performance Test)

B. Verbal Retrospective Memory

Individuals with verbal memory deficits may report difficulty recalling conversations or verbal instructions. Following are the various aspects of verbal memory and examples of appropriate measures to include in any assessment.

- **List learning** may be assessed by the California Verbal Learning Test or the Hopkins Verbal Learning Test.

- **Narrative memory** is measured by the Logical Memory subtest of the Wechsler Memory Scale–III (WMS-III) and stories from the Rivermead Behavioral Memory Test.
- **Immediate memory**, which is recall of verbal information immediately following presentation, is assessed by most verbal memory tests. A selective deficit in immediate recall in the presence of good retention of material across a time delay may suggest a problem with encoding.
- **Delayed memory (recall and recognition)** is measured by recall of verbal information, typically after a 20- to 30-minute delay period. Poor retention of material is indicated by a substantially worse performance on delayed compared with immediate recall and may suggest a problem with storage. A selective deficit in recall as opposed to recognition may suggest a particular problem with retrieval of verbal material.

C. Visual Retrospective Memory

Visual memory deficits may be manifested in everyday life as difficulty recalling routes as well as objects or individuals in visual form. Types of visual memory important to assess and examples of appropriate measures follow:

- **Concrete visual memory** may be assessed by the Recognition Memory Test–Faces.
- **Abstract visual memory** is measured by the Visual Reproduction subtest of the WMS-III and the Rey-Osterreith Complex Figure.
- **Immediate memory**, which is recall of visual information immediately following presentation, is assessed by most visual memory tests.
- **Delayed memory (recall and recognition)** is measured by recall of visual information after a 20- to 30-minute delay period. The same patterns of performance and associated implications for the nature of memory impairment that are seen across various verbal memory tasks also apply to visual tasks.

D. Prospective Memory

Individuals with prospective memory deficits typically report difficulty remembering to do things in the future. For example, they frequently have trouble remembering to perform errands and to attend doctor appointments. The Prospective Memory

Screening Test (Sohlberg & Mateer, 1989a) is one of the few available validated instruments (also see Cockburn, 1996).

III. REHABILITATION

The following rehabilitation strategies are organized on the basis of the four processes critical for memory: attention, encoding, storage, and retrieval. Neuropsychologists can teach these strategies to their patients, choosing specific exercises on the basis of weaknesses identified during assessment. Many of the examples are worded as though addressing the patient for simplicity of presentation.

A. Improving Attention

As we mentioned earlier, attention is a requisite ability for successful remembering. If one does not devote attention to information at the time of presentation or encoding, it will likely not be accurately recalled later. There are a variety of methods to help patients increase their attention to information (see Higbee, 1993; Morse, 1994).

Verbal mediation: talking to oneself either aloud or silently when intending to perform or while performing a task
Purpose: To keep intentions (e.g., locking the front door) in mind until they are carried out or to help recall whether tasks have been accomplished.
Example: Saying "I am placing the keys on the table" to aid later recollection of the location of the keys.

Repetition: repeating back what has been said, paraphrasing the material
Purpose: To focus on conversations or verbal instructions.
Example: After being told the date, time, and location of an upcoming event, repeating back these details to the person who provided this information.

Controlling and reducing the rate at which information is presented: taking rest periods and small breaks within and between tasks
Purpose: To encode substantial amounts of information.
Example: Reading new information for 20-minute periods interspersed with short breaks, during which one engages in a different activity.

Reducing interference: eliminating distractions in the environment as much as possible
Purpose: To maintain focus when other external stimuli compete for attention.

Example: Turning off the television set when engaging in conversation.

Increasing the salience of the information: focusing on the consequences of not recalling the conversation at a later time

Purpose: To increase arousal and focus on conversations or verbal instructions.

Example: When informed about an upcoming event (such as a social gathering) focusing on the consequences of not recalling this information such as angering one's spouse.

B. Improving Encoding

1. GENERAL STRATEGIES

The following strategies can improve encoding in individuals with mild-to-moderate memory deficits. The choice of particular strategies and techniques should be guided by both the individual's reported failures in everyday memory and the assessment results. That is, techniques should take advantage of and build on an individual's cognitive strengths to compensate for weaknesses. For those with visual memory deficits, therefore, training should focus on verbal techniques, and for those with verbal memory impairment, visual techniques should be emphasized. Within each general encoding strategy (organization, association, visualization, and verbalization), a number of examples of specific techniques are described (see Higbee, 1993).

a. Organization

Individuals frequently have difficulty recalling information because it was not encoded in an organized manner. Recall can be enhanced by improving organization of the material as it is presented and encoded. Specific organizational techniques follow:

Categorization: Group items into categories that can later act as retrieval cues.

Purpose: To encode and recall lists of items that can be grouped by category.

Example: Group grocery store items by category (e.g., fruit, vegetables, meats, or canned goods) at the time the list is generated and encoded. Later, at the store, use the categories as cues to recall the items on the list.

Number of items: Count the number of items on the whole list or in each category at the time of encoding, and use this information at the time of retrieval.

Purpose: To encode and recall lists of information.

Example: If using a shopping list, count the number of items within each category (e.g., vegetables). Then, at the store, check to be sure that the correct number of items has been gathered. If the number is incorrect, scan the foods until the additional items are recognized.

Chunking: Group information into meaningful clusters.

Purpose: To recall number series (e.g., telephone numbers).

Example: Group the numbers in the series 6 7 7 3 4 5 6 into 677, 34, 56.

PQRST: Acronym for performing the steps Preview, Question, Read, State, and Test.

Purpose: To organize and recall prose or narrative information.

Example:

• *Preview* or skim the material prior to reading the text.

• Generate *questions* on the basis of the preview that can be answered by the material, including questions involving the five *wh's: who, what, where, when, and why.* For example: Who is the story about? What is the story about? Where did the events take place? When did the events take place? Why is this information useful to me?

• *Read* the text with the goal of answering the questions.

• *State* aloud or in written form the answers to the questions.

• *Test* memory by answering the questions without referring to the text.

b. Association

Another useful strategy to increase depth of encoding and thus facilitate recall is association. The concept involves connecting new information with previously stored material. Specific techniques to aid in forming associations follow:

Analogies: Find a similarity between new and old information.

Purpose: To encode and recall new information (e.g., concepts or relationships).

Example: If one is explaining how memory works, a useful analogy would be a large filing cabinet containing numerous bits of information to be filed, stored, and retrieved.

Compare and contrast: Compare and contrast the new information with related, stored information.

Purpose: To encode and recall new information.

Example: When meeting a new person by the name of Sally, compare and contrast her characteristics with those of other people named Sally.

c. Visual imagery

Use of imagery is a general strategy that involves forming a mental image of the information to be remembered. Imagery increases the depth of encoding and is particularly useful for individuals with verbal memory deficits. Imagery can be used to encode information that is typically processed visually (e.g., concrete objects, people's physical characteristics) as well as to encode verbal material that can be translated into visual images (e.g., verbal descriptions of actions). The more vivid and bizarre the image, the more likely it will be recalled at a later time. Visualizing objects or individuals moving or interacting makes the image more vivid, and exaggerating the size of objects makes them more bizarre. To remember to perform two errands, such as going to the bank and the dry cleaner, one might form a logical visual image such as money in a cash register at the dry cleaner. A more bizarre and thus more memorable image would be large dollar bills hanging from the dry cleaner's revolving rack in place of clothing. Other, more specific visual imagery techniques include the following:

Method of loci: Visualize to-be-remembered items placed along a familiar route, such as a walk through one's house. To recall items, take a walk through the house noting the new items that were visualized in each room.

Purpose: To encode and recall discrete items, especially in a specified order (e.g., lists of errands, topics in a speech).

Example: To remember a speech about general strategies for memory rehabilitation (e.g., organization, association) form a visual association between one's living room and the concept "organization" (e.g., decorative items in the living room rearranged by color or size); between one's dining room and the concept "association" (e.g., a friend or "associate" dancing on the dining room table); between one's kitchen and the concept "visualization" (e.g., eyeballs covering the kitchen counter), and so on. Later, imagine walking through the rooms of the house, noting the items that were "placed" there by visualization.

Pegword method: Using imagery, associate to-be-learned items with a pegword list that consists of previously learned nouns that rhyme with successive numbers. One standard pegword list is one-bun, two-shoe, three-tree, four-door, five-hive, six-sticks, seven-heaven, eight-gate, nine-wine, ten-hen.

Purpose: To encode and recall a list of items, especially in a specified order.

Example: To encode an errand list, associate bun with the first errand (e.g., going to the bank) by imagining a sandwich made out of a hamburger bun with a stack of bills instead of a hamburger patty. Then imagine the second errand interacting with a shoe, and so on. To recall the items, proceed by recalling the overlearned Number 1, which acts as a cue for "bun." The hamburger is revisualized along with the stack of bills inside it.

Link method: Form a visual association or link between items that follow one another in a series.

Purpose: To encode and recall lists of concrete objects.

Example: To encode a list of items that includes *dog, hat, flower,* and *table,* first form a visual association between dog and hat by imagining a dog wearing a straw hat, then form an association between hat and flower by imagining a hat with a large purple flower on it, and last, link the flower and the table by imagining a card table imprinted with purple flowers. When it is time to recall the list, only dog must be recalled independently; once *dog* is recalled, it acts as a cue for the hat, which cues the flower, and so on down the list.

Face–name association: Relate a person's name to a prominent physical feature through imagery.

Purpose: To learn and remember people's names.

Example: If *Butters* is the name to be recalled, transform it into a concrete image (e.g., butter), identify a prominent physical feature of the person (e.g., light, wavy hair), and then form a visual image associating the feature with the name (e.g., butter dripping from the hair). Later, to recall the name when confronted with the person, recognize the prominent physical feature (the person's hair), use this feature as a retrieval cue to recall the image–name association (butter dripping), and transform the image into the name *Butters.*

d. Verbalization

There are a variety of verbal techniques that increase depth of encoding and that are particularly useful for individuals who have weak visual abilities along with relatively strong verbal skills.

Rhyming: Rhyme new information with previously stored material.

Purpose: To learn and recall simple verbal information.

Example: If a car is parked on the fourth floor of a garage, a rhyme could be four-door.

Keyword method: Transform a to-be-learned term into words already in one's lexicon, and relate them to one another in a meaningful way.

Purpose: To acquire new vocabulary words and associated meanings.

Example: To learn the word *Zoloft* (trade name of a commonly prescribed antidepressant drug), transform the word into

Zoe and *loft,* and associate the two words with each other: "My friend Zoe is happy living in a loft."

Acronyms: Create a word using the first letter of each item or step in a to-be-remembered list or task.

Purpose: To encode and recall a list of items or steps in a task.

Example: To remember a shopping list of bread, eggs, apples, and milk, use the first letter of each item to generate the word *beam.* Later, recall the word *beam,* and use each letter in the word as a cue to recall each item in the list.

Acrostics: Use the first letter of each item to generate a word, then form a sentence using the created words.

Purpose: To encode and recall a list of items or steps in a task.

Example: A sentence using the previously mentioned list (bread, eggs, apples, and milk) could be "better [bread] eat [eggs] all [apples] of the meal [milk]," and the first letter of each word in the sentence is a cue to recall each item in the list.

Story method: Create a story out of the list of items.

Purpose: To encode and recall a list of items or steps in a task.

Example: To remember the list *dog, hat, flower, table,* make up a story such as the following: My *dog* put on my big straw *hat,* picked a pretty purple *flower,* and sat on the *table* to eat it.

2. TRAINING DOMAIN-SPECIFIC TASKS

The techniques described in this section largely rely on implicit rather than explicit memory systems. Individuals with severe explicit memory deficits frequently have normal implicit memory ability. Therefore, memory that relies on implicit processes can be useful for individuals with moderate-to-severe memory impairment in whom improvement of general memory functioning is unlikely to occur. These techniques can be used to train performance in a broad range of specific tasks, from making a sandwich to using a computer.

Spaced retrieval: To strengthen encoding, practice retrieving items at gradually increasing intervals (see Schacter, Rich, & Stampp, 1985).

Purpose: To learn specific information or tasks.

Example: To learn a grooming skill, an individual might perform the task once, then again after 1 minute, then after 5 minutes, 10 minutes, and so on, with progressively longer intervals between repetitions.

Errorless learning: To speed and strengthen encoding, prevent the occurrence of errors during learning (see Baddeley, 1992).

Purpose: To learn the steps to perform a new task.

Example: To learn how to use a computer, the individual performs the task with close guidance, one step at a time, repeatedly, with as much information as necessary to complete each step without error. Each step must be completed without error several times before proceeding to the next step.

Vanishing cues: Gradually withdraw cue information across learning trials (see Glisky, Schacter, & Butters, 1994).

Purpose: To acquire domain-specific knowledge, including steps to perform a new task.

Example: To learn a new task, break it down into steps and teach each step separately. Present as many cues as necessary for correct responding. Gradually withdraw the cues across trials until the individual completes the task successfully without aid.

C. Improving Storage and Retention

Once information has been encoded, employing the following techniques may help to maintain the information until it is retrieved and thereby increase the probability of recall (see Higbee, 1993). These techniques are most useful for individuals with mild-to-moderate memory impairment. They can also be helpful for those with moderate-to-severe deficits if material has been successfully encoded.

Distributed practice: To increase the strength of the memory trace, distribute practicing of a new task or material across time. That is, practice the material for shorter, more frequent periods, rather than for longer, less frequent sessions.

Purpose: To learn specific information or new tasks.

Example: To learn to play a specific piece for the piano, practice it daily for a half hour rather than for three and a half hours once a week.

Review: Review information periodically.

Purpose: To maintain new information in storage.

Example: Carry index cards containing new information and read them periodically throughout the day.

Overlearning: Continue to practice newly learned tasks or information well beyond the first correct performance or recitation.

Purpose: To increase the strength of a memory trace and maintain it in storage.

Example: When studying for an examination, continue to quiz oneself on the new information well after the first time it is correctly recited.

D. Improving Retrieval

1. GENERAL STRATEGIES

Memory impairment is often at least partially attributable to retrieval failure. The following strategies are useful for most individuals who have difficulty retrieving well-known information such as familiar names or aspects of their daily routine (see Higbee, 1993).

Relaxation: Use relaxation techniques such as deep breathing at the time of retrieval. Relaxation techniques are particularly useful for individuals who are able to recall information in certain situations but not in others.

Purpose: To reduce retrieval difficulties caused by anxiety.

Example: Use deep breathing to reduce anxiety and maximize retrieval performance during an examination or a presentation.

Structuring the environment and routine: Keep items in the same place all the time, and perform routine actions and tasks in a consistent manner.

Purpose: To recall the location of objects and to remember to perform specific tasks.

Example: Keep eyeglasses or wallet in one designated location. Pair a new task (e.g., taking new medication) with another, overlearned task in the daily routine (e.g., brushing one's teeth) by keeping the medication with the toothpaste so that the latter task will act as a visual cue to perform the former task.

2. SEARCH TECHNIQUES

Search techniques are self-initiated ways for systematically generating cues that trigger retrieval of stored information (see Higbee, 1993).

Mental retracing: Reconstruct the events leading up to and occurring after an item was misplaced.

Purpose: To find missing items.

Example: To find lost keys, mentally reenact the events of the day.

Alphabetic searching: Systematically go through the alphabet, generating words beginning with each letter until the correct word is retrieved.

Purpose: To retrieve specific verbal information.

Example: To retrieve a forgotten name, start with the letter *a* and generate names beginning with that letter, continuing through the alphabet until the correct name is recalled.

Recreating context: Recreate the environmental and contextual factors that were present at the time of encoding.
Purpose: To retrieve all kinds of information.
Example: To recall a conversation held with another individual during a meal at a restaurant, recreate the environment and context either mentally, through imagery, or physically, by returning to the restaurant.

3. CUING TECHNIQUES

Cuing can be used by the caregiver of a memory-impaired individual to trigger retrieval of stored information. These techniques can be useful for memory-impaired individuals who are not able to generate cues independently but who are able to benefit from cues provided by others (see Van der Linden & Van der Kaa, 1989). Although retrieval through cueing does not necessarily increase one's level of functioning or independence, it can help a memory-impaired individual experience some success in coping with the environment.

First-letter cueing: Provide the first letter of the object or name.
Purpose: To recall specific information.
Example: During a visit to the doctor's office, the caregiver provides the memory-impaired individual with a first letter as a cue, to create an opportunity to recall a new symptom or problem.

Category cuing: Provide the category of the information.
Purpose: To recall specific information, especially information that has been categorically organized at the time of encoding.
Example: While shopping, the caregiver provides the memory-impaired individual with category cues such as "clothing" or "hardware" to aid recall of specific items to purchase.

4. EXTERNAL AIDS

External aids are physical instruments used to enhance everyday functioning by circumventing memory. They are especially useful for performing tasks that rely on prospective memory, or memory for future intentions (see Harris, 1992; Higbee, 1993).

Written reminders (e.g., instructions, memos, checklists): Write information down and place it in a prominent location.
Purpose: To provide cues to perform a future act or to serve as a reminder of a past act.
Example: To remember to pass along a phone message, write a note and place it on the refrigerator.

Timers (e.g., watch alarms, alarm clocks, cooking timers): Set timer to go off when a task needs to be performed.

Purpose: To provide an auditory cue or reminder to perform a future act.

Example: Set a cooking timer to go off when the washing machine cycle is completed as a cue to take the laundry out of the washer and place it in the dryer.

Computerized paging system: Program a paging system (e.g., Neuropage; Hersh & Treadgold, 1994) so that the pager vibrates or produces a tone that acts as a cue to look at the display. The display contains a message about an event or action to be performed.

Purpose: To provide cues to perform a future act.

Example: Program into the system various medication names and times the drugs should be taken so that the pager reminds one to take specific medications when the appropriate times arrive.

Appointment books, diaries, and calendars: Record actions to be performed in the future and review past actions.

Purpose: To remember to perform future actions and to recall past actions.

Example: To retreive information regarding a previous meeting, refer to one's appointment book.

Electronic organizers: Enter personal information as well as actions to be performed into organizer and set electronic timer.

Purpose: To remember to perform future actions as well as to retrieve personal information.

Example: Personal information such as insurance policy numbers or driver's license number can be stored for simple access when away from home.

Memory notebook: A comprehensive notebook system has been developed by Sohlberg and Mateer (1989b). The notebook is carried throughout the day and is used to record information about past and future actions, as well as personal information and other useful material. It is individualized and contains separate sections relevant to one's life. Sections can be referred to and information can be recorded as frequently as hourly or only when new information (such as appointments or phone numbers) is presented.

Purpose: To retrieve information, provide cues to perform future acts, and provide structure and organization to an individual's daily routine.

Example: The notebook may include sections such as these:

(1) Orientation: Record personal information (e.g., owner's address, phone number, medications, names of physicians, name of pharmacy).

(2) Memory log: Record the events of the day (e.g., phone conversations, tasks completed).

(3) Calendar: Keep track of holidays and schedule appointments and other personal events.

(4) Things to do: Record tasks to be completed, and cross them off as they are performed.

(5) Transportation information: Include relevant material for public transportation (e.g., bus schedules, phone numbers for taxi services).

(6) Feelings log: Record feelings about the changes experienced since the injury.

(7) Relevant people: Record names and addresses as well as identifying information about people with whom one has regular contact (e.g., physical descriptions, photographs, or personal interests).

(8) Work-related information: Include names of coworkers, instructions on how to complete work-related tasks, and locations.

IV. CONCLUSION

Losing the ability to recall information can be devastating and often affects nearly all aspects of life. Clearly, all the techniques described in this chapter are not appropriate for everyone. Some techniques are too complex to be acquired or too cumbersome to be applied by many patients. Nevertheless, learning and using just one or two methods can greatly improve independence or quality of life. For example, if an individual with a focal, severe memory impairment is unable to remember to perform many activities of daily living, a computerized paging system that provides cues to perform tasks could substantially increase his or her independence. An individual with a relatively mild memory deficit who remains employed but has a problem making required presentations because of difficulty remembering the content and consequent anxiety may learn to use the method of loci along with deep breathing; these techniques may greatly improve his or her performance and ultimately help maintain employment.

Individuals with more severe cognitive deficits in addition to memory impairment pose the greatest challenge. It is usually impossible to improve their memory functioning substantially. However, applying a few simple methods (e.g., caregiver cuing, labeling drawers) in a few situations (remembering complaints during a doctor visit, finding clothes to dress oneself) that are particularly distressing for the individual can improve coping and thus quality of life.

BIBLIOGRAPHY

Baddeley, A. D. (1992). Implicit memory and errorless learning: A link between cognitive theory and neuropsychological rehabilitation? In L. R. Squire & N. Butters (Eds.), *Neuropsychology of memory* (2nd ed., pp. 309–314). New York: Guilford Press.

Cockburn, J. (1996). Assessment and treatment of prospective memory deficits. In M. Bradimonte, G. O. Einstein, & M. A. McDaniels (Eds.), *Prospective memory: Theory and applications.* Monwak, NJ: Erlbaum.

Franzen, M. D., & Haut, M. W. (1991). The psychological treatment of memory impairment: A review of empirical studies. *Neuropsychology Review, 2,* 29–63.

Glisky, E. L., Schacter, D. L., & Butters, M. A. (1994). Domain-specific learning and remediation of memory disorders. In M. J. Riddoch & G. W. Humphreys (Eds.), *Cognitive neuropsychology and cognitive rehabilitation.* Hillsdale, N.J.: Erlbaum.

Harris, J. E. (1992). Ways to help memory. In B. A. Wilson & N. Moffat (Eds.), *Clinical management of memory problems.* San Diego, CA: Singular.

Hersh, N. A., & Treadgold, L. G. (1994). Neuropage: The rehabilitation of memory dysfunction by prosthetic memory and cuing. *Neurorehabilitation, 4,* 187–197.

Higbee, K. L. (1993). *Your memory: How it works and how to improve it* (2nd ed.). New York: Paragon House.

Little, M. M. (1987). The remediation of everyday memory deficits. In J. M. Williams & C. J. Long (Eds.), *The rehabilitation of cognitive disabilities.* New York: Plenum Press.

Morse, P. A. (1994). Cognitive remediation in a neuropsychiatric setting. In J. M. Ellison, C. S. Weinstein, & T. H. Malinofsky (Eds.), *The psychotherapist's guide to neuropsychiatry: Diagnostic and treatment issues* (pp.107–143). Washington, DC: American Psychiatric Press.

Schacter, D. L., Rich, S. A., & Stampp, M. S. (1985). Remediation of memory disorders: Experimental evaluation of the spaced retrieval technique. *Journal of Clinical and Experimental Neuropsychology, 7,* 79–96.

Sohlberg, M. M., & Mateer, C. A. (1989a). *Prospective Memory Screening*. Puyallup, WA: Association for Neuropsychological Research and Development.

Sohlberg, M. M., & Mateer, C. A. (1989b). Training use of compensatory memory books: A three stage behavioral approach. *Journal of Clinical and Experimental Neuropsychology, 11*, 871–891.

Sunderland, A., Harris, J. E., & Baddeley, A. D. (1984). Assessing everyday memory after severe head injury. In J. E. Harris & P. E. Morris (Eds.), *Everyday memory actions and absent-mindedness* (pp. 191–206). New York: Academic Press.

Van der Linden, M., & Van der Kaa, M. (1989). Reorganization therapy for memory impairments. In X. Seron & G. Deloche (Eds.), *Cognitive approaches in neuropsychological rehabilitation* (pp. 105–158). Hillsdale, NJ: Erlbaum.

Wilson, B. (1992). Assessment and management of memory problems. In N. von Seinbuchel, D. Y. von Cramon, & E. Poppel (Eds.), *Neuropsychological rehabilitation* (pp. 194–202). New York: Springer-Verlag.

CHAPTER 23

Mieke Verfaellie

Neglect Syndromes

I. CLINICAL MANIFESTATIONS OF NEGLECT

Unilateral neglect is an acquired disorder that dramatically affects an individual's ability to acknowledge or respond to stimulation on the side contralateral to a lesion. A diagnosis of neglect is made only when the disorder cannot be attributed to elementary sensory or motor deficits, such as impaired acuity, clumsiness, or weakness (Heilman, Watson, & Valenstein, 1993). Neglect can be manifested in a variety of ways, and it is now generally acknowledged that different subtypes of the disorder may have their own underlying neuropathology. It may be more appropriate, therefore, to consider the neglect syndrome as representing a diverse group of disorders that have in common spatial selectivity. Patients may tend to dress only one side of their body or may fail to eat food from one side of their plate; they may read only parts of words or sentences and may have difficulty negotiating their wheelchair without bumping into obstacles. Although the acute signs of neglect may remit

Preparation of this chapter was supported by Grants NS29342 and NS26985 from the National Institute of Neurological Disorders and Stroke.

spontaneously, many patients continue to manifest signs of neglect for months or even years after onset. These manifestations can have devastating consequences for daily living and significantly affect the prognosis for functional recovery. Efficient remediation of neglect requires accurate diagnosis of its different forms and the ability to link these manifestations to underlying processing deficits.

Because in most contemporary theories of neglect, the disorder is interpreted as an attentional deficit, a useful way to classify subtypes of neglect is according to the level of processing at which attention is disrupted. A second, orthogonal classification takes into account the sector of space that is affected. Although patients may show deficits in more than one component of attention or more than one sector of space, these subtypes of neglect can occur in isolation, which suggests that they reflect processing disruptions in distinct neural systems (see Table 1 for overview).

A. Subtypes of Neglect

Sensory neglect is a failure to detect stimuli presented contralaterally to a central nervous system lesion. This deficit is not due to a sensory disturbance but rather to a disruption of the mechanisms responsible for attending to the contralateral side of space. Because attention modulates perception of incoming information, this form of neglect is also referred to as **perceptual neglect**. Sensory neglect may manifest in the following ways:

• **Unawareness of contralateral stimuli.** Patients with sensory neglect may ignore visual, tactile, or auditory stimuli presented to the contralateral side. Neglect may also be

Table 1. Varieties of Neglect

Type of neglect	Manifestations	Sectors of space
Sensory neglect	Unawareness of contralateral stimuli; allesthesia; extinction	Personal; peripersonal; far extrapersonal
Premotor neglect	Akinesia; hypokinesia; motor impersistence; motor extinction	Personal; peripersonal; far extrapersonal

present for stimuli presented in ipsilateral space, but this is generally less severe. This finding has been interpreted as evidence for the existence of an attentional gradient (Kinsbourne, 1987). This gradient can be conceptualized as an orienting bias to the most ipsilateral of several stimuli, regardless of whether stimuli are presented in both sides of space or are restricted to a single hemispace. A similar orienting bias can be seen in search tasks in which patients scan the display starting from the ipsilesional side.

- **Allesthesia.** Occasionally, stimuli are misperceived as having been presented on the ipsilateral side. This can be seen, for instance, when patients are addressed by an examiner on the contralateral side but respond by orienting to the ipsilateral side.

- **Extinction to double simultaneous stimulation.** In less severe cases, deficits may not be apparent with the presentation of single stimuli. When two stimuli are presented simultaneously, however, patients may fail to report the stimulus on the contralesional side. Extinction is most obvious when a contralateral stimulus is presented simultaneously with an ipsilateral stimulus, but it can also occur when two stimuli are presented ipsilaterally. Multimodal extinction is commonly seen during the course of recovery from neglect. Unimodal extinction, in contrast, may occur in the absence of other manifestations of neglect and may be the result of different neuropathological mechanisms. Some clinicians consider extinction to be a useful method of diagnosing neglect, but the relationship between neglect and extinction remains controversial.

Premotor neglect is a failure to respond appropriately to stimuli in the contralateral side of space in the absence of obvious weakness. This response failure is striking because it occurs despite patients' awareness of the presence of a stimulus. It can affect movement of the head and eyes as well as movements of the limbs bilaterally, but testing of the contralateral limbs is often impossible owing to the co-occurrence of hemiparesis. In the acute phase, patients may show a marked deviation of the head, eyes, and trunk to the ipsilesional side. This motor bias can also be seen during examination of eye movements, with scanning saccades restricted to the ipsilateral side of space, even though patients may be capable of making full extraocular movements to command (Halligan & Marshall, 1993).

Impairments in intention or response preparation can be manifested in a number of different ways:

- **Akinesia** is a failure to initiate movements in and toward contralateral space. This problem is often manifested as a lack of oculomotor or manual exploration in search tasks. It can also be accompanied by a directional motor bias, which is a tendency to deviate the eyes or the limbs ipsilesionally when asked to fixate or point to a target in midline.
- **Hypokinesia** refers to a delay in the initiation of contralateral movements. As a consequence, latencies in detecting a target in contralateral space are slower than corresponding latencies in ipsilateral space.
- **Motor impersistence** is a failure to sustain a movement or posture in or directed toward contralateral space. In addition to limb commands, a variety of facial movements of the eyes, mouth, and tongue can elicit impersistence.
- **Motor extinction** is a failure to move or maintain movement of the contralateral limb when the ipsilateral limb is moved simultaneously. Like sensory extinction, motor extinction often occurs during the course of recovery and represents a mild form of premotor neglect.

B. Sectors of Space

Findings from both animal and human studies (e.g., Rizzolatti & Berti, 1993) have suggested that the representation of space can be parsed into at least three distinct sectors corresponding to personal (body), close extrapersonal (also called peripersonal), and far extrapersonal space. Accordingly, neglect can differentially affect one or more of these spatial representations. Patients with **personal neglect** show attentional disturbances for the contralateral side of their body. They may fail to discriminate the position of their contralateral limb or neglect to use objects such as a comb or razor on the contralateral side of their own body. They often also have an impairment in the representation of the contralateral side of their body. For instance, when asked to identify pictures of the left or right hand seen from the palm or from the back, they perform poorly, which suggests that they are unable to match perceptual information to body representations. Patients with **peripersonal neglect** show attentional disturbances within reaching or grasping space. They may perform poorly when line bisection or search tasks are presented 30–60 cm away from their body but not when the stimuli are presented further away. The opposite pattern occurs in patients with **far extrapersonal neglect**, in whom attentional disturbances may be detected only when stimuli are presented out of reach and responses are made by means of a light pointer.

II. NEUROPATHOLOGICAL MECHANISMS UNDERLYING NEGLECT

Neglect is most commonly seen in patients with focal disease resulting from vascular insufficiency (hemorrhagic or embolic stroke), but it is occasionally seen with tumors, as an ictal manifestation in patients with seizures, and in patients with collosal lesions. Although neglect can occur following lesions of either the left or right hemisphere, its frequency of occurrence and severity are greater following right than left hemisphere lesions. Persistent right-sided neglect is extremely rare, and when present it should raise the suspicion of bilateral lesions. The association between neglect and right hemisphere lesions has led to theories of right hemispheric dominance in the mediation of different components of attention (Heilman, Bowers, Valenstein, & Watson, 1987; Mesulam, 1985).

Neglect can be caused by a variety of cortical and subcortical lesions (see Table 2), a finding in keeping with the notion that there are multiple neural circuits that mediate the distribution of attention in space (Rizzolatti & Camarda, 1987). The most common site of damage is the inferior parietal lobe, but lesions of frontal cortex, cingulate gyrus, basal ganglia, thalamus, and reticular formation may also cause neglect (Heilman et al., 1993; Vallar & Perani, 1987). Electrophysiological studies have suggested that the inferior parietal lobe is critical for directing attention to information coded in a spatial framework, whereas the frontal lobes, including the frontal eye fields, are critical for coordinating the motor programs for explo-

Table 2. Anatomic Substrates of Neglect

Anatomic substrate	Putative contribution
Parietal lobe	Orienting of attention, spatial representation
Prefrontal lobe	Motor intention
Basal ganglia	Motor control
Reticular formation, intralaminar thalamic nuclei	Arousal
Anterior cingulate	Motivation for action
Posterior cingulate	Stimulus significance

ration, scanning, and navigation in space. The contribution of the cingulate gyrus lies primarily in the evaluation of the motivational significance of stimuli, whereas the thalamus and mesencephalic reticular formation are critical for the modulation of the overall level of arousal and vigilance. In light of these findings, it has been suggested that sensory neglect results from a disruption in the parietal and limbic (posterior cingulate) components of this attentional network and that premotor neglect results from a disruption in the prefrontal, basal ganglionic, and limbic (anterior cingulate) components. Given their role in arousal, the thalamus and reticular formation are thought to be important for both sensory and premotor components of attention. In agreement with this framework, several researchers have reported premotor neglect following frontal lesions and sensory neglect following parietal lesions (e.g., Coslett, Bowers, Fitzpatrick, Haws, & Heilman, 1990; Daffner, Ahern, Weintraub, & Mesulam, 1990). Other investigators, however, have failed to find a similar pattern. This is because infarcts in the territory of the middle cerebral artery often produce extensive damage in frontal as well as parietal regions. Even in cases with restricted lesions, however, it is sometimes difficult to isolate sensory and premotor components of neglect. This may be due to limitations in the assessment techniques, but it also may reflect the tight connectivity between these two areas.

The neuroanatomic fractionation of subtypes of neglect that affect different sectors of space is much less clear. Animal studies have shown that lesions of discrete cerebral areas may cause isolated neglect for "far" or for "near" extrapersonal space (Rizzolatti & Camarda, 1987). Although similar behavioral dissociations have been obtained in humans, there has not been a clear neuroanatomic counterpart. This endeavor is complicated by the limited number of dissociated cases with sufficient neuroanatomic detail, as well as the fact that naturally occurring lesions in humans are likely to be much larger than experimentally induced lesions in animals.

III. COGNITIVE MECHANISMS UNDERLYING NEGLECT

A. Nature of the Attentional Disorder

The most commonly accepted class of theories concerning neglect are those that propose some form of attentional deficit (for reviews, see Heilman et al., 1993; Robertson & Marshall,

1993). These theories are based on the notion that each hemisphere mediates attention and response preparation (intention) in the contralateral side of space. A unilateral lesion affecting these attentional control centers thus results in a contralateral orienting deficit, with the consequence that information in the corresponding side of space is inadequately explored or does not become the focus of further processing. Cognitive theories of attention distinguish between a reflexive form of orienting that is automatically evoked by salient stimuli and an internally controlled form of orienting that is under voluntary control. Neglect is thought to be due primarily to a deficit in reflexive orienting, such that novel or significant stimuli do not automatically attract attention when they are presented in the contralesional side of space. This deficit can be overcome to some extent when cues are provided that help patients voluntarily to redirect attention. For instance, a substantial decrease in neglect may be seen when patients are cued and instructed to report a contralateral stimulus prior to performing a line-bisection task. Information inherent in an ipsilesional stimulus display may also function as an attentional cue; depending on its meaning or internal coherence, it may further guide attention to the contralateral side.

A contralateral orienting deficit disrupts the attentional balance between the two hemispheres, and consequently it also manifests itself as an orienting bias to the ipsilateral side of space. This orienting bias has also been described as **attentional capture**, or **hyperattention.** This conceptualization emphasizes the notion that the intact hemisphere may be hyperactive because it is released from inhibition (Kinsbourne, 1993). Consistent with this view patients with neglect may sometimes perform better than normal individuals when they have to detect or respond to information presented in the extreme ipsilateral side of space. More important, this view also suggests that neglect can be ameliorated when ipsilesional information is rendered less salient. Indeed, patients' performance generally improves when there are fewer distracting stimuli on the ipsilesional side, when these stimuli are erased after they are responded to, or when testing takes place in the dark.

The combination of impaired contralateral orienting and enhanced ipsilateral capture affects not only the direction of attention, but also the initiation of eye and limb movements from the ipsilesional to the contralesional side of space. Therefore, this framework can account for most of the impairments seen in patients with neglect. For instance, in tasks that require exploration of space, patients spontaneously orient to the ipsilateral side. Even though the use of strategies can help with exploration of the contralateral side, when patients move their head and eyes, progressively more information is presented in the ipsilateral space. This information will again attract attention, and consequently exploration will be stopped prematurely. A similar account can be given for the devastating effect of presenting cues ipsilaterally: Such cues strongly capture attention and thus compound the already existing difficulty patients have orienting attention to the contralateral side.

A striking feature in patients with neglect is that they ignore the contralateral side, not only of externally presented information, but also of internally generated images. For instance, in imagining the layout of their home, they may fail to describe rooms on the contralateral side. This is not due to a lack of knowledge; the deficit can be reversed when such patients mentally view their home from the opposite perspective. Findings such as these have led some theorists to suggest that neglect reflects a representational deficit, that is, an inability to construct the contralateral side of mental representations (Bisiach, 1993). Such a view need not be seen as contradicting an attentional viewpoint, however, because attentional networks are critical in the creation and scanning of internal representations.

An attentional interpretation also can explain why some perceptual and even meaning-based processes remain preserved in the face of severe neglect. At a perceptual level, the visual field is rapidly parsed on the basis of primitive features such as colors, shape, and orientation to define regions of interest for subsequent analysis. This early level of analysis, which includes processes for figure–ground segregation and symmetry analysis, occurs preattentively and is largely intact in patients with neglect. Likewise, activation of meaning-based representations may occur automatically and preattentively, a finding that may account for a variety of recent reports of preserved processing of "neglected" information (e.g., McGlinchey-Berroth, Milberg, Verfaellie, Alexander, & Kilduff, 1993).

B. Spatial Coordinates of Attention

An important issue in understanding hemispatial neglect concerns what marks the division between the "good" and the "neglected" side of space. Clinical evidence demonstrates that hemispace is not rigidly defined by an absolute egocentric midline. Each patient has his or her own attentional boundary that may vary according to the method of testing, and this boundary not uncommonly extends into the ispilateral side of space. To understand this finding it is important to realize that hemispace is a dynamic construct that is defined not only by the position of the trunk, but also by the position of the head and eyes. Thus, as the head and eyes move, the right and left hemispace move accordingly. As a consequence, neglect commonly affects the side contralateral to a viewer's focus of attention. When attention operates on a global spatial array, the contralateral side of the array is ignored; when attention operates within segregated figures, the contralateral side of each figure may be ignored, because the spatial framework is now successively centered on each figure. Although different in their attentional focus, these forms of neglect are similar in that the spatial framework in which attention operates is defined by the position of the viewer in space, hence the term **viewer-centered neglect.**

In some instances, however, the contralateral side of an object can be dissociated from the contralateral side of space, such as when an object is rotated by 90 degrees. Under such conditions, patients may still neglect the contralateral side of the object as defined by its principal axis or its intrinsic orientation, even though in terms of the viewer, this information is presented ipsilaterally from other information that is appropriately attended. This phenomenon has been termed **object-centered neglect** to indicate that spatial coordinates intrinsic to an object can form the frame of reference within which attention operates. Under most ordinary circumstances, the object-centered and viewer-centered frames of reference coincide with each other, because objects are usually presented in their upright position. Methods aimed at disentangling these frames of reference, however, have demonstrated that some patients neglect primarily the contralateral side of space, whereas others neglect primarily the contralateral side of objects they encounter.

IV. DIFFERENTIAL DIAGNOSIS

To allow a definitive diagnosis of neglect, it is crucial to rule out primary sensory disorders such as hemianesthesia or hemianopia as the cause of a patient's behavioral deficits. In contrast to attentional deficits, primary sensory deficits are not ameliorated by attentional cues or by conditions that limit the number of distracting stimuli. Thus, patients with hemianopia fail to identify stimuli in the contralateral field even when tested in the dark, without conflicting stimuli. Although this might be considered a more severe problem than neglect, these patients do better in everyday life because they compensate by means of eye movements and generally fully explore the visual field. Consequently, they typically perform better on search and cancellation tasks than patients with neglect.

Despite these behavioral differences, it is often difficult to distinguish between neglect and primary sensory deficits without accurate knowledge of lesion localization. Following are a number of findings that can help in making the differential diagnosis:

Unilateral hearing loss does not occur following unilateral lesions because the auditory pathways from the ear to the primary auditory cortex are bilateral. A failure to report or orient to contralateral auditory stimuli, therefore, must necessarily be due to inattention.

Visual field cuts are not affected by the position of the eyes in space, whereas attentional deficits are. Therefore, if patients are unable to detect contralateral stimuli when they are looking straight ahead, but they are able to do so when their gaze is directed to the ipsilateral hemispace (placing the contralateral visual field in the ipsilateral head and body hemispace), this points to an attentional deficit. Likewise, when the position of a patient's limb in space affects detection of somatosensory stimuli, inattention rather than a primary sensory defect can be inferred.

Patients with neglect show **normal sensory evoked potentials** (up to P25) to visual and somatosensory stimuli contralateral to their lesion, whereas patients with primary somatosensory or visual loss do not.

Many patients who have neglect, as evidenced by auditory inattention or by the fact that they continue to be inattentive when allowed to move their eyes or head freely, are also diagnosed as having hemianopia. Although these deficits can co-occur, the diagnosis of hemianopia is probably not justified in many instances, because the formal evaluation of the visual fields is biased toward showing defects in patients with neglect. In standard visual field testing, patients are asked to maintain fixation on a central fixation cross while stimuli are briefly presented in different parts of the visual field. When patients fail to report stimuli presented in the contralesional visual field, a visual field defect is inferred. However, because these presentation conditions in effect represent conditions of double simultaneous stimulation, these findings are likely due to extinction rather than to a primary sensory deficit. To avoid this con-

Exhibit 1. Evaluation of Neglect

Neglect rather than primary sensory deficit:
Auditory inattention
Effects of position of the eye or limb in space
Normal sensory evoked potentials

Bedside evaluation:
Extrapersonal neglect
    Single stimulation: verbal and nonverbal responses,
       crossed responses
    Double simultaneous stimulation
Personal neglect
    Orienting to contralateral body parts
    Movement to contralateral body parts
    Matching body parts to external representations

Tests of spatial neglect:
Cancellation
Line bisection
Drawing
Reading and writing

founding influence, alternative perimetry procedures are needed in which the lateralized stimuli are presented asynchronously with a central fixation cross (see, e.g., Walker, Findlay, Young, & Welch, 1991).

V. ASSESSMENT OF NEGLECT DISORDERS

In many cases of acute neglect, observation of spontaneous behavior when the patient is interacting with an examiner, handling objects in the environment, or using a wheelchair may reveal the presence of contralateral orienting deficits. Simple bedside testing may allow the examiner to specify more clearly the nature of the disorder. In milder cases, deficits may be detected only with more taxing cognitive tasks. Regardless of severity, however, a thorough assessment of different manifestations of neglect is necessary for an adequate understanding of the nature of a patient's deficits (see Exhibit 1).

Before the discussion of common assessment techniques is begun, a comment should be made regarding the variability often seen in patients' performance. Patients with neglect may perform well on some tasks and poorly on others because the tasks are sensitive to different components of neglect (e.g., disorders of attention vs. intention). It is the pattern of performance across different tasks that commonly leads to the diagnosis of a particular subtype of neglect. However, patients may also show high variability in their performance on a single task across repeated observations (or on different tasks thought to measure the same component of neglect). Such variability may be due to fluctuations in a patient's general arousal state, distractibility, or fatigue. Performance is also commonly influenced by the attentional load of a task, with patients performing more poorly as the attentional demands of a task increase (Rapscak, Fleet, Verfaellie, & Heilman, 1989). Finally, stimuli in the environment that function as distractors or as spatial cues may affect performance and should be avoided as much as possible. For this reason, testing should take place in a quiet room with the examiner positioned in front of (or behind) the patient to avoid lateral orienting biases.

A. Bedside Examination

1. EXTRA-PERSONAL NEGLECT

An elementary examination consists of presentation of auditory, visual, or tactile stimuli to the ipsilateral and contralateral side in random order and asking patients to respond to these stimuli. Responses can be made verbally, by means of pointing, or by means of head or eye movements to the side of the stimulation. Patients with neglect may fail to respond to contralateral stimuli in one or more modalities. To disentangle the input (attention) from output (intention) components of neglect, a crossed response task can be used (Watson, Miller, & Heilman, 1978). In this task, patients are asked to respond with the right extremity when stimulated on the left side and with the left extremity when stimulated on the right side. If patients fail to respond to contralateral stimuli (with the ipsilateral extremity), an attentional deficit can be inferred. If they fail to respond to ipsilateral stimuli (with the contralateral extremity), an intentional deficit can be inferred. A similar approach can be used to test the head or eyes by having patients move away from the side of stimulation.

Following testing for unilateral neglect, patients should also be tested for extinction by intermixing unilateral trials with trials on which two stimuli are presented simultaneously to homologous areas of space. This testing also can be done in different sensory modalities. In the visual modality, patients are asked to fixate their gaze centrally, but one should note spontaneous gaze attraction to the ipsilateral side, which may occur when the examiner raises his or her hands to present the stimuli.

2. PERSONAL NEGLECT

Different commands that require orienting to or awareness of contralateral body parts can be used to test for personal neglect. For instance, patients can be asked to touch their contralateral side with the ipsilateral extremity. Patients with neglect may interrupt their movement before the target is reached or may fail to initiate a movement to the contralateral limb. Another task consists of asking patients to match parts of their body with external representations, for example, to touch on their own body the body part pointed out on a model or to point to a body part on a model when it is touched on their own body.

B. Standardized Assessment Techniques

Most standardized tests of neglect consist of visual tasks performed in peripersonal space, but several can be easily adapted to the tactile modality or can also be performed in far extrapersonal space. Despite the surface similarity among many tasks, several investigators (e.g., McGlinchey-Berroth et al., 1996) have suggested that these tasks tap more than a single neuropsychological construct, with line-bisection and cancellation tasks, in particular, showing low correlations in performance. For this reason, a broad-based assessment is needed.

1. CANCELLATION TASKS

There are a variety of tasks that require patients to mark or cross out items presented in an array. These tests are commonly scored in terms of the number of omissions, but they also provide valuable information regarding a patient's search strategy. They vary in difficulty from simple tests in which patients are asked to cancel all items, such as Albert's (1973) Line Cancellation task, to more demanding ones in which patients have to find targets embedded in a dense field of distractors, such as the Bells Test (Gauthier, Dehaut, & Jeanette, 1989). Two tests on which normal individuals rarely make errors and that are highly sensitive to the presence of neglect are the Starr Cancellation test (Wilson, Cockburn, & Halligan, 1987) and Mesulam's Verbal and Nonverbal Cancellation tests.

Contralateral omissions in a cancellation task can be due either to an attentional failure causing imperception of the contralateral side or to an intentional failure causing a reluctance to move to the contralateral side. Consequently, several investigators have tried to disentangle these components by decoupling the direction of movement and the direction of attention so that the patient has to move his or her hand to the left to initiate a movement to the right. This can be done relatively easily by presenting the test on an overhead projector, because this arrangement mirror-reverses the display of visual information (Nico, 1996). Patients cancel the targets on a transparency presented on the overhead projector, but direct view of the transparency is prevented so that the stimuli can be seen only displayed on the opposing wall. If a patient with left neglect on a standard cancellation task omits stimuli on the right side of the transparency, an attentional deficit is inferred because the omitted information is displayed on the left side on the opposing wall. If the same patient omits stimuli on the left side of the transparency, an intentional deficit is inferred, because the patient can see this information displayed on the right but fails to move to the left to cancel the stimuli.

2. LINE BISECTION

In this task, patients are asked to cut lines in half by placing a mark in the center of each line. Normal individuals tend to mark lines quite accurately, with small deviations (on the order of 1–2 mm) occurring to the left of center. Patients with neglect, on the other hand, often demonstrate much larger deviations to the ipsilateral side. In both normal individuals and patients with neglect, deviations from center increase with increasing line length. The position of the line in space also systematically affects the performance of patients with neglect, with performance in ipsilateral space more accurate than that in midline or contralateral space. A version of the test developed by Schenkenberg, Bradford, and Ajax (1980) incorporates the features of both line length and line position.

To disentangle sensory from premotor neglect, similar arrangements can be used to those in the cancellation tasks. An alternative technique (Milner, Harvey, Roberts, & Forster, 1993) is to present patients with lines that are pretransected at the midline and to ask them to point to the end of the line closer to the transection mark. Patients who have sensory neglect point to the contralateral end of the line, because the contralateral extent of the line is perceived as being shorter. However, patients who have premotor neglect point to the ipsilateral end of the line, because there is a reluctance to move to the contralateral side.

3. DRAWING

Spatial neglect can be assessed by asking patients to copy or draw spontaneously simple symmetrical figures (e.g., a cross) or figures that contain equally important details bilaterally (e.g., a flower). Patients with right hemisphere lesions frequently have visuoconstructional deficits that affect their drawings. A test that is less affected by visuoconstructional deficits is the Clock-Drawing Test, in which patients are asked to place numbers on a clock. It should be noted, however, that verbal intelligence may compensate for neglect on this test. Another way to disentangle visuoconstructional from attentional deficits is to compare patients' standard figure copy with a "hidden figure copy" (McGlinchey-Berroth et al., 1996). Here, patients are asked to copy onto a piece of carbon paper placed over a blank sheet of paper using a stylus rather than a pencil. This arrangement does not produce a visible result to the patient, but it does produce a drawing on the underside of the blank sheet of paper that is exposed to the carbon paper, thus allowing the drawing to be evaluated later. In this condition, copy performance is not affected by the appearance of increasing amounts of ipsilateral information by which attention may be captured. Consequently, patients with neglect often perform much better in this condition. Visuoconstructional deficits, on the other hand, are not ameliorated by this manipulation.

4. READING AND WRITING

Assessment of reading should include both single words and compound words as well as paragraph-length passages that require scanning across the entire page. Two useful reading tests are part of the Behavioral Inattention Battery (Wilson et al., 1987): Menu Reading, in which 10 food items, one or two words long, are presented for reading in two columns, and Article Reading, in which two paragraphs are presented in a columnar arrangement, similar to a newspaper article. In evaluating writing, attention should be paid to the use of the space on a page. Typing on a keyboard may also elicit neglect, as patients may fail to use the keys on the contralesional side.

In patients with right hemisphere lesions, a number of disorders may co-occur with neglect. Whether these disorders are functionally related or are theoretically independent currently remains controversial. The most commonly associated deficits follow.

VI. ASSOCIATED DISORDERS

A. Anosognosia

Neglect can be associated with denial of illness. Patients may explicitly deny their hemiparesis or sensory loss, or they may avoid responding to questions that make reference to their impairments. Occasionally, patients have delusions that their affected limb belongs to someone else or does not exist. These phenomena are most often seen during the acute phase of illness, when patients may also exhibit confusional behavior.

B. Anosodiaphoria

Although patients with neglect usually acknowledge their illness, they may appear unconcerned about it or may even joke about their disabilities.

C. Other Visuospatial Deficits

Patients with right hemisphere lesions often have deficits in the processing of global information and, consequently, show a bias toward processing of local objects. In contrast, patients with left hemisphere lesions have difficulty processing local information and, consequently, show a bias toward processing global scenes. These visuospatial deficits may exacerbate neglect, especially in patients with right hemisphere lesions. Typically, a visual display contains more local than global information. Because patients with right hemisphere lesions are biased toward local information, it becomes even more difficult for them to move their attention away from local objects in ipsilesional space.

VII. CONCLUSION

Neglect refers to a class of disorders in which patients fail to attend or respond to stimuli presented in the contralateral part of space. Attentional disturbances can affect the processing of incoming information (sensory neglect) as well as responses to these stimuli (premotor neglect), and it can selectively affect one or more sectors of space. Because there are multiple neural circuits that mediate the distribution of attention in space, neglect can be caused by a variety of lesions, although right hemisphere parietal and frontal lesions predominate. In diagnosing the disorder, care should be taken to rule out sensory disorders as the cause of a patient's deficits. Bedside evaluation in the acute phase and standardized testing once a patient's condition has stabilized are required to document adequately the nature and severity of the disorder and to devise an appropriate management and rehabilitation plan.

BIBLIOGRAPHY

Albert, M. L. (1973). A simple test of visual neglect. *Neurology, 23*, 658–664.

Bisiach, E. (1993). The twentieth Bartlett Memorial Lecture: Mental representation in unilateral neglect and related disorders. *Quarterly Journal of Experimental Psychology, 46A*, 435–461.

Coslett, H. B., Bowers, D., Fitzpatrick, E., Haws, B., & Heilman, K. M. (1990). Dissociated neglect hypokinesia and hemispatial inattention in neglect. *Brain, 113*, 475–486.

Daffner, K. R., Ahern, G. L., Weintraub, S., & Mesulam, M. M. (1990). Dissociated neglect behaviour following sequential strokes in the right hemisphere. *Annals of Neurology, 28*, 97–101.

Gauthier, L., Dehaut, F., & Joanette, Y. (1989). The Bells Test: A quantitative and qualitative test for visual neglect. *International Journal of Clinical Neuropsychology, 11*, 49–54.

Halligan, P. W., & Marshall, J. C. (1993). The history and clinical presentation of neglect. In I. H. Robertson & J. C. Marshall (Eds.), *Unilateral neglect: Clinical and experimental studies* (pp. 3–25). Hillsdale, NJ: Erlbaum.

Heilman, K. M., Bowers, D., Valenstein, E., & Watson, R. T. (1987). Hemispace and hemispatial neglect. In M. Jeannerod (Ed.), *Neurophysiological and neuropsychological aspects of spatial neglect* (pp. 115–150). New York: North-Holland.

Heilman, K., Watson, R., & Valenstein, E. (1993). Neglect and related disorders. In K. Heilman & E. Valenstein (Eds.), *Clinical neuropsychology (3rd ed.*, pp. 279–336). New York: Oxford University Press.

Kinsbourne, M. (1993). Orientational bias model of unilateral neglect: Evidence from attentional gradients within hemispace. Mechanisms of unilateral neglect. In I. H. Robertson & J. C. Marshall (Eds.), *Unilateral neglect: Clinical and experimental studies* (pp. 63–86). Hillsdale, NJ: Erlbaum.

McGlinchey-Berroth, R., Bullis, D. P., Milberg, W. P., Verfaellie, M., Alexander, M., & D'Esposito, M. (1996). Assessment of neglect reveals dissociable behavioral but not neuroanatomical subtypes. *Journal of the International Neuropsychological Society, 2*, 441–451.

McGlinchey-Berroth, R., Milberg, W., Verfaellie, M., Alexander, M., & Kilduff, P. (1993). Semantic processing in the neglected field: Evidence from a lexical decision task. *Cognitive Neuropsychology, 10*, 79–108.

Mesulam, M. M. (1985). Attention, confusional states and neglect. In M. M. Mesulam (Ed.), *Principles of behavioral neurology* (pp. 125–168). Philadelphia: Davis.

Milner, A. D., Harvey, M., Roberts, R. C., & Forster, S. V. (1993). Line bisection errors in visual neglect: Misguided action or size distortion? *Neuropsychologia, 31*, 39–49.

Nico, D. (1996). Detecting directional hypokinesia: The epidiascope technique. *Neuropsychologia, 34*, 471–474.

Rapscak, S. Z., Fleet, W. S., Verfaellie, M., & Heilman, K. M. (1989). Selective attention in hemispatial neglect. *Archives of Neurology, 46*, 178–182.

Rizzolatti, G., & Berti, A. (1993). Neural mechanisms of spatial neglect. In I. H. Robertson & J. C. Marshall (Eds.), *Unilateral neglect: Clinical and experimental studies*, (pp. 87–105). Hillsdale, NJ: Erlbaum.

Rizzolatti, G., & Camarda, R. (1987). Neural circuits for spatial attention and unilateral neglect. In M. Jeannerod (Ed.), *Neurophysiological and neuropsychological aspects of spatial neglect* (pp. 289–313). Amsterdam: North-Holland.

Robertson, I. H., & Marshall, J. C. (1993). *Unilateral neglect: Clinical and experimental studies*. Hillsdale, NJ: Erlbaum.

Schenkenberg, T., Bradford, D. C., & Ajax, E. T. (1980). Line bisection and unilateral visual neglect in patients with neurologic impairment. *Neurology, 30*, 509–517.

Vallar, G., & Perani, D. (1987). The anatomy of spatial neglect in humans. In M. Jeannerod (Ed.), *Neurophysiological and neuropsychological aspects of spatial neglect* (pp. 235–258). New York: North-Holland.

Walker, R., Findlay, J. M., Young, A. W., & Welch, J. (1991). Disentangling neglect and hemianopia. *Neuropsychologia, 29*, 1019–1027.

Watson, R. T., Miller, B. D., & Heilman, K. M. (1978). Nonsensory neglect. *Annals of Neurology, 3*, 505–508.

Wilson, B., Cockburn, J., & Halligan, P. (1987). *Behavioral Inattention Test*. Titchfield, England: Thames Valley Test Company.

CHAPTER 24

Russell M. Bauer and Sarah R. Kortenkamp

The Agnosias

The **agnosias** are a relatively rare set of disorders in which a patient with brain damage becomes unable to recognize or appreciate the nature of sensory stimuli. Clinical examination of the patient reveals a profound, modality-specific recognition impairment that cannot be fully explained by problems in elementary sensory processing, mental deterioration, attentional disturbances, aphasic misnaming, or unfamiliarity with the stimuli used to assess recognition abilities. Classically, a distinction between **apperceptive** and **associative** forms of agnosia has been made whereby the patient with **apperceptive** agnosia is said to have deficits in early stages of perceptual processing, whereas the patient with **associative** agnosia either does not display such problems or does so to a degree not sufficient to impair substantially the ability to perform perceptual operations. Clinically, the associative agnosic typically can draw, copy, or match unidentified objects, whereas the apperceptive agnosic cannot. This distinction has been clinically useful, although it is a complicated distinction, and it should be remembered that adequate copying or matching by itself does not indicate normal perceptual processing (see Bauer, 1993; Farah, 1990).

Clinical assessment of the putative agnosic patient requires performance of two specific tasks. First, the possibility that the recognition disturbance exists because of elementary sensory disturbance, dementia, aphasia, or unfamiliarity with the stimulus should be ruled out with standardized neuropsychological testing instruments. Second, the scope and nature of the patient's recognition disturbance should be determined. Does the recognition disturbance exist only for certain stimuli or classes of stimuli? Is it restricted to a particular sensory modality? Under what conditions can the patient recognize stimuli? This phase of the evaluation often requires detailed testing using specially formulated testing materials, and it should be conducted from the point of view of cognitive models of recognition disturbance. Appropriate referrals for neurological, neuroradiological, and basic sensory–perceptual (e.g., ophthalmologic, audiological) testing are also critical in formulating a diagnosis at the initial stages of case formulation.

I. BASIC DEFINITIONS

Several types of agnosia have been identified in the literature. The basic subtypes, clinicoanatomic correlations, and neurobehavioral mechanisms producing disturbances in recognition are summarized by Bauer (1993) and Farah (1990). Humphreys and Riddoch (1987) have provided an excellent book-length description of a visual agnosic written from a cognitive neuropsychology perspective. "Pure" forms of these disorders are quite rare, and the etiology of the patient's disorder (e.g., focal stroke or a more diffuse condition such as carbon monoxide poisoning) and the stage of recovery (if acute onset) together determine the observed pattern of deficits. Defining characteristics of the basic subtypes of agnosia are given in the following outline and in Table 1. The outline method of presentation is intended to stimulate attempts at differential diagnosis, but it should not discourage attempts at more in-depth analysis of presenting syndromes.

A. Visual Agnosias

1. VISUAL OBJECT AGNOSIA

a. Key features

1. Patient cannot recognize the meaning of visually presented objects.

2. Disorder is not restricted to naming (e.g., patient cannot point to the object when named or describe or demonstrate its use).

Table 1. Subtypes of Agnosia: Defining Characteristics and Key References

Subtype	Affected stimulus category	Varieties	Basis for distinction	Suggested reference
Visual agnosias				Farah, 1990
Visual object agnosia	Objects	a. Apperceptive	a. Drawing, matching –	Benson & Greenberg, 1969
		b. Associative	b. Drawing, matching +	Rubens & Benson, 1971
Simultanagnosia	Multiple objects or pictures	a. Dorsal	a. Cannot see multiple items	Hecaen & Ajuriaguerra, 1954
		b. Ventral	b. Can see multiple items	Kinsbourne & Warrington, 1962
Prosopagnosia	Faces	a. Apperceptive	a. Match, categorize faces –	DeRenzi et al., 1991
		b. Associative	b. Match, categorize faces +	Pallis, 1955
Color agnosia	Colors	a. Achromatopsia	a. Failure of color vision	Damasio et al., 1980
		b. Color anomia	b. Can succeed at nonverbal color tasks	Geschwind & Fusillo, 1966
		c. Color aphasia	c. Disproportionate deficit with color names	Kinsbourne & Warrington, 1964
Auditory agnosias				Vignolo, 1969
Cortical deafness and cortical auditory disorder	All sounds	a. Cortical deafness	a. Subjective deafness?	Michel et al., 1980
		b. Agnosia	b. Patient claims not to be deaf	Kanshepolsky et al., 1973
Pure word deafness	Speech sounds	a. Prephonemic	a. Auditory acuity generally impaired	Buchman et al., 1986
		b. Phonemic	b. Disorder of phonemic discrimination	

(Continued)

Table 1. Subtypes of Agnosia: Defining Characteristics and Key References *(Continued)*

Subtype	Affected stimulus category	Varieties	Basis for distinction	Suggested reference
Nonverbal auditory agnosia	Nonspeech sounds	a. Perceptual b. Associative	a. Misidentifications primarily acoustic b. Misidentifications primarily semantic	Spreen et al., 1965
Sensory (receptive) amusia	Musical sounds			Bauer & Zawacki, 1996
Tactile agnosias				
Cortical tactile disorders	Tactually presented objects and object qualities	a. Object based?[a] b. Spatial?[a]	a. Fail on object discrimination tasks b. Fail on tasks requiring spatial discrimination	Delay, 1935 Caselli, 1991 Corkin, 1978 Semmes, 1965
Tactile agnosia	Tactually presented objects	a. Disconnection b. Agnosic	a. Unilateral; can demonstrate object use b. Bimanual; cannot demonstrate object knowledge	Geschwind & Kaplan, 1962 Hecaen & David, 1945

Note. + = function is spared; – = function is impaired.
[a]Question marks signify that the varieties are meant to be suggestive, as little data exists.

3. Recognition sometimes is better for real objects than for pictures or line drawings.

4. Patient can recognize objects when presented in other modalities.

b. Varieties

1. ***Apperceptive.*** Patient cannot demonstrate adequate perception of objects through drawing, copying, or matching tasks.

2. ***Associative.*** Drawing, copying, or matching tasks bring more success, although performance is sometimes "slavish."

c. Recognition disturbance may be worse for certain categories of objects (e.g., living things, tools); recognition testing should employ various categories of objects.

2. SIMULTANAGNOSIA

a. Key features

Patient cannot apprehend the overall meaning of a picture or stimulus but may be able to appreciate and describe isolated elements.

b. Varieties

1. "Dorsal" simultanagnosia (bilateral occipitoparietal lesions); patient cannot see more than one object at a time.

2. "Ventral" simultanagnosia (left inferior occipital lesions); patient may be able to "see" more than one object at a time.

3. Often considered a variant of apperceptive agnosia.

3. PROSOPAGNOSIA

a. Key features

1. Patient is unable to recognize the identity of viewed faces.

2. Patient often can appreciate aspects of faces such as age, gender, or emotional expression.

b. Varieties

Apperceptive and associative forms have been identified on the basis of matching tasks.

c. Associated features

Within-class recognition of other types of visually similar objects (e.g., recognition of individual chairs, cars, or animals) may be impaired.

4. COLOR AGNOSIA

Because colors can only be appreciated visually, the status of color agnosia as a true agnosic deficit has been difficult to establish. Nonetheless, three classes of patients have been identified with disproportional impairment in recognizing, naming, or otherwise using color information.

a. Central achromatopsia

Acquired deficit in color vision owing to central nervous system (CNS) disease. Patient cannot match, discriminate, or name colors. Suspect bilateral occipital lesion, although lesions may be unilateral.

b. Color anomia

Specific difficulty in naming colors, usually found in the context of right homonymous hemianopia and pure alexia (Geschwind, 1965). Other aphasic signs are generally absent; suspect posterior left hemisphere lesion.

c. Specific color aphasia

Seen in the context of aphasia; represents a disproportionate difficulty in naming colors; suspect left (dominant) parietal lobe damage.

5. OPTIC APHASIA

a. Key features

1. Patient cannot name a visually presented object.

2. Patient can demonstrate its use by gesture or can point to it when named (variable).

b. Condition is not regarded as a true agnosia.

c. It may represent a visual–verbal disconnection.

B. Auditory Agnosias

Subtypes of auditory agnosia have been distinguished on the basis of the type of auditory stimulus the patient has difficulty recognizing. Although much remains to be understood about these disorders, which have not been studied as exhaustively as have cases of visual agnosia, three general classes of deficits have been described.

1. CORTICAL AUDITORY DISORDER AND CORTICAL DEAFNESS

a. Key features

1. Patient has difficulty recognizing auditory stimuli of many kinds, verbal and nonverbal.

2. Basic audiological testing results are abnormal.

b. Varieties

1. *Cortical deafness.* Patient complains of a subjective sense of deafness.

2. *Cortical auditory disorder.* There is no subjective sense of deafness.

c. Condition may evolve to one of the more selective types of auditory agnosia described in the following section; longitudinal assessment is important.

2. PURE WORD DEAFNESS

a. Key features

1. Inability to comprehend spoken language, but patient can read, write, and speak in a relatively normal manner.

2. Comprehension of nonverbal sounds is relatively spared.

3. Patient is relatively free of aphasic symptoms found with other disorders affecting language comprehension (Buchman, Garron, Trost-Cardamone, Wichter, & Schwartz, 1986).

3. AUDITORY SOUND AGNOSIA (AUDITORY AGNOSIA FOR NONSPEECH SOUNDS)

a. Key features

1. Inability to comprehend meaning of common environmental sounds, with relative sparing of speech comprehension.

2. Condition is far rarer than pure word deafness.

b. Varieties (Vignolo, 1969)

1. *Perceptual–discriminative form.* Patient makes predominantly acoustic errors (e.g., "whistling" for birdsong).

2. *Semantic–associative form.* Patient makes predominantly semantic errors (e.g., "train" for automobile engine).

4. SENSORY (RECEPTIVE) AMUSIA

a. Key features

1. Inability to appreciate various characteristics of heard music.

2. Impairment in perceptual versus conceptual aspects of music should be evaluated.

b. Impaired music perception occurs to some extent in all cases of auditory sound agnosia and in most cases of aphasia and pure word deafness; the exact prevalence is unknown.

c. Condition is probably underreported because a specific musical disorder rarely interferes with everyday life.

d. Perception of pitch, harmony, timbre, intensity, and rhythm may be affected to different degrees or in various combinations.

C. Tactile Agnosias

Compared with visual agnosias, somatosensory (tactile) agnosias have received scant attention and are poorly understood. Several distinct disorders have been identified, and many classifications of tactile agnosia have been offered. Delay (1935) distinguished three disorders, including (a) **amorphognosia**, the impaired recognition of the size and shape of objects; (b) **ahylognosia,** the impaired recognition of the distinctive qualities of objects such as weight, density, texture, and thermal properties; and (c) **tactile asymbolia**, the impaired recognition of tactile objects in the absence of amorphognosia and ahylognosia. Although it is only tentative, a clinically useful distinction can be made between "cortical tactile disorders," which probably encompass the first two of Delay's deficit classes, and "tactile agnosia," which represents an inability to appreciate the nature of tactually manipulated objects.

1. CORTICAL TACTILE DISORDERS

a. Key features

Deficits are in appreciating distinct object qualities such as size, shape, weight, or spatial configuration of tactually presented objects.

b. Varieties

Some patients have especially obvious defects of size discrimination, whereas others fail in tasks that emphasize the spatial character of tactually manipulated objects.

c. No hemispheric specialization exists in elementary somatosensory function, but patients with right hemisphere disease may have difficulty in performing the spatial component of many tactile discrimination tasks.

2. TACTILE AGNOSIA

a. Key features

1. Patient cannot identify objects placed in the hand.
2. Elementary sensory function is intact.

b. Varieties

1. *Deficit exists in both hands.* An "agnosic" deficit (an inability to appreciate the nature of stimuli because of a central defect in processing the nature of a stimulus); patient cannot demonstrate use of object through gesture.

2. *Deficit exists in one (usually left) hand.* A "visual–verbal disconnection"; patient can demonstrate use of the object and can name the object if it is placed in the other hand.

II. NEUROANATOMIC CORRELATES

Lesion localization on the basis of individual case studies and recent reviews of the agnosic syndromes described previously is presented in Table 2. In general, apperceptive agnosias involve more extensive damage to sensory association cortex, whereas

Table 2. Lesion Localization for Various Forms of Agnosia

Disorder	Lesion localization	Reference
Visual agnosias		
1. Apperceptive visual object agnosia	Diffuse, posterior damage to occipital lobes and surrounding regions	Benson & Greenberg, 1969
2. Associative visual object agnosia	Bilateral; inferior occipitotemporal	Rubens & Benson, 1971
3. Simultanagnosia		
a. Dorsal	Bilateral parietal and superior occipital	Farah, 1990
	Localized bilaterally to either superior occipital or inferior parietal lobes	Hecaen & Ajuriaguerra, 1954
b. Ventral	Dominant occipitotemporal junction	Kinsbourne & Warrington, 1962
4. Prosopagnosia		
a. Apperceptive	Traditionally seen as bilateral in all or nearly all cases; cortex and white matter in occipitotemporal gyrus or projection system	Bauer, 1993
	More recently, a few cases of apparently unilateral damage to right visual association cortices within occipital and parietal lobes	Damasio et al., 1990 DeRenzi, 1986
b. Associative	Bilateral anterior temporal regions compromising hippocampal and other regions	Damasio et al., 1990

(Continued)

Table 2. Lesion Localization for Various Forms of Agnosia *(Continued)*

Disorder	Lesion localization	Reference
5. Color agnosia		
a. Achromatopsia	Unilateral or bilateral inferior ventromedial region of occipital lobe—involves lingual and fusiform gyri—superior field defects	Damasio et al., 1980
b. Color anomia	Dominant occipital infarction with corpus callosum involvement	Geschwind & Fusillo, 1966
c. Specific color aphasia	Dominant parietal damage coincident with posterior aphasia	Kinsbourne & Warrington, 1964
6. Optic aphasia	Unilateral; dominant occipital lobe and splenium	Riddoch & Humphreys, 1987 Geschwind, 1965
Auditory agnosias		
1. Cortical auditory disorder	Variable; can involve superior temporal gyrus and efferent connections of Heschl's gyrus or bilateral subcortical lesions	Kazui et al., 1990 Oppenheimer & Newcombe, 1978
2. Pure word deafness	Bilateral; symmetrical lesions of anterior section of superior temporal gyri; most often bilateral disconnections of Wernicke's area from auditory input	Buchman et al., 1986
	Unilateral (rare); deep subcortical in dominant superior temporal region damaging primarily auditory cortex or pathways to and from medial geniculate gyrus or both	Weisenburg & McBride, 1935/1964

3. Auditory sound agnosia		
a. Perceptual–discrimination type	Nondominant hemisphere	Vignolo, 1969
b. Semantic–associative type	Dominant hemisphere—linked with posterior aphasia	Vignolo, 1969
4. Sensory (receptive) amusia	Unilateral temporal lobe—if comorbid with aphasia, lesion is on dominant side	Bauer & Zawacki, 1996
Tactile agnosias		
1. Cortical tactile disorders	Severe and long lasting—contralateral postcentral gyrus. Less severe—bilateral lesions of secondary somatosensory area	Corkin, 1978
2. Unilateral tactile anomia	Corpus callosum (affecting crossing somatosensory fibers minimally; actual lesion may be more extensive)	Geschwind & Kaplan, 1962
3. Tactile agnosia	Contralateral primary somatosensory projection area in postcentral gyrus	Caselli, 1991

associative agnosias result from lesions of corticocortical pathways or from impairment in areas where semantic representations of objects are stored. In most published cases, lesions are reported to be caused by ischemic stroke, although cases of carbon monoxide poisoning, posttraumatic hematoma, and neoplasm have been reported (Bauer, 1993; Farah, 1990). It is becoming increasingly recognized (most prominently in the visual domain) that apperceptive agnosia can result from degenerative disease, with particular attention being devoted to dementia syndromes presenting with predominant visuoperceptual disturbance (Mendez, Mendez, Martin, Smyth, & Whitehouse, 1990).

III. DIFFERENTIAL DIAGNOSIS OF AGNOSIA

A. Basic Decision-Making Process in Differential Diagnosis

Diagnosis of the agnosias begins with identification of the basic characteristics of the patient's recognition defect. The process of reaching a tentative initial diagnosis is outlined in flowchart form in Figure 1. In applying the flowchart, clinicians should remember that "pure" forms of agnosia are not particularly common. The first part of the flowchart (Figure 1A) presents three "streams" representing visual, auditory, and tactile agnosias, respectively, and outlines basic questions that should be asked in making a tentative initial diagnosis. The second part of the flowchart (Figure 1B) deals specifically with visual agnosias, which are more common and better understood than their auditory and tactile counterparts.

The flowchart assumes that simple materials for bedside testing are available (or can be manufactured) and that the clinician consults professionals from other disciplines to document further the extent of neuroanatomic damage and to characterize the status of the patient's sensory–perceptual function. In many cases, such referrals are made by the physician or the treatment team, but the informed neuropsychologist can serve as an advisor in ensuring that appropriate referrals are made. In addition to an extended behaviorally oriented neurological examination, it is potentially useful to include neuroimaging consultations (CT and MRI), evoked potential studies, and referrals to professionals in ophthalmology, speech pathology–audiology, or other fields for more detailed evaluation of sensory–perceptual status. Of course, referral decisions should not be made in "knee-jerk" fashion but should depend on the likely cost-effectiveness of obtaining the requested information.

Figure 1A. Flowchart for Clinical Decision Making for the Agnosias: Differential Diagnosis of Agnosia

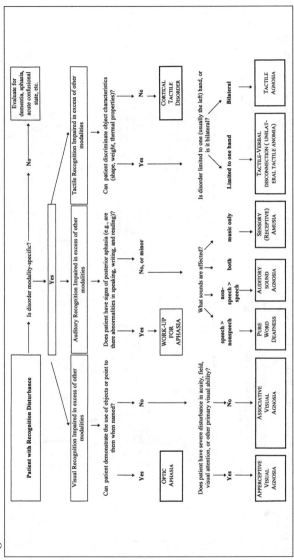

Figure 1B. Flowchart for Clinical Decision Making for the Agnosias: Differential Diagnosis of Visual Agnosia

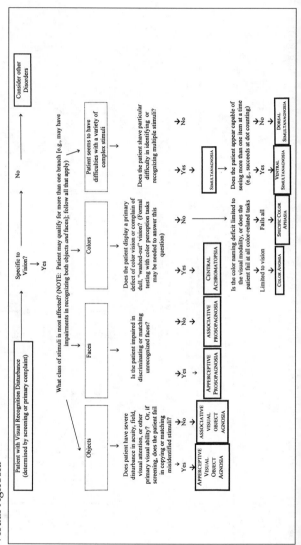

B. Neuropsychological Assessment in Differential Diagnosis

Once a tentative diagnosis has been reached (or the clinician has narrowed the differential diagnosis to a subset of possible disorders on the basis of the clinical presentation), formal assessment of neuropsychological skills is indicated. As discussed earlier, neuropsychological assessment of the putative agnosic seeks to (a) rule out alternative explanations of the patient's deficit and (b) characterize in more precise terms the nature of the patient's deficit so that its underlying mechanism and its relationship to pathological anatomy can be understood.

1. RULING OUT ALTERNATIVE EXPLANATIONS

As suggested earlier, disturbances of "recognition" can occur in a variety of neurological conditions, but they are considered agnosic only if they exist in the relative absence of aphasia, generalized dementia, or impaired attentional capacity. Therefore, one critical aspect of the assessment of the agnosic patient involves assessment of these "bracketing" conditions to rule them out as explanations for the recognition defect. A review of available case reports has revealed considerable variability in the methods used for this portion of the assessment. Table 3 presents a reasonable strategy for achieving this goal; it is recognized that many other tests are available for achieving this purpose.

In general, patients should receive a basic neuropsychological examination designed to determine general intellectual status, memory function, linguistic competence, and sensory–perceptual processing. The clinician may wish to perform a comprehensive neuropsychological test battery to understand better the patient's cognitive strengths and weaknesses, to document baseline functioning, or to assist in treatment planning. Assessment of language ability (naming, auditory comprehension, fluency, repetition, reading, writing, and praxis) is especially important in understanding the possible role that linguistic factors might play in the patient's recognition defect. A comprehensive aphasia battery (e.g., **Boston Diagnostic Aphasia Examination;** Goodglass & Kaplan, 1983; **Multilingual Aphasia Examination;** Benton & Hamsher, 1989; **Western Aphasia Battery;** Kertesz, 1982) is useful for achieving this goal, although it may be necessary to perform supplementary tests to ensure that naming and recognition are tested in all sensory modalities.

Table 3. Ruling Out Alternative Causes of Recognition Disturbance

Condition or problem	Assessment instruments	Domains tested	Reference
Generalized dementia	Dementia Rating Scale	Memory, attention and concentration, construction, initiation and perseveration	Mattis, 1988
Aphasia	Boston Diagnostic Aphasia Examination Multilingual Aphasia Examination Western Aphasia Battery	Fluency, comprehension, naming, repetition, reading, writing, praxis	Goodglass & Kaplan, 1983 Benton & Hamsher, 1989 Kertesz, 1982
Disturbances of attention or orientation (e.g., delirium)	Temporal Orientation Test Visual Search and Attention Test WAIS-R Digit Span Sentence Repetition WMS-R Mental Control Line Bisection	Time orientation Visual search and selectivity Focused attention span Focused attention span (sentences) Mental tracking, sustained attention Spatial attention, hemispatial neglect	Benton et al., 1994 Trenerry et al., 1990 Benton & Hamsher, 1989 Schenkenberg et al., 1980

Unfamiliarity with stimuli	Determined subjectively; the examiner needs to ensure that failures of naming or identification are not based on experiential, cultural, or other factors that lead to the patient's unfamiliarity with stimuli tested; use of frequently encountered items typically circumvents this problem.	Visual, auditory, and tactile object identification with common objects should be tested in each patient to determine familiarity statistics and to determine modality specificity; patients who cannot name objects should be encouraged to divulge anything they know about them or to group items into familiar and unfamiliar categories.	Familiarity must be determined, even informally, on an individual basis. In creating in-house stimulus sets, general references containing relevant statistics on item frequency, imageability, and so on should be consulted to ensure a balanced set of items.

Note. WAIS-R = Wechsler Adult Intelligence Scale–Revised; WMS-R = Wechsler Memory Scale–Revised.

2. CHARACTERIZING THE NATURE OF THE AGNOSIC DEFICIT

Once the patient's general neuropsychological status has been determined, the clinician performs further testing to characterize more precisely the nature of the patient's recognition deficit. At this stage, cognitive neuropsychological models of the perceptual-recognition process become helpful in guiding the approach to assessment. A representative model, adapted from the work of Ellis and Young (1988), is presented in Figure 2. Consulting the individual case reports referred to in Tables 1 and 2 will also assist in planning an appropriate assessment.

Figure 2 draws on a diverse literature in perceptual psychology and neuropsychology (Ellis & Young, 1988); it is presented to the clinician because such models have succeeded in fractionating the process of object recognition into clear information-processing components or stages. The left side of Figure 2 represents dissociable stages of the object recognition process suggested by clinical and experimental research. The right side of Figure 2 presents the most important implications of the model for clinical assessment, with suggestions of some commonly available tests that can be used in "localizing" the defect at a particular processing level. Defects before the level of the "object recognition unit" can be roughly considered **apperceptive** in nature, whereas subsequent deficits correspond to **associative** forms of agnosia. The model presented in Figure 2 is clearly best suited to evaluating a visual recognition disturbance, but it should provide guidance in assessing auditory and tactile agnosias as well. A comprehensive evaluation proceeds with evaluation of all levels of the model, even in situations in which "early" deficits are found.

IV. RELEVANT LABORATORY, EEG, AND NEUROIMAGING CORRELATES

As a general neuropsychological classification, agnosia is not associated with any definitive pattern of abnormality in laboratory tests. EEG and neuroimaging findings vary with the type of agnosia, as might be anticipated from the lesion localization data presented in Table 2. The most common etiologies of agnosia include cerebrovascular accident (CVA), tumor, carbon monoxide poisoning, closed head injury, and central nervous system infection; however, as indicated earlier, it is becoming increasingly recognized that some cases of degenerative dementia with primary involvement of posterior cortex can present with prominent signs of (primarily apperceptive) agnosia

Figure 2. Clinical Application of Cognitive Neuropsychological Model

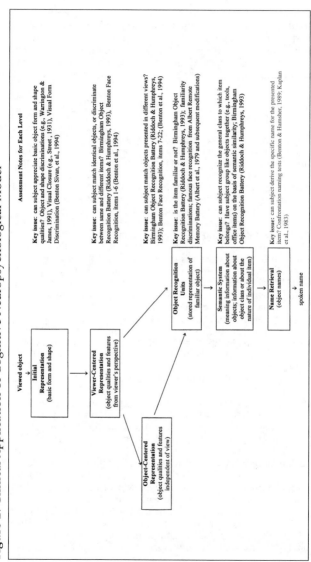

(Mendez et al., 1990). Medical findings vary with etiology and localization. Because of these considerations, laboratory, EEG, and neuroradiological findings per se do not play an integral role in differential diagnosis. Instead, the clinician should rely on behavioral factors and should consider the physical findings as confirmatory.

V. PSYCHOLOGICAL AND PSYCHIATRIC COMORBIDITY

The lesions most likely to produce agnosic defects spare limbic, paralimbic, or frontal regions, which, when damaged, produce prominent affective or personality changes. For this reason, specific forms of psychopathology are not obligatory accompaniments of agnosic syndromes. However, secondary emotional reactions to the real-life consequences of agnosia are common. Factors such as unemployment, social life changes, dependency on others for help in everyday activities (e.g., dressing, transportation, eating), and boredom are seen. These major lifestyle changes may lead to depression or adjustment disorders in some individuals, whereas others may find adaptive ways to cope. Providing an excellent example of coping, Humphreys and Riddoch (1987) described in detail how their patient, John, and his wife both cope with John's visual agnosia. Their description contains evidence of both adaptive and maladaptive compensations. Although epidemiological studies have yet to be conducted, auditory and tactile agnosias seem less likely to produce major life changes; therefore, such disorders may have less deleterious consequences. Such speculations await definitive research.

Another trait sometimes seen in agnosics is sensory compensation. This is an interesting and as yet unresearched phenomenon reported in the animal literature (Horel & Keating, 1969) in which the agnosic comes to rely on intact sensory modalities (e.g., audition and touch in the case of visual agnosia) in exploratory activity. Whether this represents an attempt to achieve an optimal arousal level through sensory stimulation or an attempt to gain understanding of the world through an intact modality remains to be seen. For example, Bauer's (1982) patient with severe visual agnosia listens to music constantly to lessen the boredom of living with the disorder. In our experience, substance abuse is a risk in the chronic period, possibly in response to the reduced stimulation that results from an agnosic deficit and possibly a result of premorbid factors. It should be emphasized that one problem in understanding psychiatric comorbidity in agnosia is that the relative rarity of these syndromes precludes an analysis of whether such problems are caused or exacerbated by the underlying neurological impairment or whether the appearance of such problems reflects preinjury factors that would have exerted themselves in any event. Such issues await systematic research.

VI. CONCLUSION

Agnosia refers to an acquired impairment in the ability to recognize the nature of sensorially presented stimuli. It is a relatively rare disorder that can produce significant everyday impairment. No specific laboratory or neuroradiological marker exists, although orderly anatomic findings have been reported in the literature on visual, auditory, and tactile agnosia that should serve, if present, to raise suspicion of the diagnosis in individual cases. Key symptoms, characteristic neuroradiological findings, and a general assessment approach based on cognitive neuropsychological models of object recognition were summarized in this chapter. Although significant progress has recently been made, much remains to be learned about these complex disorders, and clinicians are encouraged to take a hypothesis-oriented approach to enlarge the available knowledge base.

BIBLIOGRAPHY

Albert, M. S., Butters, N., & Levin, J. (1979). Temporal gradients in the retrograde amnesia of patients with alcoholic Korsakoff's disease. *Neurology, 36,* 211–216.

Bauer, R. M. (1982). Visual hypoemotionality as a symptom of visual–limbic disconnection in man. *Archives of Neurology, 39,* 702–708.

Bauer, R. M. (1993). Agnosia. In K. M. Heilman & E. Valenstein (Eds.), *Clinical neuropsychology* (3rd ed., pp. 215–278). New York: Oxford University Press.

Bauer, R. M., & Zawacki, T. (1996). Auditory agnosia and amusia. In T. Feinberg & M. J. Farah (Eds.), *Behavioral neurology and neuropsychology.* New York: McGraw-Hill.

Benson, D. F., & Greenberg, J. P. (1969). Visual form agnosia. *Archives of Neurology, 20,* 82–89.

Benton, A. L., & Hamsher, K. deS. (1989). *Multilingual aphasia examination.* Iowa City, IA: AJA Associates.

Benton, A. L., Sivan, A. B., Hamsher, K. deS., Varney, N. R., & Spreen, O. (1994). *Contributions to neuropsychological assessment* (2nd ed.). New York: Oxford University Press.

Buchman, A. S., Garron, D. C., Trost-Cardamone, J. E., Wichter, M. D., & Schwartz, M. (1986). Word deafness: One hundred years later. *Journal of Neurology, Neurosurgery, and Psychiatry, 49,* 489–499.

Caselli, R. J. (1991). Rediscovering tactile agnosia. *Mayo Clinic Proceedings, 66,* 129–142.

Corkin, S. (1978). The role of different cerebral structures in somesthetic perception. In C. E. Cartarette & M. P. Friedman (Eds.), *Handbook of perception* (pp. 105–155). New York: Academic Press.

Damasio, A. R., Damasio, H., & Tranel, D. (1990). Impairments of visual recognition as clues to the processes of categorization and memory. In G. M. Edelman, W. E. Gall, & W. M. Cowan (Eds.), *Signal and sense: Local and global order in perceptual maps* (pp. 451–473). New York: Wiley.

Damasio, A. R., Yamada, T., Damasio, H., Corbett, J., & McKee, J. (1980). Central achromatopsia: Behavioral, anatomic, and physiologic aspects. *Neurology, 30,* 1064–1071.

Delay, J. (1935). *Les Astereognosies. Pathologie due Toucher. Clinique, Physiologie, Topographie.* Paris: Masson.

DeRenzi, E. (1986). Prosopagnosia in two patients with CT scan evidence of damage confined to the right hemisphere. *Neuropsychologia, 24,* 385–389.

DeRenzi, E., Faglioni, P., Grossi, D., & Nichelli, P. (1991). Apperceptive and associative forms of prosopagnosia. *Cortex, 27,* 213–221.

Ellis, A. W., & Young, A. W. (1988). *Human cognitive neuropsychology.* Hillsdale, NJ: Erlbaum.

Farah, M. J. (1990). *Visual agnosia: Disorders of object recognition and what they tell us about normal vision.* Cambridge, MA: MIT Press.

Geschwind, N. (1965). Disconnexion syndromes in animals and man. *Brain, 88,* 237–294, 585–644.

Geschwind, N., & Fusillo, M. (1966). Color-naming defects in association with alexia. *Archives of Neurology, 15,* 137–156.

Geschwind, N., & Kaplan, E. F. (1962). A human disconnection syndrome. *Neurology, 12,* 675–685.

Goodglass, H., & Kaplan, E. (1983). *Boston Diagnostic Aphasia Examination (BDAE).* Philadelphia: Lea & Febiger. (Distributed by Psychological Assessment Resources, Odessa, FL)

Hecaen, H., & Ajuriaguerra, J. (1954). Balint's syndrome (psychic paralysis of visual fixation) and its minor forms. *Brain, 77*, 373–400.

Hecaen, H., & David, M. (1945). Syndrome parietale traumatique: Asymbolie tactile et hemiasomatognesie paroxystique et douloureuse. *Revue Neurologique, 77*, 113–123.

Horel, J. A., & Keating, E. G. (1969). Partial Klüver-Bucy syndrome produced by cortical disconnection. *Brain Research, 16*, 281–284.

Humphreys, G. W., & Riddoch, M. J. (1987). *To see but not to see: A case study of visual agnosia.* London: Erlbaum.

Kanshepolsky, J., Kelley, J., & Waggener, J. (1973). A cortical auditory disorder. *Neurology, 23*, 699–705.

Kaplan, E. F., Goodglass, H., & Weintraub, S. (1983). *Boston Naming Test.* Philadelphia: Lea & Febiger.

Kazui, S., Naritomi, H., Sawada, T., & Inque, N. (1990). Subcortical auditory agnosia. *Brain and Language, 38*, 476–487.

Kertesz, A. (1982). *Western Aphasia Battery.* San Antonio, TX: Psychological Corporation.

Kinsbourne, M., & Warrington, E. K. (1962). A disorder of simultaneous form perception. *Brain, 85*, 461–486.

Kinsbourne, M., & Warrington, E. K. (1964). Observations on color agnosia. *Journal of Neurology, Neurosurgery, and Psychiatry, 27*, 296–299.

Mattis, S. (1988). *Dementia Rating Scale (DRS).* Odessa FL: Psychological Assessment Resources.

Mendez, M. F., Mendez, M. A., Martin, R., Smyth, K. A., & Whitehouse, P. J. (1990). Complex visual disturbances in Alzheimer's disease. *Neurology, 40*, 439–443.

Michel, J., Peronnet, F., & Schott, B. (1980). A case of cortical deafness: Clinical and electrophysiological data. *Brain and Language, 10*, 367–377.

Oppenheimer, D. R., & Newcombe, F. (1978). Clinical and anatomic findings in a case of auditory agnosia. *Archives of Neurology, 35*, 712–719.

Pallis, C. A. (1955). Impaired identification of faces and places with agnosia for colors. *Journal of Neurology, Neurosurgery, and Psychiatry, 18*, 218–224.

Riddoch, M. J., & Humphreys, G. W. (1987). Visual object processing in optic aphasia: A case of semantic access agnosia. *Cognitive Neuropsychology, 4*, 131–185.

Riddoch, M. J., & Humphreys, G. W. (1993). *Birmingham Object Recognition Battery.* Mahwah, NJ: Psychology Press.

Rubens, A. B., & Benson, D. F. (1971). Associative visual agnosia. *Archives of Neurology, 24*, 304–316.

Schenkenberg, T., Bradford, D. C., & Ajax, E. T. (1980). Line bisection and unilateral visual neglect in patients with neurological impairment. *Neurology, 30*, 509–517.

Semmes, J. (1965). A non-tactual factor in astereognosis. *Neuropsychologia, 3*, 295–314.

Spreen, O., Benton, A. L., & Fincham, R. (1965). Auditory agnosia without aphasia. *Archives of Neurology, 13*, 84–92.

Street, R. F. (1931). *A Gestalt completion test* (Contributions to education Technical Rep. No. 481). Bureau of Publications, Teachers College, Columbia University, New York.

Trenerry, M. R., Crosson, B., DeBoe, J., & Leber, W. R. (1990). *Visual Search and Attention Test.* Odessa, FL: Psychological Assessment Resources.

Vignolo, L. A. (1969). Auditory agnosia: A review and report of recent evidence. In A. L. Benton (Ed.), *Contributions to clinical neuropsychology.* Chicago: Aldine.

Warrington, E. K., & James, M. (1991). *Visual Object and Space Perception Battery.* Bury St. Edmunds, Suffolk, England: Thames Valley Test Co. (Distributed by National Rehabilitation Services, Gaylord, MI)

Weisenburg, T. S., & McBride, K. L. (1964). *Aphasia.* New York: Hafner. (Original work published 1935)

CHAPTER 25

Kenneth M. Heilman, Robert T. Watson, and
Leslie J. Gonzalez-Rothi

Limb Apraxias

Limb apraxia is defined as an inability to perform learned skilled movements with the forelimbs correctly (Heilman & Rothi, 1993). Limb apraxia may be developmental or induced by neurological dysfunction, and such a diagnosis is typically made by excluding other causative factors. To be classified as apraxic, the inability to perform learned movements cannot be directly secondary to (a) sensory loss or more elemental motor disorders such as weakness, tremors, dystonia, chorea, ballismus, athetosis, myoclonus, ataxia, or seizures or (b) severe cognitive, memory, motivational, or attentional disorders. Although the presence of these disorders does not preclude apraxia, before making this diagnosis the clinician should be certain that these behavioral disorders do not fully account for the patient's inability to perform skilled acts.

Although limb apraxia is a common, disabling, and enduring sequela of brain damage, it may be the least recognized neuropsychological disorder associated with cerebral disease. It is most commonly associated with strokes and degenerative dementia of the Alzheimer type, but it may be seen with many other diseases of the central nervous system. For example, apraxia may be associated with cerebral trauma and tumors and may be the presenting symptom in corticobasal degeneration and focal atrophies.

There are several reasons that apraxia often goes unrecognized. When apraxia is associated with hemispheric injury such as stroke or trauma, patients often also have a right hemiparesis. When these patients attempt to perform skilled acts with their nonpreferred arm and find that they are impaired, they often attribute their difficulty to premorbid clumsiness of the nonpreferred arm. In addition, apraxic patients are often anosognosic for their apraxia (Rothi, Mack, & Heilman, 1990). In addition, caregivers of chronically impaired individuals may find it easier to anticipate needs and perform mechanical tasks than to await failures. Last, and perhaps most important, many health professionals do not test for limb apraxia, are not fully aware of the nature of errors associated with apraxia, and do not know what these errors imply.

I. TYPES OF LIMB APRAXIA

There are several types of limb apraxia. In this chapter we discuss six types: limb kinetic, ideomotor, dissassociation, conduction, ideational, and conceptual. Each of these disorders is defined by the nature of errors made by the patient as well as by differing underlying anatomic substrates. Although constructional apraxia and dressing apraxia also involve the limbs, these disorders are strongly associated with visuoperceptual and visuospatial disorders as well as neglect; therefore these two disorders are not discussed here. The most common errors associated with each of the apraxic syndromes described here are summarized in Table 1.

A. Limb Kinetic, or Melokinetic, Apraxia

1. CLINICAL PRESENTATION

Patients with limb kinetic apraxia demonstrate a loss of the ability to make finely graded, precise, individual finger movements. The patient may have difficulty picking up a straight pin from the top of a desk using a pincher grasp of the thumb and forefinger. Limb kinetic apraxia usually affects the hand that is contralateral to a hemispheric lesion. Recommended tasks include (a) the Rapid Finger Oscillation Test and (b) the Grooved Pegboard Test.

2. PATHOPHYSIOLOGY

Animal models have shown that lesions confined to the corticospinal system result in similar errors.

Table 1. Errors Associated With Each of the Apraxic Syndromes

	Error type				
Syndrome	Gesture to command	Discrimination–comprehension	Imitation	Series	Mechanical knowledge
Ideomotor					
Anterior	+++	O	++	O	O
Posterior	+++	+++	++	O	O
Conduction	+	O	+++	O	O
Disassociation	+++	O	O	+++	O
Ideational	O	O	O	++	O
Conceptual	O	O	O	O	+++

Note. This table lists the error types that define each syndrome. However, patients often have more than one apraxic disorder. + indicates presence of errors; ++ indicates greater errors; +++ indicates the greatest number or most serious errors.

B. Ideomotor Apraxia

1. CLINICAL PRESENTATION

Patients with ideomotor apraxia (IMA) make the most errors when asked to pantomime transitive acts to verbal command, and their performance typically improves with imitation. When using tools their performance may improve even further, but it often remains impaired. Patients with IMA make primarily spatial and temporal production errors. Spatial errors include errors of postural (or internal configuration), spatial movement, and spatial orientation. Goodglass and Kaplan (1963) noted that when apraxic patients were asked to pantomime, they often used a body part as the tool (a form of postural error). For example, when asked to pantomime using a pair of scissors, they may use their fingers as if they were the blades. Because many normal persons make similar errors, it is important that the patient be instructed not to use a body part as a tool. Unlike normal persons, in spite of these instructions, patients with IMA may continue using their body parts as tools. When not using their body parts as tools, patients with IMA often fail to position their hands as if they were holding the tool or object.

When normal persons are asked to use a tool, they orient that tool to an imaginary target of the tool's action. Patients with IMA often fail to orient their forelimbs to an imaginary target. For example, when they are asked to pantomime cutting a piece of paper in half with a pair of scissors, rather than keeping the scissors oriented in the sagittal plane, these patients either may orient them laterally (Rothi, Mack, Verfaellie, Brown, & Heilman, 1988) or may not maintain the scissors in any consistent plane.

When patients with IMA attempt to make a learned skilled movement, they often make the correct core movement (e.g., twisting, pounding, cutting), but their limb movements through space are often incorrect (Poizner, Mack, Verfaellie, Rothi, & Heilman, 1990; Rothi et al., 1988). These spatial trajectory errors are caused by incorrect joint movements. Patients with apraxia often stabilize a joint that they should be moving and move joints that should not be moving. For example, when pantomiming the use of a screwdriver, a patient with IMA may rotate his arm at the shoulder and fix his elbow. Shoulder rotation moves the hand in arcs when the hand should be rotating on a fixed axis. The patient with apraxia may be unable to coordinate multiple joint movements to get the desired spatial trajectory. For example, for a person to pantomime slicing bread with a knife, the shoulder and elbow joints must be alternately flexed and extended. When the shoulder joint is being flexed, it also needs to be adducted, and when the shoulder joint is being extended, it also needs to be abducted. If joint movements are not well coordinated, the patient may make primarily chopping or stabbing movements.

Poizner et al. (1990) noted that patients with IMA may also make timing errors, including a long delay before initiating a movement and brief multiple stops (stuttering movements). When normal persons make a curved movement, they reduce their speed of movement, and when they move in a straight line, they increase their speed of movement. Patients with IMA, however, do not demonstrate a smooth sinusoidal hand speed when performing cyclic movements such as cutting with a knife. The recommended tasks are pantomime to command imitation of transitive movements, use of actual objects, and comprehension and discrimination of transitive movement.

2. PATHOPHYSIOLOGY

In right-handed individuals, IMA is almost always associated with left hemisphere lesions, but in left-handed persons IMA is usually associated with right hemisphere lesions. IMA is associated with lesions in a variety of structures, including the corpus callosum, the inferior parietal lobe, and the supplementary motor area. IMA has also been reported with subcortical lesions that involve the basal ganglia and the hemispheric white matter. Specifically, IMA may result from lesions located in the corpus callosum, the inferior left parietal lobule (Heilman, Rothi, & Valenstein, 1982; Rothi, Heilman, & Watson, 1985), and the supplementary motor area (Watson, Fleet, Rothi, & Heilman, 1986).

C. Conduction Apraxia

1. CLINICAL PRESENTATION

Ochipa, Rothi, and Heilman (1990) reported on a patient who, unlike patients with ideomotor apraxia who improve with imitation, was more impaired when imitating than when pantomiming to command. Because this patient was similar to patients with conduction aphasia who repeat poorly, Ochipa et al. (1990) termed this disorder *conduction apraxia*. The recommended task is imitation to command.

2. PATHOPHYSIOLOGY

The patient of Ochipa et al. (1990) with conduction apraxia could comprehend the examiner's pantomimes and gestures. We believe, therefore, that the patient's visual system could access the movement representations, or what we have termed praxicons, and that these activated movement representations could activate semantics. It is possible that decoding a gesture requires accessing of different movement representations than does programming an action. Therefore, there may be two different stores of movement representations, an input praxicon and an output praxicon. In the verbal domain, a disconnection of the hypothetical input and output lexicons induces conduction aphasia, and in the praxis domain a disconnection between the input and output praxicons could induce conduction apraxia. Whereas the lesions that induce conduction aphasia are usually in the supramarginal gyrus or Wernicke's area, the location of lesions that induce conduction apraxia is unknown.

D. Disassociation Apraxia

1. CLINICAL PRESENTATION

Heilman (1973) described patients who when asked to pantomime looked at their hand but did not perform any recognizable actions. Unlike the patients with ideomotor and conduction apraxia described earlier, these patients' imitation and use of objects were flawless. De Renzi, Faglioni, and Sorgato (1982) reported not only on patients similar to those reported on by Heilman (1973) but also on patients who had a similar defect in other modalities. For example, they may have been unable to pantomime in response to visual or tactile stimuli but able to pantomime to verbal command. The recommended tasks are pantomime to visual or tactile stimuli, pantomime to verbal commands imitation, and use of actual object.

2. PATHOPHYSIOLOGY

Not only may callosal lesions be associated with IMA, as discussed earlier, but callosal disconnection may cause disassociation apraxia. For some patients, movement representations may be bilaterally represented, and thus a callosal lesion may induce a disassociation apraxia (e.g., only of the left hand because the verbal command cannot get access to the right hemisphere movement representations). Whereas the patient with callosal disassociation apraxia cannot correctly perform skilled learned movements of the left arm to command, patients with callosal disconnection can imitate and use tools and objects with their left hand, because these tasks do not need verbal mediation and the movement representations stored in their right hemisphere can be activated by visual input.

Right-handed patients who have both language and movement formulas represented in their left hemisphere may show a combination of disassociation and ideomotor apraxia with callosal lesions (Watson & Heilman, 1983). When asked to pantomime with their left hand, they may look at it and perform no recognizable movement (disassociation apraxia), but when imitating or using tools and objects, they may demonstrate the spatial and temporal errors seen with ideomotor apraxia.

Left-handed patients may demonstrate ideomotor apraxia without aphasia from a right hemisphere lesion. These patients are apraxic because their movement representations are stored in their right hemisphere and their lesions have destroyed these representations (Heilman, Coyle, Gonyea, & Geschwind, 1973; Valenstein & Heilman, 1979). These patients are not aphasic because language is mediated by their left hemisphere (as in most left-handed people). If these patients have a callosal lesion, they may demonstrate disassociation apraxia of their left arm and ideomotor apraxia of their right arm.

The disassociation apraxia described by Heilman (1973) caused by left hemisphere lesions was unfortunately incorrectly termed *ideational apraxia*. The patients reported on by Heilman (1973) and those described by De Renzi and associates (1982) probably had an intrahemispheric language–movement formula, visual–movement formula, or somesthetic–movement formula disassociation. The locations of the lesions that cause these intrahemispheric disassociation apraxias are not known.

E. Ideational Apraxia

1. CLINICAL PRESENTATION

The inability to carry out a series of acts, or formulate an ideational plan, has been called *ideational apraxia* (Pick, 1905). When performing a task that requires a series of acts, these patients have difficulty sequencing the acts in the proper order. Unfortunately, use of the term *ideational apraxia* has been confusing; the term has been used erroneously to label other disorders. For example, Heilman (1973) used this term when he first described disassociation apraxia. Patients with ideomotor apraxia usually improve when using tools and objects, but De Renzi, Pieczuro, and Vignolo (1968) reported on patients who made errors with the use of tools and objects. He also termed these patients *ideationally apraxic*. Although the inability to use tools and objects may be associated with a conceptual disorder, a severe production disorder may also impair object use. The term has also been used to describe patients who make conceptual errors; however, we term this problem *conceptual apraxia*, and we discuss the disorder in the next section. The recommended task is assessment of ability to perform multistep tasks (as described earlier).

2. PATHOPHYSIOLOGY

Pick (1905) noted that most patients with this type of ideational apraxia have a degenerative dementia. Frontal lobe dysfunction also is often associated with temporal order processing deficits.

F. Conceptual Apraxia

1. CLINICAL PRESENTATION

To perform a skilled act, two types of knowledge are needed: conceptual knowledge and production knowledge. Whereas dysfunction of the praxis production system induces ideomotor apraxia, defects in the knowledge needed to select and use the tools and objects successfully are termed *conceptual apraxia*. Therefore, patients with ideomotor apraxia make production errors (e.g., spatial and temporal errors), and patients with conceptual apraxia make content and tool selection errors. Patients with conceptual apraxia may not recall the types of actions associated with specific tools, utensils, or objects (tool–object action associative knowledge) and therefore make content errors (De Renzi & Lucchelli, 1988; Ochipa, Rothi, & Heilman, 1989). For example, when asked to demonstrate the use of a screwdriver either pantomiming or using the tool, the patient with the loss of tool–object action knowledge may pantomime a hammering movement or use the screwdriver as if it were a hammer.

Content errors (i.e., using a tool as if it were another tool) can also be caused by an object agnosia. However, Ochipa et al. (1989) reported on a patient who could name tools (and therefore was not agnosic) but often used them inappropriately. Patients with conceptual apraxia may be unable to recall which specific tool is associated with a specific object (tool–object association knowledge). For example, when shown a partially driven nail, they may select a screwdriver rather than a hammer from an array of tools. This conceptual defect may also be in the verbal domain: When a tool is shown to a patient, the patient may be able to name it, but when asked to name or point to a tool when its function is described, he or she cannot. Patients with conceptual apraxia may also be unable to describe the functions of tools.

These patients may also have impaired mechanical knowledge. For example, if they are attempting to drive a nail into a piece of wood and there is no hammer available, they may select a screwdriver rather than a wrench or pliers (which are hard, heavy, and good for pounding; Ochipa et al., 1992). Mechanical knowledge is also important for tool development, and patients with conceptual apraxia may be unable to develop simple tools correctly (Ochipa, Rothi, & Heilman, 1992). Recommended tasks include (a) gesture to holding and seeing tools, associate tools with objects, and mechanical knowledge.

2. PATHOPHYSIOLOGY

De Renzi and Lucchelli (1988) argued that the temporoparietal junction is integral to the mediation of conceptual knowledge. The patient reported on by Ochipa et al. (1989) was left-handed and rendered conceptually apraxic by a lesion in the right hemisphere, which suggests that both production and conceptual knowledge have lateralized representations and that such representations are contralateral to the preferred hand. Further evidence that these conceptual representations are lateralized contralateral to the preferred hand comes from the observation of a patient who had a callosal disconnection and demonstrated conceptual apraxia of the nonpreferred (left) hand (Watson & Heilman, 1983). However, conceptual apraxia is perhaps most commonly seen in degenerative dementia of the Alzheimer type (Ochipa et al., 1992). Ochipa et al. also noted that the severity of conceptual and ideomotor apraxia did not always correspond. The observation that patients with ideomotor apraxia may not demonstrate conceptual apraxia and patients with conceptual apraxia may not demonstrate ideomotor apraxia provides support for the postulate that the praxis production and praxis conceptual systems are independent. However, for normal function these two systems must interact.

II. THE EXAMINATION FOR LIMB APRAXIA

To diagnose the specific forms of approval that we have discussed one must perform a series of diagnostic tests. The examiner should determine whether the patients perform these tests incorrectly as well as note the type of errors made by the patient.

A. Perform a Proper Neurological Examination

Because the diagnosis of apraxia is in part a diagnosis of exclusion, the clinician must perform a neurological examination to determine whether the abnormal motor performance can be completely accounted for by any of the nonapraxic motor, sensory, or cognitive disorders listed in the introduction to this chapter. The presence of elemental motor defects does not prohibit or preclude praxis testing, but the examiner must interpret the results of praxis testing with the knowledge gained from the neurological examination. **Whenever possible, both the right and left arms and hands should be tested.** When one arm is weak or is the site of another motor disorder that would preclude testing, the nonparetic limb should be tested.

B. Tests

1. **Gesture to command.** Testing praxis involves selectively varying input and task demands. When possible, the same items should be used for all subtests. First, patients should be requested to pantomime to verbal command (e.g., "Show me how you would use a bread knife to cut a slice of bread"). Both transitive (i.e., using a tool and instrument) and intransitive (i.e., communicative gestures such as waving good-bye) gestures should be tested.

2. **Gesture imitation.** Patients should be asked to imitate the examiner performing both meaningful and meaningless gestures.

3. **Gesture in response to seeing and holding tools and objects.** Regardless of the results of the pantomime to command and imitation tests, the patient should be asked to hold tools or objects and to demonstrate how to use these implements. In addition to having the patient pantomime to verbal command, the examiner may want to show the patient pictures of tools or objects and ask him or her to pantomime their use. The examiner may also want to show the patient real tools or the objects that tools work on (e.g., nail) and, without having the patient hold the tool or object, request that the patient pantomime the action associated with the tool or object.

4. **Pantomime recognition and discrimination.** It may be valuable to see if the patient can name or recognize transitive and intransitive pantomimes made by the examiner and

discriminate between well-performed and poorly performed pantomimes done by the examiner.

    5. **Sequential acts.** The patient should be asked to perform a task that requires several sequential motor acts (e.g., making a sandwich).

    6. **Associative tool–object knowledge and mechanical knowledge.** The patient may be asked to match tools with the objects on which they operate (e.g., given a partially driven nail, will the patient select a hammer from an array of tools?) and to fabricate tools or select alternative tools to solve mechanical problems.

III. TYPES OF ERRORS

The types of errors made by patients with apraxia often define the nature of their praxis defect; therefore, it is important to qualify errors. We use a scoring system in which we first classify praxis errors as either production or content errors. Content errors include semantically related productions (e.g., pantomiming playing a trumpet rather than a trombone) and unrelated productions (e.g., making hammering movements rather than those associated with playing a trombone). Production errors include assuming the wrong posture, incorrect orientation of the limb, timing errors, moving the incorrect joints, or improperly coordinating multijoint movements. Each gesture produced by the patient may contain one or more praxis errors. For details concerning this scoring system, see articles by Rothi et al. (1988) and Poizner et al. (1990).

IV. CONCLUSION

Apraxia is defined as an inability to perform skilled movements. In this chapter we have discussed the clinical presentations and pathophysiology of six forms of apraxia. These forms of apraxia are distinguished by the profile of praxis tests that patients fail to perform correctly and by the type of praxis errors the patients exhibit.

BIBLIOGRAPHY

De Renzi, E., Pieczuro, A., & Vignolo, L. (1968). Ideational apraxia: A quantitative study. *Neuropsychologia, 6*, 41–52.

De Renzi, E., Faglioni, P., & Sorgato, P. (1982). Modality-specific and supramodal mechanisms of apraxia. *Brain, 105*, 301–312.

De Renzi, E., & Lucchelli, F. (1988). Ideational apraxia. *Brain,* *113,* 1173–1188.

Goodglass, H., & Kaplan, E. (1963). Disturbance of gesture and pantomime in aphasia. *Brain, 86,* 703–720.

Heilman, K. M. (1973). Ideational apraxia: A re-definition. *Brain, 96,* 861–864.

Heilman, K. M., Coyle, J. M., Gonyea, E. F., & Geschwind, N. (1973). Apraxia and agraphia in a left-hander. *Brain, 96,* 21–28.

Heilman, K. M., & Rothi, L. J. G. (1993). Apraxia. In K.M. Heilman & E. Valenstein (Eds.), *Clinical neuropsychology.* New York: Oxford University Press.

Heilman, K. M., Rothi, L. J., & Valenstein, E. (1982). Two forms of ideomotor apraxia. *Neurology, 32,* 342–346.

Ochipa, C., Rothi, L. J. G., & Heilman, K. M. (1989). Ideational apraxia: A deficit in tool selection and use. *Annals of Neurology, 25,* 190–193.

Ochipa, C., Rothi, L. J. G., & Heilman, K. M. (1990). Conduction apraxia. *Journal of Clinical and Experimental Neuropsychology, 12,* 89.

Ochipa, C., Rothi, L. J. G., & Heilman, K. M. (1992). Conceptual apraxia in Alzheimer's disease. *Brain, 114,* 2593–2603.

Pick, A. (1905). *Sudien uber Motorische Apraxia und ihre Mahestenhende Erscheinungen* [Studies of motor apraxia]. Leipzig, Germany: Deuticke.

Poizner, H., Mack, L., Verfaellie, M., Rothi, L. J. G., & Heilman, K. M. (1990). Three dimensional computer graphic analysis of apraxia. *Brain, 113,* 85–101.

Rothi, L. J. G., Heilman, K. M., & Watson, R. T. (1985). Pantomime comprehension and ideomotor apraxia. *Journal of Neurology, Neurosurgery, and Psychiatry, 48,* 207–210.

Rothi, L. J. G., Mack, L., & Heilman, K. M. (1990). Unawareness of apraxic errors. *Neurology, 40,* 202.

Rothi, L. J. G., Mack. L., Verfaellie, M., Brown, P., & Heilman, K. M. (1988). Ideomotor apraxia: Error pattern analysis. *Aphasiology, 2,* 381–387.

Valenstein, E., & Heilman, K. M. (1979). Apraxic agraphia with neglect induced paragraphia. *Archives of Neurology, 36,* 506–508.

Watson, R. T., Fleet, W. S., Rothi, L. J. G., & Heilman, K. M. (1986). Apraxia and the supplementary motor area. *Archives of Neurology, 43,* 787–792.

Watson, R. T., & Heilman, K. M. (1983). Callosal apraxia. *Brain, 106,* 391–403.

Clinical Evaluation of Visual Perception and Constructional Ability

The evaluation of visual perception and constructional ability is a necessary component of the comprehensive neuropsychological examination. A focal lesion or incipient dementia may cause a profound deficit of visuoperceptual discrimination, visuospatial judgment, or constructional ability in an otherwise articulate patient with normal verbal functioning and visual acuity. This chapter provides an outline of the major visual perceptual deficit syndromes and their neuroanatomic correlates. Practical methods of measuring visual perception and constructional ability are provided, and examples of the error types commonly observed in patients with constructional deficits are described.

I. VISUAL AND CONSTRUCTIONAL DISORDERS

A. Definition of Terms

1. VISUAL PERCEPTION

Visual perception is the process through which sensory information derived from light is interpreted for object recog-

The authors gratefully acknowledge their indebtedness to Sherry Buffamonte, OTR, -L (occupational therapist, registered and licensed) for her contribution of clinical examples of constructional deficit.

nition or spatial orientation. Visual perception consists of visuoperceptual and visuospatial ability, two functionally independent processes that have separate neuroanatomic substrates.

a. Visuoperceptual ability

Visuoperceptual ability subsumes form or pattern discrimination. Color, shape, and other instrinsic features are processed by the visuoperceptual system, regardless of the location of the perceived object in space. This system arises from the dorsal layers of the lateral geniculate nucleus and proceeds to the visual areas of the inferior occipital and temporal cortices.

b. Visuospatial ability

Visuospatial ability is the processing of visual orientation or location in space. Depth and motion are subsumed by this system, which arises from the ventral layers of the lateral geniculate nucleus and proceeds to the visual areas of the superior occipital and parietal cortices.

2. CONSTRUCTIONAL ABILITY

Synonymous with *constructional praxis*, **constructional ability** is the capacity to draw or assemble an object from component parts, either "on command" or "to copy" a model. The concept measures the integrative aspect of construction. Patients with a constructional deficit may be able to reproduce component parts of a design, but they will be unable to produce a design that represents an integrated whole.

B. Etiology

Posterior right hemisphere disease is the most frequent cause of deficits in visual perception and constructional ability. Left hemisphere lesions and conditions causing bilateral multifocal or diffuse disease may also produce deficits on tests of visual perception, although careful evaluation typically shows that these visual deficits are subsumed under overarching neurobehavioral syndromes such as aphasia, dementia, or confusion. See the section "Competing diagnoses," following, for differential diagnosis of these conditions.

C. Specific Disorders

1. VISUOPERCEPTUAL DEFICITS

a. Visual agnosia

Visual agnosia is a deficit in recognition of common objects or familiar faces. Intact naming in the tactile mode differentiates patients with visual agnosia from those with aphasia. The apperceptive versus associative basis for the disorder can be determined using the methods described later in this chapter for evaluating the intactness of visual perception and constructional ability. Visual agnosia as a syndrome independent of dementia is uncommon. Bilateral temporo-occipital lesions damaging the visual association cortices of both hemispheres are usually necessary for the manifestation of visual agnosia.

b. Deficits in form or pattern discrimination

Deficits of form discrimination may be found on a variety of tasks including the following:

(1) Matching of complex patterns

(2) Discrimination of unfamiliar human faces

(3) Visual analysis, which involves the identification of overlapping or hidden figures

(4) Visual synthesis, which involves the ability mentally to combine disparate parts into an integrated whole.

The typical neuroanatomical substrate for these deficits is a lesion in the right temporo-occipital area. A left superior quadrantanopia is frequently seen as a correlated sign.

c. Deficits in color vision

Congenital color blindness is relatively common and has a retinal basis. In contrast, achromatopsia, an acquired deficit in color vision, is caused by a lesion in the inferior temporo-occipital junction, with sparing of the optic radiations and the primary visual cortex of the fusiform gyrus. A bilateral lesion of this type will produce a "full" achromatopsia in both visual fields, whereas a unilateral lesion may produce a "hemiachromatopsia" affecting only the contralateral field. Right hemiachromatopsia is often accompanied by color anomia or alexia.

2. VISUOSPATIAL DEFICITS

a. Balint-Holmes syndrome

Balint-Holmes syndrome is associated with bilateral lesions of the superior parietal lobule and is composed of the following symptom tetrad:

(1) Oculomotor apraxia

(2) Misreaching (optic ataxia or visuomotor apraxia)

(3) Impaired visual attention (simultanagnosia)

(4) Defective judgment of distances

b. Visual neglect

Visual neglect is inattention to objects or events positioned in the visual space contralateral to a brain lesion; it is a disorder of the integrated functioning of vision and attention. Neglect is often correlated with, but is functionally unrelated to, the presence of visual field defects or hemianopia; neglect can be seen in the context of completely full visual fields. It is most often apparent in the acute stage of recovery from a cerebral insult. Neglect occurs more frequently, and with greater severity, following right hemisphere lesions than following unilateral left hemisphere lesions. Visual neglect has been observed following unilateral lesions of the parietal lobe, dorsolateral frontal lobe, putamen, cingulate gyrus, thalamus, and mesencephalic reticular formation.

c. Deficit in visuospatial judgment

Deficits in judging the position and orientation of objects are frequently observed in the context of posterior right hemisphere disease. Relatively low frequencies of defective performance are observed in patients with right anterior or left hemisphere lesions.

d. Topographic disorientation

Difficulties on navigational tasks may be seen with lesions of either parietal lobe, although posterior right hemisphere disease is strongly suggested. The "amnestic" form of topographic disorientation has particular association with lesions of the right hippocampus and its overlying temporal neocortex. The inability to navigate may be caused by a number of mechanisms including:

(1) Visual neglect, causing a patient to turn always in one direction

(2) Deficit in landmark recognition

(3) A memory disorder specific to spatial schema such as "cognitive maps"

3. CONSTRUCTIONAL DEFICITS

Constructional deficits are typically measured using graphomotor tasks, two-dimensional (2-D) mosaic block designs, or three-dimensional (3-D) block designs. Correlational studies have indicated that scores on graphomotor copying tasks have a low correlation with scores on the other constructional tasks and that scores on 2-D and 3-D block design tests are modestly correlated. Right parietal disease is the most frequent etiology for constructional apraxia, although both right frontal disease and aphasia with comprehension deficit may also lead to constructional deficits.

a. Graphomotor copying

Qualitative aspects of performance on graphomotor copying tasks may differ depending on the laterality and anterior versus posterior locus of lesion.

(1) **Left hemisphere lesions.** Performance of right-handed patients with left hemisphere lesions may be affected by poor motor control in the preferred right hand or by use of the nonpreferred left hand forced by an acquired hemiparesis. Patients with left hemisphere lesions may reproduce the spatial elements or outer configuration of a figure successfully, but their reproductions tend to be oversimplified and with significant omission of internal details.

(2) **Right hemisphere lesions.** Patients with right hemisphere lesions often neglect to draw the left side of the figure, or they may crowd details from the left side of the figure into the right side. They may reproduce individual details accurately but with distortion of the spatial relations of design elements. Misplacement of design features is also frequently seen.

(3) **Dementia.** Patients with dementia often show both simplification and spatial distortion of designs. A tendency to copy their production directly onto the stimulus model is often apparent.

b. Two-dimensional block designs

The Wechsler Adult Intelligence Scale–Revised (WAIS-III) Block Design subtest is the most frequently used version of the 2-D, or mosaic block task. Performance on this task is sensitive to lesions of either hemisphere, because the task is complex and demands diverse cognitive resources such as visual analysis, visual synthesis, planning ability, visual intelligence, and psychomotor speed. In the easier designs, each block corresponds to a specific feature of the stimulus model, as in the "pinwheel" design of the WAIS-III. In contrast, the features of the more difficult designs transcend individual blocks and must be assembled from combinations of blocks, as in the "chevron" design of the WAIS-III (Walsh, 1985).

(1) **Left hemisphere lesions.** Patients with left hemisphere lesions often construct block designs with the correct 2×2 or 3×3 configuration, but they often make errors concerning the internal details of the design (see Figure 1). Correct placement of the center block of the 3×3 designs often presents particular difficulty. Patients with left, as opposed to right, hemisphere lesions are more likely to have insight that their reproductions are incorrect.

Figure 1. Mosaic block design error. The external 2×2 configuration of the stimulus model (A) is reproduced in the patient's solution (B), but with errors of internal detail apparent.

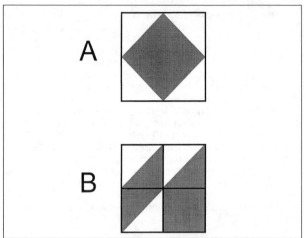

(2) **Right hemisphere lesions.** Patients with right hemisphere lesions often construct designs that preserve internal features of the design, but they may "break" the external 2×2 or 3×3 configuration of their construction (see Figure 2). When blocks are disproportionately skewed into right hemispace, this may be an artifact of visual neglect. Patients with right, as opposed to left, hemisphere lesions often demonstrate a dramatic lack of insight into the fact that their reproductions may be grossly distorted and incorrect.

Because relative weakness on the WAIS-III Block Design subtest is present as a normal variant in the intellectual profiles of many patients, the presence of a low score should not be interpreted in isolation as a sign of brain disease without corroborating evidence or an appropriate rationale for the presence of cerebral dysfunction.

c. Three-dimensional block construction

This task makes little demand on intellectual capacity and has the advantages of face validity, task familiarity, and use of real depth, which is present in neither graphomotor tasks nor 2-D block designs. Deficits in 3-D block construction are most frequently seen with posterior right hemisphere lesions.

Figure 2. Mosaic block design error. The stimulus model (A) demands that nine blocks be assembled into a 3 × 3 design with an internal diagonal band. The patient's solution (B) maintains the diagonal concept, but creates an incorrect 1 × 4 external configuration.

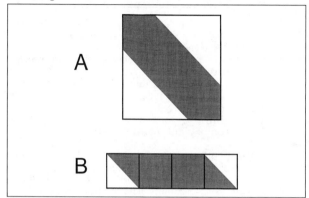

Frontal lobe lesions may also produce constructional deficits, which are related to perseveration and deficits in planning and self-monitoring.

d. Error types on constructional tasks

A number of clinically informative error types may be apparent on constructional tasks. Some error types have already been discussed, such as the internal detail versus configural errors commonly seen on 2-D mosaic block design tests. Error types should not be interpreted as pathognomonic of lesion laterality, because the error type observed is often confounded with the severity of constructional deficit. Many of the following error types may be observed in graphomotor, 2-D, or 3-D block design tests.

(1) **Attentional error.** This is the only error type that is frequently seen in normal individuals. Design elements may be carelessly omitted on graphomotor copying. On 2-D block design tests, one or two blocks may be oriented incorrectly, especially on the "pinwheel" item of the WAIS-III Block Design subtest. On 3-D block design tests, one or more blocks may be omitted or rotated, or a minor substitution of a wrong-size block may be apparent. The patient may produce a completely accurate solution that is carelessly rotated 180 degrees.

Although this rotational error may represent a deficit in visuospatial judgment in some patients, the careless patient will usually correct the rotational error when the examiner asks the patient to check if the solution is correct. These error types typically represent attentional lapses, and they do not reflect true constructional apraxia, which is better represented by the following error types.

(2) **Neglect.** Half of the design may be constructed, or elements from both halves of the design may be crowded into unilateral hemispace (see Figure 3). On 3-D constructions, designs may be produced in which blocks repeatedly fall off into the neglected hemispace.

(3) **Simplification.** All three dimensions of the design may be represented, but the solution does not reflect the complexity of the stimulus model (see Figure 4).

(4) **"Closing-in."** An attempt is made to construct the solution directly onto, or integrated with, the stimulus model (see Figure 5).

(5) **Vertical "piling-up."** Only the vertical dimension of the design is recognized (see Figure 6). Blocks are piled straight up in the vertical dimension, often continuing until the design collapses owing to its instability. The patient may then react with bewilderment.

Figure 3. Left-sided neglect. The patient's design (at left) shows crowding of design elements into right hemispace.

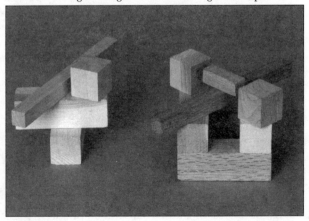

Figure 4. Simplification error. All three dimensions of the stimulus model (at left) are reproduced in the patient's design (at right) in a grossly simplified manner.

Figure 5. Closing-in error. The patient's design (in the foreground at left) is built directly onto the stimulus model.

(6) **Horizontal "stringing-out."** Only the horizontal dimension of the design is recognized (see Figure 7). Blocks are strung out in one plane, and the depth or height of the design is generally ignored.

Figure 6. Vertical "piling-up" error. Cubes rise in the vertical dimension from the patient's simplified design reproduction (at right).

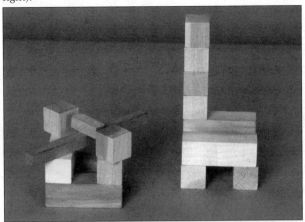

Figure 7. Horizontal "stringing-out" error. The patient's design (in foreground) is predominantly horizontal with additional "closing-in" through a bridging block built onto the stimulus model.

(7) **Dismantling.** An attempt is made to deconstruct the stimulus model, rather than to construct a solution.

(8) **Nonpurposeful activity.** Seemingly random behavior, such as repeatedly moving blocks around without assembling any substantive object, is frequently observed in severely demented or globally aphasic patients. The patient either fails to grasp the task to be performed despite repeated demonstration or fails to execute purposeful behavior toward a goal.

The following two frequently observed error types often reflect executive, or "frontal lobe systems," deficits in self-monitoring and self-correction:

(9) **Perseveration of design elements.** A correct component of the solution may be repeated as the patient fails to terminate what may initially have been appropriate behavior (see Figure 8). The vertical piling-up error and horizontal stringing-out error may be variants of perseveration; the patient becomes mentally fixed on building within a single dimension.

(10) **Failure to self-correct.** A patient may commit a serious error early in the construction, which, unless corrected, will prevent him or her from achieving an accurate solution. These patients often are observed to puzzle over the problem, realizing that they are not reaching their goal, yet it does not occur to them to correct their initial error. Instead, they produce a solution that is an approximation of the stimulus model but is built around the initial error.

Figure 8. Perseveration of design elements. The stimulus model (at left) was successfully reproduced by the patient, who then continued the pyramidal theme until she ran out of cubes. After that, she simply began piling up blocks in the vertical dimension.

4. POSITIVE VISUAL PHENOMENA

Neuropsychologists are typically concerned with areas of deficit, which represent "negative" symptoms of disease, or areas of reduced function. Occasionally, however, patients present with **positive visual phenomena**, which represent new onset of experiences that were not present premorbidly. These phenomena may have diagnostic significance.

a. Visual hallucinations

(1) **Simple hallucinations.** These phenomena range from simple flashes of light (photisms, photopsias, or phosphenes) to complex and scintillating geometric patterns. Lesions anywhere from the retina to the primary visual cortex may cause these phenomena. Ischemia in the occipital lobe, such as found in migraine, is an especially common etiology.

(2) **Complex (formed) hallucinations.** The content of these phenomena is usually of people or animals, often of a lilliputian (reduced) size. Common etiologies are as follows:

- **Toxicometabolic confusion.** The most common etiology for complex visual hallucinations is toxicometabolic confusion, frequently induced by drug intoxication or withdrawal.
- **Focal vascular lesions.** Strategically placed lesions of the mesencephalon, cerebral peduncles, diencephalon, and occipitotemporal and occipitoparietal regions may cause Lhermitte's hallucinosis, in which vividly colored and animated formed hallucinations occur in an otherwise clear sensorium.
- **Dementia.** Demented patients often suffer from complex hallucinations, particularly during episodes of nocturnal confusion. The demented patient often regards the hallucinations as a nuisance and reacts to them with a mild annoyance.
- **Psychiatric disorders.** Visual hallucinations are rare in patients with psychiatric (psychotic) disorders, whereas they are commonly reported by malingering patients.

b. Visual illusions

Visual illusions represent either distortions or misinterpretations of seen objects; these occur both in normal persons and in patients with psychopathology. Most of these phenomena are rare. These positive symptoms are usually caused by areas of neuronal irritation (e.g., subictal electrical abnormalities) or partial deafferentation (Jacobs, 1989). The locus of dysfunction is typically in the parieto-occipital region, and the phenomenon usually occurs in a visual field defect created by the lesion.

(1) **Metamorphopsia.** This phenomenon subsumes alteration in size (micropsia or macropsia), form (dysmorphopsia), and color of objects. A viewed object may also be perceived as a different object or as a more complex version of the viewed object.

(2) **Spatial illusions.** Illusions of depth may occur through experience of distorted perspectival cues. Lesions of the tegmentum or brain stem involving the vestibular pathways are frequently responsible.

(3) **Palinopsia.** This phenomenon represents the persistence or reappearance of a recently viewed object. Development or resolution of a visual field defect is usually in progress. Neoplastic or vascular lesions of the posterior cerebrum are usually present.

(4) **Polyopia** is the perception of multiple, simultaneous visual images while viewing a single object. Parieto-occipital lesions are usually present, although ocular, cerebellar, and vestibular dysfunction may also cause this phenomenon.

(5) **Visual allesthesia.** The transposition of a visual image from one visual half-field to the opposite, usually defective, half-field. The etiology is unknown, although it is found commonly with bilateral cerebral lesions, dementing conditions, and severe psychiatric disorders. Certain hallucinogenic drugs produce this effect in some patients.

(6) **Oscillopsia** is the perception of back-and-forth movement in a stationary object. Nystagmus is the typical cause.

(7) **Visual synesthesia** is the experience of a visual sensation in response to a stimulus in another sensory modality, most typically an auditory startle stimulus. Visual synesthesia can occur in otherwise normal persons or in the context of a visual field defect caused by a lesion of the optic nerve or chiasm. It also occurs with the use of hallucinogens.

c. Nonpathological hallucinations and illusions

Hallucinations occurring while falling asleep (hypnogogic) or awakening (hypnopompic) may be seen in normal persons, who frequently report the experience of an illusory moving object, such as a small fleeting animal, in the visual periphery. These visual false alarms are normal phenomena secondary to the high concentration of motion-sensitive photoreceptors in the retinal periphery. Catching a fleeting glimpse of a deceased relative is common during bereavement.

II. COMPETING DIAGNOSES

In the differential diagnosis of a visual perception or constructional deficit syndrome, a number of competing diagnostic possibilities should be ruled out.

A. Psychiatric Disorder

As part of the attentional disturbance often seen in psychiatric patients, numerous minor or careless errors may be apparent on tests of visual perception and constructional ability. Attentional dysfunction is particularly common in patients with psychiatric disorder, and a pattern of greatest deficit on other tasks demanding focused concentration, sustained effort, and cognitive efficiency may help to differentiate the patient with psychiatric disorder from the patient with frank neurological disease.

B. Dementia

Whether from a primary or secondary etiology, diffuse or multifocal in localization, dementia often is accompanied by deficits in visual perception and constructional ability. Occasionally, the initial presentation of an incipient degenerative dementia takes the form of an isolated deficit in visual perception or constructional ability. This clinical situation is relatively rare; Alzheimer's disease is the most common etiology, and in this disease memory is the cognitive domain that usually is first and most seriously affected. Unless there is evidence for focal right hemisphere disease, serial testing may be necessary, with deterioration or stability of other cognitive domains confirming or refuting the possibility of a progressive dementia process.

C. Confusional States

Confusion, or delirium, whether acute or subacute, is likely to cause deficits on tests of visual perception and constructional ability (Lee & Hamsher, 1988). History of a recent toxicometabolic disturbance and fluctuating level of alertness are signs that confusion should be considered in the differential diagnosis. In confusion, as in psychiatric disorder, deficits on the neuropsychological battery as a whole are more contingent on attentional demands and on task complexity than on the type of cognitive domain tested.

D. Aphasia With Comprehension Deficit

Defective performances on tests of visual perception and constructional ability are frequently observed in aphasic patients with comprehension deficit. Globally aphasic patients, in particular, frequently are unable to perform any type of purposeful or conceptual activity.

III. SENSORY AND MOTOR SYMPTOMS

A. Visual Acuity

Although adequate visual acuity is necessary for performance on tasks of visual perception and constructional ability, it is clear that disorders of visual perception are independent of visual acuity.

B. Visual Field Defects

Left-sided visual field defects often accompany deficits in visual perception and constructional ability. This relationship is correlative, rather than causative, in that a right posterior lesion frequently results in both left-sided visual field defects and perceptual deficits. There is no relationship between right-sided visual field defects and disorders of complex visual perception.

C. Left Hemiparesis

Constructional deficits are frequently associated with left hemiparesis, but as in visual field defects, the association is correlative rather than causative. As noted previously, left hemisphere lesions can cause particular difficulty on graphomotor constructional tasks, because these tasks demand fine motor control that may be difficult for premorbidly right-handed patients, who are forced to use a hemiparetic preferred hand or their nonpreferred left hand.

IV. THE NEUROPSYCHOLOGICAL EXAMINATION

There are three clinical situations in which it is essential that visual perception or constructional abilities be evaluated: (a) in the context of known or suspected posterior right hemisphere disease, (b) in the presence of aphasia with comprehension deficit, and (c) during dementia evaluations, when a sampling of all major cognitive domains is sought.

A Posterior Right Hemisphere Disease

It has been emphasized that patients most likely to have deficits in visual perception or constructional ability are those with posterior right hemisphere disease. For these patients, the core neuropsychological examination should be supplemented by a complete examination of the functioning of the visual system.

1. VISUAL ACUITY SCREENING

A pocket chart such as the Rosenbaum Visual Screener can be used to determine whether a valid examination of visual perception can be obtained. As a convention, corrected near-point visual acuity of 20/70 or better is considered adequate for the purposes of neuropsychological evaluation.

2. VISUAL NEGLECT

The presence of hemispatial neglect is easily assessed by cancellation tasks, which demand that the patient visually scan an array and cancel designated targets. Line bisection tasks, in which patients are asked to draw a mark through the midpoint of a horizontal line, may also be used. A variety of these tasks are illustrated by Lezak (1995), or they can be easily improvised on a sheet of unlined paper if a standard version is not readily available to the examiner. The patient with neglect will fail to cross out the target stimuli on one side of the cancellation task, and on line bisection tasks, the center mark will grossly deviate from the actual midpoint of the line. If the patient has a motor limitation that does not permit administration of these tasks, two-syllable words may be used. For example, the patient with left-sided neglect may read "football" as "ball." If visual neglect is apparent, the examiner may attempt to help the patient compensate by placing stimuli eccentrically in the intact hemiattentional space, with frequent demonstrations to the patient of the necessity of scanning the entire stimulus field. This approach is often of limited value, however, because patients may ignore everything to one side of their center of visual attention no matter where an object is situated. To place all stimuli directly to the center of a patient converts every test into a measure of visual neglect.

3. VISUOPERCEPTUAL DISCRIMINATION

Benton, Sivan, Hamsher, Varney, and Spreen's (1994) Test of Facial Recognition is a valid and reliable test of visuoperceptual discrimination.

4. VISUOSPATIAL JUDGMENT

Benton et al.'s (1994) Judgment of Line Orientation task is a valid and reliable test of visuospatial judgment.

5. CONSTRUCTIONAL ABILITY

a. Graphomotor tasks

A number of standardized approaches to measuring graphomotor performance follow:

(1) **Developmental Test of Visual-Motor Integration** (Beery, 1989). This is the test of choice for adult patients in whom severe deficit is suspected, and the developmental norms are useful in pediatric populations as well. The test has a wide range of stimuli, which vary from single lines that demand no integrative constructional ability to complex two-dimensional figures such as a Necker cube and interlocking triangles.

(2) **Benton Visual Retention Test** (Sivan, 1992). The copy trial of this task provides a range of stimuli of varying size and difficulty. This test is especially useful when normative data corrected for premorbid intellectual status are needed.

(3) **Rey-Osterreith Complex Figure**. For patients in whom subtle constructional deficits are suspected, the Rey-Osterreith Complex Figure Test is the task of choice. The stimulus model (Lezak, 1995) demands ability to reproduce both a geometric spatial framework and a variety of internal details. Numerous scoring systems and normative samples exist (e.g., Lezak, 1995; Loring, Martin, Meador, & Lee 1990; Spreen & Strauss, 1998), and a recall trial can be used to measure visual memory.

b. WAIS-III block design

Age-corrected scaled scores should always be used on the Block Design subtest because performance on this task plummets with old age. Motor deficit or slowing of thought processes may substantially affect performance owing to the timed nature of the test. The Object Assembly subtest also purportedly measures constructional ability, although there is a recognition as well as a constructional component. The Object Assembly subtest would ordinarily have a low priority in the neuropsychological examination because it has the lowest reliability and validity of any WAIS-III subtest.

c. Three-dimensional block construction

The first design of this test by Benton et al. (1994) is two-dimensional, consisting only of width and height but not depth. The other two designs measure constructional ability in all three dimensions. An advantage of the test is its simplicity, allowing evaluation of constructional ability even in poorly educated patients. The relatively large size of the blocks and generous time limits allow evaluation of patients who are slow or who have difficulty with motor dexterity.

6. COLOR VISION

The Ishihara Pseudoisochromatic plates are the standard for evaluation of color deficits, although most of the plates measure red–green vision, and only two of the plates measure blue–yellow vision. The test is also confounded with form discrimination: The patient must fuse an array of isochromatic circles together to perceive a target number. Administration of plates that have been rendered monochromatic by photocopying can help determine whether a deficit in form discrimination is confounding the test. Ordinary crayons or common objects can be used to examine for gross color vision deficits if color plates are not readily available.

B. Aphasia With Comprehension Deficit

Examination of visual perception and constructional ability is useful in the aphasic patient to measure the intactness of nonverbal performance. Because of its simple task demands, the Three-Dimensional Block Construction task can be informative. If the patient fails to comprehend verbal instruction, the examiner may resort to building the first design in view of the patient, then having the patient imitate this performance. If the patient cannot construct even these simple designs, it is clear that the aphasia has caused a pervasive cognitive deficit such that the patient is incapable of performance even on tasks that make no overt demands on verbal comprehension.

C. Dementia

It is relatively common for older patients to present for dementia evaluations after a distressing episode of topographic disorientation. Measurement of visual memory should be given top priority in this clinical situation, although further testing of visual perception and constructional ability frequently reveals a wider syndrome of visual deficit.

V. CONCLUSION

The clinical evaluation of visuospatial and visuoconstructive functions forms an integral part of any neuropsychological examination. A broad range of focal lesions and neurological disorders may lead to either subtle or profound deficits as outlined in this chapter. This chapter provides a practical framework with which to isolate specific visual perceptual and constructive deficits in both hospital and outpatient settings.

BIBILIOGRAPHY

Beery, K. E. (1989). *Developmental Test of Visual-Motor Integration* (3rd rev.). Cleveland, OH: Modern Curriculum Press.

Benton, A. L., & Tranel, D. (1993). Visuoperceptual, visuospatial, and visuoconstructive disorders. In K. M. Heilman & E. Valenstein (Eds.), *Clinical neuropsychology* (3rd ed., pp. 165–213). New York: Oxford University Press.

Benton, A. L., Sivan, A. B., Hamsher, K. deS., Varney, N. R., & Spreen, O. (1994). *Contributions to neuropsychological assessment* (2nd ed.). New York: Oxford University Press.

Bender, M. B., Rudolph, S. H., & Stacy, C. B. (1982). The neurology of the visual and oculomotor systems. In R. J. Joynt (Ed.), *Clinical neurology* (Vol. 1, pp. 1–132). Philadelphia: Lippincott-Raven.

Capruso, D. X., Hamsher, K. deS., & Benton, A. L. (1995). Assessment of visuocognitive processes. In R. L. Mapou & J. Spector (Eds.), *Clinical neuropsychological assessment: A cognitive approach* (pp. 137–183). New York: Plenum Press.

Gainotti, G. (1985). Constructional apraxia. In J. A. M. Frederiks (Ed.), *Handbook of clinical neurology.* Revised series (45): Clinical neuropsychology (pp. 491–506). Amsterdam, North Holland: Elsevier.

Jacobs, L. (1989). Comments on some positive visual phenomena caused by diseases of the brain. In J. Brown (Ed.), *Neurophysiology of visual perception.* Hillsdale, NJ: Erlbaum.

Kaplan, E. (1990). The process approach to neuropsychological assessment of psychiatric patients. *Neuropsychiatry, 2,* 72–87.

Kirk, A., & Kertesz, A. Hemispheric contributions to drawing. *Neuropsychologia, 27,* 881–886.

Lee, G. P., & Hamsher, K. deS. (1988). Neuropsychological findings in toxicometabolic confusional states. *Journal of Clinical and Experimental Neuropsychology, 10,* 769–778.

Lezak, M. D. (1995). *Neuropsychological assessment* (3rd ed.). New York: Oxford University Press.

Loring, D. W., Martin, R. C., Meador, K. J., & Lee, G. P. (1990). Psychometric construction of the Rey-Osterreith Complex Figure: Methodological considerations and interrater reliability. *Archives of Clinical Neuropsychology, 5,* 1–14.

Sivan, A. B. (1992). *Benton visual retention test* (5th ed.). San Antonio, TX: Psychological Corporation.

Spreen, O., & Strauss, E. (1998). *A compendium of neuropsychological tests* (2nd ed.). New York: Oxford University Press.

Walsh, K. W. (1985). *Understanding brain damage: A primer of neuropsychological evaluation.* Edinburgh, Scotland: Churchill Livingstone.

Wechsler, D. (1997). *Wechsler Adult Intelligence Scale–III* (WAIS-III). San Antonio, TX: Psychological Corporation.

CHAPTER 27

Ronald A. Cohen, Paul F. Malloy, and
Melissa A. Jenkins

Disorders of Attention

Impairments of attention are among the most common manifestations of brain damage. In contrast to rare neuropsychological syndromes that result from specific, focal brain lesions, disorders of attention occur following damage to a variety of different cortical and subcortical brain systems as well as from nonspecific neurophysiological factors that affect arousal and metabolic state. Alterations in level of consciousness associated with acute brain dysfunction invariably have a direct impact on attention. It is essential, therefore, that attention be assessed as a standard part of a neuropsychological evaluation.

Patients with attentional dysfunction have an inability to allocate cognitive resources effectively to the task at hand. Clinical examination reveals that the patient fails to perform at optimal levels even though primary cognitive resources, such as sensory registration, perception, memory, and associative functions, are intact. Patients with primary attentional disorders are able to perceive sensory input, comprehend language, form and retrieve memories, and perform other cognitive functions, yet they fail to do so consistently. The performance inconsistency that is a hallmark feature of attentional disturbances stems from the fact that attention consists of a set of dynamic processes that influence the interaction between other core cognitive functions, such as perception and memory, and the external environment.

Whereas perception and memory form the substrates of cognition, attention governs the processing flow of these cognitive substrates. Attentional processes facilitate, enhance, or inhibit other cognitive processes. Attention enables people to respond to particular information while either consciously or unconsciously ignoring other potential stimuli. Attention implies cognitive or behavioral withdrawal from some things so that others can be effectively dealt with. Attention results in behavioral orientation toward particular stimuli or response demands associated with the task at hand. Therefore, a primary function of attention is to facilitate selection of salient sensory information for further processing **(sensory selective attention).** Attentional processes also serve to facilitate responding by influencing the tendency to respond in particular ways to task demands (i.e., response bias). Through the processes of **response intention, selection,** and **control,** attentional selectivity relative to available response alternatives is possible.

In addition to being selective, attention governs the intensity of cognitive allocation directed toward a particular stimulus or task. This intensity of attentional allocation is often conceptualized as **focus,** and subjectively it is experienced as the ability to concentrate. Attentional focus is a direct function of **capacity** limitations, influenced by both energetic (e.g., arousal) and structural (e.g., processing speed) factors. When attentional capacity is reduced by either brain damage or neurophysiological dysregulation, patients become less able to focus and concentrate. Attention also has a strong temporal dynamic. Whereas the content of associations, language, and percepts can be considered to be independent of the variable of time, what is attended to is usually a direct function of the time period that one examines. Furthermore, the ability of people to attend and focus selectively changes over time. Variations in attention over time is a function of the individual's capacity for **sustained attention.**

Attention was once conceptualized as a single process, similar to a filter or bottleneck, that restricted the flow of sensory input subject to higher cognitive operations, thereby limiting the amount of information to be processed to manageable levels. Although this model has intuitive appeal, compelling evidence now exists that attention is not a unitary process but a function of the interaction of at least four component processes under the influence of multiple brain systems. A variety of attentional disorders exist that differentially affect the underlying component processes of **sensory selective attention,**

response selection and control, capacity and focus, and sustained attention (Cohen, 1993; Mirsky, 1989). Figure 1 depicts the primary factors underlying attention.

I. COMPONENTS OF ATTENTION

A. Sensory Selective Attention

Sensory selective attention refers to the processes by which sensory input is chosen for additional cognitive processing and focus. Perceptual processes are engaged relative to target stimuli and are disengaged from nontargets. It occurs at a very early stage of processing, often before a clear task demand is present. The orienting response (OR), the most elementary behavioral response identified during classical conditioning, is a simple form of automatic sensory selection. Stimuli that are novel, salient, or potentially significant elicit an OR, whereas nonsalient "old" stimuli fail to do so. Salience may reflect perceptual factors, such as figure–ground contrast, or informational value derived from past experience. Sensory selection is contingent on the integration of the following elementary operations:

1. **Filtering.** At early stages of perceptual processing, selection occurs on the basis of sensitivities to or preferences for certain types of sensory features. Input that has these features receives additional processing, whereas input that does not is filtered.

2. **Enhancement.** Prior to the presentation of a stimulus to a particular spatial location, cortical neuronal sensitivity to that location is increased by information that creates an expectancy that an event will occur there. Attentional readiness and expectancy to spatial position form the basis of spatial selective attention. The neuronal substrates of enhancement have been demonstrated in primates (e.g., Goldberg & Bushnell, 1981).

3. **Disengagement.** Once attention has been focused on a particular stimulus, it remains fixed until another stimulus or internal event signals a shift of attention to another spatial location or perceptual feature. This attentional shift requires disengagement from the initial stimulus, before attention can be allocated to new stimuli. Attentional disengagement requires processing resources, and it takes time.

B. Response Selection and Control (Intention)

Attentional processes also serve to facilitate action through the selection and control of behavioral responding. **Intention**

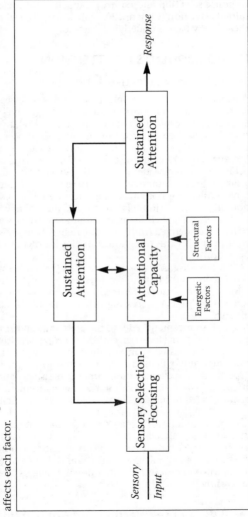

Figure 1. Primary factors underlying attention. Flow of information is shown through the four major components of attention: sensory selection and focusing, response selection and control, capacity, and sustained attention. Attentional capacity is influenced by energetic and structural components. Sustained attention is a product of the information flow through the system and the resulting feedback that affects each factor.

refers to allocation of attentional resources for response selection and control.

1. Although sensory selective attention is sometimes viewed as an antecedent to responding, in many cases response intention and selection precede sensory selection. For instance, if one loses one's keys, an intent to search and a search strategy may be generated before the perceptual act of selectively attending to a particular spatial location is initiated.

2. Intention depends on the individual's being prepared to make a response. The following functional states influence the generation of intention as well as sensory selective attention:

a. **Readiness.** The individual must be ready to make a response for optimal performance to occur. Readiness is mediated by arousal and reinforcement associated with a task.

b. **Expectancy.** In addition to being ready to respond, one has the expectation that a response will need to be made at a particular time.

c. **Anticipatory response.** Preparatory responses in anticipation of the need to respond often serve to facilitate intentional response selection and control.

3. Response selection and control are usually controlled and effortful, in contrast to sensory selective attention, which often is performed more automatically.

4. Conscious awareness usually occurs with response selection and control, whereas sensory selection often occurs without awareness.

5. Sequential processing is usually associated with response selection and control, whereas sensory selection often occurs as a result of parallel processing.

6. **Executive functions** are strongly linked to response selection and control. Specific executive functions that have direct attentional underpinnings include:

a. Intention: processes by which response set and preparation are established

b. Initiation: processes by which the response is started

c. Generative capacity: processes that facilitate production of the response

d. Persistence: processes that enable sustained responding

e. Inhibition: processes that prevent or enable cessation of the response

f. Switching: processes that enable a shift from one response to another

C. Attentional Capacity and Focus

Once a stimulus has been selected for further processing, attention is allocated in accordance with the demands of the task at hand. For many cognitive operations, quality of performance is a function of the intensity of directed attention.

1. **Focused attention** controls the intensity and scope of attentional allocation and, consequently, the cognitive resources devoted to a particular task or cognitive operation.

2. Conversely, focus is a function of processing **capacity limitations** (Kahneman, 1973).

3. Attentional capacity is governed by both **structural** and **energetic** limitations (Cohen, 1993). Energetic capacity limitations tend to be state dependent, composed of factors such as **arousal** and **motivational** state. Structural capacity tends to be less state dependent, is determined by factors intrinsic to the individual, and varies greatly across people.

4. Structural factors that provide attentional capacity limitations include the following:
   a. **Neural transmission** and **processing speed**
   b. **Working memory capacity**
   c. **Temporal processing constraints**
   d. **Spatial processing constraints**

D. Automatic Versus Controlled Processing

An important distinction exists between automatic and controlled attention. In many instances, attention is elicited automatically when particular environmental signals occur. Furthermore, some tasks can be performed without the need for much attentional capacity (e.g., typing).

1. *Automaticity* refers to the capacity to attend to and perform particular cognitive operations with minimal effort and without the need for controlled intensive serial processing (Hasher & Zacks, 1979; Schneider & Shiffrin, 1977).

2. Increasing attentional focus relative to the task at hand usually results in a reduction in automaticity.

3. With automaticity, there is usually relatively little demand placed on attentional capacity, and often attention can occur without much awareness or subjective effort (e.g., attending to other cars while driving on a highway with light traffic).

4. Once a task is learned, less working memory is required, and demands for controlled effortful processing are reduced.

5. Automaticity occurs most commonly in the context of sensory selective attention, particularly when involving single-frame parallel processing, in which rapid selection of relevant

targets from the larger set of potential stimuli in the environmental field can be accomplished at a very early stage of processing (single frame). Visual selective attention is particularly well suited for single-frame parallel processing. Visual information typically occurs in parallel with a vast array of information reaching the brain almost instantaneously. Automaticity is more difficult to achieve for tasks that require sequential cognitive operations, although greater automaticity is often attainable through practice.

6. Selective response attention (intention) is less likely to occur with automaticity than is sensory selective attention. One reason is that motor responding often requires the sequencing of complex responses. The development of well-learned motor programs (e.g., typing, musical performance) often enables attentional automaticity. Increasing memory demands usually decrease the capacity for attentional automaticity (Schneider & Shiffrin, 1977).

7. Sustained attention often can be performed with automaticity. Yet when long durations of sustained attention or vigilance are required, automaticity decreases and greater demand for controlled attentional processing results. Demands for concurrent attention on more than one task or unit of information often cause a rapid decrease in automaticity.

E. Sustained Attention

The maintenance of optimal performance over time requires **sustained attention.** When one considers most other cognitive processes, a consistent level of performance is usually assumed. For instance, in a neurologically healthy person, visual perception always occurs when certain psychophysical parameters are met. Similarly, language competence usually implies that once individuals have achieved comprehension, they will always comprehend particular information. In contrast, temporal inconsistency is a defining characteristic of attention, because the ability to attend and focus selectively varies over time.

1. The variability of performance over extended time periods illustrates an important feature of attention that distinguishes it from other cognitive processes.

2. **Vigilance** is a special form of sustained attention in which there is a demand for a high level of anticipatory readiness for low-probability targets or stimulus events (Parasuraman & Davies, 1984).

3. Sustained attention is a direct function of the task duration. Any task can be extended to the point that a failure of sustained attention will occur.

4. Sustained attention is dependent on the target:distractor ratio. Generally, sustained performance is most difficult in situations in which target stimuli are rare.

5. Tasks that demand high levels of attentional focus and capacity are usually more difficult to sustain.

6. **Energetic capacity**, including arousal, is a strong determinant of sustained attention performance.

7. Reinforcement greatly influences sustained attention. Incentive and internal motivational state are important determinants of how attention is maintained over time.

II. FUNCTIONAL NEUROANATOMY OF ATTENTION

Attention cannot be localized to one discrete brain system; rather, multiple brain systems interact in a network to control attention (Cohen, 1993; Heilman, Watson, & Valenstein, 1993; Mesulam, 1981). However, the specific attentional processes are controlled by different brain systems within this network (see Figure 2).

The *inferior parietal cortex* plays a central role in spatial selective attention (Heilman, Watson, Valenstein, & Goldberg, 1988; Heilman et al., 1993; Mattingley, Bradshaw, Bradshaw, & Nettleton, 1994; Mesulam, 1981; Posner, Walker, Friedrich, & Rafal, 1987). In primates, area PG of the nondominant hemisphere contains neurons that enhance attentional responses to particular spatial positions. Damage to this area results in impaired spatial attention (e.g., hemineglect). Other posterior cortical areas also appear to be involved in selective attention. For example, the inferior temporal lobes, which are involved in processes of higher order sensory analysis such as object recognition, exhibit enhancement responses relative to focal attributes of visual information. Such enhancement probably enables attentional focus on relevant visual features.

The *frontal cortex* is an important part of the attentional network. Although the most obvious function of the frontal cortex concerns response selection and control, it also plays a role in most other aspects of attention, including sustained attention and capacity. Even sensory selection seems to be influenced by the frontal cortex, as evidenced by findings of spatial hemi-inattention following unilateral nondominant hemisphere damage. The frontal cortex plays an integral role in switching and search for sensory selective attention.

Figure 2. Functional neuroanatomy of attention. Multiple brain systems interact in a network to control attention.

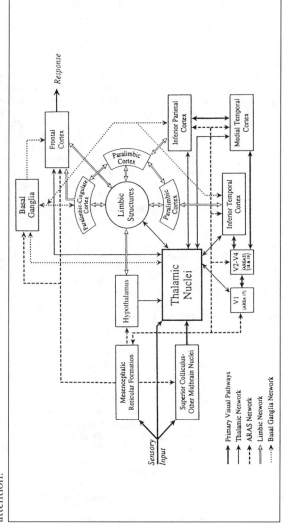

The **orbital frontal region** plays a major role in response initiation and inhibition. Damage to this area causes go/no-go impairments, which have direct implications for attention (Fuster, 1989). The medial frontal lobe, including the paralimbic cingulate cortex, plays an important role in the formation of intent to respond, the temporal consistency of responding, and focused attention (Cohen, 1993). The dorsolateral frontal cortex also appears to play a role in attention, although this is less well understood. This region seems to influence response sequencing, persistence, switching, and focus, particularly with respect to integration and responding relative to semantic representations. The frontal eye fields control saccadic eye movements and are important for visual search and looking. Neuronal response of this region is influenced by attention neurons in the parietal cortex. The premotor cortex facilitates planned movements; although it is not in its own right an attentional system, it influences response automaticity.

Limbic system structures, such as the amygdaloid and septal nuclei, play an important role in attention. These nuclei help to establish salience, which in turn determines the priority given new information as well as existing associations. The limbic system plays an essential role in defining the limits of attentional capacity and focus, and it also is instrumental in determining response biases and propensity (Cohen, 1993; Pribram & McGuinness, 1975). Memory encoding and retrieval functions of the hippocampus constrain attentional capacity. The rate at which short-term memories are encoded into long-term representations influences the ease with which attentional operations can be performed (Schneider & Shiffrin, 1977). Interactions of the amygdaloid, septal, and hypothalamic nuclei are responsible for the creation and experience of motivation and emotions, and ultimately they govern the salience associated with information.

Subcortical systems play a critical role in attention. Thalamic nuclei are involved in both sensory and response selective attention, and they have a gating function as sensory input is relayed through the thalamus to cortical areas. Furthermore, motor control signals sequenced within the basal ganglia are processed through the thalamus and then relayed to supplementary motor and frontal areas prior to motor output, with the thalamus serving as a gatekeeper. The caudate nucleus of the basal ganglia is critically important not only for the selection of motor responses but also for the selection and coordination of sensory information relative to these responses.

Midbrain systems, particularly the mesencephalic reticular system, are essential for production of arousal and activation

(Cohen, 1993; Pribram & McGuinness, 1975). Arousal establishes a tonic energetic level, which in turn influences the responsivity and attentional bias of the system. The reticular system activates the thalamus, limbic system, and cortical areas, and it is therefore critical for maintaining consciousness. Midbrain nuclei are also involved in the control of saccadic movements for visual search.

III. NEUROLOGICAL AND NEUROPSYCHIATRIC DISORDERS OF ATTENTION

A. Stroke

Focal lesions associated with embolic or hemorrhagic cerebrovascular infarction often produce the most dramatic form of attentional disturbance. **Hemineglect, extinction,** and **hemi-inattention** syndromes are among the disorders of attention that are common after stroke. These syndromes are discussed in considerable detail elsewhere in this text and are not extensively reviewed. However, several key summary points regarding these syndromes are in order.

1. Hemi-inattention and neglect are manifestations of unilateral brain lesions. Striking spatial asymmetry in attentional performance is a central feature of these syndromes.

2. Neglect usually occurs relative to the left side of space, which illustrates the importance of the nondominant cortical hemisphere in spatial attention.

3. Although most patients with neglect have a number of common symptoms, the specific attentional disturbance depends on the exact location of the lesion.

a. Lesions affecting the reticular system that produce neglect also involve significant arousal and activation impairments.

b. Unilateral basal ganglia damage often results in both hemi-attention and intention impairments, reflecting the importance of this system to sensorimotor integration.

c. Cingulate lesions are more likely to affect intention than sensory selective attention.

Although hemineglect syndrome is one of the most dramatic forms of attentional disturbance, focal lesions secondary to stroke commonly produce disorders that do not involve hemineglect.

4. Focal frontal lesions may produce impairments of focused attention in addition to the common finding of attentional impairments of response selection and control.

5. Thalamic lesions may result in problems with informational gating and selection regardless of whether unilateral neglect is present.

6. Subcortical lesions often produce impairments of arousal, activation, and information-processing speed, which in turn may limit attentional capacity.

7. Subcortical small vessel disease secondary to cerebral hypoperfusion may result in dementia; this type of dementia seems to affect attention and information-processing efficiency most dramatically.

B. Dementia

Alzheimer's disease and other neurological diseases that result in diffuse global cortical dysfunction often have significant associated attentional impairments. Yet patients with dementia are often able to sit and sustain a general attentional orientation toward the examiner, and automatic attention is usually preserved until relatively late stages of the illness. Therefore, clinicians often conclude erroneously that attention is preserved in these patients.

1. Attentional capacity and focusing ability are almost always impaired early in the disease course, although sensory selective attention tends to be intact.

2. Simple response selection and control are affected to varying degrees in early stages of dementia.

3. Executive functions often fail relatively early.

4. Sustained attention may appear adequate with respect to a patient's ability to sit and respond to the examiner. Yet sustained performance on structured tasks is usually quite impaired, and there may be problems with impersistence.

C. Multiple Sclerosis

Of the cognitive impairments that often accompany multiple sclerosis (MS), the most common disorders involve attention (Cohen, 1993).

1. Fatigue is the most common of all symptoms in MS. Fatigue is associated not only with motor effort but also with attending to and performing cognitive tasks.

2. Subcortical lesions secondary to demyelination may disrupt attentional control.

3. Subcortical white matter lesions also reduce neural transmission speed. Slowed processing time reduces attentional capacity and creates processing bottlenecks.

D. Hydrocephalus

Hydrocephalus often creates pressure on periventricular white matter–subcortical systems, and attention and information-processing problems are quite common. Because ventricular pressure often fluctuates, attentional difficulties frequently exhibit a fluctuating course with this disorder.

E. Head Trauma

Whereas diffuse neuronal injury often results from moderate or severe head trauma, the most common areas of bilateral damage are the frontal lobes, basal temporal lobes, and subcortical brain systems. Brain damage to these areas occurs not only as a by-product of an object hitting the cranium, but also as a result of shearing forces, especially when an accident has involved rapid acceleration–deceleration.

1. Attentional impairments of the type described previously for patients with focal frontal lesions are often observed.

2. The shearing effects that damage subcortical white matter often result in arousal and activation deficits.

3. Slowing of information processing is also common.

F. Schizophrenia

Severe attention impairments are common.

1. Problems with informational filtering or gating often exist.

2. Selective attention is often impaired with increased information load.

3. Problems distinguishing relevant from irrelevant input are quite common and seem to belie a problem with the tagging of semantic value of informational input or associations that are attended to.

4. Sustained and focused attention are often poor, and capacity is often limited, particularly for divided attention (concurrent task performance).

G. Affective Disorder

Attentional disturbance is the most common cognitive symptom associated with major affective disorders.

1. Subjective complaints of problems with concentration and focus are among the symptoms that are considered in a diagnosis of depression.

2. Problems with reduced energetic capacity (focused attention) and sustained attention are most common. Response selection and control is often more moderately impaired. Sensory selective attention is usually less affected.

3. Attentional performance is often quite variable over time.

4. The quality of attentional impairments varies as a function of affective state. Manic patients tend to make more errors of commission and failure to inhibit responding, whereas depressed patients make more errors of omission and are likely to show low levels of arousal with psychomotor slowing. Great effort is often required for attention.

5. Given the strong likelihood of attentional disturbance in patients with affective disorders, it is essential that depression be ruled out or factored in when one is assessing attention associated with other brain disorders.

H. Attention Deficit Disorder

The most commonly diagnosed disorder of attention, attention deficit disorder (ADD) has become one of the most frequently diagnosed disorders within U.S. society. Although a diagnosis of ADD is now sometimes made on the basis of patient self-reported symptoms, there is considerable evidence that self-reported symptoms do not always correspond well with evidence of attentional impairments observed on assessment. This is particularly true for adults presenting with new concerns about possible ADD but without a history of childhood ADD.

1. Patients with ADD often exhibit milder forms of attentional impairment than patients with neurological and other neuropsychiatric disorders.

2. High comorbidity with depression, other psychiatric disorders, substance abuse, and learning disabilities exists.

3. A thorough attentional assessment in patients with suspected ADD is strongly suggested, but the workup should also include a thorough history (including childhood school records or behavioral reports), thorough diagnostic interview, and evaluation of comorbid conditions.

IV. ASSESSING DISORDERS OF ATTENTION

Although it is an essential cognitive process, attention is difficult to observe directly or to measure. Attention fluctuates in accordance with changes in task demands and the processing capacity of the patient over time. Unlike other cognitive functions, performance may differ greatly at different points in time; it is this variability that in fact defines attention. Attention is often situation specific, which may account for the observation that some children with ADD perform well in a controlled laboratory setting despite reports of gross problems of inattention in school or at home. Attention primarily serves to facilitate other cognitive functions; it enhances or inhibits perception, memory, motor output, and executive functions, including problem solving. Yet attentional performance is measured as a function of performance on tasks that also load on one or more other domains. A number of methodological issues need to be considered, therefore, when attention is assessed.

A. Methodological Issues

1. Pure tests of attention do not exist.

2. Attention usually must be assessed within the context of performance on tasks that load on one or more other domains.

3. Attentional performance is often a function of a derived measure obtained by comparing performance across tasks that load differentially with respect to key attentional parameters (e.g., target:distractor ratio).

4. Absolute performance often proves less informative than measures of performance inconsistencies in the assessment of attention. For example, how performance varies as a function of time, spatial characteristics, or memory load provides more information about attentional dynamics than does the total number of errors on a visual detection task.

5. Because attention is not the by-product of a unitary process, it cannot be adequately assessed on the basis of findings from one specific test. For example, conclusions about attention based solely on digit span performance are misguided.

6. Attentional assessment requires a multifactorial approach.

The specific measures used in an evaluation depend on the overall level of functioning of the patient.

1. For patients with global cognitive dysfunction, it may be difficult to use tasks that require complex responses.

2. For patients with relatively high overall cognitive abilities, tasks should be chosen that require multiple component processes. If the patient is able to perform well on these tasks,

severe attentional disturbance involving specific attentional component processes can be ruled out. The Stroop and Trail Making tests are examples of tasks that require multiple attentional processes.

3. If impairments are found on such tasks, more extensive testing of specific component processes can be conducted.

4. Whenever possible, efforts should be made to use tasks that incorporate **signal detection methods**, even when one is not evaluating sensory selective attention per se. These methods provide the best means of accurately summarizing performance relative to all possible types of errors. Also, tasks using a signal detection approach can often be easily integrated with response time measures.

B. Attentional Parameters That Should Be Considered

A thorough assessment of attention should be based on analysis of data from a comprehensive battery of attentional tests (Cohen, 1993) that sample the various component processes of attention (see Table 2). These tasks should enable evaluation of performance as a function of different stimulus, response, and task parameters. Tasks should be differentially sensitive to the following attentional parameters:

1. Spatial characteristics
2. Temporal dynamics
3. Memory demands
4. Processing speed requirements
5. Perceptual complexity
6. Demand for different levels of control and sequencing
7. Demand for various types and complexity of cognitive operation
8. Effortful demands
9. Task salience, relevance, and reward value
10. Demand for single-frame parallel and multiframe serial processing

C. Levels of Assessment

Although multifactor neuropsychological assessment provides the best means of evaluating attentional impairments, a comprehensive attentional evaluation may not be feasible in everyday clinical practice because (a) the patient is too ill to partici-

Table 1. Neuropsychological Taxonomy of Attention:
Component Processes With Associated Variables
Substitute to Each Component

Attentional component	Task variables
Sensory selective attention	
Filtering	Stimulus complexity
Focusing and selection	Computational demands
Automatic shifting	Orienting-response parameters
Response selection and control	
Intention	Task and information salience
Initiation and inhibition	Multiple response onsets (e.g., go/no-go demands)
Active switching	Alternation of responding
Executive regulation	Categorical switching
	Rule-governed decisions
Attentional capacity	
Energetic factors	
Arousal	Intrinsic biological state
	External stressors
Motivational state	Consequences and payoff
Effort	Task demands and salience
Structural factors	
Memory capacity	Short-term memory demands, rehearsal, and so on
Processing speed	Individual differences
	Testing different modalities
Temporal dynamics	Serial or multiframe designs
Spatial characteristics	Spatial frame design
Global resources	General cognitive demands
	Complexity of operations
Sustained performance	
Vigilance	Signal:target ratio
	Task duration
	Arousal
Fatigability	Salience, payoff
	Intrinsic biological state
Reinforcement contingency	Schedule of payoff and costs

Table 2. Component Processes of Attention-Associated Neuropsychological Tests

Component	Tests
Sensory Selective Attention	Letter and symbol cancellation Line bisection Cued spatial detection (Posner task) Spatial search tasks (span of apprehension) Dichotic listening CPT (D′) Line orientation
Response selection and control	Go/no-go Complex motor programs Rampart figures Trail Making CPT(F+) Porteus Mazes—breaks Sorting tasks—failure to maintain response set Fluency measures (COWAT, design fluency)
Capacity and focus	Digit symbol (Stroop) Paced Serial Addition Test (PASAT) Stroop tests (interference) Reaction time measures Levels of processing (working memory tasks) Timing tasks (motor continuation, duration discrimination) Spatial rotation tasks Dichotic listening (divided attention paradigms)
Sustained Attention	CPT vigilance decrement Motor persistence tasks (sustained finger tapping) Variation across session on repeated administration of task

pate for long time periods, (b) other functions in addition to attention must be assessed, or (c) there are time constraints in the clinical context. Consequently, clinicians should be aware of the information that can be obtained from different levels of attentional assessment.

1. CLINICAL INTERVIEW

The most common source of information regarding a possible attentional disorder is the clinical interview. A number of structured interview procedures exist for assessing subjective reports of attention deficit (e.g., WURS). Although the clinical interview often provides useful information, the following key problems arise if one relies only on this source of information:

a. Subjective complaints of attentional problems often do not correlate well with actual impairments on attentional tests.

b. Patients with the most severe attentional problems often have little awareness of their impairments.

c. Family members frame their experience of symptoms on the basis of their own tolerance for certain types of behavior, which results in questionable validity for this source of data.

d. Because of the preceding problems, interview and even questionnaire data should be treated with caution, as a starting point in the assessment of attention.

2. BEHAVIORAL OBSERVATION

Observation of the patient's behavior during the clinical interview and subsequent testing provides useful information. Use of a behavior symptom checklist for some of the key symptoms of attention disturbance described previously may facilitate such observation and improve validity.

a. Behavioral observation methods enable systematic recording during the examination of behavioral events that reflect attentional problems. These methods include **event recording** of behavioral frequency, **interval recording** of the presence of an event at certain times, and **scan sampling** of duration of events per unit of time.

b. Behavioral observation methods often provide the most ecologically valid measures of attention. However, the following limitations exist relative to their use:

(1) Behavioral observation methods can be quite labor intensive.

(2) The methods require long recording periods to detect low-frequency events.

(3) Behavioral observation does not directly measure or provide much information regarding the cognitive processes underlying inattention symptoms.

3. TRADITIONAL PSYCHOMETRIC APPROACHES

Many psychological tests that were not designed specifically to assess attention have been used for this purpose. For instance, the Wechsler Adult Intelligence Scale–Revised (WAIS-R), originally developed as an intelligence test, is widely used to provide information about specific cognitive functions including attention.

a. A subtest pattern based on scores on three WAIS-R subtests has long been used by clinicians as an indicator of attentional problems. The **Digit Span**, **Arithmetic**, and **Digit Symbol** subtests are intercorrelated and have been shown to correspond with a common factor that seems to reflect "freedom from distractibility." Impaired performance on this WAIS-R triad has been considered to be an indicator of attentional impairment.

b. This triad is not particularly sensitive to problems with sustained or selective attention.

c. The Picture Completion subtest may be helpful for detecting visual selective attentional problems in some cases, although evidence of impairment needs to be interpreted with caution because task performance is influenced by various factors, including perceptual and inferential ability and cultural knowledge.

d. On the Wechsler Memory Scale (WMS-R), the Mental Control and Digit Span subtests have been consistently identified as part of a "concentration" factor (Prigatono, 1978). These tasks require short-term memory retention (i.e., working memory) and cognitive operations that demand attentional focus, such as serial arithmetic computations.

e. On the WAIS-R and WMS-R, attentional problems may also be identified on the basis of the patient's response characteristics, as follows:

(1) Excessive interitem variability may reflect fluctuations in attentional focus and problems with sustained attention.

(2) Intertest variability, particularly when inconsistencies are noted among subtests measuring the same cognitive function, may also suggest impaired attention.

(3) Caution should be used when interpreting attentional impairments on the basis of performance variability, because variability may also reflect the standard error of measurement and subtle psychometric factors associated with test construction.

4. NEUROPSYCHOLOGICAL ASSESSMENT OF ATTENTION

Ideally, the assessment of attention should include neuropsychological tests that have been developed to be sensitive to the different component processes of attention. With the use of these tests, impairments of attention can be more easily dissociated from other cognitive problems. Norms exist for many of these tests.

a. Sensory selective attention

Tests used in the assessment of neglect syndromes provide a foundation for the assessment of sensory selective attention.

(1) Letter and symbol **cancellation tasks** are useful for detecting abnormalities in both the spatial distribution of visual attention and general signal detection capacity.

(2) **Line bisection** may also provide evidence for a hemispatial attentional disturbance.

(3) The paradigm of **double simultaneous stimulation (DSS)** provides a method for detecting **extinction** and neglect of stimuli in impaired hemispace.

(4) The analysis of the spontaneous drawings of objects and copying of figures may point to lateral differences in attention to detail or spatial quality.

(5) Although paper-and-pencil tests and simple behavioral tasks such as DSS provide the best method for initial assessment, computerized tests based on experimental paradigms provide for a more thorough evaluation of sensory selective attention.

(a) **Dichotic listening** paradigms, which involve the presentation of different information to the two ears, provide a way of assessing auditory attentional selection under different conditions of discriminability and response bias. However, this paradigm also involves divided attention and reflects capacity limitations as well. Dichotic listening has been employed in **shadowing** paradigms, which require the participant to repeat material being presented auditorily in one ear while processing a competing message in the other ear. Participants have great difficulty extracting information from the nonshadowed ear during dichotic listening, but they can detect physical changes in the stimuli to that ear. Participants also show little memory of material presented to the nonshadowed ear, although they attend better to the nonshadowed channel when different modalities were used and after they have learned to attend to the nonshadowed channel.

(b) **Spatial search tasks** provide an excellent means of assessing the spatial distribution for visual attention. Tachistoscopic or computerized presentation of an array of visual stimuli enables attentional search to be evaluated as a function of the time taken to scan the visual array for a particular target (**visual–spatial search tasks**). By mapping this spatial distribution as a function of attentional parameters, it is possible to determine what factors influence search. Search accuracy tends to be best above the fixation point, whereas extreme points in the vertical dimension are the least likely to be accurately searched. Selection has also been shown to vary greatly along the horizontal axis, and search times are greatest when there is high similarity between targets and distractors. The accuracy of visual search depends on the attentional demands of the task. Accurate detection should occur at an almost perfect rate when the location of the target is obvious and not difficult to discriminate. Reduced speed and accuracy occur when targets are shifted in the visual field and the location is uncertain.

(c) **Spatial cue** paradigms, which measure the influence of attentional bias in anticipation of spatial position, provide another important method for assessing visual selective attention (Posner et al., 1987). Although a variety of spatial cue paradigms exist, the principles underlying these tasks are generally the same. A neutral cue is presented at some spatial location prior to the onset of a target. On some trials, the cue correctly signals the future position of a target stimulus, whereas on other trials the information provided by the cue is incorrect. The accuracy of detection and reaction times can then be measured as a function of the anticipatory cue to either correct or incorrect spatial position.

b. Response selection and control

A large number of tasks are available for use in assessing response selection and control. Many of these tasks fall within the rubric of tests of executive functions. These tests are differentially sensitive to the executive functions of intention, initiation, generation, persistence, inhibition, and switching that were described previously. Simple motoric response control may be assessed by tasks such as double alternating movements, alternating graphic sequences (e.g., Rampart Figures), motor impersistence, and the go/no-go paradigm. Tests such as Trail Making, the Stroop tasks, the Wisconsin Card Sorting Test (WCST), and the Porteus Mazes provide a means for assessing higher order executive functions such as goal-directed behavior, response planning, and active switching of response set.

c. Intention

1. Response selection and control is predicated on the formation of intent to act. Although intent is often inferred rather than measured directly, there are ways of assessing intentional impairments.

(a) A failure to initiate a search or goal-directed behaviors despite motivational feedback that provides incentive for such action suggests an intention impairment.

(b) Failure to persist in a search strategy (impersistence) may also reflect impaired intention.

(c) The quantity and quality of spontaneously initiated behaviors, including the ability to generate alternative creative solutions to problems, may provide the best intention index.

2. Capacity for initiation, generation, and persistence can be measured in a number of different ways.

(a) Verbal and design fluency not only indicate the total quantity of response output for a circumscribed time period, but also can point to problems with initiation and persistence.

(b) Simple and choice reaction time may help to characterize response initiation problems.

(c) Tests of motor functioning such as the Grooved Pegboard Test measure generation of and persistence in fine motor response production.

(d) Motor system deficits need to be considered when one is assessing whether a response generation deficit relates to attentional–executive impairments; occasionally, problems in the motor domain may present a confounding variable in the interpretation of neuropsychological results. Deficits in the ability to persist on motor tasks may also reflect problems with attention and executive functioning. For instance, patients suffering from multiple sclerosis show fatigue that extends beyond their motor deficits. This fatigue has been shown to be related to attentional deficits in these patients.

3. **Response inhibition.** The ability to inhibit responses can be measured through a number of different tasks. Interference tasks such as the Stroop test determine the ability to inhibit attentional response to one stimulus characteristic while responding to another characteristic. The go/no-go paradigm and continuous-performance tests (CPTs) also provide information regarding the patient's ability to inhibit false positive responses. Intrusion errors on these tests point to failed response inhibition.

4. **Response alternation and switching.** Several of the tasks described previously (alternating graphic sequences,

go/no-go) require the alternation of response pattern and therefore provide information about this capacity. The Trail Making Test is one of the most commonly used tests of response-switching ability and mental control. Errors occur when the patient fails to alternate between letters and numbers or when there is a break in the sequence and a particular item is omitted.

d. Attentional capacity and focus

Many paradigms are available for assessing attentional capacity and focus. Although these tasks are similar in that they require attentional focus, the cognitive operation that is necessary to perform the task may vary. Therefore, patients may exhibit performance inconsistencies across tasks according to their ability to perform certain cognitive operations.

1. Tests of focused attention

(a) Among the standard measures used to assess attentional focus are tests that require "mental arithmetic and control." Digit Span Backwards, Backwards Spelling, the Arithmetic subtest of the WAIS-R, and serial addition and subtraction tests are examples of such tasks. All of these tasks are also quite sensitive to brain dysfunction.

(b) The Paced Auditory Serial Addition Test (PASAT) is an example of a highly controlled test of attention that requires both focused and sustained attention. The PASAT is quite sensitive to subtle attentional impairments. Because considerable effort is required for adequate performance, however, the PASAT cannot be used with patients with severe brain dysfunction. Also, poor motivation or reduced arousal greatly affects performance on the PASAT.

(c) The Symbol Digit Modality Test (SDMT) and Digit Symbol subtest of the WAIS-R are also excellent measures of focused attentional capacity. Because these tasks require rapid processing of symbolic information and the coding of symbol–number pairs, they collectively can be considered **symbol coding** tests. Focused attention is required because the number–symbol pairs to be coded are not familiar to the patient. Therefore, attentional capacity is taxed in accordance with the memory demands of the task and the requirements of visual tracking, perceptual-motor integration, and time pressure.

2. Some tasks place demands on attentional capacity and focus because of the requirement for **divided attention.** Dichotic listening is the best example of such a task.

(a) The ability to inhibit interfering stimulus characteristics while responding to a target feature is another example of divided attention that taxes capacity limitations. The Stroop test fits this category, because the patient is required to inhibit responses to words that are presented but to name the color that the word is printed in. Interference is created by the fact that the color of the printed word conflicts with the color denoted by the word itself.

(b) Concurrent production tasks (e.g., finger tapping while demonstrating verbal fluency) provide a vehicle for assessing capacity limitations associated with divided attention. Such tasks are extremely effortful and require controlled focused attention. The task of finger tapping with fluency is useful for assessing response to the demands associated with two forms of response production. Alternatively, dichotic listening paradigms provide a way of assessing focused attention in the context of sensory selective attention.

(c) Focused attention associated with demand for specific cognitive operations can be assessed through a number of different paradigms. For example, levels of processing memory paradigms create semantic activation with an associated level of attentional activation and effort. In principle, most cognitive tasks can be modified such that the fundamental cognitive operation remains constant but the demand for focused attention is controlled. For instance, by comparing digit–symbol to symbol–symbol coding performance, the effects of different levels of attentional focus can be assessed.

3. **Brief attention span.** Tests of attention span provide a means of assessing capacity limitations associated with short-term or working memory. Digit Span Forwards is an example of such a test that also illustrates a problem associated with the traditional interpretation of attentional deficits. Digit Span Forwards has often been used as a general index of attention, yet strong performance is usually possible with minimal demand for attentional focus.

(a) Performance on this test is most strongly associated with short-term memory (STM), working memory, and the language requirement of repetition. Performance is dependent on the ability to hold a string of items for a brief interval until a response is required.

(b) Encoding of this information into more permanent memory storage is not necessary for task completion, and typically people are unable to retain the material soon after initial recall. Tests of brief attention span, therefore, bridge attention and STM.

(c) Weak performance on Digit Span Forwards is not very informative in its own right, although when analyzed relative to other findings, it may provide clinical information about working memory as well as the motivation of the patient.

(d) Considerable interitem variability, such as missing some short sequences but correctly repeating longer sequences, is significant, because it suggests a lapse of attention.

(e) Other tests, such as the Corsi Blocks and the Knox Cube Test, provide an opportunity to measure brief span in the visual–spatial modality. However, poor performance on spatial span tests may reflect spatial selective attentional deficits as well.

e. Sustained attention and vigilance

Tests that provide a measure of performance over time provide a means of assessing sustained attention and vigilance.

1. **Continuous-performance tests** (CPTs), which measure signal detection performance over blocks of trials, are the most commonly used tests of sustained attention. Many versions of the CPT exist, all consisting of the same basic paradigm. Either visual or auditory stimuli (usually letters) are presented sequentially. Intermixed among distractor stimuli are particular target stimuli, such as the letter *A*. The task is to respond to the target and the distractors. The attentional demands of the task can be modified on many CPT tests by changing the ratio of targets to distractors, total number of stimuli, total time of the test, perceptual complexity of the stimuli and background, interstimulus interval, and use of anticipatory stimuli. A variety of signal detection measures, such as misses, false positives, inconsistency, and vigilance decrement, can be determined that help to quantify impairments of sustained attention.

2. Information about sustained attention can also be derived from other neuropsychological measures. For instance, symbol cancellation tests require the patient to scan a sheet of paper to detect a particular stimulus or sequence of stimuli and to mark all target stimuli with a pencil. Performance is measured as a function of total time for task completion and of target stimuli missed. Failure to detect stimuli is considered to be an indicator of inattention. This type of task also provides information about sensory selective attention, including the presence of neglect.

3. Symbol coding tasks such as the Digit Symbol subtest may also be used to assess sustained attention by comparing performance during the early and late stages of the task. Similar modifications can also be made on tasks that involve more complex cognitive operations to make them more sensitive to impairments of sustained attention.

4. Tests of sustained attention, such as CPTs and symbol cancellation tests, can be modified to increase the demand for focused attention and effort. On the CPT this can be done by increasing the complexity of rules governing target selection (e.g., respond to *x* only when preceded by *A*). Also, by adjusting parameters such as memory load, interstimulus times, or the presence of more than one stimulus in a target field on a trial, other attentional factors besides sustained attention can be examined. This is particularly useful in experimental studies, although it is somewhat problematic for clinical use because modifying task demands invalidates comparison to standardized, normative performance.

D. Assessment Strategy

The primary disadvantage of most traditional neuropsychological tests of attention stems from their reliance on a paper-and-pencil format. Although such methods typically provide useful data about error characteristics, they are not well suited for response time measurement, and they do not provide adequate information about interitem variability or change in performance across the task duration. For these reasons, it is recommended that efforts be made to use some computerized tests of attention that enable greater experimental control over stimulus and response parameters, such as the rate of stimulus presentation, the spatial characteristics of visual stimuli, and response times. Among the methods that enhance the assessment of attention are the following:

1. SIGNAL DETECTION METHODS

Error types associated with attentional processing can be best assessed using signal detection methods. Besides providing information about the relationship between errors caused by missing targets and false positive errors caused by responding to nontargets (β) and discriminability (d'), these methods enable a determination of expected response characteristics given the ratio of targets to distractors. Other attentional indices such as vigilance decrement and response inconsistency are also easily derived using signal detection methods.

2. CHRONOMETRIC ANALYSIS

Reaction time (RT) provides a useful index of the processing time involved in an attentional selection or response on particular tasks. Greater processing demands relative to capacity limitations tend to be associated with increased RTs. The costs and benefits of attentional allocation and disengagement (e.g., spatial cueing) can be determined through RT methods as well.

3. PHYSIOLOGICAL METHODS

Psychophysiological measurement provides a potentially rich source of information regarding the neurobiological substrates of attention. Although these methods have not yet been well integrated into standard neuropsychological practice, physiological findings can help to confirm clinical hypotheses by providing an independent index of attentional allocation.

a. Autonomic measures are particularly useful in characterizing elicitation and habituation of the orienting response. These measures can also provide an index of the intensity of attentional focus and effort.

b. Measures of central nervous system activity, such as electroencephalography, also provide indices of attentional processes.

c. Event-related potentials yield waveforms that correspond to specific attentional processes, such as initial registration, attentional allocation, and response to stimulus salience.

d. Recently developed functional imaging techniques such as positron emission tomography (PET), single photon emission computed tomography (SPECT), and functional magnetic resonance imaging (fMRI) enable dissociation of component processes of attention and undoubtedly will be clinically useful in the future.

E. Recommended Measures for Initial Assessment

In many clinical situations, it is not possible to administer a comprehensive battery of tests of attention. Therefore, it is important to use a small set of measures that will provide some information about each attentional component process. As a core set of measures, we recommend the Digit Symbol subtest, Trail Making, a letter cancellation task, and a CPT. The Digit Symbol subtest provides information about focused attention, working memory, and processing speed. Trail Making provides information about spatial search and response-switching ability. Letter cancellation provides information about visual search and sensory selective attention. The CPT is the best available means of assessing sustained attention.

F. Steps in Decision Making When Assessing Attention

Regardless of the battery that is chosen, the assessment of attention depends on a logical, stepwise decision process. A decision tree for evaluation of attention disorders is provided in Figure 3.

Figure 3. Interrelated functions to be evaluated systematically according to the recommended steps and decision making during an examination of attention.

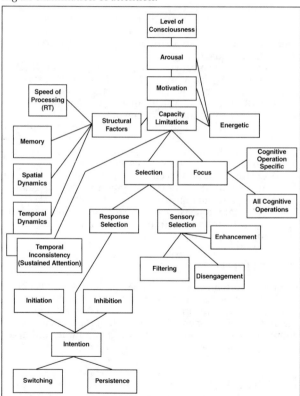

Step 1: Level of consciousness. Is the patient fully alert? Is lethargy or fatigue evident?

Step 2: Arousal. Is activity level within normal limits, or is the patient slowed or agitated?

Step 3: Motivation. Does the patient seem to exert adequate effort?

Step 4: Are sensory, perceptual, and motor functions intact? If not, it is essential to factor in the contribution of these impairments.

Step 5: Is attentional capacity reduced? Do impairments consistently appear on tasks requiring high levels of focus, working memory, or effort?

Step 6: Is reduced capacity general or limited to specific operations or modalities? If it is operation specific, attentional effects may be secondary to the greater effort required for tasks that are more difficult cognitively for the patient.

Step 7: If a general capacity problem is present, limiting factors should be examined in detail. This involves assessing factors such as processing speed and memory influence.

Step 8: Is attentional performance temporally inconsistent? Is there a performance decrement?

If so, a more thorough assessment of sustained attention is in order.

Step 9: Is the attention problem limited to sensory selection or to response selection and control?

Step 10: If sensory selective attention impairment is suggested, is spatial distribution of attention abnormal? Is attention also impaired in nonspatial visual or auditory tasks?

Step 11: Are response selection problems related to specific problems with intention, initiation, inhibition, persistence, switching, or other executive functions?

V. CONCLUSION

Disorders of attention are common sequelae of a wide variety of brain injuries or diseases. The components of attentional control are complex and are mediated by an elaborate and highly integrated series of neural systems. The proper evaluation of attentional dysfunction forms an integral, routine, and necessary portion of a complete bedside or outpatient examination.

BIBLIOGRAPHY

Cohen, R. A. (1993). *Neuropsychology of attention*. New York: Plenum.

Colquhoun, W. P., & Baddeley, A. D. (1967). Influence of signal probability during pretraining on vigilance decrement. *Journal of Experimental Psychology, 73*, 153–155.

Desimone, R., & Gross, C. G. (1979). Visual areas in the temporal cortex of the macaque. *Brain Research, 178*, 363–380.

Fuster, J. M. (l989). *The prefrontal cortex: Anatomy, physiology, and neuropsychology of the frontal lobe.* New York: Raven Press.

Gibbon, J., & Allan, L. (1984). Timing and time perception. *Annals of the New York Academy of Sciences, 423.*

Goldberg, M. E., & Bushnell, M. D. (1981). Behavioral enhancement of visual response in monkey cerebral cortex: II. Modulation in frontal eye fields specifically related to saccades. *Journal of Neurophysiology, 46*, 783–787.

Hasher, L., & Zacks, R. T. (1979). Automatic and effortful processes in memory. *Journal of Experimental Psychology: General, 108*, 356–388.

Heilman, K. M., Watson, R. T., & Valenstein, E. (1993). Neglect and related disorders. In K. M. Heilman & E. Valenstein (Eds.), *Clinical neuropsychology* (3rd ed., pp. 279–336). New York: Oxford University Press.

Heilman, K. M., Watson, R. T., Valenstein, E., & Goldberg, M. E. (1988). Attention: Behavior and neural mechanisms. *Attention, II*, 461–481.

Kahneman, D. (1973). *Attention and effort.* Englewood Cliffs, NJ: Prentice-Hall.

Kahneman, D., & Treisman, A. (1984). Changing views of attention and automaticity. In R. Parasuraman & D. R. Davies (Eds.), *Varieties of attention.* New York: Academic Press.

Kaplan, R. F., Verfaellie, M., DeWitt, L. D., & Caplan, L. R. (1990). Effects of changes in stimulus contingency on visual extinction. *Neurology, 40*, 1299–1301.

Mattingley, J. B., Bradshaw, J. L., Bradshaw, J. A., & Nettleton, N. C. (1994). Residual rightward attentional bias after apparent recovery from right hemisphere damage: Implications for a multi-component model of neglect. *Journal of Neurology, Neurosurgery, and Psychiatry, 57*, 597–604.

Mesulam, M. A. (1981). A cortical network for directed attention and unilateral neglect. *Archives of Neurology, 10*, 304–325.

Mirsky, A. F. (1989). The neuropsychology of attention: Elements of a complex behavior. In E. Perelman (Ed.), *Integrating theory and practice in neuropsychology.* Hillsdale, NJ: Erlbaum.

Parasuraman, R., & Davies, R. B. (1984). *Varieties of attention.* New York: Academic Press.

Pardo, J. V., Fox, P. T., & Raichle, M. E. (1991). Localization of a human system for sustained attention by positron emission tomography. *Nature, 349*, 61–64.

Posner, M. I., & Cohen, Y. (1984). Facilitation and inhibition in shifts of visual attention. In H. Bouma & D. Bowhuis (Eds.), *Attention and performance*. Hillsdale, NJ: Erlbaum.

Posner, M. I., Walker, J. A., Friedrich, F. A., & Rafal, R. D. (1987). How do the parietal lobes direct covert attention? *Neuropsychologia, 25*, 135–145.

Pribram, K. H., & McGuinness, D. (1975). Arousal, activation, and effort in the control of attention. *Psychological Review, 82*, 116–149.

Prigatano, G. P. (1978). Wechsler Memory Scale: A selective review of the literature. *Journal of Clinical Psychology, 34*, 816–834.

Schneider, W., & Shiffrin, R. M. (1977). Controlled and automatic human information processing: I. Detection, search, and attention. *Psychological Review, 84*, 1–66.

Verfaellie, M., Bowers, D., & Heilman, K. M. (1988). Attentional factors in the occurrence of stimulus-response compatibility effects. *Neuropsychologia, 26*, 435–444.

CHAPTER 28

Paul F. Malloy, Ronald A. Cohen, and
Melissa A. Jenkins

Frontal Lobe Function and Dysfunction

Historically, frontal lobe functions have been poorly understood. Although their role in emotion and psychopathology
was emphasized early on (Moniz, 1940), this area was not
believed to play a major role in cognition. For many years, clinicians persisted in referring to the prefrontal lobes as *silent areas,*
because sensorimotor signs were often absent after prefrontal
damage. The lack of a thorough understanding of the functioning of the frontal lobes was also due to the functional diversity
of this phylogenetically recent area and the resultant variety of
clinical syndromes that emerge following damage to the frontal
lobes.

The extensive connections to and from the frontal lobes
have become clearer through animal studies (Goldman-Rakic,
1987; Nauta, 1972; Pandya & Barnes, 1987). Clinical syndromes
have been better described following observation of patients
with disease or injury affecting the frontal lobes (Luria, 1980;
Malloy, Webster, & Russell, 1985) and study of patients undergoing psychosurgery (Stuss et al., 1983; Valenstein, 1990).
Recent advances in structural and functional neuroimaging
have also been important in advancing the understanding of
frontal functions in normal persons (Marenco, Coppola,
Daniel, Zigun, & Weinberger, 1993; Martin, Friston, Colebatch,

& Frackowiak, 1991) and in patients (Andreasen et al., 1986; Weinberger, Berman, & Zec, 1986).

I. FRONTAL LOBE FUNCTIONS

A. General Functions

The frontal lobes subserve pyramidal motor functions, sensorimotor integration in complex volitional movement, and executive and self-regulatory abilities. Self-regulation is essential for modulation of affect and socially appropriate conduct. The term *executive* refers to the role of these systems in response choice and execution. **Executive functions** include the following abilities:

1. Formulating goals with regard for long-term consequences
2. Generating multiple response alternatives
3. Choosing and initiating goal-directed behaviors
4. Self-monitoring the adequacy and correctness of the behavior
5. Correcting and modifying behaviors when conditions change
6. Persisting in the face of distraction

Patterns of limbic activation, along with sensory association signals, are processed by the frontal regions and sequenced with regard to the anticipated response possibilities. This system has an important function in regulating the flow of behavior into a "stream" of continuous behavior and cognition. The course of this stream is dictated by changes in the environment on the basis of affective–motivational data perceived by the sequencing system. The organism selects from the available response alternatives; broadens or narrows environmental search and monitoring parameters; and sustains, discontinues, or adjusts ongoing behaviors in relation to environmental demands. Thus, the monitoring of the junction between organism and environment, with ensuing self-regulation, is crucial to the executive control of behavior.

B. Frontal Systems

In humans the frontal lobes constitute about one third of the cerebral cortex (Goldman-Rakic, 1987). They lie anterior to the central sulcus and may be divided into a number of anatomic–functional subsystems. **Functional frontal subdivisions** include the following:

1. Primary motor area
2. Premotor area
3. Frontal eye fields
4. Dorsolateral area
5. Orbital and basal areas
6. Supplementary motor and anterior cingulate gyrus areas

Each of these frontal zones has extensive connections with specific posterior cortical structures, thalamic nuclei, and basal ganglia (see Table 1). Frontal zones act in concert with these other structures to form **frontal lobe systems.** Only a few of the major pathways are listed in Table 1; the frontal cortex has a multitude of interconnections that allow communication with most other areas of the brain.

II. FRONTAL LOBE DYSFUNCTION

A. General Dysfunctions

Primary motor area lesions result in flaccid hemiplegia in the contralateral side of the body, which typically resolves into spastic hemiplegia. Less severe lesions to this area or its connections result in hemiparesis and incoordination of the contralateral side.

Premotor area lesions result in apraxia (difficulty programming complex volitional movements) and the inability to make use of sensory feedback to modify movements smoothly. Disruption of connections with sensory areas of the parietal lobe to this area can also result in difficulty in integrating sensory information into ongoing motor plans.

Frontal eye field damage can result in the inability to control volitional eye movements in the contralateral visual field, inability to direct complex attention during defensive behaviors, and problems guiding eye movements during goal-directed behavior involving memory.

Prefrontal damage impairs more complex behaviors and "metacognition." These higher prefrontal functions are generally of greater concern to the neuropsychologist. Conceptually, deficits caused by prefrontal lobe damage can be divided into disorders of executive control, behavioral excess, and diminished response.

B. Specific Syndromes

Three prefrontal syndromes have been associated with damage to these anterior subsystems (a) a dysexecutive syndrome—

Table 1. Functions and Primary Connections of Frontal Subsystems

Subsystem	Major functions	Afferent connections
Primary motor	Fine motor movement	Primary somatosensory area of parietal lobe Ventrolateral thalamic nucleus
Premotor	Praxis (complex volitional movement) Sensorimotor integration	Secondary somatosensory area of parietal lobe Extrapyramidal motor system Primary motor area Ventroanterior thalamic nucleus
Frontal eye fields	Voluntary gaze Visual search Directing complex attention	Dorsomedial thalamic nucleus
Dorsolateral prefrontal	Executive functions	Posterior association cortex Angular and supramarginal gyri Dorsomedial thalamic nucleus
Orbital prefrontal area	Smell discrimination Behavioral inhibition	Cingulate Anterior temporal lobes Limbic system Dorsomedial and intralaminar thalamic nuclei
Supplementary motor and anterior cingulate	Initiation and inhibition of exploratory search	

the dorsolateral convexity, (b) a disinhibited syndrome—the orbital area, and (c) an akinetic syndrome—the medial area.

1. DYSEXECUTIVE SYNDROME

Lesions of the dorsolateral prefrontal area can result in an inability to integrate disparate sensory elements into a coherent whole, a stereotyped or limited response repertoire, easy loss of task set, perseverative or inflexible behavior, and lack of self-monitoring of errors. In the realm of memory, executive problems result in decreased working memory, inefficient learning, failure to make use of active learning strategies, reduced memory for temporal or situational context information, and inefficient free recall despite normal recognition of newly learned information. Problems with behavioral switching cause a lack of response flexibility, such that the patient becomes "stuck in set."

2. DISINHIBITED SYNDROME

Anosmia, disinhibited personality change, amnesia with confabulation, and failure on neuropsychological tests of inhibition are signs of orbitofrontal damage (Malloy, Bihrle, Duffy, & Cimino, 1993). Lesions of this subsystem result in disruption of inhibitory and emotional mechanisms, with impulsive and socially inappropriate behavior resulting. A patient may be aware that a particular behavior is inappropriate but unable to inhibit the behavior. Disorders of emotional reactivity can include emotional incontinence, affective lability, and situationally inappropriate emotional reactions. Perseveration may also result from a failure of inhibition, as can the inability to release from the current stimulus despite a change in its salience (stimulus-bound behavior). Related cognitive problems include difficulties with attention, most commonly, increased distractibility by irrelevant stimuli and diminished sustained and divided attention.

3. APATHETIC–AKINETIC SYNDROME

Lesions to the anterior cingulate gyrus can result in **akinetic mutism**, in which the patient fails to respond to environmental stimuli and remains inert. When the lesion is unilateral, akinesia is typically transient, whereas persistent akinesia usually results from bilateral lesions. Conversely, lesions to the supplementary motor area and corpus callosum result in "alien hand syndrome," in which the patient may grab objects, throw things, and otherwise explore the environment in a disinhibited way (Goldberg & Bloom, 1990). The patient feels that he or she has no control over movements of the left hand. In reality, these movements are probably attributable to the actions of the right hemisphere in initiating behaviors while disconnected from the verbal left hemisphere.

Diminished responsiveness can manifest itself in problems with initiating or persisting in behavior. Patients may have lowered responsiveness to environmental triggers or a preserved motivation to act but be unable to organize these impulses into directed drives, action plans, or response sequences. Impersistence refers to the failure to maintain a particular response despite reinforcement, feedback, cues, or other signals indicating that additional responding is necessary. Flat or diminished affect may be seen. Some patients become docile, apathetic, or even akinetic. Social changes (divorce, job loss, difficulty initiating or maintaining friendships) often occur in the wake of a frontal lobe injury. Personality changes are commonly reported. Inability to follow through with tasks at work is a typical problem.

C. Nonlocalized Frontal Deficits

The frontal lobes normally inhibit a number of primitive reflexes (e.g., grasp, snout, glabellar). The presence of these **frontal release signs** may be another indication that frontal damage has occurred. However, frontal release reflexes are also seen in elderly persons without neurological disease and in patients with generalized neurological conditions such as degenerative dementias.

Environmental dependency is a syndrome in which the patient responds in a habitual way to stimuli in the surrounding area without regard for the current necessity or appropriateness of the response (Hoffmann & Bill, 1992). A subtype is **utilization behavior**, in which the patient uses objects without a specific goal or need (e.g., sipping from an empty cup when satiated; Lhermitte, 1983). Environmental dependency has been conceptualized as the release of parietal exploratory behavior owing to absence of frontal inhibition (Lhermitte, Pillon, & Serdaru, 1986).

A variety of neuropsychiatric disorders have also been linked to frontal lesions, including **reduplicative paramnesia** (the delusion that a place has been duplicated; Benson, Gardner, & Meadows, 1976), **Capgras syndrome** (the delusion that a person has been duplicated; Malloy, Cimino, & Westlake, 1992), and **secondary depression** and **secondary mania** (Cummings & Mendez, 1984).

III. DISEASES THAT COMMONLY AFFECT FRONTAL FUNCTIONS

Conceptualizing brain–behavior relationships in terms of systems rather than discrete centers is nowhere more important than in executive and self-regulatory functions, occupying as they do the apex of the behavioral hierarchy. It follows that "frontal lobe" dysfunction can occur with lesions to any part of these systems (Cummings, 1993), including (a) cortical frontal areas, (b) subcortical nuclei having connections with the frontal lobes, and (c) white matter lesions disrupting the connections.

Traumatic brain injury (TBI), for example, may cause dysfunction owing to damage to the frontal lobes themselves or to white matter connections. The orbital surface and frontal poles are particularly vulnerable to focal damage from TBI because of their close proximity to the bony prominences of the skull (Mattson & Levin, 1990), but patients with TBI often suffer damage to multiple frontal zones. Diffuse axonal injury can also result in dysexecutive syndromes owing to disruption of white matter connections affecting widely distributed frontal systems.

Neoplasms can cause gradual or abrupt changes in mood and personality that may or may not be accompanied by dramatic cognitive complaints (depending on size, location, and rate of progression). Intrinsic tumors such as gliomas are most common; they often begin unilaterally in frontal white matter but can spread bilaterally by invading the corpus callosum. Extrinsic tumors, such as meningiomas, are frequently located subfrontally or in the falx cerebri, where they compress mesial frontal lobes bilaterally.

Vascular lesions can occur secondary to stroke, aneurysm, or microvascular disease. Large vessel strokes commonly cause unilateral damage. Left frontal damage may be accompanied by speech and language deficits (Broca's or transcortical motor aphasia), right-sided sensory and motor deficits, and secondary depression. Right hemisphere damage may result in diminished performance on spatial tasks as well as elevated mood, pressured or disorganized speech, and grandiosity. Another major category of vascular lesion affecting the frontal lobes results from ruptured aneurysms of the anterior communicating artery (ACoA), producing personality changes and a characteristic amnesic syndrome with prominent confabulation. Microvascular disease involves damage to the small blood vessels found in subcortical brain regions. These small changes may appear as hyperintense areas on T2- or proton density–weighted magnetic resonance imaging (MRI) scans. Risk factors for microvascular disease include advancing age (it is found in many normal elderly persons), hypertension, cardiovascular disease, and possibly smoking and diabetes. Microvascular disease can occur in the frontal lobes themselves and also can disrupt major cortical and subcortical connections to the frontal lobes.

Certain **dementing illnesses** (Pick's disease, Lewy body disease, dementia of the frontal type) cause gradual deterioration of frontal lobe functioning. Early in the course of these frontal dementias, there is typically disturbance to personality and social behavior out of proportion to deficits in memory (Neary, Snowden, Northen, & Goulding, 1988). This pattern is in contrast to the usual impairment in Alzheimer's disease, in which dramatic memory loss typically precedes change in personality and emotional function. Subcortical dementing processes such as Parkinson's and Huntington's diseases also commonly cause executive dysfunction along with changes in motor functioning (Gotham, Brown, & Marsden, 1988).

IV. ASSESSMENT OF FRONTAL LOBE FUNCTIONING

Both informal and psychometric methods of assessing frontal deficits can be useful. Table 2 summarizes common bedside maneuvers and formal tests for assessment of each frontal system.

A. Primary Motor Functions

The clinician can test basic motor functions at bedside using the familiar maneuvers of the elementary neurological examination. Motor strength can be tested by having the patient squeeze the examiner's fingers and attempting to extricate the fingers from the patient. This maneuver allows the comparison of the relative strengths of the two hands, which should be approximately equal. Motor speed and dexterity can be assessed by having the patient perform rapid movements with the hands and feet. Neuropsychological tests of simple motor abilities include the Reitan **Grip Strength Test** and the **Finger Tapping Test** (Reitan & Wolfson, 1985).

B. Premotor System Functions

Deficits in this subsystem can be tested at bedside by having the patient touch each finger to the thumb sequentially and

Table 2. Bedside and Neuropsychological Tests of Frontal System Dysfunction

Subsystem	Bedside maneuvers	Neuropsychological tests
Primary motor	Patient squeezes the examiner's fingers; compare relative strength of the two hands. Patient performs rapid movements with the hands and feet.	Retain Grip Strength Test and Finger Tapping Test
Premotor	Patient touches each finger to the thumb sequentially; observe for clumsiness, slowing, or inaccuracies. Patient commanded to perform single and serial limb movements, whole body movements, and buccofacial movements. Luria reciprocal motor tasks and alternating graphic sequences (Luria, 1980, No. 26).	Grooved Pegboard Boston Diagnostic Aphasia Examination tests of praxis
Frontal eye fields	Observe patient in direct gaze to command versus passive following of a moving stimulus.	Visual search tasks

(Continued)

Table 2. Bedside and Neuropsychological Tests of Frontal System Dysfunction *(Continued)*

Subsystem	Bedside maneuvers	Neuropsychological tests
Dorsolateral prefrontal	EXIT (Royall et al., 1992, No. 20).	Word fluency Figural fluency Wisconsin Card Sorting Test
Orbital prefrontal	Go/no-go tasks (Malloy et al. 1985, No. 5). Informal tests of smell discrimination.	University of Pennsylvania Smell Identification Test Stroop Color–Word Test Frontal Lobe Personality Scale (FLOPS)

Note. EXIT = Executive Interview.

observing for clumsiness, slowing, or inaccuracies. Callosal connections between premotor systems can be assessed by placing the fingers of one of the patient's hands in certain positions and requiring the patient to reproduce the positions using the other hand with eyes closed (Luria, 1980). Psychometric tests for evaluating complex movement and its disturbances include the **Purdue Pegboard** (Purdue Research Foundation, 1948) and the **Grooved Pegboard** (Lafayette Instrument Company, n.d.), which require the patient to place as many pegs into holes on a board as possible within a time limit. Praxis can be assessed by requiring the patient to perform single and serial limb movements, whole body postures, and buccofacial movements. Examples of such tasks can be found in the Boston Diagnostic Aphasia Examination manual (Goodglass & Kaplan, 1972).

C. Frontal Eye Fields Functions

Lesions in the frontal eye fields (FEF) result in transient ipsilateral eye deviation and more persistent contralateral gaze paresis. Secondary to these deficits in eye movement, the patient is unable to pursue a target or search visual space efficiently. Patients with FEF lesions are unable to search actively the side of the page contralateral to their lesion, although they are capable of passive eye movements in the same visual field. The intactness of passive gaze distinguishes such patients from those with hemispatial neglect.

D. Dorsolateral Prefrontal Functions

Dorsolateral functions encompass a variety of aspects of behavior, and numerous assessment methods are available for examining this domain. For example, Royall, Mahurin, and Gray (1992) developed a brief bedside test for measuring a variety of these functions, called the **Executive Interview** (EXIT). The EXIT includes tasks derived from a number of sources, including so-called frontal release signs from the neurological examination, abbreviated versions of neuropsychological tests such as word fluency, and Luria's complex motor tasks.

Generation of multiple response alternatives can be measured by word and figure fluency tasks. The most widely used word fluency task is the **Controlled Oral Word Fluency Test** (COWA; Benton, 1968). Other categorical fluency tasks (e.g., naming animals, fruits, and vegetables) have been shown to be more sensitive and specific than COWA in detecting dementia, but they may not tap executive functions to the same extent as the COWA. The COWA requires not only multiple response generation but also maintenance of a complex task set: The words must not include proper names and must not consist of previously used words with a suffix. In addition, there is the opportunity to observe perseverative intrusion errors and the use of vulgar or socially inappropriate words by patients with disinhibitory deficits. A nonverbal, or figural, fluency task was developed by Jones-Gotman and Milner (1977), who demonstrated that whereas patients with left frontal lobe dysfunction failed in verbal fluency tasks, those with right frontal lobe dysfunction differentially failed in figural fluency tasks. Ruff and colleagues developed a figural fluency task incorporating some constraints to enhance reliability. The **Ruff Figural Fluency Test** has been shown to be sensitive to right versus left frontal lesions, and large-scale norms are available for adults (Ruff, 1988).

Luria described a number of bilateral hand movements and alternating graphic sequences that theoretically require intact motor, premotor, and executive functions, particularly the ability to produce alternating response sets (Luria, 1980; Malloy et al., 1985). In administering these tasks, it is important to ensure that a response set is established and then changed and that the task is sustained long enough to allow observation of subtle executive dysfunction (within-task perseverations, cross-task perseverations, simplification of the movements, and intrusions of habitual responses such as writing letters rather than drawing the required shapes).

The **Wisconsin Card Sorting Test** (WCST; Heaton, 1981) has been considered the premiere test of executive functions for many years. It taps a variety of executive abilities, including maintenance of task set, flexibility in response to feedback or changing circumstances, and perseverative tendencies. The WCST has been shown to be sensitive to effects of frontal lobe lesions in a number of studies, but negative findings have also been reported regarding the frontal specificity of the test (van den Broek, Bradshaw, & Szabadi, 1993).

The **Category Test** and **Trail Making Test** have generally been considered measures of abstraction, set maintenance, and cognitive flexibility. Hence, clinicians frequently employ these tests as measures of dorsolateral frontal functions. However, research has indicated that these tests are failed by patients with nonfrontal as well as frontal lesions (e.g., Pendleton & Heaton, 1982).

E. Orbital Prefrontal Functions

Relatively few measures of orbital frontal functions in humans exist. Clinicians may therefore have difficulty detecting common behavioral sequelae of orbital frontal damage.

Anosmia can be assessed clinically by having the patient identify common aromatic substances such as coffee, tobacco, or cocoa. Psychometric assessment of smell discrimination is possible using the University of Pennsylvania **Smell Identification Test** (Doty, 1983), which provides age-corrected norms (major declines in smell thresholds are seen with normal aging). There are many other medical causes of reduced smell discrimination, however, such as infections of the nasal passages, smoking, and medication use.

Go/no-go tasks require the patient to make a response to a *go* signal and withhold or inhibit the response to the *no-go* signal. The task can be made more difficult by changing the habitual meaning of the signals (e.g., *go* to a red light, *no-go* to a green light). A bedside example of this task can involve asking the patient to tap his or her fist when the examiner says *stop* and not tap when the examiner says *go* (Malloy et al., 1985). The **Stroop Color–Word Test** (Stroop, 1935) is another task that places demands on inhibitory abilities. Orbital frontal zones are activated in normal persons during this task (Bench et al., 1993), but patients with orbital lesions have particular difficulty with the inhibitory portion (i.e., naming the color and ignoring the word during the color–word trial).

Disinhibited or socially inappropriate behavior can be observed informally on the treatment unit, and family reports should always be sought. Patients with orbital frontal dysfunction may display such behaviors as facetious humor, inappropriate sexual behavior, and labile emotionality. The **Frontal Lobe Personality Scale** (FLOPS) provides a psychometric means of assessing patient, staff, and family ratings of behavioral change caused by frontal lesions (Paulsen et al., 1996).

F. Cingulate and Supplementary Motor Area Functions

Lesions to the anterior cingulate gyrus and supplementary motor area (SMA) can result in **akinetic mutism** and **alien hand syndrome**, respectively (Goldberg & Bloom, 1990). Utilization behavior and the more general class of behavior called environmental dependency have been commonly reported with large bilateral frontal lesions and in unilateral mesial frontal lesions, although the precise localization remains unclear. These dramatic syndromes require no special assessment techniques beyond the ability of the examiner to make the appropriate anatomic–clinical correlations.

G. General Observations

Most neuropsychological tests are fairly well structured and call for a limited sample of behavior. Much of the planning and organization of the task are performed by the examiner in presenting instructions and rules. This may limit the opportunity to observe dysexecutive problems. A number of abnormal behaviors may be more apparent during the relatively unstructured interview, including reduced initiative and drive, poor insight into deficits, inappropriate social behavior, environmental dependency, poor self-monitoring of errors, easy agitation, and hypomanic-like state. The examiner should pay particular attention to discrepancies between patient and caregiver reports of problems.

The qualitative or process aspects of performance may nonetheless be informative in a patient with frontal dysfunction. On memory testing, for example, patients often display impoverished learning strategies, intrusions and perseverations, poor retrieval strategies, and difficulty with temporal tagging of learned information. The **California Verbal Learning Test** (CVLT; Delis, Freeland, Kramer, & Kaplan, 1988; Delis, Kramer, Kaplan, & Ober, 1987) is an excellent tool for examining these process dimensions. Using the CVLT, it is possible to observe patients with frontal lobe dysfunction producing a shallow learning curve across the five trials (owing to inefficient encoding strategies), mixing up the first and second lists (owing to problems in temporal tagging), showing inordinate gains from cued or recognition recall in comparison to free recall (owing to inability to formulate a retrieval strategy), and producing large numbers of perseverations and intrusions. This is a markedly different pattern from that of Alzheimer's disease, for example, in which patients typically do not benefit from cueing or recognition to a significant degree.

Patients with frontal lobe dysfunction often perform well on simple attentional tasks such as digits forward but display characteristic errors on complex attentional tasks requiring active manipulation of information. This deficit is often most apparent when the patient is required to overcome overlearned or habitual behavioral patterns (e.g., saying the days of the week backward rather than forward).

Dysexecutive and disinhibitory problems may affect the performance of these patients throughout the assessment session. Poor organization may lead the patient to fail to plan number placement on clock drawings. Perseverative tendencies may cause him or her to reuse an earlier item during a confrontational naming test. The examiner must be aware of the underlying frontal deficit lest these errors be mistaken for primary difficulties in visuospatial or language functions. Hence, it is usually desirable to assess frontal functions early in the assessment session.

V. CAUTIONS IN EVALUATING FRONTAL FUNCTIONS

The examiner must remember that most complex behaviors require that various frontal subsystems act in concert to produce adaptive functioning. Sustained and directed attention is an example of an ability involving multiple frontal zones (including dorsolateral, orbital, and cingulate areas). Second, many patients show combinations of the frontal syndromes described because naturally occurring lesions damage multiple subsystems.

Some deficits may be the result of either frontal or nonfrontal lesions. For example, abstract reasoning can be viewed as a measure of ability to shift mental set from the specific (i.e., more concrete or tangible) to the general (i.e., abstract) principle. It is often measured through proverb interpretation or similarities tests at bedside. However, abstract reasoning is strongly dependent on innate intelligence and education as well as general intactness of the brain. Although abstraction is quite susceptible to the effects of injury involving frontal systems, poor ability to abstract is not specific to frontal injury.

VI. CONCLUSION

The skilled clinician must be guided by a knowledge of frontal lobe subsystems and their roles in determining specific types of abnormal behavior. Bedside maneuvers can then be designed to discriminate dysfunction, and the clinician will be alerted to changes in incidental behavior that indicate frontal impairment. Neuropsychological assessment can provide an invaluable tool for testing frontal lobe functions taking into account the complexity of these behaviors and the profound effects of maturation and aging on frontal functions.

BIBLIOGRAPHY

Andreasen, N., Nasrallah, H. A., Dunn, V., Olson, S. C., Grove, W. M., Ehrhardt, J. C., Coffman, J. A., & Crossett, J. H. (1986). Structural abnormalities in the frontal system in schizophrenia: A magnetic resonance imaging study. *Archives of General Psychiatry, 43,* 136–144.

Bench, C. J., Frith, C. D., Grasby, P. M., Friston, K. J., Paulesu, E., Frackowiak, R. S., & Dolan, R. J. (1993). Investigations of the functional anatomy of attention using the Stroop test. *Neuropsychologia, 31,* 907–922.

Benson, D. F., Gardner, H., & Meadows, J. C. (1976). Reduplicative paramnesia. *Neurology, 26,* 147–161.

Benton, A. L. (1968). Differential behavioral effects in frontal lobe disease. *Neuropsychologia, 6,* 53–60.

Cummings, J. L. (1993). Frontal-subcortical circuits and human behavior. *Archives of Neurology, 50,* 873–880.

Cummings, J. L., & Mendez, M. F. (1984). Secondary mania associated with focal cerebrovascular lesions. *American Journal of Psychiatry, 14,* 1084–1087.

Delis, D. C., Freeland, J., Kramer, J. H., & Kaplan, E. (1988). Integrating clinical assessment with cognitive neuroscience: Construct validation of the California Verbal Learning Test. *Journal of Consulting and Clinical Psychology, 56,* 123–130.

Delis, D. C., Kramer, J. H., Kaplan, E., & Ober, B. A. (1987). *The California Verbal Learning Test: Research edition.* New York: Psychological Corporation.

Doty, R. L. (1983). *The University of Pennsylvania Smell Identification Test administration manual.* Philadelphia: Sensonics.

Goldberg, G., & Bloom, K. K. (1990). The alien hand sign: Localization, lateralization and recovery. *American Journal of Physical Medicine and Rehabilitation, 69,* 228–238.

Goldman-Rakic, P. S. (1987). Circuitry of the primate prefrontal cortex and regulation of behavior by representational memory. In F. Plum & V. Mountcastle (Eds.), *Handbook of physiology, the nervous system, and higher functions of the brain* (Sec. 1, Vol. 5, pp. 373–417). Bethesda, MD: American Physiological Society.

Goodglass, H., & Kaplan, E. (1972). *The assessment of aphasia and related disorders.* Philadelphia: Lea & Febiger.

Gotham, A. M., Brown, R. G., & Marsden, C. D. (1988). "Frontal" cognitive function in patients with Parkinson's disease "on" and "off" levodopa. *Brain, 111,* 2.

Heaton, R. K. (1981). *Wisconsin Card Sorting Test manual.* Odessa, FL: Psychological Assessment Resources.

Hoffmann, M. W., & Bill, P. L. (1992). The environmental dependency syndrome, imitation behaviour and utilisation behaviour as presenting symptoms of bilateral frontal lobe infarction due to moyamoya disease. *South African Medical Journal, 81,* 271–273.

Jones-Gotman, M., & Milner, B. (1977). Design fluency: The invention of nonsense drawings after focal cortical lesions. *Neuropsychologia, 15,* 653–674.

Lafayette Instrument Company. (n.d.). *Instructions for the Grooved Pegboard.* Lafayette, IN: Author.

Lhermitte, F. (1983). "Utilization behavior" and its relation to lesions of the frontal lobes. *Brain, 106,* 237–255.

Lhermitte, F., Pillon, B., & Serdaru, M. (1986). Human autonomy and the frontal lobes: Part I. Imitation and utilization behavior. A neuropsychological study of 75 patients. *Annals of Neurology, 19,* 326–334.

Luria, A. R. (1980). *Higher cortical functions in man.* New York: Basic Books.

Malloy, P. F., Bihrle, A., Duffy, J., & Cimino, C. (1993). The orbitomedial frontal syndrome. *Archives of Clinical Neuropsychology, 8,* 185–202.

Malloy, P. F., Cimino, C., & Westlake, R. (1992). Differential diagnosis of primary and secondary Capgras delusions. *Neuropsychiatry, Neuropsychology, and Behavioral Neurology, 5,* 83–96.

Malloy, P. F., Webster, J. S., & Russell, W. (1985). Tests of Luria's frontal lobe syndrome. *International Journal of Clinical Neuropsychology, 7,* 88–94.

Marenco, S., Coppola, R., Daniel, D. G., Zigun, J. R., & Weinberger, D. R. (1993). Regional cerebral blood flow during the Wisconsin Card Sorting Test in normal subjects studied by xenon-133 dynamic SPECT: Comparison of absolute values, percent distribution values, and covariance analysis. *Psychiatry Research, 50,* 177–192.

Martin, A. J., Friston, K. J., Colebatch, J. G., & Frackowiak, R. S. (1991). Decreases in regional cerebral blood flow with normal aging. *Journal of Cerebral Blood Flow and Metabolism, 11,* 684–689.

Mattson, A. J., & Levin, H. S. (1990). Frontal lobe dysfunction following closed head injury. A review of the literature. *Journal of Nervous and Mental Disease, 178,* 282–291.

Moniz, E. (1940). Prefrontal leucotomy in treatment of mental disorders. *American Journal of Psychiatry, 93,* 1379–1385.

Nauta, W. J. H. (1972). Neural associations of the frontal cortex. *Acta Neurobiologiae Experimentalis, 32,* 125–140.

Neary, D., Snowden, J. S., Northen, B., & Goulding, P. (1988). Dementia of frontal lobe type. *Journal of Neurology, Neurosurgery, and Psychiatry, 51,* 353–361.

Pandya, D. N., & Barnes, C. L. (1987). Architecture and connections of the frontal lobe. In E. Perecman (Ed.), *The frontal lobes revisited* (pp. 41–72). New York: IRBN Press.

Paulsen, J. S., Stout, J. C., DelaPena, J., Romero, R., Tawfik-Reedy, Z., Swenson, M. R., Grace, J., & Malloy, P. F. (1996). Frontal behavioral syndromes in cortical and subcortical dementia. *Assessment, 3,* 327–337.

Pendleton, M. G., & Heaton, R. K. (1982). A comparison of the Wisconsin Card Sorting Test and the Category Test. *Journal of Clinical Psychology, 38,* 392–396.

Purdue Research Foundation. (1948). *Examiner's manual for the Purdue Pegboard.* Chicago: Science Research Associates.

Reitan, R. M., & Wolfson, D. (1985). *The Halstead-Reitan Neuropsychological Test Battery.* Tucson, AZ: Neuropsychology Press.

Royall, D. R., Mahurin, R. K., & Gray, K. F. (1992). Bedside assessment of executive cognitive impairment: the executive interview. *Journal of the American Geriatric Society, 40,* 1221–1226.

Ruff, R. M. (1988). *Ruff Figural Fluency Test administration manual.* San Diego, CA: Neuropsychological Resources.

Stroop, J. R. (1935). Studies of interference in serial verbal reactions. *Journal of Experimental Psychology, 18,* 643–662.

Stuss, D. T., Benson, D. F., Kaplan, E. F., Weir, W. S., Naeser, M. A., Lieberman, I., & Ferrill, D. (1983). The involvement of orbitofrontal cerebrum in cognitive tasks. *Neuropsychologia, 21,* 235–248.

Valenstein, E. S. (1990). The prefrontal area and psychosurgery. *Progress in Brain Research, 85,* 539–553.

van den Broek, M. D., Bradshaw, C. M., & Szabadi, E. (1993). Utility of the Modified Wisconsin Card Sorting Test in neuropsychological assessment. *British Journal of Clinical Psychology, 32,* 333–343.

Weinberger, D. R., Berman, K. F., & Zec, R. F. (1986). Physiologic dysfunction of dorsolateral prefrontal cortex in schizophrenia. I. Regional cerebral blood flow evidence. *Archives of General Psychiatry, 43,* 114–124.

CHAPTER 29

Daniel N. Allen and Rhonda K. B. Landis

Neuropsychological Correlates of Substance Use Disorders

The lifetime prevalence rate for any substance use disorder is 16.7%, with lifetime rates for alcohol and drug use disorders of 13.5% and 6.1%, respectively (Regier et al., 1990). Substance use disorders are often chronic and debilitating. They are associated with increased mortality rates, increased homelessness, and increased use of health care systems. As a result, substance use disorders are enormously costly in human and economic terms. Evaluation of cognitive functioning in patients with substance use disorders has received increasing attention because of the recognition that substance use can cause a wide range of cognitive deficits and that these cognitive deficits are either directly or indirectly related to treatment outcome (Allen, Goldstein, & Seaton, 1997). Also, because of the localizing properties of neuropsychological tests, neuropsychological investigations have provided some information relevant to the etiology of various substance use disorders.

Partial support for this project was provided to Dr. Allen by a Theodore and Vada Stanley Foundation Research Award.

I. GENERAL ISSUES

A. Diagnostic Categories

Although there is no universally accepted definition of substance use disorders, the most popular diagnostic system is the category of substance-related disorders of the *Diagnostic and Statistical Manual of Mental Disorders* (4th ed., *DSM-IV*; American Psychiatric Association, 1994, pp. 175–272).

1. The **substance-related disorders** include the following:

a. **Substance use disorders**, which are divided into the subcategories of substance abuse and substance dependence

b. **Substance-induced disorders**, which include substance intoxication, substance withdrawal, substance-induced delirium, substance-induced persisting dementia, substance-induced persisting amnestic disorder, substance-induced psychotic disorder, substance-induced mood disorder, substance-induced anxiety disorder, substance-induced sexual dysfunction, and substance-induced sleep disorder

c. **Not all substances cause all substance-related disorders.** For example, substance abuse, substance dependence, and substance intoxication are associated with cannabis use, whereas substance withdrawal, substance-induced persisting dementia, and substance-induced persisting amnestic disorder are not.

B. DSM-IV Diagnostic Criteria

To meet DSM-IV criteria for **substance abuse**, an individual must exhibit maladaptive use that leads to significant negative consequences (e.g., substance-related arrest, driving while intoxicated, poor performance at work, relationship problems). This maladaptive substance use must be present during any given 12-month period. **Substance dependence** is diagnosed when, in addition to negative life consequences, there is a pattern of compulsive substance use, increased tolerance, or symptoms of withdrawal. Presence of increased tolerance or withdrawal symptoms is not required to make the diagnosis of substance dependence.

C. DSM-IV Substance Classifications

The *DSM-IV* also classifies drugs according to 11 categories including alcohol; cannabis; cocaine; opioids; amphetamines; hallucinogens; caffeine; inhalants; nicotine; phencyclidine; and sedatives, anxiolytics, or hypnotics. The neuropsychological sequelae associated with long-term substance abuse have not been adequately investigated for many substances.

D. Diagnosis of Substance Use Disorders

To diagnose substance use disorders accurately, a thorough history is needed. However, a number of factors can interfere with accurate history taking.

1. **Potential impediments to accurate substance use history**

a. Individuals who have substance abuse or substance dependence are sometimes hesitant to report the extent of their substance use.

b. Individuals who are intoxicated, delirious, or otherwise incapacitated are often unable to provide an accurate history.

c. Individuals with persisting cognitive impairment secondary to substance abuse may not be able to provide information on recent or remote substance use.

d. Clinicians who are unaware of possible substance abuse will fail to take adequate histories.

2. **Methods to ensure accurate substance use history**

a. Obtain histories from significant others when possible.

b. Recommend alcohol and drug screening when there is any suspicion of substance use.

c. Consult medical records for patterns of physical problems consistent with substance abuse, listings of prescription medications with high potential for abuse (e.g., benzodiazepines), and past history of substance use disorders (see chapter 1, this volume, for more information on review of medical records).

3. **Psychometric assessment and screening.** In addition to a thorough history and routine laboratory tests, there are psychometric instruments that may assist the clinician in arriving at a diagnosis of substance abuse. For example, there are self-report measures designed specifically to assist in the diagnosis of alcohol use disorders. These include the CAGE questionnaire (Ewing, 1984) and the Michigan Alcohol Screening Test (MAST; Selzer, 1971). These questionnaires are brief, assess a range of alcohol use behaviors and symptoms, and have defined cutoff scores for classification of problem drinking. These measures are often used as screening instruments to assist in identifying individuals at high risk for alcohol or drug abuse. Further evaluation of symptoms is necessary (e.g., through clinical or standardized interviews) before a final diagnosis is made.

4. **Concurrent abuse or dependence.** Finally, it is important to remember that substances are often abused concurrently (e.g., cocaine dependence accompanied by alcohol and cannabis abuse).

E. Neuropsychological Assessment of Substance-Induced Cognitive Deficits

1. **Cognitive deficits in substance use disorders.** Cognitive deficits noted in individuals with substance use disorders may vary in severity over time and from one individual to the next. Factors that may contribute to this variability include quantity, duration, and frequency of substance use; acute versus chronic effects of substance use; cognitive deficits caused by comorbid or preexisting psychiatric disorders; poor educational achievement; and medical conditions resulting from substance use (e.g., cirrhosis of the liver) and their deleterious effects on cognitive functioning. Concerning factors that contribute to cognitive deficits, two general areas that deserve close assessment are comorbid medical and comorbid psychiatric disorders. These areas must be clarified before extant cognitive deficits can be attributed to direct neurotoxic effects of a particular substance.

a. **Diagnosis of comorbid medical disorders.** In all patients who have substance use disorders, a thorough physical examination is necessary to rule out comorbid disorders that could affect neurocognitive functioning, such as the following:

(1) Disorders resulting from malnutrition (e.g., thiamine deficiency leading to Wernicke-Korsakoff disorder).

(2) Cirrhosis of the liver leading to hepatic encephalopathy.

(3) Subdural hematoma secondary to head injury.

(4) Epileptic seizures (alcohol use is one of the most common causes of adult-onset seizures).

(5) Infectious diseases associated with substance use (e.g., human immunodeficiency virus resulting from intravenous drug use).

b. **Diagnosis of comorbid psychiatric disorders.** In addition to comorbid medical disorders, a number of psychiatric disorders have high comorbidity with substance abuse and dependence (see Alterman, 1985). Comorbidity for some illicit substances, such as opiates and hallucinogens, has not been systematically investigated. Comorbid psychiatric disorders that can also contribute to decrements in neuropsychological functioning include the following:

(1) Attention deficit hyperactivity disorder, which has an increased incidence in patients with alcohol and heroin use disorders and early-onset (adolescent) substance use disorders.

(2) Major depression, which has a greater prevalence in patients with alcohol, cannabis, and polysubstance use disorders.

(3) Anxiety disorders, which occur with greater frequency in patients with alcohol use disorders.

(4) Antisocial personality disorder, which has an increased incidence in patients with alcohol, cannabis, cocaine, and polysubstance use disorders.

2. **Choice of neuropsychological tests.** In this section, we briefly describe some of the available instruments for cognitive screening as well as address other issues relevant to neuropsychological evaluation of individuals with substance use disorders. Because this is a summary, we do not discuss specific instruments in depth. We recommend that clinicians who are unfamiliar with the assessment instruments or wish to learn more about specific tests consult one of the standard texts that describe neuropsychological tests (e.g., Lezak, 1995; Reitan & Wolfson, 1985; Spreen & Strauss, 1991).

a. **Cognitive screening.** Because many clinicians do not have the time or expertise to administer and interpret full neuropsychological batteries, cognitive screening instruments have been developed. Two of these instruments are Cognistat (formerly the Neurobehavioral Cognitive Status Examination; Kiernan, Mueller, Langston, & Van Dyke, 1987) and the Mattis Dementia Rating Scale (MDRS; Mattis, 1988). Each of these instruments has advantages and disadvantages. General advantages are that they require little time to administer (about 30 minutes or less in most cases) and relatively little training to administer properly.

(1) Cognistat has been used with all age groups. Cognistat subtests assess orientation, attention, language comprehension, language repetition, confrontational naming, construction, memory, calculation, verbal abstraction, and judgment. Some investigators suggest that it overdiagnoses cognitive dysfunction in elderly individuals.

(2) The MDRS was designed specifically to assess for dementia, although the instrument assesses a variety of cognitive domains (attention, initiation, perseveration, construction, conceptualization, and memory). The usefulness of the MDRS in nondemented individuals who have cognitive deficits has not been thoroughly demonstrated.

b. **Full neuropsychological evaluation.** For a comprehensive discussion of full neuropsychological assessment see Lezak (1995). The subsequent sections focus on the typical neuropsychological deficits of individuals who abuse specific substances. A number of issues need to be kept in mind when reading this information:

(1) The harmful effects of some substances on cognitive functioning are not known. Because most of the available neuropsychological data are for alcohol, cannabis, cocaine, opiate, benzodiazepine, and polysubstance abuse, we restrict our discussion to these disorders.

(2) Of all the disorders of licit and illicit substance use, the neuropsychology of alcoholism is by far the most thoroughly investigated. Also, alcohol is the most widely abused substance. Because of this, we direct most of the discussion toward alcohol-related disorders and the cognitive deficits associated with them.

II. ALCOHOL

In the United States, more than 90% of individuals older than 18 have used alcohol, a central nervous system (CNS) depressant, at some time in their life.

A. Intoxication and Withdrawal

Common neurological symptoms of alcohol intoxication are slurred speech, ataxia, incoordination, and nystagmus. Behavioral symptoms include increased aggression. Psychological symptoms associated with intoxication include fluctuations in mood state and impaired cognitive abilities (e.g., memory, attention, and judgment). Physiological dependence on alcohol develops after heavy and prolonged consumption. Withdrawal usually occurs within 4–12 hours of drinking cessation (almost always within 48 hours). Most withdrawal symptoms resolve within 1 week. Withdrawal symptoms vary in severity; common mild symptoms include anxiety, irritability, increased heart rate, perspiration, and insomnia. More severe symptoms include grand mal seizures, delirium, and hallucinations.

B. Neuropsychological Findings

The research not only has characterized enduring cognitive deficits but has provided time periods during which cognitive abilities recover following cessation of alcohol consumption (see Parsons, Butters, & Nathan, 1987). In addition, investigators have characterized the cognitive deficits associated with specific syndromes, including Wernicke-Korsakoff syndrome, alcohol-induced persisting dementia, and hepatic encephalopathy associated with alcoholism. In the following sections, we first discuss cognitive deficits noted in individuals without dementia or Wernicke-Korsakoff syndrome. This discussion is broken down according to three time periods following alcohol cessation and the deficits noted during these time periods: acute deficits (present during the first week of abstinence), short-term deficits (present 2–5 weeks after the start of abstinence), and long-term deficits (present 13 months to 3 years after the start of abstinence). We then discuss alcohol-induced persisting dementia, Wernicke-Korsakoff syndrome, and hepatic encephalopathy.

1. **Acute cognitive deficits.** Neuropsychological functioning is the most significantly impaired immediately after cessation of alcohol consumption. In younger alcoholics (age <40), this impairment gradually improves over 3–4 weeks. Older alcoholics exhibit slower recovery curves (Goldman, Williams, & Klisz, 1983). During the first 2 weeks following drinking cessation, performance on tasks assessing intellectual functioning, memory, and visual motor skills often show marked improvement.

2. **Short-term cognitive deficits.** Studies of recently detoxified alcoholics (2–5 weeks) have indicated the presence of impairment across a number of cognitive domains, although there appears to be an age effect. For younger individuals (less than 35 years old) with relatively short drinking histories (5–10 years), those who consume more alcohol over the course of their lives exhibit poorer performance on neuropsychological measures, and those who are abstinent for longer periods of time exhibit better performance on neuropsychological tests. However, when these younger individuals are abstinent for an average of 4–6 weeks, cognitive functioning appears to return to expected, or "normal," levels (Eckardt, Stapleton, Rawlings, Davis, & Grodin, 1995). It may be that the cognitive deficits that persist after drinking cessation are the result of the cumulative effects of a lifetime pattern of alcohol abuse. When cognitive deficits persist, the most prominent areas of impairment are as follows:

　　a. Abstraction ability and problem solving

　　b. Perceptual-motor ability

　　c. Short-term and long-term verbal and nonverbal memory, with nonverbal memory relatively more impaired

3. **Long-term cognitive deficits.** Studies examining alcoholics who were abstinent for longer periods of time have been less conclusive regarding the nature and severity of impairment. In general, it appears that verbal abilities recover more quickly and that nonverbal learning and memory recover more slowly. Also, there is evidence indicating that even after long-term abstinence, deficits persist in the following areas:

　　a. Problem solving

　　b. Perceptual-motor abilities

c. Symbol–digit paired-associate learning and, possibly, visual learning and memory

4. **Wernicke-Korsakoff syndrome.** This syndrome is caused by a deficiency in thiamine, to which some alcoholics are particularly susceptible because of poor dietary practices. Thiamine deficiency causes hemorrhages in white matter structures (third and fourth ventricles and the aqueduct of Sylvius), which then cause impairment of motor and cognitive functioning. Ataxic gait, nystagmus, ophthalmoplegia, and confusion are present during the acute phase of the disorder (Wernicke's encephalopathy). These symptoms resolve within 4 weeks if patients are given large doses of thiamine. Most patients then go on to develop severe retrograde and anterograde amnesia as well as impairment in other areas of cognitive functioning, including executive functions (Korsakoff's syndrome). However, general intellectual functioning and semantic memory are typically preserved. Because cognitive deficits caused by thiamine deficiency are severe and debilitating, clinicians should always evaluate the patient's nutritional status and consider giving thiamine prophylactically.

5. **Alcohol-induced persisting dementia.** Although controversy exists regarding the etiology of alcohol-induced persisting dementia, Victor (1994) contends that the large majority of suspected cases of alcohol-induced dementia can be explained more adequately by other disorders, such as Korsakoff's disorder, rather than as a result of neurotoxic effects of alcohol. However, accumulating evidence suggests that this disorder accounts for a significant proportion of dementia cases, with as many as 25% of elderly alcoholic patients having alcohol-induced dementia and up to 24% of institutionalized elderly having alcohol-induced dementia (see Salmon, Butters, & Heindel, 1993, for review). Also, the DSM-IV includes a diagnosis of alcohol-induced persisting dementia. Onset of alcohol dementia is insidious.

a. **Characteristics of alcohol-induced dementia**

(1) Cognitive dysfunction affects general intellectual abilities as well as memory, visuospatial abilities, and abstraction and problem-solving abilities.

(2) Cognitive impairment is permanent, persisting long after alcohol consumption has ceased.

(3) Cognitive deficits significantly interfere with daily functioning.

b. **Differential diagnosis**

(1) Language abilities remain relatively well preserved in alcohol dementia. Knowing this may help clinicians distinguish

between patients with alcohol-related dementia and those with Alzheimer's dementia, in which prominent aphasic language disturbances are present (see chapter 12, this volume, for more information on assessment of dementia).

(2) Individuals with alcohol dementia tend to be younger (by approximately 10 years) than individuals with other dementias and have twice the average length of institutionalization.

6. **Hepatic encephalopathy.** Up to 30% of individuals with alcohol use disorders develop cirrhosis of the liver (Rehnstrom, Simert, Hanson, & Vong, 1977), which produces cognitive deficits. Results of recent research have suggested the following (Arria, Tarter, Starzl, & VanThiel, 1991; Moss, Tarter, Yao, & VanThiel, 1992; Tarter, Moss, Arria, & VanThiel, 1990):

a. Individuals with cirrhosis resulting from alcohol use disorders perform similarly to individuals with cirrhosis from other factors, although individuals with alcohol-induced cirrhosis have performed worse on tests of short-term memory, eye tracking, and hand–eye coordination.

b. Although many cognitive deficits improve following liver transplantation, memory capacity does not.

c. Subclinical hepatic encephalopathy (i.e., typical alterations in mood, cognition, and consciousness are not present) can produce significant neuropsychological impairment and is associated with memory impairment and motor slowing.

d. Initial evidence has suggested that biochemical indices of liver dysfunction are associated with specific types of cognitive dysfunction:

(1) Elevated nitrogenous compounds (in serum) are associated with impaired visuospatial abilities.

(2) Impaired protein synthesis is associated with impaired psychomotor ability, language efficiency, and perceptual abilities.

(3) Decreased hepatic blood flow is related to decreased language efficiency.

e. General intellectual functioning and abstraction abilities do not appear to be adversely affected by subclinical hepatic encephalopathy.

C. Neuroimaging, Event-Related Potentials, and Autopsy Findings

Cerebral abnormalities in alcoholics have been studied using a variety of techniques including autopsy studies; electrophysiological methods such as event-related potential (ERP) studies; and neuroimaging techniques, including computed tomography (CT), magnetic resonance imaging (MRI), and positron emission tomography (PET). Of these findings, the MRI and CT results are well established.

1. In recently detoxified alcoholics, CT and MRI results have shown cerebral atrophy and white matter and gray matter loss (most pronounced in older alcoholics), although prolonged abstinence (3–6 months) appears to cause white matter volume increases and cerebrospinal fluid volume reductions (see Mann, Mundle, Strayle, & Wakat, 1995, for review).

2. Initial PET studies have suggested that neuropsychological impairment is associated with overall decreased glucose metabolism and decreased metabolism in the frontal cortex and subcortical structures (hypometabolism significantly associated with performance on "frontal lobe" tests; Adams et al., 1993).

3. ERP evaluations have suggested that deficits in abstinent alcoholics do not improve over time (Glenn, Parsons, & Sinha, 1994).

4. Brain autopsy studies have indicated significant (40%) decreases in muscarinic cholinergic receptors in frontal and temporal cortex and putamen, as well as decreased benzodiazepine receptors in the frontal cortex (30%) and hippocampus (25%).

III. CANNABIS

Cannabinoids are the most widely used of the illicit substances. All cannabinoids are obtained from the cannabis plant, with the most common form being marijuana. Some studies have suggested that U.S. lifetime prevalence rates are as high as 33% for marijuana, with 10% of the population using it at least once a year and 1% using it monthly. The psychoactive effects resulting from cannabis use are caused by delta-9-tetrahydrocannabinol, or THC.

A. Intoxication and Withdrawal

Common physiological symptoms of cannabis intoxication include increase in appetite, bloodshot eyes, and dry mouth. Psychological symptoms associated with cannabis intoxication include fluctuations in mood state (euphoria or anxiety), thought disorder (grandiosity, paranoia, or hallucinations), and impaired cognitive abilities (e.g., memory, sensory perception, and judgment). Because it is not clear whether cessation of cannabis use leads to withdrawal, the DSM-IV does not include a diagnostic category for cannabis withdrawal. Most evidence suggests that cannabis withdrawal occurs only with very heavy and prolonged use and, even then, not in all cases. Symptoms of withdrawal may be psychological (anxiety, irritability), physiological (insomnia, nausea, tremor), or both. A number of psychosocial factors are associated with cannabis abuse or dependence, including poor motivation and work records, lower employment status, poor social relationships, higher incidence of legal problems, affective blunting and apathy, and decreased libido.

B. Neuropsychological Findings

Investigators have examined the cognitive deficits caused by cannabis during intoxication, as well as acute (24 hours after cessation) and long-term deficits.

1. **Cannabis intoxication.** Studies have consistently demonstrated that cannabis intoxication produces significant and widespread cognitive deficits. Investigators have demonstrated deficits in (a) problem solving, (b) abstraction, (c) attention, (d) expressive and receptive language, and (e) memory.

2. **Acute deficits.** Some deficits persist during the 24 hours following cessation of cannabis use (see Pope & Yurgelun-Todd, 1996). These include impairment of (a) attention, (b) executive functions, (c) mental arithmetic, and (d) immediate recall of verbal information.

3. **Long-term deficits.** There have been relatively few studies of the long-term neurocognitive effects of cannabis abuse or dependence, and many of the studies that have been done are methodologically flawed. Most of the well-controlled studies have failed to demonstrate consistently any significant cognitive differences between cannabis users and controls. On the basis of existing studies, it is clear that cannabis abuse does not lead to significant deficits on tests of intelligence or on comprehensive neuropsychological batteries such as the Halstead-Reitan in most users. However, individuals with heavy and prolonged use have exhibited deficits on tasks requiring attention, perceptual-motor abilities, reaction time, and short-term memory. Because of the equivocal nature of the literature, it is not clear whether these deficits reflect actual neurological damage caused by cannabis use or simply represent premorbid cognitive differences between users and nonusers (see Fals-Stewart, Schafer, Lucente, Rustine, & Brown, 1994).

C. Neuroimaging Findings

The effects of cannabis on structure and function of the cerebrum have not been thoroughly investigated. Few CT studies are available in which structural changes induced by cannabis use have been examined, and MRI, PET, and single photon emission computed tomography (SPECT) studies are lacking. Also, little information is available on cannabis-induced electrophysiological changes. Available information suggests the following:

1. There are no consistent differences between CT scans of users and nonusers after neurological and medical risk factors are controlled.

2. For individuals with significant historical use of cannabis but no current use, ERP studies have indicated that the ability to focus attention, avoid distraction, and process information quickly is decreased.

IV. COCAINE

Cocaine is a stimulant that causes cerebral vasoconstriction and hypertension, which, in turn, can cause ischemic stroke; cerebral vasculitis; cerebral, subarachnoid, and parenchymal brain hemorrhage; and seizures. Use of cocaine can also lead to death from respiratory or cardiac failure. Because cocaine use can cause multiple medical disorders that can adversely affect neurocognitive function, we suggest that readers consult the chapters in this volume that address cerebrovascular accidents (chapter 19) and nonepileptic seizures (chapter 16) to gain a more thorough understanding of the neuropsychological consequences of these disorders.

A. Intoxication and Withdrawal

Cocaine intoxication is accompanied by physiological, behavioral, and psychological symptoms. Physiological symptoms of intoxication include pupil dilation, increased blood pressure, increased psychomotor activity, tachycardia, and perspiration. Behavioral changes induced by cocaine include restlessness, hyperactivity, and stereotyped behavior. Psychological symptoms induced by cocaine include euphoria, increased alertness, anxiety, depression, and grandiosity. Cocaine dependence develops after heavy chronic use. Withdrawal begins within hours after cessation and almost always within 2–3 days. During withdrawal, individuals typically experience feelings of sadness, depression, or anxiety. This dysphoria is accompanied by disrupted sleep, appetite, or psychomotor functioning. These symptoms typically abate after physiological withdrawal is complete (1–5 days), although some symptoms may last much longer. Anhedonic symptoms have been reported to last up to 10 weeks with continued abstinence in some individuals.

B. Neuropsychological Findings

In most cases, gross intellectual abilities remain intact. Also, long-term memory, verbal fluency, semantic processing, and constructional abilities are preserved. A number of investigators (O'Malley, Adamse, Heaton, & Gawin, 1992; Strickland et al., 1993) have suggested that moderate-to-heavy cocaine users who are drug free and beyond cocaine withdrawal exhibit impairment in the following areas:

1. Mental flexibility and control
2. Attention and concentration
3. Visuomotor ability
4. Verbal and visual learning and memory

C. Findings on Imaging and Electrophysiological Tests

1. There is a strong correlation between amount of cortical atrophy and length of cocaine use, which suggests that increased use causes increased cerebral damage.

2. SPECT studies have indicated that during acute use, cocaine causes widespread hypoperfusion in periventricular areas. These lesions are not always evident on MRI and CT scans.

3. Initial results of SPECT studies also have suggested that women have fewer cerebral abnormalities than men and that women's SPECT scans often appear normal.

4. On SPECT, long-term cocaine users exhibited cerebral hypoperfusion in the frontal, temporoparietal, or periventricular regions.

5. In patients abstinent from cocaine for several months, PET studies have indicated decreased glucose metabolism in the frontal cortex, which appears to be related to dose and length of cocaine use.

6. A small percentage of cocaine users develop seizures; these individuals have been found to have brain atrophy on CT scans as well as diffuse electroencephalographic (EEG) slowing.

7. Some perfusion abnormalities apparently normalize with abstinence.

V. OPIOIDS

The DSM-IV category of opioids includes naturally occurring substances such as opium and morphine, semisynthetic substances such as heroin, and synthetic substances such as methadone and codeine. The most commonly abused illicit opioid is heroin. Medical and psychosocial factors associated with heroin abuse include a history of head trauma, poor school or occupational performance, and hyperactivity or attentional problems. Opioid abuse and dependence are much less common than substance use disorders associated with alcohol or cannabis, although some evidence suggests that heroin use disorders are increasing in prevalence.

A. Intoxication and Withdrawal

Opioid intoxication is characterized by feelings of euphoria, impaired attention and judgment, lethargy, slurred speech, and constriction of the pupils. Dysphoria often follows the initial euphoria. Less common symptoms include hallucinations and delirium. Withdrawal symptoms from opioids such as heroin typically occur within 24 hours of cessation. During opioid withdrawal, dysphoric feelings occur, including anxiety and depression. In addition, opioid withdrawal is characterized by malaise, nausea, dilation of pupils, sweating, insomnia, and muscle aches. Although most of these withdrawal symptoms abate within 1 week, some can continue for several months (e.g., dysphoria).

B. Neurocognitive Profiles

Researchers evaluating residual cognitive deficits in long-term opioid abusers have reported conflicting results. Some have found significant differences between heroin abusers and controls (Hill & Mikhael, 1979), whereas others have reported negligible differences (Rounsaville, Novelly, Kleber, & Jones, 1981). Cognitive effects of long-term heroin use, like those of other drugs, are difficult to evaluate because heroin is infrequently the only substance of abuse or dependence. Studies of cognitive abilities during acute administration of opioids are less equivocal and suggest that heroin impairs delayed verbal and visual memory as well as some measures of attention and concentration (Hanks, O'Neill, Simpson, & Wesnes, 1995). In some studies of current users, investigators have also found impairment of fine motor speed, visuospatial and visuomotor abilities, attention, verbal fluency, and memory, as well as a great deal of diffuse cognitive impairment. Again, conclusions about the severity of cognitive impairment are highly tentative because of methodological limitations. Deficits that persist following cessation of heroin use in chronic users may include impairment of executive functions and nonverbal reasoning. However, cognitive deficits noted in individuals with histories of chronic heroin use may also reflect the effects of other drugs (e.g., cocaine and alcohol), childhood factors (e.g., ADHD, poor education), or comorbid medical and psychiatric disorders.

C. Findings on Imaging Tests and EEG

Neuroimaging studies of individuals with opioid use disorders are limited. Existing studies have suggested the following:

1. No CT scan differences were found between abstinent heroin addicts and controls.

2. Individuals who use heroin and cocaine concurrently exhibited more perfusion abnormalities on SPECT than individuals who abuse cocaine only.

3. Decreased glucose metabolism in the whole brain was found after morphine administration.

D. Human Immunodeficiency Virus and Intravenous Drug Use

Because many individuals who use heroin administer it intravenously, these persons and other intravenous drug users (e.g., cocaine users) are at significantly higher risk for contracting human immunodeficiency virus (HIV). Individuals with HIV exhibit a number of neurocognitive symptoms that range from mild to severe. As a result, it is important to consider the role HIV could play in the cognitive deficits of individuals with disorders of heroin or other intravenous drug use. The cognitive symptoms associated with HIV have been well characterized; for additional discussion, we suggest that readers consult chapter 17, this volume.

VI. BENZODIAZEPINES

Benzodiazepines are classified as sedative–hypnotic drugs and are often used to treat anxiety, insomnia, and agitation. They are among the most widely prescribed medications in the world. These medications have a high potential for abuse because of their calming and sometimes euphoric effects. Although rates of substance use disorders are significantly higher among younger individuals, benzodiazepines are more often abused by elderly individuals for at least two reasons. First, elderly individuals receive almost 40% of benzodiazepine prescriptions (Juergens, 1993). Second, benzodiazepines are often used to treat disorders that increase with age (e.g., insomnia). Surveys of community-dwelling elderly individuals have indicated that up to 16% use hypnotics for sleep. Of these individuals, 19% report using hypnotics for 5–10 years, and 25% report using hypnotics for 10 or more years (Morgan, Dallosso, Ebrahim, Arie, & Fentem, 1988). In addition to the increased potential for abuse in the elderly, benzodiazepines can produce more serious reactions in elderly than in younger individuals. Because of this, we recommend that clinicians pay special attention to the assessment of benzodiazepine use disorders in the elderly. In some of these individuals, delirium can be induced by even small doses, and sudden discontinuance of benzodiazepines can cause confusion (see Tune & Bylsma, 1991, for review).

A. Intoxication and Withdrawal

Physiological side effects of benzodiazepine use include ataxia, dysarthria, incoordination, diplopia, vertigo, and dizziness. Benzodiazepines also induce relaxation, calmness, euphoria and, less frequently, feelings of hostility and depression. Long-term use of benzodiazepines can lead to development of tolerance to their therapeutic effects. Physiological dependence can appear after only a few days or weeks of use. Symptoms of withdrawal can include anxiety, irritability, insomnia, muscle twitching or aching, sweating, concentration difficulties, depression, and derealization. More severe withdrawal symptoms include seizures, delirium, and confusion. Withdrawal symptoms may be more intense when shorter acting benzodiazepines are discontinued. However, abrupt discontinuance of benzodiazepines with long half-lives (e.g., diazepam) can cause seizures within 3 days of discontinuation.

B. Neuropsychological Findings

Investigators have examined changes in cognitive function during benzodiazepine use. Benzodiazepines with both short and long half-lives have been examined. Also, young and elderly samples have been compared. These studies have suggested that elderly individuals tend to be more sensitive to the negative effects benzodiazepines can have on cognition. The acute cognitive effects of low-dose benzodiazepines appear negligible in younger individuals. In older individuals, however, even low doses can impair cognitive abilities. In addition, cognitive impairment increases as the dose increases, and cognitive deficits become less pronounced with chronic administration. Few researchers have examined residual cognitive deficits after benzodiazepine cessation.

1. **Acute effects.**

a. **Long-acting benzodiazepines** can cause impaired immediate and delayed verbal recall, impaired delayed visual recall, slowed reaction time and psychomotor performance, and an increase in intrusion errors on list-learning tasks.

b. **Short-acting benzodiazepines** can cause impairment of a variety of memory functions including explicit, implicit, working, and semantic memory and attention.

2. **Benzodiazepine discontinuance.** Individuals with suspected or actual cognitive impairment exhibit improved cognitive functioning after discontinuing benzodiazepines.

3. **Long-term use.** Cognitive deficits noted in chronic long-term benzodiazepine users may not improve even after 6 months of abstinence. Deficient cognitive performance was noted in middle-aged patients withdrawn from diazepam on tasks requiring verbal memory, visuospatial abilities, and psychomotor abilities (Tata, Rollings, Collins, Pickering, & Jacobson, 1994).

C. Findings on Imaging and Electrophysiological Tests and EEG

1. CT studies have suggested that there are no structural differences between long-term benzodiazepine users and controls.

2. PET studies have suggested that benzodiazepine administration decreases regional cerebral glucose metabolism.

3. Results of ERP studies have indicated that acute administration of benzodiazepines slows information processing.

4. Results of EEG studies have indicated that benzodiazepines decrease cortical arousal in frontal and central regions during acute administration.

VII. POLYSUBSTANCE USE

The DSM-IV includes a diagnosis of polysubstance dependence. To be assigned this diagnosis, the individual must have been repeatedly using three substances (excluding caffeine and nicotine) over a 1-year period, and the symptoms produced by this multiple substance use must meet criteria for substance dependence. However, to make this diagnosis, none of the substances used can meet criteria for substance dependence in and of themselves. A broader definition of polysubstance abuse would be abuse of or dependence on more than one substance; in such cases, if DSM-IV nomenclature were used, multiple diagnoses of abuse and dependence would be given, rather than a single diagnosis of polysubstance dependence. In the studies examining the neuropsychological concomitants of polysubstance use reviewed here, the investigators have employed the broader (non-DSM-IV) definition.

A. Intoxication and Withdrawal

Symptoms of intoxication and withdrawal reflect the specific symptoms associated with each substance. However, some substances can potentiate the effects of others. For example, using alcohol and benzodiazepines together produces increased sedation and euphoria than use of either one alone. In assessing individuals who abuse multiple substances, consideration of substance interactions is warranted.

B. Neuropsychological Findings

Up to 50% of current polysubstance users exhibit cognitive deficits (Grant & Judd, 1976). However, because of the varying effects of different substances on cognitive function, it is difficult to make any definitive statements regarding the general category of polysubstance users. In this group, cognitive deficits represent not only the combined neurotoxic effects of the substances use disorders, but also the unique comorbid factors associated with each substance (e.g., medical and psychiatric disorders). The literature examining individuals who have multiple substance use disorders suggests that the most consistently impaired cognitive abilities are as follows:

1. Perceptual-skills
2. Motor ability
3. Visuospatial abilities
4. Problem solving
5. Visual and verbal memory

C. Neuroimaging

The neuroimaging results of individuals who abuse multiple substances, like their neuropsychological profiles, are largely dependent on the substances they abuse. Multiple substance use can create a host of neurological abnormalities on neuroimaging tests or, conversely, may have a relatively benign presentation. When examining the neuroimaging studies of individuals with polysubstance use, the reader may wish to consult the previous sections on imaging to determine the types of abnormalities that are likely to be present.

VIII. CONCLUSION

There is growing recognition of the importance of evaluating cognitive deficits in individuals who have substance use disorders. At this time, the greatest amount of information is available concerning cognitive deficits associated with prolonged and excessive alcohol consumption. This literature suggests that some cognitive deficits improve with abstinence, whereas others do not. Also, the cognitive deficits associated with alcoholism are not always the result of the neurotoxic effects of alcohol; they are often produced by comorbid medical or psychiatric conditions or may reflect premorbid differences. On the basis of the relatively limited information available regarding other substances, it is apparent that associated cognitive deficits are multiply determined. Because multiple factors produce cognitive deficits, trying to determine the etiology of cognitive deficits in these individuals requires thorough physical, psychiatric, and psychosocial evaluation. More information is necessary before firm conclusions can be drawn about the long-term cognitive effects of most illicit substances. Also, further investigation is necessary to determine how these deficits interact with different types of substance abuse treatments to produce positive or negative outcomes.

BIBLIOGRAPHY

Adams, K. M., Gilman, S., Koeppe, R. A., Kluin, K. J., Brunberg, J. A., Dede, D., Berent, S., & Kroll, P. D. (1993). Neuropsychological deficits are correlated with frontal hypometabolism in positron emission tomography studies of older alcoholic patients. *Alcoholism: Clinical and Experimental Research, 17*, 205–210.

Allen, D. N., Goldstein, G., & Seaton, B. E. (1997). Cognitive rehabilitation of chronic alcohol abusers. *Neuropsychology Review, 7*, 21–39.

Alterman, A. I. (Ed.). (1985). *Substance abuse and psychopathology.* New York: Plenum Press.

American Psychiatric Association. (1994). *Diagnostic and Statistical Manual of Mental Disorders* (4th ed.). Washington, DC: American Psychiatric Association.

Arria, A. M., Tarter, R. E., Starzl, T. E., & VanThiel, D. H. (1991). Improvement in cognitive functioning of alcoholics following orthotopic liver transplantation. *Alcoholism: Clinical and Experimental Research, 15*, 956–962.

Eckardt, M. J., Stapleton, J. M., Rawlings, R. R., Davis, E. Z., & Grodin, D. M. (1995). Neuropsychological functioning in detoxified alcoholics between 18 and 35 years of age. *American Journal of Psychiatry, 152*, 53–59.

Ewing, J. A. (1984). Detecting alcoholism: The CAGE Questionnaire. *Journal of the American Medical Association, 252*, 1905–1907.

Fals-Stewart, W., Schafer, J., Lucente, S., Rustine, T., & Brown, L. (1994). Neurobehavioral consequences of prolonged alcohol and substance abuse: A review of findings and treatment implications. *Clinical Psychology Review, 14*, 755–778.

Glenn, S., Parsons, O. A., & Sinha, R. (1994). Assessment and recovery of electrophysiological and neuropsychological functions in chronic alcoholics. *Biological Psychiatry, 36*, 443–452.

Goldman, M. S., Williams, D. L., & Klisz, D. K. (1983). Recoverability of psychological functioning following alcohol abuse: Prolonged visual–spatial dysfunction in older alcoholics. *Journal of Consulting and Clinical Psychology, 51*, 370–378.

Grant, I., & Judd, L. (1976). Neuropsychological and EEG disturbances in polydrug users. *American Journal of Psychiatry, 133*, 1039–1042.

Hanks, G. W., O'Neill, W. M., Simpson, P., & Wesnes, K. (1995). The cognitive and psychomotor effects of opioid analgesics. II. A randomized controlled trial of single doses of morphine, lorazepam and placebo in healthy adults. *European Journal of Clinical Pharmacology, 48*, 455–460.

Hill, S. Y., & Mikhael, M. (1979). Computerized transaxial tomographic and neuropsychological evaluations in chronic alcoholics and heroine abusers. *American Journal of Psychiatry, 136*, 598–602.

Juergens, S. M. (1993). Benzodiazepines and addiction. *Psychiatric Clinics of North America, 16*, 75–86.

Kiernan, R. J., Mueller, J., Langston, J. W., & Van Dyke, C. (1987). The neurobehavioral cognitive status examination: A brief but differentiated approach to cognitive assessment. *Annals of Internal Medicine, 107*, 481–485.

Lezak, M. D. (1995). *Neuropsychological assessment* (3rd ed.). New York: Oxford University Press.

Mann, K., Mundle, G., Strayle, M., & Wakat, P. (1995). Neuroimaging in alcoholism: CT and MRI results and clinical correlates. *Journal of Neural Transmission: General Section, 99*, 145–155.

Mattis, S. (1988). *DRS: Dementia Rating Scale professional manual.* New York: Psychological Assessment.

Morgan, K., Dallosso, H., Ebrahim, S., Arie, T., & Fentem, P. H. (1988). Prevalence, frequency, and duration of hypnotic drug use among the elderly living at home. *British Medical Journal Clinical Research Edition, 296,* 601–602.

Moss, H. B., Tarter, R. E., Yao, J. K., & VanThiel, D. H. (1992). Subclinical hepatic encephalopathy: Relationship between neuropsychological deficits and standard laboratory tests assessing hepatic status. *Archives of Clinical Neuropsychology, 7,* 419–429.

O'Malley, S., Adamse, M., Heaton, R. K., & Gawin, F. H. (1992). Neuropsychological impairment in chronic cocaine abusers. *American Journal of Drug and Alcohol Abuse, 18,* 131–144.

Parsons, O. A., Butters, N., & Nathan, P. E. (Eds.). (1987). *Neuropsychology of alcoholism: Implications for diagnosis and treatment.* New York: Guilford Press.

Pope, H. G., & Yurgelun-Todd, D. (1996). The residual cognitive effects of heavy marijuana use in college students. *Journal of the American Medical Association, 275,* 521–527.

Regier, D. A., Farmer, M. E., Rae, D. S., Locke, B. Z., Keith, S. J., Judd, L. L., & Goodwin, F. K. (1990). Comorbidity of mental disorders with alcohol and other drug abuse: Results from the Epidemiologic Catchment Area (ECA) study. *Journal of the American Medical Association, 264,* 2511–2518.

Rehnstrom, S., Simert, G., Hanson, G., & Vong, J. (1977). Chronic hepatic encephalopathy. A psychometrical study. *Scandinavian Journal of Gastroenterology, 12,* 305–311.

Reitan, R. M., & Wolfson, D. (1985). *The Halstead–Reitan Neuropsychological Test Battery: Theory and clinical interpretation.* Tucson, AZ: Neuropsychology Press.

Rounsaville, B., Novelly, R., Kleber, H., & Jones, C. (1981). Neuropsychological impairment in opiate addicts: Risk factors. In R. B. Millman, P. Cushman, & J. H. Lowison (Eds.), *Research developments in drug and alcohol* abuse (pp. 79–90). New York: New York Academy of Sciences.

Salmon, D. P., Butters, N., & Heindel, W. (1993). Alcoholic dementia and related disorders. In R. W. Parks, R. F. Zec, & R. S. Wilson (Eds.), *Neuropsychology of Alzheimer's disease and other dementias* (pp. 186–209). New York: Oxford University Press.

Selzer, M. L. (1971). The Michigan Alcohol Screening Test: The quest for a new diagnostic instrument. *American Journal of Psychiatry, 127,* 1653–1658.

Spreen, O., & Strauss, E. (1991). *A compendium of neuropsychological tests.* New York: Oxford University Press.

Strickland, T. L., Mena, I., Villanueva-Meyer, J., Miller, B. L., Cummings, J., Mehringer, C. M., Satz, P., & Myers, H. (1993). Cerebral perfusion and neuropsychological consequences of chronic cocaine use. *Journal of Neuropsychiatry and Clinical Neurosciences, 5*, 419–427.

Tarter, R. E., Moss, H., Arria, A., & VanThiel, D. (1990). Hepatic, nutritional, and genetic influences on cognitive process in alcoholics. *National Institute on Drug Abuse Research Monograph series: 1990 Research Monograph, 101*, 124–135.

Tata, P. R., Rollings, J., Collins, M., Pickering, A., & Jacobson, R. R. (1994). Lack of cognitive recovery following withdrawal from long-term benzodiazepine use. *Psychological Medicine, 24*, 203–213.

Tune, L. E., & Bylsma, F. W. (1991). Benzodiazepine-induced and anticholinergic-induced delirium in the elderly. *International Psychogeriatrics, 3*, 397–408.

Victor, M. (1994). Alcoholic dementia. *Canadian Journal of Neurological Sciences, 21*, 88–99.

CHAPTER 30

Christopher Starratt

Emotional Disorders Associated With Neurological Diseases

The assessment of emotional status in a patient with possible brain dysfunction is essential because of the potential influence of emotional status on the performance of tasks that are used to assess other functional strengths and limits. In addition, a patient's emotional status, in and of itself, may be of neurodiagnostic significance. This area, however, is unlike many of the other areas of functional ability that neuropsychologists routinely evaluate. There is no arsenal of reliable, valid, commercially available instruments for testing the various aspects of emotion that are of potential neuropsychological significance.

Because emotional alterations can be associated with a wide range of neurological disorders, only neurological disorders for which a component of emotion is a particularly striking feature of symptom presentation are discussed here. Reference is made to the work of investigators who have developed or described methods of emotion evaluation that have been applied specifically to well-defined groups of patients with neurological disorders.

I. DEFINITION OF THE EMOTIONAL PROBLEM

A. Is It a Problem of Affect, Emotion, or Mood?

Affect is considered to be a fundamental, irreducible emotional feeling state. The experience of affect is, by definition, subjective. At the most basic level, it is experienced as either a pleasant or an unpleasant feeling state. Affect is generally regarded as temporally limited, that is, as a fleeting or momentary emotional state.

Emotion lends itself to more definitional variability. Despite disagreements about the range and types of experiences that should be included in a definition of emotion, most investigators are in general agreement that emotions are object focused. That is, the experience and expression of an emotion is related to some specific environmental event or cognitive representation of an event. Emotions function to signal the presence of a personally relevant environmental situation and to prepare the person for a specific action. Whereas an affective experience is always a private event, an emotion is an observable, "public" event (although behavioral expression can be suppressed or masked). It is generally accepted that the number of core, or basic, emotions is limited and finite. A representative listing of basic emotions, each of which has unique behavioral qualities, such as a characteristic facial expression, include happiness/joy, sadness, fear, anger, disgust, and, more equivocally, surprise. There is strong empirical evidence that these are universally experienced and recognized emotions. More complex emotions such as jealousy or guilt are thought to be based on differing combinations of the basic emotions. A relatively prolonged sequence of transactions between an individual and an environmental event of particular salience or relevance is described as an emotional sequence. Regardless of the complexity of the feeling state or environmental condition, the essential, defining feature of an emotion is rooted in its properties as a signal of a specific event that requires a specific action.

Mood is defined as a more generalized, diffuse, feeling state that has no specific object or referent associated with its experience. Whereas individuals can generally identify the object of their emotional state (e.g., one feels angry at someone or happy about something), they are hard-pressed to identify the specific reason for a mood state (the cause of the angry or happy mood). In addition, a mood state is generally considered more enduring than either an affective or emotional state. There has been much less empirical investigation of mood states than of emotions. Some research has indicated that moods can function to moderate either emotional experience or affective appraisal of specific environmental events. For example, one may be more likely to experience anger if one's mood is depressed. Similarly, one is more likely to attend to the more unpleasant aspects of the environment during a depressed mood.

B. Is It a Problem of Perception, Expression, or Experience?

This characterization, called mode of processing, also refers to the nature of the demand placed on the patient during a structured interaction with the examiner (i.e., what is required of the patient during a particular task). Most clinical research has focused on the perception and expression of emotion. A somewhat separate body of literature has focused on the experience of emotion, which includes the experience of basic emotions as well as of mood states.

C. What Is the Channel of Communication?

Channel of communication refers to the sensorimotor system used to display the target emotion. The preponderance of clinical investigation has focused on four communication channels:
- Facial display of emotion
- Vocal intonation of emotion (emotional prosody)
- Gesture of emotion
- Speech content (lexicon of emotion words)

II. DEVELOPMENT OF DISRUPTIONS IN EMOTIONAL FUNCTIONING

The disruption of emotional functioning is not specific to a particular neurological disorder. Emotional dysfunction can occur in association with an acute focal condition such as a cerebrovascular accident (CVA), an acute diffuse disorder such as traumatic brain injury (TBI), a progressive focal disorder such as a localized tumor, or progressive neural degenerative disorders such as senile dementia of the Alzheimer's type (SDAT) or Huntington's disease (HD).

In contrast to the extensive literature on cognitive functioning, there is relatively limited information regarding the course of emotion symptoms associated with the onset of neurological disorders. The literature that does exist, however, suggests that symptom course may be related to mode of emotional processing. For example, alterations in the perception of emotion may follow a course similar to that seen for cognitive processing, such as perceptual processing of nonemotional stimuli or language processing. Expression and experience of emotion, however, may exhibit a more complex pattern of presentation than does perception. Because environmental conditions play a larger role in the elicitation of emotional expression, and probably in emotional experience, there is more variability in their manifestation. The relative contribution of neurological and environmental factors in the expression and experience of emotions remains an unresolved issue.

III. VARIANTS OF EMOTIONAL DYSFUNCTION

Emotional valence (i.e., positive vs. negative emotions) may be of lateralizing significance, although there is no clear consensus on this issue at present. The right hemisphere *may* be specialized for the *expression* and *experience* of negative emotion, whereas the left hemisphere *may* be specialized for the *expression* and *experience* of positive emotion. Models of contralateral neural inhibition have been proposed to account for the expression of specific emotions in the presence of lateralized neurological dysfunction. Thus, a left hemisphere lesion may lead to the expression or experience of a negative emotional state such as depression through the release of contralateral inhibition of right hemisphere (i.e., negative emotion) processes. An alternative view of hemisphere-specific emotional expression is that lateralized emotional valence can best be understood from the perspective of disruptions in ipsilateral, cortical–subcortical neural processes. Interested readers are referred to Tucker (1981) for a more thorough discussion of this issue. Finally, some researchers have suggested that these asymmetries in emotional valence may extend to *perception* of emotions as well, although there is even more debate about the lateralized specialization for emotional valence for this mode of processing.

IV. NEUROPATHOLOGICAL CORRELATES OF DYSFUNCTION IN THE PERCEPTION, EXPRESSION, AND EXPERIENCE OF EMOTION

This section is organized by mode of processing. For each mode of processing (perception, expression, and experience), the most commonly reported site or sites of neuroanatomic dysfunction are presented. Each subsection concludes with a list of the neurodiagnostic groups that have reportedly demonstrated impairment within that mode of processing. Diagnostic groups that have not been reported in the literature to have been specifically evaluated for performance on a particular dimension of emotion are not included. The purpose of offering a brief listing of neurodiagnostic groups is to emphasize the range of neurological disorders that can present with symptoms of emotional disruption, not to provide an exhaustive list of all possible neurological disorders that might exhibit a particular emotional symptom.

A. Perception of Emotion

Focal lesions of the right hemisphere, particularly the right posterior region, have been most consistently associated with deficits in the perception of emotion for facial, prosodic, and lexical stimuli. However, mode of response may interact with side of lesion. For example, facial emotion matching deficits have been associated with right hemisphere lesions, whereas facial emotion naming deficits have been associated with both right and left hemisphere focal lesions.

Patients with nonfocal or multifocal lesions can also be impaired in the perception of emotion, although there is less association with side or site of lesion. For example, among TBI patients with bilateral lesions, the anterior–posterior axis does not appear to be related to performance in this task, although this dimension has been shown to be related to performance among TBI patients without bilateral damage.

Individuals with the following diagnoses have demonstrated impaired performance on a variety of emotion perception tasks:

- Cerebrovascular accident (right and, less commonly, left)
- Traumatic brain injury
- Senile dementia of the Alzheimer type
- Parkinson's disease
- Huntington's disease
- Complex-partial seizures (Temporal lobe epilepsy)

B. Expression of Emotion

1. STRUCTURED CONDITIONS

Lesions of the right hemisphere, particularly the right anterior region, have been associated with impaired expression of basic emotions under both posed (e.g., requiring the patient to demonstrate a target emotion) and spontaneous but structured (e.g., during a structured or semistructured interview) conditions. Expressions are usually diminished in intensity, frequency, or accuracy.

The following neurological disorders have been reported to be associated disruptions in the expression of emotion under structured or posed conditions:

- Cerebrovascular accident
- Traumatic brain injury
- Parkinson's disease (impaired facial expression but not prosody)

2. UNSTRUCTURED CONDITIONS

Disruptions in the spontaneous expression of emotion under unstructured conditions have been identified, and have been associated with greater variety of neuropathological sites, although lesions along the frontolimbic pathways are most frequently reported.

- Diminished emotional expression (e.g., apathy and indifference) is most commonly associated with dorsolateral frontal lesions.
- Excessive emotional expression (e.g., affective lability, impulsiveness, irritability) has been associated with orbitofrontal lesions.
- Spontaneous, unprovoked, intense expression of emotion (specifically, pathological laughing or crying) has been associated with subcortical lesions, particularly those that encroach on the corticobulbar tracts. Such states have also been reported among individuals with lesions in virtually any brain region. The particular emotion expressed *may* be of lateralizing significance: There have been reports of "silent" lesions of the right hemisphere eliciting pathological laughing and "silent" lesions of the left hemisphere eliciting pathological crying. This symptom should not be considered pathognomonic, however.
- Unprovoked expression of fear or intense anxiety, with or without the concomitant subjective experience, has also been reported among some individuals with temporal lobe epilepsy. However, positive emotional expressions (gelastic seizures) are rarely reported as part of the ictus of a temporal lobe seizure.

Disruption in the expression of emotion under unstructured or spontaneous conditions has been reported for the disorders in the list that follows. A brief description of the most frequently reported manifestation of emotional expression is included.

- Focal lesions (e.g., CVA, tumor)
  Diminished expression—dorsolateral frontal lesions
  Exaggerated expression—orbitofrontal lesions
- Traumatic brain injury—irritability or anger
- Parkinson's disease—masked facies (a hallmark of this disorder)
- Huntington's disease—apathy, indifference, outbursts of anger
- Senile dementia of the Alzheimer type—coarseness and shallowness of emotional expression
- Temporal lobe epilepsy—ictal fear or anxiety and, more rarely, ictal laughter

C. Experience of Emotion

Disruption in mood state is the most commonly reported aspect of dysfunction in emotional experience among brain-injured individuals. Although psychiatric classification of affective disorders and self-report measures of specific mood states (e.g., depression, anxiety, and anger inventories) generally do not distinguish between affective, emotional, and mood states, these approaches form the basis of the understanding of disruptions in emotional experience following brain injury. An overview of such states is provided in this section.

1. DEPRESSION

The most frequently cited disruption in mood state following any type of brain insult, depression usually is associated with left anterior or right posterior lesions; the latter are more frequently reported among patients with a family history of affective illness. The specific symptoms present in clinical depression may vary by hemisphere of lesion; however, this is an extremely complex issue that is not yet clearly resolved. The following is a brief, partial list of neurodiagnostic groups that have been reported to be associated with the experience of depressed mood:

- Cerebrovascular accident
- Tumor
- Traumatic brain injury
- Senile dementia of the Alzheimer type
- Parkinson's disease
- Huntington's disease
- Progressive supranuclear palsy
- Multiple sclerosis

2. EUPHORIA

Excessively positive emotional experiences, ranging from mild euphoria to frank mania, have been reported following brain insult. Disruptions in right hemisphere processing, particularly within the right orbitofrontal or basotemporal regions, have been associated with euphoric and manic states. Indifference to one's medical condition and associated life circumstances can be a concomitant feature. Euphoric reactions have been reported to be associated with the following disorders:

- Cerebrovascular accident (right hemisphere)
- Traumatic brain injury
- Huntington's disease
- Multiple sclerosis

3. ANXIETY

Ranging from mild apprehension to major fear reaction and panic episodes, anxiety has been reported to be a sequelae of brain insult. Both cortical and subcortical structures have been implicated, including lesions in the left dorsolateral cortical regions and discharging lesions (i.e., seizures) in the amygdala and anterior cingulate cortex. The amygdala is purported to be a particularly critical structure in the process of fear conditioning. Anxiety reactions have been reported for the following diagnostic groups:

- Cerebrovascular accident
- Traumatic brain injury
- Seizure disorders
- Senile dementia of the Alzheimer type

V. COMPETING DIAGNOSES THAT MUST BE RULED OUT

In the case of emotional disruption following brain injury, the most obvious competing diagnoses are associated with psychiatric disorders. Neuropsychologists are often faced with the task of determining whether a patient is suffering from a primary psychiatric disorder or is experiencing psychiatric symptoms that are the direct result, or an associated feature, of an acquired brain disorder. This distinction is particularly important because characteristic patterns of cognitive deficit can be associated with psychiatric disorders in and of themselves, such as a dementia-like presentation among some clinically depressed elderly (see chapter 10, this volume). In addition, comorbid psychiatric and neurological disorders can yield more pronounced cognitive deficits and perhaps different patterns of cognitive deficit than would be expected on the basis of the presence of a given neurological disorder by itself. This factor can result in errors in diagnosis as well as overestimation of the severity of cognitive sequelae associated with neurological insult.

Both depression and schizophrenia (per criteria of the *Diagnostic and Statistical Manual of Mental Disorders* (4th ed.; DSM-IV; American Psychiatric Association, 1994) have also been associated with impairment on direct measures of emotion perception. Patients with schizophrenia have been reported to be more broadly and severely impaired, whereas depressed patients reportedly have greater difficulty with emotion naming as opposed to emotion matching. In addition, depressed patients may overidentify emotional stimuli as representing a sad emotion and may be less likely to identify happy emotional stimuli correctly.

VI. THE NEUROPSYCHOLOGICAL EXAMINATION

A. Areas of Emphasis

The logic of examining a patient for evidence of disruptions in emotional functioning should follow the logic of any neuropsychological examination. A clinical screening of the perception, expression, and experience of emotion can be incorporated into a neuropsychological examination with minimal additional time burden. Specifically, in the clinical interview one should directly inquire about changes in emotion. Third-party reports of alterations in general mood, as well as emotional reactions to specific events, should be pursued.

Systematic evaluation of all aspects of emotional functioning is particularly important in any situation in which there has been an abrupt change in mood or behavior, especially if there is no prior history of such behavior. Similarly, uncooperative or oppositional patients who are referred for evaluation warrant particular attention, because such behavior may reflect impaired functioning in one or more of the emotional domains. Systematic evaluation is critical because emotional processes are interrelated in complex ways. For example, without careful assessment, it is impossible to know if an individual with intermittent angry outbursts is having difficulty with the modulation of emotional expression, is responding appropriately to a misperception of the emotional context of the situation, or is manifesting features of a dysfunctional mood state (e.g., depression).

B. Methods of Assessment: Response and Stimulus Alternatives

The following is an overview of the various methods that have been used in the clinical and clinical research literature to evaluate the perception, expression, and experience of emotion, with a focus first on the types of responses that are typically required of the patient, followed by the kinds of stimuli that are most often used.

1. PERCEPTION OF EMOTION

a. Response alternatives

When choosing the method of response, it is important to keep in mind that some clinical researchers have reported that response mode can influence performance in patients with some types of lesions. For example, patients with both right and left hemisphere focal lesions have been reported to be equally impaired when naming the emotion of a facial display, whereas those with right focal lesions have been reported to perform more poorly than those with left focal lesions when matching facial displays (e.g., Blonder, Bowers, & Heilman, 1991).

Naming emotional stimuli. Emotion naming is generally conducted using a multiple choice format in which several, if not all, of the names of the basic emotions are printed in a vertical array on a cue card. The patient is asked either to state or point to the name that corresponds to a displayed emotional stimulus. Because of the language demands associated with this response mode, it is recommended that the examiner confirm that the patient can read, name, and point to the response options prior to presenting any emotion stimuli.

Identifying named emotions. An array depicting several different emotions is presented either simultaneously (e.g., a vertical array of four faces, each depicting a different emotion) or sequentially (e.g., the repetition of a sentence expressing the prosody associated with different emotions). The patient is asked to identify a target emotion that has been specified by the examiner (e.g., point to the happy face; raise your hand when you hear the sentence spoken in a sad tone of voice).

Matching emotional stimuli. This task is loosely analogous to a discrimination procedure in which pairs of emotion stimuli are presented either simultaneously or sequentially and the patient is asked to indicate only whether the pair represent the same emotion or different emotions. This procedure has been most often reported for use with facial and prosodic stimuli. Some cross-modality studies have also been reported (e.g., a face depicting anger is displayed along with an audiotape of a sentence spoken in a fearful tone).

b. Types of stimuli

Facial display. Slides of adult men and women depicting basic emotions (happiness, sadness, fear, anger, surprise, disgust, neutral) are presented to the patient, who is expected to provide a response that identifies the depicted emotion. Slides are commercially available (e.g., Ekman & Friesen, 1976) with norms for each slide. Given the large number of slides per emotion, it is fairly easy to select slides that have been accurately identified by at least 80% of non-brain damaged individuals.

Videos of adult men and women displaying basic emotions have also been developed, usually for use within specific research laboratories. An advantage of video stimuli is their ecological validity, which allows the patient to observe an emotion as it unfolds. Equipment constraints and relative difficulty obtaining stimulus tapes reduce the clinical usefulness of video stimuli.

Bedside examination can be conducted by a clinician displaying the facial expression associated with each of the basic emotions. This approach requires practice on the part of the clinician. It is useful to obtain independent ratings of facial displays by colleagues before use with patients.

Regardless of the type of stimulus used, multiple trials (at least five) of several different emotions are generally presented to the patient to obtain sufficient sampling of patient performance for meaningful interpretation. O'Sullivan (1982) has reviewed a number of tests, both static and video, that have been developed to measure perception of facial emotion.

Vocal intonation. Audiotapes of adult men and women reciting sentences that are neutral in emotional content (e.g., the book is on the desk) using the emotional expression, or prosody, associated with basic emotions (happiness, sadness, fear, anger, surprise, disgust, neutral) are used to assess a patient's ability to comprehend vocal intonation.

Bedside examination can be accomplished using the same procedure. Ross (1981) provided an excellent description of how to conduct a bedside examination of emotional prosody. As recommended for facial stimuli, multiple trials per emotion should be presented.

Gestures. Bedside examination is the most typical setting for the evaluation of emotional gesturing. The clinician pantomimes basic emotions (happiness, sadness, fear, anger, surprise, disgust) in the presence of the patient. Ross (1981) provided a description of this procedure and specifically recommended that emotional gesturing be evaluated separately from emotional prosody.

Examination of emotional gestures has been incorporated into videos of emotional communication. For example, the Profile of Nonverbal Sensitivity (PONS; Rosenthal, Hall, DiMatteo, Rogers, & Archer, 1979) includes gestures as a separate dimension of emotional communication. However, the PONS was not initially developed for use with patients with neurological disorders; it can be difficult for some patients to complete because segments are relatively short (about 2 seconds) and they are not intended to display single basic emotions.

Speech content (lexicon). **Emotion words** that are semantically related to the basic emotions (e.g., *terror* and *dread* for the basic emotion *fear*) are presented to the patient. A list of emotion words and nonemotion words of similar frequency of use in the language of examination are typical stimuli for evaluating the emotion lexicon. Words are often selected from a general word source that also provides information about frequency of use, such as the Thorndike and Lorge (1944) list. Any of the modes of response previously described could be used to assess the integrity of the emotion lexicon.

Short **emotion sentences** are presented to the patient that infer a basic emotion either by the use of an emotion word in the sentence (e.g., he was elated by his victory) or by context alone (e.g., his eyes were full of tears as he left the funeral). In the assessment of lexicon, stimuli can be presented in a written format, by audiotape, or by using a combination of the two methods. Borod, Andelman, Obler, Tweedy, and Welkowitz (1992) have provided a detailed description of the methods associated with the evaluation of emotion words and sentences.

2. EXPRESSION OF EMOTION

a. Response alternatives

Posed responses are the channel-specific actions produced by the patient in response to a specific direction by the examiner (e.g., make a happy face; make a face that looks like the one I am making). Posed responses are judged primarily for accuracy. Spontaneous responses are generally multichannel actions produced by the patient that have been elicited by either a structured or an unstructured stimulus condition. Spontaneous responses to structured stimuli are judged for both accuracy and frequency, whereas spontaneous responses to unstructured stimuli are often judged for accuracy, frequency, and appropriateness to the situation.

Regardless of the type of stimulus condition or response alternative used, it is optimal to videotape the patient's responses and to have independent judges rate the dimensions of interest. However, for clinical purposes, the examiner can (with practice) conduct clinically useful ratings during the examination.

b. Stimulus conditions

In general, the examiner attempts to create a condition that will elicit an emotional response from the patient. This can be accomplished using a relatively structured or unstructured format. Structured conditions include **direct commands** (e.g., show me an angry face), **displays** of basic emotions (e.g., make a face like the person in the picture), or **emotion-eliciting** stimuli (e.g., picture or video of a surgical procedure). An array of emotion-eliciting pictures has been developed and normed by the University of Florida Emotion and Attention Research Group (Center for the Psychophysiological Study of Emotion and Attention, 1994). In contrast to structured stimulus conditions, unstructured conditions are not intended to elicit a particular emotion directly or discretely. Clinical observation during an interview or during a patient activity that is not directed by the examiner is most representative of this approach.

3. EXPERIENCE OF EMOTION

There is considerably less systematic information in the neuropsychological literature on the experience of emotion compared to the perception and expression of emotion. The inability to identify or describe one's feeling has been reported primarily in the psychiatric literature as **alexithymia.** This concept generally does not appear in the neurological or neuropsychological literature, and its usefulness for elucidating neurologically relevant problems in the experience of emotion has yet to be established.

Whereas specific instruments have been developed to assess the experience of emotion, few have been used with groups of patients with neurological disorders. For example, Lang (1980) described a procedure using a series of manikin drawings that depict affective valence (pleasant to unpleasant) and affective arousal (calm to intensely aroused). Similarly, visual analogue scales have been applied to the self-rating of mood states (Cowdrey, Gardner, O'Leary, Leibenluft, & Rubinow, 1991). Such scales can be either bipolar or unipolar. Bipolar scales include opposing mood states represented pictorially at the anchor points of a line. A vertical display is typically used to reduce the potential biasing effects of visual neglect or visual field cuts on self-ratings of mood. The patient indicates, by pointing or marking with a pencil, the position along the line that best represents his or her current mood state. Conversely, single mood state scales use a "thermometer" approach of measurement. A single mood is represented pictorially at the base with a vertical line extending up the page. The patient represents the degree or magnitude of that feeling state along the vertical line. Responses can be quantified by measuring the distance from the center (neutral response) of bipolar scales or from the base of unipolar scales. Such instruments are particularly useful when assessing individuals with language disorders.

Mood states are often evaluated with the self-report and clinical rating instruments commonly used with nonneurologically impaired individuals (e.g., Beck Depression Inventory, Hamilton Rating Scale, State-Trait Anxiety Inventory). At best, they are imperfect measures of the putative mood state when used with neurologically impaired groups, and the results should be interpreted with caution.

Despite the limited research in this area, the experience of emotion is an important dimension to include in a comprehensive evaluation of the emotional status of a patient with a neurological disorder. Anecdotal reports have indicated that a dissociation can occur between the expression and experience of emotion among some clinical groups. For example, a patient may not display an emotion such as anger when provoked but may report an intense feeling of anger associated with the situation. Conversely, a clinician may observe an intense expression of emotion when there is no concomitant report of the subjective emotional experience, as has been described in cases of pathological laughter or pathological crying. Such dissociations may be of diagnostic significance.

VII. CONCLUSION

It is difficult to convey within a guidebook format the full richness and complexity of the construct of emotion as it applies to neuropsychological assessment. Additional readings that may be of assistance in developing a conceptual understanding of the neurology of emotion include those by Bear (1983), Borod and Koff (1989), Campbell (1982), Derryberry and Tucker (1992), Heilman, Bowers, and Valenstein (1985), and Le Doux (1995). More detailed descriptions of clinical assessment batteries that evaluate the perception and expression of emotion can be found in writings by Borod et al. (1990) and Blonder, Bowers, and Heilman (1991). Finally, for those interested in more methodologically rigorous assessment approaches, Lang (1995) has described a startle reflex technique using eyeblink measurement that may have potential applications in the effort to uncover the neural mechanisms of emotion and to understand the ways in which emotion can become disrupted as the result of various neuropathological conditions.

BIBLIOGRAPHY

American Psychiatric Association. (1994). *Diagnostic and statistical manual of mental disorders* (4th ed.). Washington, DC: Author.

Bear, D. M. (1983). Hemispheric specialization and the neurology of emotion. *Archives of Neurology, 40*, 195–202.

Blonder, L. X., Bowers, D., & Heilman, K. M. (1991). The role of the right hemisphere in emotional communication. *Brain, 114*, 1115–1127.

Borod, J. C., Andelman, F., Obler, L. K., Tweedy, J. R., & Welkowitz, J. (1992). Right hemisphere specialization for the identification of emotional words and sentences: Evidence from stroke patients. *Neuropsychologia, 30*, 827–844.

Borod, J. C., & Koff, E. (1989). The neuropsychology of emotion: Evidence from normal, neurological, and psychiatric populations. In E. Perecman (Ed.), *Integrating theory and practice in clinical neuropsychology* (pp. 175–215). Hillsdale, NJ: Erlbaum.

Borod, J. C., Welkowitz, J., Alpert, M., Brozgold, A. Z., Martin, C., Peselow, E., & Diller, L. (1990). Parameters of emotional processing in neuropsychiatric disorders: Conceptual issues and a battery of tests. *Journal of Communication Disorders, 23*, 247–271.

Campbell, R. (1982). The lateralization of emotion: A critical review. *International Journal of Psychology, 17*, 211–229.

Center for the Psychophysiological Study of Emotion and Attention. (1994). *The International Affective Picture System* [Photographic slides]. Gainesville, FL: Center for Research in Psychophysiology, University of Florida.

Cowdrey, R. W., Gardner, D. L., O'Leary, K. M., Leibenluft, E., & Rubinow, D. R. (1991). Mood variability: A study of four groups. *Americal Journal of Psychiatry, 148*, 1505–1511.

Derryberry, D., & Tucker, D. M. (1992). Neural mechanisms of emotion. *Journal of Consulting and Clinical Psychology, 60*, 329–338.

Ekman, P., & Friesen, W. V. (1976). *Pictures of facial affect.* Palo Alto, CA: Consulting Psychologists Press.

Heilman, K. M., Bowers, D., & Valenstein, E. (1985). Emotional disorders associated with neurological diseases. In K. M. Heilman and E. Valenstein (Eds.), *Clinical neuropsychology* (pp. 377–402). Oxford, England: Oxford University Press.

Lang, P. J. (1980). Behavioral treatment and bio-behavioral assessment: Computer applications. In J. B. Sidowski, J. H. Johnson, & T. A. Williams (Eds.), *Technology in mental health care delivery systems* (pp. 119–137). Norwood, NJ: Ablex.

Lang, P. J. (1995). The emotion probe: Studies of motivation and attention. *American Psychologist, 50*, 372–385.

Le Doux, J. E. (1995). Emotion: Clues from the brain. *Annual Review of Psychology, 46*, 209–235.

O'Sullivan, M. (1982). Measuring the ability to recognize facial expressions of emotion. In P. Ekman (Ed.), *Emotion in the human face* (2nd ed., pp. 281–317). New York: Cambridge University Press.

Rosenthal, R., Hall, J. A., DiMatteo, M. R., Rogers, P. L., & Archer, D. (1979). *Sensitivity to nonverbal communication: The PONS test.* Baltimore: Johns Hopkins University Press.

Ross, E. D. (1981). The aprosodias: Functional-anatomic organization of the affective components of language in the right hemisphere. *Archives of Neurology, 38*, 561–569.

Thorndike, E. L., & Lorge, I. (1944). *The teacher's word book of 30,000 words.* New York: Bureau of Publications, Teachers College.

Tucker, D.M. (1981). Lateral brain function, emotion, and conceptualization. *Psychological Bulletin, 89*, 19–46.

APPENDIX

Selective Listing of Medical Record Abbreviations

a	arterial
Aa	alveolar/arterial
āā	of each
abd	abdomen
ABG	arterial blood gas
abn	abnormal
ac	before meals
A/C	assist control
ACE	angiotensin-converting enzyme; adrenocortical extract
ACLS	advanced cardiovascular life support
ACT	activated clotting time
ACTH	adrenocorticotropic hormone
ADH	antidiuretic hormone
ADL	activities of daily living
ad lib	as desired, freely
adm	admission
AF	atrial fibrillation
AIDS	acquired immunodeficiency syndrome
AJ	ankle jerk
AKA	above-knee amputation
AL	arterial line

alb	albumin
ALL	acute lymphoblasic leukemia
ALS	amyotrophic lateral sclerosis
AM	morning
AMA	against medical advice
AMI	acute myocardial infarction
AML	acute myelogenous leukemia
amp	ampule
AMP	adenosine monophosphate
amt	amount
amy	amylase
ANA	antinuclear antibody
ANLL	acute nonlymphocytic leukemia
AODM	adult-onset diabetes mellitus
AOP	aortic pressure
AP	anteroposterior
appt	appointment
aq	water
ARC	AIDS-related complex
ARDS	acute respiratory distress syndrome
ARF	acute renal failure
ARM	arterial rupture of membranes
ART	assessment, review, and treatment
AS	atriosystolic; aortic stenosis
asa	aspirin
ASHD	arteriosclerotic heart disease
at fib	atrial fibrillation
ATC	around the clock
ATN	acute tubular necrosis
AV	arteriovenous; atrioventricular
AVM	arteriovenous malformation
B	black
ba	barium
BBB	blood–brain barrier; bundle branch block
BC	blood culture
BCP	birth control pill
BE	barium enema
BEE	basal energy expenditure
bid	two times per day
bilat	bilateral
bili	bilirubin
BKA	below-knee amputation
Bl s	blood sugar
BM	bowel movement
BMR	basal metabolic rate
BP	blood pressure

BPH	benign prostatic hypertrophy
bpm	beats per minute
BR	bed rest
BRP	bathroom privileges
BS or bs	breath sounds
BSA	body surface area
BSO	bilateral salpingo-oophorectomy
BTL	bilateral tubal ligation
BUN	blood urea nitrogen
BW	body weight
Bx	biopsy
c̄	with
C	centigrade
Ca	cancer
Ca^{+2}	calcium
CAB	coronary artery bypass
CABG	coronary artery bypass graft
CAD	coronary artery disease
cal	calorie
cap	capsule
CAT	computerized axial tomography
cath	catheterization
CBC	complete blood cell count
CBD	common bile duct
cc	cubic centimeter
CC	chief complaint
CCr	creatine clearance
CCU	coronary care unit
CD4	helper–inducer T cells
CD8	suppressor–cytotoxic T cells
CEA	carcinoembryonic antigen
CF	complement fixation; conversion factor
CHD	congenital heart disease
CHF	congestive heart failure
cho	carbohydrate
CI	cardiac index
CK	creatine kinase
CK-MB	creatine kinase, myocardial band
cl	clear
Cl$^-$	chloride
CLL	chronic lymphocytic leukemia
cm	centimeter
CM	costal margin
CNS	central nervous system
CO	cardiac output; carbon monoxide
c/o	complains of

CO_2	carbon dioxide
CoA	coenzyme A
conc	concentrate
COPD	chronic obstructive pulmonary disease
CPAP	continuous positive airway pressure
CPK	creatine phosphokinase
CPR	cardiopulmonary resuscitation
cps	cycles per second
Cr	creatinine
CR	cardiorespiratory
CRH	corticotropin-releasing hormone
C/S	culture and sensitivity
CSF	cerebrospinal fluid
C/sec	cesarean section
CT	computed tomography
Cu	copper
CV	cardiovascular
cva	costovertebral angle
CVA	cerebrovascular accident
CVP	central venous pressure
CXR	chest X-ray
cysto	cystoscopy
D&C	dilation and curettage
D/C	discontinue
D&S	dilation and suction
DAT	diet as tolerated
Dial	dialysis
dil	dilute
dl	deciliter
DLE	drug-related lupus erythematosus
DM	diabetes mellitus
DNA	deoxyribonucleic acid
DOA	dead on arrival
DP	dorsalis pedis
DPT	diphtheria, pertussis, tetanus
DFR	delivery room
ds	double strand
DSD	dry sterile dressing
FS	frozen section
FSH	follicle-stimulating hormone
FWB	full weight bearing
fx	fracture
g	gram
Ga	gallium
GA	general anesthesia
GB	gallbladder

Gc	gonoccocus
GERD	gastroesophageal reflux disease
GI	gastrointestinal
glu	glucose
gr	grain
GSW	gunshot wound
gtt	drop
GTT	glucose tolerance test
GU	genitourinary
GVHD	graft-versus-host disease
Gyn	gynecology
H/A	headache
HAV	hepatitis A virus
Hb	hemoglobin
HBP	high blood pressure
HBV	hepatitis B virus
hct	hematocrit
HCV	hepatitis C virus
HD	hospital discharge
HDL	high-density lipoprotein
HDV	hepatitis D virus
HEENT	head, eyes, ears, nose, and throat
Hg	hemoglobin
H/H	hemoglobin/hematocrit
HIV	human immunodeficiency virus
H&L	heart and lungs
HLA	human leukocyte antigen
H_2O	water
H_2O_2	hydrogen peroxide
H&P	history and physical examination
HPI	history of present illness
HR	heart rate
HRS	hepatorenal syndrome
hs	hour of sleep (at bedtime)
HSV	herpes simplex virus
ht	height
HTN	hypertension
hx	history
I&D	incision and drainage
IABP	intraaortic balloon pump
IBC	iron-binding capacity
IBD	inflammatory bowel disease
IBS	irritable bowel syndrome
ICP	intracranial pressure
ICU	intensive care unit
ID	intradermal

IDDM	insulin-dependent diabetes mellitus
Ig	immunoglobulin
ILD	interstitial lung disease
IM	intramuscular
Imp	impression
inf	infusion
inh	inhalation
inj	injection
I&O	intake and output
IOP	intraocular pressure
IQ	intelligence quotient
IUD	intrauterine device
IV	intravenous
IVC	inferior vena cava
J	joule
JVP	jugular vein pulse
K+	potassium
Kj	knee jerk
kg	kilogram
KUB	kidney, ureter, and bladder
l	left
L	liter
LA	left atrium
lab	laboratory
lac	laceration
LAD	left axis deviation
lap	laparotomy
lb	pound
LBP	low back pain
LBBB	left bundle branch block
LDL	low-density lipoprotein
LFT	liver function test
LH	luteinizing hormone
LHRH	luteinizing hormone–releasing hormone
Li	lithium
Lip	lipid
liq	liquid
LLL	left lower lobe
LLQ	left lower quadrant
LMD	local medical doctor
LMP	last menstrual period
LNMP	last normal menstrual period
LOC	level of consciousness
LP	lumbar puncture
LPN	licensed practical nurse
LSk	liver, spleen, and kidney

LUL	left upper lobe
LUQ	left upper quadrant
LVH	left ventricular hypertrophy
L&W	living and well
m	murmur
M	midnight; monoclonal
MAO	monoamine oxidase
MAP	mean arterial pressure
MAT	multifocal atrial tachycardia
MCA	middle cerebral artery
MCV	mean cell volume
med	medication
MED	medical
mets	metastases
MF	maturation factor
mg	milligram
Mg^{2+}	magnesium
MI	myocardial infarction
min	minute
mixt	mixture
ml	milliliter
ML	malignant lymphoma
µmol	micromole
mm	millimeter
mM, mmol	millimole
mod	moderate
MOM	milk of magnesia
MRI	magnetic resonance imaging
MS	mitral stenosis; mental status; multiple sclerosis
MVA	motor vehicle accident
MVP	mitral valve prolapse; mitomycin; vinblastien, cisplatin (Platinol)
N	normal
NA	not applicable
Na^+	sodium
NAS	no added sodium
NB	newborn
NCP	nursing care plan
ng	nanogram
NG	nasogastric
NH^3	ammonia
NHL	non-Hodgkin's lymphoma
NIDDM	non-insulin-dependent diabetes mellitus
NIH	National Institutes of Health
NKA	no known allergies
NKDA	no known drug allergies

NM	neuromuscular
no	number
noc	night
NPH	normal pressure hydrocephalus; neutral protamine Hagedorn (insulin)
NPO	nothing by mouth
NS	normal saline
NSAID	nonsteroidal antiinflammatory drug
NSR	normal sinus rhythm
NTG	nitroglycerin
OA	oral airway
OB	obstetrics
OD	overdose
OD	right eye
OETT	oral endotracheal tube
oint	ointment
OOB	out of bed
OOP	out on pass
OPD	outpatient department
opt	optimum
ophth	ophthalmology
OR Oral	operating room
Orth or ortho	oral surgery orthopedics
OS osm	left eye
OT	osmolality
OU	occupational therapy
oz	each eye
p	ounce
p	after pulse
PAP	pulmonary artery pressure
para	number of pregnancies
PASP	pulmonary artery systolic pressure
PAT	paroxysmal atrial tachycardia
PAWP	pulmonary artery wedge pressure
pc	after meals
Pco_2	carbon dioxide tension
PE	physical examination; pulmonary embolism
PEARL	pupils equal and reactive to light
ped	pediatric
PEEP	positive end-expiratory pressure
PEFR	peak expiratory flow rate
per	by
PERRLA	pupils equal, round, reactive to light and accommodation
PFT	pulmonary function test

pg	picogram
PGE	prostaglandin E
PH	past history
phos	phosphorus
PHR	peak heart rate
PI	present illness
PKU	phenylketonuria
PM	afternoon
PMP	previous menstrual period
PM&R	physical medicine and rehabilitation
PO	by mouth
postop	postoperative
Po_2	oxygen tension
PP	postpartum
preop	preoperative
prep	preparation
prn	as needed
psi	pounds per square inch
Psych	psychiatry
pt	patient
PT	prothrombin time; physical therapy; posterior tibia
PTA	prior to admission
Pth	pathology
PUD	peptic ulcer disease
PX	physical
q	every
qd	every day
qh	every hour
qhs	every bedtime
qid	four times a day
qns	quantity not sufficient
qod	every other day
qs	quantity sufficient
r	right
R	respiratory rate)per minute)
RA	rheumatoid arthritis; right atrium
RAI	radioactive iodine
RAN	resident's admission note
RAP	right atrial pressure
RBC	red blood cells
RDW	red cell distribution width
R&E	round and equal
readm	readmission
REM	rapid eye movement
RF	rheumatoid factor

Rh	Rhesus blood factor
RIA	radioimmunoassay
RL	Ringer's lactate
RIND	reversible ischemic neurological deficit
RLL	right lower lobe
RLQ	right lower quadrant
RML	right middle lobe
RN	registered nurse
RNA	ribonucleic acid
R/O	rule out
ROM	range of motion
ROS	review of systems
rpt	repeat
RPT	registered physical therapist
RR	recovery room
RSR	regular sinus rhythm
rt-PA	recombinant tissue plasminogen activator
R/T	related to
RTC	return to clinic
RUL	right upper lobe
RUQ	right upper quadrant
RV	right ventricle; residual volume
RVH	renovascular hypertension; right ventribular hypertrophy
Rx	therapy; treatment; prescription
S/A	sugar and acetone
SA	sinoatrial
SAH	subarachnoid hemorrhage
sat	saturated
SB	stillbirth
SC	subcutaneous
SCP	standard care plan
SGA	small for gestational age
SL	sublingual
SLE	systemic lupus erythematosus
SLR	straight leg raising
SMI	suggested minimum increment
SMS	somatostatin
SNF	skilled nursing facility
SO_2	oxygen saturation
SOB	shortness of breath
SOC	state of consciousness
sol	solution
S/P	status post
SQ	subcutaneous
SR	slow release

SRM	spontaneous rupture membranes
ss	half
S/S	signs and symptoms
SS	Sjögren's syndrome
stat	immediately
STD	sexually transmitted disease
STS	serologic test for syphilis
subcu, SC	subcutaneous
supp\	suppository
Surg	surgery
susp	suspension
SVC	superior vena cava
SVR	systemic vascular resistance
SVT	supraventricular tachycardia
Sx	symptoms
syr	syrup
T&A	tonsillectomy and adenoidectomy
tab	tablet
TAH	total abdominal hysterectomy
TB	tuberculosis
TBIL	total bilirubin
TBNa	total body sodium
Tbsp	tablespoon
TBW	total body water
T/C	throat culture
temp	temperature
TENS	transcutaneous electrical nerve stimulation
TIA	transient ischemic attack
tid	three times daily
tinc	tincture
TLC	total lung capacity
TM	tympanic membrane
TNM	tumor-nodes-metastases
TO	telephone order
top	topical
tPA	tissue plasminogen activator
TP	total protein
TPN	total parenteral nutrition
TPR	temperature, pulse, and respiration
TRIG	triglycerides
tsp	teaspoon
TTS	transdermal therapeutic system
Tx	therapy
U	unit
UA	umbilical artery
U/A	urinalysis

UGI	upper gastrointestinal
ung	ointment
U/P	urine:plasma ratio (concentration)
URAC	uric acid
URI	upper respiratory tract infection
UTI	urinary tract infection
UV	ultraviolet
v V	mixed venous
vag	volume
hyst	vaginal hysterectomy
VD	venereal disease
VER	visual evoked response
VF	ventribular fibrillation
VO	verbal order
vs	visit
VS	vital signs
VSD	ventricular septal defect
VT/VF	ventricular tachycardia–fibrillation
W	white
WBC	white blood cell count
w/c	wheelchair
WD	well developed
WF	white female
WHO	World Health Organization
WN	well nourished
WNL	within normal limits
wt	weight
y/o	years old
X	times

SYMBOLS

@	at		>	greather than
++	moderate amount		<	less than
+++	large amount		μ or μm	micron (micrometer)
0	zero, none		+	positive, presence
°	degree		"	minute
♀	female		'	second
♂	male		∅	absence of
#	number		✔	check
↑	increased		–	negative, absence
↓	decreased		Δ	changes

Index

About the Editors

Peter Jeffrey Snyder, PhD, graduated with high honors from the University of Michigan in 1986, after completing an undergraduate major in psychology. His PhD degree in clinical psychology, with an emphasis in behavioral neuroscience, was awarded by the Michigan State University in 1992, following an internship in clinical neuropsychology at the Long Island Jewish Medical Center (Albert Einstein College of Medicine). Dr. Snyder received a Wilder Penfield Research Fellowship in 1992 from the Epilepsy Foundation of America for his research on quantitative MRI studies of language disorders in epilepsy patients, and he served as a Behavioral Neurosciences Fellow in the NIMH Clinical Research Center for the Study of Schizophrenia at Hillside Hospital (Albert Einstein College of Medicine). He also served as a visiting scientist at the National Institutes of Health in 1991.

Dr. Snyder publishes regularly in peer-reviewed scientific journals and has delivered many presentations at international scientific conferences. His academic interests range from neuroembryological markers of cognitive and motor differences to the functional neuroanatomic substrates of emotion and prosodic speech. Dr. Snyder's clinical interests bridge a wide variety of neurological and neuropsychiatric conditions, and he has specialized in the diagnosis and treatment planning of complicated, medically refractory seizure disorders.

Dr. Snyder is the director of the Division of Behavioral Neurology, Department of Neurology, at the Allegheny Campus of the MCP◆Hahnemann School of Medicine (Allegheny General Hospital, Pittsburgh, PA), and he maintains an active research program. He holds the rank of associate professor of neurology and neuroscience at the MCP◆Hahnemann School of Medicine, Allegheny University of the Health Sciences.

Paul David Nussbaum, PhD, graduated with high honors from the University of Arizona in 1985, after completing an undergraduate major in psychology. His PhD degree in clinical psychology, with an emphasis in clinical neuropsychology and minor in gerontology, was awarded in 1991 following an internship in clinical neuropsychology at the Highland Drive Veterans Medical Center (Pittsburgh, PA). Dr. Nussbaum then completed a 1-year postdoctoral fellowship in geriatric neuropsychology in the Department of Psychiatry, University of Pittsburgh School of Medicine.

Dr. Nussbaum publishes regularly in peer-reviewed scientific journals and has delivered many presentations at national and international scientific conferences. His academic and clinical interests include normal aging, age-related cognitive change, depression in the elderly, dementia, and cognitive correlates of functional capacity. Dr. Nussbaum was nominated for an Early Career Contribution to Clinical Neuropsychology award by the National Academy of Neuropsychology in 1993.

Dr. Nussbaum is the director of the Aging Research and Education Center for Lutheran Affiliated Services, a continuum of care system that specializes in the acute and long-term care of the elderly. He holds the rank of adjunct assistant professor of psychiatry (neuropsychology) and neurology at the MCP◆Hahnemann School of Medicine, Allegheny University of the Health Sciences.